Hearing the Scriptures

Hearing the Scriptures

Liturgical Exegesis of the Old Testament in Byzantine Orthodox Hymnography

EUGEN J. PENTIUC

OXFORD
UNIVERSITY PRESS

OXFORD
UNIVERSITY PRESS

Oxford University Press is a department of the University of Oxford. It furthers the University's objective of excellence in research, scholarship, and education by publishing worldwide. Oxford is a registered trade mark of Oxford University Press in the UK and certain other countries.

Published in the United States of America by Oxford University Press
198 Madison Avenue, New York, NY 10016, United States of America.

Library of Congress Control Number: 2021912232
ISBN 978-0-19-023964-0 (pbk.)
ISBN 978-0-19-023963-3 (hbk.)

DOI: 10.1093/oso/9780190239633.001.0001

1 3 5 7 9 8 6 4 2

Paperback printed by Marquis, Canada
Hardback printed by Bridgeport National Bindery, Inc., United States of America

To Flora, Daniel, and Cristina, with love.

Contents

Contents

Preface

This is a book on the use and interpretation of Scriptures in Byzantine Orthodox hymnography. The idea of writing such a book emerged with the publication of my *The Old Testament in Eastern Orthodox Tradition* (Oxford University Press, 2014). In the last two chapters of that work, I dealt with two media through which liturgists have interpreted the Scriptures, namely, the "aural" (e.g., hymnography, lectionaries, homilies, etc.) and "visual" (e.g., portable icons, mosaics, frescoes, liturgical acts, etc.) modes of interpretation, which I coined "liturgical exegesis."

In that work, I made a general remark about liturgical exegesis: "The condensed liturgical exegesis is again a challenge to hearers and readers to locate the texts, events, images, and figures woven into the hymnography."[1] I took on that challenge myself, having researched and written the present book, which seeks to identify Scriptures in Byzantine hymnography, a challenge as difficult as finding the proverbial needle in a haystack. Through a comprehensive and minute analysis of selected hymns, I have strived to make sure that no scriptural needle, as tiny and unobservable as it might be (i.e., scriptural *hapax legomena* [Gr., forms "occurring once" in the Bible] or rare words), remains hidden in the depths of the hymnic tapestry.

Therefore, the first goal of my research was to find Scriptures, primarily Old Testament, in Byzantine Orthodox hymnography. The selection criteria for which hymns to consider rested fundamentally upon the presence of references and hints of the Old Testament in the targeted hymns. However, due to the resilient "hiddenness" of scriptural material within the poetic fabric of the hymns, it took me quite some time to decide which hymns should be selected and then thoroughly analyzed.

The second goal of my research was to identify key features and hermeneutical procedures characteristic of "liturgical exegesis" in comparison to "discursive exegesis" (i.e., the interpretive method of ancient biblical commentaries).

Another important factor that encouraged me to pursue this project was the very scarcity of studies on the subject matter of Scriptures and Byzantine hymnography. Moreover, those few studies dealing with this topic were carried out by experts in Byzantine and liturgical studies, from a historical perspective, and focused not so much on Scriptures as on matters concerning Byzantine liturgy, society, and culture.[2]

A noteworthy exception is Bogdan G. Bucur's contribution to the study of early Christian biblical interpretation (i.e., patristic commentaries and Byzantine hymnography) in its theological-hermeneutical frame-work.[3] Seeking to reconstruct the theological presuppositions of the early interpreters, Bucur's view is that Christophanies (Christ's appearances in the Old Testament) are epiphanic, denoting not a simple hermeneutical proce-dure but a "real presence" of the Logos. Nevertheless, Bucur's treatment of Scriptures and hymnography is more from a patristic-theological point of view than from a biblical scholarly perspective.

Jack Custer rightly notices, "Oddly, philologists, liturgists and theologians alike have largely ignored this rich corpus of poetry and, until recently, modern biblical scholarship took scant interest in patristic prose, much less in poetry. Nevertheless, it may be safely asserted that Byzantine liturgical hymns are as much products of biblical interpretation as they are of poetic inspiration and therefore stand as important documents of Greek patristic exegesis."[4]

Since there are no comprehensive studies on this topic from a biblical scholarly point of view, I embarked as a biblical scholar (with primary focus on the Old Testament) and philologist (interested in Septuagint Greek and Semitic languages) on a research journey to identify Scriptures in Byzantine hymnography as well as to reconstruct the hermeneutics beyond the litur-gical exegesis.

The methodology followed in this volume can be briefly described as a critical lexical-biblical analysis of the hymnic material with special emphasis on Scriptures and the ways in which they are recontextualized in a liturgical setting and what influenced hymnographers in their choice of favorite scrip-tural texts or terms as they interwove these with poetry and theology.

Given the vast corpus of Byzantine hymnography, I have narrowed the scope of my research to selected Holy Week hymns. Why did I expressly choose the hymns of the Holy Week cycle as a case study? First, much of the Old Testament is found in the Triodion and Holy Week liturgical services if one considers both the lectionary and hymnography. Second, Holy Week is replete with gospel material concerning Jesus's last week in Jerusalem, hence my curiosity to see how the interplay between texts belonging to the Old and New Testaments unfolds at the level of Byzantine hymnography.

I titled the volume *Hearing the Scriptures: Liturgical Exegesis of the Old Testament in Byzantine Orthodox Hymnography* to indicate that my research was done on "aural" interpretations as attested by hymnography, leaving the analysis of "visual" interpretations as found primarily in iconography for a future endeavor. The phrase *Byzantine Orthodox* in the title underlines the continuity between Byzantine hymnography and what is chanted today in Orthodox churches.[5] This continuity, in spite of all modifications and screenings, may be seen in present-day Orthodox Holy Week hymns that represent essentially and illustratively what we call "Byzantine hymnography."

The book is divided into two parts, with an introduction. In the introduction, "Brief Overview of Byzantine Orthodox Holy Week," the reader is introduced to Byzantine Holy Week functioning as a bridge between Great Lent and Pascha or the Easter vigil.

Part I, "Hearing the Scriptures through Holy Week Hymns," contains six chapters, each of which corresponds to a specific day of Holy Week (Monday through Saturday) and follows a similar structure: a brief overview of the day's theological themes(s) followed by a lexical-biblical-theological analysis of selected hymns prescribed for that day, occasionally supplemented with hymnic material from outside the Holy Week cycle, in order to underline an idea or theme primarily found in an analyzed Holy Week hymn. Additionally, each of the six chapters opens with the brief *synaxarion* notice for the day taken from the Triodion which identifies the specific themes liturgically commemorated for each day of Holy Week.

The single chapter in Part II, "Liturgical Exegesis," is a compilation of key features of liturgical analysis and hermeneutical procedures employed by hymnographers in using and interpreting the Scriptures.

While writing this book, I have had in mind a twofold readership: biblical scholars and liturgiologists interested in the history of biblical interpretation on the one hand and, on the other, common readers, belonging or not belonging to a faith community, who want to acquire a deeper understanding of these mini masterpieces of poetical beauty, biblical reflection, and theological inquiry that are the Byzantine hymns.

Acknowledgments

The six years of research and writing materialized in the present volume require a proper recognition of those who have assisted me to complete this project.

First and foremost is my own home institution, Holy Cross Greek Orthodox School of Theology, with its president, George Cantonis, and interim dean, Maximos Constas, which granted me a sabbatical so necessary to conclude this volume and submit it for publication.

Second, is the Archbishop Demetrios Chair for Biblical Studies and Christian Origins along with its generous donor, the Jaharis Family Foundation, which supported me financially during summer sabbaticals at École Biblique et Archéologique Française (EBAF) in Jerusalem, where I did most of the research.

Third, EBAF in Jerusalem and the Dominican friars, especially director Jean-Jacques Pérennès, who welcomed me into their famous biblical school and library. The EBAF extended me the invitation to teach, as a visiting professor, a course on "Byzantine Orthodox Modes of Interpretation" (spring semester 2021), based on the research I did for the present volume.

Fourth, I thank St. Joseph's Catholic Seminary in Yonkers, New York, its former rector Peter Vaccari and current rector Bishop James Massa and vice rector William Cleary, and the entire faculty, who invited me as "scholar-in-residence" for the academic year 2020–2021, where I completed the final touches for the book.

I am in debt to the following colleagues and friends who read drafts of my work, sending me their helpful suggestions and comments at various moments of this journey. Here they are in alphabetical order: Stefanos Alexopoulos, Matthew Baker (in memoriam), John Behr, Harald Buchinger, Maximos Constas, Michael Coogan, Kevin DiCamillo, Stamatia Dova (special assistance on ancient Greek), Allan Emery, Mary Funchion, Alexander Lingas, James C. Skedros, Gregory Tucker, Olivier-Thomas Venard, Philip Zymaris.

My special thanks go to my good and reliable friend and colleague whom I have known for almost twenty-five years, James C. Skedros, who constantly encouraged me to pursue this project until its completion.

I am indebted to Seraphim Dedes and Michael Colburn for their assistance with the Greek text of the hymns, digitally stored with search capabilities by AGESInitiatives (www.agesinitiatives.org).

Cynthia Read, Executive Editor at Oxford University Press has my special thanks for her professionalism and great patience. I would be remiss if I did not mention other people involved in the publication of my book: Drew Anderla, team leader, Narayanan Srinivasan, project manager, and Wendy Keebler, copy editor.

In addition, I would like to thank Elias (Bogue) Stevens and Malbis Foundation for their financial support.

Mea culpa in case I have left someone off this list.

My heartfelt thanks go to my family—my wife, Flora, and our children, Daniel and Cristina—who had to cope with my unpardonable absences during the writing of this book. To them I dedicate the book with love.

I would be remiss if I did not mention here the most reliable companion I have had during the research and writing journey, through shadowy valleys and shining mountain peaks, namely, the Lord of Passion (*Kyrios tōn Pathōn*), who inspired, encouraged, and protected me with his humble, self-offering, and "mighty love" (*agapēsin krataian*, Hab 3:4 [LXX]), nailed on a cross two millennia ago, as an unshakable testimony. To him and his unique saving Passion, I reverently and gratefully dedicate this volume.

Abbreviations

General

Akk.	Akkadian
ANE	Ancient Near East
Byz.	Byzantine text-type (New Testament)
En	Enoch (book)
Gk.	Greek
Heb.	Hebrew
kativ	See *qere* below. The terms *kativ* and *qere*, found on the margins of Hebrew Bible manuscripts, indicate what is written (*kativ*) and what is read (*qere*), as preserved by scribal tradition.
Lat.	Latin
LXX	Septuagint (the Greek Old Testament)
MT	Masoretic Text
NT	New Testament
OT	Old Testament
Q	Qumran (scroll)
qere	See *kativ* above.
S	Peshitta (the Syriac Old Testament)
Tg(s).	Targum(s)
Theod.	Theodotion
V	Vulgate (the Latin Old Testament)

Primary Sources

Hebrew Bible/Old Testament

Gen	Genesis
Exod	Exodus
Lev	Leviticus
Num	Numbers
Deut	Deuteronomy
Josh	Joshua
Judg	Judges
Ruth	Ruth
1–2 Sam	1–2 Samuel

1–2 Kgdms	1–2 Kingdoms (LXX)
1–2 Kgs	1–2 Kings
3–4 Kgdms	3–4 Kingdoms (LXX)
1–2 Chr	1–2 Chronicles
Ezra	Ezra
Neh	Nehemiah
Esth	Esther
Job	Job
Ps/Pss	Psalms
Prov	Proverbs
Eccl	Ecclesiastes
Song	Song of Songs
Isa	Isaiah
Jer	Jeremiah
Lam	Lamentations
Ezek	Ezekiel
Dan	Daniel
Hos	Hosea
Joel	Joel
Amos	Amos
Obad	Obadiah
Jonah	Jonah
Mic	Micah
Nah	Nahum
Hab	Habakkuk
Zeph	Zephaniah
Hag	Haggai
Zech	Zechariah
Mal	Malachi

New Testament

Matt	Matthew
Mark	Mark
Luke	Luke
John	John
Acts	Acts
Rom	Romans
1–2 Cor	1–2 Corinthians
Gal	Galatians
Eph	Ephesians
Phil	Philippians
Col	Colossians
1–2 Thess	1–2 Thessalonians

1–2 Tim	1–2 Timothy
Titus	Titus
Phlm	Philemon
Heb	Hebrews
Jas	James
1–2 Pet	1–2 Peter
1–2–3 John	1–2–3 John
Jude	Jude
Rev	Revelation

Septuagint Additions

Bar	Baruch
Pr Azar	Prayer of Azariah
Sus	Susanna
1–2 Esd	1–2 Esdras
Ep Jer	Epistle of Jeremiah
Jdt	Judith
1–2 Macc	1–2 Maccabees
3–4 Macc	3–4 Maccabees
Pr Man	Prayer of Manasseh
Sir	Sirach/Ecclesiasticus
Tob	Tobit
Wis	Wisdom of Solomon

Mishnah and Talmud

b.	*Talmud Bavli* (Babylonian Talmud)
m.	*Mishnah* (Mishnah)
Sanh.	*Sanhedrin*

Secondary Sources

ABD	*Anchor Bible Dictionary*, edited by D. N. Freedman, 6 vols. (New York: Doubleday, 1992)
ACCS	Ancient Christian Commentary on Scripture
ANF	*Ante-Nicene Fathers*
BAR	*Biblical Archaeology Review*
BHS	*Biblia Hebraica Stuttgartensia*
CBQ	*Catholic Biblical Quarterly*
GOTR	*Greek Orthodox Theological Review*
HTR	*Harvard Theological Review*
JBL	*Journal of Biblical Literature*
JECS	*Journal of Early Christian Studies*
JETS	*Journal of the Evangelical Theological Society*

JPS	Jewish Publication Society
JSOT(Sup)	(Supplements to) *Journal for the Study of the Old Testament*
JTS	*Journal of Theological Studies*
KJV	King James Version
NETS	*A New English Translation of the Septuagint*, edited by Albert Pietersma and Benjamin G. Wright (New York: Oxford University Press, 2007)
NPNF²	*The Nicene and Post-Nicene Fathers*, Series 2
NRSV	New Revised Standard Version
NTSup	*Novum Testamentum* Supplements
ODB	*The Oxford Dictionary of Byzantium*, edited by Alexander P. Kazdhan (New York: Oxford University Press, 1991)
PG	*Patrologia graeca* [= *Patrologiae cursus completus*: Series graeca], edited by J.-P. Migne, 162 vols. (Paris, 1857–1886)
PL	*Patrologia latina* [= *Patrologiae cursus completus*: Series latina], edited by J.-P. Migne, 217 vols. (Paris, 1844–1864)
RB	*Revue biblique*
RQ	*Revue de Qumran*
RSR	*Revue des Sciences Religieuses*
SBL	Society of Biblical Literature
SC	*Sources chrétiennes* (Paris: Cerf, 1943–)
SVTQ	*St. Vladimir's Theological Quarterly*
TDNT	*Theological Dictionary of the New Testament*, edited by Gerhard Kittel and Gerhard Friedrich, translated by Geoffrey W. Bromiley, 10 vols. (Grand Rapids, MI: Eerdmans, 1964–1976)
TDOT	*Theological Dictionary of the Old Testament*, edited by G. J. Botterweck and H. Ringgren, translated by J. T. Willis, G. W. Bromiley, and D. E. Green, 15 vols. (Grand Rapids, MI: Eerdmans, 1974–2006)
TLG	*Thesaurus Linguae Graecae*, Digital Library, edited by Maria C. Pantelia, University of California, Irvine, http://www.tlg.uci.edu
TNK	Tanakh, Jewish Publication Society
VT	*Vetus Testamentum*
VTSup	Supplements to *Vetus Testamentum*

Notes on Editions and Translations

Bible

For practical purposes, biblical citations follow the NRSV in terms of book name and numbering; e.g., 1 Sam (NRSV) corresponds to 1 Kgdms (LXX).

Specifically, the first number indicates the NRSV, and the second number (placed in parentheses) denotes the LXX. For instance, Ps 22:16 (21:17) means Ps 22, v. 16, according to the NRSV numbering, or Ps 21, v. 17, following the LXX numbering. With respect to Dan 3, beginning with v. 24, the citations will read: Pr Azar 1:1–68 (NRSV) = Dan 3:24–90 (LXX/Theod./*NETS*).

For uniformity, the spelling of biblical proper names follows the NRSV, even in those portions translated from the LXX.

The transliteration of Hebrew forms follows Thomas O. Lambdin, *Introduction to Biblical Hebrew* (New York: Charles Scribner's Sons, 1971), with slight alterations. The transliteration of Greek and Syriac forms is according to *The SBL Handbook of Style: For Biblical Studies and Related Disciplines*, directed by Billie Jean Collins, Bob Buller, and John F. Kutsko (Atlanta: SBL Press, 2016).

Bible translations belong to the author, unless otherwise indicated.

Hymnography

Hymnographic citations are taken from the following editions:

Lenten Triodion (in Greek *Triōdion Katanyktikon*), edited by the Church of Greece. 2nd ed. Athens: Apostoliki Diakonia, 2003.

Papagiannis, K. *Corrections and Observations on the Triodion* (in Greek *Diorthōseis kai Paratērēseis eis to Triōdion*). 2nd ed. Thessaloniki: University Studio Press, 2008.

Translations of hymns used in this volume belong to the author, unless otherwise indicated. For lexical-analysis purposes, these renditions are occasionally more literal than literary. During the translation process, the author consulted closely the following available renditions, listed here in alphabetical order. Of great use and inspiration were Dedes's and Lash's translations.

Dedes, Seraphim. "Ecclesiastical Translations, Texts, and Music." https://www.agesinitiatives.com/dcs/public/dcs/dcs.html.

Holy Week, translated from Greek by the Holy Transfiguration Monastery. Brookline, MA: Holy Transfiguration Monastery Press, 2016.

Lash, Ephraim. "Holy Week Translations." http://web.archive.org/web/20060911201927/http://anastasis.org.uk/.

The Lenten Triodion, translated from the original Greek by Mother Mary and Archimandrite Kallistos Ware. Service Books of the Orthodox Church. London: Faber and Faber, 1978.

The Services for Holy Week and Easter, translated by Leonidas C. Contos and edited by Spencer T. Kezios. San Francisco: Narthex Press, 1994.

Introduction

Brief Overview of Byzantine Orthodox Holy Week

Given that Holy Week is the case study of the first and longest part of this volume, which consists of lexical-biblical-theological analyses aimed at identifying Scriptures in the "great ocean" of Byzantine Orthodox hymnography—before gathering a number of hermeneutical procedures the hymnographers used in interpreting the Scriptures in the book's second part—a brief introduction to the Orthodox Holy Week is well warranted.

As the title of this introduction states, this is solely a "brief overview" for readers who have little or no knowledge of the history and structure of Holy Week as it is celebrated today in Eastern Orthodox communities. For this reason, the information here is general and relies heavily on the works of some contemporary liturgiologists.

This introduction covers the history of Pascha and Holy Week from its earliest attestations to the Byzantine synthesis, the structure of today's Orthodox Holy Week along with the liturgical services held on each day (Monday through Saturday), and ends with a cursory exposition of Byzantine hymnography and some of its main genres.

From the outset, one needs to keep in mind Robert Taft's caveat: as ancient as it might look, the Byzantine Orthodox rite is not a museum of unchanged content and practices.[1] The following historical overview of the Orthodox Holy Week will show that what one experiences today with respect to this important liturgical period is astonishingly the result of a lengthy and intricate process of borrowing, adaptation, synthesis, renewal, and symbiosis.

Hearing the Scriptures. Eugen J. Pentiuc, Oxford University Press. © Oxford University Press 2021.
DOI: 10.1093/oso/9780190239633.003.0001

Past
The Origin of Christian Pascha

The "Lord's Day" and Jesus's Resurrection

There is no evidence in the New Testament of any commandment of Jesus directed to his disciples to commemorate his crucifixion, death, and resurrection with a *synaxis* ("gathering").

Nonetheless, there is a single occasion when Jesus asks his disciples to share bread and wine in his remembrance (Luke 22:17–20: "Do this in my remembrance [*anamnēsin*]" [v. 19]; cf. Matt 26:26–29; Mark 14:22–25)—which later became the Eucharist, held primarily on Sunday, as the "day of the Lord" (*kyriakē hēmera*, lit. "lordly day," Rev 1:10) or the "eighth day," that is, the day of his resurrection.

Paul, following Luke 22:19 (*anamnēsin*), explains to the Christians in Corinth that having bread and wine when they gather together fulfills an *anamnetic* ("commemorative") function, namely, reminding Jesus's followers of the "Lord's death" until his coming again (*parousia*): "For as often you eat this bread [*arton*], and drink this cup [*potērion*], you herald [*katangellete*] the death of the Lord [*thanaton tou kyriou*] until he comes [*achri hou an elthē*]" (1 Cor 11:26).

Both names used for Sunday, "Lord's day" (Rev 1:10) and "eighth day"[2] (*Epistle of Barnabas* 15.8–9), are helpful in reconstructing the early Christians' view of Sunday as a liturgical *synaxis* (Gk., "gathering, assembly"). The first Christians saw Sunday as the beginning of a New Creation (i.e., a proleptic experience or an eschatological understanding) or as the day when Jesus rose from a tomb belonging to one of his secret disciples, Joseph of Arimathea (i.e., a historical understanding of Sunday, a commemoration of a past, historical event in a concrete historical-geographical context).

The two meanings of Sunday coalesce neatly especially in the current Eastern Orthodox understanding of the Eucharistic service held on Sunday aiming at a twofold goal: to enter into communion with the suffering and risen Lord throughout this earthly life's journey while looking forward with a deep sense of eschatological expectancy to meeting the Lord upon his Parousia at the end of time. History and eschatology in Eastern Orthodox liturgical life are tightly interwoven. The dichotomy between past and future attested in the post-Reformation West is absent in Eastern Orthodoxy, where the anamnesis and prolepsis, historical commemoration and anticipatory celebration, do coexist.

Summing up, Sunday was the only commemoration of Jesus's resurrection before the introduction of an annual celebration of Pascha in the second century. The primitive Church was more interested in the week than in the year as a liturgical cycle. So Sunday from the very beginning was associated with the Paschal events. Sunday became a commemoration of Jesus's resurrection.[3]

The Christian Pascha: Quartodeciman and Dominical Traditions
The Christian Pascha derived, as name and theology, from the Jewish Passover held on the fourteenth day of the month Nisan. The name *Pascha* is the Greek transliteration of the Aramaic word *pasha'* going back to the Hebrew *pesaḥ*, "passing over," with reference to God who "passed over" (*pāsaḥ*), saved, the Hebrew houses during the last plague over Egypt (Exod 12:27).[4] With respect to its theological meaning, if the Jewish Passover commemorates the liberation of ancient Hebrews from Egyptian slavery through Moses's agency, the Christian Pascha celebrates humans' liberation from Satan's slavery through Jesus's salvific work culminating with his Passion, death, and resurrection.

Christian Pascha, with Jewish Passover as its model, was a "nocturnal festival"—a vigil was held from Saturday evening until Sunday at dawn. The vigil began after lighting lamps and consisted essentially of a series of lections interwoven with chants.

From Melito of Sardis's poetical homily *Peri Pascha* ("On Pascha," ca. 190), one may surmise that Asia Minor's practice and Rome's practice had something in common: the readings from Exod 12. The presence of this lection in both rites (Asia Minor and Rome) testifies to a common earlier origin of Paschal practices going back to a Jewish prototype, the Passover. Another lection was from the gospel of John (from the trial in front of Pilate [chap. 18] to the end of John's account of resurrection [chap. 21]). According to Harald Buchinger, the antiquity of this custom is difficult to prove. The gospel resurrection narratives as liturgical readings for Pascha (Easter) are not attested prior to the late fourth century.[5] After the readings, there was a homily delivered by a bishop, followed by the baptism of catechumens and confirmation of the neophytes joining the faithful in prayers and in the Paschal Eucharist.[6]

The *Armenian Lectionary* (fifth century, based on fourth-century sources) prescribes as readings for the Pascha vigil the following themes (among others): creation (Gen 1:1–3:24), the binding of Isaac (Gen 22:1–18), and the Passover narrative (Exod 12:1–24). According to Thomas J. Talley, these three readings correspond to three of the four themes (the fourth being the coming of the Messiah) associated with Passover in a "Poem of the Four Nights" found in the Palestinian Targum on Exodus.[7] These readings indicate continuity between the Christian Paschal vigil and the Passover tradition.

The practice of Quartodecimanism (i.e., celebrating the Pascha on Nisan 14) was observed by Asia Minor churches as well as those churches consisting of relocated Asia Minor Christians in Italy and other western areas. Pope Victor I, Bishop of Rome (189–199) sought to excommunicate those Asia Minor Christians who celebrated the Pascha on the evening of Nisan 14 in alignment with the Jewish Passover meal. These Christians were called Quartodecimans, "Fourteeners." Pascha could have fallen on any weekday, and Quartodecimans needed to wait for the rabbis in Jerusalem to set the day for the beginning of Passover (the afternoon Nisan 14 when the lamb was sacrificed) and the vigil with the Passover meal beginning after sunset. A lamb was chosen out of the flock on Nisan 10 to be slain on the afternoon of Nisan 14 (Exod 12:6). The Passover meal was to be eaten on Nisan 15 (Exod 12:8).

One may add that the Quartodecimans were not intentionally seeking to imitate the Jewish Passover but rather following the Johannine view that Jesus died on the "day of preparation" (Gk. *paraskeuē*), Friday in the afternoon (John 19:14–31), when the Paschal lambs were slaughtered; they wanted to make sure that they keep the vigil on Nisan 14 when Jesus, the "Lamb of God" (John 1:36), was crucified and died.[8]

According to the gospel of John, Jesus died on a Friday afternoon almost at the time when the Paschal lambs were slain and prior to the beginning of the Passover feast (at sunset); the Last Supper in John was an ordinary supper. Unlike John, the synoptic gospels set Jesus's death on the cross on the very first day of Passover, and the Last Supper was the Passover meal. John is probably the correct one: Jesus died on a Friday, around three p.m., a few hours before the Passover meal held at sunset in anticipation of Nisan 15, the first day of Passover and Sabbath at the same time.

Here is Eusebius's (d. 339) account of Quartodecimans in Asia Minor:

> A question of no small importance arose at that time. For the parishes of all Asia, as from an older tradition, held that the fourteenth day of the moon, on which day the Jews were commanded to sacrifice the lamb, should be observed as the feast of the Savior's Passover. It was therefore necessary to end their fast on that day, whatever day of the week it should happen to be. But it was not the custom of the churches in the rest of the world to end it at

this time, as they observed the practice which, from apostolic tradition, has prevailed to the present time, of terminating the fast on no other day than on that of the resurrection of our Savior. Synods and assemblies of bishops were held on this account, and all, with one consent, through mutual correspondence drew up an ecclesiastical decree, that the mystery of the resurrection of the Lord should be celebrated on no other but the Lord's day, and that we should observe the close of the paschal fast on this day only. (*Ecclesiastical History* 5.23.1–2)[9]

The *Epistula Apostolorum* composed in Asia Minor in the second century introduces the risen Lord who urges his disciples: "Therefore, you should celebrate the remembrance of my death, i.e., the Passover."[10]

The Asia Minor Quartodeciman bishops led by Polycrates of Ephesus wrote to Pope Victor, arguing to keep their old Paschal practice that dated back to the apostle John (cf. Eusebius, *Ecclesiastical History* 5.24). Melito of Sardis was one of the first well-known Quartodecimans, and his *Peri Pascha*, "On Pascha," is a midrash on Jesus's Passion, suffering, and death.

Pope Victor, disturbed by the Ephesians' claim on apostolic authority (John and the "great lights" of Ephesus such as Polycarp and Papirius) with respect to their Paschal practice, acted hurriedly by excommunicating the churches in Asia Minor, while asking the other bishops to do the same. Nonetheless, one of them, Irenaeus of Lyon (115–202), did not follow his direction and criticized Victor for his harsh attitude toward the Quartodecimans. Irenaeus reminded the pope that some of his liberal predecessors of the see of Rome allowed a variety of Paschal practices.[11]

The Quartodecimans overlooked Victor's excommunication and continued their practice until 325, when the Council of Nicaea decreed Sunday as the day of annual celebration of Pascha—and the vast majority of Quartodecimans complied with the council's decision. The Council of Nicaea condemned Christian views that bridged Pascha with the beginning of Jewish Passover. The council also noted that Christians in the West (primarily at Rome) traditionally commemorated Pascha on the first Sunday following the Jewish Passover. The Council of Nicaea decided that Easter[12] should be celebrated on the first Sunday after the first full moon following the spring equinox, i.e., March 21. It is noteworthy that the Quartodeciman controversy and its follow-up (i.e., the adoption of a Sunday as the date of Pascha) reflect a change in emphasis from "Passion" (Nisan 14) to "Resurrection" (Sunday).[13]

Origen (185–254) reminds the faithful that the Lord's resurrection is commemorated weekly on the "eighth day," i.e., Sunday, and annually on Pascha, when primarily one commemorates Jesus's Passion, including its outcome: "There is now a multitude of people on account of the Preparation day, and especially on the Sunday which commemorates Christ's Passion. For the resurrection of the Lord is not celebrated once in the year, but also always every eighth day" (*Homily on Isaiah* 5.2).[14]

The Paschal Vigil

It is noteworthy that, according to the orthodox practice adopted at Nicaea, the nocturnal vigil and Eucharist service was moved from a fixed date (Nisan 14) to Saturday night toward Sunday. During the nocturnal vigil, the faithful continued to fast until the "cockcrow" (around three a.m.) after the Jewish meal was over (cf. third-century *Epistula Apostolorum* 26 and late-fourth-century *Apostolic Constitutions* 5.18.2). What is the meaning of the nocturnal vigil? Most likely, the Paschal vigil was observed initially in the hope of Jesus's return, hence its eschatological dimension.[15]

The third-century Syriac *Didascalia* 21, reflecting a dominical celebration of Pascha yet containing traces of Quartodeciman practices, sees in the Paschal vigil an opportunity for "prayer and intercession for those who have sinned" but also for "the expectation and hope of the resurrection of our Lord Jesus until the third hour in the night after the Sabbath." According to Buchinger, the time for ending the fast (i.e., the evening "third hour" corresponding to nine p.m.) in a dominical celebration is quite early and can be explained only as a remnant of an earlier Quartodeciman practice polemicizing with the simultaneous Jewish Passover.[16]

The "Historicization" of Pascha

The liturgical services had in the pre-Nicene period an eschatological orientation (e.g., Sunday and Pascha services were offering a proleptic experience of resurrection), but this eschatological orientation was historicized in the fourth century, especially in Jerusalem, during the time of Cyril of Jerusalem (ca. 375–444). Gregory Dix associates this historicization with the Jerusalem liturgy.[17] The precursor of this historicization is the "quasi-historic cycle of the martyrs" commemorated in the third century side by side with the eschatological meaning of Sunday. After Nicaea, liturgical observances began to have a commemorative function.[18]

The historicization process began when the eschatological celebration of Pascha in Jerusalem came to be associated with Jesus's Passion. The earliest evidence for this can be found in Egeria's *Diary*, which describes in detail the main processions performed during the Holy Week of 384, all having a commemorative character. This "historicization," along with the demise of eschatological interest among Christians in general, should be understood in the context of the legalization of the Christian Church by the emperor Constantine. Jesus's Passion on Good Friday turned the Pascha, originally conceived as a "feast of redemption," into a "historical commemoration" of a historical episode: Jesus's resurrection from the tomb in the garden of Joseph of Arimathea.[19]

It is generally agreed that at least in its earliest phase, the Church showed little concern for matching a liturgical synaxis to its corresponding point on the "salvation history" axis, with some exceptions, such as the feasts of Ascension and Pentecost, for which Acts 1–2 provides a fair historical background, but in many local churches, the commemorative dimension of these feasts was not underscored until the fourth century or later.[20]

The Emergence of Great Lent

The Origin of Great Lent
Since it is a truism that there is no accurate description of Pascha without mentioning Great Lent and Holy Week, some brief general comments on the emergence of Great Lent as a preparatory period leading to Holy Week are quite warranted at this juncture.

Today the Byzantine Orthodox Holy Week is prefixed by a lengthy and austere forty-day Lenten period (Gk. *tessarakostē*, Lat. *quadragesima*, "fortieth [day]"), functioning as a preparatory interval of time, ending with the Vespers of Saturday of Lazarus, held on the preceding Friday evening: "Having completed the soul-profiting forty-day [fast of Lent] [*tēn psychōphelē plērōsantes tessarakostēn*], we ask [you] [*aitoumen*] O Lover of Humanity that we may behold [*katadein*] the Holy Week of your Passion" (Saturday of Lazarus, Vespers, Idiomelon).

Great Lent is a period of fasting and penitence. It is called "great" to differentiate it from the other three less important Byzantine "lents" preceding major feasts (i.e., Lord's Nativity on December 25, Theotokos's Dormition on

August 15, and Holy Apostles Peter and Paul on June 29). The word *lent* is a shorter variant of Old English *lencten* (current *lengthen*), meaning "spring-time, spring" (lit. "lengthening" [of days]).

The first evidence of Great Lent is found in the *Paschal Letter* 2 of Athanasius the Great (297–372), Patriarch of Alexandria, dated to 330:

> We begin the fast of forty days on the 13th of the month Phamenoth [March 9]. After we have given ourselves to fasting in continued succession, let us begin the holy Paschal week on the 18th of the month Pharmuthi [April 13]. Then resting on the 23rd of the same month Pharmuthi [April 18], and keeping the feast afterwards on the first of the week, on the 24th [April 19], let us add to these the seven weeks of the great Pentecost, wholly rejoicing and exulting in Christ Jesus our Lord, through Whom to the Father be glory and dominion in the Holy Ghost, for ever and ever. Amen. (*Paschal Letter* 2.8)[21]

Eusebius of Caesarea, in his *On the Paschal Feast* (composed between 325 and 337), notes that Christians undertake these forty days of fasting as an "exercise" (*askēsin*) in preparation for the Paschal feast, thus imitating the "zeal" (*zēlon*) of the prophets Moses and Elijah (*On the Paschal Feast* 4, *PG* 24:700B–C). Eusebius uses Old Testament exempla overlooking Jesus's fasting after baptism. Cyril of Jerusalem (toward the middle of the fourth century) addresses the catechumens about the need for repentance before receiving baptism, using the phrase *hagia tessarakostē*, "holy forty days" (*Catechetical Lectures* 4, 3). In Jerusalem in 384, nun-pilgrim Egeria (*Diary* 27–29) speaks of an already codified fasting period of eight weeks (seven weeks plus the "Paschal week" [Lat. *septimana paschale*], i.e., the Great/ Holy Week). The Armenian Lectionary 19–32 (fifth century) mentions a six-week fasting period followed by the "Paschal fast" (Holy Week).[22] In the fifth century, John Cassian (ca. 360–435) noted that although the same fast with the same meaning occurred in both the East and the West, the fast differed in terms of the number of weeks: six weeks in Rome, seven weeks in Constantinople (*Conferences* 21.27).[23]

How did the Great Lent emerge? There are two main explanations. The first sees Great Lent developing from a short Paschal fast. Beginning in the third century, the Paschal fast expanded from a fast of one (Paschal vigil), two, or three days to a week, and after the Council of Nicaea (325) to a forty-day period (Quadragesima), with each of these fasting periods having its own independent history.[24] During the fourth century, a forty-day Paschal fasting period became the universal practice, along with variants in terms of duration and the beginning and end of Lent.[25] However, these short fasting periods should not be taken as direct predecessors of the forty-day period of the Great Lent.

The second explanation of Great Lent's origin is to be found in a "preparatory" period (initially three weeks) that catechumens observed prior to receiving the sacrament of baptism. According to this hypothesis, if Holy Week and Pascha were "due to an initiative of the Jerusalem Church"[26] with an established catechetical period prior to baptism, the pre-Paschal Quadragesima emerged not as a growth in preparation for Easter but as an independent occurrence in Egypt (Athanasius, *Paschal Letter* 2) following Epiphany (the liturgical celebration of the Lord's baptism), thus imitating Jesus's forty-day fasting following his baptism and preceding his threefold temptation (Matt 4:1–2). This Quadragesima served as a fasting preparatory time for baptism in mid-February. Quadragesima and Holy Week are independent phenomena, each having its own history. Holy Week has a mimetic function to imitate Jesus's Passion, which in the gospels can be framed within a one-week period, whereas Quadragesima has a penitential character, first connected with Epiphany and as a preparatory period for those receiving baptism, then as a preparatory period for receiving baptism at the Easter vigil, and today a penitential period with an eschatological dimension, to encounter the risen Lord.[27] However, later, most likely after the Council of Nicaea, this Quadragesima was connected to Easter, and along with this preparatory period, baptism was transferred to the Easter vigil.[28]

According to Maxwell Johnson, the replacement of adult baptism with infant baptism in the fifth century and afterward made the preparatory period of forty days of fasting and catechesis pointless; hence the shift from baptismal to Paschal in the nature and scope of the forty-day fasting period.[29] Thus, from a preparation for baptism, the forty-day fast became a preparation for encountering Jesus, the Lord of the Passion and the Resurrection.

The emergence of an annual Pascha commemoration during the second century occurred almost at the same time as an increasing need for a baptismal Eucharist different from the weekly Sunday Eucharist. Those wishing to be baptized had to go through a preparatory period of fasting, prayer, and learning culminating with the day of baptism, which was commonly set for the Easter. What could be a better fit for baptism—restoration of humanity in Christ—than the Lord's resurrection? Here one should note Jesus's identification of his own suffering and death with baptism shortly before his crucifixion (Mark 10:38–39).

In the mid-second century, Justin Martyr (100–165) mentions such a baptismal Eucharist in comparison to the Sunday Eucharist, when God began his creative work and when Jesus rose from the dead (*First Apology* 65–67). But since in this passage there is no indication that at that time the baptismal Eucharist was the Pascha, one may assume that the fusion of the baptismal Eucharist and Pascha occurred in Rome sometime after 165. Based on Tertullian's (160–220) testimony, this fusion was already in place by the end of the second century. Tertullian (*On Baptism* 19) writes: "The Pascha affords a more solemn day for baptism, when also the Passion of the Lord, in which we are baptized, was completed."[30]

Gradually, Lent acquired a penitential dimension leading to forgiveness of the penitent during Holy Week. Throughout the history of Christianity, Great Lent has exhibited various distinct traditions, most notably in Jerusalem, Rome, and Egypt, just to mention a few. As regard to duration, the initial six weeks of fasting turned into an eight-week Lent due to the fast-free Saturdays and Sundays during Lent. Thus, in order to have a strict number of forty fasting days, two weeks were added to the initial six weeks of lent, namely, the week preceding the beginning of Lent, called "Cheesefare Week," and Holy Week ending with the Easter vigil. Great Lent was well established in Jerusalem when Egeria attended the Holy Week stational services[31] in 384 or when Cyril of Jerusalem, nearly contemporaneously, delivered his baptismal catecheses. The fifth-century Armenian Lectionary of Jerusalem confirms this fact.[32]

According to Buchinger, the raison d'être of the Quadragesima remains obscure.[33] On the one hand, there is no evidence for a "genetic connection" between a one-week preparation for Easter and the Quadragesima (a hypothesis embraced by traditional scholarship). On the other hand, the second hypothesis (reflecting modern scholarship), the transfer of an initially independent forty-day period to the Paschal cycle, lies on "shaky foundations" being supported by only a few, late documents. Considering the Quadragesima a fasting period loaded with biblical symbolism (e.g., the fasts of Moses and Elijah and, later, Jesus's post-baptismal fasting), Buchinger eschews assuming "genetic dependence" between Quadragesima, a one-week pre-Pascha, and a three-week preparatory period prior to baptism.

The Structure of Today's Orthodox Great Lent

Great Lent is preceded by three weeks of spiritual preparation (the pre-Lent period) consisting of four Sundays, each with a specific theme as the gospel reading at the Liturgy intimates: (1) Sunday of the Publican and Pharisee (Luke 18:10–14, humility), (2) Sunday of the Prodigal Son (Luke 15:11–32, repentance), (3) Sunday of the Last Judgment (Matt 25:31–46, preparation for final judgment), (4) Sunday of Forgiveness (Matt 6:14–21, forgiveness).

Consisting of six weeks of fasting, Great Lent begins on Monday after the Sunday of Forgiveness and ends on Friday evening before the Saturday of Lazarus and Palm Sunday. Actually, the Saturday of Lazarus and Palm Sunday function as a transition between Great Lent and Holy Week.

The recitation of the Great Canon of Saint Andrew of Crete (d. 740) is a feature of the first week of Great Lent. Andrew was born in Damascus, and at the age of fifteen, he entered a monastery in Jerusalem, then moved to Constantinople and was ordained deacon at Hagia Sophia (Gk., "Holy Wisdom") Cathedral (consecrated in 537). Later he was elevated and appointed Archbishop of Gortyna in Crete. Andrew is credited with the invention of *kanon* ("canon") as a genre of hymnography consisting of nine odes arranged in stanzas (four or more lines with a fixed meter).

The Great Canon sets the tone for the entirety of Great Lent: repentance over a life spent loosely with little or no attention to the inner cry of a soul stifled by transient pleasures and self-overrated trials. The Great Canon is read four times during Lent, in four sections on Monday, Tuesday, Wednesday, and Thursday of the first week and as a whole on Thursday of the fifth week.

> How shall I begin to deplore the deeds of my miserable life? What beginning shall I make, O Christ, to this lament? But since you are compassionate, grant me remission of my trespasses. Like as the potter gives life to his clay, you have bestowed upon me flesh and bones, breath and life; today, O my Creator, my Redeemer and my Judge, receive me a penitent.... I have lost my first made beauty and dignity, and now I lie naked and covered with shame ... (The Great Canon)[34]

Another feature of Great Lent is the recitation of the Penitential Prayer, attributed to Saint Ephrem the Syrian (306–373), on the weekdays of Lent at the end of each church service: "O Lord and Master of my life, give me not a spirit of sloth, vain curiosity, lust for power and idle talk, but give to me, Thy servant, a spirit of soberness, humility, patience and love. O Lord and King, grant me to see my own faults and not to condemn my brother: for blessed art Thou to the ages of ages. Amen. O God, cleanse me, a sinner."[35]

The Psalter is read during Great Lent twice a week, mostly in monastic communities.

The lectionary, i.e., the biblical readings assigned to Great Lent, contains pericopes from the Old Testament, which are not to be found in the Eucharistic service (Liturgy) and are mostly absent outside Lent except for the Vespers for the great feast days (Nativity of the Lord, Nativity and Dormition of the Theotokos, etc.). Old Testament readings, on every single day of Lent, are taken from three books: Genesis and Proverbs at Vespers and Isaiah at the sixth hour. Interestingly, these three books of the Lenten lectionary represent the three sections of the Jewish tripartite division of the Hebrew Bible (Old Testament): Torah "Instruction" [LXX: Law] (Genesis), Prophets (Isaiah), and Writings (Proverbs). The Old Testament lectionary ascribed for Great Lent intimates the "preparatory" role of the Old (Elder) Testament. The book of Genesis through the story of creation and "primeval history" (Gen 1–11) is the preamble of salvation history unfolded through and out of the Pentateuch. The book of Proverbs shows the role of Wisdom in salvation history as well as in everyday life. And finally, the reading from the book of Isaiah, replete with messianic prophecies, evokes Jesus, the suffering Messiah.

The hymnography contained in the Triodion, the hymn book of Great Lent, contains hymns to be chanted at daily Vespers and Orthros (Matins) services. The Byzantine hymnography of Great Lent and particularly of Holy Week, as this volume will show, is a treasure trove of biblical motives, verbatim quotations, and hidden hapax legomena (words or phrases occurring only once in the entire Greek text of the Old Testament).

The Sundays during Lent are titled according to an important theme or figure. The first Sunday of Lent, called the Sunday of Orthodoxy, commemorates the victory of the iconodules against the iconoclasts (843). The second Sunday is dedicated to the great fourteenth-century theologian Gregory Palamas, the herald of *theosis* (deification) teaching. The third Sunday's theme is the Veneration of the Holy Cross (at Orthros, the cross is brought out of the sanctuary and placed in the middle of the church to be venerated by the faithful). The fourth Sunday makes remembrance of Saint John of the Ladder, the author of *Spiritual Ladder*, a popular ascetic book. And the fifth Sunday is dedicated to Saint Mary of Egypt, a model of penance.

During Great Lent, a special Liturgy of Presanctified Gifts replaces the regular Eucharist service (Saint John Chrysostom Liturgy) that is not celebrated on the weekdays, for Liturgy pointing to Jesus's resurrection would be in sharp contrast with Lent's penitential tenor. The Presanctified Liturgy is celebrated attached to Vespers on Wednesday and Friday evenings during Great Lent. The gifts (elements) are consecrated on the previous Sunday, and during this special Liturgy, clergy and faithful commune with the presanctified gifts.

The Triduum Question

Before dealing with the Byzantine Holy Week, its origin and development, a few words about the so-called Triduum (Latin "three-day" [fast]) are warranted. In his article "In the Bridegroom's Absence: The Paschal Triduum in the Byzantine Church," Taft uses the phrases "Jerusalem Triduum" and "Byzantine Paschal Triduum services" with reference to both the past and present liturgical practices of the Eastern Orthodox tradition.[36] Taft speaks of a Jerusalem Triduum with a "full-blown system of stational services following the sequence of the events of Jesus' Passion" by the time of Egeria's presence in Jerusalem (384). Taft's line of thought is that from an one-day Paschal commemoration (the Pascha vigil), the Paschal fasting increased to two[37] and finally three days, thus leading to a Triduum as an independent liturgical period and then to a full-blown six-day Holy Week linking Great Lent, via the Saturday of Lazarus and Palm Sunday, to Easter Sunday.

However, as Buchinger surmises, based on a meticulous analysis of the primary textual sources brought repeatedly into the debate over the antiquity of the Triduum period, such a brief liturgical cycle is much later than previously assumed.[38] Buchinger shows convincingly that the general opinion about an early Triduum, as intimated in Taft's article, is due to a confusion between "theological" and "liturgical" imports that the Triduum acquired throughout history.

Here are the three main earliest sources related to a "three-day" period.

In the fifth homily on Exodus, dealing with the exodus of ancient Hebrews from Egypt and crossing of the sea (Exod 12–14), Origen refers to Exod 5:3 (i.e., the "way of three days") in conjunction with Hos 6:1–2: "Hear what the prophet says: 'God will revive us after two days, and on the third day we will arise and live in his sight' [Hos 6:1–2]. The first day is the Passion of the

Savior for us. The second day is the day on which he descended into hell. The third day is the day of resurrection."[39]

As one may notice, there is no reference to the Easter Liturgy but rather an allegorizing interpretation of the ordinal number "third" with respect to the "third day" resurrection that fulfilled the "Scriptures" (1 Cor 15:4; cf. Hos 3:2).

According to Ambrose of Milan (d. 397), these are "the three holy days . . . within which he [Christ] suffered, lay in the tomb, and arose, the three days of which he said: 'Destroy this temple and in three days I will raise it up' [John 2:19]."[40] Again, "three days" in Ambrose's letter is not *expressis verbis* connected to a concrete celebration, although a liturgical context cannot be entirely denied. Ambrose reiterates a three-step sequence (i.e., suffering [death], entombment, resurrection) handed down by the apostolic *kerygma* (Gk., "proclamation") on Jesus's salvific work (1 Cor 15:3–4).

Similarly, Augustine (d. 430) notes: "Since it is clear from the Gospel on what days the Lord was crucified and rested in the tomb and rose again, there is added, through the councils of the fathers, the requirement of retaining those same days, and the whole Christian world is convinced that the pascha should be celebrated in that way" (*Letter* 55.15.27).[41] Triduum blends the two fundamental aspects of Pascha, Jesus's Passion culminating in crucifixion (or, as Augustine rightly puts it in his sermon, "death"), and his resurrection: "Since the Lord Jesus Christ made one day dolorous by His death and another glorious by His Resurrection, let us, by recalling both days in solemn commemoration, keep vigil in memory of His death and rejoice in celebration of His Resurrection" (*Sermon* 221.1).[42]

The three-step sequence of Jesus's salvific work (i.e., crucifixion, entombment, resurrection) reappears in Augustine's letter but this time within a somehow "liturgical setting," namely, the Paschal celebration. Augustine mentions some "days" commemorating the three-step sequence of events recorded in the "gospel" (liturgical) days prescribed by "councils" and required to be observed by Christians worldwide. However, there is no clear indication that in fifth-century Hippo there was such an autonomous liturgical Triduum. Augustine is most likely referring to the most important three days (Friday, Saturday, and Sunday) as part of the Holy Week–Pascha period.

According to Buchinger, the best proof that the "theologoumenon of the Triduum" emerged and developed outside a liturgical setting, that is, within a literary exegetical context, is found in Origen's above-quoted lines.[43] Originating in the area of exegesis, though, the idea of Triduum may have influenced the liturgical life in the West. The East had never known of a Paschal Triduum. The Holy Week liturgical cycle that most likely originated in Jerusalem spread somehow uniformly all over the Byzantine world, but the adoption of the hagiopolite (Jerusalem) Paschal celebrations in the West was more complicated.

The Byzantine Holy Week

Prior to the emergence in the late fourth century of Holy Week as a six-day liturgical unit (cycle), the Easter vigil was the only service commemorating Jesus's sufferings, death, and resurrection. Unlike the Quadragesima introduced to Palestine by the middle of the fourth century, which had a penitential character—a period of fasting, prayer, and penance—the Holy Week that emerged in Palestine had from the very beginning a mimetic role, aimed at imitating the last week in Jesus's life as recorded in the canonical gospels.[44]

In the Byzantine tradition, the six-day period preceding Easter is called "the Great Week" (Gk. *hē megalē hebdomas*).[45] The first attestation of a "Paschal fast" of sorts is found in Dionysius of Alexandria's (200–265) *Epistula ad Basilidem* 1,[46] ca. 260. In the following fragment from *Ad Basilidem* 1, Dionysius deals with timing and intensity of fasting practices held by various Christian communities of his time related to the "six days" before Easter, what is known today as Holy Week (a liturgical development dated to the third quarter of the fourth century): "For all do not continue during the six days of the fast either equally or similarly: but some remain without food till cockcrow on all the days, some on two, or three, or four, and some on none of them . . . and then, when they come to the last two and prolong their fast on them alone, viz. on Friday and Saturday, think they are performing some great feat by continuing till dawn."[47]

In considering the emergence and development of the Byzantine Holy Week, the following are the main literary sources that need to be taken into account.

For the Jerusalem rite: Egeria's *Diary* (384) (see discussion below), Armenian (fifth century) and Georgian (fifth to eighth centuries) lectionaries, and codex Stavrou 43, which is more a rubric book than a lectionary (dated to 1122 but reflecting earlier phases prior to the destruction of the holy places by Caliph al-Hakim in 1009).[48]

For the Constantinopolitan rite: codex Stavrou 40 (the Typikon of the Great Church [Hagia Sophia] found in manuscripts of the ninth and tenth centuries).

What one calls today the Byzantine rite is the result of a complex process of synthesis and symbiosis between the Palestinian rite with its two important centers—Jerusalem and St. (Mar) Sabas Monastery—and the Constantinopolitan rite represented by the Great Church and Stoudios Monastery (located in Constantinople near the Golden Gate).

Here is a brief summary of the intricate history of the Byzantine rite.

From the outset, one may say that there has been a long-lasting and reciprocal influence between Jerusalem and Constantinople in terms of Holy Week practices.[49] Jerusalem had the aura of *hagiopolis* (Gk., "holy city"), with pilgrims coming from different regions. The pilgrims' purpose was not solely to see the sacred sites where biblical events occurred or to walk in Jesus's footsteps but also to visit the monasteries and interact with holy monastics living there. Upon returning to their homes, these pilgrims shared with their own communities some of the liturgical practices they remembered seeing in Jerusalem or in others parts of the Holy Land, such as St. Sabas Monastery, an important monastic community settled in the Judaean desert somewhere between Jerusalem and the Dead Sea. This process of Jerusalem influencing Christian liturgical practices was geographically broad in scope, but it had a particular impact on Constantinopolitan services. This influence reached the climactic point with the demise of the cathedral Liturgy of Constantinople soon after 1204 and its replacement by the so-called monastic rite.

This shift from cathedral[50] to monastic rite in Constantinople was possible due to the great influence of Theodore the Studite (759–826), Abbot of Stoudios Monastery, who invited monks from St. Sabas Monastery in the Judaean desert to come to Constantinople and assist them in their battle against the iconoclasts. This was the very time when monks of Stoudios Monastery synthesized the borrowed office from the Sabaitic community by adding elements from the Asmatike Akolouthia (Gk., "sung office," the cathedral rite of the Great Church of Constantinople). The result of such an intricate synthetizing effort was a hybrid "Studite" office, a mix of Palestinian Horologion (collection of "hours") containing psalmody and hymns with the Great Church's Euhologion (collection of "prayers") made up of litanies.[51]

In its turn, Constantinople, the "New Rome"—the capital of the Christian Roman Empire, with its Great Church (Hagia Sophia)—exercised a great deal of authority in all ecclesiastical matters including liturgical developments over lesser episcopal sees located throughout the empire. In a nutshell, for the first millennium, there was an ongoing tandem of reciprocal exchanges between Jerusalem and Constantinople pertaining to liturgical praxis. The ninth-century codex Vatican Gr. 2282, containing the Liturgy of Saint James, exhibits obvious signs of Byzantinization of the Jerusalem Eucharistic service.

The Constantinopolitan-Sabaitic synthesis spread throughout Byzantine monastic communities, including those in Palestine where it underwent further hagiopolite refinements. By the end of the first millennium, the literary evidence for Holy Week exhibits an interesting symbiosis between a monasticized Constantinopolitan rite and a Byzantinized Palestinian rite. This hybrid neo-Sabaitic monastic rite reached Mount Athos Hesychastic communities and was fully codified by the fourteenth century and gradually adopted by the entire Orthodox world. The current Orthodox Holy Week codified in the Byzantine liturgical book the Triodion[52] reflects this neo-Sabaitic rite.[53]

Egeria's *Diary* (384 C.E.)

Among the literary sources mentioned above, the Spanish nun-pilgrim Egeria, who visited Jerusalem during Holy Week of the year 384, occupies a place of honor. In her well-known *Diary* (chaps. 30–38),[54] Egeria journalized lavishly and in careful detail her experience with the cycle of stational services,[55] covering the Passion Week services held on the premises of the Holy Sepulcher Church (initially called *Anastasis* [Gk., "Resurrection"]) that was built by the emperor Constantine the Great on the site of Jesus's tomb and consecrated in 335.

According to Eusebius, Constantine built a large basilica to the east of the tomb and arranged a courtyard with colonnades between the basilica and the tomb (Eusebius, *Vita Constantini* 3.35). The altar of the basilica was oriented toward the tomb, then to the west, with the entrance from the Cardo Maximus, the colonnaded boulevard (on the east side). The basilica, in Greek, was called *Martyrion*, Gk. "testimony, proof" (cf. Matt 24:14). Later, *martyria* (plural of *martyrion*) would refer to the tombs of martyrs, those who confessed Christ and died for him; however, for Egeria (*Diary* 30:1), the word *martyrion* refers to the Passion of Christ—a church as a testimony of Christ's Passion. Golgotha, the place of crucifixion and including a baptistery, was incorporated at the corner in the very large basilica of the Martyrion.[56]

Egeria's *Diary* divides clearly into two parts: chaps. 1–23, a travelogue in the proper sense of the words, and chaps. 24–49, a detailed description of the services attended and the liturgical cycle observed at Jerusalem. Probably initially, due to the lack of a smooth transition, the two parts were distinct works.

As for the author of this famous travelogue, Egeria, originally from northwestern Spain, was most likely a nun (or an abbess), a person of substance, having the necessary means to travel far and long (i.e., through Palestine, Egypt, Syria, Mesopotamia, and Asia Minor), probably with a large retinue. She belonged to the upper socioeconomic class, given her ability to read and write as a woman living in a time when illiteracy was its paramount stamp. Although not at home with classical literature, Egeria betrays a good grasp of the Scriptures, tilting toward a literal rather than allegorical interpretation.

During her travels, Egeria attended a good number of liturgical services from Holy Week to Sunday Eucharist, or daily prayer synaxes ("gatherings")—the hot spot being always Jerusalem, and primarily the Holy Sepulcher Church (the Anastasis complex)—in the presence of a varied group of worshipers, including laypeople, clergy, and ascetics. All these services are chronicled in Egeria's travelogue.

A good portion of Egeria's description of liturgical services has to do with Holy Week. Each day of the "Great Week" follows similar rubrics: a vigil done in the Martyrion of the Holy Sepulcher Church, between the ninth hour (three p.m.) of the day and the first hour (seven p.m.) of the night—this was the case for Monday, Tuesday, and Wednesday.

On Thursday, the vigil was held at Eleona Church on the Mount of Olives, between the first hour (seven p.m.) and the fifth hour (eleven p.m.) of the night, followed by a procession from there to the city commemorating the main events of that grisly night (i.e., Jesus's prayer, betrayal, and arrest):

> And then everyone hurries to return to their home to eat, because as soon as they have eaten, they all go to Eleona [Mount of Olives], to the church in which there is the cave in which on this day the Lord was with the apostles. And there until about the fifth hour of the night hymns and antiphons appropriate to the day and place are continually recited, similarly also readings; prayers are interspersed; those passages also from the gospel are read in which the Lord addressed the disciples that very day, sitting in the same cave that is in that church. And from there at about the sixth hour of

the night they go up with hymns to the Imbomon, to that place where the Lord ascended into heaven. And there again similarly readings and hymns and antiphons appropriate to the day are recited; also whatever prayers there are that the bishop says are always appropriate both to the day and to the place. (*Diary* 35:2–4)[57]

On Friday, there were no services in the morning, and worshipers could venerate the cross and other treasured relics around it, but there was a vigil held in front of the cross from the sixth to the ninth hour (twelve p.m. to three p.m.). The vigil consisted of psalms, readings, and prayers. There followed another vigil held in the Martyrion and a Liturgy in the Anastasis for the burial of Christ (*Diary* 37.8).[58]

Here is the description by Egeria of the procession and veneration of the cross that was held on Good Friday:

So, after this the dismissal from the Cross is done, that is, before the sun rises, and everyone immediately goes eagerly to Sion to pray at that pillar at which the Lord was scourged. Having returned from there, they sit down a little while in their homes, and soon all are ready. And then a chair is placed for the bishop on Golgotha behind the Cross, where he now stands; the bishop sits in the chair; a table covered with a linen cloth is placed before him; the deacons stand around the table and a silver-gilt casket is brought, in which is the holy wood of the cross; it is opened and [the wood] is brought out; both the wood of the cross and the inscription are placed on the table. So, when it has been placed on the table, the bishop, sitting, grips the ends of the holy wood with his hands, and the deacons who stand around guard it. It is guarded thus because the custom is that all the people coming one by one, both the faithful and the catechumens, bowing at the table, kiss the holy wood and pass through. And because, I don't know when, someone is said to have bitten off and stolen a piece of the holy wood, therefore it is now thus guarded by the deacons who stand around lest anyone dares to come and do so again. Thus, all the people pass through one by one, all bowing, touching the cross and the inscription first with their forehead, then with their eyes, and then kissing the cross, they pass through, but no one raises a hand to touch. (*Diary* 37.1–3)[59]

On Good Friday,[60] a Liturgy of the Word was observed before the cross between the sixth hour (twelve p.m.) and the ninth hour (three p.m.) of the day on Golgotha, part of Constantine's ecclesiastical complex but left unroofed under open sky. Another vigil took place in the Martyrion between the ninth hour (three p.m.) and the twelfth hour (six p.m.), followed by an elective vigil in the Martyrion beginning at the first hour (seven p.m.) of the night. On Holy Saturday,[61] a Paschal vigil in the Martyrion was scheduled for the afternoon. The vigil was probably the oldest liturgical form Christians observed in preparation for Pascha. Later, the vigil practice became "stational," namely, associated with various sites where biblical events had occurred. The ninth hour (three p.m.) was the usual starting time for a vigil, for it marked the end of a working day and a daily fast throughout the year. On Thursday, there were two Eucharist services, one at the eighth hour (two p.m.) in the Martyrion, followed by another behind the cross (only once a year was the Eucharist celebrated in this location; *Diary* 35.1–2).

As one can glean from Egeria's *Diary*, though the tendency of the Jerusalem Great Week seems to be stational, imitating Jesus's last week in Jerusalem, some of the most important moments and sites were overlooked, such as the house of Caiaphas or the Praetorium where the trial in front of Pilate took place. In addition, the enactments via the liturgical procession were not dramatic but quite sober, not to mention that the gospel chronology does not always match its liturgical counterpart.

Present
The Byzantine Holy Week Today

As we saw in the previous section, Holy Week, originating in mid-fourth-century Jerusalem, became the Byzantine Holy Week through a long and complicated process of synthesis and symbiosis between the two liturgical rites, Palestinian and Constantinopolitan. It is this composite that spread eventually all over the Eastern Orthodox world.

Today's Orthodox "Holy and Great Week" (Gk. *hagia kai megalē hebdomas*) is preceded by a two-day festal unit consisting of Saturday of Lazarus and Palm Sunday, functioning as both a bridge with Great Lent and a biblical-theological prelude to the Great Week itself, namely, Jesus's last week in Jerusalem culminating with his Passion and resurrection.

Even though, as we saw above, there is no Byzantine Orthodox Triduum as a special liturgical unit, the most important events recorded in the canonical gospels and commemorated liturgically during Holy Week, such as the

Mystical Supper, crucifixion, burial, and resurrection, are all clustered on Holy Thursday, Good Friday, Holy Saturday, and Easter Sunday.

Below is a brief presentation of the main features of the Orthodox Byzantine "Holy and Great Week" (Holy Monday through Holy Saturday), along with its daily services. My hope is that this will be an appropriate and useful mise en scène for the lexical-biblical-theological analyses of selected hymns gleaned from each day of Holy Week and displayed in the part I of this volume.

Orthodox Holy Week begins with Holy Monday[62] and culminates with the Paschal vigil of Saint Basil Vesperal Liturgy celebrated on Holy Saturday morning, preceding and paralleling the nocturnal Paschal vigil, namely, the Orthros (Matins) of Pascha or Easter Sunday, observed around midnight on Holy Saturday preceding the Easter Sunday Liturgy held shortly after midnight.

The central theme of the Orthodox Byzantine Holy Week is the "Pascha of the crucifixion and the resurrection" (Gk. *staurōsimon kai anastasimon Pascha*)—the "saving tension of joyous-sorrow (*charmolypē*)."[63] This paradoxical blend of joy and sorrow may be found in the selection of Old Testament readings for Holy Week. During Great Lent, the Old Testament readings are taken from the books of Genesis and Proverbs, while during Holy Week, the readings are from Exodus and Job. These biblical writings are central to Old Testament theology: the book of Job is about suffering and its intrinsic relation to the human predicament, and the book of Exodus places liberation and freedom as the highest aspiration of any human being and community.

In addition to the overarching theme of Holy Week, each day has a special theme. These daily themes are like planets revolving in their own orbits around the sun, namely, the central theme of Holy Week. The liturgically selected theme of each day is condensed in the few lines of the *synaxarion* ("collection" [of details regarding the person/event commemorated on that day]) and will be pointed out in part I of this volume at the very beginning of each chapter, under the heading "Overview."

Holy Week divides into two equal parts: Monday, Tuesday, and Wednesday, followed by another three-day sequence, Thursday, Friday, and Saturday.

Characteristic of the first part is its theological-eschatological outlook. The second part of Holy Week functions more like a liturgical "commemoration" (Gk. *anamnesis*) of some concrete biblical events. Notwithstanding, this division needs some refining or nuancing. Even though the second part of the week is obviously anamnetic in its liturgical retelling of the biblical stories of Jesus's last week in Jerusalem, one should not overlook its profound theological content eschatologically oriented where Jesus's Passion and resurrection are relived with an intense sense of expectation for the new creation of God. Parenthetically, Holy Week is a good example of Constantinopolitan-Sabaitic synthesis and symbiosis where theology/eschatology meets salvation history.

The first three days form a distinct liturgical unit, as each day consists of the same number and type of services: Orthros (Matins), held in anticipation at evening on the previous day (e.g., Matins of Holy Monday is held on the evening of Palm Sunday), followed by a Presanctified Liturgy in the morning of that specific day.

It is noteworthy that the first three days deal more with Jesus's sayings (i.e., parables and discourses) than concrete actions done by him or being part of them, obviously with a few exceptions, e.g., the cleansing of the Temple on Holy Monday or the episode of the sinful woman anointing Jesus along with Judas's reaction leading to betrayal on Holy Wednesday.

The Orthros (Matins) of each of these three days is called the "Service of the Bridegroom" (Gk. *Akolouthia tou Nymphiou*), a title inspired by the parable of ten virgins (Matt 25:1–13). The opening troparion ("Behold the Bridegroom comes in the middle of the night . . .") introduces the worshipers to a twofold setting, of Passion and Parousia. The main theme is watchfulness in light of the past history of salvation (e.g., Jesus's Passion) while looking forward with a deep sense of expectancy to the Parousia, the coming in glory, yet unexpectedly, of the Church's Bridegroom, who suffered in order to eradicate the source of evil. The "Bridegroom" (*Ho Nymphios*) icon is placed at the front of the nave, where it will remain for veneration until Holy Thursday. The icon, representing Jesus as humiliated by Pilate's soldiers (Matt 27:27–31), with a crown of thorns on his head, a reed in his hand, ropes around his wrists, and a scarlet cloak on his shoulders, is the Eastern variant of the Western pictorial representation *Ecce Homo*, "Behold the human being." The Bridegroom hymn along with its iconic supplement invites the worshipers to look at Jesus, the Lord of Passion, as their loving Bridegroom, who in spite of all their shortcomings, weaknesses, and disloyalties, loves them with the same passionate love as he did when he accepted to suffer on their behalf.

Holy Monday

The Orthros (Matins) is held on Palm Sunday evening. Besides the main theme of "Bridegroom" pointing to watchfulness, the service directs the worshipers' attention to the patriarch Joseph (Gen 37–50), a model of chastity and endurance in temptations and trials—a much-celebrated type or foreshadowing of Christ by patristic commentators.

In addition to Joseph, Holy Monday commemorates an unmatched biblical episode where Jesus curses a fig tree for being fruitless. Behind the almost anecdotic character of this quite brief episode (Matt 21:18–22) lies the same eschatological tenor attested in each of the first three days of Holy Week: those listening to Jesus's teaching who do not bear fruit will share the fate of the fig tree when the day of judgment comes. The story was inserted into the Holy Monday service due to the note in Matt 21:18 (cf. Mark 11:12) that the fig tree was cursed on the day following Jesus's entrance into Jerusalem (i.e., Palm Sunday).

One may note that according to the synoptic gospels (Matt 21:12–17; Mark 11:15–19; Luke 19:45–48; cf. John 2:13–16 [which probably referred to a different episode]), this is the day when Jesus cleansed the Temple. However, as noted above, the first three days of Holy Week are focused on theological and not historical matters.

The Vespers and Presanctified Liturgy are celebrated on Holy Monday morning. The gospel reading at the Liturgy is Matt 24:3–35, dealing with signs of the end of time, including the "sign of the Son of Man" (v. 30).

Holy Tuesday

The Orthros (Matins) service for this day is held in anticipation on Holy Monday evening. The main theme of Holy Tuesday is watchfulness in light of the Parousia, as both lections, the parable of the ten virgins (Matt 25:1–13) and the parable of the talents (Matt 25:14–30), intimate.

The Vespers and Presanctified Liturgy are celebrated on Holy Tuesday morning. The gospel reading at the Liturgy is a cento of pericopes: Matt 24:36–51; 25:1–46; 26:1–2.

Holy Wednesday

Holy Wednesday is a bridge from the theological-eschatological outlook of Holy Monday and Holy Tuesday to the commemorative outlook characterizing the last three days of Holy Week.

This is the day when "a woman" entered the house of Simon the Leper in Bethany and anointed Jesus's head, to the indignation of his disciples (Matt 26:6–16), leading to Judas's act of betrayal. However, Kassia's hymn, the most important hymn in the lyric repertoire of the day, relies on a different anointing, done by a "sinful woman," which occurred in the house of Simon the Pharisee in Capernaum at the beginning of Jesus's ministry (Luke 7:36–50).

The Vespers and Presanctified Liturgy are celebrated on Wednesday morning; the gospel reading at the Liturgy is Matt 26:6–16 (the anointment in Bethany).

The Mystery (Sacrament) of the Holy Unction (Gk. *Euchelaion*), aiming at the healing of physical and spiritual ailments and based on Jas 5:14–17, is celebrated for the health and well-being of the entire community on Holy Wednesday evening. It is noteworthy that Holy Unction may be celebrated at any time during the liturgical cycle.

Holy Thursday

On Holy Thursday, the oils for Holy Chrism or Myron (Gk. *myron*, "myrrh, perfumed oil") to be used in the baptism of the catechumens, which in antiquity took place on Pascha (Easter Sunday), are consecrated. In later times, after the practice of the Easter baptism vanished, the consecration of the oils lost its initial annual regularity. The service is held at the end of the Liturgy on Holy Thursday. The bishop is the one who consecrates the oils for Chrism, and the priests use it when they administer the Sacrament of Chrismation which follows and is closely connected to the Sacrament of Baptism.

The Service of the Nipter (foot washing) (John 13:3–17) is held also on Holy Thursday morning.

The Liturgy was initially celebrated in the evening of Holy Thursday as anamnesis of the Last Supper, being preceded by the Service of the Nipter. This special Liturgy has two sections: Great Vespers, with Old Testament readings, and the Liturgy of Saint Basil, starting with the Trisagion prayer. The gospel readings (Matt 26:1-20; John 13:3–17; Matt 26:21–39; Luke 22:43–45; Matt 26:40–27:2) recap the events from Wednesday evening up to the early morning of Friday (anointing in Bethany, betrayal, washing of the disciples' feet, institution of the Eucharist, Peter's denial prophesied, prayer in the Garden of Gethsemane, Judas's kiss, the arrest, Jesus before the high priest, Peter's denial, and Jesus before Pilate).

On Holy Thursday, the icon of the "Mystical Supper," replacing the icon of the "Bridegroom" (exposed for the first three days of Holy Week), is displayed for veneration.

At the *Proskomede* (Gk., "preparatory" service preceding the Liturgy) on Holy Thursday morning, the priest removes from the *prosphora* (Gk., "offering" bread) a second *Amnos* (Gk., "Lamb," symbolizing Christ) piece of bread that will be consecrated along with the first *Amnos* during the Holy Thursday Liturgy and preserved in the *Artophorion* (Gk., "carrier of the bread") on the altar table as default or "reserved" communion throughout the year.

Good Friday

Good Friday focuses on Jesus's trial, crucifixion, taking down from the cross, and entombment. But how is this series of biblical events commemorated liturgically? Theologically, this is the day when sin has reached its climax (i.e., humans killing their Creator) and the day when God through Jesus has reached extreme humility (i.e., God accepting to die for humans). Due to the biblical richness and theological intensity, Good Friday is graced with an exquisite synaxis of hymnography and dramatic liturgical actions worthy of the message of this uniquely sacred day.

There are three services held on Good Friday: Orthros (Matins), Royal Hours, and Great Vespers.

The Orthros of Good Friday, the longest among the liturgical services of the Byzantine Orthodox Church, is celebrated by anticipation on Holy Thursday evening. It is a special Orthros with a number of extra features, such as the twelve Passion gospel readings, hence the popular name for this Orthros service, the "Service of the Twelve Gospels" (Gk. *Akolouthia tōn Dōdeka Euangeliōn*).[64] The first and the longest reading is from John 13:31–18:1 and is about Jesus's discourse at the Last Supper. The following ten pericopes deal with Jesus's sufferings and crucifixion, while the last reading covers his burial with the sealing of the tomb and assigning a guard to keep watch over it. After each gospel reading, the choir's response is the same, "Glory to your long-suffering [*makrothymia*], Lord, Glory to you," reminding the worshipers that Good Friday is the sacred time of extreme humility, long-suffering, and perfect obedience that Jesus showed to his heavenly Father and fallen humanity. Another hallmark of this special Orthros is the procession of a massive cross taken out from the altar by the serving priest, who installs it in the middle of the church. The symbolic action is known as the "Service of the Crucified One" (Gk. *Akolouthia tou Estaurōmenou*); according to an old tradition, the image of the crucified Christ was painted directly on the wood of the cross that was taken out in procession—currently occurring shortly after the reading of the fifth gospel lection.[65]

Another peculiar feature of this Orthros is that during the procession with the cross, the last of fifteen hymns (known as antiphons) is sung—"Today is hanged on a tree the one who hanged the earth in the waters"—which heightens the emotional register of this dramatic representation of Jesus's crucifixion by placing it within or at the very beginning of God's creation.

The Royal or Great Hours read currently on Good Friday morning are four in number: first (six a.m.), third (nine a.m.), sixth (noon), and ninth (three p.m.); each "hour" has its distinct theological theme, covering the day's most important moments, namely, Jesus's crucifixion, death, and entombment. Characteristic of the hours of Good Friday are the three lections read at each of the hours: prophecy, epistle, and gospel, along with selected psalms pertaining to the central theme of Good Friday, Jesus's Passion.

Great Vespers, held currently on Good Friday afternoon, is called in Greek *Apokathēlōsis* (lit. the "Un-nailing"), known also as the "Service of Deposition" or "Taking Down from the Cross," and refers to the time, shortly after the ninth hour (three p.m.), when Jesus's lifeless body was taken down from the cross, wrapped in a linen shroud, and hastily buried in a new tomb provided by Joseph of Arimathea. Besides "un-nailing" Jesus's image from the cross and its deposition on the altar table symbolizing the tomb hewn in the rock, this special Vespers features a small "burial procession" of Jesus depicted lifeless on the *Epitaphios*[66] carried by the priest out from the altar in procession throughout the church and deposited on a table in the center of the nave (*naos*) symbolizing the tomb of Christ. The other, greater procession takes place in the evening, at the Orthros service of Holy Saturday. Three Old Testament readings are followed by the epistle and gospel readings.

When there is a single officiating priest, he carries the Epitaphios over his head, and, arriving in the center of the church, he places it in the *Kouboukleion* ("bed-chamber," Lat. *cubiculum*, a euphemism for "tomb"), a wooden structure consisting of two detachable pieces (i.e., a table and a "dome"-like upper component) symbolizing Jesus's body being laid in the tomb.

On Good Friday, the icon *Akra Tapeinōsis* ("Extreme Humility," representing the bust of a lifeless Christ submerged in the tomb with a cross behind him) is displayed besides the cross and the gospel book in the Kouboukleion.

Holy Saturday

Holy Saturday services zoom in on the tomb and the underworld as a locus and time of transition between Jesus's death and resurrection. It is a time of sheer silence, troubling mystery, and tensed expectation, when sadness coexists paradoxically with joy; it is what the Greek word *charmolypē* conveys, a "joyful-sadness."[67]

Great Saturday is the Christian liturgized version of the biblical Sabbath, "cessation of work, rest." Similarly to the Creator who marked the end of his creative work by instituting the Sabbath, Jesus indicates the end of his salvific work through "sabbatizing" in the tomb. Nevertheless, Sabbath is not a complete stop but rather the end of an activity and the beginning of something new. The Creator puts an end to his creative work, which coincides with the beginning of another work, that is, his providence in taking care of his creation. The same with Jesus: his death on a cross means the end, the completion of his salvific work. This end or Sabbath "observed" in the tomb coincides with the beginning of another work, defeating the source of evil, first within the latter's own realm, through Jesus's descent to Hades, and then continuing through the Church's efforts to implement Jesus's gospel of love and forgiveness in a corrupted and disoriented creation.

Holy Saturday introduces the worshipers to a "parallel universe." On the one hand, there is a visible, tiny, dark, and cold tomb hewn in a rock outside the walls of Jerusalem, where, beyond any imagination, the source of life is at sleep. On the other hand, there is the unseen, yet intuitively sensed, farfetched, and vast domain of Hades, fastened with copper gates and iron bolts, an awe-inspiring kingdom swayed only by the utter silence and hopelessness of its invisible though apperceived denizens, a decrepit domain whose master cannot be identified or pinpointed yet whose stifling presence is diffidently suspected almost everywhere.

The main theme of Holy Saturday is conveyed by the stark contrast between the motionlessness of Jesus's dead body in the tomb and Jesus's disarming and liberating journey to Hades. It is noteworthy that Jesus is not besieging the well-protected Hades by strategizing or putting up a good fight—not at all. The mere presence of a dignifyingly humble Jesus, the "deified mortal being," lifeless in the tomb yet descending in spirit to Hades, is enough to disorient and paralyze the omnipresent deceiving master of the underworld that has never been visited by God the Creator of "heavens and earth." The same humble presence of the crucified one is enough to liberate all the hopeless captives of Hades, even those lingering in the foremost corners of that vast domain. Jesus's effortless, silent, yet real victory over Hades matches his unique endurance of suffering, humility, and faithfulness on Good Friday.

Holy Saturday reminds the worshipers that in spite of death that still reigns in this world, through his extreme humility and endurance, Jesus defeated the source of evil within its realm while liberating Hades's denizens forever.

Thus, Jesus's resurrection, his return to life incorruptibly, celebrated on Easter Sunday, would be incomplete without Holy Saturday, this "Sabbath of Sabbaths"—the Sabbath par excellence, understood as the end-beginning process of Jesus's death and defeat of evil, the unseen "sign of the prophet Jonah" (Matt 12:39) that gives Jesus's resurrection meaningful content and clear direction. The Orthodox Byzantine icon of *Anastasis* ("Resurrection") depicts Jesus coming out of Hades grasping Adam and Eve and other Old Testament righteous ones out of the underworld prison. Hades's broken gates and bolts are spread everywhere over the dark deep, where a chained monster representing Hades lies beneath Jesus's steady feet. This icon, so representative of the Orthodox view on resurrection, speaks volumes on Holy Saturday's deep and complex theological meaning.

The best known among the Holy Week services to the Orthodox and non-Orthodox is the Matins of Holy Saturday, held in anticipation on Good Friday evening. The central theme of this popular and beautiful service is a reflection on Jesus's hidden "journey" from death to resurrection. As Taft rightly notes, "this is the least 'anamnetic' and most dogmatic of the present Byzantine services."[68]

The Orthros is celebrated by anticipation on Good Friday evening and contains a special service, *Encomia* (Gk., "Praises"). This service is better known as the "Lamentations" (Gk. *Epitaphios Thrēnos*, lit. "funeral song, lament over a tomb"), divided into three sections (*staseis*) and commemorating Jesus's Passion, death, and entombment.[69] The priest, while standing in front of the Kouboukleion during the Encomia, chants the first verse of each of the three sections, censing cross-wise each time the Kouboukleion and the Epitaphios.

The chanting of Encomia is followed by a procession with the Epitaphios outside around the church. During the procession, the priest makes four stops for a brief litany each time. The popular practice is to have the faithful pass under the Epitaphios that is raised over the heads while re-entering the church. This represents symbolically the passage along with Christ from death to life.

Inside the church, the priest takes the Epitaphios from the Kouboukleion and brings it back to the altar, placing it on the Holy Table, symbolizing the entombment. The Epitaphios will remain there for forty days until the feast of Ascension.

Beginning with the Orthros of Holy Saturday, the priest wears bright vestments showing that the transition from death to life has just begun.

Today, the Vesperal Liturgy of Saint Basil is celebrated on Holy Saturday morning, but in the past, this Liturgy was officiated on Holy Saturday evening and marked the beginning of the Paschal vigil. As a matter of fact, Holy Saturday used to be the only day when faithful did not gather at the church for the Eucharist service but observed a strict fast at home.

The service consists of two parts, Vespers of Pascha and Saint Basil Liturgy, whose readings and hymns abound in baptismal and resurrectional motifs, a memento of the past when catechumens were baptized on the Paschal vigil. At the Vespers, out of fifteen Old Testament lections prescribed by the Triodion, only three are now read, from Genesis, Jonah, and Daniel, ending up with the chanting of the "Hymn (Song) of Three Youths." Among these lections, the reading of the full book of Jonah points to the "Sign of Jonah" and Jesus's descent to Hades.

Prior to the gospel reading, the priest chants the refrain "Arise, O God, and judge the earth . . ." (anasta ho theos krinon tēn gēn . . .), while the choir sings Ps 82 (81):8. During the singing, the priest spreads laurel leaves throughout the church, pointing to Jesus's victory over death and the Lord's bodily resurrection.

This is, in short, the structure of today's Byzantine Orthodox Holy Week.

Byzantine Hymnography

This section presents a few general comments on Byzantine hymnography.[70]

Structurally speaking, the liturgical services of the Holy Week cycle, with respect to the variable elements, consist primarily of hymns and scriptural readings. Both components are found in the Triodion (by default the liturgical book of Great Lent) or, since the beginning of the twentieth century, in the liturgical book titled *The Holy and Great Week*.

As a hallmark of Orthodox Byzantine hymnography, most of this corpus is anonymous, that is, most hymns are "orphans," unassigned to an author.

Many of the Holy Week hymns, and in fact the Triodion itself, were composed in various regions outside Constantinople, e.g., Palestine, Syria, Greece, southern Italy, and Asia Minor.

The hymnography we find today in the Triodion with respect to Holy Week belongs primarily and mostly to the hagiopolite rite of Jerusalem. Constantinople's influence on hagiopolite hymnography can be seen in the Typikon of the Anastasis Church in Jerusalem, based on codex Savrou 43 of the Holy Cross Monastery in Jerusalem, dated 1122 and published by A. Papadopoulos-Kerameus as *Analekta Hierosolymitikes Stachyologias ē Sylloge Anekdoton* (5 vols., St. Petersburg, 1898).[71] The Sabaitic-Constantinopolitan synthesis spread throughout the Byzantine Empire, as evidenced by the eleventh- to twelfth-century Typikon of the Euergetis Monastery in Constantinople (Codex 788 of the University Library of Athens) which represents the "Byzantine rite."[72]

Troparion

A *troparion* is the simplest and oldest Christian hymn. The troparion played an important role since the beginning of Christian worship. Initially, the term designated a short prayer written in poetical prose and inserted after each verse of the Psalms recited at Vespers and Orthros. Gradually, it came to designate a strophic unit (stanza) of a *kontakion, kanon,* or *sticheron.* A troparion can take different names, based on the delivery time (e.g., *apolytikion,* at the end of Vespers), feast day (e.g., *anastisimon,* on the resurrection), or type of melody (e.g., *idiomelon,* sung on a unique melody).[73]

One of the most well-known troparia dates to the sixth century, attributed to Emperor Justinian (527–565) and sung at Saint John Chrysostom Divine Liturgy: *Ho Monogenēs Hyios* (Gk., "The Only Begotten Son").

Although the troparion is the oldest of the hymnic structures, the kontakion and the kanon (canon) remain the two most important poetical forms of Orthodox Byzantine piety and liturgy.

Kontakion

The reign of Justinian contributed to an increasing activity in hymn writing using models from Jerusalem, Antioch, and Alexandria. By the beginning of the sixth century, another genre, longer than a troparion, emerged: the kontakion. A kontakion consists of eighteen to thirty stanzas and is a homily (sermon) in verse. The greatest hymn writer associated with the new genre is Romanos the Melodist (485–560), who, according to tradition, wrote one thousand kontakia—doubtless an exaggeration, though pointing to his uncontestable fame as a hymn writer. Romanos's most well-known kontakion is that on the nativity of Christ: "Today, the Virgin gives birth to the One who is above the being [*hē Parthenos sēmeron ton hyperousion tiktei*] . . ." Other two famous melodists (*melodoi*) contemporary with Romanos are Anastasios and Kyriakos.

Kontakion, widely used between the fifth and seventh centuries, consists of an introduction (*prooimion*) and several stanzas (*oikoi*) linked to the introduction by a refrain; the stanzas were interconnected with one another by an alphabetical sequence (acrostic). A *heirmos*, or model stanza, opens each kontakion.[74] Kontakia were composed for the Orthros (Matins) of important feasts and saint days. After the assigned scriptural lection was read, a preacher or psalter (singer), along with the choir, chanted the kontakion, the homily in verse focusing on that respective lection.

Melito's homily *Peri Pascha*, written in "oratorical prose" and influenced by Semitic poetry, may be considered an example of poetical homily.[75] Syriac poetry (especially *Mēmrā*, or poetical homily) contributed greatly to the development of kontakion. Like the Mēmrā, the kontakion was used in the morning service after the gospel reading.[76] It is noteworthy that the demise of this old genre of poetical homily and its replacement by a regular, in-prose homily led to the end of the kontakion and the emergence of a new liturgical genre, the canon.[77]

It is a truism that the synagogue was for most Christians their first place of worship, so earliest Christian hymns were either a calque of or heavily influenced and patterned by synagogue hymnography and chanting. Only gradually, though steadily, this religious poetry was replaced by genuine Christian hymns. Nonetheless, early Christian hymnography underwent another influence from pagan Hellenistic poetry triggered by the first encounters between the emerging Church and paganism with its wide variety of beliefs.

The Council of Laodicea (ca. 363), canon 59, and the Council of Braga, Spain (563), both regional (local) councils, sought an obstacle to various influences by forbidding the use of hymns without a basis in canonical books of the Bible. Given these limitations, one should admire much more the artistry of these hymnographers. In any event, one need not assess them through the lenses of classical poetry, where personal expression is the artistic ideal. Church hymns, with rare exceptions of mild personal touches here and there, represent the voice of the community and not that of the artist.

For this reason, it was liturgiologists such as Jean-Baptiste-François Pitra,[78] and not classicists, who first evaluated these hymns in their original liturgical setting and consequently appreciated their theological and artistic value. However, W. Christ, co-editor of the *Anthology of Greek Ecclesiastical Poetry*, found it necessary to apologize to the classicists for the alleged lack of artistry on the part of the hymnographers who abandoned the freedom and elegance of the classical Greco-Roman poets.[79]

The work of Pitra, *L'hymnographie de l'église grecque* (Rome, 1867), a detailed presentation based on his discovery that the strophes of the Byzantine hymns are of equal meter, marks the beginning of the analytic study of Byzantine hymnography. The most complete anthology of ecclesiastical poetry (from early Christianity to Byzantine times) is *Anthologia Graeca Carminum Christianorum*, edited by W. Christ and M. Paranikas (Leipzig, 1871).

Assessing Byzantine hymnographers solely against the benchmarks of classical poetry is to miss the main point, namely, that they are at the same time artists, biblical interpreters, and theologians. As I hope the reader will note from this volume, their distinguishing contribution surpasses the lyrical domain, being relevant to the history of biblical hermeneutics and theological ideas. The uniqueness of these medieval writers lies in their ways of fusing poetry, Scripture, and theology into one single final product that we generically call a hymn.

Kanon (Canon)

Byzantine hymnography ranging from fifth to eleventh centuries may be divided into two phases: the first phase, from the fifth to seventh centuries, is marked by the emergence of the kontakion as the liturgical poetical genre; and the second phase, from the seventh to eleventh centuries, is characterized by the replacement of the kontakion with the kanon, a new liturgical genre.

A mini collection of poetical paraphrases, the kanon (canon) began to replace the nine biblical odes[80] chanted during Orthros, while preserving the same number of nine for its own odes. For instance, ode 1 is a paraphrase of the first biblical ode, Moses's hymn of praise in Exod 15:1–19; and ode 9 reflects on the eighth and ninth biblical odes, i.e., Mary's *Magnificat* in Luke 1:46–55 and the prayer of Zacharias (*Benedictus*) in Luke 1:68–79. Each ode of the kanon consists of a heirmos and several stanzas (troparia). Among the known composers of canons are Andrew of Crete, with his famous "Great Canon," which is read during the first and fifth weeks of Great Lent; Patriarch Germanos I (d. ca. 730); John of Damascus (675–756) of St. Sabas Monastery, located halfway between Jerusalem and the Dead Sea, who is best known for the Easter Canon; Kosmas of Jerusalem, or the Hymnographer (the brother of John of Damascus) (d. 760); George of Nicomedia (d. after 860); and Joseph the Hymnographer (d. 886), perhaps the most prolific hymnographer of the Greek Church.[81]

The difference in content between kontakia and canons is that the former are poetical homilies, while the latter are hymns of praise patterned according to the nine biblical canticles. Another difference is that no matter what the goal of the canon is (i.e., to praise Christ, the Theotokos, a saint, etc.), its odes should always relate to Scriptures in search of subject-models. At the beginning, canons were composed only for the Great Lent.

A question arises: why were the beautifully elaborated kontakia replaced by shorter canons? According to Pitra, the canons were composed in the midst of the iconoclast controversies, when hymn writers did not have their predecessors' luxury of peaceful times so necessary for the production of complex ecclesiastic liturgical poetry.[82] Given the religious and ecclesiastical context of the eighth to ninth centuries, the doctrinal content and simple passionate poetry of the canons were preferred to the poetical elegance and sophistication encountered in the earlier kontakia. Moreover, the development of rituals and the addition of icons to the liturgical decor made the transition from lengthy kontakia into much shorter canons almost unnoticeable.

Nevertheless, the most important reason kontakia were replaced by canons lies with the development of liturgical services and the obligation of clergy to preach a sermon as stipulated at the Council of Trullo in 692. The emergence of homilies in the narrow sense of the word made the kontakia, whose initial function was to serve as poetical expositions on the scriptural lections, forfeit their very purpose.

At the beginning of the ninth century, the Stoudios Monastery in Constantinople became the center of Byzantine hymnography. The monastery was founded by Stoudios in 462 and shortly became the fortress of Orthodoxy during the iconoclastic controversy. Theodore the Studite's work marks the revival of the kontakia. His kontakia are more elaborate stylistically than those authored by Romanos the Melodist, his hymn-writing model. Other kontakia writers from Stoudios Monastery are Theophanes (d. 842) and his brother Theodorus and Methodius (d. 846). This is the time when the *hegoumena* (abbess) Kassia composed her hymns and canons.[83]

Due to the development of the liturgical services, other small hymns, much like the early troparion, were created to respond to the length and diversity of these services. One may list the following poetical liturgical genres: katabasia, oikos, hypakoe, kathisma, idiomelon, sticheron, Theotokion, Staurotheotokion.[84]

Summing up, the most important part of Byzantine hymnography pertains to the four hymnographers who were active between the seventh and eighth centuries, John of Damascus, Kosmas of Jerusalem, Andrew of Crete, and Germanos of Constantinople (with respect to Holy Week, feasts, and Sundays); and the two hymnographers of the ninth century, Theodore and Joseph the Studites (with respect to the Great Lent).[85]

PART I
HEARING THE SCRIPTURES THROUGH HOLY WEEK HYMNS

1

Chastity

Joseph and the Midnight Bridegroom—Holy Monday

Overview

On Holy Monday, two scriptural pericopes are brought into focus: one from the Old Testament, the "Joseph cycle" (Gen 37–50), and a short yet intriguing episode from Jesus's last week in Jerusalem, the cursing of a fig tree (Matt 21:18–22).

> On Holy and Great Monday, we make the remembrance of the blissful [*makariou*] Joseph the handsome [*pankalou*]; and also of the fig tree that was cursed by the Lord and withered. (Synaxarion)

Chastity is one of the main themes of Holy Monday, which opens the week of Christ's Passion. On this day, a sharp contrast emerges between a chaste and noble person, Joseph, and a fruitless fig tree, symbolizing idleness and carelessness. However, Joseph the chaste and handsome is the result of a gradual transformation from youthful arrogance and self-entitlement to mature endurance, self-control, and altruism. Contrarily, the fruitless fig tree is the mark of stagnation, carelessness, and uselessness under the unavoidable sign of divine judgment.

Joseph endured trials and resisted temptations, thus becoming a type of Christ's singular fortitude in the face of pleasures, suffering, and pain, all of which is defined so appropriately by the word *chastity*. From being sold by his brothers, resisting the pleasant lures of his master Potiphar's wife, and thrown in jail unjustly, to being elevated to a position of power and in the end refusing to hold any grudge against his brothers, Joseph's remarkable story is poetically and concisely rendered by the hymns of Holy Monday.

The lections prescribed for the Vesperal Presanctified Liturgy on Holy Monday subtly tie Joseph's chastity to the trials the ancient Hebrews endured during their Egyptian oppression and those that Job underwent at Satan's

Hearing the Scriptures. Eugen J. Pentiuc, Oxford University Press. © Oxford University Press 2021.
DOI: 10.1093/oso/9780190239633.003.0002

prosecutorial investigation. All of this is seen through the perspective of eschatological duress: "The one who endures to the end will be saved" (Matt 24:13). Chastity is reached only through continuous endurance.

Holy Monday is about chastity tested in the fire of trials and temptations. On this day, endurance is an arch linking the past (Joseph, Hebrews in Egypt, Job) to the eschatological future with its trials via a "liturgical present" featured by Jesus's exemplary endurance during his last week of "trials and scourges" (2 Macc 7:37).

Although in a transient appearance, Jacob, Joseph's father, lamenting over the loss of his son (Gen 37:34–35), directs the hearers' attention to the Father in heaven who, through his hard-to-understand yet dignifying silence, shares his son's indescribable bitter experience of being human.

On this day, there is another, almost ubiquitous presence, the mysterious presence of the "Midnight Bridegroom"—an outgrowth of biblical marital imagery (e.g., Hos 1–3), the Parousia-projected Jesus whose unexpected "visitation" is an urgent call to vigilance, endurance in life's struggles, and resistance to various decoys (Matt 25:1–13, the parable of the bridesmaids). In the meantime, during the "Bridegroom's absence," prayer and fasting are the only weapons against assaults from the adversary (Luke 5:33–35), and "blissful [makarios] is the servant whom the Bridegroom will find watching [grēgorounta]" (Holy Monday's hymn; cf. Luke 12:37) when he comes in the dead of the night.

Timeline: On Holy Monday, during his short trip from Bethany to Jerusalem (around two miles), Jesus curses a fruitless fig tree. Arriving at the Temple, more precisely in the "Court of the Gentiles," Jesus expels the moneychangers, sending them back to their place outside the premises of the Temple area, in the gospel episode commonly known as the "Cleansing of the Temple" (Matt 21:12–17).

Services and lections for Holy Monday: Matins (officiated by anticipation on Palm Sunday evening), Matt 21:18–43; Vespers and Presanctified Liturgy (officiated on Holy Monday), Exod 1:1–20; Job 1:1–12; Matt 24:3–35.

Analysis
The Midnight Bridegroom

Behold, the Bridegroom [ho Nymphios] is coming in the middle of the night; and blissful [makarios] is the servant whom he will find watching [*grēgorounta*]; but, on the other hand, unworthy [*anaxios*] is the servant whom he will find being indolent [*rhathymounta*]. Beware [*blepe*], my soul, be not overcome [*katenechthēs*] by sleep, so that you will not be handed over to death and be shut [*kleisthēs*] out of the kingdom. But rather, come to your senses [*ananēpson*] crying out: "Holy, holy, holy are you our God." (Holy Monday, Matins, Troparion)

"Behold [*idou*]"

The interjection *idou* ("behold, lo, there is") gives this opening troparion a biblical flavor. The LXX *idou* corresponds to the Hebrew *hnnh*, both terms introducing something out of the ordinary, some unusual, unexpected reality.[1] The element of surprise opens the suite of hymns for the first day of Holy Week. "Behold" the Bridegroom (who will come unexpectedly as a robber) is *now*—liturgically—"coming" (*erchetai*, a generic present) in the middle of the night. The service of Matins, also known as Vigil, was originally officiated at around one a.m.

"The Bridegroom [*ho Nymphios*]"

The Bridegroom is a well-established metaphor reflecting the early Church's expectation for the unpredictable return of Jesus (Matt 9:15; 25:6, 10; Mark 2:19–20; Luke 5:34–35; John 3:29 [here pointing to John the Baptist as the Bridegroom's friend]).

The marital imagery between God and his people was first used by the eighth-century North Israelite prophet Hosea[2] and re-employed by Jeremiah and Ezekiel. Besides Jesus's sayings (e.g., Matt 9:15, the bridegroom and the wedding guests), the imagery was employed by Paul in referring to the relationship between Jesus Christ and his Church (e.g., Eph 5:31–32).[3]

There are two basic ideas in the New Testament texts mentioned here. First, there will be a time when the Church will experience a gloomy period characterized by the Bridegroom's absence.[4] Second, the Bridegroom will return unexpectedly, hence the need and duty of the faithful to wait patiently and wisely so that the coming of the Lord will find them awake and well prepared for such a unique event.

Here is, perhaps, the saying that inspired the liturgist. It speaks of a period of fasting in the Bridegroom's absence—which is the point of Holy Week, to remind the faithful that they are still in the Bridegroom's absence, hence the need for fasting and praying: "Then they said to him, 'John's disciples, like the disciples of the Pharisees, frequently fast and pray, but your disciples eat and drink.' Jesus said to them, 'You cannot make wedding guests fast while the bridegroom is with them, can you? The days will come when the bridegroom will be taken away from them, and then they will fast in those days'" (Luke 5:33–35 [NRSV]). The passage is embedded in the Lucan pericope, the question about fasting.[5]

The liturgical announcement "Behold, the Bridegroom is coming" echoes the clamor and even shouting in the parable of the ten bridesmaids: "But at midnight there was a shout, 'Behold, the Bridegroom [ho Nymphios] is coming [erchetai]![6] Come out to meet[7] him!'" (Matt 25:6 [Byz.]). In our hymn, the liturgist combines the narrative detail with the "shout" leading to a shorter[8] yet more powerful proclamation, "Behold, the Bridegroom is coming in the middle of the night!"

The proclamation is immediately followed by a twofold beatitude-wise observation, "Blissful[9] is the servant whom he [i.e., the Bridegroom] will find watching [grēgorounta]." Creatively, the liturgist brings here in a slightly modified form another saying of Jesus, a beatitude, preserved in Luke 12:37: "Blissful [makarioi] are those servants whom the Lord will find watching when he comes." The context of the pericope on watchful servants (Luke 12:35–40) is quite similar to the one found in the parable of the ten bridesmaids. This time, the owner of a house returns from, significantly, a wedding banquet, unexpectedly, either at the second or third watch of the night,[10] but "blissful" are the servants who are watching for him, ready to open the door when he knocks: "You should also be ready [hetoimoi] for the Son of Man comes at an hour you do not expect" (Luke 12:40).

The parenetic interest of the liturgist is seen in the use of the singular, more personal ho doulos, "servant" (instead of the impersonal ekeinoi douloi, "those servants"). The singular is much easier to appropriate personally. Using the singular "servant," the liturgist is inviting anyone participating in the liturgical services of Holy Week to identify himself with the careful, watchful "servant" who is undoubtedly longing for the return of the Lord. The parenetic emphasis is also seen in the "reward" the liturgist pencils in for the one who is willing to watch, namely, happiness as a personal, dynamic, and daring relationship with the Lord on the convoluted paths of human history and daily life.

The virtues commended here are "watchfulness, vigilance,"[11] lying in sharp contrast (de palin, "but, on the other hand") to "idleness, indolence." The hymnographer is quite unapologetic when describing the opposite attitude, "But, on the other hand, unworthy [anaxios] is the one whom he will find indolent [rhathymountas]." The term rhathymountas[12] contrasts sharply with *grēgorountas*. If the former servant is praised for "watchfulness, vigilance," the latter is chastised for "indolence, hesitation."

As one may notice—not that it is exactly hard to miss—the opposite of "blissful, happy" (understood as a relational, process-centered key concept) is "unworthy, unfit" [*anaxios*], which might describe someone or something as unfit, incompetent.[13] The servant who was "indolent, inconsiderate" in relation to the Lord and his unpredictable yet sure return is considered by the same Lord to be an "unfit servant" (*anaxios doulos*). In other words, the "unfit servant" is not being admitted into the company of, or into a personal relationship with, the Lord, whereas the "blissful, happy servant," by a persistent vigilance, has become rightly worthy of such a reward.

Through these two antitheses, "blissful, happy" vs. "unworthy, unfit" and "watching" vs. "being indolent," the hymnographer reinterpreted creatively Jesus's parable of the ten bridesmaids (Matt 25:1–13) as well as his beatitude on the watchful servants (Luke 12:35–40). If, in the parable of the ten bridesmaids, the contrast is between the "foolish, careless" (*mōros*) and the "wise, calculated" (*phronismos*), both terms defining various ways of thinking or reflecting, the new contrast created by the liturgist is now between "watchful, vigilant" and "indolent, hesitant," both terms belonging to the creative sphere of attitude, of *doing*. The accent is moving from theory to practice, from reflection to action. The liturgist takes a parable, a paradigmatic story, and turns it into a rhetorically powerful exhortation. To become a "blissful, happy servant," someone interested and involved in a personal relationship with the "Midnight Bridegroom," takes more than a reflective stance. To be a "watchful servant" requires courage, resolution, commitment, and action while continually resisting that agonizing temptation of becoming an incorrigible, inconstant, hesitant servant,[14] deemed in the end unworthy of being in the company of his returning Lord.

The admonitory tone reaches its full expression in the second part of the hymn, when the paradigmatic story turned into an exhortation becomes a personalized and interiorized counsel and advice: "Beware,[15] my soul, be not overcome by sleep, so that you will not be handed over to death and be shut out of the kingdom." The dialogue with one's soul may be read as a positive twist on the dialogue of the rich foolish man with his soul in the parable with the same name (Luke 12:13–21).[16] The warning "Be not overcome by sleep" (*mē tō hypnō katenechthēs*)[17] sounds very close in tone to Jesus's advice to his sleepy disciples in Gethsemane prior to his arrest: "Watch and pray so that you may not enter into temptation: the spirit is indeed eager [*prothymon*], but the flesh is weak [*asthenēs*]" (Matt 26:41). According to this hymn, lack of vigilance may result in two unwanted situations: being handed over to death and self-exclusion from God's kingdom. In the latter predicament, one may discern the echo of Jesus's harsh warnings regarding the subjects of the kingdom who due to their slothfulness will be cast out of God's kingdom (Matt 8:12; Luke 13:25, 28).

The hymn closes with an invitation to the believer, through the hymnographer's voice and addressed to oneself, to become sober again (*ananēpson*)[18] by crying aloud, proclaiming[19] God's threefold holiness (or transcendence),[20] in fact, rehearsing the seraphic Trisagion heard by the prophet Isaiah in the Jerusalem Temple (Isa 6:1–3).

This hymn is repeated two times, thus setting the tone for the Holy Monday liturgical continuum: a watchful longing for the Bridegroom's unpredictable ("in the middle of the night") return, which should be regarded as the prize for all faithful struggles in this transient life, struggles whose enigmatic and paradoxical value is intimated in and substantiated by Christ's willful Passion and death, enacted liturgically throughout the holiest period of the Byzantine rite's yearly cycle, that is, Holy Week.

The First Fruits of the Lord's Passion

The present day [*parousa hēmera*] carries resplendently the first fruits [*aparchas*] of the Lord's Passion. Come, O feast lovers, to encounter [him] [*hypantēsōmen*] with canticles [*asmasin*]! For the Creator comes to accept [*katadexasthai*] cross, trials [*etasmous*] and scourges [*mastigas*], being judged by Pilate, by reason of which he is struck [*rhapistheis*] by a servant on the head [*korrēs*]. He accepts [*prosietai*] it all so that he may save humanity. Therefore, let us cry: "O Lover of Humanity, Christ the God, give forgiveness of failings [*ptaismatōn*] to the ones who worship in faith your undefiled Passion [*ta achranta Pathē*]." (Holy Monday, Matins, Kathisma, Sticheron)

"The present day carries resplendently the first fruits of the Lord's Passion [*tōn Pathōn tou Kyriou tas aparchas, hē parousa hēmera lamprophorei*]"
From the outset, this hymn sets the tone for Holy Monday in particular and for Holy Week in general. Holy Monday brings "resplendently"[21] the "first

fruits"[22] of the Lord's Passion, introducing the participants, the faithful, to the sacred drama of the Passion. The plural neuter noun *tōn Pathōn*,[23] "Passion," connotes the Passion of Christ as a multifaceted and intricate narrative beginning with Jesus's agony and arrest, his betrayal, trials, sufferings, and death on the cross and ending with his burial.

"Come, O feast lovers, to encounter [him] with canticles [*deute oun phileortoi hypantēsōmen asmasin*]"
The hymnographer invites the faithful to come and meet the saving Lord. The verb used here, *hypantaō*, "to encounter," echoes John 12:18, where a Jerusalem crowd came forth to meet (*hypēntēsen*) Jesus on Palm Sunday, for they heard that he had resurrected Lazarus of Bethany. Thus, the faithful are urged by the hymn's composer to imitate the gospel's protagonists, to actualize the gospel message at the level of liturgical performance and participation. Anyone present at the Matins service of Holy Monday is about to encounter the Lord of Passion with canticles (*asmasin*),[24] thus carrying on the Palm Sunday festal tenor into Holy Week.

"For the Creator comes to accept cross [*ho gar Ktistēs erchetai, stauron katadexasthai*]"
The hymnographer equates the "Lord" (*Kyrios*) from the previous line with the "Creator" (*Ktistēs*).[25] The newness lies not with this very correlation[26] but rather with the qualifier of the word "Lord" in our hymn. He is not simply the "Lord" (Heb. YHWH, "Yahweh"—the invisible and almighty God worshiped by the ancient Hebrews); nor is he solely the Son of God before incarnation, as on the dome mosaic of St. Mark in Venice, where the Creator is portrayed as Christ.[27] What is shocking, and here the daring creativity of the liturgist stands out, is the dramatic correlation, or rather the sharp and ticklish contrast, between the Creator of all, emanating power and forethoughtfulness, and the "Lord of Passion" (*Kyrios tōn Pathōn*), Jesus Christ, the incarnate Logos, the Son of God made man, *willing* to accept the cross, displaying weakness and humility at the hands of an anonymous and petty mob within a seemingly God-forgotten time and place.

And this suffering Lord, identified with the powerful Creator, "is coming" (*erchetai*),[28] in a liturgical way, to willfully and generously accept (*katadexasthai*)[29] the cross (*stauron*),[30] a catch-all term for all Christ's sufferings including the agonizing and horrifying death by crucifixion.

"Trials and scourges [*etasmous kai mastigas*]"

The terms *etasmos*[31] and *mastix*[32] occur in the same text (Jdt 8:27). However, as a lexical collocation or compound, that is, next to each other, they appear only in 2 Macc 7:37 ("the martyrdom of seven Maccabee brothers"),[33] where a strikingly resolute mother urges her youngest son "to accept death" (*epidexai ton thanaton*)[34] (2 Macc 7:29) as his six brothers did, thus refusing to obey King Antiochus IV Epiphanes's order to deny the God of Israel.[35]

The unnamed son replies: "Like [my] brothers, I give up [*prodidōmi*] [my] body and soul for our ancestral laws [*patriōn nomōn*] calling upon [*epikaloumenos*] God to be quickly merciful to [our] nation and with trials [*etasmōn*] and scourges [*mastigōn*] to make you acknowledge [*exomologēsasthai*] that he alone is God" (2 Macc 7:37).

The Byzantine hymn carries on the theological idea of 2 Macc 7 where the martyr's death has a substitutionary value: the youngest brother's death along with the deaths of his brothers will "bring to an end the Almighty's wrath [*pantokratoros orgēn*] which fell on the whole nation" (2 Macc 7:38). Similarly, in our hymn, the Lord's willful and obedient acceptance of cross, "trials and scourges" (*etasmous kai mastigas*), will bring salvation to a fallen humanity ("so that he may save humanity").

There is a good chance that the hymnographer barrowed the lexical collocation "trials and scourges" from 2 Macc 7:37, the only place in the entire LXX where this phrase may be found. However, "trials and scourges," remarks the hymnographer, are accepted graciously and willfully by the Lord, while in the biblical text, the youngest son hopes that through "trials and scourges," God will make the tyrant king confess that he alone is God.[36] Thus, the discrepancy between 2 Macc 7 and the hymn concerns the recipient of these "trials and scourges": the persecuting king in the former, the humble suffering Christ in the latter, who, ironically, is labeled "The *King* of the Jews" (Matt 27:37; Mark 15:26; Luke 23:38; John 19:21; emphasis added). Since the phrase "trials and scourges" is borrowed directly from 2 Macc 7, a text about martyrdom and the underlining substitutionary role of the sufferings and death of these proto-martyrs, one may assume that the hymnographer saw in the seven brothers, and primarily in the youngest one, a prefiguration of the "Lord of Passion."[37]

In all likelihood, the poet created a sui generis typology by transposing a biblical phrase into a liturgical hymn, while diverting the initially intended recipient of "trials and scourges"—the king—and applying this phrase to Christ.[38] Even though the collocation "trials and scourges" in 2

Macc 7:37 describes God's disciplinary punishment of a tyrant, Antiochus IV Epiphanes, the hymnographer employs it as a redirected pointer to the proto-martyrs, the Maccabean brothers, a foreshadowing of Jesus, the Lord of Passion. It is not any longer the tyrant king who will endure the plagues but rather the Lord of Passion who will accept them voluntarily and generously to save humanity.

The hymnographer saw another parallel between Jesus and the seven brothers: both parties were judged by foreign pagan rulers, Antiochus IV Epiphanes, the Seleucid king, and Pilate, the Roman governor. There is, perhaps, another reason the liturgist borrowed the phrase "trials and scourges" from 2 Macc 7:37 and applied it to the hymn. In both cases, Jewish saintly individuals, the seven brothers and Jesus, were tried and tested with pain ("scourges")[39] at the behest of foreign authorities ruling over Palestine at their respective times.

The plural *etasmous*, "trials," in the hymn hints at Jesus's several trial (i.e., testing) appearances. On the night of his arrest, Jesus was taken in front of the high priests Annas and Caiaphas and the Sanhedrin, the Jewish religious court (John 18:19–24; Matt 26:57). Later, he was brought before Pilate, the Roman governor (John 18:28), and "King" Herod (Luke 23:7) and back to Pilate (Luke 23:11–12), who ultimately sentenced him to death by crucifixion (Mark 15:15).

The noun *mastigas*, "scourges," alludes to the flagellation Jesus received from the Roman soldiers on Friday morning in the Praetorium[40] courtyard: "So Pilate, wishing to satisfy the crowd, released Barabbas for them; and after flogging Jesus, he handed him over to be crucified" (Mark 15:15); "Then, Pilate took Jesus and scourged [*emastigōsen*] [him]" (John 19:1). Note that John 19:1, referring to the same flagellation episode, uses the verb *mastigoō*, "to scourge, to flog" whence the noun *mastigas*, "scourges," derives. According to Roman law, scourging was administered prior to the crucifixion (Matt 27:26).

"Being judged by Pilate by reason of which, he is struck by a servant on the head [*Pilatō krinomenos hothen kai ek doulou rhapistheis epi korrēs*]"
According to the Passion narrative in the canonical gospels (Matt 26:30–27:66; Mark 14:26–15:47; Luke 22:39–23:56; John 18:1–19:42), the trial, with its two phases, political and religious, represents an important aspect or moment on the Via Crucis. If the plural noun *etasmous*, "trials," discussed above alludes to Jesus's two-phase trial (political and religious), the phrase "judged by Pilate" refers to Jesus's two appearances in front of the Roman

governor (John 18:28; Luke 23:11–12). In this hymn, "judged [*krinomenos*] by Pilate" precedes "by reason of which is he struck [*rhapistheis*] by a servant on [his] head."

The presence of the adverb *hothen* ("whence, hence, that is why, by reason of which, consequently") between the two details ("being judged by Pilate" and "struck by a servant on [his] head") makes one read these details consequentially, with the latter as part of or, more precisely, a consequence of the former. This can be seen in the following canonical gospel account: "Then the soldiers led him into the courtyard of the palace (that is, the governor's headquarters); and they called together the whole cohort. And they clothed him in a purple cloak; and after twisting some thorns into a crown, they put it on him. And they began saluting him, 'Hail, King of the Jews!' They struck his head with a reed, spat upon him, and knelt down in homage to him" (Mark 15:16–19 [NRSV]).

"He accepts it all so that he may save humanity [*ta panta prosietai, hina sōsē ton anthrōpon*]"
There is an important difference between the verb *prosiēmi* and a similar verb, *katadechomai*, used a bit earlier in the hymn. *Katadechomai* implies "to accept generously/willfully," that is, to accept (*dechomai*) it all "down" (*kata-*) there in the heart, as a first move of the heart. So the first step was Jesus's acceptance of the cross, out of his heart's immense generosity. *Prosiēmi* means "to accept as reasonable (true, valid, right, feasible, tolerable)." This verb appears in classical and patristic literature[41] but is absent from the Bible. One can notice a gradation in Jesus's acceptance of the cross: from the emotional/volitive to the rational level. The hymn depicts Jesus's acceptance of the Passion as perfect, involving *all* of his personality: heart, mind, soul, and will.

"Therefore, let us cry: 'O Lover of Humanity [*Philanthrōpe*], Christ the God'"
The invitation to participate in the liturgical chorus is followed by a strong proclamation of Jesus's divinity: "Christ *the* God." The definite article *ho* in front of *theos*, "God," is meant to reiterate that Christ, the Lord of Passion, who accepted *all* for the salvation of *all* humanity, is *the* very God. This line and the above-quoted one where the Lord of Passion is identified with the Creator echo Gregory of Nazianzus's (ca. 325–389) powerful words, "We needed a God who took flesh and was put to death, so that we might live, and we were put to death with him," a "crucified God" (*Oration* 45.28).[42]

"Give forgiveness of failings [*ptaismatōn*]"
The noun *ptaisma* ("failing," from the verb *ptaiō*, "to cause to fall, stumble, fail," sinning as falling away from God's path) occurs only once in LXX (1 Sam 6:4, "offense" [NETS]). Sin is here described as failing, shortcoming.

"Your undefiled Passion [*ta achranta Pathē sou*]"
The theological gist of this hymn is condensed in the adjective *achrantos*, "spotless, undefiled, immaculate," as singling out Christ's Passion.[43] Any human suffering, even the most painful or terrifying, is unavoidably tainted by a natural propensity for self-victimization or individualistic spirituality. Christ's sufferings, alone, are pure, immaculate, spotless, undefiled. For he alone, as Son of God made flesh, can—and in fact *did*—accept the cross with the entire mourning cortège, out of pure generosity, free will, and thoughtfulness. He alone, with no constraint from outside, neither precalculated intent nor cautiously projected goal, but merely out of genuine love, unshakable willfulness, and mature thoughtfulness, accepted it to save all of humanity with no gender, racial, or national constraints—but the *very* humanity (*anthrōpos*) concentrated in the first human being shaped by God (Gen 2:7), the primordial Adam—both collectivity and individuality, and reconfigured for eternity by Christ, the *eschatos Adam* (1 Cor 15:45), the "final (version of) Adam," through his willful, thoughtful, and generous Passion to be again and again, both collectively and individually, a restored humanity.

Joseph the Chaste

Jacob lamented [*ōdyreto*] Joseph's loss [*sterēsin*] while the noble [one] [*gennaios*] was seated on a chariot, honored as a king. For by not enslaving [*douleusas*] himself then to the Egyptian woman's lusts [*hēdonais*], he was glorified in return [*antedoxazeto*] by the one who looks at humans' hearts and freely bestows [*nemontos*] the indestructible crown [*stephos aphtharton*]. (Holy Monday, Matins, Kontakion)

With this hymn, featuring Jacob and Joseph, as well as with the thematically similar hymns that follow, the listener is introduced to the core of the "Joseph Cycle" (Gen 37–50), the largest narrative block of Genesis 12–50 ("Patriarchal History").[44]

The basic structure of the Joseph Cycle is as follows:[45]

37:2–36	Joseph sold by his brothers into Egypt	
38:1–30	Tamar and Judah	
39:1–20	Joseph and Potiphar	A
39:21–40:23	Joseph in prison	B
41:1–57	Joseph in the palace	C
42:1–38	First visit of Joseph's family to Egypt	A′
43:1–45:28	Second visit of Joseph's family to Egypt	B′
46:1–47:31	Third visit of Joseph's family to Egypt	C′
48:1–50:26	Last days of Jacob and Joseph	

As one can see (and read), the Joseph story is a "long short story" displaying "suspense, irony, and romance embedded in a plot that features sibling rivalry, unwanted affection, false rape charges, a heroic rise to power, a recognition scene, a famine, family survival, and ultimate redemption."[46]

Regarding the hymn under examination, it has a sort of chiastic structure, i.e., ABB'A'. There are four ideas:

A Jacob lamenting the loss of his son
B Joseph being honored as a sort of second king over Egypt
B′ Joseph resisting the temptations of Potiphar's wife
A′ God, the one who looks at and into men's hearts, glorifying Joseph

As mentioned, this is a sort of chiastic structure, because A′ does not obviously match A, unless one considers Jacob a symbol or type for God himself. I would label this a "chiastic typology." By such a "limping" chiasm, the liturgist invites the listener or reader to ponder a little bit more over the relationship between A and A′ and eventually see in Jacob a *type* of God, with Joseph's saga unfolded between his own father's kind love and his God's providence.

Let us take a closer look at this interesting chiasm.

A Jacob lamented Joseph's loss
B while the noble [one] was seated on a chariot, honored as a king

In A–B, the author of this hymn strikes a sharp contrast between Jacob's lament over Joseph's loss (Gen 37:34–35) and the latter's ascension to power in Egypt (Gen 41:41–43). Juxtaposing (i.e., *kai*, "and, while") these two moments, many years apart from each other, the hymnographer emphasizes the father's unalleviated and continuous pain caused by the sudden and mysterious disappearance of his beloved son. It is as if one is watching a wide movie screen equally divided into two panels—a "split screen"—with a father bewailing and a son in full glory, neither of the two knowing about the other's welfare but both being painfully unable to intercommunicate. A question arises: what is the poet's intention beyond these frozen contrasting screenshots?

Prior to answering this question, let us examine how the hymnographer depicts Jacob. He is not merely "weeping" (*klaiō*) or "mourning" (*pentheō*), as the Bible suggests: "Then Jacob tore his garments and put sackcloth on his loins, and he mourned [*epenthei*] for his son many days. And all his sons and daughters gathered together and came to comfort him, and he would not be comforted, saying, 'I shall go down to Hades mourning [*penthōn*] my son.' And his father wept [*eklausen*] for him" (Gen. 37:34–35).

But in the hymn, Jacob is "lamenting" (verb *odyrō*).[47] By such a lexical preference, the hymnographer turns Jacob's mere weeping into a lengthy and profound lament with theological and spiritual overtones, thus fully incorporating a biblical episode into its new liturgical matrix dominated by various lamentations over Christ's Passion.[48]

Another kontakion of Matins of Holy Monday expounds the theme of the father lamenting over his son, using the same lexical toolkit ("lamenting," "un-enslaving," "lording over Egypt," and "indestructible crown") as in the already quoted hymn, while heightening the emotional level of the lament by adding two powerful brushes: "pouring out tears" and being thoroughly "crushed" over a lost "praiseworthy and chaste" Joseph: "To lament let us add now lament, and with Jacob let us pour out tears [*ekcheōmen*], crushed [with him] [*synkoptomenoi*] over Joseph, the praiseworthy [*aoidimon*] and chaste [*sōphrona*], who was enslaved in body, but kept his soul un-enslaved, and lorded over the entire Egypt. For God grants his servants an indestructible crown" (Holy Monday, Matins, Kontakion).

At this point, one may raise the question: did the liturgist really intend to create a typology[49] between A (Jacob) and A´ (God), or is this simply an educated guess of a modern reader? Upon a minute search of the hymnic material spread over various services of the Byzantine rite, no precise evidence of a Jacob–God typology has been detected, though there are some liturgical depictions of Jacob that might suggest such a daring analogy.

Among Church Fathers dealing with the Joseph story, Caesarius of Arles (470–543) is perhaps the boldest by striking a typological link between Jacob and God the Father. Thus, he writes in one of his sermons *On Blessed Joseph*: "Behold, we have heard that blessed Jacob begot a son and called his name Joseph, and that he loved him more than the rest of his sons. In this place, blessed Jacob prefigured God the Father; holy Joseph typified our Lord and Savior. Therefore, Jacob loved his son because God the Father loved His only begotten Son, as He Himself said: 'This is my beloved Son' [Matt 3:17]" (*Sermon* 89.1).[50]

Likewise, Ambrose of Milan sees in Jacob a type of God the Father: "Therefore, Joseph was sent by his father to his brothers, or rather by that Father 'who has not spared his own Son but has delivered him for us all,' by that Father of whom it is written, 'God, sending his Son in the likeness of sinful flesh' [Rom 8:3]" (*On Joseph* 3.9).[51]

For Ambrose, Jacob typifies God the Father, who in a mystical way worked through Jacob when the latter sent out Joseph to check on his brothers' fate with their flock. Nevertheless, Ambrose acknowledges that there is a problem with Jacob–God typology. How could Jacob be a type of God by sending out his son and at the same time rebuking Joseph for interpreting his dreams of greatness? By doing this, remarks Ambrose, Jacob is even a *better* type of God, for the latter loves everyone, including the lost sheep of Israel represented by Joseph's brothers—and perhaps by extension the flock they are watching.[52]

Relying on the primary and well-established Joseph–Christ typology, Cyril of Alexandria (376–444) subtly parallels Jacob's deeds to God's works in Jesus Christ, thus inclining himself toward a Jacob–God sort of analogy: "And Joseph was loved by his father a great deal. And he gave him a multicolored garment as an excellent gift and a proof of the love with which he accompanied him. . . . The multicolored garment is the symbol of the multiform glory with which God the Father clothed the Son made similar to us through his human nature" (*Glaphyra on Genesis* 6.4).[53]

Gleaning from the patristic evidence just mentioned, and taking into account the chiastic structure of the hymn, one may conclude, at least as a working hypothesis, that the hymnographer's intention was to build a parallel between Jacob lamenting his son's loss and God the Father surveying human history and preparing an indestructible crown for Joseph and his Son, whose typological relationship is well evidenced throughout patristic writings[54] and liturgical hymns, as we will see.

For John Chrysostom (347–407), God's "silence" during Joseph's trials resulted in Joseph being crowned by God with a "resplendent garland (crown)":

> After hearing this, let us never despair in the midst of distress or become frustrated by following our own reasoning. Rather, let us give evidence of sound endurance and be buoyed up by hope, secure in the knowledge of our Lord's resourcefulness and the fact that instead of ignoring us and abandoning us to the experience of troubles, he wants to crown us with a resplendent garland for our struggles. . . . Far from being surprised or troubled, let us endure developments with complete fortitude and endurance, having regard not to the distress but to the gain accruing to us from it. (*Homilies on Genesis* 63.19–21)[55]

Returning to the two aforementioned frozen screenshots, namely, those of Jacob lamenting and Joseph lording over Egypt, there is a nagging question—or, rather, a brace of questions—to be answered. *Why* did Joseph not inform his mourning father about his life's twist? And *why* did Joseph want to prolong his aging father's suffering by not telling him the truth that he was alive and well?

A common explanation, though not entirely satisfying, is to see here again Joseph's trust in God who knows and controls everything in this world, hence his silence or passive attitude to allow God to do as he wills. In support of such an interpretation, one may adduce the whole story of Joseph and his brothers along with the message ingrained in it that everyone needs to self-correct before human and divine forgiveness and reconciliation may be effectuated. Jacob's weakness is his love for Joseph (Gen 37:3) at the expense of the other children, which, as any contemporary book on parenting will underline, is a terrible approach to being a good father. Through a series of meetings between an as-yet-unrecognized Joseph and his brothers, Jacob comes to realize and appreciate the unique value of each son about to be lost.[56]

B   While the noble [one] was seated on a chariot, honored as a king
B′   for by not enslaving himself then to the Egyptian woman's lusts

The lines B and B′ in the analyzed hymn refer to Joseph in two different moments: his accession to power in Egypt and resisting the sexual overtures of Potiphar's wife.

Reading the Joseph Cycle, one notices that Joseph is *not* the typical patriarch who would bring sacrifices to his God or raise loud prayers and make
solemn promises as his forefathers did. Unlike the great patriarchs Abraham,
Isaac, and Jacob, who embody the people of Israel as a whole, Joseph may be
identified rather with *any* individual human trying to do the best with his or
her lot in life.[57]

Nonetheless, Joseph exudes a firm trust[58] in God who has a plan replete
with various opportunities, and human beings should be ready to grasp them
when the time comes by using their minds and God-given gifts. Through
patience and perseverance, Joseph comes to discern, even in the most troublesome times of his life, God's subtle presence, his plan, and providence.[59]
God is in control of history, and humans need to live their lives as Joseph
did, with respect toward other human beings, always ready to forgive others'
trespasses, while having a deep fear of God whose plan has been set in
motion.

Here are Joseph's wise and reconciling words addressed to his brothers at
the end of this tear-jerking novella: "And now do not be distressed, or angry
with yourselves, because you sold me here; for God sent me before you to
preserve life" (Gen 45:5 [NRSV])" and "You took counsel [*ebouleusasthe*]
against me [*kat'emou*] for evil things [*ponēra*], but God took counsel for
me [*peri emou*] for good things [*agatha*], that many people might be fed
[*diatraphē*] as today [*hōs sēmeron*]" (Gen 50:20).[60]

Returning now to the hymn, there is a slight yet quite significant reversal
in the order of events regarding Joseph's journey through life. If in the Joseph
Cycle, the accession to power follows Joseph's refusal of the pleasant lures
of Potiphar's wife, in the hymn, the latter precedes the former: "the noble
[one] was seated on a chariot, honored as a king. For by not enslaving himself then [*tote*] to the Egyptian woman's lusts." The two episodes are linked
together by the adverb *tote*, "then, at that time," which functions here as a
pointer. In other words, the hymnographer seems to tell a slightly different
story from the one found in the Bible. "At that time" (*tote*) points to the time
when Joseph was honored as a king, when he acceded to power (Gen 41:41–
44). Thus read, the Joseph story gains a momentous ethical overtone: Joseph,
though rich and powerful, was reserved and made use of the God-given gift
of self-restraint, continence, purity, or chastity and avoided succumbing or
"enslaving himself to the Egyptian woman's lusts."[61] The gist of this hymn
is Joseph's self-restraint and chastity in front of temptations coming from a
woman of lust.

Byzantine hymnography,[62] as well as patristic literature, has always seen in Joseph a model of self-restraint (*sōphrōn*). The first recorded text where *sōphrōn* occurs with Joseph, 4 Macc 2:2, explicates why this patriarch was so popular at that time and afterward: "The chaste [*ho sōphrōn*] Joseph is lauded [*epaineitai*] for by mental effort [*dianoia*] he controlled [*periekratēsen*] self-indulgence [*hēdypatheias*]."

There is no equal to Romanos the Melodist among Byzantine hymnographers exposing in so much detail the temptation Joseph successfully resisted. In the past, based on manuscript evidence, two kontakia by Romanos and an anonymous third, each entitled "On Joseph," were to be chanted or intonated on Holy Monday. In spite of the fact that Holy Monday has two main themes, the "chaste Joseph" and the "cursing of the fig tree," there is no evidence in the lectionary tradition that Gen 39 (Joseph being tempted by Potiphar's wife) has ever been a lection for Holy Monday.

In one of Romanos's kontakia, the confrontation between the seducing woman and the chaste young man translates into a fight between the devil, on the side of Potiphar's wife, and the female personification of "Temperance" or "Chastity" (*sōphrosynē*): "with his hands [the devil] grabbed the dashing athlete tightly, but then Sophrosyne too moved into the battle, eager to untie their grip; and she said: 'Let his clothes be torn off, but let not the body of the temperate man be violated!' "[63]

In a letter addressed to Gregory of Nazianzus, Basil of Caesarea (330–379), in speaking about reading the Scriptures for models of moral and ethical living, praises Joseph's chastity and virtuous life: "The lover of chastity [*sōphrosynēs*] constantly peruses the story of Joseph, and from him learns what chaste conduct [*tas sōphronikas*] is, finding Joseph not only continent as regards carnal pleasures [*enkratōs pros hēdonas*] but also habitually inclined towards virtue [*ektikōs pros aretēn*]" (*Letter* 2.6.12–15).[64]

For Chromatius of Aquileia (d. 407), Joseph is the premier biblical model of chastity: "But the holy man considered that prison to be a palace; and Joseph himself was a palace in his prison, because where faith, chastity and modesty are, there the palace of Christ is, the temple of God, the dwelling of the Holy Spirit. . . . In the church there are three models of chastity that everybody must imitate: Joseph, Susanna [Sus / Dan 13] and Mary. May men imitate Joseph, women Susanna and the virgin Mary" (*Sermon* 24.2).[65]

Caesarius of Arles remarks that Joseph could even be considered a martyr because he *suffered* in defense of chastity: "Now when Joseph was accused by his [would-be] mistress, he refused to say that she was guilty, because as a

just man he did not know how to accuse anyone; . . . I might have said Joseph
was more blessed when he was cast into prison, for he endured martyrdom
in defense of chastity. The gift of purity is a great thing, even when it is preserved without danger, but when it is defended, although at the risk of personal safety, then it is crowned still more fully" (*Sermon* 92.4).[66]

Now, if one correlates Joseph's chastity and resistance to this temptation
with the patriarch's patient and humble endurance[67] in situations of pain
(e.g., becoming a slave sold by his brothers to the Ismaelites and his stay in
the Egyptian dungeon, mentioned in Gen 37–50 yet mysteriously absent
in liturgical material), then a possible connection with Jesus's similar experience may loom at the horizon of our investigation. The synoptic gospels
witness Jesus being tempted three times by the devil in the wilderness after
his baptism (Matt 4:1–11; Luke 4:1–13). Moreover, Jesus walks through the
"midst of death's shadow" (Ps 23 [22]:4) with patient endurance. Recapping
both, Joseph and Jesus were tempted with two kinds of temptations, *pleasurable* and *painful*, and both, through self-restraint and patient endurance,
emerged victorious from this circle.[68]

There is yet another possible similarity between Joseph and Jesus in enduring patient suffering. Both drank their bitter chalice's potion, both had
their share of suffering, and both displayed a profound and genuine meekness and humility. Ordinary human beings are inclined, while experiencing
pain, to blame others, including God, for their misfortunes. Nevertheless,
both Joseph and Jesus refused that ultimate "pleasure" or relief of the one
who suffers unjustly that Job's wife pointed to in her request to a suffering
and rejected husband: "Are you still strong in your integrity [*b-tmmtk*]?
Blaspheme [*brk*][69] God and die!" (Job 2:9 [MT]; cf. Isa 8:21; Rev 16:11).[70]
However, of course, neither Joseph nor Jesus took that path. Instead, both
accepted suffering patiently, humbly, while strongly believing that God was in
control and they were part of a divine plan or will. Moreover, having endured
suffering, they were able to forgive those who inflicted suffering on them
(Joseph forgives his brothers, and Jesus does the same with those who crucified him).[71]

Both, Joseph and Jesus displayed pure and perfect obedience to God's
will—no complaint, no accusation, not even a grief-relieving lament such
as the one imagined by Nikephoros Basilakes, a twelfth-century Byzantine
writer, who depicts Joseph lamenting over the misfortunes he experienced
because of others' envy[72] or unchaste love: "Surely, I was born for misfortune!
Though committing no wrong, I have become a slave, and though being

chaste, I am nonetheless being punished! A band of my brothers has betrayed our natural ties, and my mistress, though a woman, has not observed the ways of chaste women. First, the envy of my brothers destroyed me, and now in turn love has taken the field against me; I am undone both by envy and by love. Alas, how unlucky I am, both when I am hated and when I am loved."[73]

Ephrem the Syrian, in his sermon in verse *On Joseph the Most Virtuous*, imagines Joseph in a similar lamenting attitude. Alone in the midst of sufferings and temptations, Joseph laments and prays to his parents, Jacob, still alive, and Rachel, already dead:

> "Weep, father, for your child, and your son for his father, for thus have I been parted from childhood from your face. Who will give me a dove, moaning to bring proof to you that it may come and announce my weeping to your old age? My tears are exhausted, father, and my groans; my voice has given out; and there is none to help. . . ." When Joseph saw the tomb of his mother Rachel, he ran forward and fell upon the grave, and lifting up his voice, with tears he raised a loud lament and cried out in the bitterness of his soul, saying, "Rachel, Rachel, my mother, rise from the dust and look on Joseph, whom you loved, what he has become. See, how he is being led as a prisoner into Egypt, handed over as a malefactor into the hands of foreigners. . . . Open to me, mother, and receive me in your tomb. Let your tomb become one bed for me and you." (*On Joseph the Most Virtuous* 236–241, 273–280, 283–284)[74]

In the following passage from Ephrem the Syrian's *On Joseph the Most Virtuous*,[75] Joseph, in resisting temptations, is compared with Jesus, who condescended to go down to Hades so that he might destroy the power of Satan: "And as Joseph within the marriage chamber trampled down all the strength of sin, putting on the bright prizes of victory, against the Egyptian woman, his mistress, so too the Lord, the Savior of our souls, by his own right hand, descending into Hades, destroyed there all the power of the dread and near invincible tyrant. When Joseph had conquered sin, he was put in prison until the hour of his crowning; so too the Lord, that he might take away every sin of the world, was placed in a grave" (lines 54–65).[76]

The typological use of the Joseph story in patristic literature,[77] and more particularly in early Syriac writings,[78] began with the Bible itself,[79] continued with later biblical writings, and spread throughout the Jewish,[80] Christian, and Islamic traditions.[81]

The last line in the above-examined hymn, mentioning the "indestructible crown" given by God to athletes against temptations, may be read in conjunction with the following lines from Ephrem's sermon in verse: "Joseph took his seat in Pharaoh's chariot, having received authority over the whole of Egypt; while our Savior, king before the ages, ascending into heaven on a cloud of light, took his seat with glory at the Father's right hand, above the Cherubim, as Only-begotten Son" (lines 78–83).[82]

The retellings of the Joseph narrative attributed to the Syriac poet-exegetes, such as Aphrahat (fourth century) and Narsai (d. 503), are labeled "dramatic dialogue poems."[83]

Aphrahat uses a technique similar to the one found in Heb 11, where its author lists several biblical examples of faith. In the same way, Aphrahat gathers a number of biblical figures and themes to illustrate a point. Joseph is found in those examples where Aphrahat wants to discuss virtue, reversal of fate, and persecution of the righteous. Joseph is seen as perfect in purity before God, as attacked by Satan through a woman, and as the one by whom the Spirit speaks.[84]

Sometimes Aphrahat's lists of examples turn into "complex *syncrisis* or comparison-series."[85] After beginning with a short line, "The persecuted Joseph is a type of the persecuted Jesus,"[86] Aphrahat offers eighteen examples in which comparisons between Joseph and Jesus unfold. Here are a few lines: "Joseph's father loved him more than his brothers, and Jesus was the friend and beloved of his Father. . . . Joseph's brothers cast him into the pit; and the brothers of Jesus sent him down in the grave. Joseph came up from the pit, and Jesus arose from the grave. . . . Now, Joseph was sold into Egypt at the advice of Judah; and Jesus was delivered to the Jews by Judas Iscariot."[87]

Using the same hermeneutical comparative procedure, Narsai puts forward a new parallel, that between Reuben and Pilate: Reuben mediated for the life of Joseph (Gen 37:22); Pilate petitioned for the life of Jesus (cf. Matt 27:2–26, 58–66; Mark 15:1–15, 42–47; Luke 23:1–25, 50–53; John 18:28–19:22, 31, 38).[88]

In the following hymn also chanted on Holy Monday at Matins, the poet elaborates further on Joseph's self-control and purity, while interpreting the Egyptian woman's attempts to seduce the young Hebrew man as orchestrated by the "serpent" (*drakōn*), the devil, who tempted Adam through Eve:

Finding in the Egyptian [woman] a second Eve, through utterances, the serpent [*ho drakōn*] hurried up [*espeude*] with flatteries [*kolakeiais*] to make

Joseph stumble [*hyposkelisai*]. But this one leaving behind [his] garment [*chitōna*], fled from sin, and though naked, he was not ashamed, like the first-fashioned one [*prōtoplastos*] was before [his] disobedience [*parakoēs*]. At his intercessions, O Christ, have mercy on us. (Holy Monday, Matins, Idiomelon)

"Finding in the Egyptian [woman] a second Eve [*deuteran Euan Aigyptian*] through utterances [*rhēmatōn*], the serpent [*ho drakōn*]"
The meaning of the first line is that the serpent (i.e., the devil in disguise) identified a second Eve as instrument of his deceptive work using the same strategy as in the case of the first Eve: initiating a dialogue (*dia rhēmatōn*, "through utterances") with the woman.[89] According to Ambrose of Milan, the explanation of why the serpent spoke with Eve and not Adam is that God's commandment was addressed to Adam and not to Eve, hence her ignorance and vulnerability: "[The devil] aimed to circumvent Adam by means of the woman. He did not accost the man who had in his presence received the heavenly command. He accosted her who had learned of it from her husband and who had not received from God the command that was to be observed. There is no statement that God spoke to the woman. We know that he spoke to Adam. Hence we must conclude that the command was communicated through Adam to the woman" (*Paradise* 12).[90]

"Through utterances,"[91] the devil identified Potiphar's wife as a fitting means to make Joseph stumble. This is an interesting idea, for the first and greatest mistake of the first Eve (as well as the Egyptian woman's mistake, according to this hymn) is that she got sucked into dialogue with the serpent, knowing that he was "the most sagacious" (LXX: *phronimōtatos*; MT: ʿrwm, "the shrewdest") (Gen 3:1). In Ephrem the Syrian's view, the devil began the dialogue with Eve because, with him living as all animals did outside the Garden of Eden, the dialogue was the *only* way for him to learn all about the garden: "The serpent could not enter paradise, for neither animal nor bird was permitted to approach the outer region of paradise, and Adam had to go out to meet them; so the serpent cunningly learned, through questioning Eve, the character of paradise, what it was and how it was ordered" (*Hymns on Paradise* 3.4–5).[92]

In contrast, Christ showed his followers the right way to cope with the devil's crafty "utterances": remaining silent, not entering into dialogue, not flirting with the idea of sinning, but rather refuting sin the moment it touches one's mind, while placing full trust in God's living, creative, and powerful word. This is the way Jesus "responded"[93] to the devil's threefold temptation at the beginning of his public ministry (Matt 4:1–11; Luke 4:1–13).

The term *drakōn*, "serpent, dragon,"[94] is here used with reference to the primordial "serpent" (*ophis*), described as the "most sagacious" (*phronimōtatos*) creature, who seduced Adam and Eve to transgress God's commandment (Gen 3:1). In the New Testament and later in Christian writings, *drakōn* becomes a technical term for the devil (Rev 12:3, 7, 9; 20:2, called also the "serpent of old" [*ho ophis ho archaios*]).

The hymnographer places Potiphar's wife on par with Eve. The serpent (*drakōn*) equated here with the first tempter—the devil—found in the Egyptian woman a new Eve and quickly through words (*rhēmatōn*) and flatteries (*kolakeiais*) made the virtuous Joseph stumble (*hyposkelisai*).[95] However, both the Egyptian woman's attempts and the serpent's machinations behind the scene remained futile due to Joseph's refusal to sin.

Joseph's purity of heart is illustrated by a comparison: a naked Joseph (running from the voluptuous woman's grasp by leaving behind his garment) and a naked "first-fashioned" (*prōtoplastos*)[96] Adam prior to his "disobedience" (*parakoē*, lit. "mishearing, partial hearing");[97] both were unashamed of their nakedness (Gen 2:25; 39:13, 15), for both were self-controlled and obedient to God, hence the transparency and purity of their hearts.

In Christ's view, the ideal human condition is a "pure heart": everything begins and ends in man's heart. The moral, social "good" begins with the purity of one's heart. That is why one of the Beatitudes praises those "pure in heart" by rewarding them with God's contemplation: "Blessed [*makarioi*, lit. "happy, blissful"] are the pure in heart [*katharoi tē kardia*], for they will see God" (Matt 5:8). And purity of heart comes with obedience, as lack of purity is the result of disobedience or unwillingness to hear and/or listen.[98]

For John Chrysostom, and likewise for our hymnographer, disobedience (*parakoē*) caused Adam and Eve to feel shame. Commenting on Gen 3:7, 10, 11, Chrysostom notes: " 'They were both naked,' the text says, remember, 'and were not ashamed.' You see, while sin and disobedience had not yet come on the scene, they were clad in that glory from above which caused them no shame. But after the breaking of the law, then entered the scene both shame and awareness of their nakedness" (*Homilies on Genesis* 15.14).[99]

Along a similar line of thought is Augustine's interpretation of the proto-parents' purity as reflecting self-control and lack of rebellion against God: "[Man and woman] were aware, of course, of their nakedness, but they felt no shame, because no desire stirred their organs in defiance of their deliberate decision. The time had not yet come when the rebellion of the flesh was a witness and reproach to the rebellion of man against his Maker" (*City of God* 14.17).[100]

A hymn from Great Lent offers another example of the Joseph–Jesus typology.

> Jacob of old prefiguring [*protypōn*] your cross [*stauron sou*], O Christ, worshiped [*prosekynei*] the tip [*akron*] of Joseph's divine staff [*theias rhabdou*], foreseeing [*proopōmenos*] that frightening scepter [*skēptron phrikton*] of your Kingdom that now we worship faithfully into the ages. (Triodion, 43rd Day, Matins, Ode 8)[101]

In writing this hymn, the author was undoubtedly inspired by Heb 11:21 (Byz.): "Through faith [*pistei*], Jacob, while dying, blessed each of Joseph's sons, and bowed down [*prosekynēsen*] on the tip [*epi to akron*] of his staff [*rhabdou*]." This verse is part of the pericope on faith from Abraham to Joseph (Heb 11:17–22), "the catalogue of the faithful resumes."[102] According to the author of Heb 11, the patriarchs showed their faith nearer to their death. Heb 11:21 combines two texts taken from Genesis: 48:8–22 (Jacob blessing Joseph's two sons, Manasseh and Ephraim, giving priority to the younger) and 47:31 (a near-death Jacob visiting Joseph).

Gen 47:31 has two different readings. MT: "And he [Jacob] said, 'Swear to me.' And he [Joseph] swore to him. Then Israel bowed [*w-yšthw*] over the head of the bed [*ʿl-rʾš h-mṭṭh*]." LXX: "Then he said, 'Swear to me.' And he swore to him. And Israel bowed [*prosekynēsen*] on/over [*epi*] the tip [*to akron*] of his staff [*rhabdou*]."

The difference between MT and LXX of Gen 47:31 lies with the vocalization of the Hebrew consonantal word *mṭh*: *miṭṭāh*, "bed" (MT), and *maṭṭeh*, "staff" (LXX: *rhabdos*). According to the MT reading, Jacob, an old man, is leaning over the head of his son's bed, while after the LXX rendition, Jacob bows down on or over the tip of Joseph's staff in a sign of respect toward his son.

The author of Heb 11:21 reproduced the LXX text of Gen 47:31 and possibly understood Jacob's bowing down over the tip of Joseph's staff as a prophecy about and veneration of Joseph or someone else coming after him.[103] The phrase was interpreted by a few Church Fathers as referring to Joseph, Mary's fiancé and the legal father of Jesus.[104]

Comparing Heb 11:21 with the hymn above, one notices a slight yet significant difference. If the former text, following Gen 47:31, has *epi*, "on/over," the latter does not—hence two different meanings. In Heb 11:21, Jacob bows down on/over the tip of Joseph's staff in a sign of respect toward the owner of that staff;[105] in the hymn, Jacob "worships"[106] the "tip" (*akron*, as direct object) of Joseph's divine staff. Thus, Jacob's respect and veneration shift from Joseph to his "divine staff," prefiguring Christ's "cross" or the future "frightening scepter" of God's kingdom.

The hymn's Jacob–Joseph dyad reappears in Exod 1:5 as part of the lection (Exod 1:1–20) to be read on Holy Monday at the Vesperal Presanctified Liturgy.

The lection reads: "But all the souls which came out from the thigh of Jacob were seventy-five" (*ēsan de pasai psychai hai exelthousai ek mērou Iakōb pente kai hebdomēkonta*). Codex Vaticanus (fourth century) and Codex Alexandrinus (fifth century) for Exod 1:5 (there is no book of Exodus preserved in Codex Sinaiticus) have: "But all the souls from Jacob were seventy-five" (*ēsan de pasai psychai ex Iakōb pente kai hebdomēkonta*).

The lection adds *hai exelthousai*[107] *ek mērou*, "which came out from the thigh of Jacob" (cf. Theod.: *hai ek mērou*, "the ones from the thigh"; MT: *yṣ'y yrk-yʿqb*, "coming out of Jacob's thigh").[108] This addition underlines an important idea: *all* the Hebrews extant in Egypt were descendants of Jacob, a patriarch in his own right as were Abraham and Isaac before him.

The term *mēros*, "thigh," found in the lection is present for emphasis, pointing to two important Scriptures where *mēros* occurs, Gen 32:25 and 47:29–31. The first text refers to Jacob wrestling with an angel who eventually touches the thigh[109] of the patriarch to let him go even though Jacob asked the angel to bless him, which will happen by changing his name from Jacob to Israel ("May God prevail!").[110] In the second text, a near-death Jacob asks Joseph to swear, by placing his hand under the father's "thigh" (*hypo ton mēron*), that he will bury him in the burial place of his ancestors Abraham and Isaac in Canaan. In ancient times, the thigh (most likely a euphemism for genitalia)[111] was considered the source of posterity. Swearing an oath by placing the hand under the thigh means taking the future descendants as witnesses of that oath.[112] By this ritual, Joseph obeyed his father by making a solemn promise.

Another reason Joseph was viewed by ancient biblical interpreters and hymnographers as a type of Christ was the episode where his brothers stripped off his long robe, cast him into a pit, and sold him to some Ismaelite merchants going down to Egypt. This episode narrated in Gen 37 was related to Jesus's betrayal, arrest, and death. In the case of Joseph, who was sold by his brothers into slavery, God turned his sufferings into a means to save the people of Israel. So, too, with Jesus, judged and crucified out of envy, God turned the Passion of the Lord, who accepted his sufferings out of humility, into a means to save all humanity.

"Joseph accepting [*stergōn*][113] the ready obedience [*eupeitheian*][114] for [his] father, being cast into a pit [*lakkō*], he was sold as a prefiguration [*eis protypōsin*] of the sacrificed [*thyentos*] Christ, who was cast into the pit" (Sunday before Christmas, Matins, Ode 6).[115] But even the "pit," and later the Egyptian "dungeon," did not stifle Joseph's thirst for a virtuous life. John Chrysostom likens the virtue to a pearl that does not lose its preciousness even if cast into mud: "You notice how even when Joseph encountered troubles he had no sense of distress; instead, the creative Wisdom of God transformed all his distress. Just as a pearl reveals its peculiar beauty even if someone buries it in the mire, so too virtue, wherever you cast it, reveals its characteristic power, be it in servitude, in prison, in distress or in prosperity. So since, even when cast into prison, he won over the chief jailer and received from him control of everything there, let us see in this case as well how Joseph reveals the force of grace coming his way" (*Homilies on Genesis* 63.2).[116]

2

Loyalty

Three Youths in a Fiery Furnace—Holy Tuesday

Overview

Holy Tuesday's central theme is loyalty (faithfulness) and vigilance (watchfulness), tightly interconnected.

> On Holy and Great Tuesday, we make remembrance of the parable of the ten virgins [*parthenōn*] from the holy Gospel. (Synaxarion)

The "Midnight Bridegroom" theme, introduced on Holy Monday, continues on Holy Tuesday with more emphasis on watchfulness clearly conveyed by the parable of the ten virgins (Matt 25:1–13) read at this day's Vesperal Presanctified Liturgy.

While conspicuously absent in the Synaxarion, the story of the three Jewish youths (Dan 3), sneaked into the hymnography prescribed for Holy Tuesday, turns this day into a celebration of human loyalty to God, which only Jesus could fully reach in the midst of the turmoil of his last week.

Another example of unconditioned loyalty is Job. After having lost property and children, the man of Uz remains faithful to God, uttering his famous words of surrender: "I came out from my mother's womb naked and [so] I will depart in that place; the Lord has given, the Lord has taken away. As it seemed [good] to the Lord, thus happened. May the Lord's name be blessed" (Job 1:21 [LXX], part of Job 1:13-22 which is prescribed as a lection for this day's Presanctified Liturgy).

Compared to the faithfulness of the seven Maccabean brothers put to death by Antiochus IV Epiphanes (215–164 B.C.E.) for their reluctance to succumb to idolatry (2 Macc 7), the faithfulness of the three Jewish youths thrown into a fiery furnace (Dan 3) by the Babylonian king Nebuchadnezzar (605–562 B.C.E.) is of a higher level. If the Maccabean brothers based their faith on the final bodily resurrection, the three youths showed an unconditioned loyalty

Hearing the Scriptures. Eugen J. Pentiuc, Oxford University Press. © Oxford University Press 2021.
DOI: 10.1093/oso/9780190239633.003.0003

to their God, who is able to save, "and if not" (Dan 3:17–18 [Theod./MT]), they will remain loyal to him—very close to Jesus's perfect, unconditioned faithfulness expressed in his prayer in the Garden of Gethsemane: "My Father, if it is possible, remove this chalice from me. However, not as I will, but as you [will]" (Matt 26:39).

Although "martyrs" in the sense that they confessed their faith (Gk. verb *martyreō*, "to bear witness") in front of the Babylonian king, the three Jewish youths did not die as the Maccabean brothers did. God, "the one who holds life in his palm" (cf. Wis 3:1), sent his messenger ("angel," "someone like God's son") to turn the flames into dew. The three youths saved from death parallel Moses saved by Pharaoh's daughter from the Nile (Exod 2:5–10), a lection prescribed for this day's Vesperal Presanctified Liturgy.

This scene reminds one of the angel of the Lord who appeared to Moses from a "burning bush" (Exod 3:2), both cases offering an example of divine "condescension" (*synkatabasis*). The saving angel in Dan 3 provokes yet another intertextuality, namely, with 2 Macc 10:29–30 and the "five illustrious men on horses" who appeared from heaven to save the Judeans during a battle. Nevertheless, there is no greater example of *synkatabasis* in the salvation history than God descending in the midst of human misery and suffering through Jesus's freely assumed Passion.

The biblical episode of the three youths has generated several typologies attested in the hymns prescribed for this day: the Marian, Marian-Christological, Trinitarian, and Cross typologies. For the Marian-Christological typology, the hymnographer uses another text from the book of Daniel (7:9–10, with a "river of fire" and "thrones" in the final judgment setting) pertaining to Jesus's "second divine sojourn" (*theian deuteran epidēmian*).

Timeline: On Holy Tuesday, Jesus spends almost the entire day in the Temple area teaching the people and debating with the Pharisees on various matters of the Law (Matt 21:23–23:39). On his way back to Bethany to spend the night at his friend Lazarus's home, Jesus makes a stop on the Mount of Olives, where he decries the fate of Jerusalem while pointing to several signs announcing the end of this age and the final judgment—the gospel pericope known as the "Eschatological Discourse" (Matt 24–25).

Services and lections for Holy Tuesday: Matins (officiated by anticipation on Holy Monday evening), Matt 22:15–46; 23:1–39; Vespers and Presanctified Liturgy (officiated on Holy Tuesday), Exod 2:5–10; Job 1:13–22; Matt 24:36–51; 25:1–46; 26:1–2.

Analysis
Searching the Scriptures

The hymns gathered under the heading "The Three Youths in a Fiery Furnace" rely heavily on Dan 3. The biblical story can be summed up as follows.[1]

King Nebuchadnezzar erects a statue and orders everyone to worship it (Dan 3:1–7). Some Chaldeans come to the king and slander the Jews for not obeying the king's order (vv. 8–12). Asked by the king why they refuse to worship the statue, the three Jewish youths reply, as if not paying attention to the king, that no matter what God will do, they will not worship the idol (vv. 13–18). Angry at their evasive response, the king orders the three youths to be bound and cast down into the blazing fiery furnace (vv. 19–23). Conspicuously, although the prophet Daniel is mentioned along with the three youths in Dan 2:17, he is entirely absent in Dan 3.[2]

Dan 3:24 marks the climax of the story: the king, looking into the furnace, is astonished at what he sees. The three youths, along with someone like a "son of God," unbound and unharmed, are walking in the midst of the fire (vv. 24–25). The king, approaching the door of the furnace, calls upon the three "servants of the Most High God" to come out (vv. 26–27). The king publicly and unequivocally declares that the God of the three youths sent an "angel" to deliver them, and the king issues a punitive decree against all who would blaspheme the God of the three youths, then promotes the latter in the province of Babylon (vv. 28–30).

Almost at the center of this story is the puzzling statement in which the three youths "respond" to the king's inquiry about their refusal to worship the statue that he just erected. The response is found in Dan 3:17–18. Here are the three main textual witnesses of this passage.

MT: "*If the God whom we worship is able* [hn ʾyty . . . ykl l-šyzbwtnʾ] to deliver us from the blazing fiery furnace and from the hand of the king, he will deliver [us]. *And, if not, be it known to you* [wə-hēn lā yədîᵃᶜ lehĕwēʾ-lāk], O king, that we will neither revere your gods, nor will we do homage to your golden image that you set up" (emphasis added).

LXX: "*For there is a God in heavens* [esti gar theos en ouranois], our one [heis] Lord, whom we fear [hon phoboumetha], who is able [esti dynatos] to take us out [exelesthai] from the furnace [kaminou] of fire, and out of your hands, O king, *he will take us out! And then it will be clear for you* [tote phaneron soi] that we will neither bring service [latreuomen] to your idol, nor will we worship [*proskynoumen*] your golden image that you set up" (emphasis added).

Theod.: "*For there is a God*, whom we serve [*hō hēmeis latreuomen*], *able* [*estin . . . dynatos*] to take us out [*exelesthai*] from the furnace blazing [*kaiomenēs*] with fire, and out of your hands, O king, he will rescue [*rhysetai*] us. *And if not, be it known to you* [*kai ean mē gnōston estō soi*], O king, that we will neither bring service [*latreuomen*] to your idol, nor will we worship [*proskynoumen*] your golden image that you set up" (emphasis added).

For v. 17, the MT reading ("If the God whom we worship is able . . ."), far from expressing doubts about God's ability to save, conveys the three youths' humble though undeterred faith in God. The LXX and the Theod. found this conditional clause hard to accept, so both versions turned it into an assertion ("For there is a God [LXX: in heavens], who is able . . .").

For v. 18, according to the LXX reading ("[he will take us out!] *And then it will be clear for you* . . ."), the three youths are convinced that God is able to save, and, in fact, he will. However, based on the MT and Theod. readings ("*And if not, be it known to you* . . ."), the three youths are convinced of God's ability to save, but "*if not*," that is, if he will not intervene, they will still not worship the golden image.

Parenthetically, one might mention here that the second-century C.E. Theod. translation came to replace the LXX version of the book of Daniel (ca. 100 B.C.E., probably known to the author of 1 Macc). While the rest of the Old Testament writings found in Greek codices such as Vaticanus, Alexandrinus, and most manuscripts of the Greek Old Testament follow the LXX (Old Greek version), the book of Daniel is the only writing in these codices that follows the Theod.[3]

Summing up, according to the Aramaic text (MT) and the Theod., the confession of the three youths expresses their strong faith in and perfect surrender to God's will. While stressing God's ability to save, the three youths, in utter humbleness, do not force God's hand to save them. Thus, their faithfulness is fully unconditioned: God can save them, but *if not*, they will still remain faithful to God's will.[4] This unconditional loyalty is similar, to a certain degree, to the faithfulness of the seven Maccabean brothers (2 Macc 7). But, while the seven martyr brothers were encouraged by their mother (2 Macc 7:5, 21), who reminded them about the powerful Creator who will return the "breath and life" to them at the end of time (2 Macc 7:23, 28–29; cf. Gen 2:7), the three youths' faithfulness is pure loyalty to God, making the former and especially the latter servants a type of Jesus's perfect faithfulness to the heavenly Father shown plainly in the Garden of Gethsemane and on the cross.

Commenting on Dan 3:17–18, Theodoret of Cyrus (393–457), based on the Theod. reading, emphasizes this idea of the three youths' full surrender to God's will and providence.

> Far from serving our Lord for payment, we are motivated by affection and longing, and at the same time prefer the service of our God to everything. Hence, instead of asking for relief from the troubles unconditionally, we embrace the Lord's planning and providence; and without knowledge of what will be of benefit, we leave the helm to the pilot, no matter what he wishes, understanding clearly that he is able to free us from the threatened evils. Whether he wishes to do so, we do not know; but we leave it to him, wise governor as he is, and accept his verdict, confident that it is to our benefit. (*Commentary on Daniel* 1322–1324)[5]

After Dan 3:23 (LXX), the versions contain three additions: Prayer of Azariah (Pr Azar 1:1–22 [LXX/Theod.: Dan 3:24–45]), a fragment in prose (Pr Azar 1:23–27 [LXX/Theod.: Dan 3:46–50]), and the Song of the Three Youths (Pr Azar 1:28–68 [LXX/Theod.: Dan 3:51–90]).[6]

The fragment in prose (Pr Azar 1:23–27 [LXX/Theod.: Dan 3:46–50]) is probably the most important addition in terms of understanding the story of the three youths. Here is the fragment that inspired the liturgical hymns to be examined below:

> When the servants of the king cast them in, they did not stop heating the furnace; and when they threw the three [men] into the furnace at once, the furnace was extremely hot, heated sevenfold; and when they threw them, those who threw them were above them, and those below them were keeping the fire on with naphtha, fiber of flax, pitch, and brushwood. And the flame poured out above the furnace forty-nine cubits and broke out and burned those of the Chaldeans who were around the furnace. But an angel of the Lord came down in the furnace to be together with those who were with Azariah, and shook the flame of the fire out of the furnace and made the middle of the furnace as if a breeze of dew were whistling and the fire did not touch them at all, neither did it cause pain to, nor annoyed them. (Pr Azar 1:23–27 [LXX/Theod: Dan 3:46–50])[7]

This passage would explain the king's "amazement"[8] (Dan 3:24–25 [MT]; 3:91–92 [LXX/Theod.]). Here is the Theod. reading: "And Nebuchadnezzar heard them singing and was amazed [*ethaumasen*] and he rose hastily and he said to his nobles, 'Did we not throw three man bound in the middle of the fire?' And they said to the king, 'Truly, O king.' And the king said, 'Behold I see four men loose and walking about in the middle of the fire and there is no destruction on them, and the appearance of the fourth one is like that of a son of God.'"

Regarding the identity of the fourth figure in the furnace (Dan 3:25 [MT]; 3:92 [LXX/Theod.]), the king, looking inside the furnace, sees four figures, the fourth one having the likeness of "*a* son of gods"[9] (Aramaic *bar-ʾĕlāhîn*, indefinite), i.e., someone belonging to the divine sphere.[10] But note the LXX reading of Dan 3:92 [MT 3:25], *angelou theou*, "angel of God," and Theod., *hyiō theou*, "son of God." The Christian interpreters, based mostly, in the case of the book of Daniel, on the Theod. reading, interpreted the phrase *hyiō theou*, "son of God," with reference to *the* Son of God,[11] as one of his pre-incarnational appearances (theophanies), or, as we are going to see in some liturgical hymns, following the LXX reading *angelou theou*, "angel of God," they saw in the mysterious number four that appeared suddenly in the furnace a type of Christ rising from the tomb. The ancient Jewish tradition saw here either an angel[12] (e.g., Gabriel)[13] or God himself saving his faithful servants.[14]

Nebuchadnezzar calls the three youths out of the furnace by addressing them with the appellative "servants of the Most High God" (Dan 3:26 [MT]; 3:93 [LXX/Theod.]).[15] Note—not that it is exactly hard to miss, given the king's sudden conversion—that the title "Most High God" (MT: *ʾlhʾ ʿllyʾ* [Aramaic]; LXX: *ho theos ho hypsistos*) is an old Hebrew epithet for God (*ʾēl ʿelyôn*; cf. Gen 14:18).[16] The juxtaposition of "servants" referring to the three youths in the furnace and "Most High God" as a divine title alludes probably to their ancestral faith going back to the days of the great patriarchs.

In Dan 3:28 (MT; 3:95 LXX/Theod.), King Nebuchadnezzar surprisingly—astonishingly, given the fact that his rage has turned to benediction—blesses the God of the three youths who sent "his angel" (MT: *mlʾkh*; LXX: *angelon autou*)[17] to deliver his faithful servants. This verse matches quite well, if not exactly, with Pr Azar 1:26 (Dan 3:49 [LXX/Theod.]), which mentions that "an angel of the Lord descended into the furnace" (*angelos de kyriou synkatebē . . . eis tēn kaminon*). One may compare this saving appearance of "an angel" in the furnace to the shining descent of "five illustrious [men]" (*pente diaprepeis*) from heaven, mentioned in 2 Macc 10:29–30, who came to help Judas the Maccabee against Timothy, the leader of the Ammonites (after 164 B.C.E.).[18] The king's rather outlandish, and almost unbelievable, confession of the almightiness of the Jewish God is followed by his even more bizarre punitive decree against those who would dare blaspheme the God of the three youths (Dan 3:29 [MT]; 3:96 [LXX/Theod.]). The story, a royal court tale, ends with the promotion of the three youths to positions of prominence, thus establishing a leitmotif of transvaluation of power (cf. Dan 3:30 [MT]; 3:97 [LXX/Theod.]).[19]

In sum, then, Dan 3:1–30 ([MT]; LXX/Theod.: 3:1–97) is a story of robust faith, humble and obedient, which seeks no immediate and extraordinary release or rewards from the part of God.[20] The same humble obedience toward God is detected in 2 Macc 7 ("Martyrdom of the Seven Brothers"),[21] a text alluded to in one of the hymns read at the beginning of the Matins service on Holy Monday.[22]

Both texts, 2 Macc 7 and Dan 3, were employed by hymnographers (by decontextualizing and reassembling the biblical stories and turning them into a *collage*-type of liturgical hymns) in order to create the fitting ambience for telling a greater, more expansive story: that of Christ, who accepted the Passion with unmeasured humility and unparalleled obedience and who on the cross did not force God's hand to intervene for an immediate release or even temporary relief but rather gave his spirit peacefully and with complete trust in his heavenly Father.[23] There is an ineluctably strong similarity between Jesus and the three youths in terms of neither compromising with the opponents nor trying to "blackmail" God. Most likely, this was one of the reasons the liturgists chose Dan 3 as their inspiring text for some of the hymns to be chanted during Holy Week.

I would like to adduce here Heb 11:35 (the last section of the encomium on faith, Heb 11:1–40) as a hermeneutical key for the understanding of both the youths' and Jesus's complete surrender: "Women received their dead by resurrection [*ex anastaseōs*]. Others were tortured [*etympanisthēsan*], not accepting [*prosdexamenoi*] redemption [*apolytrōsin*], in order to obtain a better resurrection [*kreittonos anastaseōs*]" (Heb 11:35).

The first part of this seemingly cryptic and almost inexplicable verse refers to some "women" who received back their "dead" by "resurrection." This *could* be an allusion to the widow of Zarephath (1 Kgs 17:17–24) and her son resurrected by the prophet Elijah, along with the Shunammite woman (2 Kgs 4:18–37) whose son was resurrected by Elijah's protégé and successor, the prophet Elisha. But in contrast with these success stories, the second part of this verse speaks of people who were "tortured" (verb *tympanizō*) refusing to accept an immediate "redemption" but hoping for a "better resurrection." The verb *tympanizō* occurs only once in LXX (1 Sam 21:13 [14]), meaning "to pound as if on a drum," and once in the New Testament (Heb 11:35), meaning "to torment, to torture."

Heb 11:35 could be read as a hint at either the priest Eleazar (2 Macc 6:18–31, where the related noun, *tympanon*, lit., "drum," with a special meaning, "torture, rack," is used [vv. 19, 28]) or the seven martyr brothers who refused the king's offer of release and accepted martyrdom for the sake of resurrection (2 Macc 7:11, 14, 23, 24, 36). The contrast between the two parts of Heb 11:35 aims at making the following theological point: instead of accepting a temporary relief (comparable to the resurrection of the two sons, mentioned above, who eventually died or, if you prefer, "died again," like Lazarus in John's gospel, which renders these "resurrections" more like "resuscitations"), the Maccabean martyrs are lauded for longing after a *better* resurrection, namely, that resurrection at the end of time, which will usher in the eternal life of God's kingdom.[24]

Returning to Dan 3 and the Byzantine hymnography, I might add that there is yet another point in a series of connecting points between these hymns and the story of the three faithful youths. Initially intended as a story of divine intervention and deliverance, Dan 3 was probably read later, during the final redaction of the book of Daniel (including 12:1–3, the first clear biblical statement on the bodily resurrection at the end of time), as "metaphors of resurrection."[25] This shift from *temporary* deliverance to resurrection can also be detected in the liturgical typology (found in some hymns) between the three youths coming out of the furnace unharmed and Jesus coming out of his tomb alive. It is worth mentioning that the lectionary for Holy Saturday's Vesperal Liturgy contains Dan 3:1–2, 4–23, and the "Song of the Three Holy Youths" (Pr Azar 1:23–68; cf. Dan 3:46–90 [LXX/Theod.]).

Confessing God in a Fiery Furnace

The tyrannical decree [*tō dogmati tō tyrannikō*], the holy three youths not obeying [*mē peisthentes*], into the furnace being cast [*blēthentes*], they confessed God, singing [*psallontes*], "Bless the Lord, you works of the Lord." (Holy Tuesday, Matins, Ode 8, Heirmos)

The hymn exhibits a basic chiastic structure ABA' underlining the contrast between "not obeying the tyrannical decree" (A) and "confessing God, singing" (A'), a contrast intensified by an inserted note "into the furnace being cast" (B). The central gloss is for emphasis: the three youths were cast into furnace *due to their resistance*[26] to the tyrant's order, but in spite of the draconic punishment, they confessed God in song.

The hymnographer retells the biblical story in verse, using both contrast and emphasis to underline its gist: the three youths' faith is not contingent on anything external; it is merely, sheerly, the pure reflection of something rooted in the heart of the Jewish exiles. That is why not even the fire of an overheated furnace—so hot that it eviscerates those very soldiers who throw Shadrach, Meshach, and Abednego into it—is able to muzzle such a strong, genuine faith.

The three youths are also seen as "models of the faith." In the Targum of Gen 38:25, Tamar, about to be punished by fire yet strong in faith, is described as the ancestress of the three youths.[27] In the same strand of thought if not lineage, Cyprian of Carthage (210–258), writing of *virtus fidei* (*Epistle* 58.5), takes the three youths as an example of martyrs who surrendered themselves to God's sovereign will. Hippolytus of Rome (170–235) underlines the idea of *total* and complete surrender by commenting, "For the king prevailed in terrestrial matters, but the three boys prevailed in faith towards God" (*Commentary on Daniel* 2.25.3).[28]

"The tyrannical decree [*tō dogmati tō tyrannikō*]"
Surprisingly, the technical term *dogma*, "decree," does not occur in the biblical story itself.[29] Instead, Dan 3:4 (Theod.)[30] reads: "And the herald [*ho kēryx*] cried out [*eboa*] aloud, 'It is said [*legetai*] to you, O peoples, tribes, languages.'"

The adjective *tyrannikos*, "tyrannical" occurs in LXX two times only, in 3 Macc 3:8 and 4 Macc 5:27. Using this adjective, the hymnographer meant to link two episodes together: the three youthful near-martyrs in Dan 3 and the Jewish martyrs under Antiochus IV Epiphanes, primarily the priest Eleazar, in 4 Macc 5:27, where the exact same form appears.

For centuries, ancient Jewish *and* Christian interpreters have seen in the three youths a type of martyrs ready to offer their lives to God as a well-pleasing offering (e.g., 3 Macc 6:6). A midrashic interpreter seeking to unpack the "hidden" meaning of Gen 8:21 ("The Lord smelled the pleasing odor" coming out of Noah's offering) brings forth the three youths, along with Abraham, as examples of living and "acceptable offerings" (a theme reaching back to that of Cain and Abel): "He smelled the savor of the Patriarch Abraham ascending from the fiery furnace [cf. *Genesis Rabbah* 38.13]; He smelled the savor of Hananiah, Mishael and Azariah [Dan 2:17] ascending from the fiery furnace" (*Genesis Rabbah* 34.9).[31]

A fourth-century pseudo-apostolic collection lists several "offerings of the righteous," among which is that of the "three youths in the fiery furnace" (*Apostolic Constitutions* 7.37.4).[32] This "martyr/offering" theme is very well attested throughout the liturgical media and genres (i.e., hymns, homilies, iconography, sacred music). For instance, depictions of the three youths are found in the ancient Christian funereal art (i.e., catacombs, sarcophaguses, tombs) for the reason that early Christians considered the three youths to have been true martyrs by whose intercessions the deceased could benefit in their afterlife journey.[33] The "martyr/offering" theme is tightly tied to the theme of "salvation" in early Christian works, beginning with *Pseudo-Cyprianic Orations* (1.2), prior to the third century, up to *Libera me* of the *Commendatio animae* (eighth century).[34]

In 4 Macc 5 is the narration of the encounter between "the tyrant [*ho tyrannos*] Antiochus" (v. 1) and Eleazar, who was a "priest" (*hiereus*) by birth and a "lawyer" (*nomikos*) by profession (v. 4). Antiochus orders Eleazar to eat pork if he does not want to be tortured. "It would be tyrannical [*tyrannikon*]," replies Eleazar, "to force us to break the law, but also to eat in such a way so you may deride us eating the unclean food that is most hateful to us" (4 Macc 5:27). Eleazar's response to the tyrant's treacherous and life-threatening words insists on ready obedience to the Law: "O Antiochus, we who are persuaded by our law to live our lives accordingly, we think that there is no compulsion [*anankēn*] more powerful than the ready obedience [*eupeitheias*] to the law" (4 Macc 5:16). In Eleazar's view, the Law is at the same time the object of Jewish piety *and* obedience as well as the main means by which Jews attain self-control (*sōphrosynē*), so needed in their fight against temptations and endurance of trials: "But it [the Law] teaches us thoroughly the self-control [*sōphrosynēn*] that overcomes all the pleasures and desires, and also trains us in courage [*andreian*] so that we endure all pain willingly" (4 Macc 5:23).

The three youths' reluctance to answer King Nebuchadnezzar, "we do not need [*ou chreian*] to answer [*apokrithēnai*] you about this utterance [*rhēmatos*]" (Dan 3:16 [Theod.]), perhaps forced the liturgist's hand to find a substitute in Eleazar's articulate and well-thought-out response to King Antiochus IV Epiphanes (4 Macc 5). The hymnographer linked Dan 3 to

4 Macc 5 through the catchword *tyrannikos*, "tyrannical," found in 4 Macc 5:27. This intertextuality could legitimately be labeled "intertextual echo."[35] Since the intertextuality is *not* between two biblical texts but rather between a liturgical hymn and a biblical text (4 Macc 5:27) meant to parallel yet another biblical text (Dan 3), I might qualify further the above notion as "liturgical-biblical" intertextual echo.[36] The "echo" (i.e., catchword *tyrannikos*, "tyrannical") invites the listener and/or participant in the liturgical performance to see the parallel between the three youths and Eleazar with respect to their ready obedience to the Law. The central, core idea of both stories, that of enduring trials with no compromising, comes into being through this intertextual echo, which becomes ever clearer.

"The holy three youths [*hoi hosioi treis paides*] not obeying [*mē peisthentes*]" Not obeying the king's decree, the "holy three youths" (*hoi hosioi treis paides*)[37] were cast (*blēthentes*)[38] into the furnace. The verbal form "obeying" (*peisthentes*)[39] is another example of "intertextual echo" linking this hymn to 4 Macc 12:4, where "the tyrant" (*ho tyrannos*, v. 2), King Antiochus IV Epiphanes, tries to persuade the youngest of the seven martyr brothers to obey his order: "If you do not obey [*peistheiēs*], you will be tortured [*basanistheis*] with suffering [*talas*], and you will die before your time" (4 Macc 12:4).

Through the catchword "obeying," the hymnographer establishes a parallel between the three youths' story (Dan 3), which inspired the liturgical hymn, and the seven martyred brothers' narrative (4 Macc 12:4). This parallel is supported by the presence of the verb *hypakouō*, "to obey," in Dan 3:12 (Theod.).[40]

Though wrapped in flames, the three youths, instead of crying out in pain, "confessed [*hōmologoun*] God, singing [*psallontes*], 'Bless the Lord, you works of the Lord.'"[41] They acknowledged God as the one who gave them strength (blessing)[42] to endure the fire while inviting the "works of the Lord" (*ta erga kyriou*), his entire creation, to join them in their awe-inspiring doxology.

Bedewed in the Midst of Flames

The youths [*hoi paides*] in Babylon were not cowered [*eptēxan*] by the furnace's flames, but cast into [*emblēthentes*] the midst of the flame, bedewed [*drosizomenoi*], they sang: "Blessed are you, O Lord, the God of our fathers." (Holy Thursday, Matins, Ode 7, Heirmos)

"The youths [*hoi paides*] in Babylon were not cowered [*eptēxan*] by the furnace's flames"

The same rare LXX verb *ptēssō*, "to cower, cringe in fear"[43] occurs in the Prayer of Eleazar, one of the Jewish martyrs who suffered death under Antioch IV Epiphanes. The old priest prays to God so that he would make the Gentiles cower by his magnificent power: "Today let the Gentiles cower [*ptēxatō*] by your unconquerable power [*dynamin anikēton*], O noble one, who have the power to save the nation of Jacob" (3 Macc 6:13).

The Prayer of Eleazar contains the earliest commentary[44] on the three youths story (Dan 3). "When the three comrades [*hetairous*] in Babylonia willingly [*authairetōs*] gave [their] soul [*tēn psychēn*] to the fire so they might not serve [*mē latreusai*] vain things, you bedewed [*drosisas*] the fiery furnace [*diapyron kaminon*] and delivered [*errysō*] them unhurt [*apēmantous*], up to a single hair, and shot the flames to all [their] opponents [*hypenantiois*]" (3 Macc 6:6).

As one can see, 3 Macc 6:6 is familiar with the Prayer of Azariah, the Greek addition to the book of Daniel. Both texts mention the miraculous "dew" (*drosos*) that God himself or an angel of the Lord brought inside the fiery furnace.

"But an angel of the Lord [*angelos kyriou*] came down in the furnace to be together with those who were with Azariah, and shook [*exetinaxe*] the flame of the fire out of the furnace and made the middle of the furnace as if a breeze of dew [*hōsei pneuma drosou*] were whistling [*diasyrizon*]. And the fire did not touch them at all, neither did it cause pain to, nor annoyed them" (Pr Azar 1:26–27; cf. Dan 3:49–50 [LXX/Theod.]).

According to the Prayer of Eleazar, it was the "mighty-in-power king, most high, almighty God" (*basileu megalokratōr hypsiste pantokratōr theos*) (cf. 3 Macc 6:2) who delivered the three youths unhurt out of the fiery furnace. Eleazar's words might be read as a later response to King Nebuchadnezzar's question directed to the three youths: "Who is the god [*tis estin theos*][45] who will deliver you out of my hands?" (Dan 3:15 [Theod.]).[46]

Based on Dan 3:92 (LXX: *angelou theou*, "angel of God"), Hippolytus of Rome, in his *Commentary on Daniel* (composed ca. 202–211), the oldest surviving Christian commentary on Scripture, writes, "Those who were within the furnace were besprinkled [*edrosizonto*] by an angel" (2.31.3).[47]

Another hymn intimates that the dew was the result of the work of the Holy Spirit: "As in the rain [*psekadi*],[48] in the midst of the flame, by the dew of the Spirit [*tē drosō tou pneumatos*], rejoicing, God's youths walked around [*periepatoun*][49]" (Sunday of the Forefathers, Vespers, Sticheron). For hymnographer Anatolios, the very three youths should be credited for turning the overheated furnace into dew: "... honoring the three youths who changed the furnace into dew [*tēn kaminon eis droson metabalontas*]" (Sunday of the Forefathers, Vespers, Sticheron).[50]

The hymn's concluding formula, "Blessed are you, O Lord, the God of our fathers," was borrowed from the Prayer of Azariah (1:3, 29; cf. Dan 3:26, 52 [LXX/Theod.]). The appellation "the God of our fathers" underlines the idea that the one and the same God delivered the three youths and strengthened the later Maccabee martyrs, including the priest Eleazar, to suffer death for their uncompromised faith.

The One Who Holds Life in His Palm

The monument of wickedness rivaling God [*stēlēn kakias antitheou*], the godly youths put [it] to open shame [*paredeigmatisan*], but the lawless Sanhedrin [*synedrion*], raging [*phryattomenon*] against Christ, plots [*bouleuetai*] vain things [*kena*], ponders [*meleta*] to kill [*kteinai*] the One who holds life in [his] palm [*ton zōēs kratounta palamē*]; the one the whole creation blesses, glorifying [him] unto the ages. (Holy Friday, Matins, Ode 8, Heirmos)

The hymnographer selected and distilled a few scriptural texts into tiny evocative pieces and then collated them all into a brand new story, a "liturgized biblical story," that is. Due to the content density and artistic mastery of this hymn, one can now hardly detect the possible scriptural sources that once inspired the poet, i.e., Dan 3, Ps 2:1, Wis 3:1, and John 11:47–53. This hymn may be considered a good example of intertextuality where various scriptural allusions are well interconnected in a literary unit integrated within the wider liturgical matrix.

"The monument of wickedness rivaling God [*stēlēn kakias antitheou*]"
The first line of the hymn draws on Dan 3:1 and the "golden image" (LXX: *eikona*[51] *chrysēn*; MT: *ṣlm dy-dhb*) that King Nebuchadnezzar "made" (*epoiēsen*) so that it might be worshiped. The hymnographer's choice for

stēlē over *eikōn* could be explained to a certain degree by cultural-religious changes. On the one hand, *eikōn*, "image," became gradually a technical term for Christian sanctified images or representations of Jesus, the incarnate Logos, his mother, and a long cortège of saints. On the other hand, *stēlē*, "pillar,"[52] has had a long negative history as mostly designating pagan monuments and statues, hence its use here for the monument the Babylonian king set up.

The hymnographer added two qualifiers, not found in the biblical story, *kakias*, "wickedness," and *antitheos*, "rivaling God,"[53] to underline the idolatrous character of the golden image whose worship the three youths resisted heroically.

"But the lawless Sanhedrin [*synedrion*], raging [*phryattomenon*]
against Christ, plots [*bouleuetai*] vain things [*kena*]"
At this point, the hymn turns into a "midrashic actualization" of Ps 2:1, 2b, "Why did nations rage [*ephryaxan*], and peoples ponder [*emeletēsan*] vain things [*kena*]? . . . and the rulers gathered together [*hoi archontes synēchthēsan*], against the Lord and against his anointed [*kata tou christou autou*]." The "rulers gathered together" changes to "Sanhedrin" (*synedrion*), and *christos* from the common noun "anointed" becomes a messianic title, *Christos*—Christ, Jesus of Nazareth.

Brilliantly, the hymnographer knits the midrashic actualization of Ps 2:1 with John 11:47–53, which narrates how the "chief priests" (*archiereis*) and Pharisees gathered the Sanhedrin (*synedrion*) in a meeting, and following the advice of Caiaphas, they "plotted" (*ebouleusanto*) how to "slay" (*apokteinōsin*)[54] Jesus.

"Ponders [*meleta*] to kill [*kteinai*] the One who holds life in [his] palm
[*ton zōēs kratounta palamē*]"
For the phrase "the one who holds life in [his] palm," I could not find anything closer than Wis 3:1: "However, the souls of the just ones [are] in God's hand and no torture will reach them [*dikaiōn de psychai en cheiri theou kai ou mē apsētai autōn basanos*]."[55] In any event, Wis 3:1 is a good thematic match to Dan 3, for God, whose "palm" (*palamē*)[56] holds the souls of the just, protected the three youths so that no torture, not even the flames, could reach and hurt them.

Nonetheless, since there is no clear, direct connection with a specific biblical text,[57] this phrase could be interpreted as a subtle allusion to Jesus's saying "That is why the Father loves me, for I lay down my life [*psychēn*], so that I may receive [*labō*] it again [*palin*]. No one takes [*airei*] it from me, but I myself lay it down of my own will [*ap' emautou*]. I have power [*exousian*] to lay it down, and I have power to take it up again. This commandment [*entolēn*] I received [*elabon*] from my Father" (John 10:17–18). Read this way, the hymn conveys the idea that the torturers of all times and flavors can kill the body but not the soul (Luke 12:4–5).

The hymn puts forward a twofold contrast: on the one hand, between the wicked, golden, God-reviling yet lifeless idol and the one who holds life in the palm of his hand, yet to be slain; on the other hand, between two groups of people, the three godly youths who openly put to shame the ancient idol and the lawless Sanhedrin who plotted to slay Christ, the one who holds life in the palm of his hand.

The Fourth One in the Furnace

The Identity of the Fourth One

Praise and highly exalt the Lord who protected [*diaphylaxanta*] the youths in the flame of fire [*en phlogi pyros*] of the burning furnace [*kaiomenos kaminou*] and came down [*synkatabanta*] to them in the form of an angel [*en morphē angelou*]. (Heirmologion, Ode 8, Heirmos, Mode 1)

The hymnographer retells the three youths story while musing over the episode of Moses at the burning bush (Exod 3:1–12). Not only is the language of the hymn reminiscent of Exod 3:2[58] ("angel of the Lord" [*angelos kyriou*], "in the flame of fire" [*en phlogi pyros*], "burning" [*kaietai*]), "came down" [*katebēn*]), but its thematic register also resonates the main points of this Old Testament theophany. For instance, the three youths living in Babylon parallel Moses/Israel living in a foreign land (Midian/Egypt); three youths in the overheated, fiery furnace yet alive remind one of the bush burning with fire yet not consumed; Nebuchadnezzar looking into the furnace and being "astonished" (*ethaumasen*) at the three youths alive in the midst of the flames (Dan 3:24–25 [MT]; cf. 3:91–92 [LXX]) points back to Moses looking at that "great sight" (*to horama to mega*) (Exod 3:3); the "fourth one" ("angel of God," *angelou theou* [LXX]/"son of God," *hyiō theou* [Theod.]; cf. "a son of gods," *bar dy-ʾlhyn* [MT]) inside the furnace along with the three youths (Dan 3:24

[MT]; cf. 3:91 [LXX/Theod.]) matches the "angel of the Lord" within the burning bush (Exod 3:2).

In using the verb *diaphylassō*, "to watch over, protect, preserve," the hymnographer may have been thinking of a similar biblical event (2 Macc 10:29–30)[59] mentioning five heavenly figures ("five illustrious men ... from heaven" [*andres pente diaprepeis ... ex ouranou*]) on golden-clad horses coming down to defend Judas the Maccabee in battle against Timothy's army. The heavenly figures were understood as angelic warriors on the side of the Maccabees. Through this narrative intertextuality, the hymnographer paints the three youths episode as a fight between God and the pagan enemy of the Jews, King Nebuchadnezzar—similarly to what happened under Judas the Maccabee when God sent his angels to fight on the side of the Jews.[60] Interestingly, in both biblical episodes, fervent intercessory prayer precedes divine intervention. So, Pr Azar 1:1 (Dan 3:24 [LXX]) [61] mentions that "Hananiah, Azariah and Mishael prayed [*proseuxato*] and sang [*hymnēsan*] to the Lord, when the king ordered them to be cast into the furnace."[62] And a miracle happened: the three youths were preserved alive in the midst of fire.[63] Similarly, 2 Macc 10:16 (cf. vv. 25–27) notes that Judas the Maccabee and his warriors "made supplication [*litaneian*], beseeching [*axiōsantes*] God to fight on their side." And a miracle occurred: five "illustrious men" came down from heaven to fight for them (vv. 29–30).

Note the difference in wording between the biblical text and the hymn regarding the way the angelophany is described. Where Dan 3:25 (3:92 [LXX]) reads *homiōma angelou*, "in the likeness of an angel," the hymn has *en morphē angelou*, "in the form of an angel." In the hymnographer's view, a divine figure took the form (of an angel), became tangible. Choosing the word *morphē*, "form," the hymnographer perhaps wanted to underline that beyond the angelic form, the mysterious person is outside the earthly realm. And that person took the form, had the freedom to do so, rather than simply being perceived by the human beholder as someone "in the likeness of an angel" (Dan 3:25 [LXX: 3:92]).

One may add that the hymn surmises the preexistence of the Logos, who during the Old Testament times, prior to its incarnation, came down on earth and took sporadically and temporarily a humanlike (angelic) form and interacted with humans. Ancient Christian interpreters used to speak of such mysterious appearances in the Old Testament times as theophanies, "God's appearances," or Christophanies, "Christ's appearances" (especially those manifestations of the pre-incarnate Christ in the form of "the angel of the Lord"), with the latter term being often understood as mere angelophanies, "appearances of angels."[64] Should one understand these appearances as "prophecy" or "real presence" of the Son, i.e., appearances of the Logos before incarnation? The proponents of the "prophecy-with-a-little-presence" approach[65] consider the Christocentricity of the Old Testament, so celebrated by the Church Fathers, as referring to both "prophecy" and "real presence" ("local and tangible") of the Son in the "before Christ" events of the Scriptures. Along the same line of thought, Charles A. Gieschen suggests renaming the dogmatic category "Christology" with another label, "Huiosology" (or "Hyiosology"), from Gk. *hyios*, "son," which would better describe the Old Testament testimony of the Son's existence "before Christ."[66]

The hymnographer's use of the same verb, *synkatabainō*, "to go down with, descend with, condescend," as in Pr Azar 1:26 (Dan 3:49 [LXX/Theod.]), to describe the coming down of a saving divine figure brings to the foreground a well-established theological notion, the divine "condescension" (Gk. *synkatabasis*, lit. "going down together with").[67] The descent of an angelomorphic being is depicted as an act of condescension in terms of divine adjustability to the human receptacle's level of understanding and communication.[68]

Someone Like the Son of God

> The ruler [*ho kratōn*] looking at the three ones cast into the furnace, he thus [*hōs*] gazed at [*etheasato*] the appearance [*thean*] of the fourth one, whom he named [*prosēgoreuse*] "Son of God" [*hyion theou*], and cried to all: "Blessed [is] the God of our fathers [*ho theos ho tōn paterōn hēmōn*]."
> (Sunday of the Forefathers, Matins, Ode 7)

Unlike the previous hymnographer, for whom the fourth one in the furnace was an angel (Dan 3:92 [LXX]), the author of this hymn identifies the mysterious appearance with the "Son of God" (Dan 3:25 [MT]; cf. 3:92 [Theod.: *hyiō tou theou*, "[like] a son of God"]). Following Gieschen's theological coinage (Hyiosology),[69] I would dare to say that according to this hymnographer, what really occurred in the fiery furnace was a *Hyiosophany*, "an appearance of the Son" before his incarnation.

By using the verb *theaomai*, "to gaze at, contemplate," and the noun *thea*, "appearance, vision," the hymnographer places the emergence of the fourth one at the crisscrossing of the earthly reality with the divine realm, in the area of visionary contemplation.[70]

In the same vein of missionary spirit with Dan 3:28–30 (MT; cf. 3:95–98 LXX/Theod.), King Nebuchadnezzar, here called "the ruler" (*ho kratōn*), not only recognizes the almightiness of the Jewish God who saved his brave martyrs ("witnesses") but goes a step further by naming[71] the fourth figure in the furnace "Son of God" and identifying him with the "God of our fathers." Unlike the biblical text, the hymnographer, by a midrashic twist, makes the "ruler," the persecutor, become part of the oppressed ones, the Jewish people, by having him call Israel's ancient patriarchs "our fathers."

Nebuchadnezzar, "the ruler," sounds in the hymnographer's view like Azariah at the beginning of his prayer, "Blessed are you O Lord, the God of our fathers [*kyrie ho theos tōn paterōn hēmōn*]" (Pr Azar 1:3 [Dan 3:26 LXX/ Theod.]). Interestingly enough, the hymnographer adds the definite article *ho* between *theos* and *paterōn* to emphasize that the fourth one in the furnace is not just any divine figure but *the very* "God of our fathers"; though such a construction is not found in LXX, the phrase *theos tōn paterōn hēmōn* occurs several times in the Bible.

The identification with the Son of God occurs in several other hymns, where the theme of incarnation is also found. In one, this identification is further qualified. The one who "saved the youths from the burning heat [*ho flogōseōs paidas rhysamenos*]" is the Son of God who "taking on flesh [*sarka proslabomenos*], came [*hēlthen*] to earth, and being nailed upon the Cross [*staurō prosēlōtheis*],[72] he granted [*edōrēsato*] us salvation" (Heirmologion, Ode 7, Heirmos, Mode 1).

Another hymn, for instance, draws on Christ's Passion, identifying the one who delivered the youths from the furnace with the one who "became human [*anthrōpos*], suffers as a mortal one [*paschei hōs thnētos*], and through Passion [*pathous*] dresses the mortality out of corruption with majesty [*to thnēton aphtharsias endyei euprepeian*]" (Heirmologion, Heirmos, Ode 7, Mode 1).[73]

Moreover, the next hymn strikes a sharp contrast between the powerful "deliverer" and the one "dead and breathless," with the furnace, as *locus salvationis*, replaced by a lifeless tomb: "Unspeakable wonder! The one delivering [*rhysamenos*] the holy youths in the furnace from the flame is laid [*katatithetai*] as dead [*nekros*], breathless [*apnous*] in a tomb [*en taphō*] for our salvation, of those who sing, 'Redeemer, God, you are blessed'" (Holy Saturday, Matins, Ode 7, Heirmos).

In the following hymn, the deliverer of the three youths is simply called "Christ": "Praise Christ God, who protected [*diaphylaxanta*] the youths praising in the furnace and who transformed the thundering furnace into dew [*tēn brontōsan kaminon metabalonta eis droson*], praise and highly extol him into the ages" (Heirmologion, Ode 8, Heirmos).

One of the most famous Syrian-Byzantine hymnographers, Romanos the Melodist, has John the Baptist, about to baptize Christ, convey the same idea found in the hymn just quoted, namely, that the Son of God, prior to incarnation, was somehow present and active in the Old Testament times: "And again [*palin*] contemplating [*theōrōn*] in the midst of streams [*en mesō tōn rheithrōn*]. The one who appeared in the midst of the three youths [*ton en mesō tōn triōn paidōn phanenta*], the Dew in the fire and fire in the Jordan [*droson en pyri kai pyr en tō Iordanē*], shining, gushing forth, the unapproachable light" (*Hymns on Epiphany* 1.4).[74]

The same intertextuality (i.e., the story of the three youths and Christ's baptism in Jordan) found in Romanos's strophe appears in the following hymn, where "fire" and "dew" in the Babylonian furnace parallel the "immaterial fire" (Christ) entering Jordan's streams: "The Babylonian furnace displayed [*edeixe*] a paradoxical mystery [*mystērion paradoxon*] gushing forth [*pēgasasa*] dew: that Jordan was to receive [*eisdechesthai*] in its streams the immaterial fire [*aylon pyr*] and hold [*stegein*] the Creator when he was being baptized [*baptizomenos*] in flesh [*sarki*]. Let the peoples bless and highly exalt him unto all the ages" (Heirmologion, Ode 8, Heirmos *Mystirion Paradoxo*).

Divine Condescension

The God who condescended [*synkatabanta*] into the furnace to the youths of the Hebrews [*tōn Hebraiōn tois paisi*] and changed the flame to dew [*phloga eis droson metabalonta*], [you his] works, praise as Lord [*hōs kyrion*] and highly exalt [him] to all the ages. (Heirmologion, Ode 8, Heirmos *Ton en kamino tou pyros*, Mode 2)

This hymn is reminiscent of the wording of the "burning bush" story: God "descended" (*katebēn*) into the burning bush as a sign of divine condescension (*synkatabasis*) and co-suffering with his people Israel, while being ready to "take [them] out" (*exelesthai*) of slavery (Exod 3:8). The hymn's peculiar genitive construction "youths of the Hebrews," instead of the simpler "youths" or "Hebrews," was likely meant to make the listener or reader think of "the God of the Hebrews" (*ho theos tōn Hebraiōn*) of Exod 3:18. In other words, God who condescended into the furnace to save the three youths is the same God of Exodus who came down to liberate the Hebrews from slavery.[75]

The hymnographer qualifies the highly exalted "God" (*theon*), who changed the flame to dew, "as Lord" (*hōs kyrion*). Nonetheless, the term "Lord" (*kyrios*) should not be considered the LXX default rendition of the Heb. Tetragrammaton YHWH (pronounced "Yahweh," "He Is/Will Be," based on a scholarly convention), revealed to Moses by the "Lord, God of the patriarchs" (*kyrios ho theos tōn paterōn*) at the "burning bush" (Exod 3:14–15).[76] Most likely, "Lord" in this hymn refers to Christ. If this identification proves to be correct, there is an interesting equivalence between Christ and God who saved the three youths and, earlier, took the Hebrews out of Egypt.

As a matter of fact, identifying Christ or rather the Son prior to his incarnation with the God at work in the early history of Israel has a long tradition going back to the apostolic Church. Paul in 1 Cor 10:4 equates the moving rock during the wandering of Israel through the wilderness, after the Exodus event, with Christ himself: "They [Hebrews] drank from the spiritual rock [*pneumatikēs petras*] which followed [*akolouthousēs*] them, and the rock was the Christ [*hē petra de ēn ho Christos*]."[77]

The gloss of 1 Cor 10:4 relies on a long Jewish tradition stretching from the first century C.E. to medieval rabbinic writings where God made provisions to Israel in the wilderness by giving them a "movable well" (mentioned in Exod 17 and Num 20–21).[78]

In the same hermeneutical framework (i.e., identifying Jesus with YHWH, God of ancient Israel), a special case obtains with Jude 5: "I want to remind you, although [you] know all this, that [the] Lord [(*ho*) *kyrios*] at one time [*hapax*], after saving [*sōsas*] the people from Egypt, on the second occasion [*to deuteron*] destroyed [*apōlesen*] those who did not believe" (Jude 5). Other textual variants for *kyrios*, "Lord," in Jude 5 (*ho kyrios*, "the Lord"; *Iēsous*, "Jesus"; and *theos Christos*, "Christ God") are found in the Bodmer Papyrus (P72), discovered in 1952 in Egypt and dating back to the third or fourth century C. E., most likely the pre-Nicene period. The P72 reading variant *Iēsous*, "Jesus," enjoys a fair acceptance from the scholarly community due to its *lectio difficilior* status as well as the presence of the phrase *kyrion hēmōn Iēsoun Christon*, "our Lord Jesus Christ," in v. 4. P72 proves that even during the pre-Nicene period, educated scribes, as those responsible for later codices (i.e., Vaticanus and Alexandrinus, which also read *Iēsous* in Jude 5), were convinced that the one who saved Israel from Egyptian slavery was none other than Jesus. Moreover, as early as the middle of the second century, the belief that the Logos, rather than God the Father, appeared to Abraham (Gen 18) or Jacob (Gen 28) was already widespread, especially through the writings of Justin Martyr.[79]

Hippolytus of Rome, in his commentary on Daniel, identifies the angel in the furnace with the God of Exodus and of other Old Testament events, so in the end, he may equate the angel with the very Son of God prior to his incarnation:

> And so it is needful to ask, who was this angel who was revealed in the furnace and who preserved the boys as his own children under his enfolding arms, and for those in the midst of the furnace he turned the fire into dew, but for those outside the fire he assigned his own standard of judgment. . . . Let me not deceive, he was not any other person, but the very one who judged the Egyptians with the water. . . . This was he who received the authority of judgment from the Father. He who also showered fire and divine retribution upon the Sodomites, and destroyed them on account of their lawlessness and wicked impiety. . . . For Scripture also likens this one to be an angel of God. For it was he himself who reported to us the mysteries of the Father. This one descended into the furnace with those who were around Azariah. The fire, seeing this Angel, recognized his master and, being afraid, fled outside of the furnace. (*Commentary on Daniel* 32.1–9)[80]

An interesting interpretation may be found in Romanos the Melodist. The hymnographer depicts the saving angel as constantly altering his form, taking on either divine or human traits, thus hinting at the two natures in Christ:

> Standing as in choir, in the midst of the furnace, the youths made [*apeirgasanto*] the furnace be a celestial Church [*ouranion ekklēsian*]; singing psalms [*psallontes*] along with the angel [*met' angelou*] to the Maker of the angels [*tō poiētē tōn angelōn*]; imitating [*ekmimoumenoi*] the whole liturgy of the bodiless ones [*asarkōn*]. Then, being borne about on [*emphorēthentes*] by the Holy Spirit out of worship [*ek latreias*], they saw something else more frightening [*phriktoteron*]; for that one [*autos ekeinos*]

whom they saw as angel [*hōs angelon*] was altering [*elloiou*] each time
[*kath' ekastēn*] [his] form [*morphēn*]; and they saw [him] at one time divine
[*theios*], at another time as a human being [*hōs anthrōpos*]; one time commanding [*ekeleue*], and then supplicating together [*syniketeuen*]. (*Hymn on
the Three Youths* 25)[81]

Romanos reflects here a more advanced, post-Chalcedon (451) version
of Christology than the temple theology found in John 1:14 (indwelling/
tabernacling of the Logos among humans) and later in Theodore of
Mopsuestia's (350–428) writings (where, based on Ezekiel's visions, God
can indwell but depart the Temple). In Romanos's Christology, informed
by *communicatio idiomatum*, the two natures interpenetrate each other;
there is more than a mere indwelling of the divine within a material medium, e.g., an angelomorph; there is a mysterious symbiosis between divine and material.

Various Typologies

A few typologies are generated by the three youths story (Dan 3).[82] Since
we dealt with Christological typologies above, I will dwell now on the other
three: Marian, Trinitarian, and Cross typologies.

Marian

In the furnace [*en tē kaminō*], in that one [*tē*] of the youths, once [*pote*],
O Lord, you pre-portrayed [*proapeikonisas*][83] your very mother [*tēn sēn
mētera*]. For the type [*ho gar typos*], unburned while entering in [*aphlektōs
embateuontas*], took those out [*exeileto*] of fire. We praise in hymns and
highly exalt to the ages of ages the one [*tēn*] who today [*sēmeron*], through
you [*dia sou*], became visible [*emphanistheisan*] unto the ends [*tois perasi*]
[of the world]. (Heirmologion, Heirmos *En ti kamino*, Ode 8, Mode 2)

Dan 3 contains two references to the "fourth one" in the furnace: the narrator's
voice (Pr Azar 1:26; cf. Dan 3:49 [LXX/Theod.]: "angel of the Lord") and
Nebuchadnezzar's observation (Dan 3:25 [MT]; cf. Dan 3:92 [LXX/Theod.],
rendered in three different ways: MT "*a* son of *gods*," LXX "angel of God," and
Theod. "son of *God*"; (emphasis added).

Most likely, the hymn echoes the biblical narrator's voice (i.e., "angel of the Lord," which in patristic interpretations is viewed as a type or foreshadow of the prior-to-incarnation Son of God).

The hymnographer sets forth two typologies. The first is between "angel of the Lord" (type 1) and Son of God (antitype 1). The second typology, embedded within the first one, is between Son of God (type 2) and his mother (antitype 2). I would call this "embedded typology," a distinctive interpretive procedure employed by liturgists.[84] Patristic biblical commentaries, due to the linearity of their exegetical discourse, do not allow such a "concentric" sort of biblical interpretation by which a typology generates or is embedded in another typology.

As one can see in the hymn above, the link between type and antitype in either typology, as well as the link between the two typologies, can be summed up as follows: the one who is unconsumed by fire can save others. The angel of the Lord enters the furnace unburned and saves the youths. Likewise, the Son of God through incarnation enters the creation unconsumed while saving humanity. Moreover, the Mother of God, the Ever-Virgin Mary, gives birth to Christ and remains unburned by the fire of his divinity while burning down the bitter matter of passions, as the next hymn enunciates:

> As the Chaldean furnace did not burn down [katephlexe] the three youths, so, O undefiled One [achrante], the very fire of the divinity [theotētos] protected [etērēsen] you unburned [aphlekton].[85] As for me [alla], I cry out to you: "Burn down [kataphlexon] the bitter matter [hylēn pikran] of my passions [pathōn], O Pure One [hagnē], so that I may glorify you."
> (Alexander and Antonina the Martyrs [June 10], Matins, Ode 7)

Notice the repetition of the verb kataphlegō, "to burn down": on the one hand, the furnace did not burn down the three youths; on the other hand, the faithful through the hymnographer's voice petition the Mother of God, whose holy womb typified by the furnace was kept unburned by the divinity of her Son, to burn down the "matter" (hylē)[86] of their passions.

Similarly, another hymn asserts that the furnace, which did not burn the three lads, "pre-molds" (protypousa) Mary's "birthing" (gennēsin) when the "divine fire" (theion pyr) of her Son's divinity will not burn her:

> The furnace did not burn the three lads [neanias], [thus] pre-molding [protypousa] your very birthing [gennēsin], for the divine fire [theion pyr]

did not burn you, [when] it dwelt [ōkēsen] in you and illumined [ephōtise] all to cry aloud: "Blessed are you O God of our fathers!" (The Holy Martyrs Adrian and Natalie [August 26], Matins, Ode 7)

The next hymn proposes a more sophisticated Marian typology, where the "furnace" (kaminos) symbolizes Mary's "womb" (gastēr),[87] a "spiritual furnace" (noētē kaminos), in which the Son of God "refashions" (anaplassō) the whole of humanity:

> We faithful consider [katanooumen] you, O Birth-Giver of God [theotoke], a spiritual furnace [noētēn kaminon]; for as he, the highly exalted [hyperypsoumenos], saved the three youths, so he refashioned [aneplasen] me, whole humanity [holon anthrōpon], in your womb [gastri], the one praised, God of [our] fathers, glorified above all. (Heirmologion, Heirmos Se Noitin, Ode 9, Mode 1)

The following hymn continues the idea of humanity being incorporated, refashioned, and bedewed within Mary's womb, where the incarnate Son of God finds an appropriate dwelling place. Even though the hymn speaks only of "furnace" (kaminos) as typifying the "new tabernacle" (nea skēnē), one may assume that the latter alludes first to Mary and then to the Church. Read this way, the hymn proposes a new typology that one could label "meta-typology":

> As in the furnace [en kaminō], [in the] God-receiving [theodochē] new tabernacle [nea skēnē], all from the spiritual [pneumatikou] Israel, bedewed [drosizomenoi], let us cry aloud: "Blessed are you in the temple [en tō naō] of your glory, O Lord." (Forefeast of the Elevation of the Holy Cross [September 13], Matins, Ode 7)

Mary is the "new tabernacle" in which all from the "spiritual Israel" are bedewed. The tabernacle/temple imagery, initially used in relationship to the Incarnation, after the Council of Chalcedon (451) was applied gradually to Mary, who houses God or, as our hymn puts it, "receives God" (theodochē) in the most intimate way. However, the Marian usage of tabernacle imagery does not begin with post-Chalcedon times; its roots actually go back to the second-century Protoevangelium of James.[88] According to Gary Anderson,[89] the emerging significance of Marian feasts in the wake of Chalcedon substantially helped the growth and spread of the tabernacle imagery in connection with Mary. Homilies and icons generated by Marian feasts contributed to a proliferation of hymns using such a rich metaphor in a variety of artistic expressions.[90]

Given the scantiness of New Testament texts referring to Mary, it is not surprising that the Church has always made use of figural interpretation of Old Testament texts done by hymnographers and homilists.[91] Thus, Mary's ecclesial portrait is a mix of "proof texts" gleaned from both testaments. One may note, though, that most of this portrait's brushes are from the Old Testament cache of texts.[92] The function of the Old Testament was not understood as a mere pointer to a New Testament "ultimate fulfillment" but more as a resource in itself of figures and metaphors used by liturgists, homilists, and iconographers in their ardent quest for the character of the Mother of God.[93]

In this context, Anderson is quite right when he pleads for reading the New Testament in light of the Old Testament, whose integrity as an independent witness should always be recognized: "The development of the temple metaphor in relationship to the Incarnation sheds considerable light on how the early church conceived the relationship between the two testaments. The relationship between the two is not primarily predictive, but figural. And in this fashion the Old Testament can do more than simply anticipate the New; it can take a necessary role in filling out what the New has not disclosed."[94] The common yet fairly deficient "prophecy fulfillment" model should be replaced with a time-honored and much-closer-to-reality interpretive view where the two testaments are in a relationship of complementarity.[95] According to this paradigm, the Old Testament text preserves its "original voice."

In any of the above-quoted hymns, it is not the story itself ("three youths" of Dan 3), not even all the aspects of that story, but rather a single detail that made the liturgist think of a type–antitype relationship with Mary. For instance, it is the fire turned into dew by a divine intervention that typifies Mary's unburned womb by her Son's divinity at the moment of conception. Through such a hermeneutical maneuver, the Old Testament story preserves its "original voice": the fiery furnace burned down neither the Jewish youths nor their obedient faith. The rationale for this approach may be summed up as follows: listening closely to the "voice" of the Old Testament story translates into a better understanding of the proposed typology's tenor. The figural use is like an echo of the "original voice": the louder the voice is, the much clearer and lengthier the echo's pitch waver is.

The following hymn is a good illustration of such a hermeneutical mastery combining two interpretations, allegorical and historical, within the same piece of poetry. The first part of the hymn proposes two typologies, Trinitarian and Christological, while the second part is a historical (plain) interpretation of what happened in the furnace. The historical interpretation, based on the liturgist's keen observation that the three youths' faith spared their lives, allows the "original voice" to be heard clearly and loudly throughout this mini composition:

> As in raindrop [*psekadi*], in the midst of the flame [*phlogos*], by the dew
> [*tē drosō*] of the Spirit, rejoicing, God's youths were walking about
> [*periepatoun*] mystically [*mystikōs*]; by this, pre-typifying [*protypōsantes*]
> the Trinity [*triada*] and the Incarnation of Christ [*sarkōsin Christou*], and
> as wise [*hōs sophoi*] through faith [*dia pisteōs*] they quenched [*esbesan*]
> the fire's power [*dynamin pyros*]. (Sunday of the Forefathers, Vespers,
> Steicheron 3)

Marian-Christological

> In the flaming furnace of fire, as in the bedewing, the faithful and your Holy
> Youths pre-painted from life [*proezōgraphoun*] mystically your coming
> [*eleusin*] from the Virgin [*parthenou*], which shone forth [*analampsasan*]
> to us without being burnt [*aphlektōs*]. And Daniel, the Just, and wonderful
> among Prophets, clearly [*tranōs*] foreshowing [*prodēlōn*] your second di
> vine sojourn [*epidēmia*], cried out: "Looking [*heōrōn*] until [*heōs hou*]
> the thrones were set [*etetēsan*], says he, and the judge [*kritēs*] sat down
> [*ekathestē*], and a river of fire [*pyros potamos*] appeared [*epestē*]"; from
> which, by their intercessions [*hikesiais*], may we be rescued [*rhystheiēmen*],
> O Master Christ! (Sunday of the Forefathers, Vespers, Sticheron *Ho en
> Edem Paradeisos*)

The hymn combines the three youths story (Dan 3) with the vision of the thrones (Dan 7:9–10).[96] The latter is part of Dan 7:1–14 which includes two other visions: the four beasts (vv. 1–8) and the judgment before the Ancient of Days (vv. 11–14).

The hymn opens with a Marian-Christological typology: the three youths in the flaming furnace "pre-painted from life" (*proezōgraphoun*) Christ's first "coming" (*eleusin*) from the Virgin, which shone forth without any burning. The central idea is that the fire of Christ's divinity did not burn either the Virgin or those who followed him.

The second typology is solely Christological in scope. The hymnographer moves from Dan 3 to Dan 7:9–10, while mentioning the "second divine sojourn" (*theian deuteran epidēmian*) of Christ, namely, his second coming and dwelling among humans. One may assume that the "judge" (*kritēs*) who "sat" (*ekathestē*) on one of the thrones is Christ. The judgment scene is dominated by the "river of fire" (*pyros potamos*) from which the hymnographer prays that the followers of Christ will be rescued through the intercessions of the three youths.

Here is Dan 7:9–10 which the hymnographer used in crafting the second typology:

> I watched [*etheōroun*] until the thrones [*thronoi*] were placed [*etethēsan*],[97] and the Ancient of Days [*palaios hēmerōn*] sat [*ekathēto*], and his mantle was white like snow and the hair of his head was like pure wool; his throne was a flame of fire [*phlox pyros*], and its wheels [*trochoi*] a burning fire [*pyr phlegon*]. A river of fire [*potamos pyros*] drew in [*heilken*] before him. Thousand thousands [*chiliai chiliades*] were serving [*eleitourgoun*] him, and ten thousand times ten thousands were attending [*pareistēkeisan*] him. A court sat in judgment [*kriterion ekathisen*], and books were opened. (Dan. 7:9–10 [Theod.])

Let us compare the second part of the hymn to its inspiring text base, Dan 7:9–10. One may notice that Daniel in the biblical text is "watching" (verb *theōreō*, "to behold, look at; to see in a vision"), while in the hymn he is merely "looking, seeing" (verb *horaō*); this lexical alteration allows the hymnographer to focus not so much on Daniel's visionary experience but rather on the occupant of the throne, who is not the "Ancient of Days" (*palaios hēmerōn*), as in Dan 7:9, but the "judge" (*kritēs*).

The image of multiple thrones (*thronoi*) on which the "court sat in judgment" (Dan 7:10) has a well-attested tradition in the ANE (e.g., the divine council of El, chief god of the Ugaritic pantheon), echoing in the Hebrew Bible (Ps 82 [81]:1, "God standing in the assembly of El(god)"; MT: ᶜdt-ʾl, "assembly of El[god]"; cf. LXX: *synagōgē theōn*, "assembly of gods"). In the New Testament, there may be an interesting parallel in the twelve apostles chosen and commissioned by Christ to sit on twelve thrones and judge the twelve tribes of Israel at the end of time (Matt 19:28; cf. Rev 20:4).[98]

The phrase "river of fire" (MT: *nhr dy nwr* [Aramaic]; Theod.: *potamos pyros*) is a hapax legomenon encountered only in Dan 7:10.[99] The biblical text is silent about the source of this "river of fire," but one may surmise that it is coming out of the already fiery throne. This river of fire "was flowing and came before him [the Ancient of Days]" (MT: *ngd w-npq mn-qdmwhy* [Aramaic]).[100] In the hymn quoted above, the "river of fire appeared" (*tou pyros epestē potamos*) when the judge sat down on his throne.

Nonetheless, the key question concerns the identity of the judge sitting on one of the thrones. Is he the Ancient of Days or perhaps the other enigmatic figure mentioned in Dan 7:13b, someone "like the Son of Man" (*hōs hyios anthrōpou*)?[101] This question is even more complicated when one takes into account the textual discrepancy between the two Greek variant readings of Daniel 7:13b.[102] For LXX,[103] the Son of Man is the same as the Ancient of Days; for Theod.,[104] these are two distinct persons. Since MT (*w-ᶜd-ᶜtyq ywmyʾ mṭʾ*, "he came as far as the Ancient of Days") is identical with the Theod., one can consider LXX the result of a (phonetic) haplography, i.e., *heōs*, "as far as" (Theod.), loses the initial epsilon and turns into *hōs*, "like."[105]

It is difficult to conclude which Greek variant the hymnographer followed, though there is a fair-to-good possibility that this was the LXX.[106] However, the hymnographer's choice for "judge" instead of "Ancient of Days" (Dan 7:9) may be explained also as reflecting the apostolic *kerygma* that the Son will preside at the final judgment: "For the Father judges no one, but has given all judgment [*krisin pasan*] to the Son" (John 5:22).[107]

Whatever might be the case with the hymnographer's choice regarding the textual variant, early Christian interpreters saw the "judge" taking a seat on one of the thrones (see the above-cited hymn) as Christ the Lord about to carry out the final judgment.

As an illustration, the *Syriac Apocalypse of Daniel*, an early-seventh-century text, in its eschatological section offers a quite elaborated description of Christ's judgment:[108]

> The Holy Cherub he will set up on Mount Zion and the throne of righteousness in the New Jerusalem. The Great Christ, the Son of Man, will sit on it, and will judge the peoples in righteousness and the nations in uprightness. He will hold [dominion] and exercise kingship for ever and ever,

and throughout generations. All the ends of the earth will worship him. A mighty fire will be around Zion, sparks of flames will be blazing around Jerusalem. And they will gather together all peoples and nations and all the just and righteous and all who fear the name of the Mighty Lord. They will come together and enter into [the city] with uncovered heads in joy in order to receive what they have been promised. And they will rejoice in the joy of Zion and in the exultation of Jerusalem. They will enter through her fiery walls, and on the sparks of fire they will set their feet. The fire will turn into dew under their feet, and fiery sparks will become holy water. (*Syriac Apocalypse of Daniel* 38–39)[109]

As in the Byzantine hymn above, so also in the Syriac apocalyptic fragment just quoted, the "fire" may have two functions: theophanic and punitive. For its theophanic function, starting with the Old Testament evidence, the fire is the distinguishing mark of God's intervention and appearances (i.e., theophanies) within the created space-time continuum (Exod 3:2–6; 19:18; 24:17; Deut 4:11–12, 15, 33; Judg 13:15–20; 1 Kgs 19:11–12). For its punitive function, fire is an instrument of punishment used by both humans and deity (Dan 3; Num 16:35; 26:10; Lev 10:2; 2 Kgs 1:10, 12, 14; Ps 97 [96]:3; Mal 4:1 [3:19]). In Dan 3, one may detect an extra function of fire: the ordeal (test) function.[110] Yet here the boundary between punitive and ordeal functions is quite slim. Nebuchadnezzar's initial intent was to punish the three youths by casting them into a fiery furnace, but eventually the fire turned into dew, and so the ordeal purpose of such a failed punishment came to the fore. Thus, the king, convinced of the Jewish youths' innocence, issues a decree against anyone blaspheming the Jewish God.

Unlike this biblical account, in Dan 7 and its later interpretations (i.e., Byzantine hymn and Syriac apocalypse), the fire has a theophanic and punitive functionality.[111] It points to God's ultimate theophany on the day of universal judgment while representing a frontier between God/New Jerusalem and the "outside" reality. As such, the fire has a punitive role, namely, consuming those who are not worthy to enter God's kingdom (Matt 13:42: *kaminon tou pyros*, "furnace of fire") while becoming inoffensive to Christ's followers. The punitive function can be surmised from the hymnographer's prayer to the three youths to intercede with God to rescue the faithful out of the "river of fire" as well as from the *Syriac Apocalypse of Daniel*, where Christ's people are depicted as entering unconsumed through New Jerusalem's fiery walls.

The hymn examined above proffers an ingenious sort of typology that I would label "meta-typology," namely, two interconnected serial typologies. The first part of the hymn, a Christological-Marian typology, opens up to a full-fledged Christological typology. The passage from one typology to the other is done via the "fire" motif: the fire in the furnace turns into the river of fire marking the judge's presence. Conspicuously, the fire does not hurt God's faithful servants (i.e., Jewish youths, the Virgin, and hopefully the faithful for whom the hymnographer prays). Moreover, the switch between Christ's first "coming" (*eleusin*) and his "second divine sojourn" (*theian deuteron epidēmian*) contributes to a smooth transition from Marian-Christological to Christological in this meta-typology.[112]

Trinitarian

Three Youths in a furnace typifying [*typōsantes*] the Trinity [*triada*], trampled down [*katepatēsan*] the fire's threat [*apeilēn*], and praising [*hymnountes*], they cried out [*eboōn*]: "Blessed [are you], God of our fathers." (Heirmlogion, Heirmos *Treis Paides en kamino*, Ode 3, Mode 3)

The hymnographer depicts the "three Youths" (*treis paides*) in a furnace as "typifying" (*typōsantes*) the "Trinity" (*triada*). Does the typological relationship between three Jewish servants and the Trinity lie with the number three solely, or could it be extended to the three youths' "trampling down" (*katepatēsan*) the fire's threat? If the latter explanation holds true, then "typifying" the Trinity empowered somehow the three servants to overlook the dangerous environment in which they were cast and to praise the God of their fathers.

In the following hymn, again the number three serves as a starting point for a Trinitarian typology. Each person of the Trinity is described with its distinguishing main attribute: God the Father is the "Maker" (*dēmiourgos*); God the Son, the Logos, is the one who "condescends" (*synkatabōn*); and the all-holy Spirit is the one who "gives life" (*zōēn parechōn*) to all:

O Three youths, same in number as the Trinity [*tēs triados isarithmoi*], bless God the Father, the Maker [*dēmiourgon patera theon*]. Praise the Word who condescended [*synkatabanta Logon*], and who changed [*metapoiēsanta*] the fire into dew [*droson*], and exult exceedingly [*hyperypsoute*], to the ages, the all-holy Spirit [*pneuma panagion*] who gives life [zōēn parechōn] to all. (Heirmologion, Heirmos *Eulogeite Paides*, Ode 8, Mode 4)

Taking these three attributes in their succession (maker, condescending, and life-giving) one may notice a gradual unfolding of caring that originates in one godhead. The three youths are preserved through God's condescension which turned the fire into dew. The unity as source and action is translated into diversity of attributes or aspects of the same divine providence. This unity in diversity of the Trinity is illustrated by the unity in faith of three youths in the furnace:

Come now all [*deute apantes*], let us celebrate [*panēgyrisōmen*] faithfully [*pistōs*] the annual memorial [*mnēmēn*] of the fathers before the Law [*pro nomou*]: Abraham and those with him. Let us honor [*timēsōmen*] worthily [*axiōs*] the tribe [*phylēn*] of Judah, and let us extol [*euphēmēsōmen*] the youths in Babylon, who quenched [*sbesantas*] the flame in the furnace as a type of the Trinity [*ōs tēs triados typon*], and also Daniel. Holding fast [*katechontes*], trustworthily [*asphalōs*], to the Prophets' predictions [*prorrēseis*], along with Isaiah, let us cry out in a loud voice [*megalophōnōs*]: "Behold the Virgin [*hē parthenos*], will conceive in the womb [*en gastri lēpsetai*] and she will bear [*taxetai*] a Son, Emmanuel, which means God is with us." (Sunday of the Forefathers, Matins, Lauds)

In this hymn, the three youths are mentioned in the middle of a list of Christ's forefathers who are liturgically remembered on the Sunday prior to the feast of Nativity. The hymn identifies among these forefathers names such as Abraham, (the tribe of) Judah, Daniel, and Isaiah and concludes with a classical messianic text, Isa 7:14 (LXX), pointing to the virginal birth of Emmanuel.

In the hymnographer's view, the three youths are a "type" (*typos*) of the Trinity simply due to their numeral identity with the number of the divine persons. One may notice, though, that the function of the "type" somehow enables the Jewish youths to extinguish the flame in the furnace. As we have seen on other occasions, being a type (foreshadow) of a future or metaphysical entity (i.e., event, figure) positions the type in an intimate relationship with the antitype, which in turn transfers to the former some of its own attributes or qualities. In our case, the Trinity (antitype) "represented" by the three youths (type) confers to the latter the blessing to quench the fire and get out of the furnace unharmed.

The juxtaposition of this Trinitarian typology with Isa 7:14 betrays a certain hymnic tradition that saw in Dan 3 a textual basis for the two typologies, Christological (Incarnation) and Trinitarian: the three youths standing for the triune God, while the flame in the furnace symbolizes the divinity of the Logos tabernacling in Mary's womb, yet leaving this holy receptacle of incarnation entirely unharmed.[113]

The Cross

The thrice-blissful [*trismakarioi*] Youths of old [*pote*], in the furnace, raising up [their] hands, they pre-typified [*proetypoun*], O Good One, your undefiled Cross [*achranton stauron*], through which, O Christ, you overthrew [*katheiles*] the rule/tyranny [*dynasteia*] of the enemy [*echthrou*]. (Sunday of the Myrrh-Bearing Women, Heirmos *Ton en ti bato Mosi*)

In this hymn, the mere "pre-representation" (*protypoō*) of the cross by the youths with their hands raised up in an orante attitude of prayer gave the youths some of the power of the cross, formerly an instrument of punishment but, due to Christ's crucifixion (i.e., his free and substitutionary offering on behalf of fallen humanity), a means of salvation and an "undefiled" object of worship able to overthrow the tyranny of the enemy. The time elapsed between type (three youths in the furnace) and antitype (cross), underscored by a few narrative elements (i.e., "of old" [*pote*], "pre-typified" [*proetypoun*]), did not hinder the transfer of power from antitype to type.

3

Bravery

A Daring Woman and a Hiding Eve—Holy Wednesday

Overview

On Holy Wednesday, the virtue of bravery takes center stage.

> On Holy and Great Wednesday, remembrance should be made of the prostitute woman [pornēs gynaikos] who anointed [aleipsasēs] the Lord with [fragrant] oil [myrō], as the most divine fathers decreed [ethespisan], that this occurred shortly [micron] before the saving Passion. (Synaxarion)

The hymns prescribed for Holy Wednesday are meant to underline the contrast between two women: the sinful woman who anointed Jesus's feet and the old Eve of Eden. Both women are depicted as sinful, but while the former dares to approach the Lord who could liberate her from the yoke of sin, the latter, out of shame and fear, hides herself among Eden's trees in a childish attempt to avoid God's presence. In addition, the tragic figure of Judas, confused, angered by his master's sayings and actions, and cowardly handing over Jesus to the high priests, overshadows this day's hymnography.

Even though the gospel lection (Matt 26:6–16) prescribed for the Presanctified Liturgy on Holy Wednesday refers to the anointment in the house of Simon the Leper of Bethany, which happened during Jesus's last week in Jerusalem, the day's hymnography is dominated by the hymn of Kassia inspired by another anointment, that one done by a sinful woman in the house of Simon the Pharisee of Capernaum at the beginning of Jesus's ministry (Luke 7:36–50). The female hymnographer contrasts the sinful woman to Eve, the feet of Jesus representing the common element linking the gospel episode to the Eden story. Jesus's feet which the sinful woman anoints are somehow the same as God's "feet" whose walking sound was perceived by Adam and Eve (Gen 3:8).

Hearing the Scriptures. Eugen J. Pentiuc, Oxford University Press. © Oxford University Press 2021.
DOI: 10.1093/oso/9780190239633.003.0004

Kassia's life intersects with the destiny of the sinful woman of the gospel, and the hymnographer's poetry seeks to mix personal memories with scriptural references. The melding of poetry, Scripture, theology, and personal reflection is at its best in Kassia's hymn.

Through her well-chosen coinage, "the woman who fell in with many sins," Kassia turns a particular sinful woman from the small Galilean fishing town of Capernaum into a paradigmatic figure epitomizing human sinfulness in all its complexity. And in universalizing the "sinful" Galilean woman, the hymnographer brings us to the foremother, Eve, a neophyte to the lexicon of sinfulness, with its keywords *frustration*, *shamefulness*, *timidity*, and *fearfulness*.

The only Old Testament scriptures detected in Kassia's hymn are from the "primeval history" (Gen 1–11), more specifically Gen 1–3. Gen 3:8 tells us that Adam and Eve, hearing the "sound" of God walking in the Garden of Eden, hid themselves, and v. 10 (Adam talking to God) is explicit about the reason for such behavior: fear of God, since they both realized that after taking from the forbidden tree of knowledge of good and evil, they were actually naked.

Kassia emphasizes God's presence in Eden by using the word *krotos*, "striking (sound)," of God's walking. In her hymn, Kassia underscores the movement from a sonic revelation prior to the Incarnation to a visual revelation through Jesus: God's feet have been "heard" in the garden; now, in Simon's house, the same divine feet are "seen," are tangible, and are within this sinful woman's very reach. One woman fearfully hides herself among the trees away from God; another woman daringly hides herself from people while coming closer to Jesus.

Collaterally, the Old Testament readings prescribed for Holy Wednesday's Presanctified Liturgy, Exod 2:11–22 and Job 2:1–10, reinforce the day's central theme of bravery and determination by supplementing it with integrity and justice: for his courageous acts of justice, such as helping the oppressed Hebrews in Egypt, Moses is repaid with an exile, while Job remains upright in the time of trials and temptations.

Timeline: On Wednesday, Jesus did not go to Jerusalem but remained in Bethany, at his friend Lazarus's home. That day, Simon the Leper of Bethany invited Jesus to his house to have supper. During supper, a woman came with an alabaster of costly myrrh and poured it on Jesus's head, a gesture interpreted by Jesus as a preparation for his burial. The episode ends with the apostles' consternation at Jesus's approval of the unnecessary money spent for his anointment instead of helping the poor. This is also the day when Judas went to the high priests in Jerusalem to negotiate the price of Jesus's delivery to them (Matt 26:6–16).

Services and lections for Holy Wednesday: Matins (officiated by anticipation on Holy Tuesday evening), John 12:17–50; Vespers and Presanctified Liturgy (officiated on Holy Wednesday), Exod 2:11–22; Job 2:1–10; Matt 26:6–16.

Analysis
The Sinful Woman: Determination and Bravery

Scripture: The Anointing of Jesus's Feet by a Sinful Woman (Luke 7:36–50)
The hymns on Holy Wednesday send one back to the Old and New Testaments, primarily to the gospels dealing with the sinful woman who anointed Jesus's feet, and Judas, who betrayed Jesus, as well as to Gen 3:8, specifically to Eve's hiding among the garden's trees at the "sound" of God's footsteps.

Let us first take a look at the gospel references. From the outset, one notices that there are three different gospel anointing episodes during Jesus's public mission:

1. the anointing of Jesus's feet in the house of Simon the Pharisee by a sinful woman ("sinner in the city"), which occurred perhaps in Capernaum (Luke 7:36–50);
2. the anointing of Jesus's feet in Bethany, perhaps in the house of Lazarus after the latter's resurrection, by Mary (John 12:1–8) as a prophetic sign of entombment; and
3. the anointing of Jesus's head in the house of Simon the Leper, in Bethany, by a unnamed woman (Matt 26:6–16; Mark 14:3–9) as a prophetic sign of entombment.

There is a certain consensus among scholars that in spite of similarities and hints, there is no sufficient ground for identifying the Lukan episode with the Bethany anointing occurrences.[1]

Since the Kassia hymn, analyzed below, is primarily centered on the anointing of "a woman who fell in with many sins," it would be appropriate first to take a closer look at Luke 7:36–50, the only gospel pericope in the

New Testament mentioning that Jesus's feet were anointed by "a woman, that was a sinner in the city" (v. 37).

Scholars generally agree that Luke 7:36–50 (as literary genre, an apothegm or "table talk")[2] is embedded within a wider literary unit (Luke 7:1–50). It comes after a pericope dealing with John the Baptist's and Jesus's ministries (vv. 18–34). Thus, v. 35 is a gloss linking the two pericopes. A good grasp of the structure and composition of Luke 7[3] assists the reader in a correct understanding of the sinful woman's daring attitude toward Jesus, the wonder teacher who proclaimed, as John had done before him, divine forgiveness to those who repent. The proverb in v. 35 ("But Wisdom is justified by all her children")[4] intimates that the sinful woman is one of Wisdom's children; through her love and faith in Jesus, she does prove that God works through Jesus, *the* divine Wisdom, who, though ignored by "the people of this generation" (v. 31), can produce concrete results.[5]

Here is a summary of the Luke 7:36–50 pericope's most salient points:

"One of the Pharisees asked him [Jesus] to eat[6] with him. And entering the Pharisee's house, he reclined [*kateklithē*] [at the table]" (Luke 7:36). Jesus's host is a Pharisee,[7] whose name (Simon) will be revealed a little later in the story when Jesus addresses him (v. 40). In spite of their differences of opinion on various *halakhoth* (law matters),[8] the Pharisees and Jesus were on reasonable terms. Some of the Pharisees invited Jesus to eat with them, as in the present case (cf. Luke 11:37; 14:1).[9]

The place where the Pharisee lived was likely Capernaum, a thriving fishing town on the northern shore of the Sea of Galilee, known as Jesus's "home" (Mark 2:1) or "his own city" (Matt 9:1) during Jesus's long ministry in Galilee (Mark 1:29–35). Capernaum was the town where some of Jesus disciples (Peter, Andrew, James, John, and Matthew) lived, and Jesus most likely spent many nights in Peter's home.[10]

"He [Jesus] reclined [at the table]." This was the common posture for eating in the Greco-Roman world. Jews and Romans did not sit but rather reclined at the table.[11] A Roman dining room was called a *triclinium* because it was usually furnished with three couches, arranged in U-shaped formation. On each couch, three or four individuals would lean on their left sides with their right hands reaching for food that was placed on the table(s) in the middle of the room. Couches were dressed with cushions so that guests could lean more comfortably. While eating, guests stretched their feet behind them. This posture explains how a woman sneaked into the dining room and then knelt at the back of the couch where Jesus was reclining and began to anoint his feet without being noticed by the host, at least for a little while.

"And, lo, a woman in the city, which was a sinner [*hamartōlos*], having learned that he [Jesus] was reclining [*anakeitai*] [at the table], in the Pharisee's house, brought an alabaster jar of [perfumed] ointment [*myrou*]" (Luke 7:37). The interjection *idou*, "lo, behold," announces a surprising, unusual, unexpected event—in this case, a sinful woman from that city (perhaps Capernaum) enters the house of a Pharisee, a person preoccupied with purity laws (*halakhoth*). How could a "woman of the streets" enter the house of a notable person, a Pharisee, without being noticed? Perhaps the house's door was left open and guests were still coming in. If so, the sinful woman could have hidden herself among guests and slipped into the house surreptitiously.

John Nolland suggests connecting *en tē polei*, "in the city," with *hamartōlos*, "a sinner"— a Semitic idiom meaning a "well-known," "public sinner," the "city's sinner."[12] The generic designation *hamartōlos*, "sinner," does *not* necessarily connote sexual depravation or prostitution, even though it could possibly designate such a person. Moreover, ancient Christian writers, beginning with Pope Gregory the Great (540–604),[13] have identified this sinful Galilean woman with Mary of Bethany—and even Mary Magdalene. Nevertheless, there is no evidence in the gospels for such identification. Mary of Bethany is not a "sinner," and Luke (10:39, 42) is aware of her praiseworthy behavior. As for Mary Magdalene, Luke significantly ranks her first in two different lists, i.e., female disciples of Christ who used their own personal resources to minister to him (Luke 8:1–3; cf. Mark 15:40–41) and the myrrh-bearing women who announced to the apostles about the empty tomb (Luke 24:10).

"She brought in an alabaster [jar] of [perfumed] ointment [*alabastron myrou*]." *Alabastron* or *alabastros* (cf. Luke 7:37; Matt 26:7; Mark 14:3) designates a vase for keeping perfume/ointment, made of alabaster (a sort of soft marmoreal stone) and with a long neck that was usually smashed (cf. Mark 14:3) when the perfumed ointment was used.[14] *Myron* (Semitic loanword: Heb. *mōr*, "myrrh," resin of *Commiphora habessinica*) means "ointment," "perfume," used for common anointing or for embalming a body (Luke 23:56).[15] The use of *myron* (and not merely olive oil, *elaion*, Luke 7:46) is a clear indication that the woman offered the *best* oil she owned.[16] In Mark 14:3, the ointment (*myron*) is identified with "spikenard" (*nard*).

"And standing behind, by his feet, weeping, she began to wet his feet with tears and she wiped them away with the hairs of her head and she kissed passionately his feet and anointed [*ēleiphen*] them with [perfumed] ointment"(v. 38). After her unnoticed and somewhat mysterious entrance, the woman was now "standing" (*stasa*) behind Jesus, more precisely "by his feet" (*para podous autou*). With the flood of tears, she moistened (*brechein*)[17] Jesus's feet. Then she probably bent over or knelt down, and, using her untied tresses as a towel, she wiped his feet while kissing them affectionately. The composite verb *kataphileō* may have this special connotation, "kissing with fervor and passion."[18] It was as if she had dreamed for some time to be close to Jesus, and now, when the moment arrived, she could not suppress her genuine love toward him except by instantaneous, ardent kisses.

The "anointing"[19] itself comes as a climax of a series of deep feelings that the sinful woman came to experience during that short, silent, yet so personal and intimate time she spent at Jesus's feet. Nevertheless, wetting Jesus's feet with tears and drying them with her hair were *not* a premeditated gesture. They were rather a spontaneous outburst of affection, remorse, and gratitude. The sinful woman's initial goal was to anoint Jesus's feet.

The woman's demeanor and body language (i.e., abundant tears, spread-out hair,[20] passionate kissing, anointing feet with costly perfume) can be interpreted as signs of intimacy.[21] If she indeed was a prostitute (the term *hamartolos*, "sinner," can be taken as a sort of euphemism for prostitute), perhaps that was the *only* way she knew to express her gratitude toward Jesus, the teacher of forgiveness and love.[22] And the latter neither stopped nor censured her. As a true prophet, Jesus understood and accepted her unconventional yet heartfelt gestures.[23]

Speaking of the sinful woman motif in Late Antique Syrian literature, Hannah Hunt remarks that its popularity is due partially to an intriguing juxtaposition of ascetic anthropology and penitence.[24] Unlike the "ravaged and neglected body of a hermit," the sinful woman is restored through penitence to God while keeping the integrity of her attractive body. There is a strikingly subtle mix of sexuality and penitence in this unique biblical character.

"When the Pharisee who invited him saw [this], he said to himself, 'This one [*houtos*], if he were a prophet, he would have known who and what sort of woman is this one who touches [*haptetai*][25] him, for she is a sinner" (v. 39). Oddly, the host could not observe the woman entering his very own house. It is now, *after* her weeping, wiping, and anointing, that he realizes (active participle *idōn*, "seeing, noticing") that he has an uninvited, unwelcome guest in his house. It is quite ironic that the host, who himself had failed to see this woman entering his house, had the effrontery and hypocrisy to judge Jesus as not being a prophet.

Instead of talking to himself and judging the "other," as the Pharisee did, Jesus chooses to be outspoken and enlighten all those present at the repast. His word to Simon, beginning in a mild, polite tone, "I have something to say to you" (v. 40), turns into a brief and somewhat moralizing story (vv. 41–42), a parable about a creditor and two debtors. One debtor owed the creditor five hundred denarii, and the other owed fifty. Since both were unable to pay back their debts, the creditor canceled the debts for both of them. At the end of the parable, Jesus raises a maieutic question (v. 42): "Now, which of them will love him more?" Simon, unsure where Jesus is going with this line of questioning, prefixes his answer with a cautious "I *suppose*" (*hypelambanō*): the one with a greater debt will love him more, for love is commensurate to forgiveness (v. 43). Looking at the woman, Jesus answers Simon while praising the uninvited guest for her self-offering and love (vv. 44–47). There is a sharp contrast between the repenting woman, who offers tears, perfumed oil, and kisses and the quick-to-judge Simon, who, as a host, failed to offer his guest the basic signs of hospitality: foot-washing, anointing, and a welcoming kiss.[26] The sinful woman, the uninvited and unwelcomed intruder, the mysterious trespasser, now becomes Jesus's real host.[27]

At the end of the pericope, Jesus turns to the woman with a brief logion in passive conjugation, "Your sins have been forgiven [*apheōntai*]" (v. 48), which, for some inexplicable reason, scandalizes those present at the table. Until this moment, they have been a mute group of people, but now, following Simon's example, they question Jesus's *authority* to forgive sins, though the logion suggests that God alone can forgive sins (cf. the theological passive "[your sins] have been forgiven"),[28] while Jesus is "simply" the herald of divine forgiveness. Luke 7:36–50 ends in a rather abrupt way, with no further discussion on forgiveness (cf. Mark 2:5–12) but rather with Jesus's final word to the woman: "Your faith saved you. Go in peace" (v. 50).

But where should this woman go? Back to the streets whence she came? Here the gospel invites its readers to stop a bit and reflect on the role of the Church as an extension of Jesus in society: "The story screams the need for a church, not just any church but one that says, 'You are welcome here.'"[29]

At the end of this summary, an important question arises: does human love precede divine forgiveness, or is it the natural response to the latter? To phrase it another way, is human love the cause or the consequence of divine forgiveness? In other terms, is it the free grace of God or our actions that save us? The final word of Jesus (v. 50), "Your faith saved you," leans toward human love as the *cause* of forgiveness. Jesus pronounces forgiveness upon a sinful woman who minutes earlier showed her love toward him. However, as Joseph A. Fitzmyer rightly points out, Luke 7:47 can be taken either way with respect to the relationship between forgiveness and love:[30] "For this reason, I say to you: 'Her sins, which are many, have been forgiven [*apheōntai*] for she loved [*ēgapēsen*] much; but to whom little is forgiven [*aphietai*], loves [*agapa*] little."

Ancient interpreters dealt in various ways with this conundrum. For instance, Origen suggests that the woman was forgiven *because* of her generous love. Origen ranks love as the sixth among seven ways through which forgiveness is granted: "forgiveness comes through the abundance of love. The Lord himself says, 'Truly I say to you, her many sins are forgiven because she loved much.' The apostle says, 'Because love will cover a multitude of sins' [1 Pet 4:8]" (*Homilies on Leviticus* 2.4.5).[31] However, for John Cassian, love is the *consequence* of forgiveness: "It happens that, whatever state of life a man has reached, he sometimes can offer pure and devout prayer. Even in the lowliest place, where a man is repenting from fear of punishment and the judgment to come, his petitions can enrich him with the same fervor of spirit as the man, who attained to purity of heart, gazes upon God's blessing and is filled with an overwhelming happiness. As the Lord said, 'The one who knows he has been forgiven more begins to love more'" (*Conferences* 2.9).[32]

Conspicuously, other biblical texts, motifs, and figures, as well as hymns from various Holy Week days, are interspersed among Holy Wednesday's remembrance of the sinful woman. For instance, the story of the three Jewish youths in the fiery furnace (Dan 3), remembered on Holy Tuesday, resurfaces here in order to highlight the virtue of courage and determination of the sinful woman who anointed Jesus's feet. Similarly to the three youths who "trampled [*patēsantes*] the royal decree," the woman overlooked and breached the rules and regulations of "high society" when she entered the Pharisee's house determined to get as close as she could to Jesus, the wonder teacher of forgiveness and love. In the same vein, Mary, the "mother of Emmanuel" (*mētera tou Emmanuēl*), is mentioned here, as a reinforcement of the belief that through Jesus's mother, *any* sinner can get close to Christ and receive forgiveness, as it obtained with the anointing woman—or, perhaps, even more efficiently than the latter, for Jesus's mother is now the premier intermediary and intercessor between sinners and the Lord. Holy Wednesday, at the middle of the spiritual journey of Holy Week, reuses the marital imagery of the bridegroom and his "decorated wedding hall" (*nymphōna kekosmēnon*) over against the unpreparedness of the lamenting worshiper who has no fitting wedding "garment" (*endyma*) as a reminder of the great chasm sin creates between God and human beings.

The parable of the talents (Matt 25:14–30) or, more precisely, "the one who hid the talent" (*tou krypsantos to talanton*), is mentioned at the service of Vespers and Presanctified Liturgy on Holy Wednesday to warn worshipers against idleness and indolence with regard to God's gifts— namely, that "God's Word" (*logon theou*) is to be turned into "wonders" (*thaumasia*), which should not be hidden but rather fully proclaimed (*katangelō*). The subsequent scene of the final judgment in Matt 25:31–46 looms at the Vespers service, along with a hymnographer's utmost and daring plea to the "good Shepherd" (*poimēn agathe*) not to "separate" (*diachōrizō*) sinners from him.

Hymnography: The Hymn of Kassia

The hymnography of Holy Wednesday revolves around three biblical figures and the sharp contrast between them: the female sinner exuding contrition, love, and determination;[33] Eve exhibiting blame shifting and impenitence, fear, and embarrassment; and Judas displaying treachery/deceitfulness (*dolios*) and avarice.

An important hermeneutical procedure used across the entire liturgical corpus is producing backstories or offering background for situations and characters found in biblical narratives.

With respect to the Lucan pericope, these backstories might have been determined by three important factors or objectives: (1) to harmonize biblical texts apparently contradicting each other (e.g., the three various accounts of female anointers spread over the four canonical gospels) using the "narrative conflation" procedure leading to a meta-story with its own life and history; (2) to fill in the gaps (e.g., the mysterious silence of the female anointer in all the three anointing episodes) by retelling or expanding on the original narrative;[34] and (3) to clarify and explain uncommon features, words, and phrases encountered in the biblical narrative (e.g., the awkward phrase describing the sinful woman in Luke 7:36–50).

As a brief illustration of the third point above, the hymnographers modify Luke 7:37's description—"a woman, that was a sinner in the city" (*gynē hētis ēn en tē polei hamartōlos*)—reducing the whole phrase to *hē hamartōlos*, "female sinner," *gynē hamartōlos*, "sinful woman," *hypeuthynos hamartiais*, "responsible for sins," or *hē bebythismenē tē hamartia*, "the one who submerges in sin," thus making the sinning or guiltiness of sin an intrinsic part of the anointing woman's personality. For the hymnographers, this woman is not simply a "sinner [known] in the city," a "public sinner," but rather *the* sinner par excellence. Moreover, the hymnographers take another step: identifying the woman's "sinfulness" with "prostitution" itself by qualifying this woman as *pornē*, a "prostitute."

The hymn of Kassia, examined in depth below, concludes the Matins service for Holy Wednesday. It is actually the last *apostichon* before Matins' concluding prayers and *apolysis* "dismissal." In its position at the end of Matins, the Kassia hymn is an exquisite summary of all other hymns having the sinful woman of Luke 7 as a central theme. Here is the hymn of Kassia (apostichon) line by line:

1. Lord, the woman [*hē gynē*] who fell in with [*peripesousa*] many sins [*pollais hamartiais*],
2. Sensing [*aisthomenē*] your very divinity [*tēn sēn theotēta*],
3. Assumed [*analabousa*] the role [*taxin*] of a myrrh bearer [*myrophorou*];
4. While lamenting [*odyromenē*],[35] she offers [*komizei*] you [fragrant] oils [*myra*] prior to entombment [*entaphiasmou*].
5. "Woe to me! [*hoimoi*]"—she said—"for night [*nyx*] is upon [*hyparchei*] me,
6. The insane passion of debauchery [*oistros akolasias*]; dark [*zophōdēs*] and moonless [*aselēnos*]
7. Lust for sin [*erōs hamartias*].
8. Accept [*dexai*] the streams [*pēgas*][36] of my tears [*dakryōn*],
9. You who use the clouds to draw [*diexagōn*] the water of the sea.
10. Bend down [*kamphthēti*] to me, toward the heart's sighings [*stenagmous*],
11. You who bowed [*klinas*] the heavens, by your ineffable self-emptying [*tē aphatō sou kenōsei*].
12. I shall kiss passionately [*kataphilēsō*],
13. I shall wipe dry [*aposmēxō*] again,
14. With the hair locks [*bostrychois*] of my head [*kephalēs*],
15. Your undefiled [*achrantous*] feet [*podas*];
16. Whose striking [*kroton*] having been sounded [*ēchētheisa*] in [her] ears,
17. Eve in paradise [*en tō paradeisō*] at twilight [*to deilinon*] hid herself [*ekrybē*] in fear [*phobō*].
18. O my life-saving [*psychosōsta*] Savior, who can explore [*exichniasei*]

19. The multitude [*plēthē*] of my sins and the depths of your judgments [*abyssous krimatōn*]?

20. Do not despise [*paridēs*] your very maidservant [*doulēn*],

21. You who have measureless mercy [*ametrēton eleos*].

(Holy Wednesday, Matins, Apostichon, Idiomelon)[37]

The Holy Wednesday chorale is highlighted by one of the most beautiful of all Byzantine hymns. It entered into the communal memory of the Eastern Orthodox Church and has been handed down through centuries as the "Hymn of Kassia." In medieval manuscripts, scribes titled this hymn *Eis tēn Pornēn* ("To the Harlot"), but in general, it is known as *To Troparion tēs Kassianēs* ("The Troparion of Kassiane").[38]

The hymn title derives from the personal name *Kassianē* carried by a ninth-century abbess and composer (another female composer known in Byzantium was Anna Comnena [d. 1153]). This name is the feminine Greek variant of the Latin name Cassius (English form Kassia).

Kassia (ca. between 805–810 and 843–867), an abbess and a saint in the Orthodox Church (commemorated on September 7) is the most prominent female hymnographer in the history of Byzantium as well as the Eastern Orthodox tradition. The Middle Byzantine period (ninth to twelfth centuries) represents a turning point in terms of women's involvement in literary practices.[39]

Only three female hymnographers from the eighth to ninth centuries are known to us: Thecla, Kassia, and Theodora.[40] Among these, Kassia is the best known due to her *Troparion for Holy Wednesday*, which came to be included, probably by the Studite monks, in the *Lenten Triodion* and dedicated to the sinful woman of Luke 7:36–50, whose commitment, bravery, and perseverance brought her forgiveness.

Biographical data about Kassia[41] may be gleaned from Byzantine chroniclers,[42] monastic correspondence,[43] and her own writings.[44]

Described by a Byzantine chronicler as *monachēs eulabeotatēs kai sebasmias gynaikos hōraias tō eidei* ("most reverend nun and most venerable woman, beautiful in appearance"),[45] Kassia was born ca. 805–810 in Constantinople into an aristocratic family.[46] Her father was a *candidatos*, that is, a high-ranking officer at the imperial court, and Kassia received a solid education, both secular and religious.

Kassia's participation in the "bride show" for the bachelor emperor Theophilus the Iconoclast (r. 828–842), which had been organized by his stepmother, the widowed empress Euphrosyne, mentioned by few chroniclers including Symeon the Logothete (tenth century), remains questionable.[47] The story says that during that show, Theophilus, awed by Kassia's beauty, approached her with an astute remark: "Through a woman, came forth the trivial things [ta phaula]," referring to Eve's sin, to which Kassia retorted, "But through a woman, spring the better things [ta kreittō]," intimating the Theotokos and the mystery of the Incarnation. Yet, out of pride, the emperor overlooked Kassia's beauty and wits and married Theodora of Paphlagonia on June 5, 830.[48] John Zonaras, a twelfth-century chronicler, in his work *Epitome Historiarum*, narrates how Kassia, after being rejected by Theophilus, set out to build a monastic convent, which she founded on the west side of Constantinople, near the Constantinian Walls, and became its first abbess. Although this action can be interpreted as a direct response to the emperor's refusal to marry her, nevertheless a letter from Theodore the Studite to Kassia shows that the latter had a long-lasting propensity and longing for the contemplative life.[49] The monastery of Stoudios played an important role in her decision. Stoudios became throughout the ninth and tenth centuries an important center where liturgical books were re-edited. Kassia's works were also preserved due to the diligent work of the monks of Stoudios.[50] Kassia's work includes liturgical poems (hymns, stichera, kontakia). Tradition attributes to Kassia 49 religious hymns and 261 secular verses in the form of epigrams and gnomes or moral sentences. She is best known for her liturgical hymns. She wrote an extensive number of hymns included in liturgical collections such as the *Menaia* and the *Triodion*.[51]

Her hymn for Holy Wednesday is the clearest expression of Kassia's high artistry, talent, and creativity. Kassia's poetical and musical compositions defending persecuted, marginalized, and depraved women, such as the unnamed female character of the Lucan pericope, position her as an eminent advocate for women in a society and age largely monopolized by male theologians, writers, or artists.

Kassia's troparion is considered a pseudo-autobiographical work. After she failed the "bride show" test, Kassia became a nun when Theophilus married Theodora. The legend says that Theophilus later tried to meet Kassia to convey his heartache and love. Kassia avoided seeing him, but deep in her heart she felt herself like a sinner torn apart between monastic vows and surfacing old passions. That is why the phrase "woman who fell in with many sins" might be read as intimating her own emotional struggles. When the emperor visited her monastery, Kassia fled, leaving the unfinished poem about the sinful woman on her desk. Entering the empty cell, Theophilus took the liberty of adding a few words to her poem, namely, "whose footfalls echoing in Eve's ears, in paradise, at the twilight, when she hid herself in fear," which could be interpreted as a reference to Eve hiding herself at the sound of God's footsteps in the Garden of Eden (cf. Gen 3:8) or to Kassia, who fled and hid herself from Theophilus.[52]

Much of the hymn is a reworking of Luke 7:36–50 material conflated with Matt 26:6–13, Mark 14:3–9, and John 12:1–8. Yet at the core of the hymn, as in the Lucan pericope, lies the intrinsic, reciprocal relationship between love and forgiveness.

The hymn of Kassia, carrying the superscription *Eis tēn pornēn*, "To the Harlot," is a "narrative poem" exhibiting the marks of narrative texts, telling a story while the narrator functions as a sort of "poetic persona."[53] The first-person supplication prayer of the sinner is embedded in a third-person narration. The narrator, not defined by gender, introduces the sinful woman to God's attention.

The monostrophic poem consisting of twenty-one lines may be divided into two parts: a brief narration (lines 1–4, description of the protagonist) and a direct speech (lines 5–21, a monologue of the protagonist).

The Narrative Section: Lines 1–4

Lines 1–4 are arranged in an embedded structure (scheme): ABB'A', with A and A' the longest lines, containing eighteen syllables each. Line A describes the woman before her encounter with Jesus; B and B' narrate the encounter between the woman and Jesus; A' turns to the worshipers who participate in the Holy Week services (lamenting and bringing fragrant oils to the Lord of Passion).

"The woman who fell in with [*hē peripesousa gynē*]" The hymnographer replaces the description given to the female protagonist in Luke 7:36, lit. "*a* woman [*gynē*] who was a sinner [*hamartōlos*] in the city," with "*the* woman who fell in with many sins." This change could have been caused by Jesus's observation, "Her sins are many" (*hai hamartiai autēs hai pollai*, Luke 7:47).

In the New Testament, the verb *peripiptō*, "to fall in with," occurs in the parable of the good Samaritan (Luke 10:30), with reference to "some human being" (*anthrōpos tis*) (the person similarly being unspecified, as in Luke 7:37, "*a* woman" [*gynē*]) who "fell among the robbers" (*lēstais periepesen*).

In the Kassia hymn, that same verb, *peripiptō*, with all its semantic nuances, "to fall in with, to be involved, to go along with," describes the woman's situation: she has become involved in many sins, found herself *entangled* with or in the company of sins, which are almost personified—they are her "companions" (who can become as hostile and hurtful as the "robbers" [Luke 10:30] in the parable of the good Samaritan). By continuously sinning, the woman gets into an almost personal relationship with her own sins, which eventually brings her to grief.

"Many sins [*pollais hamartiais*]" By using "many sins" (*pollais hamartiais*), instead of "sinner" (*hamartōlos*, Luke 7:37), the hymnographer aims at two goals. On the one hand, she seeks to underline the truth that there are no "absolute" sinners, hence such a label is quite artificial. Humans are frail by nature, hence they cannot be persistent even when they sin.[54] On the other hand, she tries to diffuse the interpretation that would reduce the whole problematic of sin to its carnal, sexual aspect (i.e., prostitute). Such a stereotype can be found in an incipient form in Simon's tacit remark on Jesus's inability to discern "what type of woman" (*potapē hē gynē*) the intruder was (Luke 7:39). Nonetheless, Kassia wants her female protagonist to epitomize any human being dealing with sin, forgiveness, and redemption. Calling her "the woman who fell in with many sins," Kassia makes her the paradigm for human sinfulness[55]—hence the tight correlation this hymnographer suggests between the sinful woman of the gospels and the sinful Eve at the dawn of human history (Gen 3).

"Sensing your very divinity [*tēn sēn aisthomenē theotēta*]" The contrast between Simon the Pharisee and the sinful woman regarding the spirit of discernment (i.e., being a prophet), already intimated in the Lucan pericope, is here enhanced by a participial phrase underlining the woman's ability to discern Jesus's divinity through her senses (*aisthomenē*).[56] Although not fully expressed in the hymn, the contrast between the woman's sense-based discernment and the Pharisee's distorted reasoning in the gospel is quite obvious. Quite ironically, in Luke 7:39, a sense-based reasoning ("seeing" [*idōn*], "he spoke to himself" [*eipen en heautō*]), led Simon to a wrong conclusion (Jesus is *not* a "true" prophet). In contrast with the sinful woman, Judas is depicted in hymns as "senseless" (*aphrōn*): "Senseless [was] the man among you [who became] a traitor [*prodotēs*]" (Holy Thursday, Matins, Troparion).

"Assumed the role of a myrrh bearer [*myrophorou analabousa taxin*]" Her perception of Jesus's divinity causes the sinful woman to assume (*analabousa*) the role or responsibility (*taxin*) of a myrrh bearer (*myrophorou*).

How did Kassia come to this conclusion that the sinful woman assumed the role of a myrrh bearer? Simply put, she conflated several biblical texts. The hymnographer couples not only three biblical characters—the unnamed sinner of Luke 7:36–50, the good unnamed woman of Bethany (Matt 26:6–16), and Mary Magdalene *at the tomb* (Matt 28:1; Luke 24:1, 10; Mark 16:1; John 20:1)—but also two different episodes: the anointing of Jesus's *feet* in the house of Simon the Pharisee (Luke 7:36–50), and the anointing of Jesus's *head* in the house of Simon the Leper in Bethany (Matt 26:6–16).[57] By creating a *chronotopos*[58] that defies both linear chronology and spatial allocation, the hymnographer places her protagonist in three places simultaneously: Capernaum (in Simon the Pharisee's house), Bethany (in Simon the Leper's house), and Jerusalem (outside the empty tomb). Thus, Kassia succeeds in fusing three women into a complex personality identifiable with any human being in its frailty but also in determination and generosity. As Andrew R. Dyck[59] remarks, "Cassia can be said to have laid bare the human soul in a poem of extraordinary concentration and power."

As an illustration of this gripping and convincing *chronotopos* created by Kassia, let us take a look at two texts, Luke 7:38 and John 20:11, describing two different situations: the sinful woman's anointing of Jesus's feet and Mary Magdalene's myrrh-bearing role at the tomb.

Luke 7:38: "And standing [*stasa*] behind, by his feet [*para tous podas*], weeping [*klaiousa*], she began to wet his feet with tears and she wiped them away with the hairs of her head and she kissed passionately his feet and anointed them with [perfumed] ointment."

John 20:11: "But Mary stood [*heistēkei*] outside by the tomb [*pros to mnēmeion*] weeping [*klaiousa*]. As she wept [*eklaien*], she bent over to look [*parekypsen*] into the tomb."

As one can clearly notice, there is the same word sequence in both verses: *histēmi—para tous podas/pros to mnēmeion—klaiō*, a place designation (feet/tomb) flanked by two actions (standing/weeping).

Moreover, both women are "weeping" (note the very same participial form, *klaiousa*) at two locations accompanied by an adverb conveying each woman's respect toward Jesus: the sinner "behind" (*opisō*) him, at Jesus's "feet" (Luke 7:38; among all the anointing gospel narrations, this is the only place where the anointer weeps), and Mary Magdalene "outside" (*exō*) the tomb (John 20:11).[60]

The textual parallel or biblical intertextuality proposed by Kassia suggests quite an attentive and original reading of the Bible as a whole.

"**While lamenting [*odyromenē*], she offers [*komizei*] you fragrant oils [*myra*] prior to entombment [*entaphiasmou*]**" Line 4 projects the sinful woman's anointing of Jesus's feet, coupled with Mary Magdalene bringing fragrant ointments to the tomb, into the "liturgical present," thus bridging past events of salvation history as recorded in the gospels to one's personal relationship with Christ via "liturgical performances."

The participial form *odyromenē*, "lamenting," does not refer exclusively to the sinful woman or Mary Magdalene (both described as "weeping" [*klaiō*], respectively, at the feet and outside the tomb of Jesus). It perhaps points to the inclusive and concurrent aspects of liturgical performances commemorating these two past events, where *anyone* can assume the role of sinful/myrrh-bearing woman. In support of this conjecture, one may adduce Kassia's preference for the verb *odyromai*, "to lament, mourn" (instead of *klaiō*, "to weep," found in the gospels), which can be taken as a liturgical "hermeneutical pointer."[61]

The use of the verb *komizō*, "to bring, to offer," in present tense, likely habitual present, is perhaps another liturgical indicator. If so, then *any* (and by extension, every) participant in Holy Week services can identify her/himself with the Magdalene at the tomb.

The word *entaphiasmos*, "entombment," does not occur in the Lucan pericope, but it does appear in Mark 14:8 (the anointing of Jesus's head in Bethany): "She has done what she could. She accepted [*proelaben*] to anoint [*myrisai*] my body beforehand for the entombment [*eis ton entaphiasmou*]."[62]

The Direct Speech (Monologue): Lines 5–21
With line 5, the narration turns into a direct speech (monologue)—a personal, passionate, and heartfelt confession of the sinful woman before Christ.[63]

If the Lucan pericope emphasizes the dialogue between Jesus and the Pharisee pertaining to the love–forgiveness relationship, the Kassia hymn gives the full stage to the sinful woman to express herself in a lengthy monologue spread over almost the entire poem. While entirely silent in the gospel, the woman's voice in the Kassia hymn is clearly heard. The woman's confession before Christ mirrors a deep and thorough soul-searching experience.

The monologue offers a detailed, high-resolution radiography of the woman of Luke 7:36–50, unveiling the inner life of a poor human being seen from outside, that is, from the perspective of the city: narrowly as a "sinner" (*hamartōlos*), the "kind of woman" (*potapē gynē*) everyone should avoid at all costs. Yet, inside her psyche, this poor woman was tortured and torn apart by a multitude of sinful feelings intertwined with good but stifled intentions.

The sinful woman's confession is so candid, so real, and so moving that it throws the listeners/readers off kilter. On the one hand, she recognizes ("Woe to me! [*hoimoi*]") that the "night is upon" (*nyx hyparchei*) her as a heavy load pressing, nearly crushing her (line 5). So addicted was she to "the insane passion of debauchery" (*oistros*[64] *akolasias*[65]) (line 6),[66] and so powerful was the "dark and moonless lust for sin" (*zophōdēs*[67] *kai te aselēnos erōs hamartias*) (lines 7–8) that it was impossible for her to imagine, let alone promise, change in her troublesome life. (See the typical case of a repenting sinner, the prodigal son, who "having come to his senses," begins examining his conscience and rehearsing in advance his confession before his father; Luke 15:17–19.) Contrariwise, the woman is so extremely cognizant of her no-return, no-exit, infernal situation that she limits herself to pleading with Christ to receive her tears as the only *good* thing she can offer. (In the days of the prophet Hosea, eighth century B.C.E., a paralyzed-by-sin Israel pleads with God to accept the "fruit of her lips" [Hos 14:2/3], a confession of sorts, as the only "good thing" that *she* could offer.) Most likely exhausted by so many unsuccessful attempts to change, she cries almost in despair:[68] "Accept [*dexai*] the streams [*pēgas*] of my tears [*dakryōn*]. You who use the clouds to draw [*diexagōn*] the water of the sea" (lines 8–9).

Lines 10–11 continue this plea by bringing forth a literary motif used at times by the Hebrew prophets known as the "moral pressure," where they try to convince God to be true to his covenant and help his people:[69] "Bend down [*kamphthēti*] to me, toward the heart's sighings [*stenagmous*], you who bowed [*klinas*] the heavens,[70] by your ineffable self-emptying [*tē aphatō sou kenōsei*]." Put more simply: In the past, you bowed the heavens by self-emptying in the act of incarnation; please do it again and bow down to listen to my heart's sighs!

Here, the theologically rich term *kenōsis*, "self-emptying" (verb *kenoō*, "to self-empty"), denotes as in the New Testament text source of Phil 2:6

the divine self-humbleness that occurred in the Incarnation. Many patristic authors do the same. However, Kassia, in the heirmos of the Tetraodion, correlates kenōsis to the cross: "Habakkuk foresaw your divine self-emptying upon the cross [tēn en staurō sou theian kenōsin proorōn Abbakoum]."[71] An engaging case occurs in Kosmas the Melodist's canon for Good Friday, where the verb kenoō, "to self-empty," is in parallel with the verb hypokyptō, "to stoop under a yoke" (similar to klinō, "lie down," in Kassia's "To the Harlot" hymn), where the divine condescension encompasses both the Incarnation *and* the Passion: "At the dawn, I rise for you, who out of mercy, without change [atreptōs], you emptied yourself [kenōsanta] for the fallen one [tō pesonti], and impassibly [apathōs] stooped under the yoke [hypokypsanta] as far as the Passion [mechri pathōn]" (Good Friday, Matins, Ode 5, Heirmos).

Lines 12–15 describe two actions taken by the sinful woman as a substitute for promises that she, in her humble honesty, sees only as empty words. So instead of making promises that she could not keep, the sinful woman offers her kissing and wiping of Jesus's feet as two expressions of self-offering and genuine love. Kassia's sinful woman is somehow resigned: appealing to Christ's mercy, offering her humility and gratitude, and leaving everything to his wise judgments.[72]

Lines 16–17 introduce, somewhat abruptly, the case of Eve. However, in a closer reading of the text, one detects the hymnographer's intention to create a contrast between the female protagonist of the Lucan pericope and Eve of Genesis.[73] Both women are silent and offer no confession of sins (only in reworking the Lucan pericope, Kassia makes her protagonist speak up and confess her sins). Nevertheless, there is a huge difference between the two women: while Eve hides herself from the presence of God, the sinful woman of Luke and the Kassia hymn gathers up her courage and approaches Christ, acknowledging by silent acts (and in Kassia's hymn, by word, too) her sinfulness.[74]

In lines 18–19, given the complexity of her feelings and thoughts, the woman raises a pertinent and trenchant question: "Who can explore [exichniasei] the multitude of my sins [plēthē hamartiōn] and the depths of your judgments [abyssous krimatōn]?"—echoing Rom 11:33.

Lines 20–21 conclude this poem with another plea similar in tome to the "moral pressure" strategy found in lines 10–11" "Do not despise [paridēs] your very maidservant [doulēn], You who have measureless mercy [ametrēton eleos]"—resonating the words of Ps 51 (50):1.

A mere browsing of Holy Wednesday services shows that a sizable number of hymns ascribed for this day that mention the sinful woman, or the religious authorities (priests, scribes), also reference the name of Judas.

In all of the lists of the twelve apostles found in the synoptic gospels, Judas occupies the last spot and is always qualified with a form of the verb *paradidōmi*, "to hand over, deliver, transmit" (and by extension, with respect to Judas, "to betray"):[75] Matt 10:4, *ho kai parados auton*, "the one will deliver him"; Mark 3:19, *paredōken auton*, "who delivered him"; Luke 6:16, *egeneto prodotēs*, "who became a traitor." John, who provides no listing of the apostles per se, has a similar qualifying phrase for Judas in 6:64, 71, *ho paradōsōn auton*, "who would betray him"—possible indications that he was not among Jesus's closest friends.[76]

Regarding Judas's *motivation* for betrayal, the canonical gospels offer two possibilities: love of money (John 12:1–8) as a subtle hint and Satan's influence (Luke 22:3; John 13:2) as a clear statement. Judas's portrait painted by the hymns of Holy Wednesday draws heavily on the gospel of John. It is a bit surprising how such a brief comment found in John 12:4–6 about the treasurer-like role of Judas within Jesus's small group coupled with the label "thief" (*kleptēs*) has had such a long and strong afterlife in older and much later Christian literature.

Note that in Matt 27:3, Judas "regretted" (*metameletheis*) seeing Jesus condemned. But his regret remained just a simple inner feeling, even though outwardly he returned the money he had received for his treachery—he did not have the courage either to admit his mistake or to express his regret to the Lord. And here is the deep separating line between him and the sinful woman of the Lucan pericope: although she was unable to *promise* anything, the woman was determined to come forward, and in fact she *did*, confessing her sin rather tacitly through simple gestures of genuine, tender love; Judas failed to express his regret, and he put an end to his torment by hanging himself.

Far from being satisfying, the monetary explanation of Judas's motivation for betrayal is still ubiquitous in the Byzantine hymnography for Holy Week.

The Johannine hint at Judas "taking away" (*bastazō*) from what people used to throw into the disciples' common box (John 12:6) becomes in the following hymn "love of money, avarice" (*philargyria*). "Intoxicated/drunk" (*paroinēsas*) by avarice, Judas "premeditates" (*emeletēsen*) how to "deliver" (*paradōsō*) Jesus to the authorities:

Being in love with the love of money [*philargyrias erōn*], the treacherous [*dolios*] Judas premeditated deceitfully how to deliver you, the Treasurer of

Life. Thus, intoxicated, he runs to the Judeans, saying to the lawless, "What do you want to give me to deliver [him] to you, so that you may crucify him." (Holy Wednesday, Matins, Kathisma 2)

Note the hymnographer's explicative gloss ("so that you may crucify him"), seeking to fill in the gospel's silence on the goal of Judas's action to hand Jesus over to the high priests.

In the hymns for Holy Wednesday, when he appears along with the sinful woman, Judas may be likened to a bass guitar keeping a steady rhythm, while the woman is the lead guitar emitting brief, sharp, melodious notes. Unlike Eve (see below), who stands in sharp contrast to the sinful woman, Judas is used merely as a backdrop for the deservedly praised woman:

The harlot approached you who love humanity [*Philanthrōpe*], pouring out [*katakenousa*] perfumed ointments and tears upon your feet. At your command she was released [*lytroutai*] from the filth of evils [*dysōdia kakōn*]. On the other hand, the ungrateful disciple, still breathing your grace [*pneōn de tēn charin*], rejected this, he commingled himself with mud, selling you for love of money [*phylargyria*]. (Holy Wednesday, Matins, Kathisma 3)

In order to further heighten the contrast, the hymnographer altered slightly the order of events found in the gospels. If in Matt 26:14 (cf. Mark 14:10), Judas's approach to the priests comes after the anointing episode, in the hymn below, these two acts are concurrent, thus better underscoring the contrast between the female anointer approaching the Lord and Judas departing from him:

When the sinner brought the perfumed ointment, the disciple made an agreement with the lawless ones. She rejoiced in pouring out the pricy [perfumed ointment], but he rushed to sell the priceless One. She recognized [*epegignōsken*] the Master, but he separated [*echōrizeto*] himself from the Master. She was liberated [*ēleutherouto*], and the treacherous Judas became a slave of the enemy [*doulos echthrou*]. How great rashness [*rhathimia*]! How great repentance [*metanoia*]! "Give me this repentance, O Savior, who suffered for us, and save us!" (Holy Wednesday, Matins, Sticheron, Idiomelon)

A Hiding Eve: Shyness and Fearfulness

Scriptures

Gen 3:8 (LXX): "And they heard the sound [*phōnēn*] of the Lord God [*kyriou tou theou*] walking about [*peripatountos*][77] in the orchard [*paradeisō*] by afternoon/evening [*to deilinon*], and both Adam [LXX: *ho Adam*; MT: *hā-ʾādām*] and his wife hid themselves [*ekrybēsan*] from the presence [*apo prosōpou*] of the Lord in the midst of the timber [*en mesō tou xylou*] of the orchard."

The account of the sin of Adam and Eve (Gen 3:1–24) tells how Eve, at the serpent's shrewd and self-serving advice, took some fruit from the "tree of knowledge of good and evil" (LXX: *xylou tou ginōskein kalon kai ponēron*; MT: *ʿēṣ ha-daʿat ṭôb wā-rāʿ*) and shared it with her husband, in spite of God's expressed prohibition (Gen 2:17).

As a first consequence of their act of disobedience, Adam and Eve realized that they were naked and, out of shame, hid themselves from God's presence, among the trees of the garden (Gen 3:8). In the "afternoon/evening" (LXX: *deilinon*),[78] God was walking in the orchard.[79] At God's somewhat rhetorical question to Adam,[80] "Where are you?" (Gen 3:9), the latter retorts defensively, "When I heard the sound of you [walking] in the garden, I was afraid, because I am naked, and I hid myself" (v. 10).

Fear of guilt *and* punishment now enter the picture. Gen 2:25 states emphatically, using the same phrase, "Adam and his wife" (same pair as in Gen 3:8), that "The two of them were naked, Adam and his wife, and they were not ashamed." The creation, represented here by the trees of the orchard, ceases to be a transparent and suitable setting for a personal relationship with God,[81] turning thus into an opaque locus, a hiding place for the first humans gripped by fear and disquiet.[82]

Answering God's brief question,[83] Adam is at least (or at most) half-honest when he acknowledges that fear made him hide himself. However, he links fear only to *shame* and does not deal directly with the root problem, which is the actual sin (i.e., the conscious neglect of God's first ban, Gen 2:17).

Also of interest is that if during Eve's dialogue with the serpent (Gen 3:1–5), the awareness of God's presence was quite quiescent, that awareness now is back but aroused by a guilty conscience. Hiding suggests admission of guilt in relation to God, at least tacitly assumed by the perpetrators.[84]

Walter Brueggemann is right on point when he notes: "The story [i.e., Gen 3] is a theological critique of anxiety. It presents a prism through which the root cause of anxiety can be understood. The man and woman are controlled by their anxiety (3:1). They seek to escape anxiety by attempting to circumvent the reality of God (3:5), for the reality of God and the reality of anxiety are related to each other. Overcoming of God is thought to lead to the nullification of anxiety about self. But the story teaches otherwise. It is only God, the one who calls, permits and prohibits, who can deal with the anxiety among us."[85]

Keeping all aspects in sight, I would add that the anxiety Brueggemann mentions was part of the human condition even beforehand in the "orchard" (LXX: *paradeisos*; MT: *gan-ᶜeden*, "Garden of Eden") (Gen 2:15–17), prior to sinning. Far from being the "icon of perfection," the primordial garden is described as an ideal place but one that is still in the making, where Adam had to experience a wide array of feelings that swayed between two extremes, happiness and anxiety, with anxiety caused by insecurity that had been prompted by God's double commandment given to the first people, to "defend" (LXX: verb *phylassō*; MT: verb *š-m-r*) the garden and the ban on the "tree of knowledge of good and evil" (an idiom for perfect knowledge and power). Tormented by the insecurity born out of fear of the unknown, while unable to grasp the forbidden knowledge in order to control and overcome the unbearable predicament, the first human couple plunges deeper and deeper into anxiety, overlooking God, the only one who could eradicate that excruciating anxiety.[86]

"Anxiety," Brueggemann notes again, "comes from doubting God's providence, from rejecting his care and seeking to secure our own well-being. Failure to trust God with our lives is death. To trust God with our lives is to turn from the autonomous 'I' to the covenanting 'Thou,' from our invented well-being to God's overriding purposes and gifts."[87] Unfortunately, instead of addressing God with that covenantal "Thou," Adam employs a self-entitled and perhaps exculpating "I" which concurrently overlooks the gravity of sin and rejects the possibility of God's forgiving intervention altogether.

Hymn of Kassia: Lines 15–17
"Whose striking [hōn kroton]*"*
Kassia proves herself to be a quite careful interpreter by avoiding the word "feet," and instead resorting to the rare form *krotos*, denoting "a striking, beating" or a loud "sound produced by striking."[88] Used in reference to Gen 3:8, the word implies a fairly powerful interaction at the sonic level between God and the primeval garden.[89] It may allude to God's "feet" beating the ground while walking, thus producing a thumping sound, which is likely

Kassia's interpretation in light of Luke's use of *podas*, "feet."[90] But *krotos* may also hint at any other sound, such as striking the tree branches as God was walking in the garden.

The hymnographer switches from the New Testament's sinful woman to the Old Testament's first woman, through another shift from the visual (Jesus's) "feet" (line 15) to the sonic (God's) "striking" (line 16).

Most likely, Kassia saw in Gen 3:8 a sort of antithetic prefiguration of the New Testament episode narrated by Luke 7:36–50. In the hymnographer's view, Christ's "feet" that the sinful woman kissed and anointed are the same feet that Eve heard walking (lit. "striking") through paradise at the dawn of history, long prior to the Logos's incarnation. Thus, the Kassia hymn is a sample of typology in which "the biblical age became at once past, present, and timeless."[91] This identification leads one to the conclusion that God the Lord "walking in the paradise"[92] was somehow the Son of God prior to his incarnation.

"Having been sounded in [Eve's] ears [tois ōsin ēchētheisa]"
By replacing the wording of Gen 3:8 (LXX), "they heard the sound [*phonēn*] of God the Lord walking to and fro [*peripatountos*]," with "the striking [*krotos*] having been sounded [*ēchētheisa*] in [Eve's] ears," the hymnographer sought, first, to downplay the biblical anthropomorphic description of God and, second, to express in a more theological way the human perception of the divine presence: God, by somehow "striking" paradise's habitat, has produced a sound or echo in Eve's ears. The emphasis falls in Kassia's wording not so much on Eve's "hearing" as a human action (cf. Gen account) but rather on the "sound" (echo [Gk. verb *ēcheō*, "to sound"]) in her ears as a result of God's sonic revelation.[93]

"In the paradise, at twilight [en tō paradeisō to deilinon]"
With respect to the place and time of God's intervention, Kassia merely quotes Gen 3:8, "in the garden, at twilight [*en tō paradeisō to deilinon*]," with the caveat that, beginning with Origen and throughout the patristic period, the Greek word *paradeisos*, "garden, orchard" (a Persian loanword; cf. Heb. *pardēs* [Song 4:13]), has been heavily encased with metaphysical and eschatological overtones.

The hymnographer eliminates the detail "among the trees" (Gen 3:8) from her description of the place where Eve hid, so that the accent falls on a more spiritualized type of paradise. In Kassia's retelling, Eve's intent was from the start doomed to failure. *How* could she hide herself from God while still living in the very same place God chose to initiate and cherish a personal relationship with Adam and Eve?[94]

"She hid herself in fear [ekrybē tō phobō]*"*
There is a stimulating aspect to the contrast Kassia creates between the sinful woman and Eve that must be mentioned here. If the sinful woman finds Jesus's feet, the "best private place," somehow hidden from the eyes of the host and other guests, Eve, at the sound of God walking, finds *her* best "private place" among the trees of the garden, somehow hidden from God's eyes. One woman hides herself from others by coming closer to Jesus, while the other woman hides herself from God. Both women carry the burden of sin on their shoulders and deep in their hearts, but each of them does this in her own particular way. The sinful woman is committed to opening herself up to Jesus, but the other closes herself in front of God, in the very first environment that the Creator offered to her. The fear of guilt and punishment made one determined, the other embarrassed.

The contrast between the sinful woman and Eve reappears mutatis mutandis in one of the hymns assigned for September 7, the day of commemoration of the "Devout Kassiane the Hymnographer." The author of this hymn replaces the sinful woman from the original composition with Kassia and contrasts the latter with Eve. As in the Kassia hymn, Eve hid herself in Eden at the sound of the footsteps of the Master of All (*pantanaktos*). Contrary to Eve, Kassia hid herself at the sound of the master's (*anax*, i.e., the emperor's) footsteps, not out of fear of disobedience but as an expression of her integrity. As noted above, Emperor Theophilus visited Kassia's monastery, long after the failed bride show, but the poet-nun hid herself from his sight:

When the sound of the Master's footsteps [*podōn tou anaktos kroton*] sounded in [your] ears [*tois ōsin ēchētheisa*], in your cell, O Blessed Kassiane, you hid yourself, like Eve at the twilight, in the Eden [at the footsteps] of the Master of All [*pantanaktos*], not out of fear of disobedience [*parakoēs*], O Venerable, but as an expression of integrity [*ekphrasin semnotētos*]. (Holy Wednesday, Matins, Ode 9)

Worthy of note is the anonymous hymnographer's high degree of creativity in moving away from Kassia's biblical cast (Eve/the sinful woman).

While using a similar vocabulary and syntax to those in the Kassia hymn, the author of this new hymn shifts from the original cast to a new, still dual, distribution: a biblical figure (Eve) and a devout Christian person (Kassia).

In perusing a few dozen hymns spread throughout the Byzantine liturgical map that mention Eve, one notices that references to the foremother (*promētōr*) are quite brief and repetitive or overlapping. She is usually referred to with a single word or phrase functioning as a mini-backdrop for a creedal type of saying on Christ's and/or Mary's salutary work and how this work relates to Old Testament types and fallen humanity yet to be restored. These hymnographic references may be summed up under three headings.

The Sin of Eve

The sin of Eve (and, for that matter, Adam) is described as a "transgression" (*parabasis*), a "disobedience" (*parakoē*, lit., "mishearing"), in which the "ancient deceiver" (*pternistēs palaios*), the "slanderous enemy" (*baskanos echthros*), used "cunning devices" (*mēchanourgiai*) to induce Eve to become an "instrument for sin" (*organon pros hamartian*).

Sin's Consequences

Here are several consequences of the first sin: "casting out of paradise" (*ekballō tou paradeisou*), "ostracizing of Eden" (*exostrakizō tēs Edem*), "grief" (*lypē*), "stumbling" (*olisthanō*), "malady of disobedience" (*nosēma parakoēs*), "loss of grace" (*tēn charin apollymi*), "bareness" (*gymnoō*), i.e., defenselessness, brought upon humans by the "dragon, author of evil" (*archekakos drakōn*), "deprivation" (*stereō*) of "incorruption" (*aphthara*), "debt" (*opheilē*), and the obligatory "curse" (*katara*).

The Restoration

Eve's (and Adam's) restoration in Christ is variously termed "deliverance" (*lytrōsis*), "liberation" (*eleutheroō*), "abolishment" (*dialyō*) of the curse, "drawing out" from the curse (*rhyomai*), "recall" (*anaklēsis*), "joy" (*chara*), "renewal" (*ananeoomai*), "leading out" (*exagō*) of the gates of death, as well as Hades being taken "captive" (*aichmalōteuō*).

In sum, Eve's occurrence in Kassia's hymn, as well as most of her liturgical avatars across the huge Byzantine hymnic corpus, is related to the sin of disobedience (*parakoē*). But what makes Eve unique in comparison with the sinful woman, at least in Kassia's view, is not the sin (all humans are frail and vulnerable) but rather her inability to express her feelings of shame *and* fear. Instead of coming forward as the sinful woman did, Eve hid herself among the trees of the garden, believing in her naiveté that somehow she could isolate herself from her Creator "walking to and fro" in a garden planted for the couple's own sake.

4

Offering

Wisdom's Freely Shared Banquet—Holy Thursday

Overview

Holy Thursday is about the Wisdom of God, who offers herself humbly and throws a lavish banquet, free of charge, to all her invitees.

On Holy and Great Thursday, the divine fathers, having arranged everything well [*kalōs diataxamenoi*], in reciprocal reception [*allēlodiadochōs*] from the divine Apostles and holy Gospels, handed over [*paradedōkasin*] to us to celebrate [*heortazein*] four [things]: the sacred Washing of Feet [*ton hieron niptēra*], the mystical Supper [*ton mystikon deipnon*] (that is, according to us, the tradition [*paradosin*] of the awesome Mysteries [*mystēriōn*]), the extraordinary [divine] Prayer [*tēn hyperphya proseuchēn*], and the Betrayal itself [*tēn prodosian autēn*]. (Synaxarion)

The Synaxarion for Holy Thursday mentions four events worthy of remembrance on this day: foot washing, mystical supper, divine prayer, and betrayal. This chapter deals only with the first two: foot washing and mystical supper.

Foot washing: The pericope of Jesus washing the disciples' feet (John 13:3–17) is one of the gospel lections prescribed for this day's Vesperal Liturgy of Saint Basil.

As with any ancient Eastern banquet, at the Last Supper hosted by Jesus, foot washing was considered a prerequisite. Nevertheless, the one who washed the feet of the guests was customarily a servant, not the host himself. The hymnographer takes this important detail and turns it, by using the old Scriptures, into a new theologoumenon: God's begotten Wisdom, the one who created the lakes and springs (Ps 114 [113]; cf. 29 [28]:3; Job 38:16), the one who controls the uncontrollable "upper waters," girds himself with a towel and washes the disciples' feet in a small basin as an expression of divine

Hearing the Scriptures. Eugen J. Pentiuc, Oxford University Press. © Oxford University Press 2021.
DOI: 10.1093/oso/9780190239633.003.0005

kenosis (Phil 2:6–8). The one who encircles the sky in clouds (Ps 147 [146]:8; cf. Job 26:8), the one in whose hands lies the breath of every human being (Job 12:10; cf. Wis 3:1), the one who bends the heavens (Ps 18:9 [17:10]; 144 [143]:5), bends his knee to wash the servants' feet. In a hymn prescribed for this day, the foot washing, besides being an expression of divine condescension, functions as an act of initiation or preparation for the gospel proclamation (cf. Rom 10:15, citing Isa 52:7).

The difficult phrase "mighty love of his [God's] strength" (Hab 3:4 [LXX]) found in one of the hymns sung on this day and dealing with the same foot-washing episode conveys God's *long-suffering* love. Pertaining to Jesus washing the disciples' feet, this "mighty love" is not a sign of weakness but the mark of infinite power, since only the almighty being of Jesus could humble himself to the extent of taking on the duty of a servant.

The hymnographers saw in Habakkuk the "watcher," a prophet standing on a watching post and awaiting God's fulminant intervention (i.e., the Logos's incarnation) in human history. He is the prophet of that faith that enlivens the "righteous" (Hab 2:4), namely, those who are loyal to God—faith rewarding the faithful.

Mystical supper: At the very center of the events commemorated liturgically on Holy Thursday is the Last Supper, with its two important moments: Jesus's last discourse and the institution of the Eucharistic mystery/sacrament (Matt 26:26–29 [and parallels], as part of the gospel lections for this day's Liturgy).

As with the case of the foot washing, so, too, with the Last Supper, the choice metaphor for Jesus in the hymnography of Holy Thursday is God's begotten Wisdom, who played a significant role in creation (Prov 8:22–31).

Wisdom building a "house for herself" (Prov 9:1), slightly altered by the hymnographer to "[she] built her house," becomes a metaphor for Christ putting on a "bodily temple" (i.e., Logos's incarnation, cf. John 1:14).

In another hymn, the same Wisdom throws a banquet with a "life-sustaining table" on which she "mixes a bowl of ambrosia [immortality]" (cf. Prov 9:2), an allusion to the institution of the Eucharist. The intertextuality between "bodily temple" and "ambrosia" directs the hearer to the Eucharist and its theological relation with the Incarnation.

The future kingdom inaugurated at the Last Supper by Wisdom's banquet will be marked by a "new drink" and Jesus among other banqueters as "God among gods." A "new drink" means not merely a renewed, refreshed old drink but a fully brand-*new* drink, something along the lines of the Pauline "spiritual drink" (1 Cor 10:4; cf. Exod 17:1–7; Num 20:7–13: the "traveling rocky well"). "God among gods" is an interpretation of Ps 82 (81):1–2, 6, which emphasizes the idea that Christ not only offers his disciples a new drink "springing up into eternal life" (John 4:14), but he, the source of this eternal life, will be with his disciples forever as God among gods (i.e., deified human beings).

The Old Testament lections prescribed for this day support the mystical supper as the making of a new covenant (Jer 31 [38]:31–34). For instance, Exod 19:10–19, the consecration of the people of Israel by Moses on the eve of the making of the Sinai covenant, parallels the foot washing and the in-stitution of the Eucharist. Moreover, Job 38:1–21 and 42:1–5, dealing with God's response (i.e., God's creation conveys the Creator's wisdom) and Job's acknowledgment of God's wisdom, hints at the eternal companionship of God's Wisdom among her invitees. Lastly, Isa 50:4–11, where the Servant of the Lord calls one to listen to his voice and imitate his life of endurance, prepares us for Good Friday.

Timeline: In the morning, Jesus sends two disciples to Jerusalem to prepare a place for a special supper to be hosted by Jesus himself (Mark 14:12–16). Before dinner, Jesus washes his disciples' feet as a model of genuine serving leadership: the master takes the role of a servant. During dinner, Jesus delivers the longest discourse recorded in the canonical gos-pels. Among the highlights of the "Farewell Discourse" are the new com-mandment, the institution of the Eucharist, the promise of the Spirit, and the subtle disclosure of the betrayer (John 13–16). After dinner, very late at night, Jesus and the disciples depart for the Garden of Gethsemane in order to spend the night there. Jesus prays three times so that his Father may spare him an imminent death, but in the end he surrenders himself to the divine will. Meanwhile, Judas, accompanied by soldiers, arrives and, through a kiss, facilitates Jesus's arrest. Jesus is brought to the house of the high priest Caiaphas. Here, Peter denies his master three times as Jesus foretold he would (Luke 22:39–62).

Services and lections for Holy Thursday: Matins (officiated by anticipation on Holy Wednesday evening), Luke 22:1–39; Vespers (officiated together with the Liturgy of Saint Basil on Holy Thursday morning), Exod 19:10–19; Job 38:1–21; 42:1–5; Isa 50:4–11; Saint Basil Liturgy, 1 Cor 11:23–32; Matt 26:1–20; John 13:3–17; Matt 26:21–39; Luke 22:43–45; Matt 26:40–27:2.

Analysis

Given space restraints, as well as the special focus of this work on Old Testament textual occurrences in Holy Week liturgical services, I will dwell on only two of the four commemorating moments of Holy Thursday: the Sacred Washing of the Feet and the Mystical Supper.

The Sacred Washing of the Feet

John 13:3–17 is one of the gospel fragments selected by liturgists to be part of the gospel reading for the Vesperal Liturgy of St. Basil for Holy Thursday.

This fifteen-verse unit is the only passage among the canonical gospels narrating the foot-washing episode that occurred at the Last Supper table. The synoptics are utterly silent about it:

> Jesus, knowing that the Father has given all the things into his hands, and that he has come from God and was going to God, rose from the supper [*deipnou*], laid aside his outer garments [*himatia*], and girded himself about [*diezōsen*] with a cloth [*lention*]. Then he poured water into a basin [*niptēra*], and began to wash [*niptein*] the disciples' feet, and to wipe [*ekmassein*] them with the cloth with which he was girded. (John 13:3–5 [Byz.])

Peter was scandalized by Jesus's unequivocal humility. Why was his teacher and Lord doing what a servant was supposed to do by washing the feet of the guests (John 13:6)? According to Jesus's very words, the foot washing was intended to be a sign, a symbol, whose full significance would not be immediately and facilely understood (v. 7). At Peter's refusal of Jesus washing his feet, the latter retorts rather enigmatically: "If I do not wash you, you have no part with me [*meros met' emou*]" (v. 8). Peter's response is a request, even though he still misunderstands the sign: "Lord, not my feet only, but also my hands and my head" (v. 9), as if personal relationship with Jesus depends on *quantity*.

In the last four verses of this Johannine pericope, Jesus gives his own interpretation of the foot-washing episode: "If I, then, your Lord and teacher [*ho kyrios kai ho didaskalos*], washed your feet, you also owe [*opheilete*] to wash one another's feet" (v. 14). So, washing the feet of others is a sign of "serving leadership" as well as an act of extreme humility. By the use of the verb *opheilō*, "to owe," John underscores an important idea: to serve others is not a matter of *choice* but a *duty*, something that we *owe* to one another following Jesus's example: "For I have given you an example [*hypodeigma*], that you should do, as I have done to you" (v. 15). The gospel fragment ends with a short beatitude: "If you know [*oidate*] these things, happy [*makarioi*] are you, if you do [*poiēte*] them" (v. 17).

By washing the feet of his disciples, Jesus gave an example to follow and a paradigm to copy, a paradigm of genuine, un-trumpeted humility, divine condescension with no pretense, discreet self-offering, and boundless love, which began with the Logos's incarnation (John 1:14) and reached its apogee on the cross in Jesus's own words: "It is completed [*tetelestai*]!" (John 19:30).

The Lord of the Lakes, Springs, and Upper Waters

I do not detect any concrete or direct scriptural basis[1] or reference for the following hymns but rather mere allusions to a recurrent theme in the Old Testament: that God is the creator and controller of the sources of water (Gen 1:2, 6–10; Job 38:16, 22; Ps 29 [28]:3). God also sets the boundaries of water (Ps 104 [103]:6–13; Jer 5:22), and his control over water is seen even in the realm of salvation history, perhaps the most dramatic example being the parting of the Red Sea (Exod 15:4–5).

> The Lord, who made the lakes [*limnas*], and the springs [*pēgas*] and the seas [*thalassas*], teaching us the best humility [*tapeinōsin aristēn*], by girding himself with a [linen] towel [*lentiō*], he washed the disciples' feet. Humbling himself [*tapeinoumenos*] with the abundance of compassion [*hyperbollē eusplanchnias*], he lifted us from the pits of evil [*barathrōn*[2] *kakias*], the one who [is] alone the lover of humanity [*philanthrōpos*]. (Holy Thursday, Matins, Ode 3, Kathisma 1)

The hymn paints an extremely evocative portrait, where the powerful Creator who made all the water sources (lakes, springs, seas) humbles himself with an abundance of compassion and washes the disciples' feet, using a small water basin, thus providing them with the best example of humility. The hymnographer shares the same line of thought with Paul in Philip 2:8 (Byz.): "And having been found in the form as a human being [*schēmati . . . hōs anthrōpos*], he humbled himself [*etapeinōsen heauton*], and became obedient unto death, even death on a cross."

The strange juxtaposition between "humility" and "abundance" found in this hymn echoes Prov 13:7: "There are some who make themselves rich while having nothing, and there are others who humble themselves [*hoi tapeinountes*] in much wealth [*pollō ploutō*]" (cf. Sir 3:18; and Jesus's logion on humbling oneself in order to be exalted, Matt 23:12; Luke 14:11; cf. Jas 4:10; 1 Pet 5:6).

In the following hymn, the singularity of the humble act of washing the disciples' feet is more deeply mined by contrasting the one who masters the lofty and uncontainable water above the visible sky—namely, God's Wisdom—and the mundane activity of pouring water into a basin:

The One [*hē*] who masters [*kratousa*] the uncontrollable [*ascheton*] and upper [*hyperōon*] water in the ether [*en aitheri*],[3] and bridles [*chalinousa*] the abysses, and rears up [*anachaitizousa*] the seas, God's Wisdom [*Theou Sophia*], [now] pours waters into a basin [*niptēri*], the Master [*Despotēs*] washes thoroughly [*apoplynei*] the feet of the servants [*doulōn*]. (Holy Thursday, Matins, Ode 5, Troparion)

Here we find Jesus himself identified with the eternal Wisdom[4] (*sophia*, feminine noun, hence the feminine form of the article [*hē*]), and God's Wisdom is depicted as "mastering" the water above the visible sky.

Instead of using the more common verb *niptō*, "to wash," attested in the gospel account of the Last Supper washing (John 13:5, 10), the hymnographer, in his known proclivity to actualize the theological message, opts for the verb *apoplynō*, "to wash off, thoroughly" (a hapax legomenon in Luke 5:2, of nets being washed off by the disciples), with its emphatic ("thoroughly") and metaphorical overtones.[5]

The phrase "upper water [*hyperōon hydōr*]" *could* be a subtle hint at the place where the washing episode took place (*anōgaion*, "upper story [room]": Mark 14:15; Luke 22:12; or *hyperōon*, "upper story, room upstairs": Acts 1:13; 9:37, 39; 20:8).[6] And in fact, one of the hymns of Holy Thursday uses the same adjective in an allegorical interpretation of the "upper room": "Let us enjoy the lordly hospitality and undying table in the upper place [*en hyperōō topō*], namely, in the high-raised hearts [*tais hypsēlais phresi*]; learning from the Word a transcendent word [*epanabebēkota logon*]" (Holy Thursday, Matins, Canon, Ode 9, Heirmos).[7]

The One Who Surrounds the Sky with Clouds

The aforementioned contrast between power and humbleness, paradoxically co-inherent in God, continues in the following hymn, where the master of the universe bends his knees to wash the servants' feet. In ancient Israel, it was the duty of a servant to wash the guests' feet as a sign of hospitality—or a basin was provided for the guest to wash himself (e.g., Gen 18:4).[8] But in this hymn, as in its scriptural basis—John 13:1–20—the roles are dramatically reversed: it is the master who washes the feet of his servants. And who is this master? The hymnographer's response, inspired by Ps 147 (146):8,[9] underlines that the master is none other than the very Creator who "wraps the sky in clouds" (*ho nephelais de ton polon periballōn*).[10]

By using the "master" (*despotēs*) and "servants" (*doulōn*) antinomy, the hymnographer exhibits a careful reading of the Johannine foot-washing episode and its authorial intent. What is so fascinating in the gospel account is not simply the fact that Jesus humbles himself, thus taking the role of a servant, but the very detail that Jesus, the teacher and master, washes the feet of his *own* disciples ("servants" in the hymn). Jesus humbles himself in front of those who were supposed to hold him in great esteem and follow his example. What Jesus did is indeed unique—unheard of, even—for no prudent teacher, especially in the Jewish cultural context of the time, would be inclined to humble himself in front of his pupils. In fact, Peter's protest (John 13:6–8) was meant to highlight further the inexplicable but amazing nature of Jesus's foot washing construed as a "status reversal."[11]

> The Master sets forth [*hypodeiknyei*] a model of humility [*tapeinōseōs typon*] to his disciples; he who surrounds [*periballōn*] the sky [*polon*] with clouds, girds himself around [*zōnnytai*] with a cloth [*lention*], and he bends [*kamptei*] the knee to wash out [*ekplynai*][12] the feet of his servants; he in whose hand is the breath of all beings. (Holy Thursday, Matins, Ode 5, Troparion)

The parallel is now quite clear. The one who surrounds (*periballōn*) the sky with clouds (*nephelais*) girds himself around (*zōnnytai*) with a cloth (*lention*). Instead of using one of the clouds with which he surrounds the sky, the master resorts to a mere piece of fabric that he girds himself with after divesting himself of his garments (John 13:4: "he laid aside [his] [outer] garments and girded himself around [*diezōsen*] with a cloth [*lention*])."[13]

A significant detail where Jesus "bends [his] knee" (*kamptei gony*) is absent in John's gospel and was added by the hymnographer probably in order to underline the idea of divine condescension (cf. Phil 2:7–9: "he humbled himself" [*etapeinōsen heauton*], v. 8). According to the hymn, the master bends his knee in front of his servants in order to wash their feet. The foot washing is more than an example of humility or ritual purity. It is *primarily* about the master's love and consideration toward his disciples. The serving leadership that the foot washing conveys comes near to an act of worship[14] of the Creator toward his creatures.

"He bends the knee" echoes God's bowing the heavens as a theophanic act (e.g., Ps 18:9 [17:10]; 144 [143]:5) as well as the sinful woman's passionate exhortation in Kassia's famous hymn: "Bend down to me, toward the heart's sighings, you who bowed the heavens, by your ineffable self-emptying" (lines 10–11). Note that the same verb, *kamptō*, "to bend down," is used in both texts.

The divine condescension, expressed by foot washing, is further emphasized in the last line of the hymn, where Jesus is identified with the very source of existence: he is "the one in whose hand [is] the breath of all existing beings" (*hou en tē cheiri pnoē pantōn tōn ontōn*)—a direct reference to the first part of Job 12:10, "Is not the life [*psychē*] of all the living [ones] [*zōntōn*] in his hand, and the breath [*pneuma*] of every human being [*anthropou*]?" (cf. Wis 3:1: "the lives of the righteous [*dikaiōn psychai*] are in God's hand").

The hymn is even more daring in tone than its scriptural underpinning. If in Job 12:10, God is the source of "all living [ones] [*zōntōn*]," in *this* particular hymn, he is the origin of existence itself ("the existing [beings] [*ontōn*]"), a great theological idea which dovetails quite well with God's personal name, Yahweh, rendered by LXX as *ho ōn*, "the one who exists" (Exod 3:14).

Why did the hymnographer single out these two texts (Ps 147 [146]:8 and Job 12:10) to endorse his theological reflection on foot washing as an example of divine condescension? Surely, the psalm reference evokes a parallel of great interest between "clouds" and "cloth" surrounding the firmament and Jesus's waist while washing the disciples' feet.

But what has Job's saying to do with foot washing, except to sharpen the contrast between the Creator's/Provider's majesty and the master bending his knees to wash his servants' feet? The contrast the hymnographer paints here is quite tantalizing: God's hand holding all living creatures is now washing thoroughly (removing all dirt from [verb *ekplynō*]) the disciples' feet. It is another way of saying that God, the source of life (and existence, according to the hymn's emphasis; see above), descends now at the concrete, mundane, quotidian level of human lives. And yet there is another question that arises: is there any subtle connection between Ps 147 (146):8 and Job 12:10 that made the liturgist use them both in the same hymn, besides the fact that both texts speak of God's majesty? First, let us take a close look at the Joban text.

Job 12:10 is part of Job 12:7–12, a "wisdom instruction speech," a parody of sorts in which Job mocks his friends' commonplace (shared with quadrupeds) wisdom. For the latter, God is absolutely unchangeable, with no foreseeable adjustments to humankind's ever-increasing and unsolvable problems and the queries that these problems might raise.[15]

Job's subtly ironic remark in v. 10[16] actually anticipates his friends' intervention that God is in control of every living creature, from animals to humans. In God's hand lies the life and breath of everything that he created. However, for the obstinately inquiring Job, the main question is "whether that hand is an open palm or a clenched fist."[17]

Job is the man who calls and receives no answer from God ("I cry to you and you do not answer me; you fell upon me with no mercy" [Job 30:20–21]). He is the typical or even archetypal "caller" with no "answerer" being provided.

By using Job 12:10, if slightly modified, the hymnographer responds indirectly to Job's pertinent question that God—the source of existence—through the Incarnation, came close to his creatures. He is not only holding life in his hand, but he bends his knees and stretches out his open arms to wash his disciples' feet as a token of deep humility and unrestrained love toward the "work of his hands" (Isa 64:8).

The Beautiful Feet of the Gospel Proclaimers

> Bonded [*syndeomenoi*] to one another with the bond of love [*tō syndesmō tēs agapēs*], the Apostles, having dedicated [*anathemenoi*] themselves to Christ, the one who is the Master of all [*despozonti tōn holōn*], and who washed thoroughly [*exapenizonto*] [their] beautiful feet [*hōraious podas*], so they may proclaim to all the gospel of peace [*euangelizomenoi pasin eirēnēn*]. (Holy Thursday, Matins, Ode 5, Heirmos)

The second part of the hymn draws on Rom 10:15 (Byz.):[18] "How beautiful [*hōs hōraioi*] are the feet of the ones proclaiming the gospel of peace [*euangelizomenōn eirēnēn*]," which actually is a quote from Isaiah: "How beautiful [*mah-nāʾwû*] upon the mountains are the feet of the one who makes a proclamation of peace [*me-baśśēr mašmîᵃᶜ šālôm*]" (Isa 52:7 [MT]). Note that Rom 10:15 does *not* follow the standard LXX (i.e., codices Alexandrinus, Vaticanus) reading of Isa 52:7 ("Like springtime [*hōs hōra*]¹⁹ upon the mountains, like the feet [*hōs podes*] of the one proclaiming a tiding of peace [*euangelizomenou akoēn eirēnēs*]"). It is, rather, a textual variant similar to the one attested by the Syro-Hexapla,²⁰ and one closer to the Heb. text (MT): "How beautiful [*hōs hōraioi*] are the feet on the mountains of the one who proclaims a tiding of peace [*euangelizomenou akoēn eirēnēs*]."

As an aside, there is a fair amount of textual evidence that the Syro-Hexapla text type *might* have been the Byzantine liturgists' favorite Greek version of the Old Testament in terms of lectionary and hymnography production.²¹

The plural *euangelizomenōn*, "the ones who proclaim," found in Rom 10:15 is one of Paul's alterations, switching from a single, providential, Messiah-type of "preacher" (MT, Syro-Hexapla) to a plurality of "preachers" of the gospel in early Christian times. Moreover, Paul's elimination of the noun "mountains" (found in MT, LXX, Syro-Hexapla) was likely motivated by the apostle's desire to extend the preaching area outside and beyond that of Mount Zion.²² The author of the present hymn has simply followed Paul's footsteps by leaving aside the word "mountains."

"Beautiful feet [*hōraious podas*]"
The word "feet" functions as a catchword between the foot washing as described in the hymn and in Rom 10:15 (cf. Isa 52:7; Nah 1:15 [2:1]).

The gospel's account of the foot washing is staged in this hymn (and herein lies the creativity of the hymnographer) *almost* as a "baptism" or "act of initi-ation," through which Jesus's disciples are endowed with the special blessing needed for the difficult mission lying ahead. On the other hand, the disciples are *required* by Jesus's example to humble themselves and thus be prepared for their listeners' stubbornness in accepting God's Word (see Rom 10:14–21, below, with respect to the difficulties with which the apostolic proclama-tion was confronted). Jesus, the hymnographer notes, "washed thoroughly" (*exapenizonto*)²³ the feet of his disciples, thus taking *all* the dirt away and turning them into fitting limbs for the proclamation of the "gospel of peace" to all people. The foot washing makes their feet "timely"²⁴ for missionary work, "appropriate," time-wise, for the proclamation of the gospel that is "among them." The final clause in the hymn ("so that they may . . .") points to the goal of Jesus's surprising action.

For the inimitable Origen, "beautiful feet" in Rom 10:15 refers to those gospel preachers who walked in Christ's way: "The beauty of the preacher's feet must be understood in a spiritual, not in a physical sense. For it would make a mockery of the apostle's meaning to suppose that the feet of the evangelists, which can be seen with the physical eye, should be regarded as beautiful in themselves.... Only those feet which walk in the way of life can make this claim. Given that Christ said that he is the way, you should understand that it is the feet of those evangelists who walk according to that way which deserve to be called beautiful" (*Commentary on the Epistle to the Romans*).[25]

"Proclaiming the gospel of peace to all"
Here the hymnographer opted for the Byz. of Rom 10:15, exhibiting the word *eirēnē*, "peace" (cf. MT, *šālôm*, but absent in other Greek New Testament text types), in order to underline the core of the apostolic *kerygma* which was the good news of reconciliation.

According to Ambrosiaster (ca. 366–384),[26] the word "peace" points to God's reconciliation with humanity: "Paul quotes the prophet Nahum [Nah 1:15 [2:1]; cf. Isa 52:7]. By talking about feet he means the coming of the apostles who went round the world preaching the coming of the kingdom of God. For their appearance enlightened mankind by showing them the way toward peace with God, which John the Baptist had come to prepare [Isa 40:3; Matt 3:3; Mark 1:3; Luke 3:4]. This is the peace to which those who believe in Christ are hastening... because the kingdom of God is peace, and all discord is taken away when everyone bows the knee to the one God" (*Commentary on Paul's Epistles*).[27]

Already prophesied in the Old Testament as a distinguishing character trait of the messianic agent (Isa 9:6 [5], MT: *śar-šālôm*, "prince of peace"; LXX: "I will bring ... peace and health to him" [*axō ... eirēnēn kai hygieian autō*]), "peace" became one of the hallmarks of Jesus's life and work. Heralded by the "heavenly host" at his birth (Luke 2:14), promised by Jesus at the Last Supper (John 14:27), and offered freely by him after resurrection (John 20:19, 21), God's "peace" (reconciliation) became the center of the gospel proclamation. This was probably the understanding of the author of this hymn as well.

The word *pasin*, "to all," is found in neither Rom 10:15 nor Isa 52:7. It was introduced by the hymnographer perhaps in response to Paul's questions in Rom 10:14–21 about the gospel being proclaimed yet rejected by his own people. It is not that God's Word somehow failed during the transmission process, but rather the blame falls on Paul's Jewish contemporaries whose contumacy against God's Word has been prophesized in the Old Testament (e.g., Isa 52:5–7). That is why, in Paul's view, at least, Israel has no excuse, and expanding the gospel of salvation to the Gentiles (i.e., "among those who did not seek" the Lord, Rom 10:20) is thus well warranted.[28]

By adding *pasin*, "to all," the hymnographer meant to say that the gospel of peace, initially directed to Israel ("lost sheep of Israel," Matt 10:5–7), should be proclaimed "to all," Jews and Gentiles alike. This is due much more to the former's rejection of the good tidings.

Moreover, alluding via Rom 10:15 to such a foundational text as Isa 52:7, the hymnographer shows a good, solid reading of Scripture. Isa 52:7–10 is one of those texts that have the cogency to shape the identity of a faith community. It offered the first Christians the literary form (*euangelion*, "good news, tidings") and the message (the coming of God's kingdom) in which they could tell the story of their founder. The two elements are found in one of Jesus's earliest sayings, "The time is fulfilled and the kingdom of God has come near: repent and believe in the good tidings" (Mark 1:15; cf. Matt 10:7). Beginning with the Pauline epistles (e.g., Rom 10:15) and extending to Byzantine hymnography (e.g., our present hymn), when Christians wanted to talk about the spreading of the good tidings and the coming of the kingdom, they have always appealed to this Isaian text.[29]

The Mighty Love of God's Strength

> Having perceived ahead [*prokatidōn*] your ineffable [*aporrēton*] mystery, O Christ, the prophet proclaimed beforehand [*proanephōnēsen*]: "You have established the mighty love of [your] strength [*ethou krataian agapēsin ischyos*], O compassionate Father; for you, O good One, sent off [*apesteilas*] your Only Begotten Son to the world as atonement [*hilasmon*]." (Holy Thursday, Matins, Ode 4, Heirmos)

The hymn cites the LXX of Hab 3:4, which is part of a larger section, commonly labeled "The Prayer of Habakkuk" (Hab 3:1–19).[30]

Hab 3:4 is one of the most difficult texts of the Old Testament, a true *crux interpretum*. According to Francis Andersen,[31] Hab 3 is probably the most rewritten text in the entire Hebrew Bible; words and phrases seem to be touched, replaced, and moved around. Moreover, the textual differences between MT and LXX are seemingly irresolvable. Given Hab 3's insurmountable textual difficulties, textual witnesses such as MT and LXX should be studied in their own right.[32]

For our concrete and immediate purpose, I will dwell briefly on the last line of this *abc* climactic colon, that is, Hab 3:4c, following the LXX version used by the hymnographers.

LXX: "And he has established a mighty love of his strength" (*kai etheto agapēsin krateian ischyos autou*).

MT: "And there he veiled his power" (*wə-šām ḥebyôn ʿuzzōh*).[33]

The LXX translator's lexical choice, "mighty love" (*agapēsin krateian*), for the Heb. (MT) hapax legomenon *ḥebyôn* (usually rendered as "covering, veil," as deriving from the verb *ḥ-b-ʾ/h*, "to cover, hide"), is explained differently by different scholars. Harper sees in LXX's phrase a "double translation" of Heb. *ʿz*, "strength, power," by two almost semantically identical words, *krataios* and *ischys*, and the Heb. hapax legomenon *ḥebyôn* as deriving from a root *ḥ-b-b*, "to love" (although attested only in Deut 33:3 [*ḥōbēb* "loving, lover"]), hence LXX *agapēsis* "love." Others consider LXX's option a "contextual improvisation," offering a descriptive, intelligible phrase, *agapēsin krateian*, for an unclear, one-time-attested Heb. word. It should be mentioned that this phrase is uniquely positioned within the context of ancient Greek literature, occurring only in Hab 3:4c and reappearing later on in Christian works dealing with this LXX text.[34]

The noun *agapēsis*, "love," with its passionate overtones, is used in the LXX Old Testament sporadically. Out of the six occurrences, this word is used only two times in reference to worldly love (2 Sam 1:26: in his moving lament, David compares his friendship with Jonathan: "your love to me was beyond women's love [*hyper agapēsin gynaikōn*; MT: *m-ʾhbt nšym*]"; Jer 2:33: of a wayward people turning its back to God). The other four occurrences point out God's love toward his people (Ps 109 [108]:5: "they rewarded me with hatred for my love"; Hos 11:4: "I stretched them out with the bands of my love"; Zeph 3:17: "he will renew you in his love"). But the closest text to Hab 3:4c remains Jer 31 (38):3: "I have loved you with an everlasting love [*agapēsin aiōnian ēgapēsa se*; MT: *w-ʾhbt ʿwlm ʾhbtyk*]"—with reference to God's eternal love, within the context of Jeremiah's famous prophecy on the "New Covenant" (Jer 31 [38]:31–37). Here, as in Hab 3:4c, divine love is further qualified as "everlasting love" (*agapēsin aiōnian*), to underline God's unique love (i.e., "eternal," long-lasting, and "mighty").

The adjective *krataios* is a poetical form of *krateros* meaning "strong, mighty, resistless." It occurs in several LXX texts, usually along with the word *cheir*, "hand," meaning "powerful, vehement" (Exod 3:19; 6:1; 13:3, 9; 1 Sam 14:52; corresponding to a nominal form of the Heb. verb *ḥ-z-q*, "to be strong, to overcome, to take hold of, to seize," intimating imposed force). In 2 Sam 22:31, *rhēma kyriou krataion*, "God's utterance [is] mighty," the same *krataios* serves as an interpretive gloss inserted by the LXX translator to explain the somewhat unclear Heb. phrase *'imrat* YHWH *ṣərûpāh*, "the Lord's saying [is] refined." In this context, *krataios* suggests verifiable, tested "strength." The adjective *krataios*, "mighty, strong," occurs only in one place in the entire New Testament, 1 Pet 5:6, where humbleness is juxtaposed with "God's mighty hand": "Humble [*tapeinōthēte*] yourselves under the mighty hand of God [*krataian cheira tou Theou*], so that he may raise you in due time." The poetical *krataios* and the common form, *krateros*, derive from the verb *krateō*, "to be strong, powerful, to rule, hold sway, to master," implying the idea of "being in control of, holding, mastering."

One question arises at this juncture: why does LXX (and, later, the hymnographer) prefer such a heteroclite collocation, *agapēsis*, "affection, (passionate) love" and *krataia*, "mighty," to convey God's "strength" (*ischys*)? The answer probably lies in a particular nuance of the qualifying adjective *krataia*, as deriving from *krateō*, "to hold, to master." Hence we have here "masterful love," namely, that type of passionate love that is held under control—or, in other words, a love that is *not* reducible to a mere feeling but rather manages to strike a balance between responsibility, affection, and passion. This is, in fact, the way the Old Testament describes God's love toward Israel, as somewhere at the crisscrossing of passionate love and covenantal duty.[35] God loves his people with a burning, long-suffering love. Yet his love does not remain a mere sentiment expressed only in words; his love translates into concrete provisions he carefully brings to completion in due time. This is probably the meaning of the LXX rendition, at least in the hymnographer's view: "He [God] established the mighty love of his strength." That is to say, in his wisdom, God chose such a riveting "covenantal love"[36] to deal with an ever-changing humanity and to show his "strength" not through fulminant acts of domineering power but rather through this "tamed," "held-under-control," though concomitant passionate love. For many, this love signals out weakness, but for many others, such a paradoxical love is the expression of God's unique personality.

However, "mighty love" in Hab 3:4c might reach another level of text polysemy, as hinting at the unyielding quality of the divine love. The more disappointed and embittered God becomes when dealing with his wayward people, the more passionate and daring his love does grow.[37] God's love dealing with humans is a long-suffering, enduring love. Here the maxim in Song 8:6 makes perfect sense: "Love [is] as strong as death" (LXX: *krataia hōs thanatos agapē*; cf. 1 Cor 13:8: "Love never falls off [*hē agapē oudepote ekpiptei*]").

Applying Hab 3:4c and the present hymn to the foot-washing episode (John 13:1–20), one may notice the ingenious and subtle way the hymnographer links the "mighty love" expressing God's "strength" with Jesus's love and humbleness shown in the washing of his disciples' feet. In the hymnographer's view, Jesus, though Son of God exuding wisdom and power, humbles himself, bending his knees in front of his disciples, showing that love is strong and gets even stronger when it serves others.

Here is a variant of the above hymn:

> You established for us a mighty love [*ethou pros hēmas krataian agapēsin*],
> O Lord; for you gave [*dedōkas*] your only begotten Son [*monogenē hyion sou*] to death for our sake. Therefore giving thanks we cry to you, "Glory to your power, O Lord!" (Heirmologion, Ode 4, Heirmos, Mode 3)

The hymnographer cites here the same text, Hab 3:4c (LXX), with slight alterations: insertion of *pros hēmas*, "for us," and removal of *ischyou*, "of strength," which reappears in a subtle way in the doxological end, *tē dynamei*, "to your power." Another peculiarity of this hymn is the conflation of the Old Testament text with John 3:16: "God so loved [*ēgapēsen*] the world that he gave [*edōken*] the Son, the only begotten one [*ton hyion ton monogenē*]." Compare the somehow more formal word order in John, "the Son, the only begotten one," with a more personal address in the hymn, "your only begotten Son."

So constructed, this hymn explains further the "ineffable mystery" (*mystērion aporrēton*) of such a "mighty love" (*krataian agapēsin*) reflecting God's "strength" (*ischyos*). It is indeed an unresolvable mystery, a paradox collapsing into itself, to willfully offer your own son for the sake of your creation. On the one hand, it requires a great deal of "passionate love" (*agapēsis*; see discussion above) for the work of your hands. On the other hand, it takes even a greater deal of strength to give away your only begotten son as atoning sacrifice for a fallen humanity and the son to respond obediently with the same love for his father and for his "least brothers" (Matt 25:40). There is an intense amount of love here, hence the somehow redundant phrase "mighty love of your strength": God loving his Son, and the Son loving his Father, and both still loving the fallen world.

Cyril of Alexandria was able to encapsulate this intense and dramatic love triangle (God–Son–world) when he wrote:

> Christ came to achieve two things: on the one hand, to destroy adversaries who led astray the whole earth under heaven, robbing God the Creator by purloining the glory due to him alone and decking their own heads with it; and, on the other, to rescue those who were deceived and subjected to a truly unbearable oppression. The fact that the power of the former was lost and completely disappeared he conveys by saying, *Horns are in his hands* [Hab 3:4], namely, those that overturn their control and strike down their arrogance with a horn, as it were. And the fact that he was destined to rescue us he demonstrates in advance by saying, *He placed a powerful love of his strength* [Hab 3:4]; in other words, we have been saved, "not by works of righteousness that we ourselves performed," not by achievements of the Law, since "the Law made nothing perfect," but from the clemency of the God and Father, who for our sake *placed a powerful*—that is, strong and mighty—*love* of the Son. The God and Father, remember, "so loved the world as to give his only Son so that everyone believing in him might not perish but have eternal life" [John 3:16]. It is therefore out of the love of the God and Father that we have been saved, as well as by the Son's enduring death for us, even if he came to life again, canceling the control of corruption and removing sin from us; accordingly, he said, "No one has greater love than this: to lay down one's life for one's friends" [John 15:13]. *The love of the strength* of the God and Father is *strong*, therefore, since through it we have been delivered from death, sin, and the oppression of the devil. (*Commentary on Habakkuk* 132–133)[38]

Reflecting on Jesus's new commandment "to love one another" (John 13:34), as well as God's paradoxical love, the hymnographer found in Hab 3:4c (LXX), "mighty love of his [God's] strength," an interpretive key, as provisional as it might seem, to appreciate at least, if not to begin to understand, God's mysterious ways of dealing with his creation.

Habakkuk, the Awaiting Prophet

Given the important place Habakkuk plays within Byzantine hymnography and iconography,[39] I will dwell briefly on a few other hymns inspired by his short yet theologically significant book.

The hymnographers saw in Habakkuk the prophet par excellence of the Logos's incarnation and Christ's birth. Perhaps the prophet's overt conversation with God (Hab 1–2) and the concluding theophany (vision) he had (Hab 3) made him a model of the "watcher" for God's intervention in human history: "I will stand on my watching post [*epi tēs phylakēs mou stēsomai*] and station myself on a rock; and will keep watching to see what he will say to me and what I will answer to my reproof" (Hab 2:1).

For Augustine, the prophet is a genuine *listener* who is not satisfied with his own reflections; he wants to listen to God's Word, hence his adamant watchfulness: "O truth, you do preside over all things, even those that take counsel with you, and you do answer in the same time all who consult you, however diverse their questions. You do answer clearly, but all do not hear clearly. All seek counsel concerning what they wish, but they do not always hear what they wish. He serves you best who does not so much expect to hear the thing from you that he himself desires, but rather to desire what he hears from you" (*Confessions* 10.26).[40]

In John Cassian's view, the "watching" prophet is the precursor of those Christians who carried out their spiritual welfare in the austerity of the wilderness: "If someone perseveres continually in this watchfulness, therefore, he will effectively bring to pass what is quite plainly expressed by the prophet Habakkuk: 'I will stand on my watch and go upon my rock, and I will look out to see what he will say to me and what I should reply to him who reproaches me' [Hab 2:1]. The laboriousness and difficulty of this is very clearly proved by the experiences of those who dwell in the desert of Calamus or Porphyrion" (*Conference* 24.4.1).[41]

Habakkuk, to a certain extent, is similar to Job, puzzled to see an almighty, just God looking passively at an unjust world. One may add in passing the high frequency of the argumentative Heb. *hălō'*, "Are [you] not?" in Job; Habakkuk runs first among the minor prophets in the use of the same construction. Nevertheless, unlike Job's puzzlement which takes the form of a continuous quarrel with God, Habakkuk's puzzlement and anguish turn eventually into a longing or watching for God's much-awaited intervention. The prophet is the perfect illustration of his own time-honored dictum, "But the righteous will live by my faith [*ho de dikaios ek pisteōs mou zēsetai*]" (Hab

2:4). When nothing is left to hold on to, there is still a grain of faith (as tiny as the "mustard seed" [Matt 17:20]), that mysteriously stubborn, unyielding faith that God's justice and goodness will at last prevail.

Jerome, as with most of the ancient Christian interpreters, sees in Habakkuk an example of persevering faith in spite of all the hindrances one may face living in this world: "'[The Lord] who keeps the truth forever' (Ps 146 [145]:6). If we are crushed by falsehood and deceit, let us not grieve over it. The Lord is the guardian of truth for all eternity. Someone has lied against us, and the liar is given more credence than we who are telling the truth. We must not despair. The Lord keeps faith forever. . . . Even if justice delays its coming, do not give up hope; 'it will surely come,' and bring salvation, securing justice for the oppressed" (*Homilies on the Psalms* 55).[42]

The following hymns are arranged around three main texts from the book of Habakkuk.

Standing on the Divine Watch

The venerable Habakkuk, standing on divine watch [*epi theias istamenos phylakēs*], had heard the ineffable mystery [*mystērion aporrēton*] of your coming [*parousias*] to us, O Christ! He clearly [*saphestata*] prophesies [*prophēteuei*] your very proclamation [*to kērygma to son*], foreseeing [*proorōmenos*] the wise apostles as horses astonishing greatly [*diatarassontas*] the sea of the nations of many seeds [*tōn ethnōn tōn polysporōn*]. (The Holy Prophet Habakkuk [December 2], Vespers, Sticheron)

The hymn refers to Hab 2:1, which lies in the middle of the prophet's conversation with God. Habakkuk, puzzled by God's reluctance to intervene in an unjust world, "stations himself" (LXX: *epibēsomai*; MT: *wə-ʾetyaṣṣəbāh*) as a soldier, watching and waiting faithfully (cf. Hab 2:4) for God's response.

The prophet's puzzlement is nicely matched by the hymnographer's remark that the multi-seed nations were "greatly astonished" by the apostles' "proclamation" (*kērygma*) of Christ to them. But this "puzzlement" can be related to the Virgin Mary's sense of astonishment at the archangel Gabriel's greeting coupled with the announcement of Jesus's birth (Luke 1:26–38). That the hymnographer perhaps had this text in mind may be supported by the fact that the verb *diatarassō*, "to greatly confuse, to disturb, to puzzle, to astonish," used in this hymn is a hapax legomenon in the entire Christian Bible, occurring only in Luke 1:29.[43] There is an interesting parallel between

Mary and the nations: both are puzzled by the novelty of the message (i.e., God's "coming" [*parousia*]) proclaimed by the archangel Gabriel and the apostles, respectively.

The hymn's "sea" (*thalassa*) imagery echoes the prophet's "second prayer" (Hab 1:12–17), where the same collocation of "sea" and "nations" occurs. The "second prayer" is dominated by the theme of an unnamed "wicked" person (v. 13b: "The wicked [MT: *rāšāᶜ*; LXX: *asebē*, "ungodly"] swallows the right-eous") while God looks on unsympathetically. This well-written poem is quite allegorical.[44] The world's foremost oppressor is depicted as a fisherman (vv. 15–16) on an expanding fishing expedition, where the "nations" are compared to the "fishes of the sea [*ichthyas tēs thalassēs*]" (v. 14).

Read through the lens of Hab 1:12–17, this hymn proposes a sharp con-trast between the Chaldeans (the world's leaders) and the apostles (Christ's followers), with the former feeding on the nations and the latter proclaiming the gospel to the nations.

A Shady Mountain

Habakkuk of old foresees [*problepei*] you as a shady mountain [*kataskion oros*], O All-blameless One [*panamōme*], carrying the Word [*pherousan ton logon*], who quite overshadows [*syskiazonta*] all [people] [*pantas*] of the burning flame [*phlogmou kausōnos*] of fallings and sins [*paraptōseōn kai hamatiōn*], O Maiden. (Holy Apostle Archipus [February 19], Matins, Ode 4)

Apparently, the hymn makes reference to Hab 3:3a (LXX): "God will come [*hēxei*] from Teman and the Holy One from a shady, thick-with-leaves mountain [*ex orous kataskiou daseos*]—interlude of strings [*diapsalma*]—his virtue [*hē aretē*] has covered [*ekalypsen*] the heavens, and the earth is full of his praise [*aineseōs*]."

MT differs in two places from LXX: "Mount Paran" (instead of "a thick-with-leaves mountain"); and "his splendor" (*hôdô*) (instead of "his virtue").[45]

The phrase *kataskion oros*, "shady mountain" (cf. LXX), with reference to the Virgin Mary[46] can be placed in parallel with *episkiazō*, "to overshadow," in Luke 1:35, describing the miraculous, powerful presence of God in the in-effable act of Jesus's conception and birth by the Virgin Mary.[47] The two bib-lical texts (Hab 3:3 and Luke 1:35) are interconnected via two lexical forms going back to a simple, basic verb, *skiazō*, "to shade." Luke 1:35: "And the angel answered her, 'The Holy Spirit will come upon you [*epeleusetai*] and the power of the Most High [*dynamis hypsistou*] will overshadow [*episkiasei*] you. Therefore, the holy *thing* born [neuter *gennōmenon hagion*] shall be called the Son of God' " (emphasis added).

Theophylact of Ohrid (before 1050–ca. 1108) is the first among the Church Fathers who makes the connection between Hab 3:3 and the Lucan Annunciation pericope (Luke 1:26–38), based on the "shadowing" (verb *skiazō*) motif. In his commentary on Habakkuk (*Expositio in prophetam Habacuc* [*PG* 126:880]), Theophylact calls Habakkuk the prophet of the Annunciation. The same textual rapprochement, but in the area of iconography, is attested by a twelfth-century illuminated Psalter, Vatican gr. 1927, where there is a representation of Habakkuk kneeling before a mountain, above which Mary and the Christ Child are depicted in a bust form.[48]

Is there any evidence or clue that ancient Christian interpreters before Theophylact were cognizant of such a plausible intertextuality? I personally think that the present hymn, though quite discreetly, hints at the Annunciation episode by the use of the word *korē*, "maiden, bride, young wife." In Christian literature, as in this hymn, *korē* is a reference to the Virgin Mary. Could *korē* be taken as a quiet allusion to Luke 1:45, where Mary calls herself "the servant of the Lord" (*hē doulē tou kyriou*)? If one takes into account Theodore the Studite's interpretation of "shady mountain" in Hab 3:3 (LXX) as alluding to Mary's virginity,[49] then the present hymn might likely be one of the earliest clues to such an intertextuality between the LXX of Hab 3:3 ("shady mountain" [*kataskion oros*]) and the Annunciation pericope in Luke 1:35 (with the Most High's power that "will overshadow" [*episkiasei*] Mary, "the servant of the Lord").

Taking another look at the hymn, read in close parallel with the Lucan Annunciation pericope, one may notice an interesting similarity between the "power of the Most High" (*dynamis hypsistou*) "overshadowing" (*episkiasei*) Mary (Luke 1:35), protecting and transforming her into a fitting vessel of the Logos's incarnation, and the incarnate "Word" (*logos*) Mary is "carrying" (*pherousan*) in this world (see the hymn). Like the "Most High," God the Father, the incarnate Son or Word, is "overshadowing" (*syskiazonta*), protecting "all [the people] from the burning flame of fallings and sins." There is an "overshadowing" continuum from the Father to the incarnate Son, via Mary. The Virgin Mary serves as a suitable conduit for such an outpouring of divine protection. Note the special nuance of the verb *syskiazō*, "to shade quite over, shade thickly, closely," used in this hymn. If the Most High "overshadows" (*episkiazō*) Mary so that she may be and remain uniquely a

"Virgin Mother," the incarnate Son of God (i.e., the "holy *thing* [entity] born" of Luke 1:35) goes a step further. Due to the divine condescension, i.e., the Incarnation, Jesus is able to "*utterly* overshadow" (*syskiazonta*) all the people, keeping them away from the "burning flame" (*phlogmou kausōnos*) of both burdensome situations, falling into and being under sin.

The Mystical Supper

At the center of the Last Supper episode lies the institution of the Lord's mystical supper or Eucharist. Paradoxically, John, who deals with the Last Supper extensively (John 13–17) has no institution account. Instead, John records Jesus's Eucharistic discourse (John 6:22–71).

The narratives of the institution of the Eucharist are to be found in the synoptics (Matt 26:26–29; Mark 14:22–25; Luke 22:15–20) and 1 Cor 11:23–25. Among these accounts, Paul's preserves the earliest formula of institution.

Note that Matthew's account is part of the composite gospel reading prescribed for Holy Thursday (Vesperal Liturgy of Saint Basil). The general view is that Matthew's account of the institution of the Eucharist was initially a nascent liturgical piece.

> While they were eating, Jesus took bread [*labōn arton*], thanked [*eucharistēsas*],[50] broke [*eklasen*] it, and gave [*edidou*] it to the disciples, saying: "Take, eat. This is my body [*to soma mou*]." And taking the chalice [*labōn to potērion*], he thanked [*eucharistēsas*], and gave [*edōken*] it to them, saying: "Drink all of you from it. For this one [*touto*] is my blood of the new covenant [*to haima mou, to tēs kainēs diathēkēs*], which is poured [*enchynomenon*] for many for the forgiveness of sins [*aphesis hamartiōn*]. I tell you: I shall not drink again of this fruit of the vine [*gennēmatos tēs ampelou*] until that day [*hēmeras ekeinēs*] when I drink it new [*kainon*] in my Father's kingdom." (Matt 26:26–29 [Byz.])

The "blood of the covenant" hints at Exod 24:4–8. The covenant between God and his people was sealed by an animal sacrifice, with the blood sprinkled on the altar symbolizing God and elders representing Israel. Similarly, Jesus's blood represents the new covenant between God the Father and human beings. However, with the institution of the Eucharist at the Last Supper, bread and wine turn mystically into Christ's body and blood.

The phrase "for the forgiveness of sins" is found only in Matthew, and it underscores the double effect of Jesus's self-offering: remission of sins and reconciliation with God. The atoning sacrifice of Christ releases humanity from the burden of sin and reconciles it with its Creator.

The Eucharist (the thanksgiving service) celebrated by the Church since apostolic times anticipates the messianic banquet Jesus alludes to at the end of Matthew's account, when he promises his disciples that he will drink again from the "fruit of the vine" renewed in God's kingdom (Matt 26:29).

God's Begotten Wisdom

Before the ages [pro tōn aiōnōn], the Father begets [genna] me, creative Wisdom [dēmiourgon sophian], [as] the beginning of [his] ways [archēn hodōn]; he created [me] [ektise] for the sake of [his] works that [are] now mystically completed [mystikōs teloumena]. For [though I am the] Logos, uncreated by nature [aktistos physei], I appropriate the [articulate] sounds [phōnas oikeioumai], of the one [nature] that now I assumed [proseilēpha].
(Holy Thursday, Matins, Ode 9, Troparion)

Conspicuously, the use of Wisdom imagery in this hymn leads one to think of Prov 8:22–31 as a scriptural basis. One of the most commented-upon pericopes of the entire Bible, Prov 8:22–31 is found in the first part of the book of Proverbs, chaps. 1–9, whose date of composition is assumed to be either the Persian or early Hellenistic period.[51] Conceived from the outset as a theological work, this unit was probably added later to chap. 8. The awkwardness of the new position was observed by the LXX translator, who added to the end of v. 21 this explanatory gloss: "If I report to you [the things] that happen [ginomena] daily [kath' hēmeran], I will remember to count [arithmēsai] the things of old [ta ex aiōnos]," meant to create a smoother transition from Prov 8:1–21 (on the current status of Wisdom) to Prov 8:22–31 (a retrospective view on Wisdom stretching back to the beginning of creation).

Prov 8:22–31 is a fascinating passage describing the role of a personified Wisdom within God's creation while focusing on the relationship between this Lady Wisdom (both Heb. [ḥokmāh] and Gk. [sophia] terms for "wisdom" are feminine nouns) and the God of creation, whose predominantly "male" profile, though not clearly stated, may be surmised from the multifaceted imagery used in classical texts dealing with the creation theme.[52]

One may detect a certain development within the Hebrew Bible, from wisdom as a theological idea not well defined (Job 28) to a personified entity in Prov 8, identified with Torah (Law) in Sir 24 and displayed as a universal abstract principle in Wis. One may note that the process of taking the somewhat vague idea of wisdom and molding it into a living entity, Lady Wisdom, is a quite extraordinary theological journey. This is one of the hallmarks of the Hebrew Bible: while firmly adhering to its monotheistic creed (e.g., Deut 6:4–5), the Hebrew Bible shows a high level of creativity by introducing a unique figure, closely aligned with God, the personified Wisdom, whose significant role in creation remains incontestable.

In Prov, Wisdom is described as a person (Prov 1:20–33; 8:1–36; and 9:1–6). The main idea of Prov 8:22–31 is quite similar to the one found in Prov 3:19, where the author rather emphatically states: "God founded [*ethemeliōsen*] the earth by Wisdom [*tē sophia*]" (LXX). In Roger N. Whybray's view, Prov 8:22–31 is a "baroque" development of Prov 3:19 (cf. Ps 104 [103]:24; Jer 10:12; 51 [28]:15, where Wisdom is a creative agent).[53] In other words, the above-mentioned former text elaborates on the general statement of the latter, by expanding on the role of Wisdom in the work of creation, as well as on the specific relationship between Wisdom and God the Creator.

Besides their similar vocabulary, these two texts are literarily interdependent, as seen in the following peculiarities detected in the MT: (a) both texts begin with YHWH, "Yahweh" (MT; cf. LXX: *ho theos*, "God"/*kyrios*, "Lord"); (b) both texts employ the Heb. verb *k-w-n*, "to establish," to describe the creation of the heavens (cf. LXX, 3:19: *ethemeliōsen*, "he founded"; cf. 8:27: *hētoimazen*, "he prepared"); (c) Prov 8:24 creates a poetical parallelism between Heb. *mᶜynwt*, "sources" (cf. LXX: *pēgas*) and Heb. *thmwt*, "depths" (cf. LXX: *abyssoi*)—nowhere encountered except in Prov 3:20 and v. 21 (MT).[54]

"The Father begets me [ho patēr genna me], *creative Wisdom* [dēmiourgon sophian], *before the ages* [pro tōn aiōnōn]"
The hymnographer reverses the verbal sequence in Prov 8:22–25 (LXX: *ktizō*, "to create" [v. 22], *themeliō*, "to found" [v. 23], *gennaō*, "to beget" [v. 25]), opening the description of Wisdom with the Gk. verb *gennaō*, "to beget" (commonly of the Father) (v. 25) so as to focus on the "birth" of Wisdom since it is more appropriate to speak of Christ, identified here with the personified Wisdom, as being "begotten" by the Father. Note that the hymn, as in the LXX of Prov 8:25, has the present tense *genna*, "he begets" (generic present), thus hinting likely at the Son's eternal generation from the Father. Note that

MT reads, "I was born, brought forth," i.e., the perfect Pol'al of the verb *ḥ-y-l*, Qal, "to be in labor, to writhe."[55] Origen is one of the first ancient Christian interpreters to see in the use of the present tense (*genna*, "he begets") in Prov 8:25 an allusion to a continual generation of the Son from the Father.[56]

The hymn also qualifies *kyrios*, "Lord" (LXX; cf. MT: YHWH), at the beginning of the biblical pericope (Prov 8:22) as being the "Father" (*patēr*), thus quickly introducing one to the Christological interpretation of this passage.

The phrase *pro tōn aiōnōn*, "before the ages" (plural vs. singular in Prov 8:23: *pro tou aionos*), was placed at the very beginning of the hymn to underscore the idea that the Father "begets" (generic present) the Son "before [all] the ages," namely, before time was created, more precisely from all eternity, eternally. The "begetting" is an eternal, unrestrained by time, essential attribute of the Father vis-à-vis the Son.

It is noteworthy that the personified Wisdom of Proverbs is described in the hymn as *dēmiourgon sophian*, "creative Wisdom." Already in Prov 8:22–31, Wisdom is introduced as a co-worker beside God, as God's creative instrument or agent. Nevertheless, the hymnographer condenses Prov's description of Wisdom as a working agent into an attributive phrase, "creative Wisdom" (*dēmiourgon sophian*)—Wisdom as God's active creative agent rather than as a passively witnessing entity. Might *dēmos*, "people," in the composition of the adjective *dēmiourgos* be a subtle hint at Wisdom's "intermediary" role between God and humanity (i.e., working for the well-being of humans)—a mediatrix role having been already assigned to Lady Wisdom by the author of Prov 8:30–31?

One may read the hymnographer's phrase *dēmiourgon sophian*, "creative Wisdom" as an interpretive attempt at v. 30, where Wisdom is further qualified as *ʾāmôn*, "artisan, artificer, crafts[wo]man" (MT)[57] (cf. LXX of Wis 7:21, where Wisdom is termed *technitis*, feminine noun, "artificer, artisan, skilled workwoman"). Note, though, that the LXX of Prov 8:30 reads *harmozousa*, "fitting [to him, God]" (verb *harmozō*, "to set in order, to arrange, prepare"). Whether one follows the MT reading ("artisan") or the LXX's interpretive choice ("fitting"), the conclusion is the same: Wisdom is a co-participant in the creative work of and a suitable partner to God.

"As the beginning of [his] ways [archēn hodōn]"
The hymnographer copies the phrase *archēn hodōn*, "[as] the beginning of [his] ways" as found in LXX Prov 8:22 (MT uses the singular, "beginning of his *way* [*darkō*]"). The plural "ways" could be a hint at God's multiple "works"

related to either creation as a hierarchy of acts or God's complex activity as unfolding throughout the Bible (e.g., creation, judgment, salvation).

The question is how to read "the beginning," which lacks the preposition "as" that would more clearly indicate the role or function of Wisdom in Prov 8:22 as a beginning/starter/principle "acquired" (MT: verb *q-n-h*)/"created" (LXX: verb *ktizō*) by God in relation to his creative work. However, the accusative *archēn* alone may lead one to such a conclusion even in the absence of *hōs*, "as." Moreover, this elliptical clause permits a slightly different interpretation, with "beginning" as Wisdom's nickname.

Following a line of interpretation like the one just mentioned, James Kugel raises an interesting question: "But if wisdom was the first thing that God had created, and if God had in fact used it to create the rest of the world, then biblical interpreters had to wonder: why did the book of Genesis leave out this crucial detail? Why didn't the first verse in the Bible read: 'In the beginning God created *wisdom*, and afterwards, the heavens and the earth'? In looking for an answer, interpreters noticed a striking coincidence. In Prov 8:22, wisdom says, 'The Lord made me the *beginning* of his work'; while the Genesis account opens, 'In the *beginning* God created the heavens and the earth.' Perhaps this was not just a coincidence. Perhaps the word 'beginning' in the Genesis verse was in fact a subtle hint, an allusion, to wisdom."[58]

In fact, this was the understanding of the author of the Fragment Targum on Gen 1:1, when he rendered Heb. *b-r'šyt*, "in the beginning," with *bḥkmh*, "with wisdom": "With wisdom [*bḥkmh*], did the Lord create and perfect the heavens and the earth." Targum Neophyti goes a step further, offering a "double translation," keeping the original word order of Gen 1:1 while inserting an explicative note: "From the beginning [*mlqdmyn*], with wisdom [*bḥkmh*], did the Lord create . . ."

As Gary Anderson points out, the same "double translation" (i.e., the word *b-r'šyt* being translated twice) encountered in Targum Neophyti is also found in the prologue to the gospel of John, "In the beginning [*en archē*], there was the Word [*ho logos*]," where *logos* "Word" stands for *ḥokmāh*, "Wisdom."[59] John and the targumist arrived at this rendition through the elliptic wording of Prov 8:22, which permits reading "beginning" as a nickname of Wisdom. More difficult to explain is how John switched from a "Wisdom theology," so well rooted in the Hebrew Bible and ancient Jewish interpretation, to an innovative "Logos theology"?

Daniel Boyarin seeks to demonstrate, first, that the Johannine logos theology has its roots in first-century Jewish thinking;[60] and, second, that the *logos* in John 1 is to be placed within a wider Jewish matrix, a sort of interpretive mosaic, consisting of three key concepts: the Hebrew Bible's understanding of wisdom, Philo's *logos*, and the Targum's *memra* (God's Word), all of which are tightly interconnected.[61]

These Jewish theological concepts mirror the difficulties biblical authors and ancient interpreters faced while trying to reconcile the two main traits of God's personality: transcendence and immanence. On the one hand, the God of the Hebrew Bible is holy, transcendent, omnipotent; on the other hand, he is approachable, revealing his personal name to Israel in order to be invoked, searched for. How can a human mortal being enter into a personal relationship with such a *mysterium tremendum et fascinosum* (Rudolf Otto), simultaneously terrifying and fascinating God? The unison answer was: by the means of an "intermediary" between God and humanity.

Thus, the three notions wisdom, *logos*, and *memra* were coined in a more or less chronological way. In essence and scope, all three are variants of the same "intermediary" idea. In spite of the minute, semitone differences between them, each intermediary was conceived as being at once "God-like" and "created," but all ended up as personified entities, very close to God. Boyarin is right when he keenly observes that the important difference between John's *logos* and the biblical Lady Wisdom, the Philonic *logos*, or the targumic *memra* lies not in how much divinity each can exhibit but rather in a much more theologically deep layer. If in Judaism, all these "personified" entities represent the Word of God "written" in a book, the Torah, that is, in the prologue to John, we are told that the same word (*logos*) of God "became flesh" (*kai ho logos sarx egeneto*, v. 14).[62] God has a human face, John proclaims. The line separating John and his Jewish theological matrix is the "incarnational Christology" he openly proclaims, which would eventually contribute to "the parting of the ways" between Judaism and Christianity, if such a thing has ever occurred in a substantial and complete way.[63]

"He created [me] for the sake of [his] works [eis erga ektise] that [are] now mystically completed [ta nyn mystikōs teloumena]"
The idea from the previous line is continued here: Wisdom was created by God not only as a "beginning" of but also as a "purpose" for God's works.

The Gk. verb *ktizō*, "to create," in the LXX of Prov 8:22 renders the ambiguous Heb. verb *q-n-h*, "to acquire, to beget, to create" attested by the MT. Note that the late Jewish translations (dating back to the second century C.E.), such as Aquila, Symmachus, and Theodotion, all opted for the verb *ktaomai*, "to acquire," likely a more suitable choice for Heb. *q-n-h*.

One may add here that the LXX *ktizō* is not to be understood exclusively as "to create"; it may also convey the idea of "founding" or "establishing" (Exod 9:18, of the kingdom of Egypt; Lev 16:16, of the Tent of Witness; 1 Esd 4:53, of the city of Babylon) or even "to perpetrate" (Prov 8:22, of wisdom; Isa 45:7, of evils). The context as well as the parallel with the verb *themeliō*, "to found," in Prov 8:23 makes one render *ktizō*, "to found, to establish," rather than "to create." According to Prov 8:22, "God" (MT: YHWH) "established" his Wisdom as the "beginning" or the "founding" principle of his ensuing creative work.

By reversing the verb sequence (i.e., *genna*, "he begets" [present] . . . *ektise*, "he created, established" [aorist]), the hymnographer likely meant to distinguish between the eternal generation of the Wisdom from the Father and the former's temporal "appointment" as creative principle or agent.

This was also the understanding of the early Christian interpreters who needed to explain the presence of the verb *ktizō* in the LXX text. As early as the mid-second century, Justin Martyr insists on the fact that while inseparable from the Father, the Son (Wisdom) is different from the Father:

> God begat before all creatures a Beginning, [who was] a certain rational power [proceeding] from Himself, who is called by the Holy Spirit, now the Glory of the Lord, now the Son, again Wisdom, again an Angel, then God, and then Lord and Logos. . . . He was begotten of the Father by an act of will; just as we see happening among ourselves: for when we give out some word we beget the word; yet not by abscission, so as to lessen the word [which remains] in us, when we give it out: and just as we see also happening in the case of a fire, which is not lessened when it has kindled [another], but remains the same; and that which has been kindled by it likewise appears to exist by itself, not diminishing that from which it was kindled. (*Dialogue*, 61)[64]

In the same line of thought, Origen equates Christ with Wisdom and the latter with the "beginning" mentioned in Prov 8:22 and Gen 1:1:

> But Christ is creator [*dēmiourgos*] as a "beginning" [*archēn*]; inasmuch as he is Wisdom [*sophia*]. It is in virtue of his being wisdom that he is called "beginning" [Gen 1:1]. For Wisdom says in Solomon, "God created me the beginning of his ways for his works" [Prov 8:22, LXX] so that the Word [*logos*] might be in a "beginning," namely, in wisdom. (*On John* 1:22)[65]

For Tertullian, as for the author of the above hymn, Prov 8:22 refers to
the Logos/Wisdom, who, inseparable from and co-eternal with God, was appointed by the Father to be his creative agent:

Now, as soon as it pleased God to put forth into their respective substances
and forms the things which He had planned and ordered within Himself,
in conjunction with His Wisdom's Reason and Word, He first put forth
the Word Himself, having within Him His own inseparable Reason and
Wisdom, in order that all things might be made through Him through
whom they had been planned and disposed, yea, and already made, so far
forth as [they were] in the mind of God. This, however, was still wanting
to them, that they should also be properly known, and kept permanently
in their proper forms and substances. Then, therefore, does the Word also
Himself assume His own form and glorious garb, His own sound and vocal
utterance, when God says, "Let there be light." This is the perfect nativity
of the Word, when he proceeds forth from God—formed by Him first to
devise and think out all things under the name of Wisdom—"The Lord created, or formed, me as the beginning of His ways. . . ." The Son likewise
acknowledges the Father, speaking in His own person under the name of
Wisdom: "The Lord formed me as the beginning of His ways, with a view to
His own works; before all the hills did He beget me." For if indeed Wisdom
in this passage seems to say that she was created by the Lord with a view
to His works, and to accomplish His ways, yet proof is given in another
Scripture that "all things were made by the Word, and without Him was
there nothing made." (*Against Praxeas* 6–7)[66]

However, beginning with the fourth century, this interpretive rapport begins
to fade away. Arius and his followers will often resort to Prov 8:22–31 in support of their subordinationist Christology. For them, the verbs in vv. 22–25
were synonymous, and thus meant to underscore the Son's inferiority in relation to the Father.

A convincing argument against the Arian exegesis is found in Eusebius of
Caesarea's comments on the same much-debated passage from the book of
Proverbs:

Even if he says that he was created, he does not mean this in the sense of
passing from non-existence into existence, not that he too, like all the other
creatures, was made out of nothing, as some have supposed in error; but

rather that he subsists and lives, being before and existing before the creation of the whole world, having been ordained to rule over all things by the
Lord, his Father, and the passage says "created" rather than "ordained" or
"appointed." (*The Proof of the Gosepl* 3.2)[67]

Nevertheless, as Maurice Dowling points out in his excellent study on Prov
8:22–31 and patristic Christology, the great merit of Eusebius is his textual-
critical work on Prov 8:22 (LXX).[68] On the one hand, Eusebius argues that the
verb *ktizō*, "to create," is sometimes used "metaphorically" (*metaphorikōs*).
On the other hand, he appeals to the Heb. text via Origen's *Hexapla*. By
doing this, he shows, first, that the Gk. versions of Aquila, Symmachus,
and Theodotion all read *ektēsato*, "acquired," rather than *ektisen*, "created"
(LXX) and, second, that their lexical choice fits better with the Heb. original (i.e., *q-n-h*, "to acquire"). Based on this piece of textual work, Eusebius
concludes: "Therefore, when the Son of God says: 'The Lord possessed
[*ektēsato*] me as the beginning of his ways for his works,' he was declaring
both his preexistence and his unique relationship to the Father, and at the
same time the value and necessity of his own personal care and control of his
Father's works" (*The Proof of the Gospel* 3.2).[69]

"For [though I am the] Logos, uncreated by nature [logos gar
aktistos ōn physei]*"*
Here the Logos is described as "uncreated" (*aktistos*), though in Prov 8:22
(and in the present hymn), the personified Wisdom states plainly that the
"Lord/Father created" (*kyrios/patēr ektise*) her. This change in language
reflects the switch from the Jewish Wisdom/Logos concept identified with
the written Torah to the Nicene-advanced Christology where the Logos, the
Word of God, who became flesh (John 1:14), is described as "begotten but
not made" (*gennēthenta ou poiēthenta*). As Brian Daley appositely puts it, the
preoccupation of the Fathers of Nicaea was not to emphasize the role of the
Son as God's agent or intermediary in creational and redemptive history but
rather to describe the relationship between the Son and the God of Israel and
of all philosophers, that Jesus and the Church call him "Father."[70] The explanatory formula "begotten but not made" was meant to eliminate any idea of
time or essence difference between the Father and the Son. The hymnographer chose *aktistos physei*, "uncreated by nature," to clarify, counterbalance,
and possibly nullify the previous line, citing Prov 8:22 which states merely
that God "created" (*ektisen*) the wisdom. To such an ambiguous wording, the

hymnographer responds that whatever the biblical text means, the Word of God is "uncreated *by nature*" (emphasis added).

I would like to note here the use of the participial form *ōn*, "being," which may point to the "uncreated" as a timeless, eternal attribute of the Word of God. But it also could be read as a hint at the personal name of God (LXX: *ho ōn*, "The One Who Is") revealed to Moses at the burning bush: "And God said to Moses: 'I am the One Who Is [*egō eimi ho ōn*]. Thus you shall say to the sons of Israel: The One Who Is [*ho ōn*] has sent me to you'" (Exod 3:14). If this interpretation is correct, then the hymnographer meant to underscore here the identity between the Word and God the Father, especially with respect to the "uncreated" attribute. It must be pointed out that such an equating between God and his Word occurs also in the Targum Pseudo-Jonathan on Exod 3:12: "Therefore, my word [*mymry*] shall be your support [*b-sᶜdk*]" for the Heb. "I will be with you." Moreover, in Exod 3:14, the same Targum equates God with his powerful, creative word through whom he created the universe, who now plays a key role in Israel's liberation from Egypt: "And the Lord said to Moses: 'He who said [*dyn dᵓmr*] and the world [*ᶜlmᵓ*] was [*hwh*]; who said and all things were.' And he said: 'This you shall say to the sons of Israel: I Am He Who Is, and Who Will Be [*ᵓnᵓ hwᵓ d-hwynᵓ w-ᶜtyd l-mykwy*] sent me to you.'"[71]

"I appropriate the [articulate] sounds [tas phōnas oikeioumai] *of the one [nature] that now I assumed* [hou nyn proseilēpha]"
At this point, though remaining close to its primary biblical basis, Prov 8:22–31, the hymn moves slowly toward John 1 and Heb 1:1–2. The incarnational tenor in these final lines of the hymn is quite obvious: "the one [i.e., nature] that now I assumed." The Logos, "uncreated by nature" (*aktistos physei*), "assumed" (perfect of *proslambanō*) at incarnation (John 1:14) human nature.

With respect to the human nature assumed by the Logos, the hymnographer, by hinting at (human) "nature" (*physei*), shares the same line of thought with the Cappadocian Fathers. Thus, Gregory of Nazianzus insists that at incarnation, the Logos assumed not just human flesh, that is, without the *nous*, "mind," as Appolinarius of Laodicea (ca. 310–390), among others, used to teach, but rather he assumed human nature in its entirety, the full *anthrōpos*, "humanity." The so called *logos-sarx* ("Logos-flesh") Christology of the prologue to John's gospel (John 1:14; cf. Phil 2:7: *morphēn doulou labōn*, "took the form of a slave") could be misleading and indeed influenced Appolinarius's views that the Logos assumed only human flesh. Gregory the Theologian responded forcefully to this erroneous teaching:

> That which he has not assumed [*aproslēpton*] he has not healed, but that which he has truly united with God is saved. If only a part of Adam fell, then that part which is assumed [*proseilēmmenon*] is saved, but if all of Adam fell, then he is completely saved only by complete union with him who has been bɵrn man in completeness. (*Epistle to Cledonius* 101)[72]

"I appropriate [articulate] sounds": through incarnation, the Word of God "appropriates" (verb *oikeioō*, middle conjugation), makes the capability of human speech his own. The word *phōnē*, "voice, sound," here in the plural, denotes articulate sounds, human language. The same word, in the plural, is used to describe the theophany on Mount Sinai (Exod 19:19). It is noteworthy that, still in the same theophanic context, Exod 20:18 notes that "all the people saw [*heōra*] the sound [LXX: *tēn phōnēn*; MT: *qwlwt*, "sounds"] and the torches [*lampadas*] and the sound [*tēn phōnēn*] of the trumpet; and the mountain was smoking. Now all the people were afraid and stood at a distance." Instead of "hearing," the people "saw" the "sound" (of God speaking).

Why such a weird collocation—the poetical term is *synesthesia*—of "sound"/"seeing"? Here is Philo commenting on this odd wording:

> And an astonishing voice [*phōnē*] sounded forth [*exēchei*] from out of the midst of the fire which had flowed from heaven; the flame became articulated speech [*arthroumenēs*] in the language [*dialekton*] familiar to the listeners [*akroōmenois*], and those [words] uttered [*ta legomena*] became evidently so clear [*etranouto*], that they seemed to see [*horan*] rather than hear [*akouein*] them. All the people "saw the voice [*heōra tēn phōnēn*]," ... for the voice of men is thought to be audible [*akoustēn*], but the voice of God is truly visible [*horatēn*]. How so? Because whatever God says is not words [*rhēmata*] but works [*erga*], whose judges are the eyes [*ophtalmoi*] before the ears [*ōtōn*]. (*The Decalogue* 46–47)[73]

In Philo's view, the "visibility" of God's speech points to the divine "works" (*erga*) as defining element for the "One Who Is," vis-à-vis human speech characterized primarily by "utterances" (*rhēmata*). Also of interest is the distinction Philo draws between "voice, articulate sound, speech" (*phōnē*), intrinsic to a person (God, humans), and "language [discussion]" (*dialectos*), as a concrete result of the former, conditioned by a group "living together" (*synētēs*).

The plural form *phōnas*, "sounds," used in this hymn may connote "articulate sounds" or "human speech" in general. What is the connection between human speech and incarnation or with the human condition itself? The hymn could be a subtle hint at an ancient Jewish interpretation of Gen 2:7 attested in the Targums. According to Gen 2:7, when God "breathed" into the nostrils of "the humanity" (MT: *h-ʾdm*; LXX: *ho anthrōpos*) that he was fashioning out of the dust of the ground, the humanity became a "living breath, soul" (MT: *npš ḥyh*; LXX: *psychēn zōsan*). Targum Onkelos renders the Heb. *npš ḥyh*, "living breath, soul," with *rwḥ mmllʾ*, "speaking spirit." Targum Pseudo-Jonathan expands Onkelos's original reading: "and [God] breathed into his nostrils the breathing of life [*nšmtʾ d-ḥyy*], and the breathing became in the body [*b-gwpʾ*] of Adam a speaking spirit [*rwḥ mmllʾ*] unto the illumination of the eyes [*l-ʾnhrwt ʿynyn*] and the hearing of the ears [*l-mṣtwt ʾwdnyn*]."

The targumist's lexical choice, *rwḥ mmllʾ*, "speaking spirit," could be explained in two ways. Either the targumist mistook *ḥwh*, "to announce, inform, speak" (Piʿel, cf. Ps 19:3 [18:4]), for *ḥyh*, "living," or he wanted to distinguish between animals (non-speaking creatures) and humans (speech-endowed beings).[74]

However, there might be another, much more profound theological explanation if one follows the canonical approach and reads Gen 1 and 2, dating back to different centuries and schools of thought, as a literary-theological continuum. This way, one may detect a subtle link between God, who creates things by the power of his "utterance" (e.g., Gen 1:3) and humanity, created in God's "image" (Gen 1:26–27), "fashioned" out of the "dust of the ground," and touched by God's "breathing of life" (Gen 2:7). In the targumic reading of Gen 2:7, the humanity was granted speech by God, not so much as a way of communication but rather as a means of imagining, deliberating, and creating. In other words, through the power of speech, humanity was empowered by God the Creator to imitate him by becoming co-creators and co-providers through the unimaginable power of "articulate sounds [*phōnai*]."

And when we think of the "mystical supper," which is remembered on Holy Thursday, and especially of Jesus's last discourse, so lavishly recorded by the gospel of John (John 13–16), we have to realize the importance of the "articulate sounds [*phōnai*]" Jesus appropriated at the Incarnation, as this hymn states so distinctly. And what is Jesus's lengthy speech at the Last Supper if not an invitation to the disciples and to us to take this imaginative and creative journey along with the Teacher on the much-trodden way toward the kingdom of God.

I would like to conclude this section with a few lines from the epistle to the Hebrews that wrap up admirably the gist of the beautiful Byzantine hymn already analyzed:

> Long ago [*palai*], God spoke [*lalēsas*] by the prophets [*en tois prophētais*] to our fathers in many [*polymerōs*] and various [*polytropōs*] ways; but at the end [*ep' eschatou*] of these days, he spoke [*elalēsen*] to us by [his] Son [*hyiō*] whom he appointed the heir [*klēronomon*] of all things and through whom also he made the ages [*aiōnas*]. (Heb 1:1–2)

Wisdom's Own House

> The boundless [*apeiros*] Wisdom of God [*sophia tou theou*], the all-cause [*pantaitia*] and creative [*parektikē*] of life, has built her house [*ōkodomēse ton oikon heautēs*], from a chaste [*hagnēs*], not-having-a-man [virgin] mother [*apeirandrou mētros*]; for she put on a bodily temple [*naon sōmatikon perithemenos*], Christ, our God, [who] is greatly glorified [*endoxōs dedoxastai*]. (Holy Thursday, Matins, Ode 1, Troparion)

Lying at the center of this hymn is Prov 9:1a, which is part of a literary unit (Prov 9:1–6 ["Lady Wisdom's Banquet"] and v. 11) that may be very briefly summed up this way: Lady Wisdom builds a house (v. 1) and prepares a feast (v. 2). She then invites people to her banquet (vv. 3–5). In v. 6, the meaning of invitation is explained, and in v. 11, Wisdom's exhortation is reinforced.

Verses 1–3a, employed by the hymns presented below, set the "banquet" scene and offer preliminary information.

Prov 9:1 (LXX) reads: "The Wisdom [*hē sophia*] built [*ōkodomēsen*] a house for herself [*heautē*] and supported [*hypēreisen*] it with seven pillars [*stēlous*]."

In Prov 9:1 (MT), "wisdom" occurs in the plural, indefinite *ḥokmôt* (cf. Prov 1:20).[75] However, the LXX has the singular along with the definite article, *hē sophia*.

Note that the MT uses the verb *ḥāṣəbāh*, "she has hewn out" (of seven pillars); the proposed amended reading *hiṣṣîbāh*, "she set up," requiring only one consonantal change (*ḥ* to *h*), is supported by the versions (e.g., LXX: *hypēreisen*, verb *hypereidō*, "to support, to prop up"), while paralleling the verb *b-n-h*, "to build" (LXX: *ōkodomēsen,* verb *oikodomeō*), in the first part of the verse.

Verse 1 is about Lady Wisdom, and Prov 14:1a concerns the wise women, with the same "house-building" imagery[76] permeating both verses. Prov 24:3: "A house is built [*oikodomeitai*] by wisdom, and rebuilt [*anorthoutai*] by understanding." It is fascinating (at least to biblical linguists) that the adjective *adiorthōtos*, "unrestored, unbuilt" (related to the verb *diorthoō*, "to restore," plus *a*-negation particle), is used in a hymn[77] touching on incarnation and restoration of humanity through Christ, with Judas who "remained unrestored" [*adiorthōtos emeinen*] for obvious reasons). Since in this hymn the imagery of Wisdom "building her house" (cf. Prov 9:1) refers to the Incarnation (i.e., putting on a "bodily temple" [*naon sōmatikon*]), the *new* theme of "rebuilding"/"restoring" (*anorthoō*) the house (in parallel to "building" [*oikodomeō*]) found in Prov 24:3 may be read as a hint at the restoration of humanity that Christ assumed at the Incarnation.

Gregory of Nyssa (about 335–394) contends that when Prov 9:1 says that Wisdom built a house "for herself," this means that the Word of God, at the Incarnation, did *not* assume someone's body but rather took on his own body from the Virgin: "We say, therefore, that when he said in his previous discourse that wisdom built a house for itself, he is speaking enigmatically about the formation of the Lord's flesh. For true wisdom did not live in someone else's building but built a home for itself from the Virgin's body" (*Against Eunomius* 3.1.44).[78]

Similarly, Hippolytus of Rome writes:

Christ, [Solomon] means, the wisdom and power of God the Father, has built his house, that is, his nature in the flesh derived from the virgin, even as [John] said beforetime: "The Word became flesh and dwelt among us" [John 1:14]. [As likewise the wise prophet Solomon] testifies: Wisdom that was before the world, and is the source of life, the infinite "wisdom of God, has built her house" by a mother who knew no man—to wit, as he assumed the temple of the body. "And has raised her seven pillars that is the fragrant grace of the all-holy Spirit, as Isaiah says: 'And the seven spirits of God shall rest upon him'" [Isa 11:2]. [But others say that the seven pillars are the seven divine orders which sustain the creation by his holy and inspired teaching: namely, the prophets, the saints and the righteous]. (*Fragments on Proverbs*)[79]

The Lady Wisdom builds her house, by supporting it with "seven pillars." Seven here, as elsewhere in the Bible, is a typological number signifying usefulness and completeness. With reference to a room, "seven pillars," besides conveying a perfect and suitable piece of work, may denote spaciousness and elegance of the dining room where Lady Wisdom sets the banquet table.

As early as the time of the Jewish midrashim, "seven pillars" were considered an allegory of the "seven days at the Beginning" (a nickname for Wisdom; see above)—an enticing piece of interpretation which accounts for the close relationship between God the Creator and Wisdom in the work of creation.[80]

A Byzantine hymn compares the "seven pillars" with the seven Maccabean brothers: "The Wisdom of God has built a temple [naon] and has supported it upon seven rational pillars [hepta stylois logikois], manifestly showing these youths to be keepers of the Law" (The Seven Holy Maccabees [August 1], Ode 6, Sticheron). The seven Maccabees are as strong as seven pillars supporting the temple, namely, Wisdom's house (cf. Prov 9:1–6), in their rigorous observance of Torah.[81]

In John Chrysostom's view, "seven pillars" represent the "seven spirits" mentioned by the prophet Isaiah (Isa 11:2):

> "Wisdom has built her house, and has set seven pillars." Since wisdom is the Son of God, once he became man he built his house, that is, the flesh from the Virgin. He [Solomon] calls the seven pillars "the spirit of God, the spirit of wisdom and understanding, the spirit of counsel and strength, the spirit of knowledge and piety, the spirit of the fear of God," as Isaiah says. [Solomon] also calls the church "house" and the apostles "pillars." The wise individual is the one who is self and self-sufficient, lacking nothing. At the house of wisdom is the church, the pillars are those who appear to be pillars in the church. (*Commentary on the Proverbs of Solomon, Fragment* 9.1)[82]

This hymn is a logical sequel to the previous one. It opens with a reinforced recap of Wisdom's role in God's creative work, then launches into a new theme, further developed over the course of the two subsequent hymns under examination. It is the theme of "Lady Wisdom's Banquet" inspired by the biblical literary unit Prov 9:1–6, 11, and vested, as customary, in a Christian theological garb.

Pertaining to her role in creation, Wisdom is described here with new adjectives such as "boundless" (*apeiros*), "all-cause" (*pantaitia*), and "creative" (*parektikē*) of life. Thus, Wisdom, "uncreated by nature" (*aktistos physei*; see the preceding hymn), is boundless, unlimited, infinite, as God the Creator is. She is also the all-cause of life, so there is no aspect of life that could avoid her. Hence Wisdom's main attribute is the creation of life: she is the co-creator along with God of all living creatures.

"She has built her house [ōkodomēse ton oikon heautēs]*"*
The Logos, namely, the Wisdom of God, has built her house. The biblical theme of Wisdom building a house serves here as metaphor for the Logos's incarnation. One notices a slight alteration, "her house" vs. "house for herself" (cf. Prov 9:1a), that finely describes the Incarnation as a process by which the Logos acquires or assumes personally (verb *proslambanō*)[83] human nature, which, one may say, becomes "his own" (i.e., "her house").

"From a chaste, not-having-a-man mother [hagnēs ex apeirandrou mētros]*"*
The Word takes on human nature via a chaste, pure (*hagnē*), and virgin (*apeirandros*) Mother. It is noteworthy that the adjective *hagnē*, "pure" (feminine singular), is used in the Bible only once with respect to a woman,[84] the mother of the seven Maccabean brothers. Here is this woman's self-description:

> I was a pure virgin [*parthenos hagnē*] and did not go outside [*hyperebēn*] my father's house, but I kept guard over [*ephylasson*] the built side [*ōkodomēmenēn pleuran*]. Neither corrupter of the wilderness [*lymeōn erēmias*], nor the seducer in the plain [*phthoreus en pediō*], nor the corrupter, the serpent of deceit [*lymeōn apatēs ophis*], spoiled [*elymēnato*] the purity of [my] virginity [*ta agna tēs parthenias*]. (4 Macc 18:7–8)

Here, the Maccabees' mother contrasts herself with Eve (emerging from Adam's built side/rib [cf. Gen 2:21–22]), who allowed the deceiving serpent to damage the purity of her virginity. These two verses echo, as Kugel rightly remarks, an ancient Jewish interpretation on the birth of Cain, the offspring of Eve and the deceiving serpent (i.e., the devil or a wicked angel), which would explain the first fratricide.[85]

Thus, if Eve did not guard the purity of her virginity, the Maccabees' mother and, later, the Holy Virgin Mary, the mother of the incarnate God, will both do so. Moreover, Mary is here described as "having-no-man" (*anandros*); that is, she is a virgin.

"For she put on a bodily temple [naon sōmatikon perithemenos]*"*
For further description of the Word of God being born from a chaste, virgin mother, the hymnographer employs the body-temple metaphor.

The phrase "bodily temple" (*naos sōmatikon*) alludes to John 1:14: "And the Word became flesh [*sarx egeneto*], and tabernacled [*eskēnōsen*] among us—and we contemplated [*ethesametha*] his glory, glory of the Only Begotten One [*Monogenous*] from the Father—full of favor [*charitos*] and truth [*alētheias*]." There are two small differences here. First, "flesh" (*sarx*) becomes "bodily" (*sōmatikon*), perhaps a subtle allusion to John 2:19–21, where Jesus compares his "body" (*sōma*) with the "temple" (*naos*). Later, Paul teaches on the body being a "temple of the Holy Spirit" (*naos tou hagiou pneumatos*; 1 Cor 6:19; cf. 1 Cor 3:16, 17; Eph 2:21–22). Second, "tenting, tabernacling" (verb *skēnoō* from *skēnē*, "tent, tabernacle") becomes "temple" (*naos*) in order to better correlate the Johannine incarnational *kerygma* with Old Testament temple theology.

Getting closer to the core of the mystery of incarnation, the hymnographer uses the participial form *perithemenos* from the verb *peritithēmi*, "to place around oneself," of one wrapping oneself all around with a garment. The image is that of the Logos who puts around himself a "bodily temple" (*naon sōmatikon*), namely, the human body assumed at incarnation. Of significance here is that the same verb, *peritithēmi*, is used in Exod 34:35, where Moses "put a veil on around his own face" (*periethēken kalymma epi to prosōpon heautou*) to hide his "glorified" face, so people might not be afraid when they wanted to approach him. In the case of Moses, as one may detect in that of the incarnate Logos, the "putting on around" a (fabric) "veil" or a "bodily temple" aims to protect those coming close (or too close) to the divine.

The word *naos* used in the hymn is found frequently in the Bible (LXX and New Testament) referring to either the most sacred part of the sanctuary, the "Holy of Holies" (MT: *qōdeš haq-qŏdāšîm*; LXX: *to hagion tōn hagiōn*), where only the high priest was permitted to enter once a year on Yom Kippur (Day of Atonement, lit. "Day of Concealment," from *k-p-r*, "to hide, to put a lid on" [see Lev 16]; 1 Sam 3:3; 2 Sam 22:7; Ps 11 [10]:4; Mark 15:38), or to the entire structure itself (Ps 5:7 [8]; Jdt 4:11), either the Tent of Witness or the Jerusalem Temple.

Etymologically, Gk. *naos* (verb *naiō*, "to abide, to dwell") conveys the idea of divine dwelling (similar to *skēnē*, "tent," and *skēnoō*, "to pitch a tent, to tabernacle," referring to the Tent of Witness). The Temple, and primarily its most sacred part, has always been imagined as the dwelling place, the topos par excellence, where the divinity lives (Tob 1:4) and makes itself accessible to human beings.

However, the Old Testament depicts God as *"The* Holy One" (e.g., in the Trisagion chanted by the seraphim in Isa 6:3), who transcends the world he created. Note that the Heb. *qādôš*, "holy," derives from the verb *q-d-š*, "to cut off, to separate" and God's modus operandi as Creator is to separate things from one another in order to bring them into reality. More than any of his ANE counterparts, this God needs an intermediary, someone at the same time close to him and to creation, to serve as a bridge and a means of communication between himself and human beings. As we have already seen, Prov 8:22–31 proposes a personified Wisdom begotten by and somewhat co-eternal with God the Creator to do this work. Later texts, the earliest interpretations of this Wisdom intermediary, show this divine Wisdom searching for a dwelling place among humans. According to Sir 24, the Wisdom of God, who is "tenting in the high places" (*en hypsēlois kateskēnōsa*, v. 4), at God's advice, chose to "pitch [her] tent" (*kataskēnōson*) in Jacob, making Israel her "inheritance" (*kataklēronomēthēti*, v. 8). Verse 23 informs us that all the blessings of Wisdom's indwelling in Israel can be summarized to the "book of covenant [*biblos diathēkēs*] of the Most High God, a law [*nomon*] that Moses commended us, an inheritance [*klēronomian*] for the gatherings [*synagōgais*] of Jacob"—in a word, to the written Torah (God's instruction).

One may detect in the following text from Sir a bit of disappointment expressed by Wisdom, who dwells in the midst of a people who have not always shown a strong affinity for divine instruction: "I will again [*eti*] pour out teaching like prophecy [*didaskalian hōs prophēteian*] and I will leave it behind [*kataleipsō*] for generations of ages [*geneas aiōnōn*]" (Sir 24:33).

In 1 En and 2 Esd (apocalyptic writings from the end of the Second Temple period), Wisdom's touch of disappointment becomes clear frustration as Wisdom realizes a partial failure on the part of Torah in being unable to bring God's word forth to the people. As a result, a frustrated Wisdom returns to God to live among the angels. Scholars see in these apocalyptic descriptions of Wisdom a sort of parody on Sir 24 and Bar 3:9–4:4: unrighteous people cause Wisdom to leave the territory of Jacob and return to God: "Wisdom found no place where she might dwell; then a dwelling place was assigned her in the heavens. Wisdom went forth to make her dwelling among the children of men, and found no dwelling place: Wisdom returned to her place, and took her seat among the angels. And unrighteousness went forth from her chambers: whom she sought not she found, and dwelt with them, as rain in a desert and dew on a thirsty land" (1 En 42:1–3).[86]

John 1:14 could be read as a Christian response to Wisdom's return to heaven.[87] The prologue in John suggests that there *is* another way Wisdom might choose, and indeed she did: to dwell among humans and make her presence more concrete and efficient, her incarnation in a human person.

Seemingly, there is no contradiction, but perhaps a sort of complementarity, between these two ancient Jewish and Christian approaches to the divine and eternal Wisdom (i.e., "before the age . . . and until the age" [*pro tou aiōnos . . . kai heōs aiōnos*], Sir 24:9), two different, yet not contradictory ways in which Wisdom was imagined to function as an intermediary between God and Israel or any human being. In general, this is the written word of God, dwelling in the Torah, and the Word of God made flesh dwelling in a human person, Jesus Christ.[88]

In sum, what the above hymn tries to convey is the Johannine teaching on the Logos made flesh and tabernacling among us (John 1:14) via his "bodily temple," i.e., human body, as being similar to the God of old, who dwelt in the midst of his people via the material structure of the temple, including all its operative panoply from furniture to vestments and liturgical objects. God's presence in his temple was real and participatory, and so is the Logos's presence in his "bodily temple," with no dichotomy between physical and metaphysical levels but rather a tight interweaving of the two.[89]

Mixing Ambrosia and Preparing a Life-Sustaining Table

> While initiating her own friends into mysteries [*mystagōgousa*], the truly existing [*ontōs*] Wisdom of God prepares [*hetoimazei*] a life-sustaining table [*psychotrophon trapezan*], and also mixes [*kirna*] a bowl of ambrosia/ immortality [*ambrosias kratēra*] for those who believe [*pistois*]. Let us draw near in piety [*eusebōs*] and call out: "Christ, our God, [who] is/has been greatly glorified!" (Holy Thursday, Matins, Ode 1)

This hymn switches from Wisdom's incarnation, depicted in the previous hymn as "putting on around a bodily temple," to the mystical supper itself, a "life-sustaining table," with the incarnate Wisdom mixing "a bowl of ambrosia/immortality."

As one can hardly miss, the hymn weaves the symbolism of a banquet thrown by Wisdom for her own friends, as it is depicted in Prov 9:2

(LXX): "She slaughtered [*esphaxen*] her own sacrificial [animals] [*thymata*]; she mixed [*ekerasen*] into a bowl [*kratēra*] her own wine [*oinon*], and she prepared [*hētoimasato*] her own table [*trapezan*]."

Noteworthy, too, is that Prov 9:2 fuses two images, a sacrificial offering (e.g., *sphazō, thymata*) and a banquet (e.g., *kerannymi, oinos, kratēr, trapeza*).

Cyprian of Carthage (d. 258 C.E.) sees here a type of Christ's sacrifice:

> The Holy Spirit through Solomon shows forth the type of sacrifice of the Lord, making mention of the immolated victim and of the bread and wine and also of the altar and of the apostles. "Wisdom," he continues, "has built a house and she set up seven columns. She has slain her victims, mixed her wine in a chalice, and has spread her table." . . . He declares the wine is mixed, that is, he announces in a prophetic voice that the chalice of the Lord is mixed with water and wine. (*Letter* 63.5)[90]

This is actually the typical biblical scenario describing a sacrifice: the animal to be offered as a "sacrifice" (*thyma*) was brought to the sanctuary, where the priest laid his hands on the victim, after which the animal was "slaughtered" (the verb *sphazō* denotes the idea of slaying an animal by cutting its throat) and its blood sprinkled over various parts of the sanctuary complex; the sacrifice itself was followed by a communal sacrificial meal (Exod 18:12; Lev 3:6–11; 1 Chron 29:21–22). This communal meal was an ancient practice going back to patriarchal times, prior to the emergence of the Levitical priesthood. Gen 31:54 (LXX) records how Jacob "offered a sacrifice [*ethysan thysia*] on the mountain and invited his kinsfolk, and they ate [*ephagon*] and drank [*epion*; MT reads only "ate"] and slept on the mountain." The sacrificial ritual succinctly described here was part of a covenant-making ceremony between Jacob and his father-in-law, Laban.

Unlike its inspiring biblical text, the hymn employs only the banquet imagery—no mention of victim slaughtering. There is no lexical evidence in this hymn to support the identification of Wisdom's banquet with a sacrificial meal. We are just simply told that Wisdom "prepares a life-sustaining table" (*hetoimazei psychotrophon trapezan*). The hymn may subtly allude to the "preparations" Jesus referred to when he advised Peter and John, in a rather enigmatic but at the same time straightforward way, where and how to meet the owner of the place where the Last Supper was to be held (Mark 14:13; Luke 22:10): "Go and prepare [*hetoimasate*] the Passover for us that we may eat it" (Luke 22:8). Note the hymn's use of the present tense "she prepares" (*etoimazei*), underscoring the "liturgical actualization" of this once-in-a-lifetime supper event.

The word *psychotrophon*, "life-sustaining," refers to Wisdom's table (*trapezan*), namely, the Last Supper,[91] where Jesus, the incarnate Wisdom, "initiated his friends into the mysteries [*philous heautēs mystagōgousa*]" of his Passion, death, and resurrection, by instituting the mystical supper (Eucharist) as a way of perpetuating his presence among his disciples. Thus, the Last Supper, as well as any liturgical enactment, has become a "life-sustaining table" for those who believe (*pistois*).

In the same line of thought, the irrepressible Origen speaks of *tou psychotrophou artou*, "the life-sustaining bread" (the Eucharist), whose efficiency in the believer's life is conditioned by purifying oneself of passions and practicing God's commandments: "He, who purifies [*kathairōn*] himself from passions and practices [*ergazomenos*] God's commandments, will be filled [*emplēsthēsetai*] with life-sustaining bread [*psychotrophou artou*] and God's wisdom [*sophias*] and knowledge [*gnōseōs*]" (*Expositio in Proverbia* [*fragmenta ex commentariis in Proverbia e catenis*] [PG 17:245]).

"She mixes a bowl of ambrosia/immortality [ambrosias kirna kratēra]*"*
Wisdom's most significant task or service is to "mix" (*kirna*) "a bowl of ambrosia/immortality" (*ambrosias kratēra*). Her work turns an ordinary table, supper, and meal into an open-ended "life-sustaining" reality.

The hymn hints at an ancient Greek custom, well established in Jesus's time. The wine that was to be served at a supper or banquet was stored in large pointed jugs (*amphorae*); when the wine was to be served, it was poured from jugs into large bowls called *kraters* (Gk. singular *kratēr*), where it was mixed with water. And from these *kraters*, the mixed wine was poured into drinking cups or *kylix* and served at table.[92]

To visualize the Last Supper, and the brief reference to it in our hymn, one has to take a look into the Tanaitic literary sources (third to seventh centuries but containing traditions going back to the first century C.E.), where one finds a description of the "liturgical order" for Jewish meals that could have been observed in Jesus's time. Here is an excerpt from a Tanaitic work describing such a Jewish supper, patterned on a Greco-Roman banquet model:

> What is the order of the meal? The guests enter [the house] and sit on
> benches, and on chairs until all have entered. They all enter and they

[servants] give them water for their hands. Each one washes one hand. They [servants] mix for them the cup; each one says the benediction for himself. They [guests] go up [to the dining room] and they recline, and they [servants] give them water for their hands; although they have [already] washed one hand, they [now] wash both hands. They [servants] mix for them the cup; although they have said a benediction over the first one, they [now] say a benediction over the second, and one says the benediction for all of them. He who comes after the third course has no right to enter. (*Tosephta* 4.8)[93]

Note that according to this particular description, the servants "mix" the wine with water directly in the guests' "cups" and not in a large "bowl" (Gk. *kratēr*), as was the general practice mentioned in our hymn. The traditional blessing over the wine was "Blessed are you, O Lord, our God, king of the universe, creator of the fruit of the vine." Note Jesus's use of the same expression, "fruit of the vine," in his discourse at the Last Supper: "Truly I say to you, I will no longer drink of the fruit of the vine [*genēmatos tēs ampelou*] until that day when I drink it new [*kainon*] in the kingdom of God" (Mark 14:25).

Wisdom "mixes a bowl of ambrosia/immortality" (*ambrosias kirna kratēra*) for "the ones who believe" (*pistois*). The Greek word *ambrosia* literally means "immortality," and it refers to the food of the gods. Ambrosia reflects a common belief in the ancient world that there is a great difference between mortal or earthly food and immortal or heavenly food. The divine food is to be kept away from humans. For instance, when the goddess Calypso dines with Odysseus, he eats human food while she is served with heavenly fare, namely, ambrosia and nectar (Homer, *Odyssey* 5.197–199), that is, the foundation of *hierophagy*, "holy food." In the ancient Greek tradition, ambrosia, food as sweet as honey, is reserved for gods as a source of, and a means for sustaining, immortality.[94]

There is a rather consuming (pun intended) similarity between the ancient mythic ambrosia and biblical manna. Although not a source of immortality or fully restricted to the divine realm as with ambrosia, the miraculous food the ancient Hebrews ate during their long journey through the wilderness (Exod 16) is like ambrosia, "heavenly food." Ps 78 (77):25 (LXX) calls it "angels' bread": "The human being ate the bread of the angels" (LXX: *arton angelōn ephagen anthōpos*; MT: "bread of the mighty ones [*'abbîrîm*]").

Similarly, the book of Wisdom of Solomon, whose composition dates to the first half of the first century C.E., labels manna as "angels' food": "You [God] spoonfed [*epsōmisas*] your people with angels' food [*angelōn trophēn*]" (Wis 16:20; cf. 2 Esd 1:19), an interpretation welcomed by the famous Rabbi Akiba (*Yoma* 75b).[95]

But the author of Wis goes even a step further, equating manna with ambrosia, a hapax legomenon in the entire Bible. In the penultimate verse of Wis, we are told that flames of fire could not destroy the manna, that "crystalline easily-melting sort of ambrosial food [*krystalloeides eutēkton genos ambrosias trophēs*]" (Wis 19:21).[96]

Moreover, in John 6, Jesus compares himself with manna, the connecting line being their common "heavenly" origin. The incarnate Logos/Wisdom, typified by manna in the Old Testament, functions as an ambrosial food offering immortality to those who mystically share in his salvific life and work: "I am the bread, the living one [*ho artos ho zōn*]," says Jesus, "who came down from heaven [*ho ek tou ouranou katabas*]; if anyone eats [*phagē*] from this bread, he will live forever [*zēsetai eis ton aiōna*]; and the bread that I shall give for the life of the world is my flesh [*hē sarx mou*]" (John 6:51). "Whoever eats [*trōgōn*] my flesh [*tēn sarka mou*] and drinks [*pinōn*] my blood [*to haima mou*], has eternal life [*zōēn aiōnion*], and I will raise him up on the last day [*tē eschatē hēmera*]" (John 6:54). One must notice in Jesus's logion the same parallel as in the Wisdom text cited above, between manna, here identified with Jesus, and eternal life (ambrosia/immortality).

This is actually what the hymn proclaims: the incarnate Wisdom, the Word of God made flesh, "mixes a bowl of ambrosia/immortality" and prepares a "life-sustaining table." This poetical depiction of the Eucharist, as a source of immortality and spiritual nourishment, may be found more discursively stylized in Clement of Alexandria (150–215): "Accordingly, as wine is blended with water, so is the Spirit with man. And the one, the mixture of wine and water, nourishes to faith; while the other, the Spirit, conducts to immortality. And the mixture of both—of the water and of the Word—is called Eucharist" (*Paedagogue* 2).[97] Similarly, Ignatius refers to the Eucharist as "medicine of immortality": "At these meetings you should heed the bishop and presbytery attentively, and break one loaf, which is the medicine of immortality, and the antidote which wards off death but yields continuous life in union with Jesus Christ" (*Letter to the Ephesians* 20).[98]

Summoning with a High Proclamation

> Let us listen, all who believe, to the uncreated [aktistou] and innate [emphytou] Wisdom of God, summoning [synkaloumenēs] with a high proclamation [hypsēlō kērygmati]. For she is crying aloud: "Taste [geusasthe], and learning [gnontes] that I am kind [chrēstos], cry out: Christ, our God, [who] has been greatly glorified!" (Holy Thursday, Matins, Ode 1, Troparion)

The "uncreated" (aktistou) and "innate" (emphytou) Wisdom of God appears in this hymn as a herald summoning to her banquet with a "high proclamation" (synkaloumenēs hypsēlō kērygmati), that is, in an impressive, stately manner.

The hymn draws nearly verbatim on Prov 9:3–5 (LXX): "She [Wisdom] sent out [apesteilen] her own servants [heautēs doulous] summoning [synkalousa] with a high proclamation [hypsēlou kērygmatos] to the drinking feast [epi kratēra]." In a straightforward manner, Wisdom invites two distinct groups, the "foolish" (aphrōn) and the ones "lacking understanding" (endeesi phrenōn), which fits quite nicely with the hymn's mystical supper theme: "Come, eat my own bread [tōn emōn artōn] and drink wine [oinon] which I mixed [ekerasa] for you" (Prov 9:4–5). Note that unlike her ANE counterparts, the Hebrew Wisdom does not limit the invitation to her customary devotees, but she includes in the guest list even those who are foolish or lack understanding.[99]

"Summoning [synkaloumenēs]*"*
Both the biblical author and the hymnographer employ the verb synkaleō, "to summon, to convoke, to call together," to underline the communal aspect of Wisdom's invitation. She summons people together, in one place (like, e.g., Jesus summoning the twelve, Luke 9:1; calling one's friends together to rejoice over the lost and found sheep or coin, Luke 15:6, 9). With respect to the semantic peculiarity of the verb synkaleō, "to call together," one may adduce here the central petition of Jesus's prayer at the end of the meal, "so they may be one, as we are one" (John 17:11), where the mystical supper both relies on and nourishes the community of believers.

According to the MT of Prov 9:3a, Wisdom dispatches "her maidservants" (nᶜrtyh),[100] while in the LXX, the messengers are "male servants" (doulous). Also, the LXX explicative gloss "to the drinking feast" (epi kratēra) has no parallel at all in the MT. The messengers' duty is to transmit not their own but, rather, Wisdom's invitation. The image of Wisdom sending out her "servants" to bring guests in might have been an inspiring text behind the parable of the great banquet (Luke 14:15–24).[101]

According to Hippolytus of Rome, the "servants" sent by Wisdom to get her message out are Christ's apostles: "'She has sent forth her servants.' Wisdom, that is to say, has done so, [and it is Christ] who summons them with lofty announcement. 'Whoever is simple, let him turn to me,' she says, alluding manifestly to the holy apostles who journeyed the whole world and called the nations to the knowledge of him [in truth, with their lofty and divine preaching]" (*Fragments on Proverbs*).[102]

"With a high proclamation [hypsēlō kērygmati]*"*
The term *kērygma* (verb *kēryssō*), "what is cried by a herald, message, public note, proclamation," could have had a special resonance in the believers' ears, namely, "proclaiming the good news [*kēryssōn to euangelion*]" (Matt 4:23; 9:35; Mark 1:14; cf. Luke 8:1) or the "proclamation [*kērygma*]" (Mark 16:8; Rom 16:25; 1 Cor 1:21; 2:4; 15:14; 2 Tim 4:17; Titus 1:3).

The phrase "high proclamation" (*hypsēlō kērygmati*) evokes an impressive, stately means of publicizing the message and summoning the invitees to the feast. Note that the Prov 9:3 MT reading differs from the LXX ("high proclamation"): *ʿal gappēy mərōmēy qāret*, "[from] the tops of the city's heights," thus emphasizing "where" rather than "how" this summoning would occur. The MT reading is supported by Prov 8:2 and 9:14, where similar words indicate the "high" location whence the invitation is delivered. Wisdom, as well as her mortal opponent, Lady Folly, chooses the most visible place of the city to deliver her message. As Michael Fox astutely observes, "The banquet is not a unique event but an ongoing occurrence in the ever-present time. . . . Wisdom is always and forever building her house, preparing her feast, and inviting people in."[103] This remark squares very nicely with the hymnographer's obvious interpretive propensity to liturgically actualize past biblical events, such as the Last Supper.

"Taste, and learning that I am kind, cry out [geusasthe kai gnontes hoti*
. chrēstos egō krazate]"
These lines are a slightly altered quote from Ps 34:8 [33:9] [LXX]): "Taste and see [*idete*] that the Lord [*ho kyrios*] [is] kind [*chrēstos*; MT: *ṭôb*, "good"]); happy [*makarios*] the man who hopes [*elpizei*] in him." As one

may notice, the only difference is that Ps 34 (33) has the imperative *idete*, "see," while the hymn exhibits a participle of another verb, *gnontes*, "learning, knowing." The hymnographer's lexical-grammatical choice was likely dictated by emphasis on "learning, getting to know" (as a diligent reflective process) vs. "seeing" (as a fleeting sense-based experience) and the need for a logically smooth transition from "tasting" to "doxologizing" via "learning."

The qualifier *chrēstos*, "kind, good" (from the verb *chraō*, "to furnish what is needful, useful"), chosen by the incarnate Wisdom to introduce herself, evokes a whole range of nuances—useful, auspicious, serviceable, worthy, propitious—of someone who is ready always to help and never says no to anyone, a kind person always on duty. Moreover, on the sonic level, this form points ineluctably to its homonym "Christ," "Anointed" (*christos*, from the verb *chriō*, "to anoint"), hence this hymn's inferred Christocentric underpinning.

As in Prov 9:3, the hymn's Wisdom invites simple folks not to a banquet of meats, spiced wines, and sexual intimacy, typical traits of an ancient royal/ divine banquet, but rather to a celebration of life and divine Wisdom. At this unusual banquet, the foolish and unlearned folks begin to realize how beautiful life is, and how much greater are Wisdom's gifts when compared to any fertility goddess's promises.[104]

One may adduce Ps 136 (135):1 as a correlative to the central idea of this hymn: Wisdom's kindness reflected in her summoning to a feast should be properly understood and genuinely acknowledged and praised. Similarly to Ps 34 (33), the hymn's partial textual base, Ps 136 (135) insists on God's kindness (the psalmist's favorite attribute for God), relating this attribute (so well attested in the book of Psalms) to "mercy" (Gk. *eleos*; Heb. *ḥesed*, "steadfast, long-suffering love"): "Acknowledge [*exomologeisthe*] the Lord for he is kind [*chrēstos*] and his mercy is forever [*eis ton aiōna*]."

The "New Drink" and "God among Gods"

"I declare [*phēmi*], in my kingdom [*en tē basileia mou*], I will drink [*piomai*] a new drink [*poma kainon*] beyond the word [*hyper logon*]," Christ, you said to [your] friends [*philois*]. "For then [*hōste*], I shall be with you [*synesomai*], God among gods [*theois theos*]; since [*epei*] the Father sent [*apesteilen*] me, the Only Begotten One [*monogenē*], into the world as an atonement [*hilasmon*]." (Holy Thursday, Matins, Ode 4, Troparion)

The first half of the hymn seems to be a free quotation from Mark 14:25 (or its parallels, Matt 26:29; Luke 22:18): "Truly [*amēn*] I say [*legō*] to you that I would drink [*piō*] no more [*ouketi*] from the fruit of the vine [*gennēmatos tēs ampelou*], until that day [*heōs tēs hēmeras ekeinēs*] when I drink [*pinō*] it new [*kainon*] in the kingdom of God [*en tē basileia tou theou*]."

Scriptures

Note Matt 26:29's extremely close resemblance to Mark 14:25, though with two significant alterations: adding "with you [*meth' hymōn*; i.e., disciples]" and replacing "God's kingdom" with "my Father's kingdom" (*basileia tou patros mou*). The other textual parallel, Luke 22:18, represents an even fuller version of Jesus's logion, with a stronger eschatological touch due to the extra phrase "until the kingdom of God comes" (*heōs hotou hē basileia tou theou elthē* [Byz.]).

Most scholars regard this logion as going back, if not to Jesus's ipsissima verba, at least to one of the earliest traditions preceding the writing of the gospel.[105] Personally, I agree with Martinus de Jonge, who demonstrates convincingly that this saying is a *prediction* rather than the Nazirite vow Jesus took to abstain from wine.[106] There is no evidence in the canonical gospels that Jesus would have taken such a vow. The logion declares prophetically that the Last Supper was the last occasion before the coming of God's kingdom when Jesus could have companionship with his disciples over food and drink—in this case, specifically wine.

There are more things unsaid than said in the Marcan passage, especially if one takes into account the imagery of the final banquet following God's complete victory over the forces of evil (Luke 13:28–29; Matt 8:11–12), which Mark 14:25 might presuppose or be related to.

Oddly, Mark 14:25 does not say anything at all about Jesus's role at the eschatological banquet. It says only that he will surely participate. There is no mention about what his relationship will be with other famous banqueters, such as the patriarchs, supposedly resurrected from the dead (Mark 12:18–27), or with the remainder of the guests, many of non-Jewish descent. Hence, one may surmise *when* but not *where* this banquet will take place. Jesus does not say that he will preside at the banquet, nor does he say he will facilitate access for his disciples; he simply declares that he will be there, drinking from a new, different "fruit of the vine."

In symphony with other early testimonies, Mark 14:25's succinct statement becomes much clearer. For instance, Luke 22:28–30 tells us that the

Father confers the kingdom on Jesus so he might invite the ones who were loyal to him during his trials. Matt 19:28 speaks of Jesus sitting on a glorious throne, while Mark 10:37, by mentioning the request of two brother disciples, John and James, to sit on both sides of Jesus's throne, again alludes to Jesus's significant role in God's future kingdom.

But perhaps the most important New Testament text underlining the role of Jesus in the past, present, and future is 1 Cor 15:20–28. After having abolished all the adverse powers—including death, man's last enemy—Jesus will hand the kingdom conferred on him back over to his Father. At the end of time (*eschaton*), Jesus will submit himself to God, who submitted everything to him, so God may become "all in all" (*ta panta en pasin*; v. 28), the climax of *theosis*, deification of the entire creation.

Nevertheless, one may underscore here that even Jesus's mere presence among banqueters, who with no other qualification are present at that glorious table initiating God's kingdom, is strong proof that his preaching (on God's approaching kingdom), his salvific work (i.e., healings and exorcisms), and his atoning trials and sufferings will *all* be fully vindicated—and publicly acknowledged.

The opening term "truly" (*amēn*) is a Gk. transliteration of the Heb. asseverative particle *ʾāmēn* (cf. LXX: 1 Chr 16:36; Neh 5:13; 1 Esd 9:47). In the New Testament, *amēn* is restricted to Jesus's words (Matt 5:18; Mark 3:28; Luke 4:24; John 1:51). In Paul, it also appears as a liturgical formula (1 Cor 14:16; 2 Cor 1:20; Gal 6:18).

The phrase "fruit of the vine" (e.g., Num 6:4; Isa 32:12; Hab 3:17) could be merely another term for "wine." However, since it is found in the Jewish prayer of blessing over wine—"Blessed are you, Lord our God, king of the universe [*mlk h-ʿwlm*], who creates the fruit of vine [*brʾ pry h-gpn*]" (cf. *m. Berakah* 6:1)[107]—the phrase might hint at Jesus's "thanksgiving" (verb *eucharisteō*) before distributing the chalice (Mark 14:23).

"That day" (*hēmeras ekeinēs*) is a calque on the Heb. phrase *yôm hā-hûʾ* (Isa 4:2) with a strong eschatological resonance, alluding most likely to *yôm YHWH*, "the day of the Lord" (Isa 13:6, 9; Ezek 13:5; Joel 1:15; Amos 5:18; Zeph 1:7, 14; Mal 4:5 [3:22]), a recurring collocation in the prophetic lexicon to describe God's powerful intervention. In the New Testament, "that day" becomes synonymous with Jesus's Parousia (Luke 7:22; 2 Thess 1:10; 2 Tim 1:12; 4:8).

In Jewish eschatology, wine symbolizes the fullness of time ushering in God's kingdom (Isa 25:6–8; 2 Bar 29:5–8; 1 En 62:13–16). The eschatological flavor of Jesus's saying in Mark 14:25 is reinforced by the presence of *kainos*, "new," referring to wine (found also in Matt, but notably absent in Luke 22:18). *Kainos* does not designate a "new, young wine, must" for which the adjective *neos* is used, but rather a new, different type of wine, perhaps more appropriate for the "kingdom" with its own structures and laws.

Hymnography

Note that what has been termed "Semitism" (by Jonge) in Mark 14:25, *amēn* ("truly"), is *not* found in this hymn.

By using the form *phēmi*, "I declare," instead of the Marcan—and more common form—*legō*, "I say," the hymnographer paints Jesus's saying in prophetic-revelatory colors.[108]

"God's kingdom" or "the kingdom of my Father" becomes in this hymn "my kingdom" (*basileia mou*), that is, Jesus's kingdom, thus presupposing the New Testament teaching of God's kingdom being conferred on Christ, so clearly proclaimed by Paul in 1 Cor 15:20–28 (see above).

The subjunctive aorist *piō*, denoting an objective possibility, "I would drink," found in Mark 14:25, turns, in this hymn, into a plain certainty by the use of the future tense *piomai*, "I *will* drink."

The hymnographer does not have Christ speaking of wine by using the liturgically and eschatologically loaded phrase "fruit of the vine" but actually calls it a "new drink (*poma kainon*)," the same nuance—a special drink, as in Mark 14:25, yet in a somehow neutral way, fitting better the already-established Christian theological framework. This "special" character of the "drink" is emphasized by the hymn's addition "beyond any word (*hyper logon*)": indescribable, ineffable, or even Beckett's "unnamable."

Note that the rare word *poma*, "drink," appears also in 1 Cor 10:4, i.e., *poma pneumatikon*, a "spiritual drink," in reference to Christ, the preexistent Word of God at work through the entirety of salvation history as unfolded in *both* Testaments (see below).

Given the paucity of the use of the term *poma*, "drink," in the Bible (only seven occurrences: 3 Macc 5:2, 45; 4 Macc 3:16; Ps 102:9 [101:10]; Dan 1:16 [Theod.]; 1 Cor 10:4; Heb 9:10), I consider its presence in our hymn a pointer to 1 Cor 10:4 and its fascinating interpretation of a "traveling well" intimated by a couple of juxtaposed Old Testament passages.

In 1 Cor 10:2-4, Paul speaks about baptism and Eucharist, using typology as an interpretive method. After him, both baptism and Eucharist were foreshadowed or typified in the Old Testament by two important experiences during the journey through the wilderness: first, the protecting cloud, a type for the Holy Spirit, hinting at the baptism through the Holy Spirit, the ancient Hebrews having been "baptized," typologically speaking, under the shadow of that miraculously sojourning cloud (Num 10:12; cf. Ps 78 [77]:14; 105 [104]:39).

The second experience Israel had was that of a continuous source of water in the wilderness. How did this happen? According to Paul and other ancient Jewish interpreters, the inexhaustible water supply was secured by a miraculous rocky well traveling with the people from one place to another during their long journey through the wilderness.[109] If one juxtaposes Exod 17:1–7 with Num 20:7–13, one comes to the same conclusion as Paul and other interpreters that the water-providing rock has *always* sojourned with Israel. In Paul's view, Christ, the one who provides his followers with a "spiritual drink" (*poma pneumatikon*) (his blood in the Eucharist), is the fulfillment of the Old Testament type, that wonderful traveling water-filled rock.

During their journey through the wilderness, the Hebrews arrived at a place called Rephidim, where Moses was instructed by God to knock on a certain rock, from which water gushed immediately (the place was nicknamed *Massah* and *Meribah*, "testing and contesting") (Exod 17:1–7). Later on, during their journey, Israel arrived at Kadesh, and the miracle from Rephidim was repeated: water came out when Moses struck a rock with his staff (Num 20:7–13). Num 20:13 reads: "These are the waters of Meribah." So if the water providing rocks at Rephidim and Kadesh are equally called Meribah, then the steady source of water "traveled" somehow miraculously from Rephidim to Kadesh. This was at least the way Paul and other ancient interpreters read the two juxtaposed passages.

As Bruce Fisk remarks, Paul, Pseudo-Philo, and other ancient interpreters inherited not only the above-mentioned passages but also the earliest poetical retellings of the same story of a steady water supply, which are found in the Hebrew Bible itself.[110] So, for instance, Ps 78 (77) (LXX) emphasizes a God who "broke asunder a rock [*petran*] in a wilderness and gave them to drink as from an abundant depth [*hōs en abyssō pollē*]" (v. 15); "when he struck the rock, waters gushed out [*erryēsan*] and the brooks [*cheimarroi*] were flooded" (v. 20); Ps 114 (113):8 (LXX): "who turned the rock into a pool of waters [*limnas hydatōn*]"; Isa 41:18 (LXX): "I will turn the wilderness into marshlands [*helē*] and the thirsty land into watercourses [*hydragōgois*]."

Here are three ancient interpretations of the "traveling rock" biblical tradition:

I do not want you to be unaware, brothers, that all our fathers were under the cloud [hypo tēn nephelēn], and all passed through the sea, and . . . all drank the same spiritual drink [to auto poma pneumatikon]. For they drank from the spiritual rock following [them] [ek pneumatikēs akolouthousēs petras], and the rock was Christ [hē petra de ēn ho Christos]. (1 Cor 10:1–4)

Now He led His people out into the wilderness; for forty years He rained down for them bread from Heaven, and brought quail to them from the sea and brought forth a well of water to follow them. And it [the water] followed them in the wilderness forty years and went up to the mountains with them and went down into the plains. (Pseudo-Philo, *Book of Biblical Antiquities* 10:7, 11:15)

And so the well that was with Israel in the desert was like a rock the size of a large container, gushing upward as if from a narrow-neck flask, going up with them to the mountains and going down with them to the valleys. (Tosephta, *Sukkah* 3:11)[111]

As we have already seen, on Holy Thursday, Wisdom is mentioned several times in correlation with the events of the "washing" and the "mystical supper." I would be remiss if I did not mention that the first century C.E. already had interpreters associating Wisdom with the "traveling rock." "They [Hebrews] became thirsty and called upon you, and water was given them out of a sharp-edged rock [ek petras akrotomou], and a remedy for [their] thirst [iama dipsēs] out of hard stone [ek lithou sklērou]" (Wis 11:4).

Since, in Paul's view, Christ assumes the role of Wisdom (1 Cor 1:24, 30), the association in 1 Cor 10:4 of Christ with the "traveling rock" could just be another variant of a Jewish-Hellenistic theme. However, as Fisk notes, the Pauline equation was probably motivated by reading the Song of Moses in Deut 32[112] (cf. Ps 81:16 [80:17] LXX: *petras*, "rock"),[113] where the living God is depicted as Israel's "rock" (v. 4; MT: *haṣ-ṣûr*; unfortunately, the LXX [*theos*, "God"; likewise in Ps 73 [72]:26; 78 [77]:35 [*boētos*, "helper"], while decoding the Hebrew wording, ran the risk of reducing the metaphor [the signifier to the signified]). In writing 1 Cor 10:4, there is a fair probability that Paul read the Hebrew text behind the LXX interpretive rendition.

The second part of the hymn refers to the well-known Ps 82 (81):1, 6, portraying God as standing among other gods in order to judge them for not doing what they were supposed to do, namely, providing justice especially to those on the fringes of society, the marginalized and dispossessed. The image of God among other "gods" is found in other psalms, e.g., Ps 29 (28):1–2; 89 (88):6–9; 95 (94):3; 97 (96):7.

Ps 82 (81):1–2, 6 (LXX) reads: "God stood [*ho theos estē*] in a gathering of gods [*en synagōgē theōn*], but in their midst he correctly judges [*diakrinei*] gods. . . . 'How long will you judge with injustice [*krinite adikian*]? . . . I said, 'Gods are you, and all sons of the Most High [*hyioi hypsitou pantes*].'"

By placing "gods" in the accusative (v. 1), the LXX seeks to harmonize the opening lines with v. 6. Depicting the God of Israel as judging the "gods," "sons of the Most High," whoever they might be, the LXX underlines God's supremacy and omnipotence. In any event, Ps 82 (81) portrays God as promoter and defender of justice.[114] Here one can detect an ANE worldview that life and the universe rely on a fundamental order of law, and the gods' first job was to defend this order. But the reality as described in Ps 82 (81) does not fit with this view. The gods are a part of the problem, for they pervert justice and abuse their power. One may add that in the religious context of the ANE, only the "law deities" were responsible for protecting the disadvantaged and afflicted. However, the Hebrew Bible depicts the God of Israel, the supreme one, as primarily a God of *justice*, following high moral standards, and more important, a God of vengeance and revenge and protector of "the least ones" of humanity (orphans, widows, strangers, the poor, the *personae miserae* according to ancient Israelite law).

The proclamation in vv. 6–7, written in divine, direct speech, is perhaps one of the most spectacular passages in the entire Bible. It decrees the death of *all* gods, except for the God of Israel, along with the cessation of the governments trusting these gods.[115]

Although a short text, Ps 82 (81) generated a significant amount of scholarship, then and now. Moreover, many Church Fathers penned their own comments on this psalm, referred to by Jesus in his saying recorded in John 10:34–36:

Jesus answered them, "Is it not written in your law, 'I said, "You are gods [*theoi este*]." If he calls those 'gods' [*theous*], to whom the Word of God came [*pros hous ho logos tou theou egeneto*], and the Scripture [*hē graphē*] cannot be destroyed [*ou dynatai lythēnai*], do you say of whom the

Father has consecrated [*hēgiasen*] and sent into the world [*apesteilen eis ton kosmon*], 'You are blaspheming,' because I said, 'I am the Son of God [*hyios tou theou eimi*]?'"

John 10:34 cites accurately Ps 82 (81):6b, "'I said [*egō eipa*], 'You are gods.'" This is Jesus's response to his contemporaries who have brought blasphemy charges against him. But who is the speaker of the words quoted by Jesus? In Ps 82 (81):6, the speaker is most likely the psalmist, who thinks of "gods" as being divine beings endowed with immortality, but now he realizes that these "gods" are simple mortal humans (v. 7).[116] On the other hand, in John 10, Jesus identifies the speaker with God, calling the common people "gods."

According to Jerome Neyrey, John 10 understood Ps 82 (81) in much the same way as did Jewish midrash, thus being the earliest preserved example.[117] Ps 82 (81) was understood in Jewish traditions as referring to angels,[118] Melchizedek,[119] judges,[120] and Israel at Sinai. All these identifications are attested in midrashic literature. In Neyrey's view, John 10:34–36 seems to equate "gods" of Ps 82 (81):1, 6, with Israel at Sinai ("to whom the Word of God came" in John 10:35 might be a hint at Israel, who received the Torah from God). In Jewish traditions, Ps 82 (81):6–7 was "historicized" to refer to Israel at Sinai when God gave his Torah to the people, and the latter became, conditionally, depending on whether or not they kept the divine command-ments (Exod 19:5–6), deathless (immortal) and holy (put aside for a special ministry). John's reading (10:34–36) of Ps 82 (81):6–7 suggests that Israel at the bottom of Mount Sinai experienced a new "creation" (similar to the first humanity, Adam, who was created in the "image of God" [Gen 1:27] for im-mortality [Gen 2:7: "to become a living breath" of God] as long as humanity kept God's one commandment [Gen 2:16–17; 3:22]).

If this midrashic type of interpretation of Ps 82 (81) by John holds true, then "gods" or being divine in the psalm means to be immortal, and, con-sequently, immortality is not a given but rather a potentiality to be turned into reality by keeping God's commandments or being obedient to him. Both Adam and Israel failed to be obedient to God, and they lost immortality (they began to die; Ps 82 [81]:7). On the other hand, Christ, "the last Adam" (1 Cor 15:45) and "the new Israel" (Matt 1:1; 2:15 [cf. Hos 11:1]), by being "obedient even unto the death" (Philip 2:8) to his Father, restored the lost immortality for all of humanity (John 10:10). In John 10, Jesus says that he has power to give eternal life to those who believe in him, and no one will be able to "snatch" his followers from companionship with him. The Johannine account of Jesus's saying is very close to the gist of our hymn: Jesus will be with those who followed him, as "I will be with you [*synesomai*], God among gods [*theos theois*]."

In John 10:30, Jesus claims, "I and the Father are one [*hen*]" (equal), hence the crowd accuses him of blasphemy. In his defense, Jesus uses Ps 82 (81) in response to the accusation. If the Scripture calls mortal human beings "gods" and "sons of the Most High" (v. 7), much more is the claim of the Son, whom the Father "sanctified" and "sent" into the world, warranted. However, the emphasis in John 10:35 does not fall on the Son but rather on Israel, to whom the (preexistent) Word came (in the form of the Torah).

This is also the understanding of a second century C.E. midrash on Exod 20:18–19: "If it were possible to do away with the Angel of Death I would. But the decree has long ago been decreed. R. Jose says, It was upon this condition that the Israelites stood up before Mount Sinai, on the condition that the Angel of Death should not have power over them. For it is said: 'I said, "You are gods"' [Ps 82:6]. But you have corrupted your conduct. 'Surely you shall die like men' [Ps 82:7]" (*Mekhilta Bahodesh* 9). In other words, while Israel was at Sinai, God restrained the power of the Angel of Death, so that Israel should not die, hence the application of Ps 82 (81):6 to this event. Israel became deathless, but later, due to the sin of idolatry (i.e., the golden calf episode, Exod 32), it became mortal (cf. Ps 82 [81]:7).[121] Obedience to God leads to holiness and deathlessness (immortality).

According to Carl Mosser, the Christian concept of deification, understood as participation of believers in God's life, in its essential aspects of holiness and deathlessness, has its roots not in a "Hellenized" Christianity (so Harnack) but rather in ancient Jewish traditions,[122] mirrored in John 10, 11QMelchizedek, and other Second Temple and Rabbinic writings.[123] Patristic interpretations of John 10 and Ps 82 (81), in correlation with deification (*theopoiēis*; the classical term *theōsis* is attested for the first time in Gregory of Nazianzus [*Orations* 25.16; cf. *PG* 35:1221B], then used by some of the most representative Byzantine theologians, such as Pseudo-Dionysius, Maximus the Confessor, and Gregory Palamas, as well as contemporary Eastern Orthodox authors),[124] found in three early patristic writers, Justin Martyr, Irenaeus of Lyons, and Clement of Alexandria, rely on this solid Jewish interpretive ground.

Justin Martyr (*Dialogue* 124)[125] seeks to respond to Jews who were scandalized by his remarks that Christians can be called "sons of God." In response, Justin makes use of Ps 82 (81), and in fact he cites it in its entirety, beginning with v. 1, where he sees Christ, "God," "in the midst of gods," his followers, rendering judgment on all men. In Justin's view, v. 7 ("But you die like human beings [*anthrōpoi*] die, and like one of the rulers [*heis tōn archontōn*] you fall") refers to all those who disobey God, beginning with the "one who was called serpent, who fell with a great overthrow, because he deceived Eve" (cf. LXX, "one of the rulers"), then Adam and Eve, and all those who came afterward. "Human beings are like God [*theō homoiōs*]," Justin continues, "free from suffering and death [*apatheis kai athanatous*], provided that they kept the commandments, and were deemed deserving of the name of his sons, and yet they, becoming like Adam and Eve, work out death for themselves." However, Justin notes, "Christ begat us unto God [*tou gennēsantos hēmas eis theon*] (cf. 1 John 2:29), so "we are called and are the true sons of God [*theou tekna alēthina kaloumetha kai esmen*]." One may note the synonymy between *theos*, "God," and *athanatos*, "deathless, immortal," throughout Justin's writings.

Irenaeus of Lyons also cites Ps 82 (81):6 (*Against Heresies* 3.6; 3.19.1; 4.38.4) in support of the Christian nomenclature "sons of God," but, unlike Justin, who relies on the Johannine testimony, Irenaeus opts for the Pauline notion of "adoption" (*hyiothesia*; Rom 8:15; Gal 4:5; Eph 1:5) into divine sonship.[126] The sacrament of baptism is for Irenaeus "the seal of eternal life and rebirth unto God, that we may no longer be sons of mortal men, but of the eternal and everlasting God" (*Demonstration of the Apostolic Preaching* 3b).

> For it was for this end that the Word of God was made man, and he who was the Son of God became the Son of man, that man, having been taken into the Word, and receiving the adoption, might become the son of God. For by no other means could we have attained to incorruptibility and immortality, unless we had been united to incorruptibility and immortality. But how else could we be joined to incorruptibility and immortality, unless, first, incorruptibility and immortality had become that which we also are, so that the corruptible might be swallowed up by incorruptibility, and the mortal by immortality, that we might receive the adoption of sons? (Irenaeus, *Against Heresies* 3.19.1)[127]

In other words, the Son of God became the Son of man, so we human beings, having received the divine sonship through adoption, may become again "incorruptible" (*aphthartoi*) and "immortal" (*athanatoi*)—a similar idea to the synonymy between *theos* and immortality found in Justin.

Clement of Alexandria cites and alludes to Ps 82 (81) especially in his *Protrepticus* and *Paedagogus*, two of his earliest writings:

> The same also takes place in our case, whose exemplar Christ became. Being baptized, we are illuminated [*phōtizometha*]; illuminated, we become sons [*hyiopoioumetha*]; being made sons, we are made perfect [*teleioumetha*]; being made perfect, we are made immortal [*apathanatizometha*]. "I," says He, "have said that you are gods, and all sons of the Most High." The work is variously called grace, and illumination, and perfection, and washing: washing, by which we cleanse away our sins; grace, by which the penalties accruing to transgressions are remitted; and illumination, by which that holy light of salvation is beheld, that is, by which we see God clearly. (*Paedagogue* 1.26.1–2)[128]

All of these things, namely, baptism, illumination, adoption into sonship, perfection, and immortalization, are various aspects of the same unique reality commonly called "salvation." As an Old Testament proof text, Clement cites Ps 82 (81):6, in which, according to him, all these aspects are to be found.[129] As with Justin and Irenaeus, Clement, too, supports the idea that through baptism, human beings become sons of God (Ps 82 [81]:6) on the way toward perfection and immortality.

I would like to draw a few concluding remarks on the last part of the hymn. First, one may note that at the end of the hymn, there is a brief quote from 1 John 4:10b, "He sent his son [as] atonement for our sins (*kai apesteilen ton hyion autou hilasmon peri tōn hamartiōn hēmōn*)," with two minor alterations; *hyion* is replaced with *monogenē*, "Only Begotten One," and "for our sins" has been deleted. In addition to 1 John 4:10b (cf. 2:2), we may adduce Rom 3:25: God presented Christ as a "sacrifice of atonement [*hilastērion*], through the shedding of his blood."

Second, moving from drinking a new drink to "being together God and gods" (eternal companionship), the hymnographer betrays a good understanding of John 10:34–36's midrashic interpretation of Ps 82 (81) with an emphasis not so much on the "divinity" of Christ but rather on Christ as the "source" of life for his believers.

The tight correlation of obedience–holiness–immortality, attested in the Church Fathers and discussed above, can also be detected in our hymn. The "drink" (*poma*) (i.e., Eucharist, yet to be "renewed" in Christ's kingdom) connects the believers to Christ so that their struggles to be obedient to God become efficient and complete through Christ's atonement (understood as the recapitulation of human history in complete obedience).[130] At the end of the hymn, the faithful are reminded that Christ will not only participate in the eschatological banquet, but he "will be together with" (*synesomai*) them, as "God among gods" (*theos theois*).

5

Suffering

The Slaughtered Lamb and the
Distraught Ewe—Good Friday

Overview

On Good Friday, the sacrificial lamb is slaughtered under the very eyes of a
distraught, devastated ewe, and a whole cortège of pain and suffering unstop-
pably unfolds, from spitting and mockery to blows, nails, spear, cross, and
death of the Lamb of God.

> On this day, Holy and Great Friday [*tē hagia kai megalē paraskeuē*], we ob-
> serve/perform [*epiteloumen*] the holy, saving, and frightening Passion [*ta
> hagia kai sōtēria kai phrikta pathē*] of our Lord and God and Savior Jesus
> Christ: the spitting [*emptysmous*], the blows [*rhapismata*], the buffeting
> [*kolaphismata*], the mockery [*hybreis*], the reviling [*gelōtas*], the purple
> robe [*porphyran chlainan*], the reed [*kalamon*], the sponge [*spongon*], the
> vinegar [*oxos*], the nails [*hēlous*], the spear [*lonchēn*], and before all, the
> cross [*stauron*] and death [*thanaton*] which he accepted [*katadexato*] to
> endure readily [*hekōn*] for us; again, also the saving confession [*sōtērion
> homologian*] of the kindhearted thief [*eugnōmonos lēstou*], who was cruci-
> fied [*systaurōtentos*] with him. (Synaxarion)

Two figures dominate the liturgical day and its original settings (i.e., the
house of Caiaphas, the Sanhedrin hall, Pilate's Praetorium, King Herod's
palace, and the rocky Golgotha): Jesus and Mary, the slaughtered lamb and
the distraught ewe.

Good Friday hymnography is a zooming-in, minute radiography of suffering as experienced by Jesus and his mother, Mary.

Through two words, "scourges" and "endure," a hymnographer linked
Isa 50:6 to its early interpretation, Psalms of Solomon 10:2 ("The one who
prepares [his] back for scourges [*mastigas*] will be purged [*katharisthēsetai*],

Hearing the Scriptures. Eugen J. Pentiuc, Oxford University Press. © Oxford University Press 2021.
DOI: 10.1093/oso/9780190239633.003.0006

for the Lord is kind [*chrēstos*] to the ones who endure discipline [*hypomenousin paideian*]"), while underscoring that Christ's endurance of suffering (i.e., the cross) was not for his own cleansing, as the latter text asserts, but for the "salvation of the world." Jesus's intensified suffering at the climax of the Passion—Good Friday, a day of trials and crucifixion— is painted with the help of "circling dogs" imagery gleaned from Ps 22:16 (21:17), the very same verse that alludes to crucifixion by nailing: "they gouged [*ōryxan*] my hands and my feet" (LXX). The "circling dogs" evoke a tireless chasing of Jesus by his enemies.

Another hymnographer reminds us, "The one who hanged the earth in the waters is today hanged on a tree." As a flashback to the dawn of creation, prior to the *Fiat lux* of the first day (Gen 1:3), the crucifixion is reflected through the lenses of creation theology, with Jesus's cross hanging over the deep waters, slowly submerging into the primeval aquatic chaos of Gen 1:2. Unlike Job 26:7 stating that the earth hangs on nothing, the hymnographer imagines the earth as hanging *within* (*en*) the waters (cf. Gen 1:2). As the earth hanging "within" the waters, the same goes for Jesus hanging "on a tree"—both earth and cross are dependent on God's almighty will and ineffable graciousness. The crucifixion in conjunction with the theme of Jesus's baptism found in the same hymn underscores the interconnection between crucifixion and Jesus's descent to Hades, the place of the last confrontation between Jesus and the evil forces.

Using the Exodus review theme/pattern (e.g., Ps 78 [77]), a hymnographer puts forward several contrasts (manna/gall, water/vinegar, pillar of fire/cross, etc.), thus bringing the whole Passion of Christ into the "liturgical present." The review concludes with a call to the "nations" along the lines of Jesus's call (Matt 21:43), where "nations" should be taken as an inclusive term referring to Jews and Gentiles—the whole of humanity.

By freely citing and collocating Jer 2:13 with 17:13, another hymnographer successfully applies the ancient Israelites' attitude (i.e., abandoning God and embracing idolatry) to the mob's reaction in the Passion episode (i.e., abandoning Jesus for Barabbas's release). The "darkness" describing the "Day of the Lord" in Amos's prophetic proclamation (Amos 5:18–20) is nature's response to the crowd's attitude, which reaches the lowest point during Jesus's Passion.

Mary's induction into Golgotha is meant to heighten the tragedy already unfolding. A distraught ewe, devastated by suffering and pain, unable to do anything to alleviate her son's agony, and Jesus being "dragged" as a lamb, still young, vulnerable, yet full of that *désir de vivre*, to a merciless slaughter. The hymn draws on Isa 53:7 (cf. Jer 11:19), while hinting at Wis 14:15 (dealing with a father's devastated grief due to his son's untimely death). Mary's plea to Jesus at the end of a hymn, "Give me a word, O Word," says it all about the bitter loneliness of a mother bereft of her son and the dignifying and freely assumed sacrifice of a son, against the backdrop of an all-embracing silence, up and down, left and right. It is a thorough radiography of a mother's indescribable grief at the terrible sight of her son nailed fast on a cross. The phrase "motherly affections," freely barrowed from 4 Macc 13:19, connects the lamenting of Mary to another mother seized by grief, the mother of the seven Maccabean martyrs.

Timeline: Good Friday's series of events begins with Jesus's multifaceted trial. First, Jesus appears very early in the morning in front of the high priests Annas and Caiaphas (John 18:13–24); then he goes before the religious court (the Sanhedrin), featuring false witnesses but no defense counselors. The trial scene parallels the denial of Peter which occurs in the high priest's courtyard (Matt 26:59–75). Then Jesus is sent to Pilate, the Roman governor, who will issue the death penalty based on a political accusation. Jesus is scourged and forced to carry his cross to Golgotha, the place of crucifixion (John 18:28–19:17). He is nailed to the cross around nine a.m. (Mark 15:25). Around noon, he utters the famous lament, "My God, my God. Why have you forsaken me?" Between noon and three p.m., when Jesus dies, there is a mysterious darkness covering Golgotha, the earth quakes, and the veil of the Temple is torn in two (Mark 15:33–39). After the centurion makes sure that he is dead, Jesus's lifeless body is taken down from the cross. Joseph of Arimathea and Nicodemus, two secret disciples of Jesus, provide the fragrant oils for anointment and a brand-new tomb where Jesus's body may be laid to rest (John 19:38–42). Good Friday ends with Jesus's entombment.

Services and lections for Good Friday: Matins with the Service of Twelve Gospel Readings (officiated by anticipation on Holy Thursday evening): (1) John 13:31–18:1; (2) John 18:1–28; (3) Matt 26:57–75; (4) John 18:28–19:16; (5) Matt 27:3–32; (6) Mark 15:16–32; (7) Matt 27:33–54; (8) Luke 23:32–49; (9) John 19:25–37; (10) Mark 15:43–47; (11) John 19:38–42; (12) Matt 27:62–66; Holy Hours (officiated on Friday morning): First Hour, Zech 11:10–13; Gal 6:14–18; Matt 27:1–56; Third Hour, Isa 50:4–11; Rom 5:6–10; Mark 15:16–41; Sixth Hour, Isa 52:13–54:1; Heb 2:11–18; Luke 23:32–49; Ninth Hour, Jer 11:17–22; 12:1–5, 9–11, 14–15; Heb 10:19–31; John 19:23–37.

Analysis
Scourges and Spittings

I gave [*edōka*] my back [*nōton*] to the ones who scourge [*mastigōsin*], and
I did not turn away [*apestraphē* my face from spittings [*emptysmatōn*].
I stood before [*parestēn*] the judgment seat [*bēmati*] of Pilate, and I endured
[*hypemeina*] the cross for the salvation of the world [*dia tēn tou kosmou
sōtērian*]. (Good Friday, Matins, Lauds, Idiomelon)

The first part of the hymn consists of a slightly altered and condensed quote
from Isa 50:6 (LXX): "I gave [*dedōka*] my back [*nōton*] to whips [*mastigas*],
and my cheeks [*siagonas*] to blows [*rhapismata*]. I did not turn away
[*apestrepsa*] my face from disgrace [*aischynēs*] of spittings [*emptysmatōn*]."
There are a few textual differences between the Isaian passage and the
hymn: the perfect verbal tense *dedōka* is replaced by an aorist *edōka*; the
plural noun *mastigas* is now a present third person plural verb. *mastigōsin*;
and the deletion of "and my cheeks to blows" and "disgrace" from the Isaian
passage underscores the contrast between "back" and "face" while heightening the emotional effect on the audience at the mere mention of two terrible actions, "scourges" and "spittings," that Jesus endured from his captors
prior to his crucifixion.

One may assume that the hymnographer, quoting from Isa 50:6, was
likely aware of Psalm of Solomon 10:2 (note the use of the verb *hypomenō*,
"to endure," in both hymn and Psalm) which is related to the Isaian passage,
as a sort of theological reflection or "inner exegesis"[1] of the latter, a newer
Scripture explaining and actualizing an older Scripture. Psalm of Solomon
10:2 seems to be one of the earliest interpretations of Isa 50:6, emphasizing
the "cleansing" or "purging" dimension of a voluntary ("enduring") suffering
(mostly understood as a means of discipline). However, Psalm of Solomon
10:2 speaks of endurance leading to a "purge" of the one who willfully
"endures" suffering, which does not necessarily apply to Jesus, whose voluntary suffering was meant not for his self-purging but rather for a fallen
humanity in need of substantive cleansing and restoration: "And I, when
I am lifted up [*hypsōthō*] from earth [i.e., crucified], will drag [*helkysō*] all
[*pantas*] to myself" (John 12:32). Note the use of the verb *helkō*, "to drag"
(usually rendered "to draw"), and *pantas*, "all," to underscore the irresistible power of Christ's voluntary atoning suffering, whose beneficiaries will
be "all," with no exceptions. Therefore, in order to grasp and appreciate

the intricate intertextuality this hymn exhibits, we need to adduce here a brief theological rumination from the first Petrine epistle which speaks of Christ's redemptive suffering: "Christ suffered [*epathen*] for you ... he himself carried [*anēnenken*] our sins on the tree [*epi to xylon*], that being dead [*apogenomenoi*] to sins, we might live to righteousness [*dikaiosynē*]. By his wounds [*mōlōpi*] you were healed [*iathēte*]" (1 Pet 2:21, 24).

Now we can reconstruct the steps of this intriguing intertextuality evidenced by our hymn. First, the hymnographer quotes from Isa 50:6, being aware of Psalm of Solomon 10:2, from which he probably borrowed the verb *hypomenō*, "to endure," with reference to Jesus. Yet he sees the difficulty Psalm of Solomon 10:2 introduces by underlining the "purging" character of individual suffering. Then the hymnographer, aware of theological statements such as John 12:32 and 1 Pet 2: 21, 24, concludes his hymn by imagining a suffering Jesus addressing the worshipers, that is, the performers of his sacred Passion drama: "I endured [*hypemeina*] the cross for the salvation of the world [*dia tēn tou kosmou sōtērian*]."

The structure of this hymn divides clearly into three parts. Part one is a reference to an Old Testament Scripture mentioning a leader (teacher, prophet) enduring insults and pains from his people (Isa 50:6, along with its seemingly inner biblical interpretation, Psalm of Solomon 10:2). Part two ("I stood before [*parestēn*] the judgment seat [*bēmati*] of Pilate") is an allusion to a New Testament text mentioning Jesus in front of Pilate, who was "sitting on the judgment seat" (*ekathisen epi bēmatos*, John 19:13). And part three has Jesus addressing the worshipers for whom the hymn is written in light of New Testament theological reflections on his redemptive endurance (John 12:32; 1 Pet 2:21, 24). Thus, the hymn meshes the foreshadowing of Old Testament testimonies with New Testament *kerygma*, culminating in a liturgical setting.

Using the same interpretive framework as with the hymn above, one can read and reflect on the following beautifully crafted hymn which offers a nearly complete list of trials and insults that Jesus endured to save the world:

Every member [*melos*] of your holy flesh [*sarkos*] endured dishonor [*atimian hypemeine*] for us: the head—the thorns [*akanthas*]; the face [*opsis*]—the spittings [*emptysmata*]; the cheeks—the blows [*rhapismata*]; the mouth—the gall [*cholēn*] mixed with vinegar [*oxei*] as taste [*geusei*]; the ears—profane [*dyssebeis*] blasphemies. The back—the scourging [*phrangelōsin*]; the hand—the reed [*kalamon*]; the whole body [*sōmatos*]— stretched [*ektaseis*] on the cross; the joints [*arthra*]—the nails [*hēlous*]; and the side [*pleura*]—the spear [*lonchēn*]. The One who suffers [*pathōn*] for us, and suffering, you freed [*eleutherōsas*] us. The One who condescends [*synkatabas*] to us with love for humanity [*philanthrōpia*], and the One who exalts [*anypsōsas*] us, "O Almighty Savior, have mercy on us!" (Good Friday, Matins, Lauds, Idiomelon)

Circling Dogs

They encircled [*ekyklōsan*] [you] like many dogs [*kynes polloi*]; they struck [*ekrotēsan*] [you], O Master [*anax*], with a blow [*rhapismō*] on your very cheek [*siagona sēn*], they kept questioning [*ērotōn*] you; and they testified [*katemartyroun*] false things [*pseudē*] against you, but you endured [*hypomeinas*] all, and saved [*esōsas*] all. (Good Friday, Matins, Ode 9, Heirmos)

This hymn dovetails smoothly with the previous one in terms of subject matter (Jesus's trial), scriptural reference (Isa 50:6), and vocabulary (*hypomenō*, "to endure," *sōtēria*, "salvation"). Moreover, the phrase "my cheeks to blows," found in Isa 50:6 and absent in the previous hymn, occurs in a slightly altered way here: "they struck [*ekrotēsan*] [you] with a blow [*rhapismō*] on your very cheek [*siagona sēn*]." A single *se*, "you" (accusative) serves three verbs: *ekyklōsan*, "encircled"; *ekrotēsan*, "struck"; and *ērotōn*, "questioned."

"They encircled you like many dogs [*ekyklōsan kynes hōsei polloi*]"
The hymnographer begins his description of Jesus's Passion with a quote from Ps 22:16 (21:17) (LXX): "For many dogs encircled me [*ekyklōsan me kynes pollai*], a gathering of evildoers [*ponēreuomenōn*] surrounded [*perieschon*]; they gouged [*ōryxan*][2] my hands and feet." Ps 22 (21) is used by all canonical gospels and given preeminence by John. The gospel writers saw in Ps 22 (21) a messianic prophecy fulfilled in the last moments of Jesus's life: "they divided my garments" (while Jesus was on the cross) (Ps 22:18 [21:19]; cf. John 19:23–24); "save yourself" (Ps 22:7–8 [21:8–9]; cf. Mark 15:29–30; Matt 27:39–40; Luke 23:35); "My God, my God" (Ps 22:1 [21:2]; cf. Matt 27:46; Mark 15:34). Oddly enough, the gospel writers did not use Ps 22:16 (21:17) (LXX), "they gouged [*ōryxan*] my hands and feet," with reference to the nailing (which is simply assumed in John 20:20 and explicitly stated in John 20:25).[3]

In Ps 22 (21), David describes his enemies with vivid metaphors: "strong bulls" (LXX: "fat bulls," v. 12 [13]), "roaring lion" (v. 13 [14]), "dogs" (v. 16 [17]), and "wild oxen" (LXX: "unicorns," v. 21 [22]).

In the ANE context of Ps 22 (21), "dogs" were half-wild animals that roamed about in packs.[4] The LXX reads here *kynes polloi*, "many dogs" (MT has only "dogs"), perhaps hinting at this pack aspect. The psalmist, and then Jesus, in the hymnographer's view,[5] is surrounded by viciously barking dogs that make their prey feel completely unprotected and hopeless. The "nearness" of the enemies, underlined by the motif "surrounded" (vv. 12 [13], 16 [17]), contrasts sharply with the "farness" of God.[6]

According to Mitchell Dahood, the imagery of Ps 22:16 (21:17) is that of a chase[7]—a pertinent suggestion supported by the early vocalization (Aquila, Theod., Jerome) of MT *kəlābîm*, "dogs," as *kallābîm*, "hunters."

For Eusebius of Caesarea, the dogs refer to several players: the Jewish authorities who instigated the mob to ask Pilate to crucify Christ, the Roman soldiers who executed the sentence, and those who, after the Passion, insulted the body of Christ, his hands and feet, that is, the Church.[8]

At the stroke of a pen, the hymnographer replaces the first-person speech (i.e., the psalmist reflecting on himself) with the narrator's speech (i.e., the hymnographer directly addressing Jesus) and the psalm's metaphor "many dogs" with a more prosaic, explicative simile, "like many dogs."

"They struck [you] with a blow on your very cheek [*ekrotēsan siagona sēn rhapismō*]"
This is an example of "augmented gospel," where elements of the gospel narrative are blended with Old Testament prophetic material, and the progressive linearity of the "prophecy fulfillment" hermeneutical scheme, so frequently employed by patristic biblical commentaries, is replaced with a composite midrash-like piece whose component parts are hardly delineated from one another.

The hymnic passage above might tempt one to read John 18:22 in conjunction with Isa 50:6b and Mic 5:1 (4:14). John 18:22 records how one of the high priest's servants, infuriated by Jesus's "impertinent" response (vv. 20–21), gave him a blow (*rhapisma*): "Having said these [things], one of the servants [*hypēretōn*] standing by [*parestēkōs*] gave [*edōken*] Jesus a blow [*rhapisma*], saying, 'Thus, did you answer [*apokrinē*] to the high priest?" In the synoptic gospels, the "servants" (*hypēretai*) (Mark 14:65) or "some" (*hoi*) (Matt 26:67) of those attending the pseudo-trial of Jesus in front of Caiaphas slapped Jesus's face.

As one may notice, the Johannine passage does not mention "cheek" (*siagona*) as the hymn does, though the word appears in Isa 50:6b (plural *siagonas*) and Mic 5:1 (4:14) (singular *siagona*): "I gave [*dedōka*] ... my cheeks [*siagonas*] to blows [*rhapismata*]" (Isa 50:6b); "Now, a daughter [*thygatēr*] shall be hedged [*emphrachthēsetai*] with a fence [*phragmō*]; he set up [*etaxen*] a siege [*synochēn*] against us; with a rod [*rhabdō*] they shall strike [*pataxousin*] upon the cheek [*siagona*] the tribes [*philas*; MT: *šōpēṭ*, "judge, ruler"] of Israel" (Mic 5:1 [4:14]). The biblical idiom "to strike on the cheek" is a gesture of humiliation (Lam 3:30; 1 Kgs 22:24; Mic 5:1 [4:14]; Ps 3:7 [8]; Job 16:10). In Babylon, such an act was punished with a fine (cf. *Code of Hammurabi* 202–205).[9]

With respect to the hymn's vocabulary, note that the verb *kroteō*, "to knock, to strike," is commonly used in LXX to designate hands clapping (2 Kgs 11:12; Ezek 6:11; 21:17; Job 27:23). The hymnographer's lexical choice aims at heightening the contrast between hands clapping as a sign of approval or empathy and striking someone's cheek with a blow as a token of disagreement or contempt. The word *anax*, attested in ancient Gk., means "master, lord," with reference to gods and heroes; it was also used to designate a master over a slave.

"They kept questioning you [*erōtōn se*]"

The hymnographer probably borrowed the form *erōtōn*, "they kept questioning," from Ps 35 (34):11, since it does not occur in the gospel narratives dealing with the false witnesses testifying against Jesus (Matt 26:59–62; cf. Mark 14:55–56).

Here is the psalmist recounting: "When unjust witnesses [*martyres adikoi*][10] rose up [*anastantes*], they kept questioning [*erōtōn*] me about things I was not aware of [*ouk eginōskon*]" (Ps 35 [34]:11 [LXX]).[11] The verbal form *erōtōn*, "they kept questioning," occurs only here in the entire LXX corpus.

Most likely, the hymnographer read Matt 26:59–62 in conjunction with Ps 35 (34):11 due to the thematic similarity between the two passages, namely, "false"/"unjust" witnesses testifying against a wrongly persecuted individual (Jesus/psalmist). The above lines draw on the gospel account supplemented with the psalmist's detail that the persecutors "kept questioning" him.

This is an interesting hermeneutical procedure aiming to augment the gospel account by adding Old Testament key words or phrases, thus creating a composite picture for emphasis and dramatic effect. The procedure does not obtain with the discursive mode of interpretation (i.e., patristic biblical commentaries) where the boundaries between prophecy and fulfillment are clearly delineated. On the contrary, in liturgical media (e.g., hymnography, iconography), prophecy and fulfillment are inextricably interwoven like the warps and wefts in a tapestry, so the result is an "augmented" narrative made of New and Old Testament passages.

"And they testified false things against you [*sou de pseudē katemartyroun*]"
The hymnographer agrees with the gospel account on the profile of those testifying against Jesus, that is, that they are "false witnesses" (*pseudomartyres*) brought in by the religious authorities so that they might build a case against the recalcitrant teacher from Galilee. "But they could not find any [testimony], even though many false witnesses [*pseudomartyrōn*] came forward" (Matt 26:60; cf. Mark 14:55–56). Nevertheless, note that Ps 35 (34):11 labels differently the "witnesses" as "unjust" (*adikoi*); cf. Ps 27 (26):12.

"But you endured all, and saved all [*kai panta hypomeinas, hapantas esōsas*]"
As an ancillary note, the verbal form *ērōtōn*, "they kept questioning," should be considered an interpretive "pointer"—an oblique invitation to read Ps 35 (34) in its entirety, including v. 19 which is quoted in John 15:25. Here Jesus addresses his disciples at the Last Supper: "But, so that the word that is written in their law might be fulfilled: 'They hated me without a cause [*emisēsan me dōrean*]'" (John 15:25 [Byz.]), quoting Ps 35 (34):19: "May those who show enmity [*echthrainontes*] to me unjustly [*adikōs*], those who hate me without a cause [*misountes me dōrean*] and wink [*dianeuontes*] with the eyes, not rejoice over me" (cf. Ps 69:4 [68:5]).

Nevertheless, by using this "pointer," the hymnographer aimed at more than a mere quotation from John 15:25. He most likely wanted to strike a sharp contrast between the spirit of retribution and retaliation so obvious in Ps 35 (34), a "psalm of imprecation," and the humility and endurance Jesus underwent willfully for the salvation of all.

As Peter Craigie rightly notices, the purpose of Ps 35 (34) is altered in the life and ministry of Christ.[12] If in the psalm, the Hebrew king prays that God may deliver him from the hatred of his enemies, in the gospels, Jesus, obedient to his Father's will, surrenders himself to that hatred. Moreover, if the psalmist-king invokes curses of a treaty to dodge hatred, Jesus endured hatred in order to remove the curses placed on human lives due to their sins.

And Jesus's death as a consequence of human hatred became the way by which a new covenant between God and humanity was to be established.

The hymnographer shares the spirit of the gospel accounts by contrasting Ps 35 (34) with Jesus's final hours when he concludes his piece with these words addressed to Jesus, "but you endured [*hypomeinas*] all, and saved [*esōsas*] all."

The verbal form *hypomeinas*, "you endured," in the last line of the hymn is found in three gospel passages where Jesus shares with his disciples their future fate: "And you will be hated [*misoumenoi*] by all for my name's sake. But the one who endured [*hypomeinas*] to the end [*eis telos*], that one will be saved [*sōthēsetai*]" (Mark 13:13; cf. Matt 10:22; 24:13). In the last line of this hymn, Jesus is depicted as a living model of his own words recorded by the gospels. Through his perfect endurance, Jesus will save all.

Hanged on a Tree

Today [*sēmeron*] is hanged [*krematai*] on a tree [*epi xylou*] the one who hanged [*kremasas*] the earth in the waters [*en hydasi*]. With a crown of thorns [*stephanon ex akanthōn*] is wrapped around [*peritithetai*] the one who is the angels' king [*ho tōn angelōn basileus*]. In a fake purple [robe] [*pseudē porphyran*] is clothed [*periballetai*] the one who clothes the skies in clouds. A blow receives back [*rhapisma katedexato*] the one who freed [*eleutherōsas*] Adam in the Jordan [*en Iordanē*]. With nails [*hēlois*] is nailed fast [*prosēlōthē*] the bridegroom [*nymphios*] of the Church. With a spear [*lonchē*] is pierced [*ekentēthē*] the son of the Virgin [*hyios tēs parthenou*]. We worship [*proskynoumen*] your Passion [*ta pathē*], O Christ [three times]. Show [*deixon*] us also your glorious resurrection [*endoxon anastasin*]. (Good Friday, Matins, Antiphon 15, Troparion)

"Today is hanged on a tree [*sēmeron krematai epi xylou*]"
The word *sēmeron*, "today," indicates the traditionally accepted day (according to the synoptic gospel evidence harmonized with John's gospel) when Jesus was crucified but, more important, the day of worship, Good Friday, when the crucifixion is remembered and liturgically re-enacted by Orthodox Christians through hymns, readings, and symbolic actions.

The phrase *kremannymi/kremazō epi xylou*, "to hang on a tree," may be found in LXX (e.g., Deut 21:22; Josh 8:29; 10:26) as designating a form of punishment (hanged on a beam), more or less similar to Roman crucifixion. The word *xylon*, unlike *dendron*, "(fruit) tree," designates primarily "(a cut piece of) wood" (Gen 6:14; 22:3), even though it is also used for "fruit tree" (e.g., Gen 1:11, 12, 29; 2:16). Hence the typology the Church Fathers established between the "tree of life" (*xylon tēs zōēs*) planted in Eden (Gen 2:9) and the piece of wood (beam) used in crucifixion (Gen 40:19: *kremasei se epi xylou*, "he will hang you on a pole"), including Jesus's crucifixion. For instance, Cyril of Jerusalem identifies the saving cross with the lost "tree of life": "Adam by the Tree [of Knowledge] fell away; thou by the Tree [of Life] art brought into Paradise" (*Catecheses* 13.31).[13]

"The one who hanged the earth in the waters [*ho en hydasi tēn gēn kremasas*]"

From the outset, one may note the use of the problematic *en*, "in" (the waters), instead of the more common *epi*, "on," which would make more sense in light of the cosmology of the Hebrew Bible where the earth appears out of the waters. See below for a few comments on this peculiar lexical choice.

Due to the juxtaposition of *gē*, "earth," with *kremazō*, "to hang," Job 26:7 (LXX) is lexically the closest scriptural text to our hymn: "The one who stretches [*ekteinōn*] the northern wind [*borean*] on nothing [*ep' ouden*], the one who hangs [*kremazōn*][14] the earth on nothing [*epi oudenos*]."

All the text witnesses of Job 26:7,[15] with slight differences, convey the same picture of an omnipotent God "hanging" the earth on an empty space (i.e., "nothing"). The targumist further emphasizes this by adding "without any support to it [earth]."

In a nutshell, Job 26:7 lauds God, who "stretches" the heavens, here represented by "north," the highest point of the celestial region, as a tent without a center pole, and "hangs" the earth on sheer emptiness.[16] In Marvin Pope's opinion, the author of this passage shares Pythagoras's advanced view of "earth being a sphere freely poised in space."[17] Or as John Milton inspiringly puts it in *Paradise Lost*: "And earth self-balanced on her centre hung."[18]

However, our hymn's view (i.e., "earth hung [by God] *in* the waters") is much closer theologically to the priestly creation account (about sixth century B.C.E.), where the earth, "invisible and unwrought," was initially submerged within the primordial aquatic chaos. Gen 1:2 (LXX) reads: "But the earth [*gē*] was invisible [*aoratos*] and unformed [*akataskeuastos*],[19] and darkness [*skotos*] was over the abyss [*abyssou*], and God's Spirit [*pneuma theou*] was being carried [*epephereto*] above [*epanō*] the water."

Is earth's "invisibility" an interpretive gloss on the earth's primordial state of being submerged within the waters all wrapped up in the abyssal darkness, or does the LXX merely harmonize Gen 1:2 ("invisible" [*aoratos*], of the earth) with Gen 1:9 ("appeared," lit. "became visible" [*ōphthē*], of the dry land)?

Gen 1:9–10 describes the creation of earth (i.e., "dry land") as a simple "appearance" (*ōphthē*) out of the waters the moment God gathers the waters beneath the sky in one place allowing for the formation of "seas." LXX: "And God said: 'Let the water that is beneath the heaven [*hypokatō tou ouranou*] be gathered [*synachthētō*] into one gathering [*synagōgēn*], and let the dry land [*xēra*] appear.' And it became so. And the water beneath the heaven gathered into their gatherings, and the dry land appeared [*ōphthē*]. And God called the dry land earth [*gēn*] and the gatherings of waters [he called] seas [*thalassas*]. And God saw that it was good."

Alternatively, Ps 24 (23):1–2 reimagines God as the one who "founded" the earth on the seas and rivers (cf. Ps 75:3 [74:4]; 136 [135]:6); LXX: "The Lord's is the earth and its fulfillment [*plērōma*], the world and all dwelling [*katoikountes*] in it. It is he who founded [*ethemeliōsen*] it on the seas [*epi thalassōn*] and prepared [*hētoimasen*] it on the rivers [*epi potamōn*]."[20]

One may detect here a tiny influence from Babylonian cosmology. However, unlike in Babylonian cosmology, where the earth created by Marduk floats as a raft on fresh water (Apsu) surrounded by salt water (*Tiamat*), Ps 24 (23):1–2 states that God "founded" (*ethemeliōsen*) the earth on the seas and rivers as a solid body that cannot be removed.

In any event, the psalmist demythologizes and depersonifies the Sea (Yam) and River (*Nahar*), featured in Canaanite/Ugaritic cosmology, by reducing both to mere cosmic elements. The image depicted here is that of God establishing the inhabited world (*oikoumenē*) on seas and rivers, the now-tamed forces of a once primordial aquatic chaos (cf. Gen 1:2).[21]

As one can easily notice, in all the examples above, the earth hangs *on* water (seas, rivers) or *on* nothing; the preposition used is *epi*, "on." Strikingly, in our hymn, the preposition is *en*, "in, within," the earth hanging *in* waters.

It is worth noting that LXX does distinguish between *en*, "in, within, amid," and *epi*, "on," when construed with the verb *kremannymi*, "to hang." The preposition *en* is used when the writer refers to the inside of a thing (within), while the preposition *epi* denotes its outside. Thus, 2 Sam 18:9–10 depicts Absalom riding a mule that "entered under the thick branches of a great oak, and his head was hung *in* the oak [*ekremasthē hē kephalē autou en tē dryi*]" (cf. v. 9). Another place where *en* occurs with the meaning "in, inside" is Ezek 27:10: "they hanged [*ekremasan*] shields and helmets *in* you [*en soi*]," that is, inside the city of Sor. An interesting situation obtains in Ps 137 (136):2, where *en*, "in," appears along with *mesō* and at variance with *epi*, "on": "On the willows [*epi tais iteais*] in its midst [*en mesō autēs*] we hung up [*ekremasamen*] our instruments." The presence of the two prepositions, *epi* and *en*, in the same verse proves indubitably that the LXX distinguishes semantically between them. Mutatis mutandis, the presence of *en*, "in, within, amid," in our hymn might evoke the image of the earth hanging not *on* but rather *in* or *amid* the waters.

I would like to suggest two possible interpretations of the use of the preposition *en*, "in." According to the first interpretation, the hymnographer's entire phrase "the one who hanged the earth *in* the waters" betrays a good reading of Gen 1:2, 6–10, in conjunction with Job 26:7, where the verb *kremannymi/kremazō*, "to hang," is used with respect to earth.

Prior to the first day of creation (Gen 1:3–5), there were a few loosely superposed entities: an "invisible and unwrought" earth, a dark deep, and waters surveyed repeatedly by God's Spirit (Gen 1:2). On the second day of creation, God made a vault (firmament) by separating the waters above from the waters beneath the firmament (vv. 6–8). The next day, God gathered the waters beneath the vault into one place, thus forming the seas; then the dry land (earth) made its appearance (vv. 9–10).

Although not any longer submerged *within* the primordial aquatic chaos, the earth may be considered still *in* the waters or, more precisely, *between* the waters beneath it and the waters above the firmament. The phrase "the one who hanged the earth *in* the waters" [22] might convey God's providence: God is the one who keeps the earth continually hanging (suspended) *within* an "aquatic" universe so that it may not be flooded by the waters as happened in Noah's days (Gen 6–7). The preposition *en*, "in," instead of the more common and expected *epi*, "on" (cf. Ps 24 [23]:2), may emphasize the earth's current ambiguous state, as entirely depending on God's will and power.

For John of Damascus (ca. 675–749), the earth is still in an unsettled state, between "submerging" *in* and "rising" *out* of the waters. John cites Ps 107 (106):24: "They themselves saw the deeds of the Lord and his wonders *in* the deep" (slightly altered, *autoi eidon ta thaumasia kyriou en tō bythō*). Then he asks the question and provides a tentative answer:

Which wonders? The open sea [*pelagos*] swelling up even to the clouds [*nephōn*]; the earth just shining [appearing] [*hypolampousan*] *in* the *middle* of the waters [*en mesois hydasin*] [as] a boat [*skaphos*] hanging [*kremamenon*] by a raised wave [*apo meteōrou kymatos*], and now exactly as either [*men*], by waters [*hydatōn*], falling into the hollows [*koilōmasi*] of the cliffs [*krēmnois*], or [*de*] by a raised wave [*koryphoumenou tou kymatos*] rising [*anasphendonoumenon*] into the air. (*Sacra Parallela* 96.49.9)[23]

As in our hymn, the earth is *in the midst* of waters just "shining (appearing)." For John of Damascus, this is one of the wonders mentioned earlier in the text (*thaumasia*). The image of earth just "shining (appearing)" *in the midst* of waters takes the reader back to Gen 1:6–10, when God, separating the waters, made the earth "appear" (*ophthē*) from *within* the waters. Moreover, in John's view, there is another miracle here: though *in the midst* of waters, menaced to be submerged by waters, the earth, by God's will and power, is still there. Likewise, Jesus, hanging on a tree in the midst of enemies, is by God's will and power still there completing his salvific work. And like the earth in John's comments, Jesus "shines" in the midst of the waters (trials).

It has been often said that our hymn was inspired by Melito of Sardis's homily *Peri Pascha* 96 ("He who hung the earth is hanging" [*ho kremasas tēn gēn krematai*]).[24] I would like to refine this assertion by showing the few similarities and differences between our hymn ("Today is hanged [*krematai*] on a tree [*epi xylou*] the one who hanged [*kremasas*] the earth in the waters [*en hydasi*]") and Melito of Sardis's homily. On the one hand, both writers compare Christ's crucifixion with the Creator's (Christ's, by extension) act of "hanging the earth." On the other hand, Melito's line is shorter ("who hanged the earth") than the hymnographer's ("who hanged the earth *in* the waters"). In addition, both texts allude to Job 26:7 by using the same imagery (i.e., God hanging the earth), while eschewing Job's novel image, namely, the earth hanging "on nothing."

James Mays remarks on Ps 24 (23):1–2:

The world is the result of an overpowering, an achievement that is *finished but never simply an accomplished fact.* Seas and rivers are names for the unstable chaos in the cosmology of the ancient Near East. The chaos is always there, hostile to the ordered world. The *world exists because the Lord is and remains sovereign.* To see the world is to behold the evidence of the reign of the Lord. *To live in the world is to be dependent on the reign of the Lord.* (emphasis mine)[25]

The second interpretation regarding the use of *en*, "in," rather than *epi*, "on," is based on the assumption that the hymn might subtly allude to the "pillars" (*styloi*) on which the earth was established, pillars thought to be submerged in the subterranean waters.

As already noted, Ps 136 (135):6 states that God "made [the earth] firm [*stereōsanti*] upon the waters [*epi tōn hydatōn*]." Ps 75:3 (74:4) goes a step further and underscores the same idea of earth's stability by asserting that God "firmed up" (*estereōsa*) earth's "pillars" (*stylous*).[26]

The "pillars" on which the earth was established occur again in Job 9:6, where God is painted as the one "who shakes [*seiōn*] what is under heaven from [its] foundations [*ek themeliōn*], and its pillars [*styloi*] tremble"; Job 26:11 speaks of "pillars of heaven." In a similar creational context, Prov 9:1 predicates that personified Wisdom, God's creative agent (Prov 8:22–31), built her own house[27] and "supported it with seven pillars" (*hypēreisen stylous hepta*).

If the hymnographer meant to use *en hydasi*, "*in* the waters," as a hint at the pillars supporting the earth, then a quite nice parallel or typology may be construed between Christ's and earth's "crucifixions." The one who "hanged the earth in the waters," on pillars, is today "hanged on a tree." There is here an intriguing theological idea: the "one" (i.e., the Creator or the pre-incarnate Logos/Christ) who "hanged the earth" on pillars in order to make it "firm" (as intimated in the few biblical texts mentioned above) is now himself hanged on a "tree" (i.e., the beam of a cross) in order to make the humanity, he assumed, firm, namely, to restore and strengthen it.

The use of the same preposition *en*, "in," but in conjunction with the verb *hedryzō*, "to establish," this time, occurs in the following hymn: "May my heart be strengthened [*stereōthētō*] in your will, Christ God, who strengthened [*stereōsas*] the second heaven [*ouranon ton deuteron*] on waters [*eph' hydatōn*] and established [*hedrasas*] the earth in the waters [*en tois hydasi*]" (Heirmologion, Heirmos, Ode 3, Mode 1).

Nevertheless, one should add that the prepositions *en*, "in," and *epi*, "on," are seemingly interchangeable, as the next hymn (where the same terms, "earth," "water," and "establish," appear) plainly shows: "You who, in the beginning [*kat' archas*], made firm [*stereōsas*] the heavens with understanding [*en synesei*], and established [*hedrasas*] the earth on the waters [*tēn gēn epi hydatōn*]" (Heirmologion, Heirmos, Ode 3, Mode 4).[28]

Moreover, the next hymn employs the same verb, *kremannymi/kremazō*, "to hang," as in our hymn, though followed by the preposition *epi*, "on": "The creation seeing [*ktisis katidiousa*] you hanged *in* the Skull [*en tō Kraniō*], you that hanged [*kremasanta*] the whole earth unconditionally (without restraint) [*aschetōs*] on the waters [*epi hydatōn*], it was seized with awe and cried, 'None is holy but you, O Lord'" (Holy Saturday, Matins, Ode 3, Heirmos).

An interesting case obtains with the next hymn, where the dative *tois hydasi* can be rendered either as "to/in the waters": "Seeing your unjust slaughter [*sphagēn*], O Christ, the Virgin [*hē parthenos*] cried out to you, lamenting [*odyroumenē*]: 'Sweetest Child, how can you suffer [*pascheis*] unjustly? How to hang to a tree [*tō xylō kremasai*], you that hanged [*kremasas*] the whole earth in/to the waters [*tois hydasi*]? I pray, Do not leave [*lipēs*] me alone, your Mother and servant, O much compassionate Benefactor!'" (Octoechos, Mode 1, Tuesday, Vespers, Staurotheotokion).

"In a fake purple [robe] is clothed the one who clothes the skies in clouds [*pseudē porphyran periballetai ho periballōn ton ouranon en nephelais*]"

The first half of this line has to be read in light of John 19:2–3: "The soldiers plaiting a crown of thorns, put it on his head, and clothed [*periebalon*] him in a purple robe [*himation porphyroun*]. And they came to him, saying 'Hail King of the Jews,' and they gave him blows [*rhapismata*]" (cf. v. 5; Mark 15:17–20). Note that in Matt 27:28, Jesus wears a *chlamyda kokkinēn*, "scarlet mantle"[29] (a cheaper garment dyed with an "imitation" purple obtained from various animals or vegetables[30] and worn by a Roman officer); and Luke 23:11 notes that Herod, having arrayed Jesus in a "shining robe" (*esthēta lampran*), sent him back to Pilate.

In the Bible, purple, a quite expensive dye, made from the mucus of sea snails exposed to air for a certain amount of time, is commonly associated with wealth, royal status, and authority (Judg 8:26; Esth 1:6; Dan 5:7, 16; 1 Macc 10:20; Luke 16:19; Rev 17:4; 18:16; cf. Josephus, *Antiquities* 14.173).

It is noteworthy that the hymnographer adds *pseudē*, "fake," to *porphyran*, "purple," as an interpretive gloss. If one accounts for Ernest Haenchen's remark, "Whoever wants to insist that this scene is historical is faced with the question: where did the soldiers get a purple robe?"[31] then "fake purple" may be an attempt to answer such a question by offering a plain interpretation of the gospel account.

In contrast with the "fake purple [robe]" (*pseudē porphyran*), Jesus, whom the soldiers have vested, wears the genuine "purple robe" (*halourgida*) as the

"King of Glory," which he received at the Incarnation from the dye of the Theotokos's blood: "The King of Glory and Maker, from the dye [baphēs] of the Theotokos's blood, dying his own purple robe [halourgida], became mystically purple [mystikōs eporphyrōsen]" (January 15, Matins, Ode 3).

The second half is a quote from Ps 147 (146):8 (tō periballonti ton ouranon en nephelais), which has already been discussed.[32] If in the other hymn, where this quote occurs, the contrast is between the two acts of the Creator/Christ (i.e., wrapping the sky in clouds and washing the feet of the disciples at the Last Supper), in the present hymn, the contrast is between the Creator's act (i.e., wrapping the sky in clouds) and the creature's improper response (i.e., vesting Jesus in a fake purple robe).

Since the next line of the present hymn mentions the Jordan, I would be remiss if I did not mention here the hymn where the Creator's act of wrapping the sky in clouds is likened to Jesus's wrapping of himself in the waters of the Jordan: "Through goodness, God appeared openly [emphanōs] embodied [sōmatoumenos], the one who truly wraps the sky in clouds does come to be wrapped in the Jordan's streams [namata]" (January 3, Matins, Ode 9, Canticle 12).

"A blow receives back the one who freed Adam in the Jordan [rhapisma katedexato ho en Iordanē eleutherōsas Adam]"
"A blow receives back" may hint at John 18:22: "One of the servants [hypēretōn] standing by gave Jesus a blow [edōken rhapisma], saying: 'Is that the way you answer the high priest?'" (cf. rhapismasin, "blows," Mark 14:65), allowing a glimpse into the fake trial in front of the high priest Caiaphas. Note the possible intertextuality between John 18:22 (cf. John 19:3, rhapismata, of Jesus in front of the Roman governor Pilate) and Isa 50:6 (rhapismata) along the lines of the prophecy-fulfillment scheme.

Noticeably, there is a sharp contrast between a Jesus, deprived of liberty, who receives a blow from one of Caiaphas's guards and a Jesus, at the beginning of his salvific work, who, through his baptism in the Jordan, freed "Adam," that is, the entire humanity contained in and represented by its homonymic forefather.

The hymnographer chose the verb katadechomai, "to receive back," to underline even further the contrast between Jesus's freedom willingly offered to an enslaved-by-sin humanity and the response of the latter, represented here by a servant striking at a defenseless prisoner. The reward or payoff Jesus receives back for freeing sinful humanity is, quite ironically, a servant's blow.

"The one who freed [*eleutherōsas*] Adam in the Jordan" points likely to Jesus's baptism in the Jordan River (Matt 3:13–17 and parallels). But on which biblical grounds did the hymnographer link Jesus's baptism in the Jordon with freeing Adam (humanity)? There are a few texts in the New Testament where truth/Son/Christ is associated with freeing humanity from sin and death (John 8:32 [truth], 36 [Son]; Rom 6:18, 22 [through baptism, sharing in Christ's death and resurrection, vv. 3–6]; 8:2; Gal 5:1) or the entire creation from corruption (Rom 8:21).

In addition to the above-mentioned Johannine and Pauline texts, there are two important Old Testament episodes where the Jordan River is connected with the idea of freedom or release: Israel crossing the Jordan under Joshua's leadership (Josh 3:13–17; cf. Ps 114 [113]:3) and Elijah being translated to heaven while Elisha looks on puzzled (2 Kgs 2).

The crossing of the Jordan under Joshua, Moses's successor, occurred close to a place called "Adam" (MT: *bā-ʾādām* [Kethib]/*mē-ʾādām* [Qere]; LXX: *Kariathiarim*) near Zeretan (Josh 3:16). As soon as the priests' soles touched the Jordan's waters (v. 13), these parted waters allowed the Israelites to walk as if on dry land. The crossing betokens the final station in Israel's journey from slavery in Egypt to freedom.

The translation of Elijah that happened also at the Jordan (2 Kgs 2:7–9, 14: Elijah strikes the waters with his mantle, and these are parted) points to Israel's release from the tyranny of idolatry if one accounts for Elijah's confrontation with Baal's prophets and the fulminant outcome on Mount Carmel (1 Kgs 18).

In the case of Jesus's baptism in the Jordan, unlike in the days of Joshua and Elijah, it was not the waters that parted, but rather the heavens "opened" (Matt 3:16). Here, the idea of freedom is concretized in release from corruption and sinfulness.

Jordan represents a *place of transition* or *transfer of authority* from Moses to Joshua (from Torah corpus to the prophetic collection), from Elijah to Elisha, from John the Baptist (last of the prophets) to Jesus (from the "old" to the "new covenant"). Similarly to Moses and Elijah, John the Baptist initiates his successor at the Jordan River. In John's case, the initiation takes the form of Jesus's baptism in the waters of the Jordan.[33]

Having received baptism from John, Jesus accepted to be numbered or identified with sinners (Isa 53:12) and placed himself under the penalty of death as "wages for sin" (Rom 6:23). Thus, Jesus's baptism prefigures his substitutionary death (Mark 10:38).

The following hymn intimates that the freeing of *Adamiaion genos*, the "Adamic race," a much clearer phrase than our hymn's generic "Adam," is due to Christ's death and resurrection, both aspects of the salvific work being prefigured by Christ's baptism in the Jordan and somehow mystically present in Christian baptism (cf. Rom 6:3–4; 1 Cor 1:13; Gal 3:27; Col 2:12; 1 Pet 3:21):

> Your Resurrection from the dead do we glorify, O Christ, through which you freed [*ēleutherōsas*] the Adamic race [*Adamiaion genos*], from the tyranny of Hades [*Hadou tyrannidos*], and as God gave the world eternal life and great mercy. (Octoechos, Mode 8, Sunday, Vespers, Sticheron)

According to the next hymn, Christ's baptism aims at the regeneration and restoration of fallen humanity back to its initial freedom:

> You accepted [*katedexō*] to be baptized in the Jordan by the hand of a servant [*doulikē cheiri*], so that you, the sinless one [*anamartētos*], having sanctified [*hagiasas*] the nature of the waters [*tēn hydatōn physin*], may craft a way [*hodopoiēsēs*] for our regeneration [*anagennēsin*] through water and Spirit and restore [*apokatastēsēs*] us to the first freedom [*prōtēn eleutherian*]. (January 6, Epiphany, Prayer for Sanctification of Waters)

How did this regeneration and restoration turn into reality? The answer is given by the following hymn: through the washing of the sins of the "Forefather" in the sanctified waters of the Jordan through Christ's baptism:

> A flower [*anthos*] from David, which blossomed from the Virgin, Christ came to the streams [*rheithra*] of Jordan, to wash away [*plynai*] in the waters the sins of the Forefather [*propatoros*]. (Forefeast of Theophany [January 2], Matins, Apostichon)

Interestingly, the waters need first to be "sanctified" (put aside, next to God) so that they may be used in baptism for regeneration of the human nature to its initial freedom. This sanctification presupposes a precarious state of these waters. The Old Testament testifies to a shift from a neutrally charged, chaotic phase of the primordial waters (Gen 1:2) to a negatively charged locus sheltering the mysterious sea monsters, such as the Leviathan (MT) or the "dragon" (LXX: *drakōn*) (Ps 74 [73]:13–14; 104 [103]:25–26; Isa 27:1; Job 41:1; cf. 3:8 [LXX: *kētos*, "sea monster, huge fish"]), symbolizing those evil powers responsible for the trials and sufferings that a fragile humanity had to experience in this world.

Freeing fallen humanity (represented in our hymn by the generic "Adam") by washing away the sins of the Forefather in the sanctified waters of the Jordan and regenerating/restoring humanity to the "first freedom" is, according to the next hymn, equal to its "refashioning" (*anaplasis*) (cf. Gen 2:7, where the verb *plassō*, "to fashion," is used to depict vividly the creation of humanity):

> He [Jesus] is about to go forward [*proerchesthai*] to the streams [*rhoais*] of Jordan to be baptized. Let us receive [*dexōmetha*] him in purity of thought [*katharotēti dianoias*], for he wants to work [*ergasasthai*] the refashioning of all [*pantōn anaplasin*]. (Forefeast of Theophany [January 3], Matins, Kathisma 11)

But the baptism also prefigures Jesus's descent into the underworld (1 Pet 3:18–20; 4:6; Eph 4:9).[34] By descending into the waters of the Jordan River, Jesus previews (foretastes) the *descensus ad infernos* ("descent into Hades"). Being sinless, Jesus does not need to be "cleansed" by waters, but rather he sanctifies the waters. The main purpose of his descent into the waters of the Jordan is to defeat, dash to pieces, the evil forces (i.e., the dragons) lurking there[35] and to "recall Adam," the one who hid himself at the Creator's call in the Garden of Eden after the Fall (Gen 3:8–10). Now, at Jesus's baptism, "recalling Adam," God gives humanity represented by the Forefather another chance to return to the eternal life.

> Prepare yourself, Jordan River, for behold [*idou*] Christ God is coming [*paraginetai*] to be baptized by John, so that he may dash to pieces the unseen heads of the dragons through [his] divinity [*drakontōn aoratous kephalas synthlasē tē theotēti*], in your very waters [*en tois hydasi tois sois*]. Wilderness [*erēmos*] of Jordan rejoice; mountains leap with joy [*skirtēsate met' euphrosynēs*], for the eternal life [*hē aiōnios zōē*] came to recall [*anakalesai*] Adam. (January 2, Matins, Aposticha)

This fragment betrays the liturgist's exquisite ingenuity by connecting Jesus's baptism with two Old Testament events occurring also at the Jordan, all together denoting the idea of freedom in its complexity, that is, freedom from social oppression, idolatry, and corruption or sin. Moreover, in our hymn, as in the New Testament, Jesus's death on the cross is connected with the very act of baptism: the opening line of the hymn parallels Jesus's crucifixion on a "tree" with the earth "hanged in the waters" (an allusion to the primordial aquatic chaos in Gen 1:2), whereas in the present fragment, the freeing of humanity through Jesus's sacrificial death is associated with the latter's baptism in the Jordan. This fragment from the hymn offers a marvelous example of biblical theology through well-grounded intertextuality.

"With nails is nailed fast the Bridegroom of the Church
[*hēlois proselōthē nymphios tēs ekklēsias*]"
This line proposes another sharp contrast, almost Kafkaesque in its nonsensical, nightmarish tenor: Jesus, the "Bridegroom of the Church" (*nymphios tēs ekklēsias*), instead of "rejoicing over [his] bride" (Isa 62:5), is "nailed fast" (*proselōthē*) to a cross. Note that the verb *proseloō*, "to nail (fast)," is a hapax legomenon in the New Testament, occurring only in Col 2:14, where Jesus is depicted as the one who "wiped out" (*exaleipsas*) the "handwriting" (*cheirographon*) against humanity "by nailing it fast to the cross" (*proselōsas auto tō staurō*).

"With a spear is pierced the son of the Virgin [*lonchē ekentēthē hyios tēs parthenou*]"
The phrase "son of the Virgin" (*hyios tēs parthenou*) might be a collocation between two famous Old Testament texts, Dan 7:13 (*hyios tou anthrōpou*) and Isa 7:14 (LXX: *parthenos*; MT: *ʿalmāh*), both interpreted Christologically by the Church Fathers.[36] The phrase aims to underline the Christ paradox: while he was a "human being" (*hyios tou anthrōpou*), his birth was supernatural, that is, from a virgin (*parthenos*) (cf. Matt 1:18–25, quoting Isa 7:14).[37]

The word "spear" alludes to John 19:34, where a soldier "pricked" (*anyxen*) Jesus's "side" (*pleuron*) with a "spear" (*lonchē*). Note that the verb *kenteō*, "to prick, to pierce," appearing in this line of the hymn is found only twice in the entire Bible, Job 6:4 and Lam 4:9, both poetical texts.

Calling the Nations

When the unlawful ones [*paranomoi*] nailed [*proselōsin*] you, the Lord of Glory [*ton kyrion tēs doxēs*], fast to the cross, you cried out [*eboas*] to them: "How did I grieve [*elypēsa*] you? Or, by what did I provoke you to anger [*parōrgisa*]? Before me, who rescued [*errysato*] you from affliction [*thlipseōs*]? And now, what do you give me back [*antapodidote*]? Evil [*ponēra*] for good [*agathōn*]; for the pillar of fire [*stylou pyros*], you nailed [*prosēlōsate*] me fast to the cross; for the cloud [*nephelēs*], you dug [*ōryxate*] me a tomb [*taphon*]; for manna, you offered me gall [*cholēn*]; for water, you gave me vinegar [*oxos*] to drink [*epotisate*]. Thus [*loipon*], I will call [*kalō*] the nations [*ta ethnē*], and they will glorify [*doxasousi*] me, together with the Father and the Holy Spirit." (Good Friday, Royal Hours, Ninth Hour, Idiomelon)

The hymn opens with the narrator's voice briefly introducing the worshiper to the crucifixion scene, where the "Lord of Glory" questions the "unlawful" folks who nailed him to the cross. It is worth noting that the rhetorical questions are not addressed to "Israel" as people but rather to a mob liable for Jesus's suffering and untimely death.[38]

Patterned on the Exodus review form, a recounting of God's interventions into Israel's plight in and deliverance out of Egypt, the hymn, through Jesus's voice, contrasts God's past benevolent acts during the Exodus with the adverse attitude of Jesus's contemporaries. As one can see, Jesus is identified here with the God of Exodus.

The Exodus review form encountered in this hymn made its first appearance in the Old Testament (e.g., Ps 78 [77]—a recital of God's marvels related to the Exodus event; Ps 106 [105] and Neh 9—where Exodus recitals are embedded within a confession of sins; Wis 10–19 exhibits a complex Exodus review form, in fact, a midrash on the Exodus review; 5 Ezra [2 Esd 1–2] contrasts God's benevolent acts with Israel's ungratefulness). Outside the Bible, this literary form is attested in some early Jewish and Christian writings (e.g., Justin Martyr's *Dialogue*, Pseudo-Clementine *Recognitions*, Melito's *Peri Pascha*, and *Didascalia apostolorum*, to mention a few). In *Gospel (Questions) of Bartholomew*, a third-century work, Jesus is the speaker; he identifies himself, as in our hymn, with God of the Old Testament: "How many miracles I did for them . . . I led them out of the land of Egypt." Unlike Melito's *Peri Pascha*, in *Gospel of Bartholomew*, Jesus speaks in the first person. I may add that early Christian authors used the Exodus review form, though Jewish in origin, as a literary motif in the ongoing anti-Jewish polemic.

On a closer examination of other hymnic material, one comes across the following antiphon quite similar to the hymn under examination. However, in this antiphon, the addressee is no longer the "unlawful" (*paranomoi*), a mob, but rather "my people" (*laos mou*) and "the Judeans" (*Ioudaiois*). Moreover, the neutral "nations" (*ta ethnē*) in the previous hymns becomes here "my nations" (*mou ta ethnē*). Also, we are told that Jesus's calling of the nations is like disclosing something kept secret, a revelation of sorts.

> Thus says the Lord to the Judeans [*Ioudaiois*]: "My people [*laos mou*], what have I done [*epoiēsa*] to you, or how have I troubled [*parēnōchlēsa*] you? I gave light [*ephōtisa*] to your blind ones; I cleansed [*ekatharisa*] the lepers; I set straight again [*ēnōrthōsamēn*] the bedridden man [*andra onta epi klinēs*]. My people, what have I done to you, and what have you given me back [*antapedōkas*]? Instead [*anti*] of manna, gall; instead of water, vinegar; instead of loving [*agapan*] me, you nailed [*prosēlōsate*] me to a cross [*staurō*]. Thus [*loipon*], I will no longer [*ouketi*] keep secret [*stegō*]: I will call [*kalesō*] my nations [*mou ta ethnē*], and they will glorify [*doxasousi*] me, with [*syn*] the Father and the Holy Spirit; and I will grant [*dōrēsomai*] them eternal life." (Good Friday, Matins, Antiphon 12)[39]

According to Theodore Bergren, the two above-quoted hymns employing the Exodus review form might go back to a common source, 5 Ezra (2 Esd 1–2), written by a Christian in the late second century.[40] Among the similarities between these two hymns and 5 Ezra and other early writings, Bergren enumerates the use of rhetorical questions, as in 5 Ezra and Melito's *On Pascha*; the speaker addressing the Jews in the first person, as found in 5 Ezra and *Gospel of Bartholomew*; contrasting the deeds of Jesus/God with the deeds of their contemporaries; and most important, Jesus calling "the nations" to praise/glorify him, as in 5 Ezra.

The idiomelon here under examination has many elements in common with *Improperia* ("Reproaches"), a series of antiphons and responses in the Roman rite chanted on Good Friday afternoon at the hour of the *Adoratio Crucis* ("Adoration of the Cross").[41]

As one may notice in the fragment below, the *Improperia* are quite elaborate. After each of the *Ego* ("I") verses, the refrain *Popule meus . . . responde mihi* ("My people . . . answer me") is repeated, e.g., *Popule meus, quid feci tibi? aut quid molestus fui tibi? Responde mihi* ("My people, what have I done to you, or in what have I troubled you? Answer me").

By this refrain, the *Improperia* changes the addressee from a mob of malefactors or transgressors, "unlawful" (*paranomoi*), as in the Byzantine hymn, to "my people" (*popule meus*) as a whole:

> I scourged Egypt with [the death of] its firstborn for your sake: and you delivered me to be scourged. I led you out of Egypt, plunging Pharaoh into the

Red Sea: and you delivered me to the chief priests. I opened the sea before you: and you opened my side with a lance. I went before you in the pillar of cloud: and you guided me to Pilate's court. I fed you manna in the desert: and you cut me down with blows and lashes. I gave you saving water from the rock to drink: and you gave me gall and vinegar to drink. I struck the Canaanite kings for your sake: and you struck my head with a reed. I granted you a royal scepter: and you granted my head a crown of thorns. I raised you up in great power: and you hung me on the gibbet of the Cross."[42]

Returning now to the hymn under examination, a few lexical notes are warranted.

"The unlawful [*paranomoi*]"

The LXX employs the term *paranomoi*, rendered here "unlawful," to designate a wide variety of deviators such as, idolaters (Deut 13:14), the sexually promiscuous (Judg 19:22), murderers (2 Sam 16:7), false witnesses (1 Kgs 20:10), renegades (1 Macc 11:21), generically all transgressors of the Law (Ps 5:6; Prov 2:22; Psalms of Solomon 4:9). This term is absent in the New Testament; only *paranomia*, a hapax legomenon, occurs in 2 Pet 2:16 with respect to Balaam's transgression (Num 22–24). In the present hymn, *paranomoi* refers to insensitive, violent folks who delight in inflicting pain on others, more precisely, a mob of malefactors responsible for Jesus's premature, agonizing death on a cross.

"They nailed fast [*proselōsin*] to the cross"

The verb *proseloō*, "to fasten," used in this hymn, is a hapax legomenon in LXX, occurring in 3 Macc 4:9, of Jews being fastened by their necks to a ship's benches. In the New Testament, the verb *proseloō* is again a hapax, found in Col 2:14, of Jesus who "nailed to the cross the handwriting [*cheirographon*]" of debts against humans. The lexeme *hēlos*, "nail," embedded in the verb *proseloō*, occurs once in John 20:25, of Thomas's statement referring to the mark of nails in the risen Jesus's hands. Thus, the use of *proseloō*, "to nail (fast)," with reference to Jesus's crucifixion is unattested in the New Testament, which, instead, uses *stauroō*, a denominative verb (from *stauros*, "cross" (NT); in Classical Gk., "upright pale or stake") meaning "to fasten to a cross, to crucify" (Mark 16:6; John 19:6, 10, 15; Acts 2:36; 4:10; 1 Cor 2:8 ["Lord of Glory"; see below]; 2 Cor 13:4; Rev 11:8; figuratively in Gal

5:24). One may note here that the New Testament authors are ambiguous in describing the way Jesus's crucifixion happened, either by tying or nailing, except for John 20:25, where the first mention of "the mark of nails" (*typon tōn hēlōn*) with respect to Jesus's crucifixion occurs.

One may mention here that Ps 22 (21), which has been read Christologically since or even prior to the writing of the canonical gospels, contains a line in LXX that could be read as a foreshadowing of Jesus's crucifixion by nailing. This is Ps 22:16 (21:17) (LXX): "For many dogs [*kynes*] encircled [*ekyklōsen*] me, a gathering of evildoers [*synagōgē ponēreuomenōn*] surrounded [*perieschon*] me; they gouged [*ōryxan*] my hands [*cheiras*] and my feet [*podas*]"; note that the MT has a different reading: "like a lion . . . my hands and my feet," seemingly missing a verb.

Although the Christological reception of Ps 22 (21) is attested by the gospel Passion narratives (i.e., Ps 22:1 [21:2] ["My God, my God, why have you forsaken me?"; cf. Matt 27:45; Mark 15:34], vv. 6–7 [7–8] [mocking; cf. Matt 27:39; Mark 15:29; Luke 23:35], v. 18 [19] [dividing clothing; cf. John 19:23–24]), the most pertinent line of this psalm, v. 16 (17), "they gouged my hands and my feet," is conspicuously absent in the canonical gospels.

There is no fully satisfying explanation for such an important oversight. However, according to Naomi Koltun-Fromm, the gospels' overlooking the LXX reading of Ps 22:16 (21:17) is due to the fact that Mark and Matthew were interested not in the details of the crucifixion but rather in God's actions through Jesus, and only later on did Christian writers begin to focus on the redemptive character of Jesus's suffering, hence the emerging link between Ps 22:16 (21:17) and the Passion narrative.[43]

The first, although indirect, Christological use of Ps 22:16 (21:17) can be traced back to the *Epistle of Barnabas* (end of the first century to the beginning of the seecond century).[44]

Nevertheless, Justin Martyr is the first Christian author who used Ps 22:16 (21:17) in conjunction with the gospel Passion narrative:

> And again in other words he says through another prophet: "They pierced my hands and my feet, and cast lots for my clothing" [vv. 16/17, 18/19]. And indeed David, the king and prophet, who said this, suffered none of these things; but Jesus Christ had his hands stretched out. . . . The expression "They pierced my hands and my feet" was an announcement of the nails that were fastened in his hands and feet on the cross. And after he was

crucified they cast lots for his clothing, and they that crucified him divided it among themselves. (*First Apology* 35)[45]

Koltun-Fromm argues that Justin, and then Tertullian and Aphrahat, embedded the Christological interpretation of Ps 22:16 (21:17) within a wider context, that of anti-Jewish Christian polemics.[46] Interestingly enough, the mention of "nailing" (*prosēlōsin*) in our hymn occurs in a similar setting, the Exodus review theme unpacked on an anti-Jewish backdrop.

"The Lord of Glory [*ton kyrion tēs doxēs*]"

The title (*ho kyrios tēs doxēs*, "the Lord of Glory")[47] and basic idea of the hymn's opening lines may be an echo of 1 Cor 2:8: "None of the rulers [*archontōn*] of this age [*aiōnos toutou*] realized [*egnōken*] this; for if they had realized, they would not have crucified [*estaurōsan*] the Lord of Glory [*kyrion tēs doxēs*]."[48] In our hymn, as in the Pauline epistle just quoted, the ones who crucified/ nailed Jesus to a cross were unable to discern in their weak victim "the Lord of Glory" or the "hidden Wisdom of God [*theou sophian apokekrymmenēn*], which God pre-appointed [*proōrisen*] before the ages for our glory [*doxan*]" (1 Cor 2:7; cf. Prov 8:22–31).

Exodus Review Pattern

"Before me, who rescued you from affliction [*pro emou, tis hymas errysato ek thlipseōs*]?"

The Exodus review opens with a rhetorical question about the identity of the one who rescued Israel from its afflictions. The two key terms used here (*rhyomai*, "to rescue," and *thlipsis*, "affliction") make Jesus's own affliction reverberate through salvation history to the days of a fugitive Jacob pursued by his brother and a wandering Israel just out of Egypt facing a vast wilderness.[49] The two somehow disoriented, quite lost entities of the remote past mysteriously foreshadow a "very distressed, to the point of death" (Matt 26:38) Jesus. The paradox is that this very Jesus, abandoned by friends, crucified by enemies, and forsaken by the heavenly Father, is the Lord of Glory who rescued Jacob and the children of Israel from their afflictions. One may underline here Jesus's self-identification with the God of the Old Testament and his acts of mercy during the post-Exodus period.[50]

"What do you give me back? Evil for good [*ti moi antapodidote
ponēra anti agathōn*]"
It is worth noting that these are the words Joseph commissions his steward
with to question his brothers: *ti hoti moi antapodidote ponēra anti agathōn*,
"Why is it that you gave me back evil for good?" (Gen 44:4), with a slight
difference: the hymnographer divides this question into two parts, with the
latter serving as incipit for a series of brief yet poignant contrasts between
God's benevolent actions and the people's inadequate responses. One may
mention here that Joseph, a Christological type of endurance in patristic exegesis,[51] had his share of "affliction" (*thlipsis*) at the hands of his envious and
insensitive brothers, as the latter came to confess their guilt among themselves while entrapped in Joseph's Egyptian household (Gen 42:21).

"For the pillar of fire, you nailed me fast to the cross [*anti stylou
pyros staurō me prosēlōsate*]"
Immediately after the Exodus event, God's first benevolent action toward
wandering Israel was to lead the people through the desert by means of a
"pillar of cloud" (*stylō nephelēs*) during the day and a "pillar of fire" (*stylō
pyros*) during the night (Exod 13:21, 22; 14:24; Num 14:14; Wis 18:3). Having
returned from the Babylonian exile, the Israelites, on the Feast of Tabernacles,
made a national confession remembering God's leading his people through
the wilderness by two miraculous pillars: "And by day you led them with a
pillar of cloud, and during the night with a pillar of fire, to light for them the
way they were to go" (Neh 9:12; cf. v. 19).

To such a gracious act of divine providence, the response of the "unlawful"
was to nail Jesus to a cross; the suffering-inducing cross stands as a sharp
graphic contrast to the beneficial pillar of fire.

"For the cloud, you dug me a tomb [*anti nephelēs taphon moi ōryxate*]"
The sequence of cloud, manna, and water from the rock that appears in our
hymn's Exodus review is also found in 1 Cor 10:1–4. According to Roger Aus,
the sequence in 1 Cor 10:1–4 has a Jewish liturgical background.[52] The four
elements (sea, cloud, manna, water from the rock) in 1 Cor 10:1–4 occur as a
cluster in Ezra's prayer (Neh 9:12 [cloud, almost a paraphrase of Exod 13:21],
vv. 15, 20 [manna and water from the rock]; vv. 9, 11 [parting of the Red
Sea]); cf. Ps 105 (104): v. 39 (cloud), v. 40 (manna), v. 41 (water from the
rock). Moreover, this series reappears later on in three consecutive Sabbath

readings of the Palestinian triennial lectionary: the reading of the third Sabbath of Nisan begins with Exod 13:21 (cloud); on the fourth Sabbath of Nisan, Exodus 15:21ff. was read, including 16:4–24 (manna); and the reading of the first Sabbath of Iyyar (following Nisan) begins with Exod 16:25ff., including 17:1–7 (water from the rock).

In this line of the hymn, "cloud" stands in parallel/contrast with "tomb." The word "cloud" (*nephelē*) here may refer to either "pillar of cloud" (*stylos nephelēs*), the means by which God led wandering Israel during the day (Exod 13:21; Ps 78 [77]:14), or the thick "cloud" associated with God's appearances on Mount Sinai (Exod 19:16 [LXX: *nephelē gnophōdēs*, "dark cloud"]; 24:15, 16, 18; 34:5; Deut 5:22), in the Tabernacle in the wilderness (Exod 33:9, 10; 40:34–38; Lev 16:2; Num 9:15; Deut 31:15), or in the Jerusalem Temple (1 Kgs 8:10–12; 2 Chr 5:13–14; 6:1; Ezek 10:3, 4). In both cases, the cloud indicates God's presence (Exod 16:10; Judg 5:4; 2 Sam 22:12; Ezek 1:4, 28; Isa 14:14; Matt 17:5; 24:30; Acts 1:9; 1 Thess 4:17; Rev 10:1); the "cloud" or, more precisely, "riding on/mounting clouds" was an essential attribute of any ANE deity (Isa 19:1 [MT: "rides"; LXX: "sits"]; Deut 33:26 [MT; LXX: "sky"]; Ps 68:4 [67:5] [MT; cf. LXX: "sunset"]; 104 [103]:3; Dan 7:13–14; Sir 24:4; Matt 26:63–64; Mark 14:62; Rev 1:7; 14:14–16).[53]

Moreover, the cloud from which God spoke to Moses and Aaron has a twofold function: screening or covering God (Job 22:14: "Piles of clouds [*nephē*] [are] his hiding place [*apokryphē*] and he shall not be seen [*horathēsetai*]; and he passes through [*diaporeusetai*] the circle [*gyron*] of heaven"; Ps 97 [96]:2) and a channel of communication (Exod 19:9; 24:16; 33:9; 34:5; Num 11:25; 12:5; Deut 5:22) between God and humans.

In the midst of woes, the author of Lamentations points to God's action of covering himself with a cloud so that no prayer might reach him. LXX: "You covered [*epeskepasas*] yourself with a cloud [*nephelēn*] for the sake of prayer [*heineken proseuchēs*]" (Lam 3:44); and more clearly in the MT: "You screened [*skkwth*] yourself with a cloud, so that no prayer pass through [*mᶜbwr*]." The idea in both of these main textual witnesses is the same: God is not willing any longer to listen to the prayers coming from a doomed Jerusalem that he has covered with his wrath.[54] Nevertheless, notes Sirach (35:21 [17]), "the prayer [*proseuchē*] of the humble [*tapeinou*] passes through [*dielthen*] clouds [*nephelas*]."

The hymnographer's lexical choice, *taphos*, "tomb," construed with *oryssō*, "to dig," matches a similar construction in Gen 50:5 ("the tomb [*mnēmeiō*] that I [Jacob] dug out [*ōryxa*] for myself in the land of Canaan"). The use of *oryssō*, "to dig" (commonly of wells, cisterns; Gen 21:30; 26:15), in our hymn might be intentional, i.e., alluding to Ps 22:16 (21:17) [LXX] ("they gouged [*ōryxan*] my hands [*cheiras*] and my feet [*podas*]"), which was read by early Christian writers as a prophecy of Christ's crucifixion by nailing.

The hymnographer contrasts the "cloud" through which God led and protected[55] a wandering people with the "tomb" that the unlawful folks "dug" for Christ, identified here with the God of Exodus.[56]

"For manna, you offered me gall [*anti tou manna, cholēn moi prosēnenkate*]"
The second contrast of this Exodus review is between manna and gall. *Manna*, the Greek transliteration of the Hebrew *mān*, connotes the heavenly food the ancient Hebrews ate during their forty-year journey through the desert (Exod 16; cf. Ps 78 [77]:25: "angels' bread").[57] An allusion to this manna might be contained in the phrase "honey from the rock" (i.e., unexpected and desirable food), found in Ps 81:16 (80:17) (cf. Deut 32:13). The hymnographer reused this metaphor of God nursing his children in the wilderness as follows: "The senseless [*agnōmones*] children of Israel, who sucked [*thēlasantes*] the honey from the rock [*ek petras to meli*] offered you gall [*cholēn*], O Christ, who worked wonders [*teratourgēsanti*] in the wilderness; in exchange for good work [*euergesian*] gave you vinegar [*oxos*] for manna [*manna*]" (Octoechos, Sunday, Matins, Mode 1, Ode 3).

Instead of manna, the miraculous yet hard-to-describe nourishment the wandering Israelites enjoyed in the desert, the unlawful folks offered Jesus, the Lord of Glory, nothing but gall. The Greek word *cholē*, "gall," appears in the Passion narratives only in Matt 27:33–34: "Having arrived to a place called Golgotha . . . they gave him [Jesus] wine [*oinon*; Byz.: *oxos* "vinegar"] to drink mixed with gall [*meta cholēs memigmenon*]; but having tasted it [*geusamenos*], he would not drink."

The gospel writer opted for this rare word from the LXX in order to connect the Passion narrative to the first line in Ps 69:21 (68:22): "And they gave gall [*cholēn*] as my food [*brōma*], and for my thirst [*dipsan*] they gave me vinegar [*oxos*] to drink." The word *cholē*, "gall, liver" (cf. Tob 6:5–7; Job 16:13), should be understood here with its generic meaning of something bitter, even poisonous. The second line of Ps 69:21 (68:22) matches Matt 27:48, where the agonizing Jesus was offered "vinegar" (*oxos*).

This mixture of "gall and wine" (Matt 27:34) is to be distinguished from the "wine mixed with myrrh" (Mark 15:23) offered to a person before crucifixion in order to decrease the pain. On the contrary, "gall mixed with wine" betrays cruelty and mockery on the part of those who crucified Jesus—corresponding to the main tenor of Ps 69 (68).[58]

"For water, you gave me vinegar to drink [*anti tou hydatos, oxos me epotisate*]"
The last contrast is between the "water" (from the rock) that the ancient Israelites drank during the long journey through the desert and the "vinegar" that the unlawful folks offered to the Lord of Glory while he was agonizing on the cross. Since I have previously discussed at length[59] the wonder of the water from the rock, here I will add just a few additional observations.

There has been a popular assumption among the ancient Jewish interpreters that the wandering people were accompanied during the lengthy journey through the desert by a traveling rock (or rocky well), an interpretation based on the mere juxtaposition of Exod 17:1–7 and Num 20:7–13.[60] This ancient interpretation is echoed by Paul in 1 Cor 10:1–4, where the great apostle equates the "traveling rock" with the pre-incarnate Christ. In Paul's understanding of this episode, Christ, who offers his followers a *poma pneumatikon*, "spiritual drink" (his own blood in the Eucharist), is the fulfillment of the enigmatic traveling rock of old.

Nevertheless, instead of that miraculous source of water that ancient Israel had surprisingly experienced during its long journey through the wilderness, the unlawful folks offered Jesus "vinegar" to relieve his thirst (Matt 27:48; John 19:29); note that in John 19:30, he drinks it, but MT 27:48 is silent about this.

In this Exodus review, the hymnographer, through Jesus's voice, contrasts God's benevolent actions in the past (pillar of fire, cloud, manna, water) with the unlawful folks' rude attitude (cross, tomb, gall, vinegar) toward the crucified Lord of Glory.

However, Byzantine hymnographers went a step further, peeking beyond the humiliation side of the crucifixion episode. They noted that God's compassion and benevolence continued to unfold.

In his ineffable graciousness, God turns the insensitive response of a group of unlawful folks who crucified the Lord of Glory into an opportunity for Christ to continue and bring God's past work to a climax through new and greater acts of divine mercy. This idea permeates patristic-liturgical interpretations. Below are a few examples of such a creative hermeneutical rehearsal.

For instance, the "bitterness" of gall that Jesus tasted turns into the "sweetness" of man's salvation which Jesus procured through his exemplary endurance:

Having been raised up [hypsōtheis] on the cross as the just judge, O sweetest Child [teknon glykytaton], [and] having tasted [geusamenos] gall and vinegar, you made sweet [eglykanas] the bitter taste [geusin pikran] of Adam of old; therefore, Master, sweeten [glykanon] me, who tasted the bitter potion [pharmachtheisan] through your passion [tō pathei sou], by rising again [anastas] as All-mighty, said the Virgin [hē parthenos] while shedding tears [dakryousa]. (Octateuchos, Friday, Vespers, Mode 1, Apostichon, Theotokion)[61]

Or:

The Long-suffering [makrothymos] is given gall to drink [potizetai], becoming for me a source of saving sweetness [pēgazōn moi glykasmon sōtērion], who by the pleasure of food [enēdonō brōsei] was deprived of the delight [tryphēs] of paradise. (Octateuchos, Friday, Matins, Mode 1)

Similarly, the "gall" and "vinegar," given to the crucified Jesus through God's salvific plan and Christ's obedience, turn into the body and blood of the Savior offered to a lost humanity in the mystery of the Eucharist:

O Savior, you are given vinegar [oxos] and gall [cholēn] to drink for our sake, you who gave us your body [sōma] and your precious blood [timion haima] as food [brōsin] and drink [posin] of your eternal life. (Pentecostarion, Sunday of the Myrrh Bearers, Matins, Ode 9)[62]

"Thus, I will call the nations, and they will glorify me, together with the Father and the Holy Spirit [loipon, kalō ta ethnē, kakeina me doxasousi, syn Patri kai Hagiō Pneumati]"
As noted by Bergren, this hymn (troparion) draws heavily on 5 Ezra, which contrasts God's mighty benevolent acts during the Exodus period with Israel's ingratitude. Finally, God decides to "call the nations" (cf. 5 Ezra 1 [2 Esd 1–2], influenced by Ps 78 [77]:59–62; Gal 4:21–31; 1 Bar; synoptic

gospels); 5 Ezra 1:24 reads: "I will go over to another nation" (*Transferam me ad gentem alterum*).[63]

If one takes a look at the prophetic corpus of the Hebrew Bible, one realizes that the *rîb* ("controversy") pattern, depicting God in dispute with an ungrateful Israel (e.g., Mic 6:1–8; Isa 5; Hos 4:1–3), may have influenced those New Testament logia where Jesus decries Jerusalem's obstinacy, lamenting its ominous future (Matt 23:37–39), or parables where the kingdom of God will be taken away from Israel and transferred to a "nation [*ethnei*] producing fruit" (Matt 21:43). It is noteworthy that all this rhetoric aims at the ungrateful Israel rather than at a new nation. This remark applies also to our hymn, whose Exodus review concludes with a divine call to the nations.

The essential question is whether this calling of the nations would necessarily suggest a "replacement theology," where Israel is to be rejected and replaced with the nations. But first, who are these nations? Based on the New Testament usage of *ethnē* along with the majority of ancient and modern biblical interpreters, "nations" does not designate exclusively "Gentiles" vs. "Jews," but rather inclusively "nations" refers to both Gentiles and Jews. The end of our hymn exudes the same spirit as the "apostolic mandate" (or "great commission") in Matt 28:19. This universalist spirit, understood more locally from house to house,[64] was anticipated (Matt 5:14; 13:38) and celebrated by the early Church (Justin, *First Apology* 31.7; *Didascalia* 23).

I need to express my dissent with Bergren, who sees in 5 Ezra (2 Esd 1–2), and implicitly the Byzantine hymns influenced by it and discussed above, "a radically supersessionist reading of the apocryphal book of Baruch (1 Bar)."[65] I think that there is not enough textual evidence to label our hymns "radically supersessionist" in their content or scope. My arguments are two in number. First, this hymn does not speak of "Israel" (or "my people") but rather of "unlawful" folks (a mob); and second, calling "the nations" does not require Israel's rejection and replacement; there is no trace of the so-called replacement theology here. "The nations" (*ta ethnē*) are summoned simply to acknowledge God's great acts which he worked during Israel's history and consequently to praise the wonderful doer of all times. Thus, "the nations" are at the most a tempting generalization—the sensitive counterpart for an obstinate and ungrateful mob/people and not its substitute for God's covenant with Israel.

Heaven Was Astonished

Two evils did my firstborn son [*ho prōtotokos hyios mou*] Israel: he abandoned [*enkatelipe*] me, the source of the living water [*pēgēn hydatos zōēs*],
and he dug [*ōryxen*] for himself a broken cistern [*phrear syntetrimmenon*].
He crucified [*estaurōse*] me on a tree [*epi xylou*], and asked for [*ētēsato*]
Barabbas, and he released [*apelysen*] [him]. Heaven was astonished [*exestē*]
by this, and the sun hid [*apekrypse*] [its] rays [*aktinas*]. But you, O Israel,
were not ashamed [*enetrapēs*], instead, you handed me over [*paredōkas*] to
death. Forgive them, O holy Father, for they do not know what they have
done. (Holy Friday, Matins, Lauds, Idiomelon)

This hymn should be read as a theological sequel to the previous hymn based
on an Exodus review set of rhetorical questions. This time, the hymnographer, again using Jesus's voice, enunciates Israel's evil deeds. Note that "my
firstborn [*prōtotokos*] son Israel" replaces here the "unlawful" (*paranomoi*)
folks (the mob) found in the previous hymn.

"My firstborn son Israel did two evils [*dyo kai ponēra epoiēsen ho
prōtotokos hyios mou*]"
This hymn commences with a phrase from Exod 4:22 (God addressing
Moses, "Then you shall say to Pharaoh: 'This is what the Lord says: My firstborn son is Israel' [*hyios prōtotokos mou Israēl*])," thus intimating God's elec-
tion of Israel, which occurred not too long after the divine revelation at the
burning bush (Exod 3). Interestingly, in this hymn, Christ (the "image of the
unseen God" and "firstborn of all creation" [Col 1:15]), who identifies himself with the God of the Old Testament, calls Israel his "firstborn son." Note
that in the psalms, King David is labeled God's "firstborn [*prōtotokon*], high
among the earth's kings" (Ps 89:27 [88:28]).
    Then the hymnographer quotes Jer 2:13, though slightly altered; Jer 2:13
(LXX) reads: "For my people [*ho laos mou*] did two evils: they abandoned
me, the source of living water [*pēgēn hydatos zōēs*], and they dug [*ōryxan*] for
themselves broken cisterns [*lakkous syntetrimmenous*] that will not be able
[*dynēsontai*] to hold [*synechein*] water."
    First, the hymnographer replaces "my people" (*ho laos mou*) with "my
firstborn son Israel" (*hyios prōtotokos mou*) to emphasize the intimate, personal relation between God and Israel. Second, the plural *ōryxan*, "they dug,"

with reference to *laos*, "people" (a collective noun), is replaced by the singular *ōryxen*, "he dug," with respect to Israel, God's firstborn son. Third, the hymnographer changes the plural *lakkous*, "reservoirs" with the singular *phrear*, "(artificial) well," again to better underscore the contrast between "source [singular *pēgēn*] of living water" and "broken well (cistern) [singular *phrear*]." The subtle way these minor alterations are interwoven in the literary texture of this hymn betrays the hymnographer's close reading of Scripture as well as his literary aptness and theological acumen.

The hymn's identification of Jesus with "source of living water" might have been prompted by the hymnographer's reading of Jer 17:13b (similar in context to Jer 2:13), "They abandoned the source of life [*pēgēn zōēs*], the Lord [*ton kyrion*]," where "the Lord" is in apposition to and equated with the "source of life."

"Two evils [*dyo ponēra*]"
The Gk. numeral *dyo*, lit. "two," is to be understood as "double, twofold" (cf. Exod 22:4 [3]: *dypla* "double"), designating an "evil" with two facets, a "double, twofold evil."

The Heb. form *rᶜwt*, "evils" (LXX: *ponēra*) of Jer 2:13, probably should be rendered here as "crimes," since abandoning God concurrent with or followed by idolatry is not a mere transgression or omission of a paragraph of law. It is actually an outrageous act of disloyalty against the God of Israel, who wants to be invoked by his personal name (YHWH) revealed to Moses at the beginning of Israel's history (Exod 3:14–15). This lexical nuance fits quite well with the context of our hymn and the hymnographer's selection of Jer 2:13 to describe what happened on the day of Jesus's trial in front of the Roman governor Pontius Pilate when the mob asked for Jesus's crucifixion and the release of Barabbas, a notorious rioter and murderer (Matt 27:15–26; Mark 15:6–15; Luke 23:13–25; John 18:38–40).

Jerome ingeniously bridges Israel's "double crime" with the opening lines of the Decalogue (Exod 20:2–3):

> Moreover, the people of God have committed two wrongs: first, they forsook God, the fountain of life, who gave to them a command saying, "I am the Lord your God, who brought you out of the land of Egypt" [Exod 20:2]; second, the issue written about in the same passage, "You shall have no other gods before me" [Exod 20:3]. But in place of God they followed demons, which are called "broken cisterns," because they are not capable

of containing the commandments of God. And one should take note of this: although God is an eternal fountain possessing living water, the land was nevertheless filled with cisterns and reservoirs drawn from torrential streams or some other turbid and rainy waters." (*Commentary on Jeremiah* 2:12–13)[66]

William Holladay wonders whether Jer 2:13 echoes Hos 10:10, which mentions Israel's "two iniquities."[67] In fact, Jerome is the first among ancient interpreters to suggest a connection between Jer 2:13 and Hos 10:10c:

Two injustices, for first they sinned in the idols of Micah, secondly in the calves of Jeroboam. Or certainly we are able to designate the two injustices of Samaria in Bethel and Dan, about which the prophet Jeremiah speaks: "My people have committed two evils; they have forsaken the fountain of living water and have dug out for themselves worthless cisterns that can hold no water" [Jer 2:13]. These two injustices are against the two precepts of the Decalogue, in which it is said: "I am the Lord your God; you shall have no other gods apart from me [Exod 20:2–3]." (*Commentary on Hosea* 10:10)[68]

Jer 2:13, quoted by our hymnographer, is part of a pericope (Jer 2:4–13) dealing with God's lawsuit against Israel, accused of "two evils," namely, apostasy (disloyalty) and idolatry.

"Broken (or leaky and cracked) cisterns" (i.e., idols) evoke the idea of worthlessness and emptiness, in vivid contrast with the idea of meaningfulness and abundance suggested by "well of living water" (i.e., the living God). The hymnographer transfers Jeremiah's divine saying from its religious-cultic context to a religious-political setting where Jesus's fate is decided in conjunction with that of a political insurrectionist. Nevertheless, the contrast between worthlessness and worth and the literary form (God's lawsuit against Israel) remain unchanged.

"The heaven was astonished by this [*exestē ho ouranos epi toutō*] and the sun hid [its] rays [*kai ho hēlios tas aktinas apekrypse*]"
"The heaven was astonished [*exestē*] by this" is a perfect calque of Jer 2:12a (LXX) and the immediate reaction of nature, represented here by "heaven" and "sun," to Israel's rejection of the "source of living water" disclosed in Jesus's crucifixion.

"The sun hid [its] rays" might be a subtle hint at the sudden darkness that occurred when Jesus was on the cross. This strange phenomenon is briefly recorded by the synoptic gospels (Matt 27:45; Mark 15:33; Luke 23:44–45a), with a bit more information in Luke, which has "And it was already about [*ēdē hōsei*] the sixth hour, and darkness began to hang [*skotos egeneto*] over the whole earth [*holēn tēn gēn*] until the ninth hour, while the sun was failing [*hēliou ekliipontos*]; and the curtain of the Temple [*to katapetasma tou naou*] was torn [in the] middle [*eschisthē ... meson*]"; cf. Amos 8:9: "And there will be on that day, says the Lord, and the sun will go down at noon [*dysetai ho hēlios mesēmbrias*], and light will turn into darkness [*syskoteasei*] upon the earth in the daytime."

According to Luke's gospel, Jesus already prophesied about this "darkness" on the night of his arrest when he enigmatically addressed the temple guards: "This is your hour [*hōra*] and the power of darkness [*exousia tou skotous*]" (Luke 22:53).

Luke describes the weird darkness that occurred in plain daylight as an eclipse, hence the use of the verb *ekleipō*, "to abandon, to fail," from which the noun *ekleipsis*, "abandonment, eclipse," derives.[69] Note Byz. of Luke 23:45a: "And the sun was darkened (*kai eskotisthē ho hēlios*)." However, as Joseph Fitzmyer remarks,[70] the best manuscripts have the genitive absolute, i.e., *ekliipontos* (aorist) or *ekleipontos* (present), "the sun was failing," as in the above-quoted textual version.

It is noteworthy that Luke's use of the verb *ekleipō*, "to abandon, to fail," with reference to the sun matches the hymnographer's use of the verb *enkataleipō*, "to forsake, to abandon," with respect to Israel abandoning God/Jesus, the source of life.

The "darkness" (*skotos*) mentioned in the synoptic gospels makes one think of the Old Testament concept of the "Day of the Lord," the *Dies irae* ("Day of Wrath") variant (cf. Zeph 1:15; Joel 2:10, 30–31 [3:3–4]). The earliest use of the phrase "Day of the Lord" is found in Isa 2:12 and Amos 5:18–20.[71]

Isa 2:12 reads: "For the day of the Lord Sabaoth [*hēmera kyriou sabaōth*][72] will be against [*epi*] everyone who is proud [*hybristēn*] and arrogant [*hyperēphanon*] and against who is lofty [*hypsilon*] and haughty [*meteōron*], and they shall be humbled [*tapeinōthēsontai*]."

Amos 5:20 has: "Is not the day of the Lord [*hēmera kyriou*] darkness and not light [*skotos ... kai ou phōs*], and gloom [*gnophos*] with no luster [*phengos*] in it?"

Lactantius (240–320) sees in Amos 8:9 a messianic prophecy regarding the unusual darkness occurring when Jesus was on the cross:

> Suspended, then, and fastened to his cross Christ cried out to God the Father in a loud voice and willingly laid down his life. In that same hour there was an earthquake, and the veil of the temple that separated the two tabernacles was cut in two, and the sun was suddenly withdrawn, and from the sixth hour until the ninth hour there was darkness [Mark 15:33]. The prophet Amos bears witness to this. "And it shall come to pass in that day, says the Lord, that the sun shall go down [*dysetai*] at midday [*mesēmbrias*], and the day shall be darkened [*syskotasei*] of light [*en hēmera*]. And I will turn your feasts into mourning and all your songs into lamentation [Amos 8:9–10]." (*Epitome of the Divine Institutes* 4.19)[73]

In our hymn, Jer 2:12a, 13, are to be considered "hermeneutical pointers."[74] The hymnographer uses v. 13 to create a synonymous parallel between old Israel and Jesus's contemporaries: they both abandoned the "source of living water" (God/Jesus) for voided substitutes ("broken cisterns": idols/insurrectionist Barabbas).

Here, the hymnographer creatively throws into the mix a subtle hint at Jer 17:13b (LXX), where the "source of life" is plainly equated with "the Lord." Then the hymnographer goes on by creating a contrast between Israel and nature with regard to their attitudes toward the crucified Jesus. For this purpose, the poet chooses Jer 2:12a, "heaven was astonished/perplexed by this," that is, by the fact that the source of life was abandoned and "crucified on a tree." Then he alludes to the weird darkness that occurred during the crucifixion as recorded by the synoptics (Matt 27:45; Mark 15:33; and especially Luke 23:44–45 hinting at a solar eclipse). "The sun hid its rays," he concludes, "but you, O Israel, were not ashamed." How did he arrive at such an interpretation of darkness? Apparently, for the hymnographer, the odd darkness is a sign of nature's participation in the sacred drama of Golgotha: the sun, astonished/puzzled by Israel's past and present attitudes toward God/Jesus, is now, during Jesus's crucifixion, hiding its face out of shame/embarrassment, while Jesus's contemporaries "were not ashamed" by their own monstrous deeds. The hymnographer uses a midrash-like hermeneutical procedure: interpreting a text by using other texts, with no obvious or direct connection among them. More specifically, the hymnographer interprets the "darkness" narrated in the gospel as a sign of "shamefulness" on the part of nature[75] and contrasting this with the "shamelessness" of the people by interconnecting Jer 2:12, 13, and 17:13.

Similarly, the Church Fathers quoted below see in the weird darkness present at Jesus's crucifixion a sign of nature's participation in the Golgotha event.

Co-suffering with the Crucified Lord

According to Ephrem the Syrian, the "darkness" indicates that the whole creation co-suffers with the crucified Christ:

> God was victorious over the Egyptians, and he lit up the way for the Hebrews with the pillar of fire in the month of Nisan [Exod 13:4, 21–22]. The sun became dark over them because they had returned evil for goodness. Just as God split the sea, the Spirit split the curtain in half, since they rejected and unjustly crucified the king of glory on the Skull [Golgotha, in Aramaic, Matt 27:33]. The curtain of the Temple was torn in two for this reason. Created beings suffered with him in his suffering. The sun hid its face so as not to see him when he was crucified. It retracted its light back into itself to die with him. There was darkness for three hours. The sun shined again, proclaiming that its Lord would rise from Sheol on the third day. The mountains trembled, the tombs were opened, and the curtain was torn [Matt 27:51–52], as though grieving in mourning over the impending destruction of the place. (*Commentary on Tatian's Diatessaron* 21.5)[76]

Lamenting over the Lord's Death

In Cyril of Alexandria's view, the creation laments over the dying of its Lord on a cross:

> When they fastened to the cross the Lord of all . . . creation itself mourned its Lord. The sun was darkened, and the rocks were split, and the Temple put on the mourners' clothes. Its veil was split from the top to the bottom. This is what God signified to us by the voice of Isaiah, saying, "I clothe the heavens with blackness, and make sackcloth their covering [Isa 50:3]." (*Commentary on Luke, Homily* 153)[77]

Covering the Lord's Nakedness, While Being Astonished
by Human Cruelty
In Melito of Sardis's view, the darkness was a sign of nature's humble witness
of Jesus's exposed nakedness on the cross:

> O mystifying murder! O mystifying injustice! The master is obscured by his
> body exposed, and is not held worthy of a veil to shield him from view. For
> this reason the great lights turned away, and the day was turned to dark-
> ness; to hide the one denuded on the tree, obscuring not the body of the
> Lord but human eyes. (*On Pascha* 97)[78]

The hymn ends with a quote from Luke 23:34 ("Father, forgive them; for
they know not what they do [*poiousin*]"), where Jesus's words on the cross are
resonating from a liturgical "today," while the action of those involved in his
crucifixion are pushed into the past.

The Slaughtered Lamb

> Beholding [*theōrousa*] [her] own Lamb [*ton idion arna*] being dragged
> [*helkomenon*] to the slaughter [*sphagēn*], the ewe [*hē amnas*] Mary followed
> [him] with other women, and [being] distraught [*trychomenē*], thus she
> cried, "Where are you going, O Child? For whose sake [*tinos charin*] are
> you finishing [*theleis*] such a fast race [*tachyn dromon*]? Is there another
> wedding in Cana? And are you rushing [*speudeis*] to make [*poiēsēs*] wine
> from the water for them? Am I to go with [*synelthō*] you, O Child [*teknon*],
> or rather wait [*meinō*] for you? Give me a word [*logon*], O Word [*loge*]! Do
> not pass [*parelthēs*] silently [*sigōn*] by me, whom you kept [*tērēsas*] chaste
> [*hagnēn*], for you are being [*hyparcheis*] my Son and my God." (Good
> Friday, Matins, Kontakion, Oikos)

In this hymn, where the emotional register of the Passion is heightened
by Mary's induction into the crucifixion scene, Good Friday is about a
slaughtered lamb and a distraught ewe; about an agonizing Jesus, dragged
and nailed fast to the cross, and a worn-out Mary, unable to help her son by
wiping out that nightmarish and grotesque spectacle resiliently unfolding on
Golgotha, "on a Friday afternoon,"[79] under her own tearing eyes.

The cast consists of the hymnographer, who introduces an inquiring Mary, and the shadowing, speechless silhouettes of Jesus, those responsible for his death, and a group of women who followed the Lord on his last trip to Jerusalem, even up to the cross (cf. Matt 27:55–56). There is a sharp contrast between a questioning mother devastated by grief and a living yet utterly silent decor.

The biblical texts quoted or alluded to in the hymn are given below in the order of their appearance.

"Beholding [her] own Lamb being dragged to the slaughter [*ton idiom arna . . . theōrousa pros sphagēn helkomenon*]"
The hymn opens with a partial quotation of Isa 53:7 (cf. Acts 8:32),[80] slightly altered: "And he (*autos*), while having been mistreated [*kekakōsthai*], did not open [his] mouth [*ouk anoigei to stoma*]; like a sheep [*probaton*] brought to the slaughter [*epi sphagēn ēchthē*], and like a voiceless lamb [*amnos . . . aphōnos*] before the one shearing [*keirontos*] it, so he does not open his mouth."

The hymnographer quotes the second colon (b) of Isa 53:7, about a "sheep" (*probaton*) being "led" (*ēchthē*) to the "slaughter" (*sphagēn*), and sets aside the first and last colons (a and c) depicting the weird "silence" of the Servant ("he" [*autos*])/"lamb" [*amnos*]), matched in our hymn by Mary's plea to her son: "Give me a word [*logon*], O Word [*loge*]! Do not pass [*parelthēs*] silently [*sigōn*] by me."

This interesting way of quoting Scripture—I would call it "paraphrase-quotation"—is a hermeneutical procedure that gives the hymnographer plenty of room in shaping the hymn in a creative manner while using the Scriptures aptly yet imaginatively so that the hymn's central theme, in this case Jesus's perfect self-offering obedience to his Father, may be better emphasized.

Returning now to Isa 53:7, one may add the Servant's conspicuous silence, which is in sharp contrast, for instance, with Job's complaining profile. They are both at prayer, but the Servant is oddly quiet, while Job is enervatingly vocal. The Hebrew language has more than twenty verbs to express crying or complaining, so the silence of the Servant seems quite insular. According to Lam 3:26–29, hope may be the cause of a petitioner's silence. Note that in Deut 3:23–29, Moses prays to God to allow him to cross the Jordan and see the promised land, but God's reply is as brief as it is chilling: "That is enough! Never speak to me of this matter again." In contrast to Moses's disobedience (Num 20:8-12, striking the rock instead of speaking to it) and divine punishment (Moses being forbidden to enter the promised land), the Servant's silence in Isa 53:7 is most likely a sign of his exemplary obeisance.[81]

In our hymn, the Servant's obedience before God and men is even more amplified and better detailed through Mary's insistence on having her son speak a word. Note the pun: "Give me a word [*logon*], O Word [*loge*]."

There are two lexical differences between Isa 53:7 and the present hymn. First, *probaton*, "sheep (to be slaughtered)," was replaced with *arēn*, "a young lamb (less than one year old)" (attested already in LXX, e.g., Gen 30:32, 33; Exod 12:5; 23:19). The term *arēn*, "lamb," is found in the New Testament once in Luke 10:3: "I send you as lambs [*arnas*; cf. Matt 10:16: *probata*] in midst of the wolves [*lykōn*]"—an antithesis between lambs and wolves emphasizing the defenselessness of Jesus's disciples (cf. Psalm of Solomon 8:23: "God's righteous [saints] are like guileless lambs in their [nations'] midst" [*hosoi tou theou hōs arnia en akakia en mesō autōn*]) and the sureness of God's protection.[82]

The term *arēn*, "young lamb (less than one year old),"[83] in the present hymn was likely chosen to underline Jesus's vulnerability—even better intensified by the fact that Mary is painted here as *amnas*, "young unweaned ewe-lamb" (instead of *probaton*, "sheep," an adult animal). Interestingly, the mother–son relationship is described with two terms designating young animals (male and female lambs) characterized by age proximity. Moreover, the use of *amnas*, for a female lamb that has not given birth, instead of *probaton*, "sheep," may be taken as a subtle allusion to the virginity of Jesus's mother. Although she is a mother, after Jesus' birth, Mary remains a virgin ("young ewe-lamb").

The second lexical difference between the Isaian text and the hymn is that the verb *agō*, "to bring," was substituted with the verb *helkō*, "to draw, to drag," to underscore the compelling aspect or cruelty of the action by which Jesus was carried, "dragged," to the place of execution.

A similar image to the one in Isa 53:7b is found in Jer 11:19, where the prophet likens himself to a "guileless lamb" (*arnion akakon*): "But I was, like a guileless lamb [*arnion akakon*], brought to be sacrificed [*agomenon tou thyesthai*], without knowing [*ouk egnōn*]. They devised [*elogisanto*] an evil plan [*logismon ponēron*] against me, saying: 'Let us cast wood into his bread [*xylon eis ton arton*] and eliminate [*ektripsōmen*] him from the land of the living, and his name will be no longer remembered.'"

Jeremiah states that he was innocent, unaware of the conspirators' plot. The term *arnion* (Heb. *kebeś*, "lamb"; five of the 116 Old Testament occurrences of this word refer to a sacrificial lamb) occurs in the LXX (e.g., Jer 11:19; 50 [27]:45; Ps 114 [113]:4, 6; Psalm of Solomon 8:23), designating a young lamb. This made the ancient translators (LXX, V, T) choose "led to sacrifice" (LXX: *agomenon tou thyesthai*) for the second colon, even though the MT has *ṭbḥ*, "to slaughter," and not *zbḥ*, "to sacrifice." Likely, Jeremiah thought of himself as a sacrificial lamb. The image of a lamb brought to "slaughter" (MT verb *ṭbḥ*), found in Jer (LXX: *thyesthai*), influenced Deutero-Isaiah in Isa 53:7 (LXX: *epi sphagēn*).[84]

The description of Jesus as a lamb occurs four times in the New Testament: John 1:29, 36; Acts 8:32 (quoting Isa 53:7); 1 Pet 1:19 (of Jesus, the Paschal lamb with no blemish; cf. Exod 12:5).

In John 1:29, John the Baptist calls Jesus "the lamb of God who takes away the sin of the world [*ho amnos tou theou ho airōn tēn hamartian tou kosmou*]," and in v. 36, simply "the lamb of God [*ho amnos tou theou*]."[85] The term *amnos*, "one-year-old lamb" (compared to *arnion* for an infant sheep [John 21:15; Rev 5:6, 8, 12]) designates a young horned ram, corresponding to Heb. *kebeś* for a young adult animal/ram, usually a sacrificial animal (Exod 12:5: *śh … mn-h-kbśym*; LXX: *arnion … ek probatōn*).

Something similar to the hymn's ewe-lamb metaphor may be found in a Jewish pseudepigraphon. In the *Testament of Joseph* 19:8–9 (Armenian version), Joseph foresees Israel's restoration (8–12 extant parallel Gk. and Armenian versions): "And I saw that a virgin was born from Judah, wearing a linen stole; and from her was born a spotless lamb [*amnos amōmos*]. At his left there was something like a lion, and all the wild animals [*ta thēria*] rushed against him, but the lamb conquered [*enikēsen*] them, and destroyed [*apōlesen*] them, trampling them underfoot. And the angels and mankind and all the earth rejoiced over him."[86]

In our hymn, is the lamb (*arēn*) to which Jesus is likened a sacrificial animal[87] or simply a metaphor for the obedient Servant of the Lord of Isa 53? Since the second century in Christian literature (e.g., *Letter of Barnabas* 2:5 [cf. Isa 1:11]), *arēn* has been used as a default term for an animal ready for slaughter.

Most likely, the hymnographer conflated several textual strands, such as Isa 53:7, John 1:29, 36, and 1 Pet 1:19 (cf. Exod 12:5; John 19:36), to paint a composite portrait with two central interweaving figures, those of a slaughtered/Paschal lamb and an obedient servant. In the context of this hymn and of the entire Good Friday liturgical hymnography, an utterly silent heavenly Father and a natural mother, Mary, who is a thoroughly distraught ewe unceasingly questioning her son about his conspicuous, quasi-mysterious silence, are magisterially put in relief with the unwavering commitment of Jesus to do God's will and die for others.

The Distraught Ewe

"The ewe . . . [being] distraught [*hē amnas . . . trychomenē*]"
During her son's sufferings that lead to the cross, Mary is likened to a "distraught ewe." The term *amnas* (feminine of *amnos*, "lamb") designates a young "ewe-lamb" (a young, usually unweaned, female sheep). Maybe the best-known biblical text where *amnas* occurs is Nathan's parable in 2 Sam 12:3, 4, 6, about a poor man and his only treasure, "one little ewe-lamb [*amnas mia mikra*]."

For a sin offering (i.e., "sins of omission" vs. "sins of commission," in Lev 4:27–35), Lev 5:6 prescribes a female from the flock (sheep or goats).[88] Most likely, the hymnographer had this text in mind when he chose *amnas* as metaphor for Mary, willing to be part of her son's atoning sacrifice.

In his Paschal homily (*Peri Pascha*),[89] Melito of Sardis, inspired by John 1:29, calls the Virgin Mary the "fair ewe-lamb" (*kalēs amnados*) from whom the "slain lamb" (*amnos phoneuomenos*) was born:

> It is he who became incarnate in a Virgin, who was hung upon the wood, who was buried in the earth, who was raised from among the dead, who was lifted up to the heights of heaven. He is the mute lamb. He is the slain lamb. He is born of Mary, the fair ewe. He is taken from the flock and delivered over to immolation, and slain in the evening, and buried in the night; who was broken on the wood, was not corrupted in the earth. He rose from the dead, and raised man from the depths of the tomb." (*On the Pascha*, 71, 11.513–520)[90]

Melito uses the "ewe-lamb" metaphor with its Old Testament connotation of sacrifice and virginal purity (Lev 5:6; Num 6:14; 7:17), thus underscoring the role of the Virgin Mary in the atoning sacrifice of her son,[91] a "Paschal duet" of sorts found also in the present hymn.

Proclus of Constantinople (ca. 385–446) proclaims in his Christological and Marian homilies that Christ, "lamb" and "shepherd," was born from the "virginal ewe-lamb" (*parthenikēs amnados*). Interestingly, both Proclus and our hymnographer place emphasis on the virginal purity of Mary, the ewe-lamb:

> Let the shepherds get together for the sake of the Shepherd who came forth from the virginal ewe-lamb [*dia ton ek tēs parthenikēs amnados proelthonta poimena*]. (Proclus, *Homily on Nativity* 4.35)[92]

> Blessed is God, who descended from heaven like "rain on the virginal fleece" [Judg 6:37–40], and was born like a lamb [*amnos*] from Mary, the ewe-lamb [*amnados*]. "You are the Lamb of God who removes the sins of the world" [John 1:29)], for you were shorn by shears of the cross [*psalidi tou staurou*], clothing [*enedysas*] the world in incorruption [*aphtharsia*] [1 Cor 15:53]. (Proclus, *Homily on Crucifixion* 29.2)[93]

In hymnography, the ewe-lamb metaphor occurs numerous times with Mary giving birth to Christ or lamenting over her son nailed to the cross. Here is an example of the former:

> O Cave, make yourself ready, for the ewe-lamb [*hē amnas*] is coming, carrying the unborn [*embryon*] Christ. O Manger [*phantē*], receive hospitably the one who released us the earthlings [*gēgeneis*] from the irrational work [*alogou praxeōs*] by [his] word. . . . For the Lord appeared [*ophthē*] from a Virgin Mother; however she, bending [*kypsasa*] over him as a servant, worshiped [*prosekynēse*] him, and she accosted [*prosephthenxato*] the one in her arms [*ankalais*]: "How were you seeded [*enesparēs*] in me, or how were you implanted [*enephyēs*] in me, O my Redeemer and God." (Eve of Nativity [December 24], Vespers, Sticheron)

One may add that the ewe-lamb metaphor is used also for female martyrs. The common denominator between them and the Holy Mother is a strong commitment to co-suffer with Christ, the Lord of Passion, as can be seen in the following hymn:

> Your ewe-lamb [*amnas*], O Jesus, cries with a great voice: "O my Bridegroom [*nymphie*], for you do I long [*pothō*], and seeking you do I contend [*athlō*]; and I am crucified and buried with you [*systauroumai kai synthaptomai*] in your baptism; and I suffer [*paschō*] for your sake, so that I may reign [*basileusō*] with you; and I die [*thniskō*] for you, so that I may live [*zēsō*]

in you. At last, accept [*prosdechou*] me like a blameless sacrifice [*thysian amōmon*] as I offer myself [*tytheisan*] to you with longing [*pothou*]." Through her prayers, save our souls, O merciful One. (Horologion/ Menaion, General Apolytikion for a Woman Martyr)

Returning to the hymn under examination, one notices that the ewe is thoroughly "distraught" (*trychomenē*), unable even to express her intense pain while beholding her son "dragged [*helkomenon*] to the slaughter [*sphagēn*]." Her pain is intensified by the fact that her son, who showed his power at the wedding of Cana (John 2), is now utterly silent, reaching willingly the lowest point of human frailty, proving that he is truly the "Son of Man."[94] Yet she still hopes that her son will eventually show his power as he did at Cana, hence her insistent pleas aimed at making her son speak and act for his own salvation.

The term *trychomenē*, tentatively rendered "distraught, devastated," might be a borrowing from Wis 14:15: "For a father distraught [*trychomenos*] by untimely grief [*aōrō penthei*], having made an image [*eikona*] of the child who was quickly taken away [*tacheōs aphairethentos*], now honored [*etimēsen*] as a god what was once a dead human being [*nekron anthrōpon*] and handed over [*paredōken*] to [his] subjects [*hypocheirois*] mysteries [*mystēria*] and initiations [in the mysteries] [*teletas*]."

The term *aōrō*, "untimely," in "untimely grief" (*aōrō penthei*) refers, in fact, to the son's death. This is an example of hypallage,[95] a figure of speech, when a modifier, in our case *aōrō*, "untimely," is syntactically linked to an item, *aphairethentos*, "taken away" (died), other than the one it modifies semantically, i.e., *penthei*, "grief." Thus, the father's devastating grief is caused by his son's "untimely death."

The connection between a mother's devastating grief and a son's untimely death may be clearly seen in the following hymn:

The spotless [*aspilos*] Virgin [*parthenos*], when she saw [*blepousa*] the One [*hon*] whom she birthed [*eteke*] from a seedless womb [*asporou . . . gastros*], unable to bear the wound of her inward parts [*splanchnōn trōsin*], distraught [*trychomenē*] she said: "How have you been hung [*enapeōrēsai*] on a cross as a condemned one [*katakritos*], you who hold fast [*kratōn*] all the creation by [your] command [*neumati*]? By all means, you want to save humanity [*anthrōpinon*]!" (Wednesday of Cheese Week, Vespers, Apostichon, Theotokion)

If the choice of the term *trychomenē*, "distraught," in the hymn was informed or inspired by Wis 14:15, then the hymnographer's intent was to express a mother's devastating grief at her son's untimely death. In this case, the hymnographer betrays a good grasp of Scriptures, by choosing such a rare term (it occurs only twice in the entire Bible, Wis 11:11 [of the Israelites in the wilderness]; 14:15) to establish an intriguing intertextuality at the level of two distinct literary corpora, Bible and hymnography.

Mary's monologue that never turns, as initially intended, into a dialogue with her son concerns two points of interest: Why did Jesus become so quiet? Will he return to the glorious beginning by offering a new miracle like the one at the wedding of Cana? In other words, will Jesus reverse the current situation dominated by silence and weakness into a different one characterized by his authoritative speech at Cana ("Woman, what do you want from me? My hour has not come yet," John 2:4) and perform another "sign" of power (i.e., "making [*poiēsēs*] wine from water," vs. the gospel's subtle wording, "the steward of the feast [*architriklinos*] tasted [*egeusato*] the water which had become [*gegenēmenon*] wine," John 2:9)? On the road to Golgotha, as at Cana, Mary is the one who talks to her son; but if at Cana, Jesus quickly retorted, on the road to Golgotha, he remains conspicuously speechless.

It is worth noting that in the gospel of John, Mary appears twice, once at the beginning (at the wedding of Cana, John 2) and once at the end (at the foot of the cross of Golgotha, John 19) of Jesus's earthly journey. At Cana as at the cross, Jesus revealed his divinity in two ways: by a miracle facilitated by his mother and by obedience toward God and men (giving his mother into the care of his disciple).

Jesus's eagerness to offer himself as a sacrifice is described in terms of a "fast race [*tachyn dromon*]." Interestingly, the same term, *dromos*, "race, course," connoting one's life journey is employed with reference to John the Baptist (Acts 13:25) and the apostle Paul (Acts 20:24; 2 Tim 4:7), both having ended their lives as martyrs.

"Do not pass silently by me, whom you kept chaste [*mē sigōn parelthēs me, ho hagnēn tērēsas me*]"

Interestingly, the Passion is connected to the virginal birth. Mary reminds her silent son that, though she gave him birth, he kept her "chaste" (*hagnēn*), hence the hymnographer's peculiar lexical choice (*amnas*, a young, unweaned lamb that has not birthed). What is the theological significance of connecting Mary's "ever-virginity" (*aeiparthenos*) to Jesus's Passion and cross?

In order to answer this question, I offer a short passage from Irenaeus's work *Against the Heresies*, where the second-century writer mentions that the "pure one" (Jesus) "opened purely that pure womb [of Mary] which regenerates human beings unto God":

> There are those who say that "He is a man, and who shall know him?" [Jer 17:9], and, "I came unto the prophetess, and she bore a son, and his name is called Wonderful Counselor, the Mighty God" [Isa 8:3; 9:6], and those who proclaimed the Immanuel, born of the Virgin [Isa 7:14]: declaring the union of the Word of God with his own handiwork, that the Word would become flesh, and the Son of God the Son of man—*the pure one opening purely that pure womb which regenerates human beings unto God and which he himself made pure*—having become that which we are, he is "God Almighty" and has a generation which cannot be declared. (*Against the Heresies* 4.33.11)[96]

According to Matthew Steenberg, Irenaeus grants Mary along with her son a "recapitulatory role" in the salvific work.[97] Through Jesus's voluntarily accepted Passion and cross, Mary becomes mother or *genetrix* of the Church. Steenberg calls this recapitulation (Lat. *recapitulatio*; Gk. *anakephalaiōsis*, cf. Eph 1:10) "social," which runs parallel to a "theological" recapitulation of Adam's children by Christ. If Christ recapitulates humanity itself, Mary does it by restoring the interrelatedness with which humanity was equipped since its creation. Mary restores what Eve damaged, that is, the social or relational defining aspect of humanity.

In our hymn, Mary declares that Jesus preserved her "chastity" (virginity), so at the foot of the cross her pure womb may regenerate unto God all those restored by her son's atoning sacrifice; hence the inspired lexical choice *amnas*, "unweaned ewe-lamb, which has not yet mothered," that underlines Mary's "ever-virginity" and her "co-recapitulatory" role.

The Last Sunset

Today, the blameless Virgin [*amemptos parthenos*] is beholding [*theōrousa*] you hanging [*anartōmenon*] on the cross, O Word! She is lamenting [*odyromenē*] with motherly affections [*mētrōa splanchna*], and [her] heart was wounded bitterly [*etetrōto pikrōs*]. She was sighing [*stenazousa*] painfully [*odynērōs*] from the depths of [her] soul. By tearing [*kataxainousa*] at [her] face [*pareias*] and hair [*thrixi*], she became utterly distraught [*katetrycheto*]. Then, beating [*typtousa*] [her] breast [*stēthos*], she cried aloud mournfully [*goerōs*]. "Woe to me [*oimoi*], Divine Child [*theion teknon*]! Woe to me, the Light of the world! Why did you go down [*edys*] from my eyes, O Lamb of God [*ho amnos tou theou*]?" Then the hosts of the bodiless [beings] [*hai stratiai tōn asōmatōn*], seized [*syneichonto*] with trembling [*tromō*], said: "Incomprehensible [*akatalēpte*] Lord, glory to you!" (Good Friday, Matins, Apostichon, Idiomelon)

This graphically detailed description of a mother's unspeakable grief at the sight of her son hanging on a cross stands as a sequel to the hymn analyzed above. Mary is introduced as "blameless Virgin" (*amemptos parthenos*) and Jesus as "Lamb of God" (*amnos tou theou*; John 1:29, 36). The mother's devastation is described here with a finite verb, *katetrycheto*, "she became utterly distraught," compared to a passive participle, *trychomenē*, "distraught, devastated," found in the previous hymn.

"She is lamenting with motherly emotions [*odyromenē mētrōa splanchna*]" The phrase *mētrōa splanchna*, "motherly affections" (*splanchna*, lit. "inward parts, womb"),[98] echoes back to "motherly womb," *mētrōas gastros*, in 4 Macc 13:19. The hymnographer uses this phrase as "hermeneutical pointer," as if inviting the listener to link the two famous biblical mothers, Jesus's mother and the mother of the seven Maccabean brothers. Both mothers are confronted with the most difficult situation a mother could encounter: to see her child dying under her helpless eyes.

Both mothers suffer enormously seeing their children in extreme pain and dying untimely deaths at the hands of their persecutors. However, their motherly affections do not diminish their resolute faith. Both mothers are depicted as strong characters marked by a visceral compassion and love for their children yet fully obedient to God's will.

The hymnographer portrays the Theotokos at the foot of the cross as lamenting and torn apart between her maternal affections and her trust in God's Word (cf. Luke 1:38). Eventually, the suffering mother becomes "thoroughly distraught/devastated" (*katetrycheto*).

One can imagine Mary's bitter experience while reading the following biblical encomium composed for the courageous mother of the seven Maccabean brothers:

O more noble [*gennaiotera*] than males in patience [*karterian*], and more courageous [*andreiotera*] than men in endurance [*hypomonēn*]. . . . Sunk [*periantloumenē*] in the deluge [*kataklysmō*] of passions from every side [*pantachothen*] and oppressed [*synechomenē*] by the strong winds of the tortures [*basanois*] of your sons, nobly [*gennaiōs*] endured [*hypemeinas*] the storms [*cheimōnas*] that befell [you] for [your] piety [*eusebeias*]. (4 Macc 15:30, 32)

"Why did you go down from my eyes, O Lamb of God [*tis edys ex ophthalmōn mou, ho amnos tou theou*]?"
Unlike the former hymn, where Mary questioned her son's odd silence, this one focuses on Jesus's "sunset." Jesus, the "light of the world," exactly like a sun, comes to his own setting, more precisely, goes down from his mother's eyes.

The sunset imagery should first be read in light of Mal 4:2 (3:20), where *hēlios dikaiosynēs*, "sun of righteousness" (a hapax legomenon phrase), will rise for those who fear God's name: "And the sun of righteousness shall rise for you, fearers of my name. Healing [is] in its wings. And you will go out and leap like calves loosened from ties" (Mal 4:2 [3:20]).

Is the "sun of righteousness" an indigenous solar epithet for Yahweh, a figurative description of the eschatological day, or a mere influence from Persian Zoroastrianism?[99] Ancient Israel has been reluctant to use "sun" as a metaphor for Yahweh, given the popularity of the sun god outside Israel (e.g., Egypt and Mesopotamia). The presence of the theologically loaded term *ṣədāqāh* (Gk. *dikaiosynē*), "righteousness," as a qualifier makes one accept this phrase as an epithet for Yahweh. Moreover, throughout the history of Christian interpretation, this title has been applied to Christ.[100]

Taking into account the divine epithet pertaining to God/Christ, I tend to believe that the hymn alludes to Amos 8:9 (already quoted and discussed in this Good Friday chapter). This explanation fits quite well with the parallel between the physical sun prophesied to "go down at noon" and the Lamb of God, the "sun of righteousness," going down from his mother's sight, perhaps concurrently with the former. Or the natural sun was darkened because Jesus, the "sun of righteousness," set down first.

Note that Amos and the hymn employ the same verb, *dynō*, "to sink, to go down," to describe the sunset, literally and figuratively: "And there will be on that day, says the Lord, and the sun will go down at noon [*dysetai ho hēlios mesēmbrias*], and light will turn into darkness [*syskotasei*] upon the earth in the daytime" (Amos 8:9).

According to Luke 23:44–45a, Amos's prophetic word was fulfilled when Jesus was on the cross, more precisely, from noon until around three p.m.: "And it was already around [*ēdē hōsei*] the sixth hour, and darkness began to hang [*skotos egeneto*] over the whole earth [*holēn tēn gēn*] until the ninth hour, while the sun was failing [*hēliou eklipontos*]; and the curtain of the Temple [*to katapetasma tou naou*] was torn [in the] middle [*eschisthē . . . meson*]."

In the hymnographer's view, the odd darkening phenomenon related by the gospel writer is surpassed in magnitude by another, odder phenomenon when Jesus, the Divine Child, the Light of the World, goes down from his mother's tearing eyes. This is the last sunset of the Lamb of God, ushering in the Sabbath of Sabbaths.

6

Overcoming

Jonah and the Never-Setting Light—Holy Saturday

Overview

Holy Saturday is the Sabbath of Sabbaths. As the Creator marks the end of his creative work by sanctifying the Sabbath (Gen 2:3), so Jesus, at the end of his salvific work, sabbatizes in the tomb, a gateway to the underworld (Hades).

> On Great and Holy Saturday [*tō hagiō kai megalō sabbatō*], we celebrate [*heortazomen*] the divine-bodily Tomb [*tēn theosōmon taphēn*] and the descent into Hades [*tēn eis hadou kathodon*] of our Lord and Savior Jesus Christ, through which he recalled [*anaklēthen*] our very family [*to hēmeteron genos*] from corruption [*phthoras*] and carried [*metabebēke*] it into life eternal. (Synaxarion)

By his body lying in a tomb, by his spirit descending to Hades, Jesus overcomes the last fortress of evil and corruption, while liberating its denizens from that realm of darkness and hopelessness. It is a Sabbath like many other Sabbaths during Jesus's earthly life, an opportunity for him to sanctify this special day by doing good to those in need.

This twofold episode, which chronologically occurred on Friday late in the afternoon, marks liturgically a transition from Good Friday to Holy Saturday. Ps 104 (103), a doxological description of God as the Creator, is used by the hymnographer to introduce his *theologoumenon*: the creator of all visible and invisible reality, the one who vests himself with light, is now dead, naked, and with no tomb. The creation participates in this unspeakable tragedy: the sun vests itself in darkness, the earth surges, and the Temple veil is torn in two.

After having been taken down from the cross, Jesus is laid to rest in Joseph's tomb. However, the lion of Judah praised by patriarch Jacob (Gen 49:9) cannot be held by death. The "sleeping lion" metaphor captures somehow the paradox of Jesus in the tomb: as human being, dead; as God,

Hearing the Scriptures. Eugen J. Pentiuc, Oxford University Press. © Oxford University Press 2021.
DOI: 10.1093/oso/9780190239633.003.0007

alive and confronting Hades. Apparently, the one who shut the abyss (Prayer of Manasseh 1:3; cf. Gen 1:2; 8:1–2) is now the prisoner of a tomb, another victim for the insatiable Hades.

The very first Sabbath at the dawn of creation was a type for the Sabbath that Jesus spent in the tomb. The first Sabbath's "blessing" (Gen 2:3; cf. Exod 20:11) was somehow transferred to Jesus's Sabbath in the tomb.

According to Church tradition beginning with the apostolic period (e.g., 1 Pet 3:18–20; Eph 4:9), the tomb was not the final destination on Jesus's itinerary. In spirit, Jesus descended to the netherworld to preach the gospel of salvation and save those who would follow him.

The "one born of Mary," being accepted by a self-deceived Hades in its realm, shows his divine power by "shattering the bronze gates" (Ps 107 [106]:16) of the realm of darkness, destroying its "rulers" (Hab 3:13–14), and "raising" its captive denizens (cf. 1 Sam 2:6; Ps 16 [15]:10).

Jesus is named in the hymnography of Holy Saturday as "a deified mortal spotted with bruises, yet still powerful in action," which conveys a shocking appearance of Jesus in Hades, still bearing the traces of wounds and suffering yet being so powerful and quick in action that everyone there was taken aback. Hades was embittered at the encounter with the divine Jesus (cf. Isa 14:9 [LXX]), the intruder who disturbed and dismantled once and for all the Hades realm.

Through his victorious descent to Hades, Jesus achieved the restoration of human "nature" (*hypostasis*) located in the "lowest parts of the earth" (Ps 139 [138]:15), in the hymn a metaphor for Hades. He made corrupted human nature "brand new" (*kainos*), not merely "new" (*neos*); not refurbished, but recreated.

The same divine, creative Wisdom who shared a free banquet (Prov 8–9) on Holy Thursday through a self-offering is now entering the tomb pouring streams of life to the ones held in captivity as far as the "impenetrable innermost parts" of Hades (Wis 17:4–5, 14[13]–15[14]). There is no noise of battle, no clash of weapons, only streams of life flooding the realm of corruption, evil, and death. A victory with no battle, just an irresistible invasion of goodness, light, and life that brings Hades to its final chapter.

The ultimate goal of Jesus's descent was reached when the "inner rooms of death" (Prov 7:27 [LXX]) were shut and Hades's royal chambers emptied, thus diminishing the power of death and Hades.

In the descent of Jesus to Hades, so minutely depicted by Holy Saturday's hymns, Jonah the prophet, swallowed by a big fish and disgorged out onto the earth after three days and nights, becomes the foreshadowing, the type par excellence, of Jesus's unseen victory.

Jonah, "enclosed but not detained," in the big fish, proclaims Jesus's survival and victory in the midst of Hades. "Jonah springing up from the beast" underscores Jesus's power to come out of Hades due to his divinity which could not be retained in the realm of corruption and death. As a bridegroom, Jonah springs up from the cetacean as from a "bridal chamber" (*thalamos*) (3 Macc 1:18), addressing over time the guards set to watch over Jesus's tomb by critiquing them for abandoning Christ, the source of all mercy (cf. Jonah 2:8 [9])

The "great light" Isaiah saw (Isa 9:2 [1]) turns into the "never-setting light" the hymnographer uses in reference to Christ the Victor. Isaiah (Isa 26:9), "having risen early in the night," was awakened from his sleep in the dead of night as if it were daylight; the same light that destroyed Hades is now filling the entire time-space continuum, making the entire creation turn to the primordial light that "appeared" at God's behest out of darkness (Gen 1:3). The dead stand up, and those living on earth rejoice; the new, endless eon is about to begin.

The Old Testament lections spread over the various services of Holy Saturday are meant to direct the worshiper's attention to what happened after Jesus's entombment and the consequences of Jesus enduring suffering and death. Dan 3 (the three youths in the fiery furnace) reminds us that Jesus's Passion is a story of faithfulness, survival, and divine intervention. Jonah 1–4 (Jonah's stay in the belly of a big fish) correlates with Jesus's logion on the "sign of Jonah" (Matt 12:40) and prefigures Jesus's descent to Hades and his proclamation of the gospel to the "spirits" (cf. 1 Pet 3:18–20). Isa 52:14–54:1 (the Servant of the Lord, deprived of form, honor, and glory, suffering for sinners and making an eternal covenant of peace) tells us that Jesus's Passion brought reconciliation between God and humanity and within humanity itself. Exod 33:11–23 (Moses's intercession to see God's "glory") and Job 42:12–17 (Job's fortunes restored twofold) are about the restoration and glorification of human nature. Ezek 37:1–14 (the vision of the dry bones revived by God's Spirit) is meant to connect Jesus's victory over death and Hades to the final and universal bodily resurrection.

Timeline: The gospels are quiet with respect to what really happened to Jesus on Holy Saturday. However, Church tradition, including hymnography, teaches that while his lifeless body was in the tomb, Jesus descended, in spirit, to the underworld to save those who were held in captivity. Jesus's "descent to

Hades" and his victory over the realm of darkness form the central theme of the Vesperal Liturgy of Saint Basil celebrated on Saturday morning.

Services and lections for Holy Saturday: Vespers of Holy Saturday (Removal from the Cross) (officiated on Holy Friday afternoon): Exod 33:11–23; Job 42:12–17; Isa 52:14–54:1; 1 Cor 1:18–31; 2:1–2; Matt 27:1–38; Luke 23:39–43; Matt 27:39–54; John 19:31–37; Matt 27:55–61; Matins and Graveside Lamentations (officiated by anticipation on Holy Friday evening): Ezek 37:1–14; 1 Cor 5:6–8; Gal 3:13–14; Matt 27:62–66; Vespers of Pascha (officiated with the Liturgy of Saint Basil on Holy Saturday morning): Gen 1:1–13; Jonah 1–4; Dan 3:1–56 (and the Hymn of the Holy Three Servants); Liturgy of Saint Basil: Rom 6:3–11; Matt 28:1–20.

Analysis
Taking Down from the Cross

It is you throwing [*anaballomenon*] the light [*to phōs*] on yourself as a cloak [*himation*], whom Joseph, along with Nicodemus, took down [*kathelōn*] from the wood [*xylou*] [of the cross]. When he beheld [*theōrēsas*] you, dead [*nekron*], naked [*gymnon*], [with] no tomb [*ataphon*], taking up [*analabōn*] a compassionate lament [*eusympathēton thrēnon*], mourning [*odyromenos*], did he say: "Ah me, O sweetest [*glykytate*] Jesus! When the sun, just a little earlier [*pro mikrou*], beheld you hanging [*kremamenon*] on the cross, it wrapped [itself] [*perieballeto*] in darkness [*zophon*]; and out of fear, the earth surged [*ekymaineto*], the curtain of the Temple [*naou to katapetasma*] was rent to pieces [*dierrēgnyto*]. And now, lo, I see [*blepō*] you undergoing [*hypelthonta*] voluntarily [*hekousiōs*] death for me. How shall I prepare you for funeral [*kēdeusō*], O my God? Or, how can I wrap [*heilēsō*] you in shrouds [*syndosin*]? With what hands shall I touch [*prospsausō*] your very undefiled [*akēraton*] body, or what songs [*asmata*] shall I sing [*melpsō*] at your very departure [*exodō*], O compassionate One [*oiktirmon*]? I magnify [*megalynō*] your Passion, I praise [*hymnologō*] also your entombment [*taphēn*], along with your resurrection [*anastasei*], crying out: O Lord, glory to you!" (Holy Saturday, Vespers, Apostichon)

This hymn makes a smooth transition from Good Friday centered on crucifixion and Holy Saturday focusing on Jesus's entombment and his descent to Hades.

"It is you throwing the light on yourself as a cloak, whom Joseph,
along with Nicodemus, took down from the wood [of the cross] [*se ton
anaballomenon to phōs ōsper himation, kathelōn Iōsēph apo tou xylou, syn
Nikodēmō*]"

The hymnographer opens his poem with a quote from Ps 104 (103):2a: "throwing [*anaballomenos*] light [upon himself] as a cloak [*himation*], spreading out
[*ekteinōn*] the sky like a hide [*derrin*]."

Ps 104 (103) paints God as the Creator of the world, a world that can be
described using different lenses (scientific, aesthetical, social, economic).
The psalmist uses the lens and language of faith: God appears in this psalm
as both Creator and provider.[1] And these are perhaps the main aspects
the hymnographer wants his hearers or readers to keep in mind when
they visualize Joseph of Arimathea taking Jesus's lifeless body and laying
it in his tomb. The Creator who gives life graciously to any creature is now
dead. The one who provides bountifully has not even a tomb in which to
be buried.

The "light" (Heb. *'ôr*; Gk. *phōs*) in Ps 104 (103):2a is the same primordial
light that appeared at God's mere command on the very first day of creation (Gen 1:3: "God said: 'Let there be [*genēthētō*] light!' And it was [*egeneto*]
light") and not the "sun" as Mitchell Dahood suggested, based on a similar
image found in Rev 12:1 ("A great sign appeared in heaven, a woman having
the sun thrown around [herself] [*gynē peribeblēmenē ton hēlion*]").[2]

Quoting Ps 104 (103):2a, with its emphasis on the primeval "light," the
hymnographer seeks to equate the dead and naked Jesus with the Creator
who majestically opened his work by commanding the light, the "corner-
stone" of the entire creation, to shine out of nothingness. And the light, the
most mysterious of God's creatures,[3] becomes the cloak of one who, on a
Friday afternoon, on the rocky Golgotha, will appear naked and lifeless.

"When he beheld you, dead, naked, [with] no tomb [*theōrēsas nekron
gymnon ataphon*]"

This line describes Jesus in the moment when Joseph was about to "take
down" (*kathelōn*; cf. Mark 15:46; Luke 23:53) his lifeless body from the wood
of the cross. The three features of this description are contrasted with three
aspects of the hymn's opening line: (1) *nekros*, "dead," mighty enough to
throw the light upon himself as a cloak; (2) *gymnos*, "naked," light as a garment; (3) *ataphos*, "[with] no tomb," the whole universe, including the light
(Gen 1:3), belongs to him.

The first contrast, between Jesus throwing the light upon himself as a cloak and his lifeless body being taken down from the cross by Joseph, reminds one of Jesus's prophetic words to Peter: "When you were younger [*neōteros*], you girded yourself [*ezōnnyes seauton*], and walked [*periepateis*] wherever you wanted; when you will be older [*gērasēs*], you will stretch [*ekteneis*] your hands and someone else will gird you and carry [*oisei*] where you do not want" (John 21:18). When you were younger, you girded yourself; when you are older, someone else will gird you.

"Taking up a compassionate lamentation, mourning, did he say
[*eusympathēton thrēnon analabōn odyromenos, elegen*]"
Another interesting contrast can be detected in Joseph's two concurring actions: he "took down" (*kathelōn*) Jesus's lifeless body from the cross while "taking up [a lamentation]" (*analabōn*)—taking down and taking up.

Joseph's "lamentation" (*thrēnos*) may be read in parallel with David's dirge for Saul and Jonathan (2 Sam 1:17: *ethrēnēsen* "[David] lamented"), as well as and on the same emotional register of a tender relationship between two friends. Note that the qualifier *eusympathēton* "[well] compassionate" describing Joseph's lamentation is absent in the LXX and the New Testament but is well attested in the Byzantine literary corpus.[4]

The lamentation is intensified by the presence of the participle *odyromenos*, "mourning," a hapax legomenon (Jer 31 [38]:18, of Ephraim's repentance), related to the noun *odyrmos*, "weeping, lamentation," found in Matt 2:18 (referring to the killing in Bethlehem of the children less than two years old by King Herod while searching for the newborn Jesus; citing Jer 31 [38]:15, Rachel's lamentation). If the hymnographer had in mind *odyrmos* of Matt 2:18 when he chose *odyromenos*, then the past lamentation for the innocent children of Bethlehem turns now into a lamentation for the innocent Jesus, who escaped the first but not the second persecution.

"When the sun, just a little earlier, beheld you hanging on the cross, it wrapped [itself] in darkness [*pro mikrou ho hēlios en staurō kremamenon theasamenos zophon perieballeto*]"
At the sight of Jesus "hanging" (*kremamenon*)[5] on the cross, the sun "wrapped [itself] in darkness" (*zophon perieballeto*). The imagery of a sun losing its light is reminiscent of other hymns based on Luke 23:44–45a, where darkness hangs over the scene of the crucifixion. However, the word for "darkness" used here (*zophos*) differs from that found in the Lucan pericope

(*skotos*).[6] This odd, unnatural "darkness" (*zophos*),[7] in which the sun seems to wrap itself, is likely an allusion to the place of damnation reserved for recalcitrant angels (cf. 2 Pet 2:4, 17; Jude 6, 13); hence a more fitting rendition of *zophos* would be "nether darkness, blackness, gloom." Jude 6, using this rare word in the Bible, though well attested in ancient Greek literature (more than fifteen hundred occurrences), draws on 1 En 6–19, the earliest (about second century B.C.E.) account of the fall of the Watchers, based on Gen 6:1–4 ("sons of God" [angels?] marrying "humans' daughters"). Since these "sons of God" corrupted the entire world, God brought the deluge, punishing the Watchers by binding them under the earth, where they had to stay in "darkness" (*zophos*)[8] until the day of final judgment, when they would be cast into Gehenna.

Through this imagery of the "sun wrapping [itself] in darkness," the hearers or readers of this hymn are progressively introduced to the central theme of Holy Saturday, Jesus's descent to the netherworld. It is as if the entire creation came under the menacing darkness or blackness of the netherworld. It was a time of ordeals and trials, a time when the one who used to throw the light upon his shoulders as a royal mantle became naked, lifeless, and without a tomb, a time when the sun that regularly used to share its light became an eclipsed luminary and, in the midst of utter confusion, wrapped itself in the weird blackness of the netherworld. It was as if a living and orderly creation was giving itself over to chaos, darkness, and death. In conjunction with 1 Pet 3:18–20—where Jesus, having died and having been "made alive in Spirit, went and proclaimed to the spirits in prison [*tois en phylakē pneumasin poreutheis ekēryxen*]" (vv. 18–19)—one may consider this *zophos*, the odd blackness covering the sun, a portent of Jesus's imminent descent to the darkness of the netherworld.

"Out of fear, the earth surged [*hē gē tō phobō ekymaineto*] and the curtain of the Temple was rent to pieces [*kai naou to katapetasma dierrēgnyto*]"

In response to what happened to Jesus on Golgotha, that unexpected, sudden switch from royal figure to criminal, from light as a mantle to sheer nakedness and lifelessness, as well as an expression of fear, the earth and its center, the Temple, reacted convulsively: the earth "surged," and the screen separating the Holy from the Holy of Holies within the Temple "was rent to pieces."

Matt 27:51 records that when Jesus yielded his spirit (v. 50), "the curtain of the sanctuary was torn in two [*to katapetasma tou naou eschisthē*] from top to bottom; and the earth quaked [*hē gē eseisthē*], and the rocks were split" [*petrai eschisthēsan*]."

There are some differences between the biblical text and its hymnic retelling: word order is reversed, first "earth," then "curtain"; there are certain lexical choices, "surged" (of the earth), "rent to pieces" (of the curtain); and "rocks were split" is left out.

The image of the earth "surging" (verb *kymainō*; cf. *kyma*, "wave"), unlike the more common and biblically attested "quaking" (verb *seiō*), evokes a sea with surging waves (Wis 5:10; Jer 46 [26]:7).

The use of *kymainō*, "to surge, rise up," was likely determined by the hymnographer's intention to underscore the reverberating sonic effect of "fear" (*phobos*) impacting the entire creation at the sight of a lifeless and naked Jesus hanging on the cross. There was so much fear floating in the air at dusk that the earth became agitated, and a loud, reverberating sound of surging waters more terrifying than the fear itself ensued. Perhaps the poet wanted to convey this overwhelming sonic experience of wild billowy waters (e.g., Isa 5:30; 17:12; Jer 6:23).

This represents the liminal stage between the noises of a crucifixion scene with creation's accompanying sonorous reaction and that subsequent odd stillness, a "vibrating silence" of sorts, filling up a cold and dark tomb on an ageless Sabbath day.

Pertaining to the Temple's "curtain" (*katapetasma*), this was "rent to pieces" (*dierrēgnyto*,[9] a violent rending, vs. *eschisthē*, "torn in two," in Matt 27:51).[10]

The Gk. term *katapetasma*, lit. "that which is spread out downward," designates in LXX a "curtain" (Heb. *pārōket* or *māsāk*) of the Tabernacle or Temple. This can be a curtain between the Holy and the Holy of Holies (Exod 26:31-35; 27:21; 35:12; 2 Chr 3:14) or between the Temple or Tabernacle and the forecourt (Exod 26:37; 1 Kgs 6:36). Josephus (*Antiquities* 8.75) uses *katapetasma* for both curtains. The evangelists (Matt 27:51; Mark 15:38; Luke 23:45) understood most likely the inner curtain, because the outer curtain had no relevance for their Passion accounts.[11] Besides the synoptics, the term occurs three times in Hebrews (6:19; 9:3; 10:20) as early Christological interpretations of this ancient Jewish cultic artifact.

Daniel Gurtner notes that in the gospel of Mark, the "splitting" (*schizō*) of heavens at Jesus's baptism (Mark 1:10) and the "splitting" (*schizō*) of the veil at Jesus's death (Mark 15:38) neatly bracket Jesus's mission, with each splitting followed conspicuously by a revelation of Jesus's divine filiation (i.e., by the heavenly Father at the baptism [Mark 1:11] and by a Roman centurion at Jesus's death on the cross [Mark 15:39]).[12] David Ulansey calls it "cosmic inclusio."[13]

Interestingly, having recorded the "rending" (*diarrēgnymi/diarrēsō*) of the curtain, the hymnographer goes on to say: "And now, lo, I see [*blepō*] you undergoing [*hypelthonta*] voluntarily [*hekousiōs*] death for me. How shall I prepare you for funeral [*kēdeusō*], O my God [*thee mou*]?" The author of this hymn recognizes Jesus's divinity after the rending of the curtain, a proof for understanding Mark's unfolding "messianic secret."

Viewed through both lenses, the occurrences in the synoptics and in Hebrews, the *velum scissum* announces the opening of a heavenly portal through which Jesus, the Son of God incarnate, returns to his glory, offering himself to the Father as a holy perfect sacrifice.

A Sleeping Lion

Come, let us see our life [*zōēn*], lying [*keimenēn*] in a tomb [*en taphō*], so that he may give life [*zōopoiēsē*] to those lying [*keimenous*] in tombs. Come, while beholding [*theōmenoi*] today the one from Judah [*ton ex Iouda*] sleeping [*hypnounta*], and let us cry aloud to him prophetically [*prophētikōs*]: "Having reclined [*anapesōn*], you slept [*kekoimēsai*] as a lion [*leōn*]. Who dares rouse [*egerei*] you, O king? But, arise [*anastēthi*] by [your own] power [*autexousiōs*], you who willingly [*hekousiōs*] gave [*dous*] yourself for us. O Lord, glory to you." (Holy Saturday, Matins, Lauds, Sticheron, Idiomelon)

This hymn allows one to cast a few glimpses into the tomb where the lifeless body of Jesus was laid after being taken down from the cross.

The participants in the Matins service of Holy Saturday are invited to relive the experience of the pious women who followed Jesus from Galilee up to Golgotha: "The women who had come with [*synelēlythyiai*] him from Galilee followed after [*katakolouthēsasai*], and beheld [*etheasanto*] the tomb [*mnēmeion*], and how his body [*sōma*] was laid [*etethē*]" (Luke 23:55).

In the hymn, as in the Lucan pericope, the verb *theaomai*, "to look, see," is employed for its particular meaning of intently looking, gazing, or observing. In the biblical text just cited, Galilean women "beheld" (*etheasanto*) the "tomb" (*mnēmeion*, as a monument, viewed from outside, vs. a *taphos*, "tomb, grave," the inside part of a tomb monument) and "how" (*hōs*) Jesus's lifeless body was laid to rest. In our hymn, the worshipers are summoned, while "beholding the one from Judah sleeping [*ton ex Iouda hypnounta*]," to cry aloud using words from Gen 49:9. There is no mention in the hymn of a "tomb" monument (*mnēmeion*), but rather there is a sudden and focused close-up view of a "sleeping" Jesus, identified with "the one from Judah."

In our hymn, "sleeping" (*hypnounta*) might be taken as a euphemism for "dying," thus continuing the well-attested biblical tradition.[14] Nevertheless, due to the "lion" (*leōn*) analogy a few lines later in this hymn, I am inclined to see in a lion who is "reclined" (*anapesōn*) and "sleeping" (*kekoimēsai*) a hint at Jesus's paradoxical experience in the tomb: as man, he was dead; as God, he was still alive.

The cruel reality of Jesus's death (absence) is signaled by the hymnographer's use of the verb *hypnoō*, "to sleep," a much stronger meaning than *koimaomai*, "to fall asleep," or *katheudō*, "to lie down to sleep." Note that the same verb, *hypnoō*, occurs in the LXX of Jer 51 (28):39:[15] "so that they may sleep a perpetual sleep and never wake [*hypnōsōsin hypnon aiōnion kai ou mē egerthōsi*]," referring to the capture of Babylon by Cyrus of Persia in 539 B.C.E. (the Battle of Opis) and the subsequent massacre of the Babylonians, whose sudden death is compared to a "perpetual sleep." Choosing *hypnounta*, "sleeping," perhaps in connection with Jer 51 (28):38–40,[16] where two images (lion and lamb, metaphors for might and vulnerability) commonly associated with Jesus in hymnography occur, the hymnographer intended to liken Jesus's death and absence with a heavy sleep, that is, the sleep of death.

A similar image conjugating strength with weakness occurs in another hymn designated for Holy Saturday,[17] where *aphypnoō* (a composite verb, from *hypnoō*, "to sleep," and *aph-* (*apo*), "away from"), with its two opposite meanings, "to fall asleep" and "to wake from sleep," seeks to underscore the paradox of concomitant death and life in Jesus's lifeless body:

"Having reclined, you slept as a lion. Who dares rouse you, O king?'
[*anapesōn kekoimēsai hōs leōn, tis egerei se basileu*]"

The text here is a quote from Gen 49:9, but as with other biblical quotations, the hymnographer uses only a portion of the biblical text, the one that suits the purpose of the hymn. In this case, the quotation is from the third colon, "Having reclined . . .," with two alterations compared with the biblical text: (1) no mention of "whelp"; (2) the third person singular pronoun is replaced with the second person "you," followed by a vocative, "O king" (*basileu*). Gen 49:9 (LXX) reads: "A lion's whelp [*skymnos leontos*] you are, Judah! From a shoot [*blastou*], my son [*hyie mou*], you went up [*anebēs*]. Having reclined [*anapesōn*], you slept [*ekoimēthēs*] like a lion [*leōn*],[18] and like a whelp. Who dares rouse [*egerei*] him?"

Gen 49:9 is part of a wider literary unit, Gen 49:2–47. Although known as "Jacob's Blessings," this unit, a poem similar to the one in Deut 33, is a "schematic presentation of the twelve sons/tribes with anticipation of their futures (cf. Gen 35:22–26)" that might be better termed a "testimony."[19]

Historically, this blessing could be a hint at King David's successful military endeavors seen as a fulfillment of Jacob's blessing prophecy. Judah, the tribe David belonged to, is likened here to a lion that, after having grasped its prey, returns to its den and no one is able to challenge its power.[20]

In the Bible, "lion" is a metaphor of power and unassailability. It is not the ferocity of the beast but rather its strength that is underscored. Along these lines one may understand Cyril of Jerusalem's comments:

> Again, he is called a Lion; not a man eater, but, as it were, showing by this title his kingly, strong and resolute nature. Then too, he is called a Lion in opposition to the lion, our adversary who roars and devours those who have been deceived [1 Pet 5:8]. For the Savior came, not having changed his own gentle nature, and yet as the mighty lion of the tribe of Judah, saving them that believe but trampling upon the adversary." (*Catechetical Lectures* 10.3)[21]

Under the influence of Gen 49:9, the "Lion of Judah" became a messianic title.[22] In Rev 5:5, the expression "Lion of Judah," borrowed from Gen 49:9, designates Jesus, who in v. 6 is depicted as the slain lamb. This messianic title is found in early Jewish (4 Ezra 11:36–46) and Christian writings (Justin, *Dialogue* 52.2; Pseudo-Epiphanius, *Testimony* 71.3).[23]

The hymnographer imagines himself in conversation with the narrator of Gen 49:9, while trying to answer the latter's question, "Who dares rouse the lion's whelp," Judah's providential offspring?

In the hymnographer's view, similar to those of many other ancient Christian interpreters, the "lion's whelp" is none other than Jesus born of the tribe of Judah. The lion's "reclining" and "sleeping" may refer to Jesus dying on the cross which was followed by his entombment.

Rufinus of Aquileia (ca. 345–411) distinguishes between the two actions (reclining/crouching and sleeping) and between the two metaphors for Jesus (lion and lion's whelp). Regarding the latter distinction, Rufinus sees in it two facets of Jesus's resurrection (the victorious descent into the netherworld and the third-day return to life):

> Having crouched, you slept as a lion and as a whelp" [Gen 49:9, LXX]. It is evident that the actions of crouching and sleeping signify the passion and death. But let us see why he sleeps as a lion and a whelp. With regard to the sleep of the whelp it has been already said above that it can very conveniently be referred to Christ, who, after being buried for three days and three nights in the heart of the earth, completed, as was expected, the sleep of death. But I believe that the expression "as a lion" must be interpreted in this way: the death of Christ marked the defeat and the triumph over the demons. In fact, our lion captured all the prey that the hostile lion had conquered [1 Pet 5:8] after destroying and crushing the man. Then, by coming back from the underworld and ascending on high, he made slavery his captive [Eph 4:8; cf. Ps 68:18 [67:19]]. Therefore in his sleep the lion won and defeated every evil and destroyed the one who had the power of death [Heb 2:14]. And like a whelp he woke up on the third day. (*The Blessings of the Patriarchs* 1.6)[24]

"But, arise by [your own] power, you who willingly gave yourself for us [*all' anastēthi autexousiōs, ho dous heauton hyper hēmōn hekousiōs*]"

"Who dares rouse the lion's whelp?" asks Gen 49:9, and the hymnographer's response takes the shape of a passionate plea: "Arise by [your own] power, you who willingly gave yourself for us."

The hymnographer' imperative *anastēthi*, "Arise!" might be a tiny reverberation from the psalmist's lexical toolkit, "Wake up [*exegerthēti*]! Why do you sleep [*hypnois*], O Lord? Arise [*anastēthi*], and do not reject [*apōsē*] us until the end" (Ps 44:23 [43:24]), thus preparing the worshiper for the surprising, jubilant in tone petition refrain that will subsequently be proclaimed at the Vesperal Liturgy of Saint Basil celebrated on Holy Saturday morning: "Arise [*anasta*], O God, judge the earth, because you will inherit all nations" (Ps 82 [81]:8 [LXX]).[25]

The presence of the adverb *autexousiōs*, "by [his own] power" (lit. "freely, out of authority"), suggests that the "rising" of the "sleeping" "Lion of Judah" will be done by his own power; in other words, Jesus's resurrection will happen through Jesus's divinity and power. This is seemingly Ambrose's understanding:

> Therefore you have become acquainted with the incarnation; learn of the passion. "Resting, you have slept like a lion." When Christ lay at rest in the

tomb, it was as if he were in a kind of bodily sleep, as he himself says, "I have slept and have taken my rest and have risen up, because the Lord will sustain me" [Ps 3:5[6]]. On this account also Jacob says, "Who will arouse him?" that is, him whom the Lord will take up. Who else is there to rouse him again, unless he rouses himself by his own power and the power of the Father? I see that he was born by his own authority; I see that he died by his own will; I see that he sleeps by his own power. He did all things by his own dominion; will he need the help of someone else to rise again? Therefore he is the author of his own resurrection, he is the judge of his death; he is expected by the nations. (*The Patriarchs* 4.20)[26]

However, for Hippolytus, Jesus's "rising" was the result of the Father's intervention:

He [Jacob] says the words "After stooping down, you slept like a lion and a whelp" in order to show Christ sleeping during the three days of his burial, when he rests in the heart of the earth. And also the Lord himself has testified such when he said, "For as Jonah was three days and three nights in the belly of the whale, so will the Son of Man be three days and three nights in the heart of the earth" [Matt 12:40]. And David by announcing him in advance said, "I lay down and slept; I awoke for the Lord will help me" [Ps 3:5 [6]]. Jacob also said, "Who will wake him?" [Gen 49:9]. He did not say "Nobody will wake him" but "Who?" in order that we may understand that the Father woke the Son from the dead, as the apostle confirms: "and through God the Father who woke him from the dead" [Gal 1:1]. And Peter said, "But God raised him up, having loosed the pangs of death, because it was not possible for him to be held by it [Acts 2:24]." (*On the Blessings of Isaac and Jacob* 16)[27]

"You who willingly gave yourself for us [*ho dous heauton hyper hēmōn hekousiōs*]"

At the end, the hymnographer underscores Jesus's willingness to offer himself as a sacrifice by resorting to a rare adverb, *hekousiōs*, "willingly, freely," found only in Exod 36:2; Ps 54:6 [53:8]; 2 Macc 14:3; 4 Macc 5:23; 8:25; Heb 10:26; 1 Pet 5:2. From these few occurrences, Ps 54:6–7 [53:8–9], which deals with the free-will sacrifice,[28] is closest to our hymn: "Willingly [*hekousiōs*], I shall sacrifice to you. I will acknowledge [*exomologēsomai*] your name, O Lord [*kyrie*], because it is good [*hoti agathon*]; because you rescued [*errysō*] me from every affliction [*thlipseōs*], and my eyes gazed upon [*epeiden*] my enemies." By using the adverb *hekousiōs*, "willingly, freely," as a hermeneutical pointer, the hymnographer indicates that he sees in Jesus's free-will sacrifice the reason he was able to rise by his own power, the power of love and self-offering for others.

The One Who Shut the Abyss

The one who shut the abyss [*tēn abysson ho kleisas*] is seen dead [*nekros horatai*], and wrapped in myrrh [*smyrnē*] and shroud [*sindoni*]; laid down [*katatithetai*] in a tomb [*mnēmeiō*] is the immortal [*athanatos*] as a mortal one [*thnētos*]. The women came to anoint him with myrrh [*myrisai*], to wail [*klaiousai*] bitterly [*pikrōs*] and cry aloud [*ekboōsai*]: "This Sabbath is the most blessed one [*hypereulogēmenon*], on which Christ having fallen asleep [*aphypnōsas*], shall rise again [*anastēsetai*] on the third day." (Holy Saturday, Matins, Kontakion)

The hymn opens with a brief quote from Pr Man 1:3 (LXX: Odes 12:3):[29] "You who shackled [*pedēsas*] the sea by your word of command [*prostagmatos*], who shut the deep [*ho kleisas tēn abysson*] and sealed [*sphragisamenos*] it by your terrible [*phoberō*] and glorious [*endoxō*] name."

Note that S, by choosing the word *təhōmāʾ* to render the LXX *abysson*, "deep," links this text to Gen 1:2, where the Heb. cognate *təhōm*, "deep, abyss," occurs:

And the earth [MT: *hā-ʾāreṣ*; LXX: *hē gē*] was [MT: *hāyətāh*; LXX: *ēn*] unformed and void [MT: *tōhû wā-bōhû*; LXX: *aoratos kai akataskeuatos*, "invisible and unformed"], and darkness [MT: *ḥōšek*; LXX: *skotos*] over the deep [MT: *ʿal-pənēy təhôm*; LXX: *epanō tēs abyssou*], and the Spirit of God [MT: *rûaḥ ʾĕlōhîm*; LXX: *pneuma theou*] hovering [MT: *məraḥepet*; LXX: *epephereto*, "being carried"] over the waters [MT: *ʿal-pənēy hammāyim*; LXX: *epanō tou hydatos*].

A *crux interpretum* throughout the history of interpretation, Gen 1:2 describes the primeval state of matter prior to the beginning of God's creative work (Gen 1:3). In its initial state, this matter (whose origin is not clearly stated, though roughly implied in the incipit/heading of Gen 1:1) is marked by shapelessness, directionlessness, and amalgamation.

Note that there is only one finite verbal form, *hāyətāh*, "was" (perfective aspect of *h-y-h*), coordinating the entire sentence, and a participle (unrestricted as to time), *mərahepet*, "hovering," pertaining to the action of "Spirit of God" (*rûaḥ ʾĕlōhîm*). In addition, there is an untranslatable idiom, *tōhû wā-bōhû*.[30] Yet, based on the context of Gen 1:2 as well as the LXX interpretive reading (*aoratos kai akataskeuatos*, "invisible and unformed"),[31] one can at least discern its basic meaning, a primeval and yet-to-be-configured state of matter.

This primeval matter consists of an unformed, invisible, or voided earth, deeply covered by darkness, and waters "all around," if one may use this spatial qualifier for a directionless pre-universe (cosmos) entity.

Having said this, one may note that one of the most celebrated expressions of the Church tradition, the Nicaea-Constantinopolitan Creed (381), states rather emphatically: "I believe in one God, the Maker of all things, visible and invisible." This is, in a nutshell, the Church teaching of *creatio ex nihilo*, "creation out of nothing," proclaiming that "all things are ontologically dependent upon God and that the universe had a beginning."[32]

The doctrine of creation out of nothing, already configured in Irenaeus's time (the second century) as the Church's response to Gnostic cosmology, clearly opposes any version of pantheism and dualism, by painting an almighty God who serenely and majestically creates everything out of nothing, an idea so well delineated in Gen 1.

Perhaps the earliest Old Testament text (late second century B.C.E.) that might support this doctrine is 2 Macc 7:28; the LXX reads: "God did not make them from things that existed [*ouk ex ontōn*]"; V, in its free rendition, *ex nihilo fecit illa Deus*, "God made all from nothing," offers the technical term *ex nihilo* "[creation] out of nothing" to those who crafted this expression.

One may add here the Isaian utterance "I am the Lord [Yahweh], who made all things" (Isa 44:24; cf. 45:7) and some New Testament texts (Rom 4:17; Col 1:16; Eph 3:8; Heb 11:3; Rev 4:11) depicting God as the Creator of all things.

But what is the meaning of "deep" (Heb. *təhôm*; Gk. *abyssos*) in Gen 1:2 in conjunction with the Pr Man?

Nicholas Tromp condensed in just a few words the semantic complexity of this key term: "Hebrew *təhôm* is a vigorous and often grim word, which never entirely renounced its mythical past. A primordial strength pervades *təhôm* throughout. It stands for: *a*) the primeval ocean; *b*) the waters round the earth after creation, which continually threaten the cosmos; *c*) these waters as a source of blessing for the earth."[33]

In spite of some linguistic relation between Heb. *təhôm*, "ocean, deep," and Akk. *tiamtum*, "ocean,"[34] Hermann Gunkel's influential view that Hebrew *təhôm* is a Judaized residue of the mythical *Tiamat* designating the chaotic sea goddess featured in the Babylonian creation epic *Enuma elish* (ca. second half of second millennium B.C.E.),[35] is now untenable.

Since in the Hebrew Bible *təhôm* designates both the cosmic waters surrounding the earth and the primeval subterranean waters (Gen 7:11; Exod 15:5, 8; Deut 33:13; Isa 51:10; 63:13; Jonah 2:6[7]; Ps 36:6 [35:7]; 104 [103]:6; 106 [105]:9)[36] and not the "sea" which is connoted by the Heb. term *yam*, corresponding to Akk. *tiamtum* (cf. the chaotic sea goddess Tiamat), the LXX renders the Heb. word *təhôm* in Gen 1:2 with *abyssos*, "deep."[37]

Pr Man 1:3 (Odes 12:3) uses a similar lexicon to that found in Gen 8:1–2. In order to put an end to the devastating deluge, God brings a "wind" (*pneuma*; redolent of Gen 1:2 lexicon) so that "the fountains of the deep were covered over" (*epekalyphthēsan hai pēgai tēs abyssou*).

Gen 1:2 also states that the "Spirit of God was being carried over the waters" (LXX: *pneuma theou epephereto epanō tou hydatos*; MT: *məraḥepet*, "hovering"), that is, over the primeval aquatic matter, perhaps aiming to keep all this agitating stuff (i.e., the waters of the primeval *təhôm*) under God's control so that everything coming out of that rough matter might be in harmony with God's will or design.[38] There is no such thing as *Chaoskampf* with respect to creation in the Hebrew Bible. Even the difficult locus of Gen 1:2, implying a chaos prior to creation, has no trace of such a battle between God and a supposedly chaotic matter; rather, there is a divine agent (God's Spirit) hovering over a unorganized state of things—this is what one can say, based on the textual and literary evidence of Gen 1:2. By consequence, one should not use the word "chaos" but rather speak of a not yet configured or shaped reality, a somehow amalgamating potentiality; "chaos" seems too strong a word, unwarranted by Gen 1:1–2 or biblical theology in general.

The imagery of shutting and sealing the abyss found in Pr Man 1:3 reappears in Rev 20:1–3. If in the Pr Man, God himself defeats, through the power of his word, the primeval "deep" (Gen 1:2), in Rev 20:1–3, an angel descends from heaven and binds "that ancient serpent" [*ho ophis ho archaios*], Satan, for a thousand years by throwing him into the abyss. V. 3 reads: "And he [i.e., the angel] threw [*ebalen*] him [i.e., Satan] into abyss [*abysson*] and shut [*ekleisen*] and sealed [*esphragisen*] it over him." Though using a similar imagery, the two texts are not directly interrelated, due to the object (primeval deep vs. Satan) and the modus operandi (God vs. angel) of God's victorious intervention.

What has this piece of biblical interpretation (i.e., Pr Man) to do with the present hymn? Quite likely, the hymnographer intended to strike a sharp contrast between the "one" (again, that recurring God–Jesus identification, so ubiquitous in hymnography) who had the power to shut and seal the primeval deep and the one who is now shut and sealed in a dark tomb. There is also a contrast between the primeval deep and the tomb; the cosmic deep as the source and expression of primeval matter contrasts sharply with a small newly hewn-in-rock tomb. God is able to "shut" and "seal" this cosmic deep with the mere power of his terrible and glorious name, while Jesus's petty enemies "sealed the stone" (*sphragisantes ton lithon*, Matt 27:66)[39] that Joseph of Arimathea previously "rolled" (*proskylisas*, Matt 27:60) to the tomb's door.

The contrast between the primeval deep and Jesus's tomb becomes even sharper if one considers Prov 8:24, where God's Wisdom declares that she was "brought forth when there were as yet no depths" (MT: *hôlāltî bǝ-ʾêyn-tǝhōmôt*; LXX, vv. 23–24: *ethemeliōsen me . . . pro tou tas abyssous poiēsai*, "he founded me before he made the depths"). If the beginning of Wisdom (identified with the Logos) precedes the primeval "deep" (*tǝhôm/abyssos*, Gen 1:2), then Jesus, the incarnate Logos, who shut the deep, according to our hymn, is wrapped in myrrh and a shroud and laid in a "tomb" (*taphos*). The preexistent Wisdom, the immortal one, becomes mortal, and the terrifying deep prior to the first *fiat* (Gen 1:3) becomes a one-room tomb. The one who shut the deep is now himself shut in a sealed stone tomb. If the "deep" cannot encompass God's Wisdom (the deep says of Wisdom: "It is not in me" [Job 28:14]), then how can a small tomb contain it?

"Wrapped in myrrh and shroud [*smyrnē kai sindoni eneilēmmenos*]"
This line may be a hint at Mark 15:46: "And he [Joseph of Arimathea] bought a linen shroud, and taking him down [from the cross], wrapped him in the linen shroud [*sindoni*] and laid him in a tomb [*mnēmeiō*] which had been hewn out of the rock; and he rolled a stone [*prosekylisen lithon*] against the door of the tomb" (cf. Matt 27:59–60; Luke 23:53).

As one can notice, the synoptics are based on a common tradition that Jesus's lifeless body was simply wrapped in a "linen shroud" (*sindoni*), with no anointing, due to the fact that Sabbath day was about to begin and all work had to stop. For the synoptics, it was after the Sabbath day that the women came to the tomb, having "brought spices [*arōmata*] in order to anoint [*aleipsōsin*] him [Jesus]."

The hymnographer conflates this tradition found in the synoptics with a different tradition attested by John 19:38–41. The Johannine tradition provides a more elaborated account of Jesus's burial. Nicodemus, another "secret" disciple of Jesus, brought a "mixture of myrrh and aloes" (*migma smyrnēs kai aloēs*) (v. 39) and "wrapped it [the body] in linen cloths with spices [*edēsan auto en othoniois meta tōn arōmatōn*]" (v. 40). Note that the word *arōmata*, "spices, aromatic oils," is a general term that includes "myrrh" (*smyrnē*), which occurs also in our hymn.

One may assume that the hymnographer borrowed the term "linen shroud" (*sindōn*) from the synoptics and *smyrnē* ("myrrh") from John, while wrapping Jesus's body in both myrrh and a funeral cloth was taken from John.

"Women came to anoint him with myrrh [*gynaikes de auton ēlthon myrisai*]"
This line hints at Mark 16:1, where the scene at the tomb is dominated by a number of female disciples who came after the Sabbath day (that is, anytime after around six p.m.) to the tomb "in order to anoint" (*aleipsōsin*) Jesus's body according to Jewish tradition.

However, the verb *myrizō*, "to anoint," used in our hymn was borrowed from Mark 14:8 (hapax legomenon), the anointing episode that occurred in the house of Simon the Leper in Bethany, where Jesus speaks of the woman who anointed him: "She has done what she could. She has anointed beforehand [*proelaben myrisai*] my body for the entombment [*entaphiasmon*]."

"Christ having fallen asleep, shall rise again on the third day [*Christos aphypnōsas, anastēsetai triēmeros*]"
The verb *aphypnoō*, "to fall asleep," is found only in Luke 8:23 (i.e., the "Stilling of the Storm" pericope): "And as they sailed [*pleontōn*], he fell asleep [*aphypnōsen*]. And a windstorm [*lailaps*] came down on the lake, and they were filled [*syneplērounto*] [with water], and they were in danger [*ekendyneuon*]."

By choosing this hapax legomenon, the hymnographer wants his listeners or readers to liken Jesus lying lifelessly in the tomb with Jesus's sleep in the boat on the Sea of Galilee during a windstorm; one may see the main parallels: boat/tomb; great windstorm/trial and crucifixion; sleep/death.

Luke 8:23 evokes two dangers: Jesus's sleeping and the unexpected onset of a windstorm. In the Old Testament, sleep may signal a presumed absence of divinity (Ps 7:6[7]; 35 [34]:23; 44:23 [43:24]; Isa 51:9). While sleeping, a person is at the same time present and absent. Note that *lailaps* in Luke 8:23 denotes a strong wind (hurricane), and Luke perhaps has in mind the western part of the Sea of Galilee beaten by such winds. In ancient times, sailors were encouraged to stay in the harbor during a storm like this (cf. Philo, *On Dreams* 2:85–86). Yet Jesus, like a tired or careless sailor, falls asleep in the boat, leaving his disciples in great danger.[40]

The hymnographer perhaps saw in the Lucan text a parallel to Jesus's death and resurrection. No one traveling with Jesus from Galilee to Jerusalem to celebrate that year's Passover could imagine that such a *lailaps*, "windstorm," would rush down over them unexpectedly and that their teacher would fall asleep during the storm, leaving them alone.

Most likely to underline this idea of concurring absence and presence during sleep, Luke—and our hymnographer—opted for the verb *aphypnoō*, which can mean both "to fall asleep" and "to wake from sleep." During his "sleep" in the tomb, Jesus was absent and present at the same time. His "sleep" (i.e., death) tacitly prepared and mysteriously announced his intervention: the descent to the netherworld and the third-day resurrection.

A Blessed Sabbath

It is this present day [*tēn sēmeron*], the great Moses mystically [*mystikōs*] expressed by a type beforehand [*prodietypouto*], when he said: "And God blessed [*eulogēsen*] the seventh day [*tēn hēmeron tēn hebdomēn*]"; for this is the blessed Sabbath [*to eulogēmenon sabbaton*], this is the day of rest [*katapauseōs*], on which the Only Begotten [*ho monogenēs*] Son of God rested [*katepausen*] from all his works [*ergōn*], sabbatizing [*sabbatisas*] in flesh [*tē sarki*], through death, according to the [divine] economy [*dia tēs oikonomias*]. And returning [*epanelthōn*] once again [*palin*] to the one he was [*eis ho hēn*], through resurrection [*anastaseōs*], he granted [*edōrēsato*] us eternal life [*zōēn tēn aiōnion*], as the only Good One and Lover of Humanity. (Holy Saturday, Matins, Lauds, Sicheron, Idiomelon)

The present hymn mentions "the blessed Sabbath" (*to eulogēmenon sabbaton*) in parallel with Jesus's "rest" (*katapausis*) in the tomb. Let us look briefly at the Old Testament institution of Sabbath and see how the hymnographer interprets it through the theological lenses of Holy Saturday.

The main key texts in the Mosaic Law dealing with the Sabbath injunction are Exod. 20:8–11 (cf. Deut. 5:12–15) (Decalogue); Exod. 23:12; 31:12–17; 34:21; 35:1–3; Lev 19:3; 23:1–3; 26:2.

According to Gen 2:3, the institution of Sabbath is connected to God's creation, more precisely to the seventh day, when the Creator "ceased" (MT: *šābat*; LXX: *katepausen*) to create. Thus, Sabbath punctuates both the climax and the end point of God's creative work. However, as the "primeval history" (Gen 1–11) shows, this cessation does not translate into God's departure from his creation. Rather, God continues working, but his work does not involve creating new creatures. After the first Sabbath, God's creative work turns into providence, taking care of his creation and especially humanity.[41]

Gen 2:3 (LXX) reads: "And God blessed [*eulogēsen*] the seventh day [*tēn hēmeron tēn hebdomēn*] and sanctified [*hēgiasen*] it, because on it [*en autē*] he stopped [*katepausen*] from all his works [*apo pantōn tōn ergōn*] that God began to do [*ērxato poiēsai*]."

Exod 20:11 (LXX) has: "For in six days the Lord made [*epoiēsen*] the heaven and the earth and the sea and all things in them, and he rested [*katepausen*; MT: *wy-yānaḥ*] on the seventh day [*tē hēmera tē hebdomē*]. That is why, the Lord blessed [*eulogēsen*] the seventh day and sanctified [*hēgiasen*; MT: *wa-yəqaddəšēhû*] it."

As seen in the above-cited texts, the Heb. verb *šābat*[42] and the Gk. verb *katepausen*[43] display two logically interconnected meanings: "to end" (working) and "to rest" (a natural consequence or expression of work's cessation).

The Gk. verb *anapauō*, "to give rest," used in the following passage, is a variant of *katapauō*, both verbs going back to the basic verbal root *pauō*, "to cause to cease." Exod 23:12: "Six days you shall do your tasks [*erga*], but on the seventh day you shall stop [working] [*anapausis*] so that your ox and your draft animal might rest [*anapausētai*], and the son of your female servant and the stranger might be refreshed [*anapsuxē*]."

Interestingly, the end of work on the seventh day translates into "resting" (*anapauō*) and "refreshing" (*anapsychō*) for animals, servants, and foreigners. Sabbath is more than a means for weekly rest. It is also a source of refreshment and revival for those involved in the weekly working cycle.

"And God blessed the seventh day [*kai eulogēsen ho theos tēn hēmeran tēn hēbdomēn*]":
This line is a quote from Gen 2:3a underscoring only the fact that God "blessed" (hymn: *eulogēsen*; vs. LXX: *ēulogēsen*) the Sabbath. However, according to Gen 2:3 and Exod 20:11, God "blessed" (*ēulogēsen/eulogēsen*) and "sanctified" (*hēgiasen*) the Sabbath day.

"Blessing" and "sanctifying" are two distinct actions corresponding to two distinct notions. The Old Testament notion of "blessing" suggests imparting a special power or gift so the recipients may exercise to the fullest their assigned roles and responsibilities. Thus, God blesses living things, sea creatures, humanity, and time (Gen 1:22, 28; 2:3). All these "created" entities were viewed as *moving* (including time), so in order to be able to move, they need some special power, a blessing of sorts, from their Creator. As for "sanctifying," this notion evokes placing aside things or persons as a sign of love, care, and appreciation. In the beginning, God sanctified the Sabbath day (Gen 2:3), a portion of time, as the most representative element of God's creation, and it was set apart by the Creator to be always next to him. Interestingly, God did not sanctify space (e.g., earth, sun, moon, or even the humanity created in his image, Gen 1:27) but rather time, setting aside the Sabbath day as a precious treasure trove of his creation.

As a matter of fact, the concept of "holiness" on which "sanctification" depends lies at the very center of the Old Testament, even biblical theology as a whole. God is "holy" (Isa 6:6; Heb. *qādôš*, from verb root *q-d-š*, "to cut off, to separate," underscores God's transcendence).

Although *Der ganz Andere*, the God of Israel is open to communion and sharing. For this purpose, he reveals his personal name (YHWH) to Moses (Exod 3:13–15) so that he might be present by his (invoked) name in the midst of his people, more precisely, in the Temple, the dwelling place of the Name (1 Kgs 3:2; 8:17, 18, 19). At Mount Sinai (Exod 19:6), Yahweh promises Israel that they may be a "holy nation" (MT: *gôy qādôš*; LXX: *ethnos hagion*) to him, provided they listen to his voice and observe his covenant. Exod 19:5-6 (LXX) reads: "If you really listen [*akoē akousēte*, a Semitism, calquing *šmwᶜ tšmᶜ*] to my very voice and observe [*phylaxēte*] my covenant [*diathēkēn*] ... you shall be to me [*moi*] ... a holy nation [*ethnos hagion*]."

It is worth nothing that after the sanctification of the Sabbath day (Gen 2:3), the next created entity God sanctified or set apart, though conditionally upon observing the covenant, was the emerging people of Israel

(Exod 19:5–6). Thus, two key pieces of God's creation, time and humanity (represented by Israel at Mount Sinai), were eventually sanctified in a state of quasi-interdependence.

Pertaining to God's sanctifying the Sabbath, one may underline that Gen 1–2 contains two creation accounts, each loaded with its defining theology: sanctification of the Sabbath (time) (Gen 1:1–2:4a) and shaping of a yet-to-be-sanctified humanity (Gen 2:4b–25).[44]

Due to the development of "salvation history" within Christian theological discourse, it is the sanctification of humanity through Jesus, the "New Israel" (Matt 2:15; cf. Hos 11:1 [MT: *bənî*, "my son"; but LXX: *ta tekna autou*, "his children"]) and the embodiment of Israel and its "covenants" and "promises" (Rom 9:4), that came to be prioritized with an unfortunate demise of the sanctification of time and Sabbath theology.

Nevertheless, early Christian writers witness a continuing duet between Saturday and Sunday theologies. The *Apostolic Constitutions* (ca. 375) urges the faithful to observe two days of weekly worship in remembrance of God's creation and Jesus's resurrection:

> Let the slaves work five days; but on the Sabbath day and the Lord's day let them have leisure to go to church for instruction in piety. We have said that the Sabbath is on account of the creation, and the Lord's day of the resurrection. Let slaves rest from their work all the great week, and that which follows it—for the one in memory of the passion, and the other of the resurrection; and there is need they should be instructed who it is that suffered and rose again, and who it is permitted him to suffer, and raised him again. (*Apostolic Constitutions* 8.33)[45]

In his magisterial work *The Sabbath*, Abraham Joshua Heschel reminds one that this theological concept of "sanctification of time" promoted by the Sabbath day has been well preserved in Judaism:

> Judaism is a religion of time aiming at the sanctification of time.... Judaism teaches us to be attached to holiness in time, to be attached to sacred events, to learn how to consecrate sanctuaries that emerge from the magnificent stream of a year. The Sabbaths are our great cathedrals; and our Holy of Holies is a shrine that neither the Romans nor the Germans were able to burn; a shrine that even apostasy cannot easily obliterate.[46]

"It is this present day, the great Moses mystically expressed by a type beforehand [*tēn sēmeron mystikōs, ho megas Mōysēs prodietypouto*]"

From the outset, the hymnographer explains that when Moses wrote Gen 2:3, he "expressed by a type beforehand" (*prodietypouto*)[47] a future reality. Thus, Jesus's "rest" (death) has been prefigured long ago when God "rested" (*katepausen*) from his work and "blessed" (*eulogēsen*) the seventh day. The adverb *mystikōs*, "mystically" (a hapax legomenon, 3 Macc 3:10, "secretly, quietly"), denotes speaking in types and prophecies,[48] the role of the interpreter being to decode this mystical speech by allegorical and typological methods of exposition. This is exactly what our hymnographer is doing: unraveling what was in Moses's mind when he wrote Gen 2:3 about God blessing the seventh day.

"For this is the blessed Sabbath [*touto gar esti to eulogēmenon sabbaton*]"

The Sabbath is "blessed" (*eulogēmenon*) not only because the Creator blessed the seventh day at the end of his six-day work. It is blessed also because "the Only Begotten Son of God rested from all his works" (*katepausen apo pantōn tōn ergōn autou ho monogenēs hyios tou theou*). Jesus's "rest" in the tomb is the cause, source, and scope of this additional blessing which the Sabbath acquires on Holy Saturday. "All his works" (*pantōn tōn ergōn autou*), echoing Gen 2:2a, designates Jesus's salvific activity paralleled here with God's creative work. The close parallel between Creator and Savior is highlighted by the title "the Only Begotten Son of God" which Jesus receives in this hymn.

As in the case of the Creator, who ceased working and "rested" (*katepausen*) not due to exhaustion but to mark that he had "completed his works" (*synetelesen ... ta erga autou*, Gen 2:2), Jesus's "rest" (*katapausis*) means not fatigue but rather that the work the heavenly Father gave him to do was "accomplished" (*tetelestai*, John 19:30) on the cross.

"Sabbatizing in flesh, through death, according to the [divine] economy [*dia tēs kata ton thanaton oikonomias, tē sarki sabbatisas*]"

Somehow ironically, Jesus, the one who healed on Sabbaths, showing his contemporaries that doing good to the needy equals sanctifying the Sabbath day, came himself eventually to observe the Sabbath "rest" when he was taken down from the cross and laid in Joseph of Arimathea's tomb. Jesus "sabbatized" (*sabbatisas*)[49] in his flesh, through death, according to God's *oikonomia* ("management plan").[50]

According to the following hymn, the seventh day was sanctified when Jesus "sabbatized" ("rested" lifelessly in the tomb). By sabbatizing, Jesus identified himself with the Creator, becoming the owner of the universe that he produced and renewed:

Today you sanctified [*hēgiasas*] the seventh [day] [*hebdomēn*], the one you blessed [*eulogēsas*] previously [*prin*], by resting from the works [*katapausei tōn ergōn*]. For you produce [*parageis*] and renew [*kainopoieis*] the universe [*ta sympanta*]; while sabbatizing [*sabbatizōn*], my Savior, you own [the universe] again [*anaktōmenos*] (Holy Saturday, Matins, Ode 4, Troparion).

Hades Defeated

Today, Hades groaning [*stenōn*], cried out: "It would have been profitable [*synephere*] for me, if I had not received [*hypedexamēn*] the one born [*gennēthenta*] of Mary beneath [into my house]; for while coming [*elthōn*] upon me [*ep' eme*], he destroyed [*elyse*] my power [*kratos*], shattered [*synetripse*] the bronze gates [*pylas chalkas*], and being God [*theos ōn*], he resurrected [*anestēse*] the souls [*psychas*], which I previously [*prin*] had in possession [*kateichon*]." Glory to your Cross, and to your Resurrection. (Holy Saturday, Vesperal Saint Basil Liturgy, Sticheron, Idiomelon)

This hymn should be read as a sequel to the previous one, where God's Wisdom, having stolen into or entered the tomb unnoticed, was able to share with the inhabitants of Hades some of her life-pouring power. The current hymn, however, goes a bit further with its description of Wisdom, equating her with "the one born of Mary" and displaying the latter's feats in the very midst of Hades.

It needs to be mentioned here that during the liturgical enactment of the Passion, Jesus, Mary, and now Hades lament from their own perspectives: Jesus laments over the people's ungratefulness, Mary for the untimely loss of her son, and Hades for its unpardonable mistake of admitting Jesus into his domain. In the case of Hades, the lament is more like a loud sighing, a "groaning" (*stenōn*).[51]

One may note the hymnographer's inspired choice of the verb *hypodechomai* describing Hades's attitude toward Jesus. The prefixed *hypo-* on the verb *hypodechomai* ("to receive beneath [the surface], to receive in one's house, to receive hospitably, to welcome, to admit") may refer to either receiving someone in one's house or beneath (the ground) or conflating the two meanings concomitantly. The latter possibility seems quite appealing. It is as if Hades considered the underworld his own house in which he welcomed Jesus while being unaware of his guest's real identity.

Jesus is portrayed by Hades in his lament as "the one born of Mary" (*ek Marias gennēthenta*), a phrase reminiscent of Matt 2:1 (of Jesus, "born [in Bethlehem]," *gennēthentos*), by which Jesus's humanity is clearly stressed.

Hades knows the brevity and finitude of human life: "as soon as we were born, we ceased to be" (*gennēthentes exelipomen*) (Wis 5:13), or "a mortal human being [*brotos*], born of a woman [*gennētos gynaikos*], is short-lived and full of trouble" (Job 14:1). He is also aware of the ominous human predicament: "if you were born [*gennēthēte*], you will be born for a curse [*eis kataran*], and if you die, you will be apportioned [*meristhēsesthe*] to a curse" (Sir 41:9). However, Hades's rush to conclusion that Jesus is a mere human being, hence subject to corruption and mortality, will cost him dearly. Having been accepted by Hades into his domain, Jesus's entrance turns into a direct attack on the master of the netherworld, the personified, quasi-deified Hades.

The gist of Hades's lament is that he was deceived by Jesus's human appearance, and by consequence, he was unable to discern his guest's hidden divine nature. Interestingly, Jesus's descent to Hades is here described as a sudden assault or attack on Hades: "He came [suddenly] upon me," in a hostile way. The verb *erchomai*, "to go, to come," construed with the preposition *epi*, "on, upon," thus "to come upon," is attested in post-Homeric Greek with this special connotation, "to attack." Thus, Hades's welcoming of Jesus turns unexpectedly into the latter's open attack against the former.

"He destroyed my power [*to kratos mou elyse*]"
Hades's first complaint is that the mysterious guest "destroyed [his] power" (*to kratos . . . elyse*)—nullified it (verb *lyō*, "to loose(n), to undo, to destroy, to put an end to, to annul") and "broke to pieces his bronze gates" (*pylas chalkas synetripse*). The Bible intimates the underworld's power by the idiom "hand of Hades" (Gk. *cheir hadou*; cf. Heb. *yad-šəʾôl*) (Ps 49:15 [48:16]; Hos 13:14; both texts witness to God's power "to redeem/ransom" [*lytroō/rhyomai*] a soul from the "hand of Hades." In a more subtle poetical way, Song 8:6 hints at Hades's strength by comparing love and zeal in terms of power and durability with death and the underworld.

"Shattered the bronze gates [*pylas chalkas synetripse*]"
The "bronze gates" (*pylas chalkas*) are the prize of Hades's powerful domain. Alas, Jesus "shattered" (*synetripse*) them by his mere appearance. In a thanksgiving prayer for deliverance from many troubles, the psalmist lauds the Lord for "he shattered [*synetripsen*] bronze gates [*pylas chalkas*] and broke off iron bars [*mochlous sydērous*]" (Ps 107 [106]:16). The psalmist praises the Lord for his *ḥesed* (Heb.), loyal steadfast covenantal love" for Israel shown on many occasions when he saved his people from troubles.

The phrase "bronze gates [*pylas chalkas*]"[52] is borrowed from Ps 107 [106]:10–16, where the exile is imagined as a prison for the Israelites to serve their sentence (cf. Isa 42:7; 49:9). However, Yahweh broke into pieces both the bronze gates and the iron bars of this prison in order to release his people.[53] The hymnographer uses this metaphor by applying it to a different sort of prison, Hades, with Jesus substituting for YHWH (LXX: *kyrios*, Ps 107 [106]:15–16). A trigger that may have prompted the hymnographer to transpose this metaphor from exile to Hades was probably v. 18 "they drew near to the gates of death" (*pylōn tou thanatou*), where the exile is equated with death. What is interesting in Ps 107 (106) and in our hymn as well is that God's deliverance occurs suddenly, unexpectedly, like a wonder. And this is what the hymnographer sought to convey by Jesus's sudden appearance in the underworld, not as another prisoner on Hades's long list of captives but, in fact, as a mighty liberator.

"Being God, he resurrected the souls, which I previously had in possession [*psychas has kateichon to prin, theos ōn anestēse*]
Based on the verb *katechō*'s wide array of meanings ("to hold fast, to have in possession, to overpower, to detain, to confine"), the main idea here is that Hades used to hold fast, to detain, the souls of mortal human beings—indirectly hinting at Hades's profile as a prison[54] for these souls.[55] Nevertheless, through his descent to Hades, hardly implied by 1 Pet 3:18–20 (cf. Eph 4:8–9), Jesus as God (*theos ōn*) "resurrected" (*anestēse*) captive souls. The literal meaning of the verb *anistēmi*, "to stand up, to raise up" and the chronology of Jesus's last moments on the cross make one think of an odd episode narrated only by Matt 27:52–53. According to this brief passage, when Jesus yielded his spirit on the cross, the tombs were opened, and many "fallen-asleep bodies of the saints were awakened, raised" (*sōmata tōn kekoimēmenōn hagiōn ēgerthē*) and after Jesus's "resurrection" (*egersin*) began to appear in the "holy city" (Jerusalem). Interestingly, the rising and

appearance of these righteous people are described as a two-phase process, beginning with the "awakening," which coincides with Jesus's death on the cross (and descent to Hades) and ending with the "appearance," which happens after Jesus's resurrection and appearance to his disciples.

The Old Testament often asserts that God has power over the underworld and that he can "raise" (*egeirō*) souls from Hades (1 Sam 2:6; Ps 16 [15]:10; 30:3 [29:4]). The hymnographer is in agreement with this creedal statement when he says that Jesus, "being God" (*theos ōn*), accomplished the destruction of the bronze gates of Hades.

The following hymn, centered on the same theme of Hades's defeat, explores further Jesus's divinity which enabled the "deathless life" (*zoē athanatos*) to mortify the underworld and resurrect the dead. Through his descent to the realm of death, Jesus gave life to the dead from "subterranean regions," prompting the doxology of the "powers of heaven." Note that the last two phrases are found in Phil 2:5–11, dealing with Jesus's humbleness and exaltation:

When you descended [*katēlthes*] unto death, the deathless life, then you mortified [*enekrōsas*] Hades through the lightning [*astrapē*] of divinity [*theotētos*]. And, when you resurrected [*anestēsas*] the dead ones [*tethneōtas*] from subterranean regions [*katachthoniōn*], all the powers of heavens [*epouraniōn*] cried out: "O Giver of Life, Christ our God, glory to you." (Holy Saturday, Matins, Lamentations, Apolytichon)

For the author of the next hymn, the cause of Jesus's victory over Hades lies with his "divine emptying" (*theian kenōsin*) on the cross:

Foreseeing [*proorōn*] your divine emptying [*kenōsin*] on the cross, Habakkuk cried out in astonishment [*exestēkōs*]: "While consorting [*homilōn*] with those in Hades [*tois en hadē*], you broke off [*diekopsas*] the power [*kratos*] of the rulers [*dynastōn*] as an almighty [*pantodynamos*], O Good One." (Holy Saturday, Matins, Ode 3, Heirmos)

The hymn quotes freely Hab 3:13–14a, found in the "Psalm or Prayer of Habakkuk" (3:1–19), one of the oldest poems in the Hebrew Bible (next to other quite old texts such as Exod 15; Deut 33; Judg 5; Ps 68 [67]), which was likely composed in the pre-monarchic period as a victory hymn of the divine warrior over cosmic and earthly enemies.[56] Using the language and imagery of a theophany, the prayer of Habakkuk depicts Yahweh as a commander-in-chief, coming from the south (Teman), fighting the "lawless" (*anomōn*), and saving the "anointed ones" (*christous*): "Having come out [*exēlthes*] for the salvation of your people, to save your anointed ones [*christous*], you cast [*ebales*] death on the heads of the lawless [*anomōn*]. . . . In a frenzy [*ekstasei*] you cut through [*diekopsas*] the heads of the mighty [*kephalas dynastōn*]" (Hab 3:13–14a).

In our hymn, the word "heads" (*kephalas*) from Hab 3:14a is replaced interpretatively with "power" (*kratos*). One can imagine Jesus, who on the cross has shown his self-accepted extreme humility, descending to the underworld and breaking or cutting off the power of the rulers who tried to protect their master, a personified Hades. As a matter of fact, Jesus's "power, made perfect in weakness" (*dynamis en astheneia teleitai*) (2 Cor 12:9), proved to be irresistible to the adverse powers of the underworld.

The above-examined hymn, as well as several others prescribed for Holy Saturday, contains the "divine deception" theme that is well attested in the writings of patristic authors. As Nicholas Constas notices, "A remarkable number of Greek patristic thinkers gave expression to the theory that Satan was deceived by Christ, who exploited his adversary's mistaken belief that the object of his desires was a mere man and not the deity incarnate. Driven by an insatiable hunger for human bodies, the demonic appetite was inexorably drawn to devour the seemingly mortal flesh of Jesus."[57]

If one takes a closer look at the canonical gospels, especially Mark, one notices Jesus's reluctance to disclose his identity. Neither the tempting "devil" (*diabolos*, lit. "slanderer") in Luke 4:3 nor the cunning "unclean spirit" (*pneuma akataron*) in Mark 5:7–8 was able to discern who Jesus really was.[58] This is why the lord of the underworld, the personified Hades in our hymn, unsure of Jesus's identity, received him as any other human soul into his feud. Once arrived there, Jesus showed his true identity by breaking the gates and bars of Hades's prison.

The famous Byzantine icon of Jesus's resurrection, Anastasis (lit. "rising up"), eternized this moment. The magnificent fourteenth-century fresco of Chora Monastery in Istanbul (Constantinople) showcases Jesus rising up from the underworld. As he pulls out and holds the wrists of the righteous of the Old Testament, beginning with Adam and Eve, the victorious Jesus is trampling over gates, locks, and keys of the underworld prison, while keeping a tied-up dragon-like Hades/Satan under his feet. "The one born of

Mary" deceives the great deceiver of old, and salvation history comes full circle to a new beginning by glimpsing beyond the curtain of time.

Hades Was Embittered

O Logos, Hades was embittered [*epikranthē*] on meeting you [*synantēsas*], seeing a deified mortal [*broton tetheōmenon*], spotted [*katastikton*] with bruises [*mōlōpsi*] yet all-powerful in action [*pansthenourgon*]; [and] being shocked [*phriktō*] at [your] appearance [*morphēs*], it perished [was lost] [*diapephōnēken*]. (Holy Saturday, Matins, Troparion)

The beginning of this hymn is a partial quote from Isa 14:9.

LXX: Hades below [*katōthen*] was embittered [*epikranthē*] on meeting [*synantēsas*] you; all the giants [*gigantes*], those who ruled [*arxantes*] the earth rose together [*synērgerthēsan*] against you [*soi*], those who rose [*egeirantes*] from their thrones [*thronōn*], all the kings of the nations.
MT: Sheol was excited [*rgzh*] to greet your coming [*l-qr't bw'k*], rousing [*ʿwrr*] for you the shades [*rp'ym*] of all earth's leaders [*ʿttwdy*, lit. "rams"], raising [*hqym*] from their thrones all the kings of nations.

Sheol acts here as a person exhibiting feelings and actions. That the underworld is often personified in the Hebrew Bible (e.g., Isa 5:14) needs no further discussion. However, scholarly opinion is split on whether there is a deity (Sheol) behind death and the underworld.[59]

Isa 14:9, part of 14:4–23 (a taut song concerning Babylon), describes the journey of the defeated and executed Babylonian king to the underworld. The reader learns starting at v. 12 about the pride of this unnamed king, who deliberates in himself how to usurp God from his throne and take his place as master of the universe. God acts immediately, casting him into the pit. This is where Isa 14:9 takes the story further. One notices a difference in tone between the MT and the LXX of v. 9 pertaining to the underworld's attitude toward this oppressing king.

According to the MT reading, as the executed king enters Sheol, the latter, being excited, summons up the shades of deceased rulers of the earth to welcome the proud oppressor. There is an obvious irony here: the rulers of nations, still sitting quasi-asleep on their thrones in a horrifyingly silent underworld, rulers who when alive were oppressed by that king, are now requested to greet his coming. They greet him, though by coercion and in jest.

In the LXX version of Isa 14:9, this irony is missing. The translator-interpreter portrays Hades as being embittered at the king's arrival. Likewise, the deceased rulers become annoyed by the intruder, who disturbs Hades's silence and stillness.

Unsurprisingly, the LXX reading would have appealed to the hymnographer, who found in Hades's bitterness a much-anticipated response to Jesus's descent to the underworld. In addition to that, the hymnographer employs Isa 14:9 to create a contrast between the Babylonian king, whose pride matches Hades's bitterness, and Jesus's unpublicized extreme humility able to defeat the master of the underworld in his own habitation.

"Hades was embittered on meeting you [*ho hades . . . epikranthē synantēsas soi*]"

If in a previously expounded hymn, Hades was depicted as "groaning" (*stenōn*), now the same Hades is construed as "embittered" (*epikranthē*) upon meeting Jesus. Both attributes pertaining to the underworld, "groaning" and "embittered," foretell Hades's unavoidable destruction and loss, which, in fact, are briefly unveiled at the end of this hymn: "[Hades] became lost/perished" (*diapephōnēken*). The verb *synantaō*, "to meet," may intimate unpredictability, i.e., "to come upon" by chance (with the dative); e.g., Deut 22:6). If this is the case here, then Hades accidentally notices Jesus among other inmates of his spooky realm. Looking closely at the new prisoner, Hades comes to realize that Jesus, though spotted with bruises, is not a simple "mortal human being" (*broton*) but a "deified" (*tetheōmenon*) character, "all-powerful in action" (*pansthenourgon*).

The Gk. word *brotos*, translated here as "mortal human being," occurs in the LXX seventeen times but limited to the book of Job. In more than half of these occurrences, *brotos* stands for the Hebrew *'ĕnôš* (Job 4:17; 9:2; 15:14; 25:4; 28:13; 32:8; 33:12; 36:25), conventionally, though approximately, understood as a generic term for "human being." However, the Heb. term is related to a Semitic verbal root, *'-n-š*, "to be week, to be mortal," attested only once in the Hebrew Bible (2 Sam 12:15: *way-yiʾānaš* [Niphʿal], "and he became sick"; LXX: *ērrōstēsen*, "he became weak," of the newborn son of David and Bathsheba) but well evidenced in the Akk. verb *enēšu(m)*, "to be weak, to be sick, to be mortal."

The Aramaic phrase *kəbar-ʾĕnāš* in Dan 7:13, containing the word *ʾĕnāš* (cf. Heb, *ʾĕnôš*, Ps 8:4; 144 [143]:3), was literally translated by the LXX (Theod.) as *hōs hyios anthrōpou*, "like a son of man," i.e., "like a human being."[60] However, since both lexical variants, Heb. and Aramaic, derive from the same verbal root, *ʾ-n-š*, "to be weak, to be mortal," *brotos* would have been a better choice than *anthrōpos* to convey the special meaning (weak, mortal) of the Heb. *ʾĕnôš* and the Aramaic *ʾĕnāš*.

A somewhat similar New Testament phrase, *ho hyios tou anthrōpou*, "the Son of Man," with the definite article, is used in all occurrences (except Acts 7:56) by Jesus as a self-referential title (e.g., Mark 2:10; 8:31; Matt 8:20; 25:31; Luke 19:10), Jesus's distinctive way of speaking, or "idiolect," as Larry Hurtado coined it.[61] One may surmise that Jesus used this phrase to show that he is identifiable with the human person in what is humanity's most defining feature, its weakness and mortality.

By using the term *brotos* (let us say, over *anthrōpos*) in the phrase *broton tetheōmenon*, "deified mortal (human being)," with respect to Jesus's descent to Hades, our hymnographer betrayed a good grasp of the LXX lexicon (i.e., those occurrences in Job where *brotos* renders Heb. *ʾĕnôš*), and accomplishment in conveying the paradoxical concurrence of mortality and divinity in Jesus's persona.

"Being shocked at [your] appearance [*phriktō tēs morphēs*]"
Hades is "shocked at the appearance" (*phriktō tēs morphēs*) of Jesus: a deified mortal spotted with bruises yet all-powerful in operation. The phrase *katastikton tois mōlōpsi*, "spotted with bruises," echoes Isa 53:5, "by his bruise [*mōlōpi*] we were healed"; in v. 4, Israel misjudged the suffering Servant as being "smitten by God" without realizing that "he was wounded because of our transgressions"; note 1 Pet 2:24, quoting Isa 53:5 with respect to Jesus's crucifixion.

Jesus's appearance is strange, to say the least—a striking blend of weakness, power, and bewilderment. How would a "deified mortal human being" have looked to our hymnographer? Might one assume some distinguishing facial or bodily features? Hades's being shocked at Jesus's "appearance" leads one to such a supposition. A similar shock-inducing fear experienced by Hades in front of the numinous Jesus is mentioned in Eliphaz's account of his nocturnal vision: "Shuddering fear [*phrikē*] fell upon [*synēntēsen*] me, and trembling [*tromos*], and my bones quaked [*synenseisen*] tremendously" (Job 4:14).[62] Note the verb *synantaō*, "to meet," found in our hymn, here has the meaning "to fall upon."

"It [Hades] was lost [*diapephōnēken*]"

As a result of that unexpectedly intense shock, Hades became lost, perished instantaneously, with no warning sign whatsoever. The same verb, *diaphōneō*, "to be lost, to perish," occurring seven times in the whole Bible, is found in Israel's statement, "Our hope perished, we are lost" (*apōlōlen hē elpis hēmōn, diapephōnēkamen*) (Ezek 37:11), uttered in the wake of the Babylonian exile.

The literary-theological motif of Hades's "embitterment" may also be found in John Chrysostom's famous *Paschal Homily* (*Sermo catecheticus in pascha*, listed among *spuria*; PG 59:721–724). The author of this sermon repeats seven times the verb *pikrainō*, "to be embittered," as a rhetorical device that underscores Hades's unquenchable anger at Jesus's appearance in his subterranean domain:

He plundered [*eskyleuse*] Hades when he descended [*katelthōn*] into Hades. He brought bitterness [*epikranen*] to him [Hades] when this tasted his [Jesus's] flesh. Anticipating [*prolabōn*] this, Isaiah proclaimed: "Hades," he said, "was embittered [*epiktanthē*] when he met [*synantēsas*] you below. It was embittered because it was abolished [*katērgēthē*]. It was embittered because it was mocked [*enepaichthē*]. It was embittered because it was mortified [*enekrōthē*]. It was embittered because it was pulled down [*kathērethē*]. It was embittered because it was shackled [*edesmeuthē*]. It took a body [*sōma*] and encountered [*perietychen*] God. It took earth [*gēn*] and came face to face [*synēntēsan*] with heaven. It took what it saw [*eblepe*] and fell by what it could not see. Death, where is your sting [*kentron*]? Hades, where is your victory [*nikos*]? Christ is risen [*anestē*] and you are overthrown [*katabeblēsai*]. Christ is risen and demons have fallen [*peptōkasi*]. Christ is risen and angels rejoice [*chairousin*]. Christ is risen and life rules [*politeuetai*]. Christ is risen and not one dead [*nekros oudeis*] is in the tomb. Christ, having risen [*egertheis*] from the dead, became the first fruits [*aparchē*] of those who slept. To him be the glory [*doxa*] and the dominion [*kratos*] forever. Amen." (Sunday of Pascha, The Catechetical Paschal Homily of John Chrysostom)

Adam's Nature Renewed

You have come down [*katapephoitēkas*] in the lowest parts of the earth [*en katōtatois tēs gēs*], in order to fill [*plērōsēs*] all things with your glory [*doxēs*]. For my substance/nature [*hypostasis*] that [is] in Adam was not hidden [*ekrybē*] from you; and being entombed [*tapheis*], you made me, the corrupted one [*phtharenta*], new [*kainopoieis*], O Lover of Humanity [*philanthrōpe*]. (Holy Saturday, Matins, Troparion)

This hymn, referring to Jesus's descent, does not use the word *hadēs*, "Hades," but rather a poetical substitute, "the lowest [parts] of the earth" (*en katōtatois tēs gēs*), borrowed most likely from Ps 139 (138):15 (LXX). It is as if the hymnographer wanted to emphasize Jesus's entombment and descent as a sign of extreme humility (going down to the lowest parts) and suffering that leads to life and newness for those dwelling in the underworld.

First, let us take a look at the inspiring Ps 139 (138):15 and its main textual witnesses.

LXX: My frame [*to ostoun*] was not concealed [*ekrybē*] from you, that you made [*epoiēsas*] in secret [*kryphē*], and my substance [*hypostasis*] in the lowest [*katōtatois*] [parts] of the earth [cf. V: *et substantia mea in inferioribus terrae*].

MT: My frame [*ʿaṣmî*] was not hidden [*nikḥad*] from you, when I was being made [*ʿuśśîtî*] in secret [*bas-sēter*], intricately woven [*ruqqamtî*] in the depths [*taḥtiyyôt*] of the earth.

The MT reads *ruqqamtî*, "intricately woven," where the LXX has *hypostasis*, "my substance" (supported by the parallel with *ostoun*, "bone" [skeleton, frame], in v. 15a). The LXX has "which you made me" (supported by the context of v. 15) vs. the MT "I was being made." By dittography of Resh, the MT produced the verbal form *(bstR) ruqqamtî*, "intricately woven." Note that in Deut 11:6, *hypostasis* is employed for the Hebrew *yqwm*, "what subsists, what is living"—close to what the MT would have had (*qmty* from the same root, *q-w-m*, "to stand up, to support") without the above-mentioned dittography.

Targum on Psalms: My frame is not concealed [*ʾtks*ʾ] from you, for I was made [*ʾtʿbydyt*] in secret [*b-ṭwmr*ʾ], I was formed [*ʾṣtyyryt*] in the womb [*krys*ʾ] of my [mother [*d-ʾwm*ʾ)].

The targumist harmonizes apparently v. 15b with v. 13 (MT: "you protected me in the womb of my mother [*bbṭn ʾmy*]").

> S: My bones [*grmy*] are not concealed [*ksyn*] from you, which you made [*d-ʿbdt*] in secret [*b-strʾ*], [when] you descended [*nḥtt*] to the lowest [parts] of the earth."

It is noteworthy that the Syriac verbal form *nḥtt*, "you descended," instead of the LXX's "nature" [*hypostasis*], brings S quite close to our hymn: "You [Jesus] have come down [*katapephoitēkas*]." Did the hymnographer have access to S or to an LXX ms. similar in reading to the former?

"You have come down in the lowest parts of the earth [*katapephoitēkas en katōtatois tēs gēs*]"
The verbal root *kataphoitaō*, "to come down constantly or regularly," attested in ancient Classical Greek (e.g., Herodotus), may describe wild beasts coming down regularly from mountains to prey. Absent in the Bible, this verb occurs in patristic writings with regard to Old Testament theophanies, the Incarnation, and Jesus's descent to Hades.

Note that the *katabasis*, "descent," motif occurs as early as Eph 4:9: "What is, 'He ascended [*anebē*],' but that he descended [*katebē*] first [*prōton*] in the lower parts [*katōtera merē*] of the earth."

Ps 139 (138): 15, whence the phrase *en* [*tois*] *katōtatois tēs gēs*, "in the lowest parts of the earth," along with the term *hypostasis*, "substance," was borrowed, underscores a deep theological idea, namely, that humans, unlike other living creatures, are created individually by God. On the one hand, the MT emphasizes the intricacy and distinctiveness of each human person being "intricately woven"[63] by the great Artist. In this psalmist's view, humans are special to God, hence his exaltation: "I will acknowledge [*exomologēsomai*] you, for I was made fearfully marvelous [*phoberōs ethaumastōtēn*]."

On the other hand, the LXX differentiates between "frame" (*ostoun*; skeleton, muscles, skin—the visible stuff) and "substance" (*hypostasis*; support, sediment—what is invisible yet defining each individual) of each human being. The common element in the textual witnesses of Ps 139 (138):15 is that God creates, shapes, each individual human being[64] and that this creation occurs in secret, in the "lowest parts of the earth" (perhaps a hint at Gen 2:7, of "humanity" [*anthrōpos*] being shaped out of "dust from the ground" [*chous apo tēs gēs*]).

The dominant belief in ancient Israel was that God shapes each individual in the mother's womb (Job 10:8–12; Jer 1:5). However, in Ps 139 (138):15, the earth imagery overlaps with that of a mother's womb (cf. v. 13 and v. 15 in the reading of Targum on Psalms). One may note that the comparison of earth with a mother was common in the ANE and Greece.[65]

One might adduce Pr Man 1:13 (Odes 12:13) as the second place where the phrase *en tois katōtatois tēs gēs*, "in the lowest parts of the earth," occurs in the LXX: "I ask you, beseeching, 'Unfasten [*anes*] me, O Lord; unfasten! Do not destroy me together [*synapolesēs*] with my lawless deeds, nor be angry always and keep evil for me, nor condemn [*katadikasēs*] me in the lowest parts of the earth [*en tois katōtatois tēs gēs*], for you O Lord are the God of those who repent [*metanountōn*]."

If the phrase in Ps 139 (138):15 appears in a creation context, in Pr Man 1:13 (Odes 12:13), it is found in a punitive framework. That is why the author of the latter text petitions God to "unfasten, release" him apparently from a prison-like underworld. Nevertheless, our hymn does not echo such a negative aspect of Hades. Jesus does not descend to some folks in chains but rather to human beings who are corrupted (or in a state of paralysis) in order to revive and renew them.

"In order to fill all things with your glory [*tēs doxēs ta panta plērōsēs*]"
The accent in this hymn falls on the glory (*doxa*) that Jesus brought to the underworld as he came down (*katapephoitēkas*) to the lowest parts of the earth; and this glory or divine manifestation translates into the restoration of humanity. Most likely, this restoration motif was the bridge linking our hymn and Ps 139 (138):15, dealing with the creation of humanity. Since God made the human frame and substance in secret, within the earth, Jesus had to come down to the depths of the earth in order to make new (*kainopoieō*) the corrupted (*phtharenta*) human being whose substance (*hypostasis*) is found in Adam, the human prototype.

"My substance that [is] in Adam was not hidden from you
[*ouk ekrybē hē hypostasis mou hē en Adam*]"
The other term that the hymnographer borrows from Ps 139 (138):15 is *hypostasis*, "substance." The word occurs some twenty times in the LXX for twelve different Hebrew equivalents. The basic meaning of *hypostasis* in the LXX is the reality behind phenomena or the foundation of life that is with God, namely, the "life plan" of a human being that is hidden with God—a

fitting meaning in Ps 139 (138):15.[66] The hymnographer suggests that the substance, that invisible yet real support that defines each individual and that is part of Adam (humanity), is well known by its Creator.

"And being entombed, you made me, the corrupted one, new [*tapheis phtharenta me kainopoieis*]"

The hymnographer identifies himself with any human being, including those who lived in Old Testament times and were in Hades when Jesus was entombed. The entombment hints at Jesus's descent to the underworld, as it obtains with the juxtaposition between "he was buried" (*etaphē*) and "and in the Hades" (*kai en tō hadē*), as happened with the rich man in the parable of poor Lazarus (in Luke 16:22–23), where the burial place functions as a portal or gateway to Hades.

The hymn ponders the ontological dimension of Jesus's descent to Hades. Through his coming down to the underworld, Jesus achieved the greatest victory, which, besides inflicting fatal wounds on Hades, is the renewal of a corrupted, paralyzed humanity, beginning with Adam and all individuals dwelling in that God-forgotten place and state of being.

In his *Explorations in Theology*, Hans Urs von Balthasar notes that "the descent into hell between Christ's death and resurrection is a necessary expression of the event of the redemption—not, indeed (as on Good Friday), within the history actually in progress, but (on Holy Saturday) in the history already accomplished of the old aeon, in the sheol of the Old Testament."[67] However, Luther and Calvin, overemphasizing Jesus's sufferings on the cross, make a suffering in the underworld on Holy Saturday superfluous.

What does our hymn have to say on the matter of Jesus's redemptive descent? There are two moments of the Passion saga that show up repeatedly in hymns: the cross and the entombment along with the descent to Hades. What Balthasar asserts with respect to Jesus's suffering in Hades on Holy Saturday (i.e., his redemptive work being accomplished in the "old aeon," the Old Testament period vs. Good Friday's suffering within the unfolding history) may be found in our hymn, where Jesus's descent impacts on all of Hades's denizens going back to the very beginning of creation, to Adam, and making new the human "substance"—past, present, and future—since all individuals come into existence (receive "substance") through the "first human being Adam" (*prōtos anthrōpos Adam*) and are restored by and in the "last Adam" (*ho eschatos Adam*) (1 Cor 15:45).

I would like to point out the kenotic approach the hymnographer follows while dealing with Jesus's crucifixion and descent to Hades. Beginning with the blood-dropping prayer of Gethsemane and the loud cry of loneliness, Jesus's agony and suffering have become continuous, lasting until the end of the world. The risen Lord still carries the wounds of his crucifixion as an unshaking banner of victory, alas, a victory achieved and expressed through extreme humility, and this is the paradox of all paradoxes.

Streams of Life in Hades

The Wisdom of God, while pouring forth [procheousa] streams of life [rheithra tēs zōēs], entering secretly [hypeisdysa] the tomb, gives life [zōopoiei] to the ones in the impenetrable [adytois] innermost parts [mychois] of Hades. (Holy Saturday, Matins, Lamentations, Stanza 2)

In this tiny poetical piece, the hymnographer portrays Jesus as the Wisdom of God pouring forth streams of life. By entering the tomb, Wisdom vivifies those held in the impassable "innermost sections of Hades." Jesus's "rest" in the tomb, lying lifeless in that dark and cold place, had an overwhelming impact on the very underworld (Hades [hadēs]), a former place of death now replete with life.

The phrase theou sophia, "Wisdom of God," would automatically send the reader to Prov 8:22–31, the much-celebrated locus on Wisdom's activity within God's creation. Since I have previously discussed this pericope in detail,[68] it suffices here to add only a few words on Wisdom's role as God's vivifying agent.

In the present hymn, the Wisdom of God pours forth streams of life and vivifies even the most "dead" (sic)—those held in Hades's innermost parts. And this is appropriate given the portrayal of Wisdom in Prov 8:22–31, where she appears as God's agent in the creation.

Although the Wisdom of God in the book of Proverbs is merely God's creating agent (and only implicitly has something to do with life), here she is introduced as a primary source and transmitter of life. The hymnographer blends the biblical phrase "Wisdom of God" with Jesus's essential attribute as giver of life, and life understood here in all its complexity, physical and spiritual, transient and eternal, as Jesus so poignantly puts it: "As for me, I came so that they may have life [zōēn echōsin], and have it abundantly [perisson]"

(John 10:10). If one couples the Johannine texts on Jesus–life association (John 1:4; 3:16; 6:33; 14:6) with the synoptic resurrection narratives (Mark 5:22–23, 35–43 [Jairus's daughter]; Luke 7:11–17 [son of the widow from Nain]) and with John 11 (Lazarus), one may determine the possible textual evidence the hymnographer might have employed when he composed this hymn. This is an interesting hermeneutical procedure by which a well-known and often-used phrase ("Wisdom of God") functioning as signifier is fused with an attribute intrinsic to the signified (Jesus) into a new image.

By choosing the form *zōopoiei*, "gives life, vivifies," the hymnographer hints at John 5:21: "For as the Father raises the dead [*egeirei tous nekrous*] and gives life [*zōopoiei*] to them, even so the Son gives life [*zōopoiei*] to whom he wills [*hous thelei*]."

One may notice the identification of the Son with the Father: both are giving life to the dead. In addition, the Johannine text emphasizes the Son's will. The Son may give life to whomever he wants. And the hymn, as if corroborating this detail, asserts that God's Wisdom "gives life" (*zōopoiei*) to those held in the "impenetrable innermost parts of Hades" (*adytous hadou mychois*).

The verb used here, *hypeisdyomai*, "to get in secretly, to slip in, to steal in," unattested in the Bible[69] though found in ancient Greek works (e.g., Herodotus, *The Histories* 1.12) and ancient Christian writings (e.g., Epiphanius, *Panarion* 76.49 [*PG* 42:621B), intimates the idea of entering a place secretly, stealthly, or stealing in unnoticed. Jesus, God's Wisdom, steals into the tomb unnoticeably, heading for Hades, his final destination.

The word *mychois*, "innermost parts," occurs two times in the Bible, Wis 17:4–5, 14[13]–15[14].[70]

At this juncture, a few words about the book of wisdom of Solomon are warranted. This, purporting to be written by Solomon, was composed during the Second Temple period, sometime between 100 B.C.E. and 50 C.E., by a writer conventionally labeled Pseudo-Solomon. Several allusions to an anti-Jewish persecution (Wis 2:10–3:19) lead one to the assumption that the book was written during Gaius Caligula's reign (37–41 C.E.).[71]

Unlike the Old Testament proto-canonical Wisdom literature, whose emphasis is on the "here and now" of life in search of wisdom that could help one observe God's law, the focus of the *anaginoskomenon* Wisdom of Solomon, especially in chaps. 1–6, is on the afterlife.[72] There are a few places where Wis (especially chap. 2) seems to be an almost sarcastic response to the skepticism on the reality of the afterlife found, for instance, in Eccl (3:19–22; 6:12).[73]

The second part of the book (Wis 10–19) is a review of "salvation history," where Exodus holds a preeminent place. Wis 17:1–18:4, to which the above two quoted passages belong, is a retelling of the ninth plague (darkness) that struck Egypt prior to the Exodus event (Exod 10:21–29).[74]

Interestingly, in Wis 17:14[13]–15[14], the word *mychos* appears together with *hadēs*, "Hades," as a qualifier, the "innermost parts of Hades," precisely as in our hymn. Note that Wis uses this phrase analogically likening the Egyptians' fate to that of the inhabitants of Hades. The Egyptians lingered idly for three days on their beds due to that "palpable darkness" (*psēlaphēton skotos*) (Exod 10:21), while the Hebrews had light wherever they were "doing their dealings" (*kateginonto*) (v. 23). Exod's quite brief description is intensified by Wis, which interprets the "darkness" as coming from "Hades's innermost chambers" and wrapping the Egyptians into a sleep haunted by "monstrous phantoms" (*terasin phantasmōn*), leading to utter paralysis. Nevertheless, in our hymn, "Hades's innermost parts" is used in a plain, literal sense, referring to the underworld's depths, conquered by the life-giving Wisdom of God.

The verbal adjective *adytos* (verb *dyō*, "to enter"), "not to be entered, impenetrable," intensifies the idea that Wisdom, according to Jewish Scriptures, so anchored in God's space-time creation, is now operating at the metaphysical level, reaching the depths of the underworld. In our hymn, the use of *mychos* with *adytos* designates the innermost part of Hades, imagined as a household or dwelling place, with a hidden, secret, inner room, where precious things, treasures, were kept safely; one may assume that in our hymn, "the ones" located in *adytois mychois*, "impenetrable innermost parts," were viewed as Hades's most valuable and securely kept treasure.

While remaining silent on the identity of "the ones" (*tous*) dwelling or presumably held by a sort of coercion in the depths of Hades, the hymnographer nevertheless alludes to their lifelessness when, upon entering into the tomb, Wisdom's streams of life and vivifying power reach the innermost parts of Hades. In addition, there is not even the slightest indication of the identity of the owner (master) of Hades. It is if as Hades became deserted, remaining only with its innermost part being occupied by some "captives," who are now touched by the unstoppable streams of life coming from God's recently entered Wisdom.

Quite stingy in description, nevertheless, the hymnographer manages to paint a grotesque image similar to scenes in Theater of the Absurd. The eerie silence and motionlessness of Hades's innermost part stands in sharp contrast to the sudden emergence of God's very Wisdom, so instrumental in creation (Prov 8) and salvation history (Wis 10–19). The divine Wisdom now enters a small tomb while pouring forth streams of life and vivifying all those in Hades.

One can read this hymn as a response to Wis 17's theme of the terrifying invulnerability of the underworld, with its retinue of monstrous phantoms and terrifying sounds reverberating from its deepest depths. The hymnographer shows the immediate concrete results of Wisdom's descent to the netherworld. By her stealth in entering the tomb, God's Wisdom, pouring forth streams of life, gives life to those dwelling in Hades.

In the following prose lament attributed to the tenth-century author Symeon Metaphrastes (though preserved in a fourteenth-century ms.), Mary laments over her lost son, while rhetorically contrasting Gabriel's promise at the Annunciation to her present experience: "Even Gabriel's greeting turns out to be almost the contrary for me. For now it is not the case that 'The Lord is with me' [Luke 1:28], as he promised to me, but you [Lord] are wandering without breath and among the dead in the innermost chambers of Hades [*alla sy men apnous en nekrois kai hadou tameia phoitas ta endotera*]."[75]

By using a similar phrase ("Hades's innermost chambers" [*hadou tameia phoitas ta endotera*]) to the one employed in our hymn (*hadou mychois*), where Jesus is found wandering lifelessly, this lament nicely complements our hymn. The lament expresses the view of a mourning mother standing by her son's tomb yet unable to see through rocks and stones and learn what is really happening deep beneath the ground in Hades—and this is precisely what our hymn discloses in a brief but poignant way: the victory of God's Wisdom, who having intruded into the tomb, was able to pour out life even to those in the underworld's recesses.

Emptying Hades's Royal Chambers

When you willingly [*thelōn*] let yourself to be enclosed bodily [*sarkikōs synekleisthēs*] in the tomb [*en tō taphō*], remaining uncircumscribed [*aperigraptos*] and undefined [*adioristos*] in the nature [*physei*] of [your] divinity [*theotētos*], then you shut up [*apekleisas*] the inner rooms of death [*thanatou tameia*], and you emptied all the royal chambers of Hades [*hadou basileia*], O Christ. Thus, you made this Sabbath worthy [*ēxiōsas*] of your divine blessing [*eulogias*], glory [*doxēs*] and your very splendor [*lamprotētos*]. (Holy Saturday, Vespers, Aposticon)

"When you willingly let yourself to be enclosed bodily in the tomb, remaining uncircumscribed and undefined in the nature of [your] divinity [*hote en tō taphō sarkikōs, thelōn synekleisthēs ho physei tēs theotētos menōn aperigraptos kai adioristos*]"

The phrase "enclosed bodily in the tomb" (*en tō taphō sarkikōs... synekleisthēs*) might be reminiscent of "being put to death in the flesh" (*thanatōtheis... sarki*) (1 Pet 3:18: "In the body, he was put to death, in spirit he was made alive, in which [spirit], having gone [*poreutheis*], he proclaimed [*ekēryxen*] to the spirits in prison [*tois en phylakē pneumasin*]"). Both writers, Peter and our hymnographer, rush to say that Jesus's death affected solely the "flesh" (*sarx*), his physical, human nature; however, "in spirit [he] was made alive" (*zōopoiētheis . . . pneumati*), Peter affirms, and the hymnographer agrees with him when he expands theologically on Jesus, who, while "enclosed bodily" in the tomb, "remained uncircumscribed [*aperigraptos*] and undefined [*adioristos*] in the nature of [his] divinity [*theotētos*]." If the Petrine text sketches solely a contrast between Jesus's suffering/death and his resurrection, while using loosely the terms *sarks*, "body" (lit. "flesh"), and *pneuma*, "spirit," with reference to Jesus as a person in two different phases (death and return to life),[76] the present hymn inserts the phrase *physei tēs theotētos*, "in the nature of [his] divinity," as a theological gloss, emphasizing Jesus's divine nature (i.e., "divinity") which did not suffer any constraint in the tomb, in sharp contrast to his humanity.

The above-cited hymn's line reverberates in the following passage from Maximus the Confessor's (ca. 580–662) *Ambigua*. For Maximus, Jesus's divinity (*ta theika*, lit. "the things of God") was made manifest through the "things of a slave" (*ta doulika*) or "means of a flesh" (*sarkikōs*), and, conversely, Jesus's humanity (*ta sarkika*, lit. "the things of the flesh") was revealed by means of his divinity (*theikōs*, lit. "as a God"). Note the same use here, as in our hymn, of the adverb *sarkikōs*, "means of flesh," indicating Jesus's human nature. And similarly to our hymn, Maximus underscores that

Jesus "remained the Lord by nature," which our hymnographer expands to "uncircumscribed [*aperigraptos*] and undefined [*adioristos*] [divinity]."[77]

> For he remained [*memenēke*] Lord [*despotēs*] by nature [*physei*], and became a slave [*doulos*] for my sake, who am a slave by nature [*physei*], so that he might make me lord over the one [i.e., the devil] who through deception [*di' apatēs*] despotically lorded it over me. It is precisely for this reason that he does the things of a slave [*doulika*] in a lordly manner [*despotikōs*], that is, he does the things of the flesh [*ta sarkika*] as God [*theikōs*], showing forth his impassible and naturally sovereign power by means of the flesh— a power which through his passion destroyed corruptibility, and which through his death created life indestructible. In doing lordly things in the manner of a slave, that is, the things of God [*ta theika*] by means of the flesh [*sarkikōs*], he intimates his ineffable self-emptying which through passible flesh divinized all humanity, fallen to the ground through corruption. (*Ambigua* 4)[78]

Might the phrase "enclosed bodily in the tomb" (*en tō taphō sarkikōs . . . synekleisthēs*) be an echo of Matt 27:62–66 on sealing the stone of Jesus's tomb? On the day following the crucifixion, i.e., on Saturday, the priests and the Pharisees came to Pilate, asking him to secure the tomb so that Jesus's disciples would not be able to steal his body: "Order the tomb to be made secure [*asphalisthēnai ton taphon*] until the third day. . . . So they went and made the tomb secure [*ēsphalisanto*] by sealing the stone [*sphragisantes*] and setting a guard" (vv. 64, 66). The details Matthew provides make the imagery of Jesus being "enclosed in the tomb" (verb *synkleiō*, "to shut, to close, to confine") even more redolent.

"You shut off the inner rooms of death, and you emptied all the royal chambers of Hades [*ta thanatou apekleisas tameia kai hadou apanta ekenōsas . . . basileia*]"
The phrase *thanatou tameia*, "inner rooms of death," is found in Prov 7:27 (LXX): "Her house—roads of Hades [*hodoi hadou*; MT: *darkēy šə'ôl*, "Sheol's roads"] leading down [*katagousai*; MT: *yōrədôt*, "descending"] to Death's inner rooms [*tamieia tou thanatou*; MT: *ḥadrēy māwet*]."

The literary unit Prov 7:24–27 begins with Wisdom's exhortation and ends with the reason for such an exhortation: the irresistible and deadly nature of the adulteress's seductiveness. As throughout the book of Proverbs, here, too, the two "ladies," Wisdom and Folly, are in a state of reciprocal enmity. Folly is depicted as a deceptive adulteress whose house is replete with various destructive ways,[79] all of them leading to Hades and Death's inner rooms.

Death is portrayed as a personified, powerful entity, somehow similar to Mot, "death" (Heb. *māwet*), the Canaanite god of the underworld. In Prov 7:27, Sheol and Death are in parallel. Death's "inner chambers" (*tameia*)[80] might be a hint at various and separate sections of the underworld. The "depths [vales] of Sheol" (MT: *ʿimqēy šəʾôl*; Prov 9:18; LXX: *peteuron hadou*, where *peteuron* is a hapax of uncertain etymology and meaning "tightrope," "roosting perch for fowls") were designed for the most wretched folks, e.g., the uncircumcised (Ezek 31:18 [LXX]: *eis gēs bathos*, "in the depth of the earth").[81]

In addition, the hymn's line cited above alludes subtly to a New Testament text that contributed to the creation of the "descent to the underworld" *theologoumenon*: "In saying, 'He ascended' [*anebē*], what does it mean but he had first [*proton*] descended [*katebē*] into the lower parts [*katōtera merē*] of the earth" (Eph 4:9 [Byz.]).[82] The reference to Jesus's descent into the lower parts of the earth[83] matches "Hades" in our hymn.

The hymnographer asserts that by "[accepting] willingly" (*thelōn*) death and descending to the underworld, Jesus accomplished the shuttering of the inner rooms of death and the emptying of the royal chambers of Hades, thus drastically weakening the power of the underworld.

One may adduce here 1 Pet 3:19 as a likely expression of an apostolic tradition (cf. Eph 4:9) on Jesus's "missionary" journey to a place of imprisonment: "And having gone [*poreutheis*][84] [in spirit], he proclaimed [*ekyrēxen*] [the Gospel?] to the spirits in prison [*tois en phylakē pneumasin*])."

The clause "you shut up [*apekleisas*] the innermost rooms [*tameia*] of death" may be a hint at Rev 1:18, where Jesus is portrayed as having the "keys of death and of Hades" (*tas kleis tou thanatou kai tou hadou*).

Because of Jesus's willingness to accept suffering and death, this special Sabbath becomes worthy of divine "blessing" (*eulogia*), "glory" (*doxa*), and "splendor" (*lamprotēs*). The word *lamprotēs*, "splendor," occurs only seven times in the Bible. In Ps 90 (89):17, it connotes God's favor (MT: *nōʿam*, "delightfulness, kindness"):[85] "Let the splendor of the Lord our God be upon us and prosper upon us the work of our hands." Holy Saturday, the Sabbath par excellence, blessed by Jesus's "rest" in the tomb, exhibits its profound theology, a theology of stillness in which worshipers are exhorted to participate amid the presence of a "still" yet "working" heavenly Father (John 5:17).

Springing up from the Beast

Jonah was enclosed [*syneschethē*], but not detained [*kateschethē*] in the cetacean chest [*sternois kētōois*]. For, bearing [*pherōn*] your type [*typon*], of the one who suffered [*pathontos*] and was given to a tomb [*taphē dothentos*], as from a bridal chamber [*thalamou*], he sprang up [*anethore*] from the beast [*thēros*], and addressed [*prosephōnei*] the guard [*koustōdia*]: "You, who cherish [*hoi phylassomenoi*] vain [*mataia*] and false [*pseudē*] things, have abandoned [*enkatalipete*] mercy [*eleon*] [intended] for them [*autois*]." (Holy Saturday, Matins, Ode 6, Heirmos)

This hymn is traditionally[86] attributed to Kosmas of Jerusalem (Hagiopolites) (675–760). The speaker in this poem is the hymnographer, who mentions Jonah in the third person and refers to Jesus in the second. The switch between the third and second person is an intriguing hermeneutical procedure used often in hymnography (but apparently absent in the patristic commentaries) and is meant to heighten the mysterious tandem of type and antitype within an unfolding salvation history. A quick, sudden, almost imperceptible change in person shows how intricate the relationship between type and antitype is, much deeper in content and wider in scope than a mere foreshadowing–fulfillment pattern would suggest.

One sees in this hymn how smoothly the author moves from Jonah (spoken of), who "was restrained, but not detained in the cetacean chest," to Jesus (alluded to), while still mentioning Jonah "bearing your [Jesus's] type, of the one who suffered." The junction between third and second person, between type (Jonah) and antitype (Jesus), is done via a participial phrase describing Jonah as the "type" of Jesus.

"Bearing your type [*sou . . . ton typon pherōn*]"
The word *typos*, "type," deriving from the verb *typtō*, "to blow, to strike," generally designates a "blow." However, among its wide array of meanings,[87] the most persistent throughout various phases of Greek literature (Classical, LXX, New Testament, patristic writings) is that of an "impression" of a seal (i.e., the effect of a blow or pressure).

Using the participial phrase *ton typon pherōn*, "bearing the type," the hymnographer neither equates Jonah with the type (i.e., impression of the seal) nor limits temporally Jonah's "bearing" to a specific period in his lifetime. The present tense participle *pherōn* may indicate an action that has begun in the past (i.e., during Jonah's lifetime) and continues into the present. With each new generation of readers of the book of Jonah, the eponym still bears the type of Jesus. Through this hymn, readers of the Jonah story are indirectly invited to discover hidden, undetected, or blurred contours of the impression corresponding to the seal's original image centered on Jesus's suffering up to the time of his entombment. What our hymn seeks to convey through this participle is that the prophet functions as the carrier of this type throughout his life and beyond.

The hymn offers a diamond-like, three-faceted typology. The three steps of parallelism between Jonah and Jesus upon which this typology is built are (1) "restrained, but not detained in the cetacean chest"; (2) "suffered and was given to a tomb"; and (3) "sprang up from the beast."

The first two type–antitype parallels revolve around two pairs of actions, and the third parallel contains just a single verb as the climactic point. However, before examining this intriguing case of intertextuality, a brief summary of the book of Jonah (composed ca. the sixth to fifth century B.C.E.)[88] which inspired our hymn is warranted.

The story of this four-chapter prophetic book runs as follows. God calls Jonah to deliver a prophecy of doom against the sinful city of Nineveh. Out of fear that God will eventually change his mind, which indeed happens, Jonah disobeys the divine command and embarks on a ship with Tarsis as its destination. God brings a sea storm. Seized with fear, the mariners cast lots to determine who is the culprit. The lot falls on Jonah, who oddly asks the mariners to cast him into the sea so that the ship might be salvaged.

While sinking into the deep blue sea, Jonah is swallowed by a big fish. Inside the fish, Jonah laments his situation, likening the sea and the fish's belly to Hades. Eventually, God pities the prophet and orders the fish to spit him out on dry land. Coming back to his senses, Jonah obeys God's command and prophesies against Nineveh, whose fasting and repenting attract God's mercy, and God spares the city from destruction. Upset with God for changing his mind and making him look like a fool, Jonah sits on the ground. God makes a plant grow over Jonah to provide him with shade, but a worm sent by God destroys the plant, and Jonah becomes upset once again. The book concludes with God's lesson to Jonah: if Jonah is upset that a plant, which he did not make, withered, how much more would God have suffered seeing the numerous citizens of Nineveh decimated? The moral of the story is that divine mercy always triumphs.

The Christian typological interpretation of this story can be traced back to Jesus's logion on the "sign of Jonah" preserved in the gospels of Matthew (12:39–40; 16:4) and Luke (11:29–32). This logion, where Jesus compares his stay in the tomb/Sheol ("heart of the earth") with that of Jonah in the belly of the fish, is a response to the Pharisees' demanding that Jesus produce a sign of authority: "An evil and adulterous generation seeks for [*epizētei*] a sign [*sēmeion*]; but no sign shall be given to it, except the sign of Jonah the prophet. For as Jonah was [*hēn*] in the belly of the cetacean [*kētous*] three days and three nights, so the Son of Man [*ho hyios tou anthrōpou*] shall be [*estai*] in the heart of the earth [*en tē kardia tēs gēs*]" (Matt 12:39–40).[89]

Jonah is the only Old Testament prophet Jesus likened himself to. From a biblical and Jewish interpretive perspective, "signs" refer to the miracles associated with the Exodus or prophetic symbols. Signs do not need to be exclusively miracles. In the gospel of Matthew, the word "sign" appears again in Jesus's "eschatological discourse" (Matt 24) with reference to the "Son of Man" at the end of time but never in the sense of a "miracle." The Pharisees asking for a sign expected something other than a mere miracle from Jesus. They wanted a "sign from heaven" (Matt 16:1), a major cosmic event similar to those mentioned in ancient apocalyptic literature, disclosing Jesus's identity.[90] As one may deduce from Jesus's response in Matt 12, the "sign of Jonah" is Jonah himself and, by extension, Jesus and his salvific work.

Early Jewish writings (e.g., midrashim) saw in Jonah the model of the prayerful believer saved by God.[91]

In early Christian art (e.g., second- to fifth-century Roman catacombs of Saint Calliste and Saints Peter and Marcellinus) and in patristic thought beginning with Justin Martyr (*Dialogue* 107) and including writers such as Cyril of Alexandria (*On Jonah*), Jerome (*Epistle* 53), Gregory of Nazianzus (*Oration* 2), and Theodoret of Cyrus (*On Jonah*), just to mention a few, Jonah always has been associated with Jesus's death and resurrection as well as God's salvific plan.[92] In the Eastern Orthodox rite, the entire book of Jonah is read at the Vesperal Liturgy of Saint Basil prescribed for Holy Saturday morning commemorating Christ's descent to Hades.

Returning to our hymn, we encounter the first type–antitype parallel.

"Enclosed, but not detained [*syneschethē, all' ou kateschethē*]"
The first verb of the hymn's opening line is *synechō*, which in ancient Gk. (from Homer) connotes "to keep something together (so as not to go apart), to enclose, to oppress." The verb occurs forty-eight times in the LXX, usually

with the main meanings attested in ancient Greek; the only Heb. verbal root constantly rendered (twelve times) by *synechō* is *ʿ-ṣ-r*, "to hold back, to close, to imprison," this being the closest Heb. lexical match for the LXX verb (e.g., Deut 11:17, held back; 1 Sam 21:7, detained). In the New Testament, the verb *synechō* occurs especially in Luke and Acts (nine times) with the meaning "to close"; the meaning "to hold prisoner" appears only in Luke 22:63 (of Jesus being held prisoner).[93]

The hymn begins by informing that Jonah "was enclosed" (*syneschethē*); his physicality was restrained inside the cetacean. In the case of Jesus, his body was restrained within the walls of the tomb.

The second verb, *katechō*, "to hold fast, to hold back, (juridically) to hold in possession" is a more emphatic variant of *echō*, "to have, to possess." In the LXX, the verb *katechō* occurs with the predominant meaning "to hold fast, to possess" (e.g., Gen 22:13) and in a few instances denotes the possession or imprisonment of human beings by foreign kingdoms. In the New Testament, it is often found with the sense "to hold fast," e.g., Luke 8:15.[94]

In our hymn, *katechō* evokes the image of someone being held (in a state of captivity); similarly in Gen 39:20, "(a place where the king's) prisoners are held [*desmōtai . . . katechontai*]"; cf. 42:19, where the same verb is qualified by *phylakē*, "prison." The poet tells us that Jonah and his antitype Jesus were not detained, held in possession. Through God's will and intervention, the big fish/Hades was not able to hold Jonah/Jesus in custody; both were enclosed, confined, but only for a limited time. God's intervention is obvious in the Jonah story: God ordered the cetacean to spit Jonah out in dry land (Jonah 2:10 [11]); note that the same God ordered the cetacean to swallow Jonah (Jonah 1:17 [2:1]). In the case of Jesus's resurrection, divine intervention transpires in a number of New Testament texts where God is portrayed as "raising" Jesus from the dead (Acts 2:32–33; 13:30; Rom 6:4; Gal 1:1).

Gregory of Nazianzus underlines that although he was swallowed by the sea beast, Jonah was not destroyed: "Hence he is tempest-tossed, and falls asleep [on the ship], and is wrecked, and aroused from sleep, and taken by lot, and confesses his flight, and is cast into the sea, and swallowed but not destroyed by the whale" (*In Defense of His Flight to Pontus, Oration* 2.109).[95]

Similarly, Irenaeus remarks: "If, however, anyone imagines it is impossible that people should survive for such a length of time, and that Elijah was not caught up in the flesh but that flesh was consumed in the fiery chariot, let them consider that Jonah, when he had been cast into the deep and swallowed down into the whale's belly, was by the command of God again thrown out safe upon the land" (*Against Heresies* 5.5.2).[96]

"In the cetacean chest [*sternois kētōois*]"
The place where the prophet was "enclosed, but not detained" is termed in our hymn "cetacean chest" (*sternois kētōois*). The term *kētos* denotes a "big fish, sea monster, cetacean" (e.g., dolphins, whales, etc.) and is found in Jonah 1:17 (2:1) (LXX): "And the Lord commanded [*prosetaxen*] a great sea monster [*kētei*] to swallow up [*katapiein*] Jonah, and Jonah was [*ēn*] in the belly [*koilia*] of the sea monster three days and three nights." Note that the MT reads *dg gdwl*, "big fish."[97] It is worth noting that the LXX uses the same term, *kētos*, to render the Heb. *tnynm gdwlym*, "big sea monsters/dragons/serpents" (Gen 1:21).

Gregory of Nyssa (*On the Soul and the Resurrection*) uses the same uncontracted spelling of *kētōos* as in our hymn and interprets the sea monster as a metaphor for Satan, who, not noticing the bait of divinity hidden in his human body, swallowed Jesus.[98]

The hymnographer's lexical preference (*sternois*, "chest," plural noun) over the choice *koilia*, "belly," of Jonah 2:1[2] was probably meant to underscore the idea that Jonah's brief imprisonment happened not in the belly but rather in the very heart ("chest" being the place of the heart) of the cetacean.

"Who suffered and was given to a tomb [*tou pathontos kai taphē dothentos*]"
The hymnographer switches from Jonah to Jesus, showing that the former, while being in the "cetacean chest," typified the latter, who "suffered and was given to a tomb." Thus, suffering and being enclosed in a tomb are the two points upon which this typological relationship is built.

The first epistle of Peter describes Jesus as the one "who suffered in flesh [*pathontos . . . sarki*] for us" (1 Pet 4:1), using the same participial (aorist) form of the verb *paschō*.[99] During his last week in Jerusalem, Jesus's suffering grows gradually with each passing moment. The "Lord of Passion" (*Kyrios tōn Pathōn*) comes to taste loneliness and desertion at its deepest level, beginning with the agony in the Garden of Gethsemane, suffering through the excruciating pain of the crucifixion amplified by God's sheer silence, and culminating (or, better, reaching the bottom) in a tomb leading to the God-forgotten realm of Hades, from which there is no return. Jonah shares via his lament (Jonah 2) a similar experience of horrific and hopeless loneliness inside the sea monster.

If one takes this line with the previous one, Jonah's cetacean parallels Jesus's tomb.

Although not buried but rather swallowed by a cetacean, the prophet describes his situation in the belly of the sea beast as if he were buried. There are a few elements that evoke this imagery. The phrase "heart of the earth" (*kardia tēs gēs*), which denotes the tomb or Hades (Matt 12:39–40), is slightly altered in Jonah 2:3 (4), due to the aquatic context, to *eis bathē kardias thalassēs*, "into the depths of the heart of the sea." This is a sinking not into the sea, as expected, but "into the crevices of the mountains [*eis schismas oreōn*]" (2:5 [6]) and descending "into the earth [*eis gēn*]" (2:6 [7]).

Cyril of Jerusalem refers to this tomb/Hades imagery intimated by Jonah 2 when he comments:

> Jonah fulfilled a type of our Savior when he prayed from the belly of the fish and said, "I cried for help from the midst of the netherworld." He was in fact in the fish, yet he says that he is in the netherworld. In a later verse he manifestly prophesies in the person of Christ: "My head went down into the chasms of the mountains." Yet he was still in the belly of the fish. What mountains encompass you? But I know, he says, that I am a type of him who is to be laid in the sepulcher hewn out of rock. While he was in the sea, Jonah says, "I went down into the earth," for he typified Christ, who went down into the heart of the earth. (*Catechetical Lecture* 14.20)[100]

Similarly, Jacob of Serug (451–521) mentions that Jonah "was buried" in order to "explain" the Lord's way to the tomb: "Three days in the heart of the earth Jonah was buried so that the road of our Lord which was to the tomb should be explained. The prophet in the fish and the Lord of the prophets in the death that he desired; the ones buried who sprang forth not being destroyed by annihilation; the dead ones who became the reason for life by their actions: Jonah to Nineveh, and the Son of God to all the earth" (*Mēmrā 122: On Jonah* 35.422:17–423:3).[101]

Speaking of similarities and differences between type and antitype, Cyril of Jerusalem distinguishes between Jonah, who was cast into the sea, and Jesus, who of his own will accepted to descend to Hades to liberate its denizens: "Jonah was cast into the belly of a great fish, but Christ of his own will descended to the abode of the invisible fish of death. He went down of his own will to make death disgorge those it had swallowed up, according to the

Scripture: 'I shall deliver them from the power of the nether world, and I shall redeem them from death' [Hos 13:14]" (*Catechetical Lectures* 14.7).[102]

"As from a bridal chamber, he sprang up from the beast [*hōs ek thalamou, tou thēros anethore*]"
The hymnographer returns now to Jonah. According to Jonah 2:10 (11), God orders the sea monster to cast Jonah out onto the dry land, but there is no mention of "springing up" or a "bridal chamber" in this brief scriptural verse. Rather, this is the hymnographer's hyperbolic language meant to weave Jesus's resurrection with the prophet's story. Jonah typifies Jesus coming out of the tomb as a bridegroom springing up from his bridal chamber, refreshed, "unhurt, with a generous leap" (* abablēs me gennea pēdēma*).[103] Type and antitype are intricately interwoven in this line.

The verb *anathrōskō*, "to spring up, to bound up, to rebound" (unattested in the Bible), is employed in Christian writings with regard to Christ's bodily ascension.[104] This is another example of a hymnographer resorting to Classical Gk. lexicon to convey an original thought or image. In this context, a Classical Gk. verb is used to describe Jesus's resurrection as a quick, energizing leap out of the tomb.

The word *thalamos*, "women's apartment, inner part of the house, bridal room," is quite close in meaning to *mychos*, used to designate the "impenetrable innermost parts of Hades" (*adytous hadou mychois*).[105] *Thalamos* is a hapax legomenon, occurring in 3 Macc 1:18 (of Jewish resistance to Ptolemy) and referring to the "inner part of the house": "virgins enclosed [*katakleistoi*] in bedrooms [*thalamois*] rushed out [*exōrmēsan*] along with their mothers [*tekousais*]." This is a similar context to the one in our hymn: being "enclosed" in a hidden place and suddenly "rushing out/springing up."

Apparently, the hymnographer chose *thalamos* for its polesymy which fittingly and simultaneously evokes several facets of the Jonah–Jesus typology: (1) "inner part," similarly to *mychos*, alluding to the inside of the "beast" (i.e., Hades); (2) "bridal chamber," evoking a joyful place whence Jesus sprang up, with renewed energy, as if after a restful sleep; (3) "lowest part of a ship," calling immediately to mind Jonah's heavy sleep in the "hold [*koilēn*] of the ship" (Jonah 1:5); (4) "grave," reminiscent of Jesus's "tomb" mentioned in the previous line.

The "bedroom" (bridal chamber) image occurs in Jacob of Serug, who plays down the horrific experience Jonah would have experienced in the belly of the sea monster by saying that the prophet was like a "bridegroom for whom the movements of the fish were like a bedroom" (*Mēmrā* 31.418:5).[106]

"And he addressed the guard: 'You, who cherish vain and false things, have abandoned mercy [intended] for them' [*prosephōnei de tē koustōdia. hoi phylassomenoi mataia kai pseudē, eleon autois enkatalipete*]"
At this point, the hymnographer introduces Jonah as speaker, who applies and addresses his own lament (Jonah 2:8 [9]) to the "guard" (*koustōdia*) set to keep watch over Jesus's tomb. The word *koustōdia*, "guard," occurs only three times in the Bible, always with reference to the tomb (Matt 27:65, 66; 28:11).

This is the lament Jonah initially uttered inside the sea beast, most likely as a comment on the mariners' inability to understand God's dealings with humans:[107] "The ones who cherish [*phylassomenoi*] vain [*mataia*] and false [*pseudē*] things have left behind [*enkatelipon*] their mercy [*eleos autōn*]" (Jonah 2:8 [9] [LXX]; cf. Odes 6:9).

The MT of Jonah 2:8 (9) exhibits a construct phrase *hablēy-šāw(ʾ)*, "empty folly" (or "empty nothings"), where the LXX inserts the conjunction *kai*, "and," for *mataia kai pseudē*, "vain and false things," but even this hendiadys may be rendered with a sort of superlative, "false vanities."[108] Moreover, the LXX renders the theologically loaded Hebrew key term *ḥesed*, "steadfast, unconditioned love, loyalty," with *eleos*, "mercy."

According to the MT reading, clinging to idolatry ("empty folly") means disloyalty toward Yahweh and his covenant.[109] For the LXX, any trivial, insubstantial activity, including idolatry, procludes the doer from enjoying God's mercy.

"You, who cherish [*hoi phylassomenoi*] vain and false things, have abandoned [*enkatalipete*] mercy [intended] for them [*eleon autois*]"
What is the meaning of Jonah's quote within the context of our hymn? Jonah offers a warning for the guard who kept watch over Jesus's tomb. Since the guardians cherish what is "vain and false," they will not be able to receive what is intended for them,[110] that is, God's mercy, which presumably is Jesus who sprang from the tomb as from a bridal room.

Commenting on the above-quoted hymn, Nicodemus the Hagiorite (1749–1809) paraphrases Jonah 2:8 (9) as follows: "And prophetically [*prophētikōs*], [Jonah] said to the guard [*koustōdia*] [i.e., the guardians [*phylakas*]): 'O mindless soldiers, as you guard the tomb of the Giver of Life [*zōodotou*] vainly [*mataiōs*] and unsuccessfully [*apraktōs*], so you abandoned [i.e., put away] your mercy, namely, Christ, the one who became incarnate, died, and was entombed so that he may show mercy and save all.'"[111]

The Never-Setting Light

[O Christ,] Isaiah seeing [idōn] the never-setting light [phos anesperon] of your theophany [theophaneias], O Christ, that compassionately [sympathōs] occurred [genomenēs] to us, having risen early [orthrisas] in the night [ek nyktos], cried aloud: "The dead shall stand up [anastēsontai], the ones in tombs shall awake [egerthēsontai], and all those in the earth shall rejoice exceedingly [agalliasontai]." (Holy Saturday, Matins, Ode 5, Heirmos)

The hymn opens with the prophet Isaiah contemplating (probably in a nocturnal vision) the "never-setting light" of the appearance (theophany) of the risen Jesus. One can imagine how such a vision woke Isaiah from his early-evening sleep in order to redeliver his own prophecy (Isa 26:19), now within a different context, that is, Jesus's resurrection.

"Never-setting light of your theophany [theophanias sou . . . phōs . . . anesperon]"
The Assyrian king Tiglath-Pileser III's 734 B.C.E. military campaign on the coast (belonging to the tribes of Zebulon and Naphtali) (2 Kgs 15:29), followed by the establishment of Dor province (from Carmel to Joppa), made the doomsayers see their current situation in dark colors (Isa 8:19–22).[112] Nevertheless, Isaiah discerns some light looming on the horizon: God will intervene on behalf of his people and turn a shameful past into a glorious future. For this reason, the prophet asks his audience to make an effort to share this hope with him: "O you people who walk in darkness [ho poreuomenos en skotei], see a big light [idete phōs mega]! O you who dwell in the country [chōra] and the shadow [skia] of death, light will shine [phōs lampsei] on you" (Isa 9:1 [8:23]).[113]

The participial phrase "Isaiah seeing the never-setting light,"[114] hinting at "a great light" (Isa 9:1 [8:23]), betrays the hymnographer's careful reading of the entire Isaian poem of hope (9:1–7 [8:23–9:6]), including a well-known prophecy on the titles of the Messiah's (vv. 6 [5]–7[6]). It is noteworthy that the poem opens with a sudden transition from the land of "darkness" (*skotos*) (8:22) and "shadow of death" (*skia thanatou*) (9:2[1]b [8:23b]) to a "big light" (*phōs mega*) (9:1a [8:23a]). If one considers land of "darkness" as a metaphor for the underworld (cf. Job 10:21–22: "dark [*skotēn*] and gloomy [*gnopheran*] land [*gēn*]"),[115] then no other such intertextuality could be more appropriate for our hymn.

The transition from gloom to light found in the Isaian text reverberates in our hymn. Out of the underworld (Hades), Jesus makes the never-setting light of his "theophany" (*theophaneia*)[116] shine on all humans, including the prophet Isaiah, who saw the light of the risen Jesus long before its historical realization.

"Compassionately happened [*sympathōs genomenēs*]"

The adverb *sympathōs*, "compassionately," might make one think of Heb 4:15, where Jesus, the high priest, is depicted as "co-suffering, sympathizing" with us in our weaknesses: "For we do not have a high priest unable [*mē dynamenon*] to suffer along [*sympathēsai*][117] with/in our weaknesses [*tais astheneiais*], but one who was tempted [*pepeiramenon*] in everything as we are, but without sin [*chōris hamartias*]."

Interestingly, through the use of this adverb, the hymnographer is able to blend two important ideas intimated by the hymns of Holy Saturday: Jesus's suffering on behalf of fallen humanity and his divine compassion for all those trapped in corruption and the depths of the underworld. The theophany of the risen Lord is the immediate result and sheer expression of his willingly assumed suffering and bountifully offered compassion.

"[Isaiah] having risen early in the night [*ek nyktos orthrisas*]"

This phrase was borrowed from Isa 26:9b, "In the night, my spirit rises early toward you, O God" (*ek nyktos orthrizei to pneuma mou pros se ho theos*), with one minor difference: the Isaian text has *orthrizei*, present tense, while our hymn has *orthrisas*, an aorist participle of the verb *orthrizō*, "to rise early in the morning" (Gen 19:2, 27; 2 Kgs 6:15; Ps 63 [62]:2).

In Isa 26:9, the prophet rises early in the night because God's "ordinances [*prostagmata*] are a light [*phōs*] upon the earth." Similarly, in our hymn, the same Isaiah rose early upon seeing the "never-setting light" in the darkness. In both cases, the light of God's presence wakes the prophet up even though it is still night.

"He [Isaiah] cried aloud [*ekraugazen*]"

The second part of this hymn (Isaiah's proclamation) is a slightly altered quote from Isa 26:19a that revolves around three essential verbs painting the decor of the final scene: *anistēmi*, "to stand up," *egeirō*, "to awaken, to wake up," *euphrainō* (*agalliaō* in our hymn), "rejoice." Isa 26:19 (LXX) reads: "The dead [*nekroi*] shall stand up [*anastēsontai*], and those who are in the tombs [*mnēmeiois*] shall awake [*egerthēsontai*], and those who are in the earth [*gē*] shall rejoice [*euphranthēsontai*]; for the dew [*drosos*] from you is medicine for them [*iama autois*], but the land of the impious shall fall [*peseitai*]."

Isa 26 consists of three sections: a pilgrim's song (vv. 1–4), the dialogue of the pilgrims (5–18), and an epiphany (19–21). One may imagine the pilgrims heading for Jerusalem to worship the living God while talking among themselves about the distress their land experiences at the hands of foreign masters such as Assyria (vv. 5–18). Their talk is suddenly interrupted by God's appearance (a similar scene occurs in Luke 24:13–31, of risen Jesus's appearance to two disciples on their way to Emmaus; and in Acts 9:1–18, of Paul on his way to Damascus), and his herald assures the pilgrims, along the same line of thought as in Isa 25:7–8, that God has power over death and "the dead shall stand up ... and they shall rejoice."[118]

Although not mentioned in our hymn, the "dew" image occurs in the second part of Isa 26:19 which inspired the hymnographer. While the LXX reads, "the dew [*drosos*] around you is a remedy [*iama*] for them," the MT reads, "your dew is as the dew of lights [*ṭl ʾwrt*], and the earth shall bring to life the shades [*rpʾym*]." So precious for the ecosystem of Syria-Palestine with its many dry months, "dew" has always been associated with life in general and eternal life in particular (Ps 133 [132]:3). In both the LXX (*iama*, "medicine") and the MT (*ṭl ʾwrt*, "dew of lights") readings of Isa 26:19, the special "dew" belongs to God and is a catalyst that enacts the bodily resurrection.

In an aggadic-midrashic work on the Torah, *Pirqei de-Rabbi Eliʿezer* 34 (mid-eighth to early ninth century C.E.), one can find this interesting intertextual gloss:

> Rabbi Yehudah said, ". . . In the time to come, the blessed Holy One will bring down a dew of revival, reviving the dead. . . . 'For your dew is a dew of lights. . . .'" Rabi Thanhum said, ". . . From where does it descend? From the head of the blessed Holy One. In the time to come, He will shake the hair of His head and bring down a dew of revival, reviving the dead, as is said: *I*

was asleep, but my heart was awake. . . . For my head is drenched with dew [Song 5:2]."[119]

Similarly, in our hymn, a recast prophet Isaiah, seeing the "never-setting light of [Jesus's] theophany," rises early in the dead of the night and, assuming the role of God's herald in the original setting of Isa 26:19, proclaims the rising of the dead as sequel to the resurrection of Jesus, whose theophany startled and prompted him to interpret his own prophetic word.

PART II
LITURGICAL EXEGESIS

7

Key Features and
Hermeneutical Procedures

The "Bible" in the Byzantine World

Prior to any discussion about the key features of "liturgical exegesis" and the main hermeneutical procedures used by the hymnographers in reading and interpreting the Scriptures, specifically Old Testament passages that are the main focus of this volume, one needs to answer the following question: what "Bible" did the hymnographers employ in creating their hymnography?

It is axiomatic that before the invention of printing (1450), the "Bible" (more correctly, the Christian "sacred Scriptures") in the East was accessible to only a limited number of people, and this was for two main reasons: mass illiteracy[1] and a few number of copies distributed at any given time or place.

It is also axiomatic to assume that Byzantine hymnographers and the Greek Fathers who wrote commentaries on various books of the Bible had access to some scriptural collections, if not to a full-fledged Bible, as preserved in the fourth- and fifth-century codices Sinaiticus, Vaticanus, and Alexandrinus, which contained all the Septuagint writings, New Testament books, and some "extras." We know from two early historians, Eusebius of Caesarea and Socrates Scholasticus (ca. 380–450), that the former was commissioned by Emperor Constantine the Great to prepare fifty copies of the "sacred Scriptures" of "portable size" aimed at the "instruction of the Church." Therefore, it is extremely difficult to imagine someone in the fourth and fifth centuries reading the "sacred Scriptures" at home. Biblical codices were destined for churches, not individuals, whose only access to Scripture was via the living tradition of the Church, especially the liturgical services, aurally (e.g., listening to the hymns, biblical readings, homilies, etc.) or visually (e.g., looking at Church iconography or liturgical acts loaded with scriptural symbolism).[2]

In these circumstances, one has to recognize the significant role played by the hymnographers along with the liturgical cantors in spreading the

Hearing the Scriptures. Eugen J. Pentiuc, Oxford University Press. © Oxford University Press 2021.
DOI: 10.1093/oso/9780190239633.003.0008

Scriptures. And if one thinks of Byzantine society being Christian in its vast majority, one might dare liken the liturgical services of Late Antiquity and the Middle Ages to the current online social media, such as Facebook or Twitter, in breaking the news faster than and prior to the nationwide traditional television channels. The impact of Scripture on such a large audience regularly attending religious services has never been sufficiently emphasized.

Two developments in the production of manuscripts had significant impact on public accessibility to the Bible. The first development was the replacement of parchment, a quite expensive writing material, with paper, much cheaper and quicker to produce, though papyrus, also inexpensive, was used for many manuscripts, including larger units (e.g., Pentateuch, Pauline epistles, etc.). This gradual process began in the eighth century following the spread of Islam through Asia Minor. The earliest codex on paper is Arabic 309, a collection of sermons in Christian Arabic, preserved at St. Catherine Monastery in Sinai and dated back to 909. The second development, the change of majuscule to minuscule orthography, resulted in more writing space, hence greater quantity in book making, and word division that would be fully implemented with the printing.[3]

Various Biblical Collections

To speak of "the Old Testament" as a single comprehensive collection extant in Byzantine times is a sheer anachronism. Christian Scriptures circulated prior to the advent of printing technology in small collections grouping together a limited number of books belonging to the one of the two current parts of the Christian Bible, the Old and New Testaments.

The Psalter
Most of the Old Testament collections that have resisted the test of time are Psalters, dating from as early as the ninth century. The Psalter played an important part in the ascetic discipline practiced in monastic communities.[4] Starting at least in the fifth century, the Psalter enjoyed much popularity in Byzantium since it was the first biblical writing to receive a "preface" ("St. Athanasius' Epistle to Marcellinus") in the Codex Alexandrinus, one of the most venerable full Bible manuscripts, consisting of almost the entire Greek Old Testament and the Greek New Testament.

Old Testament Manuscripts

Besides the Psalter, the other widely spread Old Testament collections in the East were the Pentateuch and the Prophets. Moreover, there were probably other book groupings or collections limited to geographical and cultural areas. So, for instance, in Syriac, there was a collection consisting of several *anaginoskomena* (1–3 Macc, Wis, Jdt, Sus, Ep Jer, Epistle of Baruch, Bar). Such a collection is also presupposed by the Byzantine Holy Week hymnography which makes copious use of the *anaginoskomena* passages (especially 1–3 Macc and Wis). The Byzantines had the first eight books of the Old Testament gathered into a single collection known as the Octateuch ("eight [book] volume"). Large full collections, consisting of the entire Old Testament (canonical and anaginoskomena writings), such as the fifth-century Codex Alexandrinus (Greek) and the sixth- to seventh-century Codex Ambrosianus (Syriac), were quite rare during the Middle Ages within Eastern Christianity.[5] Among the few exemplars, mention should be made of an Old Testament, originally in three volumes, dated to 978 and preserved at Iveron Monastery on Mount Athos.[6]

Lectionaries

Reading scriptural passages has always been the practice at liturgical synaxes. The earliest written evidence may be found in the scribal notations in the gospel books indicating the passages that were to be read at various liturgical services—as early as the end of the sixth century (e.g., the Rabbula Gospels). A fragmentarily preserved Georgian codex from the seventh century is considered the earliest lectionary. However, eleventh-century Constantinopolitan lectionaries became the normative codices used in Byzantine Orthodox churches. There were three types of lectionaries:[7] the Old Testament (especially Prophets, Prophetologion) lectionary, the Acts and Epistles (Praxapostolos) lectionary, and the Gospel (Euangelion) lectionary.[8]

Prophetologion

Through public liturgical use, the lectionaries in general, and the Prophetologion in particular, individual Old Testament writings would have been more accessible to common folks than the full Old Testament manuscripts so rare at the time and mostly associated with libraries sheltered by monastic communities. The Prophetologion was probably the default "Old Testament" in Byzantine Christianity.[9]

The lectionary tradition of the Prophetologion is still observed in today's Byzantine Orthodox worship. According to Sysse Engberg, the Old Testament lections have never been used for the Eucharistic service (i.e., Liturgy), and the Prophetologion has been always limited to the non-Eucharistic services (i.e., Vespers, Matins), even prior to the earliest manuscript attestation (ninth century) of this lectionary.[10] Thus, the emergence of the Prophetologion tradition (perhaps coinciding with the oldest manuscripts and originating from the Stoudios Monastery in Constantinople) should not be considered indicative of a liturgical reform aimed at the exclusion of Old Testament lections from the Eucharistic service.[11]

Around the sixteenth century, marking the end of the Byzantine manuscript tradition, the Old Testament lections that once constituted the Prophetologion were transferred to various liturgical books such as the Triodion (used during Great Lent), the Pentecostarion (during the Pentecost season), and the Menaion. As for the content of the Prophetologion, it consists of a limited number of Old Testament books, with the following not represented: Ruth, 1–2 Sam (LXX 1–2 Kgdms), 1–2 Chr, 1–2 Esd (in English Bibles Ezra and Neh), Esth, Jdt, Tob, 1–4 Macc, Eccl, Song, Hos, Obad, Nah, Hab, Hag, and Lam.[12]

The Greek Text

Translations of the Old Testament into Syriac, Armenian, Arabic, or Ethiopian for their respective faith communities in the Christian East were made from the Septuagint, and extremely rarely, which tells one that in the East, the default text of the Old Testament was the Septuagint.[13]

According to the literary evidence, the Greek text of the Bible was not fully standardized until the middle of the tenth century—evidence for this comes from 948 in the monk Ephraem's notation on John 7:53–8:11 (i.e., the pericope of the woman caught in adultery) at the end of a gospel book, where he mentions several of the exemplars he was aware of: "The Chapter about the Adulteress: in most exemplars it is not in the text of the Gospel according to John, and it is not mentioned by the holy fathers who interpreted [this gospel], namely John Chrysostom and Cyril of Alexandria, nor by Theodore of Mopsuestia and the others. I omitted it in the text above. It reads, shortly after the beginning of Chapter 76 [i.e., John 8], following 'Search and you will see that no prophet is to arise from Galilee' [John 7:53]."[14]

The literary sources, as reflected in Ephraem's *Gospel*, are witness to a certain biblical textual fluidity between the ninth century and the end of the first millennium, which would gradually decrease and fully fade out by the fifteenth century. The gradual acquired textual uniformity occurred by frequent copying of the Scriptures.

Based on the lexical analysis of selected Holy Week hymns done in the first part of this volume, one may assume that the Greek text of various collections used by hymnographers was quite close to the text exhibited by the fourth- to fifth-century Bible codices known today as Sinaiticus, Vaticanus, and Alexandrinus. Moreover, my preliminary work on Old Testament lections prescribed for Holy Week shows a slight yet consistent tendency toward the Syro-Hexapla text preserved in the sixth- to seventh-century Codex Ambrosianus. Syro-Hexapla is the Syriac translation of the fifth column, Quinta—the revised Old Testament Septuagint text of Origen's monumental work *Hexapla*.

Cubist Art Analogy

The first impression one gathers when looking at the multitude of Byzantine hymns taken from a wide variety of liturgical contexts is that these hymns are biblical in language, content, form, and tone.

As noted above, the "Bible," more precisely, the "Old Testament," was extant in the Byzantine world and at times in the form of "collections," mostly liturgical in purpose, such as the Psalters, Old Testament lectionaries, the Prophetologion, and other book "groupings."

A question may arise, though: what is the appropriate terminology to describe the harmonious marriage among Scripture, doctrine, and poetry that these Byzantine hymns so adroitly exhibit?

More than a decade ago, Bogdan G. Bucur pointed out the distinction between patristic exegesis and Byzantine hymnography in terms of biblical interpretation.[15] Bucur's article, dealing with Old Testament theophanies as interpreted in hymns and patristic commentaries, is a survey of Old Testament theophanies from the perspective of a patristic scholar and historian of theological ideas, with little focus on hermeneutical and methodological differences between patristic exegesis and what he calls "hymnographic exegesis." Interesting is the author's slight propensity toward an identification of Byzantine hymnography with the "rewritten Bible" commentary genre.

Can Byzantine hymnography be considered a rewritten Bible? Let us take a quick look at the Second Temple Jewish book of Jubilees dated to the second century B.C.E., which neatly falls into the rewritten Bible category. Perhaps one of the most representative key hermeneutical features of the rewritten Bible type of commentary is the "textual expansion," a gradual process of "actualizing" interpretive work done on a particular biblical text through additions, omissions, and explicative glosses, just to mention a few of the midrashic techniques at work.[16] The final product, what one calls the rewritten Bible, such as the book of Jubilees, is a composite work made of small pieces of "rewritten" biblical texts coming from different times and interpreters. At first sight, one has the tendency to consider Byzantine hymnography taken as a whole as a sort of rewritten Bible consisting of various pieces of "rewritten" biblical texts (i.e., individual hymns) exhibiting a variety of dates of composition and authorial profiles. However, when analyzed closely and, more important, separately, these hymns reveal an entirely different hermeneutical methodology from the one at work in rewritten Bibles, such as the book of Jubilees.

The most important distinction between Jubilees and Byzantine hymnography is that the former's method of interpreting Scriptures is discursive, linear, and sequential. Thus, Jubilees can be rather likened to the patristic commentaries marked by the same three benchmarks—discursivity, linearity, and sequentiality—and not to hymnography, characterized by allusiveness, circularity, and unpredictability, some of poetry's essential features.

Let us take a closer look at Jubilees, a pseudepigraphal writing dating to the second century B.C.E., which was preserved among the Dead Sea Scrolls manuscripts. This book "rewrites" the Pentateuch up to the Sinaitic revelation. The "rewriting" process makes use of additions, omissions, etc., thus altering and reshaping the biblical text, transforming it into a new book.

The book of Jubilees follows mostly the sequence of events attested in the Pentateuch.[17] Such a relative linearity and sequentiality of the expanded and commented biblical text encountered in Jubilees[18] is not to be found in Byzantine hymnography, considered either as a corpus or individual hymns. Instead of a one-layer sequential horizontality of the interpretive movement attested in Jubilees, Byzantine hymnography exhibits a multilayered and multidimensional "galaxy" of quanta or tiny bits of biblical text as well as "hermeneutical pointers."

A hymn is a "galactic" universe where time and space coalesce and are warped by various "bodies" (words as rare hapax legomena, phrases, or half verses of biblical quotes), all revolving around a central "star" (the hymn's gist or main theme) on their own orbits at different layers of the tapestry-like fabric of the hymn. Imagined this way, the interpretive universe of a hymn is so complex that any strategy of reducing the variety of interpretations to one or a few means ignoring probably the most significant feature of hymnic hermeneutics, that is, the irreducibly multifaceted richness of liturgical interpretation of the biblical material. Another peculiarity of this liturgical interpretation is the wide variety of biblical interpretations generated by a dual network: first, the relation between "planets" (biblical quanta) orbiting the "sun" (central theme) and, second, the relation between the "planets" themselves with respect to the "sun."

Thus, a rewritten Bible analogy will not be able to account for this intricate, "galactic," multi-orbit biblical interpretation exhibited by the hymns. Thus, we need a different, more complex analogy to take into consideration all the intricacies of this liturgical interpretation.

I argued in *The Old Testament in Eastern Orthodox Tradition* that patristic commentaries follow a "discursive" (linear) interpretive methodology (hence the title of chapter 5 of that volume, "Discursive," dealing with patristic exegesis), while the Byzantine hymns represent a more "intuitive," holistic, and imagistic mode of interpretation.

In the present volume, I seek to show the difference between patristic commentaries and Byzantine hymns by promoting the notion of liturgical exegesis in conjunction with that of "liturgized Bible." Thus, for me, Byzantine hymnography is the expression of a liturgized Bible, and the hymnographers are the practitioners of liturgical exegesis by following a set of hermeneutical strategies and procedures, which will be briefly discussed in this final chapter.

I would like to propose a new analogy which will be more appropriate to Byzantine hymnography and its two collateral tracks, liturgized Bible and liturgical exegesis, than the rewritten Bible analogy.

I dare to liken Byzantine hymnography and liturgical exegesis of the sacred Scripture to cubist art.

Cubism is an avant-garde art movement of the early twentieth century that has left an undeniable mark on music, literature, painting, and architecture. In the area of visual arts, Pablo Picasso, Georges Braque, and Juan Gris are three of the most representative cubist painters. A precursor of cubism was Paul Cézanne, who daringly sought to represent three-dimensional reality in his late paintings. Although its origins are still debatable, cubist art can be said to have begun with Picasso's *Les Demoiselles d'Avignon* (1907).

Since the Renaissance, painters have been interested in presenting reality from only a single point of view or perspective. The canvas was a transparent screen through which one could contemplate reality—a type of unedited video shooting (or a still picture) with no postproduction alterations at all; the artistic representation is so close to (almost a calque), yet so far from, reality. Paradoxically, as "realistic" as the pre-cubist paintings might look, they are "illusionist" when approaching and representing reality. In their desire to accurately *re-produce* reality, the Renaissance artists had to resort to various techniques (e.g., dimming an object to simulate perspective), thus creating an "illusionary reality" on their canvases, so far-fetched and different from the actual reality. Therefore, pre-cubist art can be cataloged as a misrepresentation of the reality that the beholders see in their every-day experiences. This type of art implies that the beholder is a motionless observer of reality from one particular point of view, with the whole image in focus. "In contrast, cubist works represent simultaneously the shapes and surfaces of objects from different perspectives. Objects are 'analyzed' in terms of facets at shallow angles to the picture surface, and they do not recede from the eye. Facets are held together by grids or scaffolding lines, a constraint that contributes to the angular geometry of the works."[19]

Analogously to pre-cubist art, patristic exegesis promotes a single angle through which one analyzes the biblical text. Linear and sequential in movement, this exegetical approach uses argumentation and reasoning, with the text under examination in full focus. However, such an exposition of Scriptures is hardly consonant with the real nature of God's Word, which cannot be reduced to a particular pericope or text and then analyzed discursively by an assiduous ancient interpreter eager to find some hidden meaning that might serve the Church's teaching ministry. By contrast, God's Word is free and alive everywhere throughout the Scriptures and is nowhere exclusively and reducibly identifiable. Georges Florovsky once noted with inspired wisdom that "Scripture is a God-inspired scheme or image (*eikon*) of truth, but not truth itself."[20]

On the other hand, liturgical exegesis, as attested in Byzantine hymnography (a substantial part of what I would term liturgized Bible) and analogous to cubist art, approaches God's Word from various angles, in an imagistic and intuitive way, within an ongoing prayerful context built and carried on by a variety of liturgical services. And these angles of God's Word, which might be biblical words, phrases, or truncated quotations, are held simultaneously by the hymnographers in their hymns, true tiny "galaxies" of poetry, Scripture, and theology, with each element kept in focus.

Through geometrizing, cubifying, and other techniques used to *re-produce* the space, the cubist artists extended the beholder's experience from seeing to an almost tactile experience. The beholder is invited to "touch," at least imaginatively, the objects represented by the artists. Here I find another similarity with the hymnographers vs. discursive commentators. The hymnographers invite the worshipers not only to "see" God's Word "written" on codices or church walls (i.e., iconography, "writing icons") but also to "hear" (i.e., heed) and, more important, to "appropriate" it via liturgical performance meant to turn the worshipers into participants in the events of "salvation history" told by Scriptures and retold by liturgical services with all their attire.

Multi-angularity and simultaneity are the two main features analogously linking Byzantine hymnography to cubist art and philosophy. The difference between naturalism (Renaissance and post-Renaissance) and cubism corresponds to a certain degree to discursive vs. imagistic (poetic) interpretations of Scriptures. There are essential similarities and differences between naturalist and cubist ways of dealing with reality. Both artistic currents rely on reality as an area of investigation, but their ways or means of recording reality, or, more precisely, their understanding of the recording means, differ: while naturalist artists see them as "absolute" means, cubist artists see them as relative and imperfect, hence their interest in "capturing" more angles, facets of reality, in a relentless effort to interpret reality while respecting the beholder's role in the collaborative act of interpretation.

Likewise in hymnography, the religious poet's propensity toward polysemy translates into the hearer's participatory role in interpreting the liturgized Scriptures in ways so as to respond more efficiently to their spiritual concerns and needs. Cubism and, analogously, liturgical exegesis emphasize the creative role of the viewer or hearer in the interpretive process.

The French poet Guillaume Apollinaire describes cubism as "not an art of imitation, but imagination."[21] One may say the same thing about liturgical exegesis, that is, biblical interpretation requiring from the hearer a great deal of imagination in order to grasp as through a powerful telescope some of the otherwise hidden side of the hymnic "galactic" universe made of poetry, Scripture, and theology.

In the case of cubist art, reality is what the artist can imagine. Similarly, with respect to hymnography, Scriptures are one with their interpretations, the respective hymns, hence my proposed coinage "liturgized Bible." In cubist art, there is no separation line between reality and artistic imagination, as is the case in pre-cubist art or, to use the analogy from the area of biblical hermeneutics, as is the case with the discursive patristic commentaries. For instance, in patristic exegesis, the commentary layout runs almost unchangeably: a biblical verse or pericope is followed by its interpretation; there is a clear-cut demarcation between Scripture and commentary. Either these two textual entities are either intermixed on a single column, or the Scripture runs at the center of the page, being glossed on margins or surrounded by comments (glosses) from Church Fathers, as is the case with the medieval *Glossa Ordinaria* (Lat., "ordinary/standard gloss"; popular in the West, the earliest exemplars date to the twelfth century).

These "Bibles with commentary" were destined for various libraries, as is the case of the Psalter with commentary dated to 984 and preserved in the library of the Laura (Gk. "alley, monastery") of St. Athanasius on Mount Athos.[22] The essential point here is that text and commentary in the "discursive" mode of interpretation (i.e., patristic exegesis) are clearly distinguished and separated, while in hymnography, Scriptures and comments are so indistinguishably interwoven, intermeshed, or interfused that there is no way to find a line of demarcation between the two within the tapestry-like density of a hymn.

While trying to debunk the thesis of a possible philosophical association between cubists and Immanuel Kant's quest for "things-in-themselves" (transcendental, metaphysical reality), Dan O'Brien argues convincingly that cubist painters, such as Picasso, Braque, and Gris, were interested in representing not the "transcendental" realities but rather the very touchable reality in its quintessential defining elements, by exposing some condensed, transformed reality (smell, texture, etc.).[23] Similarly, the hymnographers are interested not in bringing forward a hidden, transcendent, spiritual sense excavated from the biblical text but rather in offering to the hearer a sample of the mystery and closeness of God's Word that was active in ancient Israel's history and is now reactivated by the imagination of these religious poets.

In its development as an artistic movement that generated other artistic currents (e.g., futurism, Dada, etc.), cubism knew two phases, the analytic and the synthetic. During the initial analytic phase, Picasso and other cubist artists deconstructed and fractured reality into small pieces to be closely analyzed, while later, during the synthetic phase, the cubists were interested in a bigger picture, re-presentation of reality, consisting of the small pieces already analyzed in the previous phase. Similarly, in Byzantine hymnography, one may detect traces of a two-phase development. When closely examining a hymn, one is amazed by the inner cohesion of tiny scriptural pieces put together in such a sophisticated assemblage. However, such a well-configured piece of liturgical exegesis presupposes a detailed analysis of separate chunks of Scripture or rare words. Although there is no way to prove such an analytic phase in the composition history of these hymns, nevertheless, the very evidence of such mini-compositions of Scripture, poetry, and theology tilts in this direction.

It will be good to conclude these brief remarks with a concise yet poignant description of what cubism, especially that of Picasso, is all about: "a melodious fabric of lines and tints, a music of delicate tones—lighter or darker, warmer or cooler—whose mystery increases the pleasure of the viewer,"[24] so true and appropriate also for Byzantine hymnography as a biblical hermeneutical exercise.

I will return to the cubist art analogy when dealing with the main features and hermeneutical procedures used by hymnographers in interpreting the sacred Scriptures.

Key Features of Liturgical Exegesis

Aural–Visual Media

Liturgical exegesis, the interpretation of Scriptures within the Church's liturgical setting, may be aural or visual. "Aural" refers to all liturgical genres delivered sonically, such as, psalmody, hymnography, homilies and orations, scriptural lections, and *synaxaria*. "Visual" covers those liturgical productions distributed visually, such as iconography.

Both liturgical media, aural and visual, were discussed in minute detail in my book *The Old Testament*.[25] The combination of two media or means of communication makes liturgical exegesis uniquely positioned vis-à-vis patristic commentaries, which remain essentially "textual" in the way they have been handed down through the centuries.

The aural–visual aspects of liturgical exegesis remind us that Scripture is not necessarily or exclusively to be memorized, but is also, most important, to be personalized and internalized. The aural–visual interplay of liturgical performances with Scripture at the center (i.e., the liturgized Bible) helps worshipers become part of the sacred history of ancient Israel, by identifying themselves with the great heroes (Joseph, Moses, the three Jewish youths, the seven Maccabean brothers, etc.) and experiencing the events and stories (e.g., resisting trials and temptations, the wandering through the wilderness under God's providence, the fire of an overheated furnace turned to dew, the first martyric death) of that history.[26]

It will suffice to add here a few lines on the originality of liturgical exegesis pertaining to this media mix of sound and image understood as two distinct hermeneutical channels. Let us take an example of the aural–visual interpretation of Scriptures from the liturgical setting of Holy Week services.

On Holy Tuesday, at Matins, worshipers hear two hymns about the three Jewish young men thrown into a fiery furnace by the Babylonian king Nebuchadnezzar (Dan 3:1–30).[27] The climax of the biblical story is in v. 25, when the king notices that in the furnace there are four instead of three men, the fourth one having the appearance of "one of the sons of gods" (MT; but LXX [Dan 3:92]: "angel of God"; Theod. [Dan 3:92]: "son of god")—some divine character. One of the hymns interprets the Aramaic phrase as referring to "God" (*theos*) himself; the other hymn explains it in terms of an angelophany, an appearance of an "angel" (*angelos*). Another hymn referring to the same episode but chanted outside the Holy Week cycle interprets the Aramaic expression in Dan 3:25 (MT) as pointing to the (pre-incarnate) "Son of God" (*hyios theou*). If we add here the usual iconographic representation (e.g., the eleventh-century mosaic "Holy Three Children" enshrined at the monastery of Hosios Loukas, Greece) of the three young men being protected by the outstretched wings of the angel, then we have a composite (aural–visual) interpretation, where the identity of the fourth figure in the furnace is simultaneously described as God, angel, and Son of God. As noted above, the interpretive simultaneity is a key feature of liturgical exegesis, absent in the discursive, linear mode of interpretation attested by patristic commentaries. In a liturgical setting, conceived as a space-time continuum, one cannot avoid this multi-angularity and simultaneity promoted by liturgists (hymnographers, iconographers, etc.).

Integration

Another important feature of liturgical exegesis, compared to the discursive mode of interpretation found in patristic biblical commentaries, is the integrative reading and interpretation of Scriptures.

In Byzantine hymnography, the distinction between "prophecy" and "fulfillment" (or to use a modern terminology, between Old and New Testaments) is replaced by an integrative use of the two, turning them into an "augmented gospel," which contains, besides information from canonical gospels, extra material, mostly from the Old Testament but also from the pseudepigrapha. This brings us to an interesting, Targum-like way of reading the Scriptures, where the text from the gospel is supplemented by insertions or additions of texts from the Old Testament.

The composite picture constructed of texts gleaned from both "testaments" makes the classical "vertical" paradigm, with the Old Testament at the base and the New Testament at the top, where prophecy is replaced by its fulfillment, almost vanish. In this vertical paradigm, the raison d'être of the Old Testament is exclusively to be a source of "prophecies," "foreshadowings," and "types," all conducive to the Christ event, central to New Testament and Christian theology as a whole. According to this paradigm, the Old Testament has some intrinsic value that lies with "moral law" and the "messianic prophecies." In other words, this paradigm somehow vacates the Old Testament of its content, thus reducing the divine revelation prior to the birth of Jesus to its prophetic dimension. It is as if this revelation was written down and enclosed in a "book" (the future Jewish scriptural corpus [i.e., the Old Testament]) to be read by Christians in light of the Christ event, thus neglecting the Jews, the initial readers and recipients of the sacred Scriptures.

Nevertheless, Byzantine hymnography proposes a different, refreshing view regarding how to read the Scriptures, now found in two distinct corpora, the Old and New Testaments. This is a "horizontal" paradigm,[28] imagined as two unequal concentric circles, with the wider outside circle representing the Old Testament and the smaller inner circle at the center symbolizing the New Testament with the Christ event at its central point.

This horizontal paradigm has two merits. First, by drawing a wider circle, it underlines the richness of the Old Testament, whose content is more than a mere collection of "messianic prophecies" and/or "moral laws." The Old (Elder) Testament is a "sacred history" (i.e., salvation history) by which God prepared a people and a place for the revelation of his Messiah, and this history represents essentially the intrinsic value of the first covenant which cannot be reduced to some "prophecies," retrospectively and only in light of the Christ event interpreted as "messianic." Moreover, referring to prophetic literature per se, the Old Testament contains a considerable number of eschatological sayings, which were not all fulfilled by Jesus, even according to classical Christian reading; they remain to be fulfilled at the "end of time."[29] Second, this paradigm, by placing the New Testament circle, with the Christ event as the starting point, at the center, emphasizes the fundamental tenet of Christian doctrine and theology, that Jesus Christ is the peak and fulfillment of God's supernatural revelation as recorded by Scripture within tradition, the latter being conceived as the life of the Church in the Holy Spirit. This horizontal paradigm strikes a neat balance between the rich content of the Old Testament and the doctrinal centrality of the New Testament while staying within the realm of a widely acceptable mild theological supercessionism.[30]

It must be noted that the vertical paradigm, well represented in ancient biblical commentaries, is attested also, to a lesser degree, in hymnography. As an illustration, I direct the reader's attention to those hymns that use the technical term *typos*, "type," as in the following: "Jonah was enclosed, but not detained in the cetacean chest. For, bearing your type [*sou gar typon pherōn*], of the one who suffered and was given to a tomb, as from a bridal chamber, he sprang up from the beast, and addressed [*prosephōnei*] the guard [*koustōdia*]: 'You, who cherish vain and false things, have abandoned mercy [intended] for them.'"[31]

Quite interestingly, this hymn exhibits both paradigms, vertical when it describes Jonah as a type of Jesus and horizontal when it mixes the two stories, of Jonah coming out of the sea beast and the guard set to watch over Jesus's tomb. Both stories are seamlessly coupled through Jonah, who, as a time traveler to the future, addresses the guard of the tomb.

Another example of the horizontal paradigm may be found in the following hymn prescribed for Holy Friday: "They kept questioning [*erōtōn*] you; and they testified [*katemartyroun*] false things [*pseudē*] against you, but you endured all, and saved all."[32]

In his quest to imaginatively reconstruct Jesus's double trial (religious [high priests and Sanhedrin] and political [Roman governor Pilate]), the hymnographer borrowed the form *erōtōn*, "they kept questioning," from Ps 35 (34):11 (absent in the gospel trial narratives [Matt 26:59–62; cf. Mark 14:55–58]): "When unjust witnesses [*martyres adikoi*] rose up, they kept questioning [*erōtōn*] me about things I was not aware of" (Ps 35 [34]:11 [LXX]). Thus, the result of combining Matt 26:59–62 with Ps 35 (34):11 is an "augmented gospel," where "messianic prophecy" is juxtaposed with its fulfillment.

A good illustration of scriptural integration as a key feature of liturgical exegesis pertaining to the hymns analyzed in this volume can be found in the hymn of Kassia. The hymnographer fuses three women, places, and times (the sinful woman in the house of Simon the Pharisee in Capernaum [Luke 7:36–50], the woman in the house of Simon the Leper in Bethany [Matt 26:6–16], and Mary Magdalene outside Jesus's empty tomb in Jerusalem [Matt 28:1; Luke 24:1, 10; Mark 16:1; John 20:1]) into a complex literary protagonist, identifiable with any human being in its intrinsic frailty. Moreover, Kassia casts into this mix the image of old Eve hiding herself among Eden's trees (Gen 3:8) out of shame for her disobedience. This intricate literary unit, termed *chronotopos*,[33] defies both linear chronology and spatial distribution.

One may add that the integration feature is not so obvious in the discursive mode of interpretation (i.e., ancient Christian commentaries), where the boundary between Old Testament "messianic prophecy" and its New Testament fulfillment is clearly delineated.

The scriptural integration feature proves that hymnographers conceived the Old Testament–New Testament relationship as a two-way street, where the one-direction arrow of time is replaced by a dual interrelation. Something similar can be detected in "reciprocal" typologies (see discussion below), where types and antitypes interchange their roles by "visiting" each other's defining space-time continuum.

Collaboration

I would like to dwell a little further on the example mentioned above, which, besides underlining the aural–visual interface of liturgical exegesis, could reveal another feature of this type of interpretation, namely, its collaborative aspect.

As already noted, Dan 3:25 (3:92: LXX and Theod.) sees in the fourth figure suddenly appearing in the fiery furnace a sort of "divine" entity, "God," or "angel"—as termed in the two hymns to be chanted on Holy Tuesday. But another hymn, outside the Holy Week cycle, identifies the fourth figure with the "Son of God," which can be taken as a type of Christ.

How did the hymnographic transition from "God"/"angel" to "Son of God" happen? Was this new nomenclature "Son of God" the result of a Christianized interpretation of Theod.s singular reading, "son of God" (*hyios theou*)? Or is this semantic shift the evidence of a genuine "intertextuality,"[34] which does not require an authorial intent but is simply the receptor's (hearer's, reader's, beholder's) construal interconnecting various corpora (textual and visual).

There are three different corpora the worshiper can encounter when trying to identify the fourth figure: Scripture (Dan 3:25: LXX: "angel of God"; Theod.: "son of God"), hymnography ("God," "angel," "Son of God"), and iconography ("angel"). The common denominator of these three corpora is the identification of an "angel."

The worshiper may think of another textual reference that can be added to the scriptural corpus for a better understanding of the hymn's "Son of God" identification. This is Isa 9:6 (5), which calls God's agent an "angel of great counsel" (LXX; but note MT: "secrete counselor"), a messianic title interpreted by the Church Fathers as referring to the second person of the Holy Trinity, the Son of God, implied by the plural "Let us make humanity" (Gen 1:26), where, according to a Trinitarian interpretation, the Creator addresses the other two persons of the Trinity, the Son and the Holy Spirit, in his deliberation to create humanity.

This intertextuality, likely considered by the hymnographer, though not necessarily required, was probably construed by not a few worshipers literate enough in the Scriptures to explain fully the nomenclature "Son of God," based on bridging Dan 3:25 (LXX: "angel of God"), supported by both hymnography and iconography, and Isa 9:6 [5] ("angel of great counsel").

Unlike the discursive exegesis (i.e., patristic commentaries), authorially and textually well configured, which convey the comments of a single interpreter, the liturgical exegesis, predominantly anonymous and part of the wider liturgical setting, is an open-ended process, leaving the door ajar to the receptor's participation through liturgical co-performance in an ongoing interpretive process. Thus, the hearer (or reader) and beholder can become co-laborers with the hymnographers and iconographers in the liturgical exegesis of the sacred Scriptures.

Actualization

Any ancient interpreter, whether Jewish or Christian, would be interested in actualizing the message of the Scriptures. This actualizing tendency is due to one of the assumptions of the pre-critical interpreters, that the Scriptures represent God's living Word, which is relevant for all people, places, and times. That is why the interpreter, a servant of the living Word, has to struggle to find ways to make God's Word "actual" for everyone and at every time.

Nevertheless, more than other modes of biblical interpretation (e.g., discursive, i.e., patristic commentaries), liturgical exegesis, through the performative function of the liturgical services, helps worshipers to engage with the liturgized Bible, thus entering and participating in salvation history. The actualization process of the Scriptures unfolds through worshipers' "liturgical immersion" into the depths of sacred history so that they may experience personally the trials of biblical figures (Joseph, three Jewish youths, seven Maccabean brothers) and God's wonderful providence (sojourning through the wilderness, walking in a fiery furnace).

Here is another example of liturgical actualization. The personified, almost deified Wisdom, God's creating and providing agent of Prov 8–9, is the metaphor for Jesus in hymns prescribed for Holy Thursday for two important episodes recorded in the gospels: the foot washing of the disciples and the mystical supper. Pertaining to the latter episode, more specifically to Jesus's institution of the Eucharist, the hymnographer tells us in poetical terms that "the truly existing Wisdom of God prepares a life-sustaining table, and also mixes a bowl of ambrosia for those who believe. Let us draw near in piety."[35] The use of present-tense verbs "prepares" (*hetoimazei*) and "mixes" (*kirna*) and the final exhortation, "let us draw near," is the sheer expression of liturgical actualization of an episode that occurred once in salvation history and now is actualized through the Holy Week services. But the liturgical actualization comes along with an interpretive procedure: the "cup" (*potērion*) containing the "fruit of the vine" (*genēma tēs ampelou*)—wine, which Jesus offered to his disciples (e.g., Mark 14:23, 25, and parallels)—is replaced by a "bowl" (*kratēr*) in which the incarnate Wisdom mixes "ambrosia" (*ambrosia*), the elixir of immortality.

Hermeneutical Procedures

What follows is a preliminary, tentative list of some hermeneutical procedures used by hymnographers in the hymns analyzed in the first part of this volume. At the risk of being redundant, I will cite only a few of them again, at least partially, so that the reader may be able to identify the procedures connected with each of these hymns.

The phrase "hermeneutical procedures" is used here in the sense of processes or means through which the hymnographers read and interpreted the Scriptures. If "interpretations are arrived at by hermeneutical (interpretative) means,"[36] then understanding liturgical exegesis (biblical interpretations by liturgists) requires a good grasp of the main hermeneutical procedures at work.

Hymnographers observed the same set of assumptions as ancient Jewish and Christian biblical interpreters, namely, that the Bible is cryptic, relevant, perfectly harmonious, and divinely inspired.[37]

I have gathered the hermeneutical procedures used by hymnographers under three headings: hermeneutical pointers, intertextualities, and typologies.

Hermeneutical Pointers

I would like to return to liturgical exegesis and the cubist art analogy, briefly discussed earlier in this chapter.

In their tireless quest for a more "real," "tangible" representation of reality than the one offered by Renaissance art, cubist artists used various means to impregnate their artistic representations with some "real feeling" of reality, hence their cubifying tendencies aimed at giving more volume and a three-dimensional sense to abstracted geometric shapes.

Picasso and Braque modified abstract art by introducing the collage (from French *coller*, "to glue," a composition consisting of different materials, such as paper, fabric, etc., glued onto a solid surface, such as a canvas) and papier collé ("pasted paper") techniques to their paintings. The collage, with its non-flat appearance, quickly became the favorite technique of the cubists who were interested in suggesting dimensionality in their works.

The papier collé is a piece of paper, previously drawn or painted on, pasted to an already painted canvas. Imagine a piece a paper on which the artist, using ink, has drawn some strings and part of a guitar. Then that paper is pasted onto the canvas so the partial, schematic representation of the guitar would match the barely visible abstract-shaped guitar in the hands of a standing man, also barely identified in the abstract cubist composition.

These collages and papiers collés, snippets of concreteness slipped into an emerging piece of art, may function as the artists' "guidelines" to show the beholders how to look at their imagined reconstructed reality.

Art critics suggest that the collage technique that emerged during the synthetic phase of cubism was used to confer a sense of hyperrealism (surrealism) to the artistic work. This aspect does not contradict the above-mentioned possible didactic, guiding function of the collage detected in cubist paintings.

A good example of papier collé and collage techniques is Picasso's *La bouteille de Suze* (*Bottle of Suze*, 1912). The artist pasted cut fragments of newsprint and construction paper (i.e., collage) and a piece of paper on which he wrote "Suze" and which he glued to an abstracted painted bottle (papier collé) to suggest a liquor bottle and the ambience of an old-fashioned Parisian cafe where folks used to read newspapers while drinking. Both the papier collé and the collage function as "guidelines" directing the beholder's imagination to the setting of the cafe. And from that point on, the spectator's imagination will progressively do its work by reconstructing a reality already imaged by the artist. The piece of art using the collage technique becomes a canvas painted again (like a palimpsest) by the beholder's own imagination.

Moreover, by using the collage technique, Picasso and Braque opened the door to multimedia (painting combined with various materials) artistic works, a feature of cubism similar to the liturgized Bible or liturgical exegesis, where the Scriptures were liturgized and interpreted by liturgists using two media of communication, aural and visual, and a number of genres pertaining to either of these media (e.g., hymns, homilies, orations, lectionaries, liturgical actions, liturgical objects, portable icons, mosaics, frescoes, etc.).

The three-dimensional collage fusing with the planar, bi-dimensional surface of a cubist painting is analogous to liturgical exegesis consisting of textual material (hymnography), bi-dimensional iconography, and three-dimensional liturgical objects that may enrich through their scripturally loaded symbolism the biblical interpretation while unfolding in the liturgical setting.

The cubist art and collage–papier collé techniques can be safely applied to a piece of liturgical exegesis. The hapax legomena and rare words or phrases detected in hymns function similarly to the collages and papiers collés used in cubist art. I would call these rare tiny scriptural pieces "hermeneutical pointers," because their role is to point one's attention to a specific scriptural text, character, or episode that the hymnographer considered significant for the hymn's central theme. Like the collages in cubist art, hermeneutical pointers in the liturgized Bible are explicative glosses or tiny evocative comments.

Let us glean two examples of hermeneutical pointers from the hymns analyzed in part I of this volume.

The first example of a hermeneutical pointer comes from a hymn prescribed for the Matins of Good Friday, where the Virgin Mary, depicted as *mater dolorosa* at the foot of Jesus's cross, laments powerlessly over her son's agonizing death: "Today, the blameless Virgin is beholding you hanging on the cross, O Word! She is lamenting with motherly affections [*mētrōa splanchna*], and her heart was wounded bitterly. She was sighing painfully from the depths of her soul. By tearing at her face and hair, she became utterly distraught."[38]

The hymnographer uses the phrase *mētrōa splanchna*, "motherly affections" (*splanchna*, lit. "inward parts, womb"), denoting a viscerally felt compassion, which only a mother can experience for her suffering children. The phrase found in this hymn functions as a hermeneutical pointer, guiding the hearer to become familiar with 4 Macc 13:19, where a similar expression, *mētrōas gastros*, "motherly womb," is used with reference to the mother of the seven martyred Maccabean brothers. By using such a hermeneutical pointer, the hymnographer invites the hearer to reflect on the parallelism between the two mothers experiencing the same array of emotions triggered by the horrifying scene of their children being murdered under their helpless eyes.

The second example of a hermeneutical pointer is found in a hymn designated for the Matins of Holy Monday, celebrated by anticipation on Palm Sunday evening: "The present day carries resplendently the first fruits of Lord's Passion. Come, O feast lovers, to encounter him with canticles! For the Creator comes to accept cross, trials and scourges [*etasmous kai mastigas*]."[39]

The hymn's phrase "trials and scourges" (*etasmous kai mastigas*) is found only once in the entire Bible, a hapax legomenon, in 2 Macc 7:37: "through trials and scourges" (*meta etasmōn kai mastigōn*). Nevertheless, there is a significant distinction between its use in the hymn and in the *anaginoskomenon* biblical text. If in the hymn, the phrase, in the accusative, refers to Jesus, who "accepted cross, trials and scourges," in 2 Macc 7:37, the same collocation, this time in the genitive, concerns the tyrant Antiochus IV Epiphanes, who murdered the seven Maccabean brothers and who eventually, "through trials and scourges," will come to realize God's almighty power.

The phrase "trials and scourges" functions here as a hermeneutical pointer directing the hearer's attention to 2 Macc 7, thus paralleling the martyrdom of the seven Maccabean brothers with Jesus's Passion; in both cases, there is a foreign leader (Antiochus, Pilate) and Jews suffering death for their strong, unshakable faith in God.

I will return to 2 Macc 7:37 and this hymn, an interesting example of "converted typology," below in the section on "Typologies."

By considering the analogy between collage and hermeneutical pointers, one can reach the following logical conclusion. If in cubism, the collage technique makes real objects cohabitate with artistic representations of reality, thus proving that art is as real as reality itself, similarly, in Byzantine hymnography, the insertion of hermeneutical pointers (i.e., hapax legomena and rare words or phrases) into hymns shows that hymnography is as scriptural as the Scriptures themselves. In both cases, there is an intriguing symbiosis between two distinct entities: (1) reality and art and (2) hymnography and Scriptures.

This analogy holds true for liturgical exegesis, where hermeneutical pointers undergo a process of osmosis, interpenetrating through the dense fabric of hymnography, and eventually, through a gradual collaborative interpretation, they end up in a strong symbiosis of Scripture with hymnic poetry.

As for discursive interpretation, that found in classical patristic commentary, this is analogous to pre-cubist, naturist art, consisting exclusively of a single entity, the artistic re-presentation of reality, functioning as a transparent screen through which the beholder is invited to contemplate reality. Similarly, in an ancient Christian commentary, the interpretation serves as a transparent medium through which the reader has access to Scriptures, gently refined and interpreted, so the commentary, like the work of a pre-cubist artist, will not dramatically change the backdrop (the Scriptures). In a nutshell, naturist art and discursive exegesis are (or meant to be) both clear and trustworthy lenses through which beholders and readers can "read" either the real world or the Scriptures.

Intertextualities

Intertextuality is a literary procedure that establishes interrelations among various texts, ultimately impacting the understanding of separate works.

These interrelations, achieved by means of quotations, allusions, calque, pastiche, and parody, may prompt the readers, who, based on their previous knowledge, experience, and spontaneous emotions, contribute to the multi-layered process of interpretation.

Intertextuality, in a narrow sense, occurs across two different literary corpora, while in a wide sense, it refers to textual interrelations within a single literary corpus. The former type of intertextuality between two different literary corpora was used first by theorists such as Ferdinand de Saussure, who argued for language's intrinsic semiotic values, and Mikhail Bakhtin, who considered language as a dialogical entity.

In her 1966 essay "Le mot, le dialogue et le roman,"[40] where she examines Bakhtin's work, focusing on the concept of dialogism, Julia Kristeva uses for the first time the term *intertextualité*, "intertextuality," with reference to textual interrelations between two distinct literary corpora.

In Kristeva's view, intertextuality does not require or presuppose necessarily the author's intent. Intertextuality is foremost a "reader-oriented" procedure. The textual interrelation is the mere result of a text being part of a network or universe of textual units where no text can escape influence from other texts. Thus, even the basic textual unit, the "literary word," is an "*intersection of textual surfaces* rather than a *point* (a fixed meaning), as a dialogue among several writings: that of the writer, the addressee (or the character) and the contemporary or earlier cultural context."[41]

The notion of intertextuality prevents one from considering "texts" as self-contained and closed systems; texts are, rather, historical and differential. As in the case of Russian dolls, there will always be a lesser doll within another doll, a tiny textual unit within a wider unit. There is no such thing as textual autonomy; all texts are subject to interrelation with other texts. And this synchronic textual interdependency has its diachronic counterpart, with textual interrelation historically determined.

Since the publication of Kristeva's essay, the text is no longer viewed as a final product with a static structure, as structuralists saw it, but rather as an open-ended entity with a certain fluidity and dynamism influenced by textual networks as well as the new layers of interpretation that readers may add to the initial multilevel corpus.

This concept of intertextuality, with its emphasis on the relative character and historical dependency of a text, applies quite well to the liturgized Bible and its hermeneutical counterpart, liturgical exegesis, where the interpretive process is still unfolding with each worshiper's participation in the act of interpretation by adding his or her previous biblical knowledge and instant emotions.

In the case of Byzantine hymnography, one may find both types of intertextuality: intertextuality proper, that is, the interrelations between two different literary corpora, namely, hymnography and Scripture (i.e., the liturgized Bible and liturgical exegesis); and intertextuality in a wider sense, that is, an "inner biblical exegesis"[42] among the biblical texts. The latter intertextuality can be embedded within the former.

One may add that patristic biblical commentaries exhibit, almost exclusively, intertextuality in its wider sense, as interconnections among biblical texts from various parts of Scripture.

With respect to Byzantine hymnography, understood as a facet of that diamond-like liturgized Bible, intertextualities are means by which biblical interpretation can be shared by hymnographer and worshiper. This hermeneutical procedure underlines the collaborative dimension of the liturgical exegesis and the significant role of the receptor (hearer or beholder) in an open-ended interpretive process.

Here are two examples of intertextuality analyzed in this volume. The first is: "The spotless Virgin, when she saw the One whom she birthed from a seedless womb, unable to bear the wound of her inward parts, distraught [*trychomenē*] she said: 'How have you been hung on a Cross as a condemned one?'"[43] The lemma *trychō*, "to wear out," occurs two times in the Bible (Wis 11:11; 14:15). In Wis 14:15, the form *trychomenos*, "distraught, devastated," describes a father overcome by grief at his child's untimely death, a graphic image similar to the one encountered in the above-cited hymn (i.e., a mother, Mary, distraught at the sight of the untimely dying of her son). Since the interrelation is between a hymn and a biblical text, thus belonging to two different literary corpora (hymnography and Bible), we may consider this hymn an example of intertextuality in the narrow sense.

The second example is: "I gave my back to the ones who scourge, and I did not turn away my face from spittings . . . and I endured [*hypemeina*] the cross for the salvation of the world."[44] This is an interesting illustration of intertextuality in the wide sense being embedded in intertextuality in the narrow sense. On the one hand, the hymnographer noticed the interrelation between Isa 50:6 and Psalms of Solomon 10:2, with the latter text functioning as a gloss on the former, a typical case of "inner biblical interpretation" (the Bible interpreting itself), hence intertextuality in the wide sense, between two texts belonging to the same literary corpus (the Bible). On the other hand, there is an interrelation between a hymn and a biblical text. The verbal form *hypemeina*, "I endured," used by the hymnographer, is also attested in Psalms of Solomon 10:2, hence an example of intertextuality in the narrow sense, as interrelation between two different corpora (hymnography and the Bible).

Typologies

The word "typology" refers to both the interpretation and the study of types and symbols, especially with reference to the Bible.[45] For a long time, it has been assumed that the linking of typology with the historical event makes it distinct from allegory. But, as Frances Young notes, "It is not its character as historical event which makes a 'type'; what matters is its mimetic quality."[46] In other words, typology is a relation between two narrative events, institutions, or figures, rather than between a narrative and a historical event. Understood this way, typology is a form of intertextuality (as discussed above).

Nevertheless, even the newer understanding of typology as intertextuality is not satisfying if one considers the earliest evidence, as recorded by the canonical gospels. I am referring to two important gospel testimonies: the Transfiguration episode and the risen Jesus's walk with two disciples on the road to Emmaus.

The Transfiguration episode is recorded in Matt 17:1–9, Mark 9:2–10, and Luke 9:28–36. According to these gospel narratives, likely going back to an earlier apostolic tradition, while heading for Jerusalem, weeks before his crucifixion, Jesus stops on a mountain, identified in Byzantine times with Mount Tabor,[47] where in the presence of three of his disciples, Peter, James, and John, Jesus was "transformed" (*metemorphōthē* [Matt 17:2; Mark 9:2]; cf. Luke 9:29: "the appearance of his face altered"). Two Old Testament figures, Moses and Elijah, "appeared to them" (*ōphthē autois*), talking with Jesus (Matt 17:3; Mark 9:4). According to Luke 9:31, Moses and Elijah "appeared in glory [*ophthentes en doxē*] and spoke of his [Jesus's] exodus [*exodon*] which he was about to accomplish in Jerusalem." Although the term *exodos* is commonly rendered "departure," suggesting that Moses and Elijah were talking of Jesus's death, it may also subtly allude to a new "exodus" that will be accomplished by Jesus, the "new Moses," not in Egypt but in Jerusalem. Considering both meanings of this key term, the Old Testament figures were conversing about Jesus's death and resurrection.

What makes this episode unique is the "appearance" in Jesus's day of two Old Testament figures long after their "departure" (i.e., Moses's death, with an unknown burial place, and Elijah's translation in a fiery chariot to heaven), thus opening the way for the interpretation of salvation history, or God's *oikonomia*, "economy, management plan" (Irenaeus), as a two-way street and not merely as a unidirectional arrow of time. Thus conceived, salvation history is a time-space continuum where time travel may happen, as noted above, from past to future.

This is an important detail when one considers the classical definition of typology as intertextuality between two narratives. If the three gospel narratives dealing with Jesus's "transformation" and the "appearance" of Moses and Elijah are based on an older, oral tradition prior to the emergence of what we today call the "New Testament," then the definition of typology as intertextuality needs to be refined. The presupposition that sees the Bible as a text with two Testaments needs to be reconsidered in light of the apostolic tradition where the sacred Scriptures referred exclusively to what we call today the "Old Testament," and the events related to Jesus of Nazareth and his disciples were considered moments in Israel's salvation history recorded in those Scriptures. In this light, typology is more complex than a mere exercise of finding intertextualities or interconnections between two parallels in two different literary corpora.

Typology, starting in the apostolic period and prior to the first New Testament writings, is actually "interpreting" Jesus's sayings and actions within the hermeneutical key of salvation history as provided by the sacred Scriptures (i.e., Old Testament writings). Moreover, the "distance" between type (Old Testament prefiguration or foreshadowing) and antitype (New Testament realization or fulfillment) presupposed by the classical definition fades away in this new understanding of typology. In the Transfiguration episode, the type (Moses, Elijah) and antitype (Jesus) are both circumscribed by the same four-dimensional time-space environment, with no considerable "distance" between foreshadowing and its realization.

In light of these observations, how should one define a typology? Put simply, typology is interpreting Jesus as part of salvation history and its "written" representation, i.e., the Scriptures (Old Testament). I may note here a very important distinction between this view of interpreting Jesus as "part" of salvation history and its sacred Scriptures and an older definition of typology, recently reactivated as a response to the classical definition of typology, that is, interpreting the Scriptures in light of Jesus. An example of this would be the attempt to understand the Scriptures through the lens of Jesus's leadership. Such a hermeneutical turn would lead to the establishment of an intertextuality between Jesus the Leader (antitype), either "historical" or "scriptural" (as recorded in the New Testament), and its foreshadowing or prefiguration (type) in the Scriptures, e.g., Moses as leader. This definition draws greatly on another important text pertaining to typology, Luke 24:25, 27, where the risen Jesus is walking with two disciples on the way to Emmaus. In this episode, the disciples, not recognizing Jesus, tell him about the death of their Master, believed by them to be the long-awaited Messiah. In response to their disappointment and sadness, Jesus reminds them of the "messianic" prophecies: "And he said to them, 'O foolish and slow of heart to believe all that the prophets have spoken [*pasin hois elalēsen hoi prophētai*]. . . . And beginning from Moses and from all prophets, he interpreted thoroughly [*diermēneusen*] to them in all the Scriptures [*graphais*] the things about him." The "prophets" spoke of Jesus, their prophecies are in the Scriptures, and they need to be "thoroughly interpreted" in light of Jesus's life. According to Luke 24:32 ("he opened [*diēnoigen*] to us the Scriptures"), Jesus is the one who can "open" the hidden Scriptures (Luke 24:44: "Law of Moses, the Prophets and Psalms"— the tripartite division of the Jewish Scriptures [Law, Prophets, Writings]). Christ is the hermeneutical key that can unlock the Scriptures.

Nevertheless, my proposed definition of typology is different from the classical definition (i.e., intertextuality between two narratives belonging to different corpora [Old Testament and New Testament]) or the one presented in the lines above (i.e., interpreting the Scriptures [Old Testament] in light of the Christ event). My definition underlines the inseparability between Jesus and Israel's salvation history as "written" in the sacred Scriptures (i.e., the Old Testament): Jesus belongs to salvation history, being in the company of and "beyond all [his] friends" (Ps 45:7 [44:8]),[48] namely, all the types, who prefigured him pertaining to his sayings and actions as handed over by the apostolic tradition and later "written" in the NT.

This definition focuses on Jesus and salvation history understood as a time-space continuum and fits quite well with the examples gleaned from Byzantine hymnography and analyzed in the present volume. Below are a few of the most popular examples of typology used in hymnography.

Converted Typology

What I call "converted typology" are examples where the attributes of a scriptural figure are "converted" to fit Jesus's salvific role while there is no type–antitype relation between the two. An example of such a pseudo-typology is the hymn prescribed for the Matins of Holy Monday celebrated by anticipation on the evening of Palm Sunday. Here is a fragment of that hymn:

> The present day [i.e., Holy Monday] carries resplendently the first fruits of the Lord's Passion. . . . For the Creator comes to accept [*katadexasthai*] cross [*stauron*], trials and scourges [*etasmous kai mastigas*], being judged by Pilate, by reason of which he is struck [*rhapistheis*] by a servant on the head [*korrēs*]. He accepts [*prosietai*] it all so that he may save humanity.[49]

Since this hymn was discussed previously in this very chapter,[50] I will underline only a few points pertaining to the present topic.

The collocation "trials and scourges" (*etasmous kai mastigas*) is a hapax legomenon, occurring in 2 Macc 7:37 with reference to the tyrant Antiochus IV Epiphanes, who because of his persecution against the Jews, including the murdering of the seven Maccabean brothers, will be punished by God "through trials and scourges" (the same phrase as in our hymn but in the genitive plural), so that he may recognize God's power.

As can be seen in the hymn, the same expression, "trials and scourges," is used with reference to Jesus during his final week in Jerusalem. For the hymnographer, it is Jesus who "accepts" ("willingly" is implied by the composite verb *katadechomai*) cross, trials and scourges, and being judged by Pilate. In 2 Macc 7, it is God who judges and punishes Antiochus IV Epiphanes. In the hymn, Jesus accepts all this debasing panoply of sufferings (e.g., "struck by a servant") for a noble cause, to "save humanity," in sharp contrast with Antiochus, where there is no mention of acceptance and the ultimate goal of "trials and scourges" is to make the tyrant recognize that God is in full control of history.

The phrase functions as a hermeneutical pointer directing the hearer's (or reader's) attention to a key (*anaginoskomenon*) text in the Bible, 2 Macc 7, on the emergence of martyrdom in Judaism as a precursor of and prelude to Christian martyrdom—an important text used in a hymn of Holy Monday, which opens Holy Week.

The conversion of the phrase "trials and scourges" in this typology is a strong proof for the creativity and originality of liturgical exegesis, the imagistic interpretations of the liturgists, more specifically for this example, the hymnographers.

Chiastic Typology

The following hymn contains a peculiar sort of textual interconnection which I coin "chiastic typology":

> Jacob lamented [ōdyreto] Joseph's loss [sterēsin] while the noble [one] [gennaios] was seated on a chariot, honored as a king. For by not enslaving [douleusas] himself then to the Egyptian woman's lusts [Old Testamentēdonais], he was glorified in return [antedoxazeto] by the one who looks at humans' hearts and freely bestows [nemontos] the indestructible crown [stephos aphtharton]."[51]

The hymn has a chiastic structure: ABB'A'. There are four ideas expressed in its lines. A: Jacob laments over his son's death. B: Joseph is honored as a king over Egypt. B'': Joseph resists the temptation of Potiphar's wife. A'': God sees all and rewards freely.

As one may notice, based on B and B', one would expect to have in the last line (A') another reference to Jacob, something along the lines of "Jacob rejoices seeing again his lost son." Instead, A' introduces a new figure, "God," who sees all and rewards freely. I would call this chiasm "incomplete" or limping due to the obvious dissimilarity between A and A'.

Nevertheless, this incomplete chiasm makes one imagine Jacob, who laments his son's death, as prefiguring God, who "looks at humans' hearts," spotting his Son as he was resisting temptations and wrestling with trials, similar to his scriptural type, Joseph the Chaste, and lamenting, like Jacob, over his Son's death, while freely bestowing the "incorruptible crown" (presumably to Joseph and his Son).

Meta-Typology

> In the flaming furnace of fire, as in the bedewing, the faithful and your Holy Youths pre-painted from life [proezōgraphoun] mystically your coming [eleusin] from the Virgin [parthenou], which shone forth [analampsasan] to us without being burnt [aphlektōs]. And Daniel, the Just, and wonderful among Prophets, clearly [tranōs] foreshowing [prodēlōn] your second divine sojourn [epidēmia], cried out: "Looking [heorōn] until [heōs hou] the thrones were set [etetēsan], says he, and the judge [kritēs] sat down [ekathestē], and a river of fire [pyros potamos] appeared [epestē]."[52]

This hymn is an example of a "meta-typology." It begins with a scriptural interconnection between the "fiery furnace," where the three Jewish youths were cast (Dan 3), and Mary's womb. The hymnographer continues this Marian typology, with a theological interconnection between the "bedewed" youths coming unharmed out of the furnace and Jesus coming from the Virgin, "shining forth" to humans without being burnt. But this meta-typology does not stop here.

The hymnographer adds another scriptural interconnection to this series, that between Jesus's first coming and his "second sojourn," triggered by his Parousia, which will happen again in a fiery setting dominated by a judge, thrones, and a "river of fire" (Dan 7:9–14). The last interconnection between two phases of Jesus's personality and mission (the first and the second advents) is a peculiar Christological typology, where type and antitype coalesce into a single person.

Reciprocal Typology

The "reciprocal typology" is probably the most interesting and defining among the hermeneutical procedures of liturgical exegesis.

> Jonah was enclosed, but not detained in the cetacean chest. For, bearing [*pherōn*] your type [*typon*], of the one who suffered [*pathontos*] and was given to a tomb [*taphē dothentos*], as from a bridal chamber, he sprang up [*anethore*] from the beast, and addressed [*prosephōnei*] the guard [*koustōdia*].[53]

In the above hymn prescribed for the Matins of Holy Saturday, the hymnographer introduces the prophet Jonah as a type of a suffering and entombed Jesus while directly addressing the latter using the second person. Furthermore, Jonah is depicted as "springing up" from the sea beast as from a bridal chamber and speaking to the guard set to watch over Jesus's tomb.

It seems as if Jonah was a time traveler to the future, and having reached the tomb of Jesus, he addressed the guard. In the scriptural interconnection between Jonah (type) and Jesus (antitype), the type moves in this multidirectional time-space continuum toward the antitype position and role, almost overlapping the latter. This is similar to the Lucan Transfiguration scene discussed above, where Moses and Elijah (types) "appeared" to the disciples as talking among themselves or with Jesus on a mountain. In both cases, Old Testament figures functioning as types of Jesus (the antitype) are time travelers to the future.

But time traveling in hymns may also occur from a narrative "present" (New Testament) or an eschatological "future" to a narrative "past" (Old Testament). In this case, the time travelers are usually Jesus and Mary.

In the next hymn, it is the antitype, the Son of God before incarnation, who travels from the future to the past or, more precisely, from out of the time-space continuum into the "past" of salvation history:

> Praise and highly exalt the Lord who protected the youths in the flame of fire of the burning furnace and came down [synkatabanta] to them in the form of an angel [en morphē angelou].[54]

The antitype's traveling is described as an act of divine condescension (synkatabasis) using the language of an angelophany: the Lord descended and took the form of an angel. The "distance" between type and antitype, so emphasized by the proponents of the older definition of typology, turns here into almost overlapping. Prior to incarnation, the Lord takes the form of an angel and makes his appearance in the "burning furnace."

Another example of antitype time traveling in the past is found in Kassia's hymn:

> I shall wipe dry again, with the hair locks of my head, your undefiled feet; whose striking having been sounded in [her] ears Eve in paradise at twilight hid herself in fear.[55]

In this fragment of superb poetry, Jesus's "undefiled feet," which were anointed and wiped by a sinful woman, are the same as God's "feet" walking in Eden, whose sound reverberated in Eve's ears, making the guilty woman hide out of shame among Eden's trees. This is an obvious example of the antitype (Jesus) traveling back in time to the dawn of humanity.

I call this kind of typology reciprocal or "role-exchanging" due to the interchangeability between type and antitype against the backdrop of a multidirectional time-space continuum marking salvation history as both a management plan and concrete history.

Embedded Typology

In the hymn below, there is a double typology. First, the antitype is a time traveler to the past, almost overlapping with its type. Second, the result of that overlapping becomes the type of a new antitype, the Theotokos. I term this theological interconnection "embedded typology":

In the furnace, in that one of the youths, once, O Lord, you pre-portrayed [*proapeikonisas*] your very mother [*tēn sēn Mētera*]. For the type [*ho gar typos*], unburned while entering in, took those out of fire.[56]

The hymnographer describes Jesus ("Lord") as the one who delivered the youths out of the furnace's fire, being unburned, while prefiguring his mother, who, like him, will not be burned by the fire of her son's divinity during pregnancy or birthing. The second antitype (Jesus's mother) is embedded within the first antitype (Jesus) time-traveling to the past.

An Open-Ended Conclusion

In the end and in a few words, how is this oft-repeated liturgical exegesis to be understood within the wider context of the liturgized Bible? Is the liturgical exegesis, that is, the ways in which liturgists interpret the Scriptures in hymnography and iconography, really that much different from what I have called the discursive mode of interpretation, that is, the interpretations of the Scriptures found in the ancient Christian biblical commentaries of the Church Fathers?

I first need to offer a clarification. While making the case for liturgical exegesis, I do not suggest that "liturgists" and "Church Fathers" are two entirely different nomenclatures. Rather, I would underline that to a certain degree, they overlap, since not a few hymnographers whose names are attached to their hymns are also well-known Church Fathers who either authored biblical commentaries or wrote comments on various Scriptures in their theological treatises. Although there are numerous anonymous hymns, even in these cases, the presumption runs rather high that their authors had some ecclesiastical or spiritual authority.

One of the main objectives of this work has been to analyze selected hymns in detail, lexically and biblically, in order to determine differences in liturgical and traditional exegesis. In my opinion, the difference, if there is a difference, is to be found in the area of key features or tenets and hermeneutical procedures emblematic of liturgical exegesis.

Since some of the defining features and hermeneutical procedures of this liturgical manner of interpreting the Scriptures were discussed above, I will conclude this part with a few general observations regarding the peculiar traits of liturgical exegesis as compared to discursive interpretation—in other words, what distinguishes Byzantine hymnography in terms of biblical exegesis from ancient Christian biblical commentaries.

Deconstructing and Reconstructing the Scriptures

By using the collocation "deconstructing and reconstructing," I do not intimate that the liturgists or, more specifically, the hymnographers deliberately deconstructed the Bible, reducing it to small constitutive pieces in order to analyze its parts individually and then put these pieces together as a new whole. On the contrary, I use "deconstructing and reconstructing" in the narrow sense in which Jacques Derrida (1930–2004) uses it.

For Derrida, French philosopher and father of deconstructionism—a semiotic analysis theory—deconstruction does not mean to take pieces apart, as understood by popular culture. In Derrida's view, deconstruction refers to dualism with respect to speech writing, where the process of writing is the very deconstruction of this dualism.

Commenting on Derrida's own definition of deconstructionism, Juliano Zaiden Benvindo notes:

> Deconstruction, after all, does not avoid tradition, but it does attack the closeness of otherness that a past or a future-present could bring forth. Hence, if negotiation is "none other than destruction itself," then it is not destruction: "If deconstruction were a destruction nothing would be possible any longer." Indeed, it is a continuum of invention and reinterpretation, which, although "[involving] the structures or the constructa, the things constructed that make life or existence possible," it is critical of it, for it does not see them as stabilized over time.[57]

Summing up Benvindo's comment, deconstructionism is against "the closeness of otherness," which, at times, traditional ways of doing things could trigger or entertain. In this way, I would like to use the term "deconstructionism" with respect to liturgical exegesis as an option for doing exegesis other than the discursive one promoted by ancient biblical commentators. By interpreting the Scriptures in a liturgical setting and establishing and following their own hermeneutical procedures, Byzantine hymnographers exposed the "otherness" of biblical interpretation. As Benvindo underlines, deconstruction is "a continuum of invention and re-interpretation," and this is what liturgical exegesis vis-à-vis discursive exegesis is all about: invention and reinterpretation in reading and using the Scriptures.

While not really deconstructing the Scriptures (i.e., a full Bible codex, a rare commodity prior to the fifteenth century), Byzantine hymnographers made the best of the fact that in their time, the "Bible" was actually preserved and transmitted as "collections" (e.g., Psalter, Prophetologion, Octateuch, etc.) that provided the scriptural lections for various liturgical services. They already had a deconstructed Bible, for practical reasons, I may add, which needed to be used and explained in liturgical *synaxes* (Gk. "gatherings"). And during this ongoing process of using and interpreting the sacred Scriptures, the "Bible" has been naturally "reconstructed," though the new version of the "Bible," or rather of Scriptures found in the above-mentioned collections looked different. This happened because the hymnographers selectively used pieces of Scripture or even single biblical words, mostly hapax legomena, and inserted them into the intricate tapestry of their hymns. Thus, the reconstructed Scriptures turned into what I call a liturgized Bible, realistically impossible to locate or circumscribe yet omnipresent in any weft thread of the uniquely designed Byzantine hymnographic tapestry.

Simultaneously, along with the emergence of the liturgized Bible, a new way of interpreting the Scriptures arose that was fully recontextualized in a worship setting. This is the liturgical exegesis, generated by the intricate process of deconstructing and reconstructing the Scriptures, just briefly discussed. One cannot talk about liturgical exegesis independently from a liturgized Bible, as we cannot have the latter without the former.

I would like to close this part and the current volume by highlighting six points that encapsulate the originality and creativity of liturgical exegesis in contrast to discursive exegesis (i.e., ancient biblical commentaries) or "learned exegetical tradition,"[58] while leaving the conclusion open-ended.

The defining points are (1) imaginative vs. discursive, (2) synthetic vs. analytic, (3) simultaneous and multi-angular vs. linear and sequential,

(4) facilitative vs. directive commentary, (5) multimedia (aural–visual) vs. textual distribution, (6) popular–global vs. limited access.

It is my strong conviction that much more analytic work is needed at both levels, aural and visual, for a better understanding of this intriguing mode of interpretation of Scripture which I have coined "liturgical exegesis."

Glossary of Liturgical Terms

The following list is compiled mostly from the glossary of liturgical and monastic terms found at the end of each of the three volumes of *The Synaxarion of the Monastery of the Theotokos Evergetis*.

Amnos: At the Proskomede service (see *Proskomede*), a piece of bread, symbolizing the body of Jesus, is taken from the prosphora (see *Prosphora*) and placed on a plate, usually made of gold, to be consecrated during the Liturgy. This piece of bread is called *Amnos* (Gk., "lamb"), pointing to the title John the Baptist used to address Jesus: "Lamb of God" (*Amnos tou Theou*, John 1:29).

Amomos: Refers to Ps 119 (118) chanted at Orthros on Saturdays and Sundays from the middle of August until the beginning of Lent.

Anamnesis: (Gk, "reminiscence, remembrance.") Refers to the commemorative aspect of liturgical services that are celebrated in remembrance of important events or figures of Church history. In the Byzantine rite, *Anamnesis* is part of the *Anaphora* (Gk., "offering."), the central prayer of the Eucharistic service (see *Liturgy*), recalling Jesus's sacrifice, death, resurrection, ascension, sitting at the right above, and second glorious coming.

Antiphon: A short scriptural refrain commonly from the Psalter that is chanted alternatively (antiphonally) by two chanting groups.

Apolysis: The dismissal prayer read at the end of each liturgical service.

Apolytikion: (Gk. *apolyō*, "to release, to dismiss.") A dismissal troparion in honor of a saint or the Virgin Mary, chanted at the end of services, such as Vespers.

Apostichon: A set of hymns (*stichera*; see *Sticheron*) accompanied by verses (*stichoi*) gleaned from Psalms, found at the end of Vespers.

Automelon: A troparion that is employed as a model melody for other troparia (see *Troparion*) and stichera (see *Sticheron*). A troparion or sticheron chanted according to the melodic design of an automelon is called prosomoion.

Canon (Kanon): A complex hymn chanted at Orthros or Matins (see *Orthros*); it consists of nine odes relying on biblical odes or canticles (see *Ode*), mostly found in the Old Testament, with the final ode taken from the New Testament (i.e., the Magnificat and Song of Zechariah). Andrew of Crete (d. 740) is credited with the invention of the canon as a liturgical poetical genre. The nine odes of the canon, with intercalated troparia, were arranged in stanzas (i.e., four or more lines with a fixed meter). Initially, the canon was used during Great Lent (e.g., the Great Canon of Andrew of Crete). With the passing of time, the second ode went out of use; currently, the canon contains eight odes. The number of troparia following the odes of the canon varies between eight and sixteen. The theme of these troparia is inspired by the event or figure commemorated on that day.

Heirmologion: The liturgical book containing the heirmoi (see *Heirmos*) for the entire liturgical year cycle.

Heirmos: Designates the first troparion that dictates the rhythm and melody for the troparia following each ode of a canon.

Horologion: A liturgical book containing the daily cycle of services (i.e., the "hours").

Hypakoe: Designates a troparion that may be chanted at Orthros (Matins) in the following instances: (a) after the *amomos* (i.e., Ps 119 [118]) or the *polyeleos* (i.e., Ps 135 [134] and Ps 136 [135]); (b) after the third ode of the canon on great feast days; (c) after the third *kathisma* (see *Kathisma*) of the Psalter.

Idiomelon: A troparion or sticheron chanted that has its own melody.

Katabasia: (Gk. *katabasis,* "going down.") The final troparion among those following each ode (see *Canon* and *Troparion*) and sung by the two chanting groups in unison.

Kathisma: (Gk. [Byzantine], "seat (of a chair), session.") Designates (1) one of the twenty sections of the Psalter, commonly recited at Vespers and Orthros (Matins); (2) a troparion (see *Troparion*) sung after each *kathisma* (see *Kathisma*) of the Psalter and after the third and sixth ode of a canon (see *Canon*), during which chanting the community sits.

Kontakion: A stanza (strophe) sung at any feast or commemoration after the sixth ode of the canon at Orthros (Matins), usually accompanied by one or more *oikoi* (see *Oikos*).

Lauds: (Gk. *ainoi,* "praises.") A part of the Orthros (Matin) service that contains Ps 148, 149, 150.

Liturgy (Eucharist service): (Gk. *leitourgia,* "work for the people, public service.") The Byzantine rite is made up of three liturgies: (1) Liturgy of Saint John Chrysostom, celebrated on most days of the liturgical year and united with Vespers on the feast day of the Annunciation; (2) Liturgy of Saint Basil, celebrated together with Vespers ten times a year (on the five Sundays of Great Lent, on the feast day of Saint Basil [January 1], on the eves of the Nativity and the Theophany, and on Holy Thursday and Holy Saturday; ; (3) Liturgy of the Presanctified Gifts (Presanctified Liturgy), celebrated usually on Wednesdays and Fridays during Great Lent and on the first three days of Holy Week, a Vesperal Liturgy which has no *Anaphora* (Eucharistic Prayer) because the gifts of bread and wine were consecrated at a previous Liturgy, hence the name "Presanctified."

Matins: See *Orthros.*

Octoechos: (Gk., "eight sounds [modes].") Designates a liturgical book where the parts (propers) of the services are arrayed according to each of the eight modes (tones).

Ode: Designates one of the nine scriptural odes making a canon. The odes are (1) Ode of Moses (Exod 15:1–19); (2) Ode of Moses (Deut 32:1–43); (3) Prayer of Anna

(1 Sam 2:1–10); (4) Prayer of Habakkuk (Hab 3:2–19); (5) Prayer of Isaiah (Isa 26:9–20); (6) Prayer of Jonah (Jonah 2:2 [3]–9 [10]); (7) Prayer of the Three Holy Youths (Pr Azar 1:2–36 [LXX/Theod.: Dan 3:26–58]); (8) Song of the Theotokos (*Magnificat*: Luke 1:46–55); and (9) Prayer of Zacharias the Father of the Forerunner (*Benedictus*: Luke 1:68–79).

Oikos: Designates the stanza (strophe) that immediately follows a kontakion (see *Kontakion*) between the sixth and seventh odes of the canon at the Orthros (Matins) service.

Orthros (Matins): Vespers and Orthros are labeled "Major Hours." Today, in most Orthodox churches, Orthros begins early in the morning, usually after sunrise.

Proskomede: Known also as *Prothesis* (Gk., "preparation"), the preparatory service that precedes the Liturgy (see *Liturgy*) and is done during the Orthros (Matins) service. The gifts of bread (see *Prosphora*) and wine are prepared on the Proskomede table and consecrated during the Liturgy.

Prosphora: (Gk., "offering.") Refers to the blessed offering bread used at the Proskomede (see *Proskomede*) service in preparation of the gifts to be consecrated during the Liturgy (see *Liturgy*).

Staurotheotokion: A troparion (see *Troparion*) honoring both the Cross and the Theotokos (see *Theotokion*).

Sticheron: A stanza (strophe) that can be chanted independently or as a group of two to three stanzas commemorating a person or event. Stichera are found between the last verses of the continuous psalmody (Vespers) and between the concluding verses at Lauds (Orthros/Matins).

Synaxarion: Known also as *Menologion*, a short account of the life of the person or a comment on the meaning of the event liturgically commemorated on a particular day. The Synaxarion is read at the Orthros (Matins) service, between the sixth and seventh odes of the canon (see *Canon*), immediately after the kontakion (see *Kontakion*). These readings are contained in a book also called the Synaxarion.

Synaxis: Designates a gathering or assembly of people for worship.

Theotokion: (Gk., "[related to] Theotokos.") A troparion (see *Troparion*) in honor of the Theotokos (Virgin Mary).

Triodion: (Gk., "three odes.") Designates (1) an older type of canon (see *Canon*) consisting of only three odes, (2) a liturgical book containing all the propers of Great Lent from the third week before Lent up to the Vespers of Holy Saturday (including the Liturgy of Saint Basil).

Troparion: (Gk., "turning.") A short hymn consisting commonly of only a single stanza and used as a refrain for the psalms, odes, and doxology.

Vespers: The evening service which indicates the beginning of a liturgical day and coincides approximately with sunset.

Notes

Preface

1. Pentiuc, *The Old Testament*, 212.
2. See Magdalino and Nelson, *The Old Testament in Byzantium*; Krueger and Nelson, *The New Testament in Byzantium*; and, more recently, Külzer and Rapp, *The Bible in Byzantium*.
3. Among Bucur's publications with relevance for my book's main topic are "Anti-Jewish Rhetoric, 39–60"; "Exegesis of Biblical Theophanies," 92–112; "The Mountain of the Lord," 129–172; "The Feet That Eve Heard in Paradise," 3–26.
4. Custer, "Inspired Word," 173. Custer's emphasis is primarily on literary (poetic) devices employed by Byzantine hymnographers, i.e., verbal, visual, and dramatic devices.
5. On Byzantine Orthodox nomenclature, see Louth and Cassiday, *Byzantine Orthodoxies*.

Introduction

1. "Popular myth sees Eastern Christianity as a living museum of early Christian usages preserved intact. The fact of the matter is that during the period of Late Antiquity practically every liturgical innovation except the 25 December Nativity feast originated in the East. This creativity remained characteristic of the so-called 'Byzantine Rite' into the Late Byzantine Period, when changes in political circumstances forced the Byzantines to give priority to the struggle for survival of empire and church. I call it the 'so-called Byzantine rite' advisedly, for the rites of both traditions, the Roman and the Byzantine, are hybrid. Like English, these two ritual languages showed during their formative period an astonishing capacity to absorb and synthetize new strains and outside influences, and to adapt themselves to new exigencies." Taft, "A Tale of Two Cities," 21. On the historical development of the current Byzantine Orthodox Holy Week, see Woolfenden, "From Betrayal to Faith," 59–44.
2. On the "eighth day" as a weekly day of worship with a strong eschatological dimension and its origin in Jewish apocalyptic literature (e.g., Enoch), see Schmemann, *Introduction to Liturgical Theology*, 59–67, 70. As early as the beginning of second century, Christians view Sunday as the "eighth day" ushering in the new world to come, as can be seen in the following passage, where Sunday, as day of jubilation (not of rest), stands in opposition to the old Jewish festal days: "but the Sabbath which I have made, when I have set all things at rest, I will make the beginning of

the eighth day which is the beginning of another world. Wherefore also we keep the eighth day for rejoicing, in which also Jesus rose from the dead, and having been manifested ascended into the heavens" (*Epistle of Barnabas* 15.8–9). It is the eschatological expectation, rather than the historical fact of the resurrection, that one celebrates on the "eighth day" (Sunday); cf. Dix, *The Shape of the Liturgy*, 336–337.

3. Talley, "History and Eschatology," location 2530.

4. On the name Pascha, its role as the central feast day of the annual Christian liturgical cycle, and the connection of this name with the Greek verb *paschō*, "to suffer," see discussion below under "Good Friday."

5. Buchinger, " 'Let the Wise Listen,' " 481–501.

6. Dix, *The Shape of the Liturgy*, 338.

7. Talley, *The Origins of the Liturgical Year*, 3, 47–50.

8. Stewart-Sykes, *The Lamb's High Feast*, 19.

9. *NPNF²* 1:241.

10. *Epistula Apostolorum* 15; cf. Talley, "History and Eschatology," location 2546.

11. From Irenaeus's letter to Victor I: "Among these were the presbyters before Soter [before 165], who presided over the church which thou now rule. We mean Anicetus, and Pius, and Hyginus, and Telesphorus, and Xystus. They neither observed it [Nisan 14] themselves, nor did they permit those after them to do so. And yet though not observing it, they were nonetheless at peace with those who came to them from the parishes in which it was observed; although this observance was more opposed to those who did not observe it. But none were ever cast out on account of this form; but the presbyters before thee who did not observe it, sent the eucharist to those of other parishes who observed it. And when the blessed Polycarp was at Rome in the time of Anicetus, and they disagreed a little about certain other things, they immediately made peace with one another, not caring to quarrel over this matter. For neither could Anicetus persuade Polycarp not to observe what he had always observed with John the disciple of our Lord, and the other apostles with whom he had associated; neither could Polycarp persuade Anicetus to observe it as he said that he ought to follow the customs of the presbyters that had preceded him. But though matters were in this shape, they communed together, and Anicetus conceded the administration of the eucharist in the church to Polycarp, manifestly as a mark of respect. And they parted from each other in peace, both those who observed, and those who did not, maintaining the peace of the whole church" (Eusebius, *Ecclesiastical History* 5.24.14–17; cf. *NAPNF²* 1:243). According to Talley ("History and Eschatology," location 2620), Irenaeus's point was that at Rome prior to Soter (i.e., before 165), there was no Paschal celebration at all, and the disagreement between Soter of Rome and Polycarp, representing the church of Asia Minor, was greater than the dissent between Victor I and the Quartodecimans.

12. Most languages use the Aramaic word *pasḥaʾ* (Heb. *pesaḥ*) to refer to Jesus's resurrection (e.g., Greek *Pascha*, French *Pâques*, Italian *Pasqua*, Spanish *Pascua*, Romanian *Paște*, Russian *Paskhal'nyy*, etc.). The English word *Easter* (German *Ostern*) may be traced back to the name of *Ostara*, the Germanic goddess of spring and dawn. Bede the Venerable (672–735), the father of English history, notes: "Hrethmonath

[March] is named for their goddess Hretha, to whom they sacrificed at this time. Eosturmonath [April] has a name which is now translated 'Paschal month,' and which was once called after a goddess of theirs named Eostre, in whose honour feasts were celebrated in that month. Now they designate the Paschal season by her name, calling the joys of the new rite by the time-honoured name of the old observance." Wallis, *Bede*, 54.

13. Calivas, *Great Week and Pascha*, 1n1.

14. Talley, "History and Eschatology," location 2562.

15. Among the earliest Christian authors who connected the Paschal vigil to hope in Jesus's return, one may mention Lactantius, *Divinae institutiones* 7.19.3; Jerome, *Commentary in Matthew* 4. See Bradshaw, "The Origins of Easter," locations 2817–2822.

16. Buchinger, "Breaking the Fast," 197–198.

17. Dix, *The Shape of the Liturgy*, 347–360; cf. Talley, "History and Eschatology," location 2508.

18. For a more nuanced view on "historicization" of Pascha, see Johnson, "Preparation for Pascha?," locations 5041–5056.

19. Ibid., location 349.

20. Talley, "History and Eschatology," locations 2522–2530.

21. *NPNF*² 4:512.

22. Buchinger, "On the Early History of Quadragesima," 101–102.

23. *NPNF*² 11:514.

24. Russo, "The Early History of Lent," 19, pertinently observes, "Today the history of Lent's origins is far less certain because many of the suppositions upon which the standard theory rested have been cast into doubt"; see also Russo, "A Note on the Role of Secret Mark," 181–197.

25. There were exceptions to this general rule. For instance, the historian Socrates Scholasticus (d. 450) mentions that "those in Rome used to fast three weeks in a row before pascha, except for Saturday and Sunday" (*hoi men gar en Rhōmē treis pro tou pascha hebdomadas plēn sabbatou kai kyriakēs synēmmenas nēsteuousin*) (*History* 5, 22, 32); cf. Buchinger, "On the Early History of Quadragesima," 100.

26. Dix, *The Shape of the Liturgy*, 353.

27. For a critical survey of this hypothesis, see Johnson, "From Three Weeks to Forty Days", 118–136, Buchinger, "On the Early History of Quadragesima," 99–117.

28. Buchinger, "On the Early History of Quadragesima," 100–104.

29. Johnson, "Preparation for Pascha? Lent in Christian Antiquity," location 5287; see Regan, "Three Days," location 3249.

30. Talley, "History and Eschatology," locations 2552–2664.

31. On stational services in Jerusalem, see Morozowich, "Historicism and Egeria," 169–182.

32. Taft, "Lent," 1205–1206.

33. Buchinger, "On the Early History of Quadragesima," 114–117.

34. Schmemann, *Great Lent: Journey*, 17–18.

35. *The Lenten Triodion*, 69.

36. Taft, "In the Bridegroom's Absence," 71–72.
37. Since the time of Tertullian (*On Fasting* 13–14; see *ANF* 4:111–112), the Latin West has observed two days of fasting, Friday and Saturday.
38. Buchinger, "Was There Ever a Liturgical Triduum in Antiquity?," 257–270.
39. Origen, *Homily on Exodus* 5.2, in *Homilies*, 278.
40. Ambrose, Letter 23.13, in *Letters 1–91*, 194.
41. Regan, "The Three Days," location 3091.
42. Ibid., location 3129.
43. Buchinger, "Was There Ever, a Liturgical Triduum in Antiquity?" 263–64.
44. Buchinger, "On the Early History of Quadragesima," 102–103, 114; see Johnson, "Preparation for Pascha?," locations 5061–5069.
45. Taft, "Holy Week," 2:943.
46. *Epistula canonica ad Basilidem episcopum* (PG 10:1282–1283); cf. Dionysius of Alexandria, *Letters and Treatises*, 76–82.
47. Dionysius of Alexandria, *Letters and Treatises*, 81–82.
48. Taft, "A Tale of Two Cities," 28. On Jerusalem lectionaries, see Janeras, "Les lectionnaires," 71–92.
49. Taft, "A Tale of Two Cities," 22.
50. On "cathedral rite," see Bradshaw, "Cathedral vs. Monastery," 123–136; Taft, "Cathedral vs. Monastic Liturgy," 173–219; Frøyshov, "The Cathedral-Monastic Distinction Revisited," 198–216.
51. Taft, "A Tale of Two Cities," 22–23.
52. The Triodion is a liturgical hymn book of "three odes" (Gk. *triōdion*) containing parts of the services held during the mobile Triodion and Easter cycle, which begins with the Vespers of the tenth Sunday before Easter and ends with the *mesonyktikon* (Gk., "midnight") service of Holy Saturday. The seventh- to eighth-century original Palestinian monastic Triodion was supplemented up through the tenth to eleventh centuries with hymns written primarily at the Studite Monastery in Constantinople; cf. Taft, "Triodion," 3:2118–2119.
53. Taft, "A Tale of Two Cities," 23.
54. Égérie, *Journal de Voyage*, 270–291. For English translation, see McGowan and Bradshaw, *The Pilgrimage of Egeria*.
55. The fifth-century Armenian Lectionary of Jerusalem confirms minutely Egeria's recording of this cycle of services; cf. Taft, "Holy Week," 2:943.
56. McGowan and Bradshaw, *The Pilgrimage of Egeria*, 66.
57. Ibid., 123–124.
58. Ibid., 91–96 and figure 6 (a summary of services during Holy Week based on Egeria's *Diary*) on p. 93.
59. Ibid., 125.
60. On the history of Good Friday, see Janeras, *Le Vendredi-Saint*.
61. On the history of Holy Saturday, see Bertonière, *Easter Vigil*.
62. Note that, based on Egeria's travelogue, the late-fourth-century Jerusalem Church began Holy Week on Palm Sunday: "So, on the next day, that is, the Lord's Day [i.e.,

Palm Sunday], when the paschal week begins, which they call here Great Week, having celebrated from cockcrow those things that are customary to do in the Anastasis and at the Cross until morning, in the morning of the Lord's Day they assemble according to the custom in the major church, which is called the Martyrium" (*Diary* 30.1); cf. McGowan and Bradshaw, *The Pilgrimage of Egeria*, 121.

63. Calivas, *Great Week and Pascha*, 16, 18.

64. Here are the gospel pericopes in the reading order: (1) John 13:31–18:1; (2) John 18:1–28; (3) Matt 26:57–75; (4) John 18:28–19:16; (5) Matt 27:3–32; (6) Mark 15:16–32; (7) Matt 27:33–54; (8) Luke 23:32–49; (9) John 19:25–37; (10) Mark 15:43–47; (11) John 19:38–42; (12) Matt 27:62–66.

65. This procession emerged first in the Church of Antioch and was transposed to the Church of Constantinople under Patriarch Sophronios in 1864. However, the roots of this symbolic liturgical action can be found in the late-fourth-century Jerusalem rite, as described in Egeria's *Diary* (37.1–3); cf. Calivas, *Great Week and Pascha*, 68 and n. 135.

66. *Epitaphios* (Gk. *epi*, "on, upon," and *taphos*, "grave, tomb") is a liturgical cloth symbolizing the bier and is made usually of silk embroidered with the image of a lifeless Jesus. It presumably appeared during the late Byzantine period. Later, the Epitaphios was embellished with texts from the Paschal hymns, especially the troparion "Noble Joseph . . ." As distinct liturgical objects, the *epitaphioi* emerged in the fourteenth century when the ritual of Holy Saturday was established. Among the oldest epitaphioi are the Epitaphios of John of Skopje (1349) and that of Syropoulos (late fourteenth century), both found at Hilandar Monastery of Mount Athos, and that of Euphemia and Eupraxia (1405), preserved at Putna Monastery (Romania); cf. Gonosová, "Epitaphios," 1:720–721.

67. Calivas, *Great Week and Pascha*, 78.

68. Taft, "In the Bridegroom's Absence," 77.

69. The Encomia appeared for the first time in the Venice 1522 edition of the Triodion, but the earliest reference to these lamentations is found in thirteenth-century manuscripts in relation to Ps 119 (118) (known as *Amomos*), the longest psalm (176 verses), which probably played a decisive role in the composition of the Encomia, initially added to Ps 119 (118) as refrains of lamentation and then becoming the collection of 185 verses that we know today; cf. Calivas, *Great Week and Pascha*, 81.

70. Those who are interested in this topic are directed to Wellesz, *A History of Byzantine Music*; and Frøyshov, "Greek Hymnody."

71. Wellesz, *A History of Byzantine Music*, 133.

72. Ibid., 134.

73. Jeffreys, "Troparion," 3:2124.

74. Jeffreys, "Kontakion," 2:1148; see also Lingas, "The Liturgical Place," 50–57.

75. Here are the opening lines of *Peri Pascha*, a poetical homily to be read after the Exodus lection during the Paschal vigil, underlining the connection between the lection's theme, "Exodus of the Hebrews," and Melito's exposition: "The Scripture of the exodus of the Hebrews has been read, and the words of the mystery have been declared;

how the sheep was sacrificed, and how the people was saved, and how Pharaoh was flogged by the mystery. Therefore, well-beloved, understand, how the mystery of the Pascha is both new and old, eternal and provisional, perishable and imperishable, mortal and immortal" (*Peri Pascha* 1–2); cf. Melito of Sardis, *On Pascha*, 37; see Wellesz, "Melito's Homily," 41–52.

76. Wellesz, *A History of Byzantine Music*, 186.

77. Thomas Arentzen makes a pertinent observation regarding Romanos's kontakion "On Joseph" for Holy Monday. Conspicuously, no lectionary mentions Gen 39 (the episode of Joseph and Potiphar's wife) among the lections for this day. Thus, as Arentzen rightly notes, kontakia have not actually been composed as comments on lections. Romanos's kontakion "On Joseph" was probably written as an independent hymn and later inserted into the service of Holy Monday; see Arentzen, "Sex in the City," 124.

78. *L'hymnographie de l'église grecque* and *Analecta sacra*.

79. Wellesz, *A History of Byzantine Music*, 146.

80. The nine biblical odes following the Psalter in the manuscript tradition are (1) Ode of Moses (Exod 15:1–19); (2) Ode of Moses (Deut 32:1–43); (3) Prayer of Anna (1 Sam 2:1–10); (4) Prayer of Habakkuk (Hab 3:2–19); (5) Prayer of Isaiah (Isa 26:9–20); (6) Prayer of Jonah (Jonah 2:2 [3]–9 [10]); (7) Prayer of the Three Holy Youths (Pr Azar 1:2–36 [LXX/Theod.: Dan 3:26–58]); (8) Song of the Theotokos (*Magnificat*: Luke 1:46–55); and (9) Prayer of Zacharias the Father of the Forerunner (*Benedictus*: Luke 1:68–79). On biblical odes, see Miller, "'Let Us Sing to the Lord.'"

81. Jeffreys, "Kanon," 2:1102.

82. Pitra, *Analecta sacra*, 37; see Wellesz, *A History of Byzantine Music*, 198.

83. Four Byzantine female hymnographers are known, three from the ninth century: *hegoumena* Kassia (twenty-five authentic works), Thecla (a canon to the Theotokos), and Theodora (a canon to Saint Ioannikios and three stichera); the fourth female hymnographer is the fourteenth-century Palaiologina of Thessaloniki, who wrote canons on a number of saints such as Saint Demetrios, but her work is lost; cf. Frøyshov, "Greek Hymnody."

84. For brief explicative notes on these genres, see the glossary of liturgical terms at the end of this volume.

85. See Frøyshov, "Greek Hymnody."

Chapter 1

1. The Hebrew interjection *hnnh* is quite frequent in narrative and prophetic writings of the Hebrew Bible. A classical example is Isa 7:14, where the prophet Isaiah delivers to King Ahaz a divine "sign" prophecy, which in the Septuagint reading reaches its full extraordinary expression, "Behold, the virgin . . ." (LXX: *idou hē parthenos* vs. MT: *hnnh h-ᶜlmh*, usually rendered "behold, the young woman" (will conceive and bear a son).

2. See Pentiuc, *Long-Suffering Love*, 81–83.

3. Long, "The Origin of the Eschatological Feast," 3, suggests that the messianic epithet "Bridegroom" was crafted by Jesus himself, who clustered three traditions gleaned from the Hebrew Bible: (1) the eschatological age inaugurated by a banquet eaten in the presence of God (Isa 25:6–8); (2) the end of the exile described as a new Exodus followed by a journey through the wilderness (Isa 40–55); and (3) the relationship of God and his people often described as a marital union (e.g., Hosea, Jeremiah). According to Jeremias, "Nymphē," 4:1102, the Messiah-Bridegroom depiction is absent in the Second Temple period.

4. See Taft, "In the Bridegroom's Absence," 71–97.

5. Current scholarship suggests that the primary aim of this saying (an etiological saying) was to explain why the early Church fasted while Christ's disciples did not; see discussion in Notley, "8 Luke 5:35," 107–121.

6. Note that the verb erchetai, "he is coming" (as in our hymn and in the lection prescribed for Holy Tuesday—Vespers and Presanctified Liturgy), occurs only in Byz. of Matt 25:6, while it is absent in other textual witnesses.

7. Lit. "in meeting [him]"; the noun apantēsis, "meeting," in Matt 25:6 has the same eschatological resonance as in 1 Thess 4:17, eis apantēsin tou kyriou eis aera, "to meet the Lord in the air," with reference to the Lord's Parousia.

8. The imperative "Come out to meet him!" is purposefully left outside so that the sense of urgency and surprise occasioned by the Bridegroom's coming might be better underlined.

9. The Greek word makarios, commonly translated "blessed," should be more accurately rendered "happy, blissful." Hebrew and Greek have specialized terms to describe two biblical concepts. On the one hand, there is the concept of "blessing/blessedness," which in the Hebrew Bible refers to a special power that "moving" creatures (i.e., animals, humans, and time represented by the Sabbath day; Gen 1:22, 28; 2:3) need from God to accomplish their duties (Heb. b-r-k / Gk. eulogeō, "to bless"). On the other hand, there is the notion of "happiness/blissfulness," which in the Hebrew Bible describes a dynamic relationship between humans and their Creator. The Heb. abstract plural noun 'šry, "happiness," may be related to the Akk. verb ešēru(m), "to advance"—as long as one is advancing toward his Creator, that person is on the path of "happiness." In light of this etymology, Ps 1:1–2 may be read as a recipe for happiness: staying away from sin while finding delight in and musing over the Word of God day and night. The liturgist is in the same vein of thought as the psalmist when he labels the one who constantly watches for the unexpected Bridegroom's return as makarios, "happy, blissful." Significantly enough, Jesus's Beatitudes (Matt 5:3–12; Luke 6:20–23), as part of the Sermon on the Mount, though recorded in Greek, still reflect the Semitic view of a fluid happiness that is a dynamic reality, a process, and not a mere point in time or an unchangeable state. For instance, "Happy [makarioi] are the ones who mourn, for these will be comforted" (Matt 5:4 [Byz.]) conveys the paradox of happiness: the mourners are labeled "happy," but their full comfort belongs to an undefined future ("these will be comforted"). Thus, happiness is a process that starts "now" as ambiguous, limited, and insignificant. This "now" might seem to some as "mourning," but it reaches its concrete, obvious, and public climax "then," when this

time and space of ours will be ushered into the never-setting light of the Lord's day. Happiness consists of a "now" and a "then" where the whole can at times be an excruciating period of waiting, that is, a period between these two points of reference.

10. The Jews in the time of Jesus used to divide the night not into hours but rather into military divisions: watches, the periods when the sentinels were on duty. The second and third watch of the night correspond approximately to the period between nine p.m. and three a.m. (cf. Matt 14:25; Mark 13:35).

11. In the Garden of Gethsemane, Jesus urges his intimate disciples to watch and pray so as not enter into temptation (Matt 26:41 [gregoreite kai proseuchesthe, "Watch and pray"]; Mark 14:38; Luke 22:40, 46). Jesus's emphasis on the need to be vigilant as a basic virtue was well treasured by the early Church, as one may note in this instruction of the Didache: "Watch over your life: let your lamps be not quenched and your loins be not ungirded, but be ready, for ye know not the hour in which our Lord comes" (16.1); cf. ANF 7:382. On "watchfulness" in the New Testament and the early Church, see Smith, "The Lord Jesus and His Coming, 363–407."

12. I.e., present participle, plural accusative, from rhathymeō, "to be careless, sluggish, indolent." This verb occurs, e.g., in LXX of Gen 42:1: "And Jacob seeing that there was a sale in Egypt said to his sons, 'Why are you indolent [rhathymeite]?'" In this example, rhathymeite renders interpretatively the Heb. question lmh ttrʾw, "Why do you look to one another" (ttrʾw, Hithpaʾel of r-ʾ-h, "to see"); in other words, "Why you do not do anything?" The rest of the occurrences of this verb are in the anaginoskomena or "Septuagint additions": Jdt 1:16; 2 Macc 6:4; Sir 32:11; and (noun rhathymia) with the meaning "to remiss, be indolent, dally"; note that the verb rhathymeō is absent in the New Testament.

13. In Jer 15:19 (LXX), anaxios renders Heb. Qal participle zwll (verb z-l-l, "to be insignificant, to be of low value," "contemptible"; cf. Aram, Syriac evidence), hence something worthless or of low value. In the New Testament, anaxios is found in only one text, 1 Cor 6:2, meaning "incompetent, unfit." The nuance "unfit," found in the latter example, fits quite well in the context of our hymn.

14. Critiquing the indolence and hesitance (rhathymountas) of the unworthy servant, the liturgist is very similar in his exhortation to the master's reproach of the one who buried his talent in the ground, instead of working, in the parable of the talents (Matt 25:14–30), which immediately follows the parable of the ten bridesmaids.

15. The imperative blepe (blepō, "to look at"), "beware," functions here as idou, "behold," at the beginning of the hymn—a call to close attention.

16. Among other biblical examples of one's dialogue with one's own soul are Ps 42:5 (41:6); 62:5 (61:6); 104 (103):1, 35; Isa 61:10.

17. From the verb katapherō, "to bring down"; a similar construction to the one in our hymn occurs in Acts 20:9, a narration about a young man, Eutychus, who, "overcome by sleep" (katenechtheis apo tou hypnou) while Paul was speaking in Troas, fell down from the third story and died.

18. The Gk. verb ananēphō, "to become sober again, to come to one's senses," occurs only once in the entire Christian Bible, at 2 Tim 2:26. Nevertheless, it is found in early Christian writings, e.g., Ignatius, Epistle to the Smyrnians 9.1.

19. The participial form *krazousa*, "crying aloud" (verb *krazō*, "to scream"), used here might allude to a public proclamation, as one notes with the usage of the same verb in early Christian writings (e.g., Clement, *Stromata* 7.9; Origen, *Homily on Jeremiah* 16.1).

20. The word *hagios* "holy" renders in LXX the Heb. word *qdwš*, "holy," from the verb *q-d-š*, "to be holy," lit. "to be cut off, to be separated," hence the basic theological idea in the Hebrew Bible that God, by his very being, is separated, cut off from, transcending his creation, the time-space continuum he created (Gen 1:1).

21. The verb *lamprophoreō* (absent in ancient classical Gk., Old and New Testaments) is a lexical creation of Byzantine Gk. from *lampros*, "radiant, bright, brilliant," and *phoreō*, "to wear, bear" (of clothes), "to carry" (cf. *pherō*). In patristic writings, *lamprophoreō* means "to wear bright robes, festal attire" (Theodoret of Ancyra, *Homily on Mary's Divine Motherhood* 1; Andrew of Caesarea, *Apocalypse* 7), "to be more resplendent" (Athanasius of Alexandria, *The Life of Anthony* 27). The noun *lamprophoria* designates "splendid attire" (Gregory of Nazianzus, *Orations* 25.2), hinting at the white garments of neophytes (Gregory of Nazianzus, *Orations* 45.2; John of Damascus, *The Life of Barlaam and Joasaph* 29). The adjective *lamprophoros* means "brilliantly arrayed" (Hippolytus of Rome, *On Theophanies* 6), especially for Easter (John of Damascus, *Carmen in Pascha* 92).

22. In LXX, the word *aparchē* denotes the first (offerings) (Deut 26:10; Heb. *r'šyt pry*, lit. "beginning of the fruit"), the first fruits of the harvest that the ancient Israelite was required to offer to Yahweh (Exod 22:29 [28]); it has the same meaning in the New Testament (Rom 11:16; figurative in 1 Cor 15:20; Rev 14:4; foretaste in Rom 8:23); in patristic writings, it means first fruits (offerings) offered by the Church (Origen, *Against Celsius* 8.34); metaphorically, it means what is best, most representative (of Christ) (Gregory of Nyssa, *Homily on 1 Cor 15:28*).

23. The Gk. neuter noun *(to) pathos* occurs in LXX with various meanings, e.g., misfortune, trouble, calamity (Prov 25:20, rendering Heb. *r'*, "evil, affliction"), mourning (Job 30:31, for Heb. *'bl*, "mourning"), emotion, passion, lust (4 Macc 1:1, 3, 4), propensity (4 Macc 1:35). In the New Testament, the same noun is used to denote a passion, primarily of a sexual nature: Rom 1:26; Col 3:5; 1 Thess 4:5. This same semantic bifurcation, "emotion, passion, affects" and "calamity, suffering," is encountered in the Christian Bible and also found in patristic literature. Moreover, the neuter plural *ta pathē* came to designate "Passion of Christ" both in patristic writings (e.g., Ignatius, *Epistle to the Romans* 6.3; Justin Martyr, *Dialogue* 74.3; 103.8; Clement of Alexandria, *Paedagogue* 2.8; Chrysostom, *Homily on John* 80.3; Hippolytus, *The Refutation of All Heresies* 8.19; Epiphanius of Salamis, *Panarion* 57.2) and in liturgical hymnography.

24. The Gk. word *asma* occurs in LXX with the generic meaning "song" (e.g., love song, Isa 5:1; harlot song, Isa 23:15); there are no occurrences in the New Testament; in patristic writings, *asma* designates song, canticle, liturgical-spiritual song, more as a religious chant (Dionysius the Areopagite, *Celestial Hierarchy* 3.3.4; Maximus the Confessor, *Mystagogia* 11).

25. See McDonough, *Christ as Creator*, 16–45, where the author examines the apostolic Church's memories of Jesus as agent of creation. For instance, the healing narratives

in the synoptic gospels paint Jesus as the agent of God the Creator by restoring creation to its primordial order and harmony (e.g., Mark 1:40–45; Luke 13:10–17). Jesus
brings the dead back to life, thus demonstrating that he controls life and death (John
5:28–29; 11:1–44). There are also passages in the New Testament that plainly discuss
Jesus's role in creating the world (e.g., John 1:3; 1 Cor 8:6; Col 1:15).

26. Note the same juxtaposition of *kyrios*, "Lord," and *ktistēs*, "Creator," in the following
biblical texts, most likely liturgical in texture and use: 2 Sam 22:32 ("Who is strong
but the Lord? Who is a creator but our God?"—David's song of thanksgiving); 2 Macc
1:24 (*kyrie ho theos ho pantōn ktistēs*, "O Lord God, the Creator of all"—a prayer).
Hurtado, *Lord Jesus Christ*, 52–53, discerns the traces of a "high Christology" in late-
first-century biblical writings, such as the gospel of John and the book of Revelation.
"Binitarianism" (two powers in heaven) is the Christian version of Jewish mono-
theism (God the Creator and Jesus) in order to avoid a ditheism; see Boyarin, "The
Gospel of the *Memra*," 243–248, noting traces of binitarianism in early Jewish inter-
pretations of the Hebrew Bible such as Prov 8 (Wisdom), Targum (Memra), and Philo
(Logos).

27. The literary (discursive) variant of this piece of visual art may be found in Ephrem
the Syrian's commentary on Gen 1:26–27 and 2:7, read canonically in their complementarity: "The Father commanded with his voice; it was the Son who carried out the
work" (*Commentary on Genesis* 1.28); cf. Pentiuc, *Jesus the Messiah*, 7.

28. The present tense *erchetai*, "he is coming," in this hymn echoes the narrator's use of
the same verbal form in the gospel pericope that was read at the Liturgy on the previous day, that is, Palm Sunday (John 12:12). Thus, *erchetai* functions as a catchword
or running head concatenating the two liturgical days into a theological continuum.

29. The verb *katadechomai* is found in Exod 35:5, with the meaning "to receive, accept" in a generous and willful way: "the one accepting [*katadechomenos*] with [his]
heart [*tē kardia*]," rendering the Heb. phrase *ndyb lbw*, "with a generous heart." In
Christian writings, the same verb is used with reference to Christ's willful acceptance
of suffering and death, e.g., Victor Antiochenus, *Catena in Marcum* 14.1; cf. Cramer,
Catena in Matthaeum et Marcum, 266; and *Liturgy of St. James*, 160.

30. The noun *stauros*, "cross," occurs in the New Testament with reference to suffering
in general and to Christ's cross (Matt 16:24; Mark 8:34; Luke 9:23; 23:26; John 19:17;
Heb 12:2); there is no nominal form in LXX, just the verb *stauroō*, "to crucify," which
occurs only two times: Esth 7:9 (rendering Heb. verb *t-l-h*, "to hang"); 8:12 (here MT
is much shorter than LXX and shows no verb at all). In patristic writings, among a
variety of possible meanings, *stauros* is used in reference to the sacrifice or death of
Christ on the cross (e.g., Chrysostom, *Homily on Jonah* 62.2).

31. The term *etasmos*, "trial, plague," appears in Gen 12:17 (Heb. *ngᶜym*, "afflictions," in
the sense of generalized illness), Jdt 8:27 ("trial"). With the latter meaning ("trial"),
the word *etasmos* occurs also in patristic writings (e.g., Origen, *Homily on Jeremiah*
20.9). The verb *etazō*, whence *etasmos* derives, means "to test, examine, investigate,
search, try" (e.g., Gen 12:17, where the noun *etasmos* and the verb *etazō* appear together: "And God tested [*ētasen*] Pharaoh with great and bad trials [*etasmois megalois
kai ponērois*], along with his house because of Sarah, Abram's wife"). Other texts

where the same verb *etazō*, "to test," occurs: 1 Chr 28:9; 1 Esd 9:16; Ps 7:9 (10); Job 32:11; 36:23; Jer 17:10; Lam 3:40; Sus 1:51.

32. The word *mastix* denotes "whip, lashes" (Prov 26:3; 1 Kgs 12:11 [Heb. *šwṭym*]), "scourge" of the tongue (Job 5:21), or "plague" (Ps 73 [72]:4); *mastix* with the meaning "whip, rod" (of discipline) occurs in Psalms of Solomon 7:9 ("and we are under your yoke forever, and the whip of your instruction [*mastiga paideias*]").

33. Note that 1 Macc 2:1–5 mentions the names of the five sons of Mattathias Maccabeus, a priest of the family of Joarib, who left Jerusalem and settled with his family in Modein (Modi'in, around twenty miles northwest of Jerusalem). The names of his sons are John (Gaddi), Simon (Thassi), Judas (Maccabeus), Eleazar (Avaran), and Jonathan (Apphus). The seven brothers mentioned in 2 Macc who suffered martyric death by defending their faith do not belong to the Maccabean family specified in 1 Macc 2:1–5, although they are referred to in Christianity as the Holy Maccabean Martyrs or the Holy Maccabees. According to an old tradition, their names are Habim, Antonin, Guriah, Eleazar, Eusebon, Hadim (Halim), Marcellus, their mother Solomonia, and their teacher Eleazar. The book of 4 Maccabees, not part of the biblical canon of the Orthodox (except Georgian Orthodox Bibles) and Catholic Churches, is a homily on piety, taking the martyric death of the seven brothers (2 Macc 7) and their ninety-year-old teacher Eleazar (2 Macc 6) as a starting point. Eleazar's speeches occupy most of the length of this homily. The book is dated between 20 C.E. and 130 C.E. Eusebius and Jerome ascribe 4 Macc to the Jewish historian Josephus Flavius based on his Hebrew name, Yoseph ben Matityahu (37–100 C.E.); cf. Bartlett, "The Books of the Maccabees," 482. The three Ethiopian books of *Meqabyan* ("Maccabees"), very different from the four books of Maccabees found in LXX mss., considered canonical in the Ethiopian Orthodox Tewahedo Church, call the seven brothers "Maccabees" and their father a Benjamite named Maccabeus. Both the Eastern Orthodox Church and the Catholic Church celebrate the feast day of the Holy Maccabean Brothers on August 1. Interestingly, whereas the Christian tradition remembers on August 1 the sacrifice of the seven brothers, who preferred to die instead of denying their faith, the Jewish tradition commemorates the victory of Judas Maccabeus against the army of King Antiochus IV Epiphanes on the feast of Hanukkah, followed by the rededication of the Jerusalem Temple. While Hanukkah, through its special emphasis on Judas Maccabeus's victory against the tyrant king, bespeaks the end of martyrdom as a form of resistance against persecution, the Christian feast day on August 1 sees the seven brothers' martyrdom as an act of high virtue, considering it a type of Christ's vicarious Passion. On the development of the cult of the Maccabean martyrs, see Schatkin, "The Maccabean Martyrs, 97–111."

34. A phrase similar to the one encountered in the hymn, *stauron katadexasthai*, "to accept willfully the cross" (pertaining to Christ).

35. Antiochus IV Epiphanes (Gk., "the one who reveals [God]"), known also as Antiochus Epimanes (Gk., "the madman"), was born in 215 B.C.E. and died in 164 in Tabae (Iran). Antiochus was a Seleucid king of the Hellenistic Syrian kingdom (which included Palestine) whose passionate promotion of Greek culture and frequent attempts to stifle Judaism resulted in a Jewish anti-Greek revolt headed by

Judas Maccabeus, known as the "Wars of the Maccabees" (167–164 B.C.E.). In 167, Antiochus IV Epiphanes "dedicated" the Temple in Jerusalem to Zeus Olympus (*Dios Olympiou*) (2 Macc 6:2). Porphyry, a third-century C.E. writer, is the first to mention the setting up of a statue of Zeus Olympus and an altar in the Temple area (Porphyry's note is preserved in Jerome's *Commentary on Daniel* 11.31 [*PL* 25:569]), which the book of Daniel, composed around the middle of the second century B.C.E., hints at (Daniel speaks of an "abomination of desolation" [MT: *šqqwṣym mšmm*; LXX, Theod.: *bdelygma tōn erēmōseōn*] set up in the holy place [Dan 9:27]). In 164 B.C.E., Judas Maccabeus conquered Judaea and reconsecrated the Temple (December). The late Jewish festival of Hanukkah, meaning "dedication" and held on twenty-fifth of Kislev (between late November and late December), commemorates liturgically the rededication of the Jerusalem Temple. The immediate historical context of 2 Macc 7, a biblical text used by the Byzantine hymnographer, is the ban by the Seleucid king on the Jewish cult to encourage the Jews to forsake their trust in the God of Israel. The seven brothers refused to deny their faith and preferred to endure death for their confession, thus becoming the first martyrs, "the greatest martyrs before martyrs [*pro martyrōn hoi megistoi martyres*]" (August 1, The Seven Holy Maccabees, Matins, Ode 6, Kontakion). For more information on the Maccabean revolt and its historical and religious echoes in the book of Daniel, see Hengel, *Judaism and Hellenism*; and Collins, *Daniel*.

36. According to 2 Macc 9, the tyrant king Antiochus IV, the one who tortured many Jews and caused them to suffer unbearable pain, experienced a similar fate and was punished by God for his superhuman arrogance. Thus, in the end, according to the prophecy of the youngest of the seven brother martyrs (2 Macc 7:37), "he came to [his] senses through divine scourge [*theia mastigi*]" (2 Macc 9:11); the same term as in 2 Macc 7:37, *mastix*, "scourge," is found in 2 Macc 9:11 to underline the perfect agreement between prophecy and its fulfillment.

37. Along the same typological interpretative vein, here is another hymn chanted on the feast day of the Seven Holy Martyrs: "O all-wise children, who rightfully guarded the teachings of Moses and devoutly strove to imitate [*zēlōsantes*] Christ's death, intercede always that we may all be saved" (August 1, The Seven Holy Martyrs, Vespers, Sticheron). With the meaning of imitating Christ's sufferings, the verb *zēloō* is found in Chrysostom, *Homily in John* 83.5. In this hymn, the seven brothers are depicted not simply as types (*typoi*) foreshadowing the suffering of Christ but, more important, as the ones who strove to imitate "Christ's death" (*Chistou ton thanaton*), as active participants in salvation history. In the following hymn, again to be chanted on their commemoration day, the seven brothers are depicted as a type of Holy Week itself: "The children who were a type of Holy Week [*septēs ebdomados typon*], yearning to treasure up life through death, resisted bravely the persecutor's threats" (August 1, The Seven Holy Martyrs, Matins, Ode 9).

38. I would call this hermeneutical procedure "converted typology." First, the hymnographer shifts the recipient of the borrowed expression from a persecutor (the tyrant king) to a victim (Christ), thus operating as a mere "literary transference" with reversal of roles. Second, the poet reinterprets the expression "trials and scourges" as covering

almost all of the Lord's Passion. Another hymnographer applies the "scourges" to the seven brothers through the voice of the martyrs: "Wild beasts, swords, fire, or scourges [*mastiges*] cannot separate us entirely from God, O Antiochus!" (August 1, The Seven Holy Martyrs, Matins, Ode 8).

39. Something similar occurs in Wis 2:19, where testing is done through pain and torture: "Let us test [*etasōmen*] him with insolence [*hybrei*] and torture [*basanō*]."

40. Since 6 C.E., the Roman governor resided at Caesarea Maritima ("Caesarea by the Sea"), the capital of the Roman province of Judaea. When in Jerusalem, as he would have been during the Passover festival, the governor resided at Herod's Palace (today's "Citadel" near the Jaffa Gate on the west side of the Old City), which became temporarily the governor's palace (*praetorium*); see O'Connor, *The Holy Land*, 23.

41. The verb *prosiēmi* occurs in patristic and Byzantine writings with the meaning "to accept as reasonable or true" (Origen, *Homily on Jeremiah* 14.3 [*PG* 13:405D]; Gregory of Nyssa, *Catechetical Oration* 9 [*PG* 45:40D]).

42. According to Balthasar, *Theo-Drama*, 226, the *theopaschist* formula ("One of the Trinity has suffered") needs some further explanation. While the pronouncement of suffering in God should be disavowed, reducing the sufferings of Christ to his human nature only (what the School of Antioch was proclaiming) should be discredited as faulty, since it does not take into account the New Testament evidence which points to the fact that the person of the Son of God made flesh suffered on the cross. By stating rather emphatically that "God died for us" (*Oration* 33.14), Gregory of Nazianzus proves himself to be an adroit theologian and an insightful biblical exegete. If in the past, the debate on the death of the incarnate Son of God concerned the area of soteriology, through works by Balthasar, Rahner, and Moltmann, the discussion has moved into the trinitarian context where the Lord's Passion is viewed in terms of the relation between the Father and the Son, with the latter suffering in his flesh the death that saved humanity; see Novello, *Death as Transformation*, 180. On the notion of divine impassiblity in patristic thought, see Gavrilyuk's engaging and original contribution, *The Suffering of the Impassible God*.

43. The Gk. verb *paschō*, "to suffer," has a steady and solid trajectory well attested throughout the history of Greek language, including LXX (e.g., to suffer [Ezek 16:5; Zech 11:5; Esth 9:26]; to suffer punishment [Wis 12:27]; to grieve over [Amos 6:6]) and the New Testament (to suffer [sometimes, suffer death]: Matt 17:12; Luke 22:15; 24:46; Acts 1:3; 1 Cor 12:26; Phil 1:29; to endure: Matt 27:19; Mark 8:31; 9:12; Luke 9:22; Acts 9:16; 2 Cor 1:6; 1 Thess 2:14). I would be remiss if I did not mention the similarity in sound between the Gk. verb *paschō*, "to suffer" (especially with reference to the Passion of Christ), and the word *Pascha*, the Gk. transliteration of the Aramaic word *pasha'* used in LXX and elsewhere to designate the Jewish feast of Passover (Heb. *pesah*, from the verb *p-s-h*, "to pass over, to skip," mentioned in Exod 12:23 [Heb. *w-psh*; LXX: *pareleusetai* and *eskepasen* in Exod 12:27] in reference to God "passing over" or "skipping" the Hebrew houses during the last plague over Egypt, the death of the firstborn). *Pesah* recalls God's punishment and suffering brought upon Egypt and the salvation offered freely and willingly to the Hebrews. In the New Testament, the Gk. transliteration *Pascha* denotes, as already in LXX, the Jewish festival (Matt

26:2; Mark 14:1; Luke 2:41; John 2:13; Acts 12:4) and the Paschal lamb (Matt 26:17; Mark 14:12; Luke 22:7; John 18:28), as well as the Passover meal itself (Matt 26:18f.; Mark 14:16; Luke 22:8, 13; Heb 11:28). Very early in Christian literature, *Pascha* was connected to the verb *paschō*, "to suffer" (Melito of Sardis, *Peri Pascha* 7.30; Irenaeus, *Against Heresies* 4.10.1; Gregory of Nazianzus, *Orations* 45.10; Chrysostom, *Homily on Pascha* 6.5), hence the interpretation of *Pascha* as type of sacrifice of Christ (*Epistle to Diognetus* 12.9; Justin Martyr, *Dialagoue* 40.1; Melito of Sardis, *Peri Pascha* 3.1.8). The Passover (*Pascha*) was fulfilled in Christ's Passion (Eusebius, *On Pascha* 5; Basil of Caesarea, *Commentary on Isaiah* 27; Didymus the Blind, *On Trinity* 2.16). However, according to another line of interpretation, Christ is the Christians' Passover (*Pascha*) (1 Cor 5:7: Christ, Paschal lamb; Irenaeus, *Against Heresies* 4.10.1; Origen, *Homily on Genesis* 14.1; Athanasius of Alexandria, *Festal Epistle* 42; John of Damascus, *Carmen in Pascha* 122). In Patristic writings, *Pascha* came to designate the festival of Easter (Origen, *Against Celsius* 8.22; Gregory of Nazianzus, *Orations* 45.2). In Byzantine hymnography, *Pascha* refers to Holy Week culminating in the Sunday of Resurrection (Easter). Interestingly enough, two different words coming from two different languages (*pasḥaʾ*, "Passover festival" [Aramaic/Heb.], and *paschō*, "to suffer" [Gk.]), due to an earlier association (note the same three consonants, *p-s-ḥ* [*p-s-ch*], found in both words), came to designate the Passion (sufferings) of Christ and the liturgical period commemorating it, Holy Week, ushering in Easter Sunday, foreshadowed, according to Church Fathers, by the old Hebrew festival of Passover (*Pesaḥ/Pascha*). I would term this phenomenon a "lexical congruence" (a more often-used term would likely be *faux amis*, French for "false friends").

44. The cast of Gen 12–50 consists of five characters: Abraham, Isaac, Jacob, Joseph, and, of course, God himself (Heb. *ʾĕlōhîm*, with the basic meaning "almighty"), who, although the most important, is never described as, but is presumed to be, the same as Yahweh, God of Israel, who reveals his personal name to Moses (Exod 3:13–15). God is actually the number one protagonist who gives unity to the entire patriarchal literary complex; cf. Moberly, *Genesis 12–50*, 19.

45. Wenham, *Genesis 16–50*, 344.

46. Brayford, *Genesis*, 389.

47. The verb *odyrō/odyromai*, "to lament," a hapax legomenon in LXX (Jer 38 [31]:18), is absent in the New Testament, where only the noun *odyrmos* occurs (Matt 2:18; cf. Jer 38 [31]:15; 2 Cor 7:7), but is well evidenced in classical works, beginning with Homer, as well as in patristic and Byzantine writings. The common verb for "lamenting" in hymnography is *thrēneō*, "to wail, sing a dirge"—hence the English term "threnody"— (cf. Judg 11:40; 2 Sam 1:17; 2 Chr 35:25; Mic 1:8), even though at times the liturgists prefer *odyromai*. Note that for the Byzantine poem known as "Lamentations," the liturgist uses the plural neuter *encōmia*, meaning "eulogies, lauds."

48. The following passage from Ephrem's *Sermon on the Most Virtuous Joseph* can carry the reader into the ambience of Holy Week and especially Holy Monday. Here is Jacob's lament imagined by the Syriac Father, a magnificent piece of spiritual poetry: "When Jacob saw the tunic he cried out with lamentation and bitter weeping, saying, 'This is the garment of my son Joseph. An evil beast has devoured my son.

Wailing he said with unbearable groans, 'Why was I not devoured rather than you, my son? Why did the wild beast not encounter me, and, having made its fill of me, left you alone, my son? Why did the wild beast not rather savage me, and I become its fodder to satiety? Alas! Alas! I am rent with anguish for Joseph! Alas! Alas! where was my son slain, that I may go and tear my grey hairs over your beauty! For I no longer wish to live, if I cannot see Joseph. I am the cause of your death, my child. I am the one who has blinded your shining eyes. I destroyed you, my child, when I sent you to journey in the wilderness to look for your brothers with the shepherds. So I will lament, my child, and grieve at every hour, until I go down to Hades, with you, my son. And instead of your body I shall place your tunic, Joseph, before my eyes, as I weep without ceasing. See once more, your tunic has brought me, my son, to another great grief; for it is still intact, so that I think that it was not a wild beast that devoured you, my beloved, but that you were stripped and slaughtered by human hands. For if, as your brothers say, you were devoured, your tunic would have been torn apart; for the wild beast would not first have stripped you and then made a meal of your flesh. If though it had stripped you and then eaten, your tunic would not have been stained with blood. There are no rents of claws, no marks of the teeth of a wild beast on your tunic. Whence then the blood? Again, if the beast who ate Joseph was alone, how did it manage to do all this? This is for me alone grief and lamentation, that I may grieve for Joseph and lament the tunic! Two griefs, two weepings and most bitter lamentations for Joseph and his tunic. Ah, how was he stripped! I shall die, Joseph, my light and my support. Let your tunic now descend with me to Hades. For without you, my son [Joseph], I no longer wish to see the light. Let my soul depart with yours, my child [Joseph]'" (lines 387–429); cf. Lash, "Ephrem the Syrian."

49. On allegory and typology, see Torrance, *Divine Meaning*, 93–129; Pentiuc, *The Old Testament*, 169–198.

50. Caesarius of Arles, *Sermons*, 39.

51. Ambrose, *Seven Exegetical Works*, 93.

52. Smith, "Ambrose," 180.

53. *PG* 69:301–304; cf. Sheridan, *Genesis 11–50*, 231.

54. Danielou, *From Shadows to Reality*, 117, 134, notes that early Christian writers saw in Jacob a type of Christ: "When he lists the names of Christ in the Old Testament in his *Dialogue with Trypho*, St. Justin writes: 'Christ is called Wisdom, Day, Orient, Sword, Stone, Staff, Israel, Jacob and many another epithet in the words of the Prophets' (*Dialogue* 4). Jacob is the only person in the Old Testament whose name is a designation of Christ. Origen's *Commentary on St John* gives the same evidence. 'Seizing the powerful enemy by the heel and alone seeing the Father, he is thus in his Incarnation both Jacob and Israel' (1.35.260). Irenaeus: 'As Jacob was to be the type of the Lord of a multitude of sons, it was necessary that he should have sons by two sisters. . . . But he did all for the sake of the younger, Rachel, who was of beautiful countenance, the type of the Church, for which Christ suffered' (*Against Heresies* 4.21.3 [*PG* 8:1045C])."

55. Cf. Sheridan, *Genesis 11–50*, 269.

56. On the theme of self-correction as a prerequisite of reconciliation in the Joseph Cycle, see Pentiuc, "Il perdono nell'Antico Testamento," 101–124. In the Talmud, one finds a

similar explanation for why Jacob had to mourn so long: the number of years that he was away from his parents (while in Laban's house) and unable to fulfill his filial duty and take care of his aging parents; cf. Talmud, *Megillah* 17a; see Ginzberg, *Legends of the Jews*, 1:342.

57. "The Joseph narrative (in its main parts)," notes Brueggemann, *Genesis*, 289, "is not a collection of unordered tribal memories which have come together in a relatively undisciplined way, as is the case with Gen 12:1–36:43. Rather, the Joseph narrative is a sustained and artistically crafted statement of considerable literary finesse."

58. Kugel, *Traditions of the Bible*, 438, correctly observes: "The Joseph story is the longest single narrative in Genesis. Through it all, what stands out is Joseph's abiding trust in God, for although he is unjustly treated on more than one occasion, he does not lose hope or give in to bitterness. As it happens, he not only ends up ruling over all of Egypt, but, in subsequent chapters, manages to use his high office to teach his brothers a lesson in proper conduct. At the end of his long adventure, he is at last happily reunited with his brothers and his father, Jacob."

59. Brueggemann, *Genesis*, 289, notes that the Joseph story "urges that in the contingencies of history, the purposes of God are at work in hidden and unnoticed ways. But the ways of God are nonetheless reliable and will come to fruition. This narrator does not express the passion of the Abraham narrative about the demand for radical trust. Nor is conflict so scandalously valued as in the Jacob narrative. Rather, this narrator is attentive to the mysterious ways of God's providence. The purposes of God are not wrought here by abrupt action or by intrusions, but by the ways of the world which seem to be natural and continuous."

60. There are quite a good number of similarities between the Joseph Cycle and the book of Proverbs, where, e.g., fear of God (Gen 39:9; cf. Prov 1:7) and self-control (manifested by Joseph and praised by Prov 14:29) are considered great virtues. Prosperity is the reward for the righteous (as obtains with Joseph at the story end and is stated in Prov 10:6). Nevertheless, Rad's thesis in "Josephgeschichte," 121–127, that the Joseph story is a sapiential text exemplifying the ideals of wisdom, hence its connection with the book of Proverbs, was rejected more recently with strong arguments by Fox in "Wisdom," 26–41. According to Fox, the Joseph story contains attitudes and assumptions different from those characteristic of didactic wisdom, marked by ethical and practical overtones, and much closer actually to the "pietistic and inspired wisdom" of Daniel.

61. By reversing the order of events narrated in Genesis, the hymn moves closer to Origen's allegorical interpretation. For Origen, Gen 45:26 ("he [Joseph] rules over all the land of Egypt") would conceal a deeper meaning. Since in Origen's homilies, Egypt stands for lusts and carnal pleasures, "ruling over Egypt" means that Joseph succeeded "to tread on lust, to flee the luxury, and to suppress and curb all the pleasures of the body" (*Homily on Genesis* 15.3); cf. Origen, *Homilies on Genesis and Exodus*, 206–207.

62. See below for liturgical and patristic evidence. Among other examples, one hymn mentions that Joseph had a "righteous [*dikaion*] and chaste [*sōphrona*] mind" (Triodion, Day 54, Matins, Ode 5).

63. Romanos the Melodist, *Canticles* 6.18.10–14; cf. Romanos le Mélode. *Hymnes I*, 286; see Arentzen, "Sex in the City," 130.

64. Basil, *Letters*, 15. Joseph's chastity is also lauded in sermons on Joseph by Chrysostom (*PG* 56:587–590; *PG* 59:615–620), Basil of Seleucia (*PG* 85:111–126), and Sophronius of Jerusalem (*PG* 87:3835–3838).

65. Cf. Sheridan, *Genesis 11–50*, 257.

66. Ibid.

67. The following hymn sees Joseph as a model of "patient endurance": "You became a pillar of patient endurance [*hypomonēs*], O holy one, striving to imitate the forefathers, Job in sufferings and Joseph in temptations [*poirasmois*], and the way of life of the bodiless, though you were in body. O holy one!" (Apolitikyon to be chanted on feast days of saints who were stylites: May 24 [Saint Symeon], September 1 [Saint Symeon], November 26 [Saint Alypios], and December 11 [Saint Daniel]). A stylite (*stylitēs*, "pillar dweller") is a type of Christian ascetic monk who lived on a platform mounted on a pillar (*stylos*) exposed to sun, rain, winds, and snow. The movement began in the fifth century with Saint Symeon the Stylite the Elder. The life of a stylite centered on fasting and prayer. See Khazdan and Patterson Ševčenko, "Stylite," 3:1971.

68. In Maximus the Confessor's view, there are two kinds of temptations, pleasurable and painful, forming a vicious circle of pleasure/pain (and, eventually, death). And the human being by nature and will is ensnared in this vicious circle (*21st Question to Thalassius* [*PG* 90:313A–B]). Human perfection is attained only by those who can stay outside this lethal enclosure, by refuting pleasurable temptations through continence and enduring the painful ones through patience (*58th Question to Thalassius* [*PG* 90:593D]). Due to the primordial fall into the sin of disobedience, no human being could break entirely this vicious circle of pleasure/pain. Only Christ, born out of the Holy Spirit and the Virgin Mary, was able to break entirely this circle. Since death came to Jesus not as a consequence of sin, he could break the circle and offer humanity, newly restored in him, the chance to be liberated/saved from this vicious circle. According to Maximus, by becoming man, the Son of God assumed human nature without sin but with its inherent "passibility"—the capacity for suffering. That "passibility" made the evil forces lurking within the human nature try to tempt Jesus to sin. In resisting the two kinds of temptations (pleasurable in the wilderness and painful at the time of the Passion), Christ succeeded in healing the human "passibility," liberating humanity from the bondage of sin, and defeating the hostile powers that tortured humanity (*21st Question to Thalassius* [*PG* 90:312B–316D]). Was Christ's temptation real? Yes. Could Christ fall into sin? No. According to Maximus, Christ is the Logos incarnate, and this Logos moves his will toward man's salvation (*Opusculum I* [*PG* 91:32A]), functioning as a guard against any possibility of sinning on the part of Christ. Christ is not merely a human being empowered by God but God-made-man, hence Christ's impossibility to sin. If those baptized in Christ can and do sin, explains Maximus, it is because they are not fully reborn to the new life in the Holy Spirit (*6th Question to Thalassius* [*PG* 90:280C–281B]); cf. Bathrellos, "The Temptations of Jesus Christ," 46–48.

69. The Heb. verb *b-r-k*, meaning "to bless" (i.e., endow someone with a special power), is used here, as in Job 1:5, as a euphemism for "to curse."

70. LXX, more extended as text, interpretatively, lowers the boorish sound of this line by replacing "blaspheme, curse" (MT: *brk*) with "Say some word [*eipon ti rhēma*] to God and die!"

71. The Old Testament offers another great example of enduring suffering with patience and humility. Although in his case, suffering is obviously God's punishment for past sins, David would take the same path as Joseph and Jesus. Instead of crushing his son Absalom's coup d'état, David, barefoot and without the Ark of the Covenant, leaves his palace with just a few men, taking the road of exile (2 Sam 15). Gary Anderson, in *Charity*, 164–168, comparing King Saul to King David in terms of their sinfulness, makes an interesting point: in spite of his notorious and grave sins (adultery, homicide), David remains God's favorite king—and this because the son of Jesse accepted suffering (i.e., God's punishment) with genuine humility, without resisting it but recognizing its cleansing and redeeming function. In Ps 132 (131):1 (LXX), one reads: "O Lord, remember David and all his meekness [*prautētos*]," and Byzantine liturgists quite often refer to him as "David the meek one" (*ton praotaton*), thus linking David via Zech 9:9 (where the ideal, messianic king is described as "meek" [*praus*]) to Christ, who invites his disciples to take upon them his "yoke" (*zygon*), for he is "gentle and humble in his heart" (*praos eimē kai tapeinos tē kardia*) (Matt 11:29).

72. Cf. Acts 7:9: "The patriarchs, being envious [jealous, *zēlōsantes*], sold Joseph into Egypt." Similarly, *Clement I* (traditionally attributed to Clement, Bishop of Rome, ca. 96), addressed to the ancient Church in Corinth which was confronted with jealousy, sees in Joseph a good biblical illustration of where this sin can lead: "Jealousy caused Joseph to be persecuted nearly to death, and to be sold into slavery" (4.9); cf. Holmes, *The Apostolic Fathers*, 51.

73. And Joseph's imaginary lament continues: "I was admired for my youthful beauty. But she saw, she admired, and she did not limit her looking to mere admiration. She was afflicted with love, and though a mistress in body she was not ashamed to be a slave in mind ["will," *tē gnōmē*]. At first she tried persuasion, but I would not consent, then she armed herself for shamelessness; she pulled me toward her by my tunic, but I resisted. A struggle ensued between a licentious love and a chaste mind. She was in love with the youthful beauty of my body, but I loved the beauty of my soul [*tēs psychēs kallous*]. But then my love won out, and having cast off my tunic, I immediately ran away. . . . She turns what happened upside down, and brings charges of rape and licentious intent against one who is chaste [*tō sōphronounti*], one who has been violated, one who has suffered. She exhibits as evidence what I left behind to preserve my chastity [*sōprosynēn*]. After this, I became a prisoner and now am suffering the fate of criminals, though I have engaged in no crime, and I am paying the penalty for wicked acts that I have not committed. . . . O envy and slavery and love and prison and all things beyond expectation! Love has had the same power over me as envy, and in all that I was unfortunate now because I am loved. My brothers' envy robbed me of my clothing then, and now a woman's love has stripped me naked. A pit held me

then, though I had done no wrong; a prison and chains hold me now, though I have committed no crime. I am outdoing you, father, in misfortunes [*tais symphorais*], and in this alone am I winning ["fortunate," *eutychēs*]. I suffered from an envy akin to his, and in this alone I am similar to my father. Rather, I actually surpass him in this regard, as well; for the misfortune that he suffered a single time at the hands of one person, I suffered many times over from many people"; cf. *The Rhetorical Exercises of Nikephoros Basilakes*, 145–149.

74. Lash, "Ephrem the Syrian."

75. The common epithet for Joseph in Byzantine liturgical texts, *pankalos*, "all-good, beautiful, noble" (found in classical writings, e.g., Plato, but absent in the Bible; cf. "all-beautiful," John of Damascus, *Homily 5* [PG 96:653C]), which encapsulates both details: physical beauty and virtues found in the biblical Joseph narratives.

76. Lash, "Ephrem the Syrian."

77. For a good summary of patristic references, see Argyle, "Joseph (Le Patriarche)," 8:1276–1289.

78. Heal, "Joseph," 29–49.

79. Lunn, "Allusions," 27–41, seeks to identify the New Testament texts where Jesus or biblical authors read the Joseph story typologically. For Lunn, the typological use of the Joseph story in the New Testament can be proved through verbal allusions, namely, the "verbal correspondences between the Joseph narratives and the writings of Luke-Acts" (p. 30). The analysis is done rightly via LXX. A good example is Acts 7:10 (with respect to Joseph): "He gave him favor [*charin*] and wisdom [*sophian*] before Pharaoh." The two attributes, "favor" and "wisdom," are also found in the Joseph narrative (e.g., "Joseph found favor [*charin*] before him" [Gen 39:4]; "A man who is discerning and wise [*phronimoteros*]" [Gen 41:39]. the same two attributes are applied by Luke to the infant Jesus: "And Jesus increased in wisdom [*sophia*] and stature, and in favor [*charin*] with God and men" [Luke 2:52; cf. v. 40]).

80. In Judaism, Joseph stands as an example of *Tsadiq*, "righteous," who is committed to do the will of God, no matter what; cf. Kugel, *In Potiphar's House*, 26.

81. An excellent study of later biblical and ancient Jewish, Christian, and Islamic interpretations is Kugel, *In Potiphar's House*; see also Kugel, *Traditions of the Bible*, 437–458.

82. Lash, "Ephrem the Syrian."

83. Lunn, "Allusions," 30; see Brock, "Dramatic Dialogue Poem," 135–147.

84. Lunn, "Allusions," 30.

85. Ibid., 31

86. Ibid.

87. Ibid., 31–32.

88. Ibid., 40.

89. The serpent's ability to speak produced much difficulty for the Church Fathers who sought to solve this conundrum in various ways. For instance, Ephrem the Syrian explains: "As for the serpent's speech, either Adam understood the serpent's own mode of communication, or Satan spoke through it, or the serpent posed the question in his mind and speech was given to it, or Satan sought from God that speech

be given to the serpent for a short time" (*Commentary on Genesis* 2.16.1); cf. Louth, *Genesis 1–11*, 75.

90. Cf. Louth, *Genesis 1–11*, 76.

91. For Irenaeus, the words can destroy or save, depending upon who uses them: "As Eve was seduced by the word of a [fallen] angel to flee from God, having rebelled against his word, so Mary by the word of an angel received the glad tidings that she would bear God by obeying his word. The former was seduced to disobey God [and so fell], but the latter was persuaded to obey God, so that the Virgin Mary might become the advocate of the virgin Eve. As the human race was subjected to death through the act of a virgin, so was it saved by a virgin, and thus the disobedience of one virgin was precisely balanced by the obedience of another" (*Against Heresies* 5.19.1); cf. Louth, *Genesis 1–11*, 78.

92. Cf. Louth, *Genesis 1–11*, 75.

93. Jesus actually quotes from Scripture with the typical introductory formula "It is written [*gegraptai*]," but he does not enter into a dialogue with the tempter; e.g., "The devil said to him, 'If you are the Son of God, command this stone to become a loaf of bread.' Jesus answered him, 'It is written, "One does not live by bread alone" ' " (Luke 4:3–4 [NRSV]).

94. In LXX, the term *drakōn* occurs in Exod 7:9, 10, 12 (of Moses's staff turned into a serpent); Isa 27:1 (of a mythical creature, Leviathan, "the crooked and fleeing serpent").

95. Cf. the verb *hyposkelizō*, "to trip up, to overthrow, to stumble" (Jer 23:12 [stumbling in the darkness]; 37 [36]:31: "The law of his God is in his heart, and his steps shall not be tripped up"; Prov 10:8).

96. The term *prōtoplastos* (from the verb *plassō*, "to fashion"), "first-fashioned/formed," hints at Gen 2:7, where the creation of humanity (*ho anthrōpos*; cf. Heb. *h-ʾdm*) is described in terms of a potter "fashioning" (verb *plassō*; cf. Heb. verb *y-ṣ-r*) his precious vessel out of the dust of the ground.

97. Note that this hymnographer shares the same line of thought with Paul in Rom 5:19, where Adam's sin is labeled *parakoē*, "disobedience."

98. The Gk. term *parakoē*, "disobedience," consists of two elements, *para*, "beside," and *akouō*, "to hear," lit. "beside/alongside/by-hearing, mishearing" which suggests a crooked way or an unwillingness to hear God's voice echoing in man's soul or more precisely inscripturated in the sacred Scriptures.

99. *PG* 53:123; cf. Louth, *Genesis 1–11*, 72. For Ephrem the Syrian, like Chrysostom, that Adam and Eve prior to their disobedience, though naked, were not ashamed was due to the "glory" God clothed the first parents with: "They were not ashamed because of the glory with which they were clothed. It was when this glory was stripped from them after they had transgressed the commandment that they were ashamed because they were naked" (*Commentary on Genesis* 2.14.2); cf. Louth, *Genesis 1–11*, 72. In Chrysostom's view, baptism brings the neophyte to that purity characteristic of the paradisiac state prior to disobedience: "After stripping you of your robe, the priest himself leads you down into the flowing waters. But why naked? He reminds you of your former nakedness, when you were in paradise and you were not ashamed. For Holy Writ says, 'Adam and Eve were naked and were not ashamed,' until they took up

the garment of sin, a garment heavy with abundant shame" (*Baptismal Instruction* 11.28); cf. Louth, *Genesis 1–11*, 72.

100. Cf. Louth, *Genesis 1–11*, 72.

101. Another hymn elaborates on the same theme, Jacob as a prefiguration of the cross, by referring to the episode in which Jacob blessed Joseph's sons Manasseh and Ephraim and favored the younger over the elder (Gen 48:13–20): "Jacob of old, blessing the children, spread [his] hands crosswise [*enallax*] signifying [*sēmainousas*] your very cross, through which, O Christ Savior, we all are delivered from a curse [*kataras*]" (Octoeuchos, Tuesday, Liturgy, Beatitudes, Mode 8).

102. Cf. Attridge, *The Epistle to the Hebrews*, 332.

103. I.e., the messianic king, as John Chrysostom ruminates: "Here we ought to set down the blessings entire, in order that both his faith and his prophesying may be made manifest. 'And worshiped leaning,' he says, 'upon the top of his staff.' Here, he means, he not only spoke, but was even so confident about the future things, as to show it also by his act. For inasmuch as another King was about to arise from Ephraim, therefore it is said, 'And he bowed himself upon the top of his staff.' That is, even though he was now an old man, 'he bowed himself' to Joseph, showing the obeisance of the whole people which was to be [directed] to him" (*Homily on Hebrews* 26.1); cf. *ANF* 14:482.

104. So Theodoret of Cyrus, *Commentary on Pauline Epistles: Hebrews* (*PG* 82:714D); and Theophylact of Ohrid, *Commentary on Pauline Epistles: Hebrews* (*PG* 125:353D); cf. Attridge, *The Epistle to the Hebrews*, 336.

105. According to Attridge, *The Epistle to the Hebrews*, 336, the intention of the author of Hebrews was to portray Jacob in an attitude of worshiping God, rather than the staff of Joseph.

106. The Gk. verb *proskyneō*, "to bow down" in a sign of respect (Gen 18:2; 19:1; 23:7; 27:29; Exod 11:8), also means "to worship" in a religious sense (Gen 22:5; Matt 18:26; Acts 24:11; Heb 1:6); see also Greeven, "*Proskyneō*," 6:758–766. In Christian literature, *proskyneō* is often found with the connotation "to venerate, revere, adore, worship" (of the cross, as in our liturgical hymn); Dorotheus Abbas (of Gaza), *Doctrinae Diversae* 4.9 (*PG* 88:1669A); Tarasius of Constantinople, *Epistulae I* (*PG* 98:1433C); Athanasius of Alexandria, *Quaestiones ad Antiochum* 39, 41 (*PG* 28:621D); John of Damascus, *De Fide Orthodoxa Libri Quattuor* 4.11 (*PG* 94:1132B).

107. The same verb form *hai exelthousai*, "those coming out," is found in a twelfth-century manuscript, Canon.gr.35 (Oxford Bodleian Library); Syro-Hexapla reads *exelthontōn* (active participle as in MT); cf. Wevers, *Exodus*, ad loc.

108. The reading from the lectionary on this specific lection, as well as several other lections that are read at the various Holy Week services, tends to be quite close to the Syro-Hexapla text or Origen's *Quinta* (the fifth column in the monumental *Hexapla*) and to a certain degree to the MT reading.

109. This episode could have been in the mind of the author of 3 Macc 6:3 (the priest Eleazar's prayer), who talks about a "sanctified Jacob" (*hēgiasmenou Iakōb*), due plausibly to the angelic touch of Jacob's "flat part of the thigh" (*platous tou mērou*).

110. Jacob's "thigh" (*mēros*) touched by the angel during that mysterious wrestling session is a sign of both defeat (crippling) and victory (a new name, Israel, for Jacob). Brueggemann, *Genesis*, 270, remarks, "The *new name* cannot be separated from the *new crippling*, for the crippling is the substance of the name. So Jacob's rendezvous in the night is ambivalent. He has penetrated the mystery of God like none before him.... And he has prevailed. But his prevailing is a defeat as well as a victory. There is a dangerous, costly mystery in drawing too near and claiming too much."

111. The English words *testify* and *testimony* are directly related to the Latin *testes*, "testicles," allowing for the possibility that ancient Rome knew a similar oath-taking procedure involving the touching of genitalia.

112. Cf. Freedman, "'Put Your Hand under My Thigh,'" 3–4, 42; see Hamilton, *The Book of Genesis*, 139.

113. The verb *stergō*, "to love," occurs once in LXX (no occurrences in the New Testament), in Sir 27:17 (love of a neighbor). In patristic literature, the same verb connotes "to feel affection, favor, accept, agree on."

114. The Gk. noun *eupeitheia*, "ready obedience" (of law, 4 Macc 5:16; of law and Moses, 9:2; of the tyrant king, 12:6; of law, 15:9), although absent in the New Testament, is found in patristic writings, especially referring to obedience of God (Clement of Alexandria, *Stromata* 7.3 [*PG* 9:425B]; Basil of Caesarea, *On Baptism* 1.1.2 [*PG* 31:1516D]).

115. Similarly, "Once Joseph was cast into a pit [*lakkō*], O Lord Master, as a type [*typon*] of your burial [*taphēs*] and resurrection [*egerseōs*]" (Triodion, Day 54, Matins, Ode 5). In another hymn, the Joseph–Jesus typology is actualized. The faithful, through the hymnographer's voice, identify themselves with Joseph's brothers in their selling of the "fruit of purity and chastity," that is, Joseph/Christ: "I confess to you, O Christ King, 'I sinned, I sinned, like once Joseph's brothers selling [*peprakotes*] the fruit of purity [*agneias*] and chastity [*sōphrosynēs*]'" (Triodion, Day 54, Matins, Ode 5).

116. Cf. Sheridan, *Genesis 11–50*, 258.

Chapter 2

1. Cf. Collins, *Daniel*, 179.

2. According to modern biblical scholars, Daniel's conspicuous "absence" in Dan 3 is due to the fact that the three youths belong to a different tradition that was not initially associated with him. An ancient Jewish interpreter argues that the king commissioned Daniel to bring fodder for cattle to Babylonia and obtain swine from Alexandria (b. Sanh. 93a), hence the latter's nonappearance during the incident narrated in Dan 3; see Collins, *Daniel*, 179. Hippolytus of Rome interprets Daniel's "silence" throughout Dan 3 as well-thought-out and purposeful: "But someone will say, 'And so was not Daniel, being a friend of the king, able to intercede on their behalf and pardon the three boys?' He was able, but it happened in this way so that the great works of God may be shown and the Babylonians may learn to fear God, and

on account of this find rest, so that also their faith may be shown and God may be glorified in them. For if this had not happened the Babylonians would be able to say, 'If Daniel did not intercede with the king on their behalf, these boys would today be destroyed in fire,' and reckon grace to be human rather than the power of God" (*Commentary on Daniel* 2:25.4–5); cf. Schmidt, "Hippolytus of Rome," 67.

3. Until the discovery in 1931 of the manuscript LXX[967] (ca. 200 C.E., thus predating Origen's *Hexapla*) in Aphroditopolis, Egypt, the LXX (Old Greek) textual witness of Daniel (OG-Dan) had been known only from the Hexaplaric witnesses, such as LXX[88] (Codex Chisianus) and the Syro-Hexapla (a seventh-century translation in Syriac [preserved in Codex Ambrosianus] of the fifth column [Quinta] of Origen's *Hexapla*); see Olariu, "Textual History of Daniel," 77–85.

4. In the midrash *Song of Songs Rabbah* 7:8, the three youths ask Daniel if God will intervene to deliver them. In spite of the negative prognostic, the three refuse to worship the idol. "Their confidence," notes Collins, "is based on the moral certainty of what they ought to do, not on the certainty of revealed foreknowledge" (*Daniel*, 184 and n. 103).

5. Cf. Theodoret of Cyrus, *Commentary on Daniel*, 75–77.

6. At this point in Dan 3, the book title and chapter/verse numbering differ. What NRSV labels "Pr Azar 1:1, etc." is for LXX, Theod., and NETS "Daniel 3:24, etc."

7. Note that for v. 46, Theod. exhibits a shorter version, excluding two details found in the LXX reading, i.e., the furnace being heated "sevenfold" (*heptaplasiōs*) and the "three [youths] being cast at once into the furnace" (*enebalosan tous treis eis hapax eis tēn kaminon*) by the king's servants who were standing on top of the furnace.

8. The Aramaic form (MT) *təwah* (with *mappiq* on final *h*) is a Pa'el of *t-w-h*, "to be startled, frightened, horrified"; LXX uses the verb *taumazō*, "to marvel, wonder at."

9. Note the appellative use "Son of God" in one of the Dead Sea scrolls (4Q246, dated first century B.C.E.), likely a messianic title. The fragment seems to narrate the dream or vision (*ḥzwn*) of a king. A mysterious figure, called "Son of God" (*brh dy ʾl*; cf. Dan 3:25) and "Son of the Most High" (*br ʾlywn*; cf. Dan 7:22), looms within a context of distress. The people of God arise; the war ends and peace begins. People of God or Son of God are receiving a kingdom from God where the nations are given under their rule; cf. Puech, "Fragment d'une Apocalypse," 98–131. Some scholars (e.g., Collins, Cross, and Knibb) indentify this "Son of God" with a Davidic king or a messianic figure; see the discussion in Reynolds, *The Apocalyptic Son of Man*, 61–67. As many scholars have noted, there are some similarities between 4Q246 and Daniel, such as the interpretation of a king's dream (Dan 2), the visions in 4Q246 and Dan 7 and their subsequent interpretations, and striking lexical similarities; see Collins, "The *Son of God* Text," 65–82.

10. This phrase hints at polytheistic beliefs well attested in ANE (cf. Gen 6:2; Ps 82 [81]; Deut. 32:8). Ancient Jewish and Christian interpreters saw in these "sons of God" (e.g., Gen 6:2; MT: *bny h-ʾlhym*; LXX: *hoi hyioi tou theou*) the angels as God's agents. Note the interpretive reading of Targum Pseudo-Jonathan, *bny rbrbyʾ*, "the sons of the great [ones]" (i.e., nobles).

11. For various patristic interpretations of the Christophany in the fiery furnace, see the detailed discussion in Bucur, "Christophanic Exegesis," 227–244. Note that Theodoret

of Cyrus, even though following the Theod. reading (i.e., "son of God"), eschews the classical Christological interpretation. The tyrant king, Theodoret notes, "was allowed a vision [*emphanē*] of an angel [*angelon*] sent to the assistance [*epikourian*] of the holy ones [*tōn agiōn*]" (*Commentary on Daniel*, 134); cf. Theodoret of Cyrus, *Commentary on Daniel*, 97.

12. So, already in Dan 3:28: "Nebuchadnezzar said, 'Blessed be the God of Shadrach, Meshach, and Abednego, who has sent his angel [MT: *ml'kh*; LXX/Theod.: *angelon autou*] and delivered his servants who trusted in him. They disobeyed the king's command and yielded up their bodies rather than serve and worship any god except their own God' " (NRSV).

13. *Exodus Rabbah* 18.5: "Gabriel, at God's behest, delivered Hananiah and his companions"; cf. Kantrowitz, *Judaic Classics Library*, ad locum. A similar interpretation may be found in the Babylonian Talmud (b. Pes. 118a–b): "Gabriel said to the Holy One, blessed be He: 'Sovereign of the Universe! Let me go down, cool [it], and deliver that righteous man [Abraham] from the fiery furnace.' Said the Holy One, blessed be He, to him: 'I am unique in my world, and he is unique in his world: it is fitting for Him who is unique to deliver him who is unique.' But because the Holy One, blessed be He, does not withhold the [merited] reward of any creature, he said to him, 'Thou shalt be privileged to deliver three of his descendants' "; cf. Kantrowitz, *Judaic Classics Library*, ad locum.

14. Cf. Ginzberg, *Legends of the Jews*, 2:1099.

15. Cf. MT: *ʿbdwhy dy-ʾlhʾ ʿlly*; LXX: *hoi paides tou theou tōn theōn tou hypsistou*, "children/servants of the Most High God of [among] the gods"; Theod.: *hoi douloi tou theou tou hypsistou*, "slaves of the Most High God."

16. Cross, *Canaanite Myth*, 51–52.

17. In the Hebrew Bible, the term *mal'ak* designates a "messenger," a herald (from the verb *l-ʾ-k*, "to send, to dispatch") and an "agent" of God, especially in light of the well-attested phrase *ml'k* YHWH, "angel of Yahweh" (LXX: *angelos kyriou*, "angel of the Lord"; cf. Gen 16:17; 22:11–15; Exod 3:2; Judg 5:23; 13:3; Mal 2:7). In some cases (e.g., Gen 22:11; Exod 3:2–6), "angel" overlaps with "God," making a precise identification quite challenging.

18. See Parker, "Judas Maccabaeus' Campaigns," 457–476.

19. According to Collins, *Daniel*, 193, Dan 3 could have been written either during the Persian period or at the beginning of the Hellenistic period.

20. Irenaeus sees in the story of the three youths a foreshadowing of what will happen in the latter days to the righteous who, similarly to the Jewish youths, will endure all kinds of trials due to their reluctance to worship the "new Babylonian king," i.e., the Antichrist (*Against Heresies*, 5.29.2).

21. That the three youths' story influenced Jewish religious life and practice during the Maccabean period may be seen in the last words of the priest Mattathias (1 Macc 2:59): "Having believed, Hananias, Azarias and Misael were saved from fire."

22. See chapter 1, Holy Monday, under "The First Fruits of the Lord's Passion."

23. One may think of the excruciating cry on that Friday afternoon, "My God, my God, why have you forsaken me?" (Ps 22:1 [21:2]), not solely as a sign of despair but more

as Jesus's surrendering his humanity assumed at conception and fully revealed on the cross to a silent yet lovingly waiting Father; see Neuhaus's inspiring meditations on Good Friday in *Death on a Friday Afternoon*.

24. Attridge, *The Epistle to the Hebrews*, 349.

25. Collins, *Daniel*, 194.

26. In another hymn, this resistance turns into scorning the royal decree: "The most blessed young men [*neoi*] in Babylon, running the risk [*prokindyneuontes*] for the ancestral laws, scorned [*kateptysan*] the ruler's irrational order [*prostagēs alogistou*]" (Holy Thursday, Matins, Ode 8, Heirmos).

27. Targum Pseudo-Jonathan expands the Hebrew text of Gen 38:24–25 interpretively: "Tamar was brought forth to be burned by fire; and she sought the three witnesses, but found them not. She lifted up her eyes on high and said: 'For mercy I pray before the Lord. Thou art he, O Lord God, who answered the afflicted in the hour of their affliction; answer me in this hour of my affliction, and I will dedicate to thee three saints in the valley of Dura, Hananya, Mishael and Azarya.' [In that hour the Word of the Lord heard the voice of her supplication and said to Mikaael, 'Descend and let her eyes be have light.' . . . When she saw them, she took them and cast them before the feet of the judges, saying: 'By the man to whom these belong, I am with child. But though I am to be burned, I declare him not, but confide in the Ruler of all the world, the Lord who is witness between me and him, that He will give to the heart of the man to whom these belong, to acknowledge whose are these ring, and mantle, and staff'"; cf. Etheridge, *The Targums*, 291–292.

28. Cf. Schmidt, "Hippolytus of Rome," 67.

29. Nevertheless, the Gk. word *dogma* occurs in Dan 6:13 in a context similar to that of Dan 3 (i.e., a royal decree).

30. Cf. MT: *ʾmryn*, "you are told." But note LXX reading, "And the herald [*ho kēryx*] heralded [*ekēryxe*] to the crowds, 'It is ordered [*parangelletai*], O nations . . .'" which by the use of the verb *parangellō*, "to order, charge, proclaim," resonates in the word *dogma*, "decree," found in the hymn.

31. Cf. Kantrowitz, *Judaic Classics Library*, ad locum.

32. *ANF* 7:475.

33. Note, inter alia, the representation of the three youths in orante attitude along with the "fourth one" in the furnace, on the fourth-century *Publilia Florentia Sarcophagus*; or in the *Catacomb of Priscilla*, ca. 280–290; cf. Seeliger, "ΠΑΛΛΑΙ ΜΑΡΤΥΡΕΣ," 259, 267; 317–328; see Dulaey, "Les trois Hébreux," 33n4.

34. The "salvation" theme is found also in *Apostolic Constitutions*, predating 280 (*Const. Apost.* 7.35.7 [*SC* 336, 79]); Ambrose of Milan (*De Virginitate* 2.27 [*PL* 16:214]); Gregory of Nazianzus (*Carmina theologica* 2.2 [*PG* 37:592]); John Chrysostom (*On Ephesians* 8.8 [*PG* 62:66]); Aphrahat (*Demonstrations* 23.54 [*SC* 359, 939]); see Dulaey, "Les trois Hébreux," 37–38.

35. See Hays, *Echoes of Scripture*," 22–23. In addition to the "intertextual echo," Moyise, in "Intertextuality," 418–431, identifies four other types of intertextuality: narrative, exegetical, dialogical, and postmodern.

36. See the section on "Intertextualities" in chapter 7.

37. The hymnographer "Christianizes" the three Jewish exiles, calling them "holy youths" (*hosioi paides*), that is, inducting them into the hall of "saints" (*hosioi*). In Dan 3:26 (MT)/3:93 (LXX/Theod.), the king calls upon them with the Aramaic phrase "servants of the Most High God" (ᶜ*bdwhy dy-*ʾ*lhᵓ* ᶜ*llyᵓ*); cf. Theod., *hoi douloi tou theou tou hypsistou*; but note that LXX utilizes the same noun as the hymnographer, *paides*, "servants [youths] of God the Most High of gods" (*hoi paides tou theou tōn theōn tou hypsistou*).

38. Verb *ballō*; a composed verb, *emballō*, "to cast, throw," is found in both LXX and Theod. of Dan 3:15.

39. The verb *peithō*, "to persuade, convince," in medio-passive voice means "to listen to, obey."

40. LXX of Dan 3:12 has *phobeomai*, "to be afraid."

41. Gk. *Eulogeite ta erga kyriou ton kyrion*. The hymnographer was inspired by a slightly different formula found in Pr Azar 1:35 (Dan 3:57 [LXX/Theod.]): "Bless the Lord, all you works of the Lord" (*Eulogeite panta ta erga tou kyriou ton kyrion*); cf. lectionary reading for Holy Saturday at the Vesperal Liturgy: *Eulogeite panta ta erga kyriou ton kyrion hymneite kai hperypsoute auton eis tous aiōnas*. This blessing formula is encountered in the Psalter, e.g., Ps 103 (102):22: "Bless the Lord all his works" (*Eulogeite ton kyrion panta ta erga autou*).

42. The liturgical formula "Bless the Lord" connotes that God is the source of all blessings. On the concept of "blessing" as a special power coming from God, see chapter 1, n. 9 on biblical concepts of "blessing" and "happiness."

43. The verb *ptēssō* could be another example of an "intertextual echo" linking 3 Macc 6 (Prayer of Eleazar) to the hymn inspired by the three youths' story.

44. 3 Macc was composed sometimes between 100 B.C.E. and 50 C.E. by a Jewish writer living in Alexandria; see Croy, *3 Maccabees*, xiii.

45. LXX reads *poios theos*, "What god?"

46. The relationship between 3 Macc 6:2 and Dan 3:15 can be considered an example of "exegetical intertextuality"; see Moyise, "Intertextuality," 422–423. The exegetical work does not show up clearly in the text of 3 Macc 6:2, but it must be assumed in order to understand the contrast between the panoply of divine attributes used by Eleazar in his speech in front of King Antiochus IV and the three youths' laconic "response" to King Nebuchadnezzar.

47. Cf. Schmidt, "Hippolytus of Rome," 74.

48. The rare LXX word *psekas*, "drop [of rain]," occurs in Song 5:2 and, again as in the hymn, in parallel with *drosos*, "dew," connoting blessing and relief, comfort.

49. In the imagination of the following hymnographer, the youths were not simply walking in the midst of the flame; they were really dancing: "Imitating [*mimoumenoi*] the Cherubim, the youths in the furnace danced [*echoreuon*] and cried out, "Blessed are you, O Lord our God" (Heirmologion, Heirmos "Imitating the Cherubim," Ode 7, Mode 2).

50. Similarly, "The Holy Youths, being cast into the furnace, turned the fire into dew through hymnography [*dia tēs chymnōdias*]" (Heirmos "The Ones in the Midst of the Fire," Ode 7).

51. In LXX, *eikōn* is used for "image of a god, idol" (2 Kgs 11:18 [for Heb. *ṣlm*, "image, statue, idol"]; Hos 13:2 [for Heb. *ᶜṣb*, "idol"). In Christian literature, *eikōn* connotes "likeness, image, picture," in an abstract or more concrete way (i.e., with reference to pagan pictures or statues as objects of worship imposed on Christians [Clement of Alexandria, *Protrepticus* 4 [*PG* 8:160B]; or Nebuchadnezzar's image [Basil of Cappadocia, *Epistles* 243.2 [*PG* 32:905A]).

52. The word *stēlē* occurs in LXX, meaning "pillar" (Gen 19:26; 3 Macc 2:27), "cultic pillar" (pagan worship, 2 Chr 33:3), "pillar to the Lord" (Isa 19:19), "gravestone" (Gen 35:20). In Christian writings, it designates a "monument"; metaphorically, "memorial, record" of deeds (Origen, *Selecta in Ps* 15.1 [*PG* 12:1209C]) or a "statue, image" in pagan worship (Clement of Alexandria, *Protrepticus* 4 [*PG* 8:160B]).

53. Not found in LXX and the New Testament, the adjective *antitheos*, "rivaling God," occurs in classical (Homer: "godlike") literature. In Christian writings, it connotes "comparable to God, godlike" (Clement of Alexandria, *Stromata* 4.26 [*PG* 8:1380B], of Gnostic poets calling the elect gods or godlike); "hostile to, against God" (Athenagoras of Athens, *Legatio* 24.2 [*PG* 6:945B]); or "rival to God" (Gregory of Nazianzus, *Orations* 30.5 [*PG* 36:108C]: "You are speaking of Logos as if he were some robber or a rival of God").

54. The last three forms, *synedrion*, *bouleuomai*, and *apokteinō*, found in John 11:47–53, match the terminology of the hymn, except for the shorter verb variant *kteinō* instead of *apokteinō*.

55. The following passage from Wis 3 can be related to our hymn. It is about testing; the three youths were tested, too, and their lives were spared because God controls ("holds") life in his palm; it could be also a hint at the other episode so intermingled with Dan 3 in these hymns, i.e., the Jewish martyrs who suffered death at the hands of the tyrant king Antiochus IV. Here is Wis 3:1–6: "The souls of the righteous are in the hand of God, and no torment will touch them. In the eyes of the foolish, they seemed to have died, and their departure was thought to be oppression, and their journey away from us to be ruin, yet they are in peace. For if in the humans' view, they were punished, their hope is replete with immortality, and having been disciplined a little, they will greatly benefit for God tested them and found them worthy of himself. As gold in the smelting-furnace, he tested them and accepted them as a sacrificial whole burnt offering."

56. The noun *palamē*, "the palm of the hand" or generally "hand" (cf. Latin *palma*, "palm"), occurs in classical literature (Homer, Pindar) but is not found in LXX or the New Testament.

57. The idea that God "holds life in the palm of [his] hand" (*ton zōēs kratounta palamē*) resonates in Dan 5:23, "God in whose hand [is] your breath" (*hē pnoē sou en cheiri autou*) (Theod.).

58. "An angel of the Lord appeared to him in the flame of fire [*en phlogi pyros*] out of the bush [*batou*], and he saw that the bush was burning with fire [*kaietai pyri*], but the bush was not burned up [*katekaieto*]" (Exod 3:2 [LXX]).

59. "When the battle became strong there appeared to them from heaven [*ex ouranou*] five illustrious men [*andres pente diaprepeis*] on horses with gold-studded bridles,

and they were leading the Judaeans. Two [so Codex Alexandrinus: *hoi dyo*; cf. Vulgate: *duo*] of them took Maccabeus in [their] midst, and protecting [*skepazontes*] him with their own armors and weapons, they preserved [*diephylatton*] him unwounded [*atrōton*]. They cast forth arrows and thunderbolts on the enemies so that, confused by blindness, they broke the line filled with commotion" (2 Macc 10:29–30).

60. Cf. Michalak, *Angels as Warriors*, 199.

61. Theod. reads differently: "They [the three youths] walked about [*periepatoun*] in the midst of flame singing hymns [*hymnountes*] to God and blessing [*eulogountes*] the Lord."

62. For patristic interpreters, the three youths represent a strong illustration of the efficacy of communal prayer. So, Nicetas, Bishop of Remesiana (ca. 335–414), advocating for congregational singing, offers the three youths as an example of praying "with one voice" (*On the Usefulness of Hymns* 13 [*PL* 3:196–197]. In Cyprian of Carthage's view, the Jewish youths exemplify Jesus's logion that when two or three are gathered in his name, there will he be also (Matt 18:19–20). Along the same line, Clement of Alexandria underscores the potency of the three youths' prayer; for the patristic examples, see Dulaey, "Les trois Hébreux," 36–37.

63. On a collateral track, yet in the same vein of thought as the story of the three youths, Dan 2:18 informs that the prophet Daniel "ordered a fast [*nēsteian*] and an intercessory prayer [*deēsin*]," so that he and his three companions (Hananias [Sedrach], Misael [Misach], Azarias [Abdenago]) would be able to interpret the Babylonian king's dream, which actually occurred during a nocturnal vision that Daniel received from the "Lord Most High" (*kyrion ton hypsiston* [LXX]; *theon tou ouranou*, "God of Heaven" [Theod.]) (v. 19).

64. See a detailed discussion on theophanies and Christophanies, primarily with regard to Dan 3, in Bucur, "Christophanic Exegesis," 227–244. Bucur notes that ancient Christian interpreters use "Christophany" to describe "a manifestation of the Logos-to-be-incarnate" (p. 227).

65. One may mention, inter alia, the doyen Ernst Wilhelm Hengstenberg, with his classical oeuvre, *Christology of the Old Testament*.

66. Gieschen, "The Real Presence," 105–126; see also Gieschen, *Angelomorphic Christology*.

67. The first one to use the term *synkatabasis* was John Chrysostom, although the idea of divine condescension is as old as the Bible itself and the first Christian writers such as Justin Martyr, Irenaeus, Tertullian, and Origen. In ancient Christian writings, the term *synkatabasis* is used with the general meaning "descent" (of Christ to Hades, of angels coming down from heaven [Caesarius of Nazianzus, *Dialogi*, 48 [*PG* 38:920]), and especially with reference to the Logos's incarnation as the most important act of divine condescension or adjustability of God to humanity. "On the one hand, [he is called] only-begotten [*monogenēs*] through the birth from the Father [*ek patros gennēsin*], on the other hand, firstborn [*prōtotokos*] through condescension [*synkatabasin*] into creation [*eis tēn ktisin*]" (Athanasius of Alexandria, *Orationes tres adversus Arianos* 2.62 [*PG* 26:280A]). For Chrysostom, God may be likened to a human being, who makes use of stratagems and ruses in order to gain his objectives;

cf. John Chrysostom, *On the Epistle to Titus* 3.2; *On Genesis* 18.3 [*PG* 62:678; 53:152; 51:36]). *Synkatabasis* is often correlated to another hermeneutical principle, that of progressive divine pedagogy, from infancy to adulthood (Chrysostom, *On Colossians* 4.3 [*PG* 62:328]); cf. Dreyfus, "La condescendance divine," 96–107.

68. For John Chrysostom and other Church Fathers, *synkatabasis* is a special meta-phor that conveys the truth that God voluntarily and graciously stoops down from his realm by accepting the limitations of human frailty; cf. Boersma, *Scripture as Real Presence*, 56–80. This notion might be understood in a rhetorical or historical-theological context. Rhetorically, *synkatabasis* refers to God's adaptability to human thought and speech—the notion is employed to describe the intricate process of di-vine inspiration of Scriptures. Historically and theologically, the idea of divine conde-scension has been employed in relation to salvation history by Irenaeus, the one who coined that famous technical term *oikonomia* ("management plan"). For Irenaeus, human history is marked by gradual development, hence God's willingness to adjust himself and become an infant when humanity was at that infancy level, culminating with the Logos's incarnation when God came to humanity as a human being. The an-thropomorphic appearance of God expresses both God's *synkatabasis* and humanity's development from the infant stage to the level of grown-up man.

69. Gieschen, "The Real Presence," 105–126.

70. The word *thea*, "appearance, vision, contemplation," is found in ancient Christian writings, with reference to vision/contemplation of God (Dionysius the Pseudo-Areopagite [sixth century], *Ecclesiastical Hierarchy*, 4.3.5 [*PG* 3:480B]); divinity of Christ (John of Damascus, *Homilies* 1.7 [*PG* 96:557A]); prophetic visions of God (Athanasius of Alexandria, *Homilies in Matthew* 11.27 [*PG* 25:217D]); appearance of the risen Christ (Gregory of Nazianzus, *Christus patiens* 245.1 [*PG* 38:328A]).

71. Based on the semantics of the verb *prosagoreuō*, "to name, to give a title," besides equating the fourth one with the Son of God before the incarnation, the ruler gives him the corresponding messianic title.

72. The verb *prosēloō*, "to fasten, to nail," occurs only once in each corpus, LXX (3 Macc 4:9, of Jewish deportees, "fastened [*prosēlōmenoi*] at the neck to the yokes of the boats") and the New Testament (Col 2:14, of Jesus, who canceled the "record/bond" [*cheirographon*] by "nailing it to the cross [*prosēlōsas auto tō staurō*]"); the same juxta-position of nailing deliverance found in Col 2:14 appears in the quoted hymn.

73. This interplay between mortality and immortality is found in a hymn where Christ is painted as a "deified mortal" (*broton tetheōmenon*): "O Logos, Hades became embittered when it met you; seeing a deified mortal, spotted with bruises [*katastikton tois mōlōpsi*], and yet all-powerful in action [*pansthenourgon*]" (Holy Saturday, Matins, Ode 4, Troparion).

74. Romanos le Mélode, *Hymnes I*, 254.

75. In a universalistic manner, the "lyre" (*lyra*) of the three youths "theologized" (*etheologei*) about the Savior as "the God and Almighty of all" (*ton pantōn theon kai pantokratora*) (Sunday of the Forefathers, Matins, Ode 7). Although closely associ-ated with the Father in creedal formulations (e.g., the Nicene-Constantinopolitan Creed) and patristic writings, *pantokratōr*, "Almighty," can describe each person of

the Trinity. In Byzantine iconography, one may notice a propensity for the "Christ-Pantocrator" identification.

76. Note that in Exod 3:14 only, the Heb. Tetragrammaton YHWH is rendered by LXX as *ho ōn*, "The One Who Is" (masculine singular active participle). Elsewhere, in LXX, YHWH is conventionally rendered *kyrios*, "Lord," so that the Decalogue injunction "You shall not take the name of the Lord your God in vain [*epi mataiō*]" (Exod 20:7 [LXX]) may be thus closely observed.

77. Similarly, 1 Cor 10:9, referring to the "deadly serpents" (LXX: *opheis tous thanatountas*; MT: *h-nḥšym h-śrpym*, "fiery serpents") episode in Num 21:1–9, identifies God of the Exodus with Christ: "We must not put Christ to the test, as some of them did, and were destroyed by serpents" (NRSV).

78. On 1 Cor 10:4, see detailed discussion in the section on "The Mystical Supper" in chapter 4.

79. King, "The Textual History," 23.

80. Cf. Schmidt, "Hippolytus of Rome," 75–76.

81. Romanos le Mélode. *Hymnes I*, 396; see Bucur, "Christophanic Exegesis," 232–233, on how the "paradox of incarnation," so magisterially penned in this kontakion, could be further elucidated.

82. See Dulaey, "Les trois Hébreux," 33–59.

83. The basic verbal form *apeikonizō* means "to represent, to reflect, to picture to oneself"; and the prefixed form *proapeikonizō* (unattested in the Bible) connotes "to represent beforehand."

84. See the section on "Typologies" in chapter 7.

85. The adjective *aphlekton*, "unburned," here matches neatly the related adverb *aphlektōs* in the previous hymn.

86. The word *hylē* exhibits an interesting semantic history. In Classical Greek works, *hylē* means "wood, firewood, forest" (so in Aristotle, Epictetus, Hesiod) or "matter" (in philosophical writings, Aristotle being the first author to use it with this meaning). Later, in the Late Antiquity and Byzantine periods, it comes to denote almost always "matter, substance." In the current hymn, given the context of a fiery furnace and the repetition of the verb *kataphlegō*, "to burn down," the word *hylē* can also connote "source" (as suggested by Maximos Constas, private communication) or, even more concrete, "fuel, firewood," the stuff that feeds the fire of, or inflames, the passions.

87. Note that in the following hymn, the three youths, not the furnace, typify Mary's womb: "He pictured [*hypegrapse*] your very womb [*sēn mētran*] through the three youths [*tous treis paidas*] of yore that the furnace could not consume [*kataphlexasa*], O Pure Maiden [*korē hagnē*] for you received [*edexō*] the fire of divinity [*theotētos*] without being burned [*aphlektōs*]" (October 10, Matins, Ode 9).

88. Louth, "John of Damascus," 156, shows that already in the *Protoevangelium*, one learns that Mary's purity was supported and enhanced by her service in the Temple. Here the Virgin was kept away from what was unclean while being prepared to become the holy vessel of the Incarnation.

89. Anderson, "Mary in the Old Testament," 49–55.

90. The major Marian feasts are the Virgin Mary's Nativity (September 8), Presentation or Entrance into the Temple (November 21), Annunciation (March 25), and Dormition (August 15). The minor feasts of Mary are Saints Joachim and Anna (September 9), the Virgin Mary's Conception (December 9), Translation of the Virgin Mary's two relics, the robe (July 2) and the belt (August 31), to Constantinople. To these feasts one may add the feast of Christ's Presentation in the Temple, known also as *Hypapante*, "Meeting" (February 2). On the induction of Marian feasts into the Constantinopolitan liturgical setting (sixth to eighth centuries), see Cunningham, *Wider Than Heaven*, 19–28.

91. See Daley, *On the Dormition of Mary*.

92. As an illustration of the use of Old Testament material in portraying Mary as God's temple, here is a fragment from Proclus's second homily on the Nativity, where he comments on the prophet Zacharia's vision of the lampstand (cf. Zech 4:4): "Who is this lampstand? It is holy Mary. Why a lampstand? Because she bore the immaterial light made flesh. And why (is the lampstand) all of gold? Because she remained a virgin even after giving birth. And just as the lampstand is not itself the source of the light but the vehicle of the light, so too, the Virgin is not herself God, but God's temple" (*Homily* 2.10); cf. Constas, *Proclus of Constantinople*, 175. Note the iconographic representation of Mary as temple in a thirteenth-century Byzantine fresco of the Dormition (St. George Monastery, Staro Nagoričane), where the prophet Ezekiel holds the Eastern Gate of the Temple (cf. Ezek 44:1–4) in his arms; see Pentiuc, *The Old Testament*, 317–319, figure 7.10A–B.

93. See Brown et al., *Mary in the New Testament*. As Anderson notes, the limitation of this otherwise quite influential and unassailable volume is that its reader is not able to conclude that the "elaboration of Mary in the church was just as much an attempt to understand her in light of the church's two-part Bible" ("Mary in the Old Testament," 55).

94. Anderson, "Mary in the Old Testament," 52; see also Pentiuc, *Jesus the Messiah*, xvi–xiii, where I voice a similar opinion by using a two-concentric-circle paradigm to describe the relationship between the Old and New Testaments, with the later as a smaller circle at the center of the former which is gradually expanding toward the eschaton when the two circles will eventually overlap.

95. In early Christian understanding, each person, figure, and event narrated in either of the two Testaments has a unique place and role in the "plan of salvation" (*oikonomia*, Irenaeus); thus, everything in salvation history has an "incarnational orientation." On such a popular theological concept and term, *oikonomia* ("divine management plan" or "salvation history"), among Byzantine writers and later Eastern Orthodox theologians, see Blum, "Oikonomia und Theologia," 281–301; Thurn, *Oikonomia*.

96. Cf. other throne visions attested in the Old Testament (1 Kgs 22:19; Isa 6; Ezek 1; 3:22–24) and early Jewish writings (1 En 14:18–23; 60:2). Dan 7:9–10 is assumed to be taken from an older poem, hence in the *BHS*, these two verses are printed as poetic lines; cf. Collins, *Daniel*, 298.

97. MT: *krswn rmyw*, "thrones were cast" (Aramaic); cf. Ps 122 (121):5: *yšbw ksʾwt* (Heb.), "thrones stood" (LXX: *ekathisan thronoi*, "thrones were set"). On movable, wheeled thrones and their ANE background, see Stokes, "Throne Visions," 340–358.

98. In Christian writings (e.g., sixth-century Syrian writer Pseudo-Dionysius's *Celestial Hierarchy*) dealing with angelology, the "thrones" (*thronoi*) are personified as a special host or order of angels. Interestingly, Paul in Col 1:16, speaking of Christ being "preeminent" (*prōteuōn*, v. 18) among all things, indirectly warns his readers to stay away from any form of "angelic" superstition. An allusion to such an exaggerated role of angels may be found in the book of Enoch. Josephus (*Jewish War* 2.8.7) imparts that the Essenes used to take a vow not to divulge the names of the angels; see Olyan, *A Thousand Thousands*; Collins, *Daniel*, 303.

99. From the time of the book of Daniel onward, the phrase has become a popular motif in describing the divine throne (cf. 1 En 14:19: "rivers of burning fire"; 4Q405.15.2: "streams of fire" [*šbwly ʾš*]); see Collins, *Daniel*, 303.

100. LXX: "went forth before him" (*exeporeueto kata prosopon autou*); Theod.: "drew in before him" (*eilken emprosthen autou*).

101. The Aramaic phrase *bar ʾĕnāš*, "Son of Man" (Gk. *hyios anthrōpou*), a hapax legomenon (Dan 7:13), initially symbolizing the Jewish people, was used as a messianic title for an individual (not a collectivity) as early as the first century B.C.E., in the book of Enoch, the section "Similitudes of Enoch"; cf. Collins, *Daniel*, 303. The Gk. phrase *ho hyios tou anthrōpou*, "*the* Son of Man" (always with definite article), is used in the gospels (e.g., Matt 9:6; Mark 2:10; Luke 5:24; John 1:51) by Jesus as a self-appellation (mostly in those places where Jesus juxtaposes his current humble position with an eschatological glorious appearance); also in Acts 7:55, where a dying Stephen sees "*the* Son of Man standing at the right side of God." Early Christian interpreters associated the "Son of Man" of Dan 7:13 with Christ. On the etymology and meaning of the form *ʾĕnāš*, see the section "Hades Was Embittered" in chapter 6.

102. On the textual distinction between LXX and Theod. with respect to the identity of the "Son of Man" figure, see Bucur, "The Son of Man," 1–27.

103. "And, behold, on the clouds, [someone] like a son of man came and like an ancient of days he was present and the attendants were present with him" (*kai idou epi tōn nephelōn hōs hyios anthrōpou ērcheto kai hōs palaios hēmerōn parēn kai oi parestēkotes parēsan autō*).

104. "And, behold, with the clouds, [someone] like a son of man was coming and as far as the ancient of days he came before and he was brought in before him" (*kai idou meta tōn nephelōn hōs hyios anthrōpou erchomenos ēn kai heōs tou palaiou tōn hēmerōn ephthasen kai enōpion autou prosēnechthē*).

105. Modern scholars such as Johan Lust and Alan F. Segal detect a "monotheizing" tendency in LXX of Dan 7:13–14. By identifying the Son of Man with the Ancient of Days, LXX translator seeks to thwart the rise of a "Two Powers in Heaven" theology. For Lust and Segal, the LXX represents the precise rendition of a lost Hebrew text, while MT is a targumic (interpretive) reading in Aramaic of that lost Hebrew text; see Bucur, "The Son of Man," 5–6.

106. Apparently, Rev 1:13–14, which portrays Jesus, "one like a Son of Man" (*homoion hyion anthrōpou*), in the image of the "Ancient of Days" (e.g., displaying "white hair" [*triches leikai*]), is based on the LXX reading of Dan 7:13b (*palaios hēmerōn*). Interestingly, the gospels rely on Theod., for here the Son of Man is different from the Ancient of Days. Note the following hymn written by Romanos the Melodist, in which Christ is described as both "Ancient of Days" and "Son of Man." This interpretation is due to LXX's one-to-one equivalence between the two Danielic figures: "Let us all raise our eyes to the Lord to the one in heaven, crying out like Jeremiah: 'The one who appeared on earth, and willfully had conversation with men' [Bar 3:37 [38], without suffering any change; the same one who showed himself to the prophets in different forms [*en morphais*], the one whom Ezekiel contemplated [*etheasato*] as a sight of man [*eidos andros*] on a chariot of fire [*epi pyrinon harma*], and whom Daniel [saw] as Son of Man and Ancient of Days, ancient [*archaion*] and new [*neon*], proclaiming [*kēryttōn*] One Lord, the one who appeared [*phanenta*] and illumined [*phōtisanta*] all" (*Hymns on Epiphany* 2.15); cf. Romanos le Mélode. *Hymnes II*, 288.

107. Up to this point in the gospel of John, God is the one who deliberates and the Son the one who carries out God's will. With John 5:22, things move dramatically in a different direction: God the Father transfers the judgment power to his Son. The Father waives his right to judgment to his Son's advantage, so that all who honor the Father will also honor the Son (v. 23); cf. Haenchen, *John 1*, 251. According to the Mosaic Law, God is the ultimate judge, for the best administration of judgment requires omniscience (Deut 1:17). John 5:22 should probably be read in parallel with Dan 7:14, which proclaims that "to him [Son of Man] was given all the dominion [*archē*; LXX: *exousia*, "authority"] and the honor [*timē*] and the kingship [*basileia*] (Theod.).

108. See the edition princeps prepared and published by Henze, *The Syriac Apocalypse of Daniel*.

109. Ibid., 115–116.

110. Methodius of Olympus (d. ca. 311) sees in the three youths a realization of what was stated by the Psalmist (Ps 66 [65]:12 [LXX]): "You mounted persons on our heads; we went through fire and through water, and you brought us out to relief." In other words, God's disciplinary actions concerning his disobedient servants will turn eventually into their "relief" (*anapsychē*). And Methodius concludes with a personal prayer: "O you, God Almighty, great, eternal, Father of Christ, let me, Methodius, also, on your Day, cross the fire unharmed"; cf. Dulaey, "Les trois Hébreux," 39.

111. Golitzin, "A Monastic Setting," 66–98, pleads for a spiritual "transformative" function of the fire in the *Syriac Apocalypse of Daniel*, arguing for a monastic Sitz im Leben for this seventh-century work. I think that the flaw of Golitzin's arguments lies in the lack of a robust contextual correspondence between the Syriac apocalypse displaying the theophanic and punitive aspects of the divine fire and the spiritual, ascetic patristic samples (e.g., Isaac of Nineveh) emphasizing the spiritual transformative power of the fire. On punitive-ordeal functionality of the fire in Dan 7 and early Jewish interpretations (e.g., 4 Ezra), see Frayer-Griggs, *Saved through Fire*, 37–38.

112. Another example of meta-typology may be found in the following hymn, where the angel is the common denominator linking two typologies centered on a situation-reversal theme: "The fire was turned into dew for the youths; the lament [*thrēnos*] was altered to joy [*charin*] for the women; for an angel ministered [*diēkonei*] in both marvels [*thaumasi*]: changing the furnace into a resting place [*anapausin*] for the former, to the latter announcing [*katamēnysas*] the resurrection [*anastasin*] on the third day [*triēmeron*]. Originator [*ho archēgos*] of our life, Lord glory to you!" (Sunday of the Forefathers, Matins, Ode 3, Hypakoe).

113. Similarly, in the following hymn, the three youths are depicted as "pre-typifying" the Trinity and the Incarnation of Christ. The verb *protypoō* used here by the hymnographer means "to pre-typify" or "to foreshadow." It is noteworthy that the third person of the Trinity, namely, the Spirit, is named and credited for turning water into dew: "As in raindrop [*psekadi*], in the midst of the flame [*phlogos*], by the dew [*drosō*] of the Spirit [*pneumatos*], rejoicing, God's Youths were walking about [*periepatoun*] mystically [*mystikōs*]; by this, pre-typifying [*protypōsantes*] the Trinity [*Triada*] and the Incarnation of Christ [*sarkōsin Christou*], and as wise [*hōs sophoi*] through faith [*dia pisteōs*] they quenched [*esbesan*] the fire's power [*dynamin pyros*]" (Sunday of the Forefathers, Vespers, Steicheron 3).

Chapter 3

1. Nolland, *Luke 1–9:20*, 686, suggests that the anointing by a woman intruder in a dining hall assumed during the oral phase of tradition various forms as attested by Mark, Luke, and John.

2. Bovon, *Luke 1*, 1:290; on table talks in Luke, see Smith, "Table Fellowship."

3. On redaction-related matters pertaining to Luke 7:36–50 ("Jesus and the Sinful Woman"), see the excellent commentary by Bovon, *Luke 1*, 1:290–293.

4. "Wisdom" (Heb. *ḥokmāh*; Gk. *sophia*) is God's principle through which he created the world; cf. Prov 8:22–23. Those who follow her in their lives are called her "children"; cf. Sir 4:11; Prov 8:32.

5. In Ambrose of Milan's view, the sinful woman's attitude of joyfully embracing Jesus's teachings is followed by the Church: "She truly kisses Christ's feet who, in reading the Gospel, recognizes the acts of the Lord Jesus and admires them with holy affection. With a reverent kiss, she caresses the footprints of the Lord as he walks. We kiss Christ, therefore, in the kiss of Communion" (*Letter* 62). Further on, in the same letter, Ambrose shows that the Church "kisses" the Lord when she takes care of everyone: "The church washes the feet of Christ, wipes them with her hair, anoints them with oil, and pours ointment on them. She not only cares for the wounded and caresses the weary, but she also moistens them with the sweet perfume of grace. She pours this grace not only on the rich and powerful but also on those of lowly birth. . . . Christ died once. He was buried once. Nevertheless he wants ointment to be poured on his feet each day. What are the feet of Christ on which we pour

ointment? They are the feet of Christ of whom he himself says, 'What you have done for one of the least of these, you have done to me' [Matt 25:40]. The woman in the Gospel refreshes these feet. She moistens them with her tears when sin is forgiven of the lowest of persons, guilt is washed away, and pardon is granted. The one who loves even the least of God's people kisses these feet. The one who makes known the favor of his gentleness to those who are frail anoints these feet with ointment. The Lord Jesus himself declares that he is honored in these martyrs and apostles" (*Letter* 62); cf. Just, *Luke*, 128.

6. "To eat [*hina phagē*]" (v. 36; cf. Luke 14:1: *phagein arton*, "to eat bread") is an informal way for a more formal manner, "to have breakfast/luncheon, to have a meal [*aristēsē*]" (Luke 11:37).

7. The rabbinic tradition (*m. Avot* 1.1) describes the Pharisees as successors of the men of the "Great Synagogue": "Moses received the Law from Sinai and committed it to Joshua, and Joshua to the elders, and the elders to the Prophets; and the Prophets committed it to the men of the Great Synagogue. They said three things: be deliberate in judgment, raise up many disciples, and make a fence around the Law"; cf. Danby, *The Mishnah*, 446. Historically, the Pharisees are the descendants of the "scribes" (*grammateis*; 1 Macc 7:12), whose roots go as far as the Persian period. The scribes were engaged in various activities, from copying and reading to interpreting the Law of Moses (Neh 8). The beginning of the Pharisaic movement should be placed around 160 B.C.E., during the time of Jonathan the Hasmonean, head of the Jewish state (160–143 B.C.E.). According to Josephus (*Jewish Antiquities* 13:171), there were three schools of thought among the Jews during Jesus's time: Pharisees, Sadducees, and Essenes. Each of these groups held different views with respect to the God–man relationship or what would later be termed *halakha*, "the way" (cf. Acts 9:2: Gk. *hē hodos*, with respect to the nascent Jewish-Christian movement). Around 150 B.C.E., the Zadokite "Teacher of Righteousness" left the Temple priestly guild and established a community from which the Qumran Yachad ("community") emerged. Thus, by the middle of the second century B.C.E., there were two *halakha* systems: the Pharisaic (influencing the Hasmonean rulers in Jerusalem) and the Sadducaic/Essenic. The Pharisaic *halakhic* system is known for its leniency with regard to ritual purity, compared with the Sadducaic/Essenic system. According to Josephus (*Jewish Antiquities* 13:298), the Pharisees enjoyed the "support of the masses," likely due to their strong beliefs in the life-changing power of the *halakhoth* (Jewish laws), supplemented by the "tradition of the fathers" (oral tradition). On Pharisaism as a Jewish social-religious movement, see Schaper, "The Pharisees," 401–427.

8. While overlooking the tendency of the New Testament writers to caricaturize the Pharisees, one may take a look at the interesting *halakha* debates between Jesus and the Pharisees. Far from being a Pharisee, Jesus seems to be in many instances similar to them; both Jesus and the Pharisees hold the "praxis" (*halakha*) higher than any doctrinal debate. Jesus recognized the Pharisees' authority in matters of *halakha* (Matt 23:2). Their conversations are not inflamed controversies but rather scholastic exchanges of ideas, with each side holding strong convictions for its own positions. The classic example remains the dispute on the inviolability of marriage, where Jesus's

view is stricter than the Pharisees'. So, Jesus either rejects divorce or acknowledges adultery as the sole reason for divorce (Mark 10:5–9; cf. Matt 19:4–9; Luke 16:18). (Here Jesus is closer to the Essenes, who favored the indissolubility of the marital union.) In their turn, the Pharisees had two diametrically opposed views: the school of Shammai considered Deut 24:1–4 to be referring to infidelity on the part of the wife as reason for divorce. The school of Hillel interprets Deuteronomy's injunction "because he finds something objectionable in her" as referring to everything that might irritate a man, even including a bad meal prepared by his wife.

9. Note that Jesus dining with Pharisees occurs only in Luke. Moreover, the third gospel writer has a more favorable view of Pharisees than Matthew, Mark, or John Having said this, one might also add that in each of the three Lucan dining stories of a Pharisee offering hospitality, Jesus always scandalizes his host.

10. Most of the town of Capernaum that Jesus knew has been restored. Today one can visit the octagonal building erected by the middle of the fifth century over a fourth-century church, which had been built by a convert Jew, Count Joseph of Tiberias (based on Epiphanius's testimony), on a primitive house church identified as Peter's house, and the basalt stone foundations of the synagogue where Jesus taught while in Capernaum (the standing walls and columns of the synagogue are dated to a later time, perhaps from the fourth to fifth centuries). The history of Capernaum begins in the second century B.C.E. During the reign of Herod Antipas, Capernaum had a customs office (Matt 9:9) and a small Roman garrison led by a centurion. That the inhabitants of this town were poor can be deduced from the fact that a Gentile (not a Jew) had to build a synagogue (Luke 7:5); see O'Connor, *The Holy Land*, 250. The famous pilgrim-nun Egeria, who visited the Holy Land, including Capernaum, between 381 and 384, gives a brief description of the town: "In Capernaum the house of the prince of the apostles [Peter] has been made into a church, with its original walls still standing. It is where the Lord healed the paralytic. . . . There also is the synagogue where the Lord cured a man possessed by the devil [Mark 1:23]. The way in is up many stairs, and it is made of dressed stone"; cf. Wilkinson, *Egeria's Travels*, 194–196.

11. Nolland, *Luke 1–9:20*, 354.

12. Ibid., 353.

13. In a sermon delivered at the basilica of St. Clemente in Rome on September 14, 591, Pope Gregory I ("the Great") identifies the unnamed sinful woman in Luke 7:36–50 with Mary Magdalene, from whom Jesus cast seven demons (Mark 16:9; cf. Luke 8:2), and identifies the latter with Mary of Bethany (Matt 26:6; Mark 14:3; John 12:3): "She whom Luke calls the sinful woman, whom John calls Mary, we believe to be the Mary from whom seven devils were ejected according to Mark. And what did these seven devils signify, if not all the vices. . . . It is clear, brothers, that the woman previously used the unguent to perfume her flesh in forbidden acts. What she therefore displayed more scandalously, she was now offering to God in a more praiseworthy manner" (*Homily* 33 on Luke 7; *PL* 76:1239–1240); cf. Schaberg, *The Resurrection of Mary Magdalene*, 82.

14. According to Pliny the Elder (*Naturalis Historia* 13.3, 19), *unguenta optime servantur in alabastris*, "ointments are very well preserved in alabaster [jars]"; see Schlier, "*Elaion*," 2:472.

15. Michaelis, "*Myron*," 4:801.
16. Clement of Alexandria writes: "She paid the Master honor with what she considered the most precious thing she had, her perfume. She wiped off the remainder of the perfume with the garland of her head, her hair. She poured out upon the Lord her tears of repentance. Therefore her sins were forgiven her" (*Paedagogue* 2.8); cf. Just, *Luke*, 126.
17. First, the verb *brechō* means "to make wet, to moisten" (through flooding), then "to rain" and "to cause to rain."
18. The same verb, *kataphileō*, is used in the parable of the prodigal son to underline the father's love for his lost son (Luke 15:20) and in Acts 20:37, where Christians in Ephesus bid farewell to Paul by kissing him. It also occurs in Matt 26:49 (cf. Mark 14:45) with reference to Judas's kiss on the night of Jesus's arrest.
19. Verb *aleiphō*, "to smear with" (vs. *chriō*, "to anoint," the technical term for anointing, rendering the Heb. verb *m-š-ḥ*).
20. Contrary to those commentators who see in the woman's letting down of her hair a sign of her "profession," Matson, "To Serve as Slave," 124, considers the same action to be an expression of penitence and grief.
21. Bertschmann, "Hosting Jesus," 43, remarks: "the woman's actions could likely be deciphered on a spectrum between intimate affection, even emotional gestures of reverence, and scandalous eroticism. But they cannot really be read as gestures of hospitality. This is something that, astonishingly, escapes most exegetes' attention." Only in retrospect and due to Jesus's imaginative interpretation, the woman's ambiguous actions may be considered gestures of hospitality.
22. That the sinful woman underwent an inner change while using the same old ways to express her new feelings can be deduced from a fanciful little story found in *Ephrem Graecus*, the Greek version of Ephrem's *memre* (narrative poem) on the sinful woman. It concerns the conversation between the myrrh seller and the sinful woman as she prepares herself to meet Jesus, her new "lover," who could liberate one from sin and corruption. The myrrh seller, unaware of the woman's inner conversion and puzzled by her strange mix of humility (expressed by her modest appearance) and luxury (conveyed by her desire to buy expensive ointments), tries to hinder her from purchasing perfume to corrupt probably another wealthy merchant. But her response, still dependent on her former profession's wording and imagery, betokens genuine renewal: "A man [Jesus] has met me today who bears riches in abundance. He has robbed me and I have robbed him; he has robbed me of my transgressions and sins, and I have robbed him of his wealth. And as to that you said of a husband; I have won me a husband in heaven, whose dominion stands for ever, and his kingdom shall not be dissolved"; cf. *NPNF*[2] 13:337. After saying this, she purchases the ointment and departs. Romanos's homily *On the Harlot* goes even further, where the harlot's monologue is permeated with erotic imagery: "As the One who loves me, I anoint him and caress him, I weep and I groan and I urge him fittingly to long for me, I am changed to the longing of the one who is longed for, and, as he wishes to be kissed, so I kiss my lover. I grieve and bow myself down, for this is what he wishes, I keep silent and withdrawn, for in these he delights" (5.4–8); see Krueger, *Liturgical Subjects*, 47. Romanos

presents a fully eroticized picture of the woman's longing for salvation; see Arentzen, "Sex in the City," 143. Similarly, Jacob of Serug (451–521) uses sensual language to describe the "fecundity of repentance" in contrast with the "sterility of sin": "The Hunter [Christ] set traps in the streets she [the sinful woman] frequented. He bound her with love so that she might not wander in vain. He was spreading out a great net of repentance before her. And she slithered and entered its great womb in naivete. The message of salvation was bait for the wild woman. And when she was engrossed in it, she came into the net of the House of God. . . . She bent her head over to wipe his feet with her hair. And just as in baptism she received holiness from the Holy One. She entered into the second womb, the place of atonement, so that in new birth she might become beautiful in a spiritual sense. She grasped his feet to find a sea of mercy at the banquet. She was baptized in him and he cleaned and polished her, and she arose pure. . . . Her love brought [her soul] into the crucible of mercy and smelted it there. Its [refined] gold showed its beauty so that it might be a case ornament of the Lord of Kings"; cf. Johnson, "The Sinful Woman," 71–72; see Hunt, "Sexuality and Penitence," 192.

23. Sir 26:22 ("A prostitute will be regarded as spittle") prohibited *any* association with a prostitute. Yet Jesus looked appreciatively at and praised the sinful woman while still addressing Simon (Luke 7:40, 44).

24. Hunt, "Sexuality and Penitence," 190. "This penitent woman," notes Hunt, "becomes a female mouthpiece of incarnational theology. This, together with the recurring and thoroughly Biblical concept of Mary as second Eve, is a powerful antidote to the dominant misogyny and patriarchal emphasis of much of the early Christian period."

25. The verb *haptō* could mean "to touch, to take hold of, to cling to" (John 20:17).

26. Washing of someone's feet was a sign of hospitality done usually by the least among a household's servants (Gen 18:4). When Jesus washed the feet of his disciples at the Last Supper as a token of "serving leadership," Peter opposed it, since in his view this undermined the teacher's dignity (John 13:12–17). Kissing on both cheeks was a way of greeting. Jacob greets Rachel with a kiss (Gen 29:10–14), and Moses kisses his father-in-law (Exod 18:7). But kissing the feet was a token of homage and deference. At least, this was the common practice in the ANE. Herodotus (*Histories* 1.134) first used the word *proskynēsis* to describe the Persian custom of prostrating oneself before persons and kissing their feet; cf. Bowen, " 'They Came and Held Him,' " 63. In the case of a prostitute, kissing someone's feet *could* have been interpreted as an erotic act. In the context of the Lucan pericope, it connotes gratitude and extreme humility (Luke 7:38); cf. Snodgrass, *Stories with Intent*, 81. Similarly, falling at someone's feet is an act of complete submission or surrender (Rev 1:17: "I fell down at his feet as though I were dead," of John the apostle falling at the risen Jesus's feet). In the Ugaritic religious context, the goddess Asherah bows down to the feet of the chief pantheon god El as a sign of reverence; Coogan, *Stories from Ancient Canaan*, 99–100. Anointing someone's head (Matt 26:7; Mark 14:3) with ordinary olive oil was a common practice (Deut 28:40; Ruth 3:3). If the anointing of feet with olive oil was unusual, using perfumed, fragrant oils (Gk. *myron*) for the same purpose was extremely uncommon. For instance, Mary of Bethany anoints Jesus's feet with "costly perfumed ointment of pure nard" (*myrou nardou pistikēs polytimou*) (John 12:3; cf. Luke 7:38, *myrō*).

27. Bertschmann, "Hosting Jesus," 30–50, shows how, throughout a few "cycles of hospitality," Simon the Pharisee, the initial host who invited Jesus to dine at his home, is replaced eventually by the unnamed woman. Bertschmann notes, "Here, the woman is singled out as somebody who has her eyes firmly on Jesus, as the *savior for sinners*. ·She is reconstructed as an able host who properly welcomes Jesus, God's visitor from on high, as the guest of honor. The woman rightly receives Jesus as God's savior who brings the gift of forgiveness" (p. 44).

28. For contemporary Aramaic formulas of forgiveness, see the *Targum of Job* found at Qumran (*11QtgJob* 38:2–3: *wšbq lhwn ḥṭ' yhwn bdylh*, "and [God] forgave them [i.e., Job's friends] their sins because of him [i.e., Job]" (on Job 42:8); cf. Fitzmyer, *The Gospel According to Luke 1–9*, 692.

29. Craddock, *Luke*, 106.

30. Fitzmyer, *The Gospel According to Luke 1–9*, 685.

31. Just, *Luke*, 129. Similarly, Ambrose wrote: "Christ is our love. Love is good, since it offered itself to death for transgressions. Love is good, which forgave sins. Let our soul clothe herself with love of a kind that is 'strong as death' [Song 8:6]. Just as death is the end of sins, so also is love, because the one who loves the Lord ceases to commit sin. For 'charity thinks no evil and does not rejoice over wickedness, but endures all things' [1 Cor 13:4–8]. If someone does not seek his own goods, how will he seek the goods of another [1 Cor 13:5]? That death through the bath of baptism, through which every sin is buried, is strong and forgives every fault. The woman in the Gospel brought this kind of love. The Lord says, 'Her many sins have been forgiven her, because she has loved much.' The death of the holy martyrs is also strong. It destroys previous faults. Since it involves a love not less than theirs, death that is equal to the martyrs' suffering is just as strong for taking away the punishment of sins'" (*Isaac, or the Soul* 8.75–76; cf. Just, *Luke*, 130).

32. Cf. Just, *Luke*, 130.

33. Ephrem the Syrian underlines the courage of the sinful woman when he writes, "She, through her love, brought into the open the tears that were hidden in the depths of her eyes, and the Lord, because of her courage, brought into the open the thoughts that were hidden in the Pharisee. . . . Our Lord, standing in the middle, worked out a parable between the two of them, so that the sinful woman might be encouraged through his pronouncing the parable and the Pharisee may be denounced through the explanation of the parable" (*Commentary on Tatian's Diatessaron* 7.18); cf. Just, *Luke*, 129.

34. For instance, the earliest retelling of the Lucan account of the sinful woman, that is, the Syriac *memre* attributed to Ephrem the Syrian (more probably from the late-fourth-century "school of Ephrem"), expands the pericope by adding a new fanciful story where the sinful woman confronts a myrrh seller intrigued by the new appearance of the well-known harlot. The drive to imagine what a silent biblical figure would have said is typical of homilists and hymnographers in their hermeneutical work. Note that the myrrh seller motif is also found in one of the hymns prescribed for Holy Wednesday: "The sinful woman ran to buy perfume [*myron*], very costly perfume, to perfume [*myrisai*] the Benefactor [*euergetēn*], and to the perfumer [*myrepsō*] she cried aloud: 'Give me the ointment so that I myself may anoint [*aleipsō*] the one who

wiped out [*exaleipsanta*] all my sins'" (Matins, Sticheron 4, Idiomelon). This hymn is most likely based on Ephrem's homily. Another example of literary expansion is found in one of the Syriac dialogue poems where Satan questions the sinful woman's desire to encounter Jesus: "Satan: He is holy, while you are unclean. With the breath of his mouth he will finish you off. You are entirely befouled with sin. Why are you going to this holy man? Woman: He is indeed holy and pure, there is nothing evil abiding in him. It is precisely because I am unclean that I go to this holy man, so that he will make me holy too"; cf. Brock, "The Sinful Woman and Satan," 46; see Hunt, "Sexuality and Penitence," 190.

35. The verb *klaiō*, "to weep, cry," in Luke 7:38 becomes *odyromai*, "to lament, mourn," in the hymn of Kassia, more dramatically adequate for the mood of Holy Week.

36. In Luke 7:38 ("she began to wet [*brechein*] his feet with her tears"), the verb *brechō*, "to rain, to wet," is used. By using the "streams of tears" (*pēgas dakryōn*; cf. Jer 9:1: *pēgēn dakryōn*, "stream of tears") image, Kassia embellishes or rather explains the choice of the verb *brechō* in the Lucan text, namely, that the woman's tears were so abundant that they turned into streams of water wetting Jesus's spotless feet.

37. For the Greek text and a good English translation, see Dyck, "On Cassia," 63–64; Tripolitis, *Kassia*, 76–79.

38. Wellesz, *A History of Byzantine Music*, 353–354.

39. Riehle, "Authorship and Gender (and) Identity," 246.

40. See the excellent survey by Topping, "Women Hymnographers," 98–111.

41. There are various spellings of this name: Kassia, Kassiane, Ikasia, etc. Regarding Ikasia, this could be a wrong spelling ("I") of the feminine article *hē*, prefixed to the name "Kasia" (*sic*), due to a scribal error; see Tripolitis, *Kassia*, xi–xii.

42. E.g., Symeon the Logothete (tenth century), *Chronographia* (*PG* 109:685C); George the Monk (eleventh century), *Chronikon* 4.264 (*PG* 110:1008B); Leo the Grammarian (tenth to eleventh centuries), *Chronographia* (*PG* 108:1046A–B); John Zonaris (twelfth century), *Ioannis Zonarae Epitome Historiarum*, Books XIII–XVII, ed. Theodore Büttner-Wobst (Bonn: Weber, 1897).

43. The three letters addressed to Kassia by Saint Theodore the Studite (*Letters* 205, 413, 541; cf. *PG* 99:903–1669).

44. See McCarty, "Illuminating the Incarnation," 165–178.

45. *Patria Konstatinopoleōs*, 276. *Patria Konstatinopoleōs* ("Patria of Constantinople"), a collection of historical writings about the Byzantine capital Constatinople, was attributed in the past to the fourteenth-century writer Georgios Kondinos. Now it is believed that the work was probably compiled much earlier, under the reign of Basil II (976–1025 C.E.); see Berger, *Accounts of Medieval Constantinople*.

46. Schiroò, "La seconda leggenda di Cassia," 303–315.

47. Zugravu, "Kassia the Melodist," 33. On the bride show and Kassia's afterlife in Byzantine and post-Byzantine works, see Rochow, *Studien zu der Person*.

48. Treadgold, "The Problem of the Marriage," 325–341.

49. Panagopoulos, "Kassia," 117–119.

50. Sherry, *Kassia the Nun*, 56.

51. See Rochow, *Studien zu der Person*, 705–715.

52. See Touliatos-Miles, "Kassia," 7.

53. Riehle, "Authorship and Gender (and) Identity," 249n21.

54. Using the same verb, *peripiptō*, as Kassia, Didymus the Blind (*Commentary on Job*; cf. *PG* 39:1132C), responding to Job 4:17 ("Can mortals be right before God?"), comments: "Do not say that you have suffered [*peponthas*] these while having no sins [*hamartēmatōn ektos*]. Because it is impossible for a man to follow with precision [*akribeian*] the laws. For due to the weakness of nature [*physeōs asthenian*], we come to grief [*peripiptomen*], sometimes [*men*] willingly [*ekousiois*], but often [*pollakis*] unwillingly [*akousiois*]." Didymus touches here on the Stoic concept of *propatheia* (Gk.; Lat. *propassio*, "pre-passion") that for him and his predecessor Origen might account for those involuntary dispositions (e.g., anger; cf. Ps 4:5: "Be angry, and do not sin") inherent in our weak nature that are not "passions" (*pathē*) per se. However, when *propathic* dispositions are entertained, feelings can turn into passions. On *propatheia* in Origen and Didymus of Alexandria, see Layton, "Origen and Didymus," 262–282.

55. In contrast, Romanos the Melodist (*Homily on the Harlot*), by depicting the sinful woman as a clichéd harlot, downsizes the meaning of sinfulness to mere sexuality; while Romanos looks at the sinful woman from outside, analyzing her deceiving look, Kassia examines her from inside as a woman, as a human being; hence the latter's portrait is marked by depth and universality, qualities that, along with the monostrophic form, endow Kassia's hymn with a "classic" aura; see Dyck, "On Cassia," 66–68, 76.

56. The verb *aisthanomai* connotes "to perceive, to apprehend by senses," but also "to understand" (of mental perception).

57. Note that Ambrose of Milan distinguishes between the two episodes: "Matthew depicts this woman pouring ointment upon Christ's head [Matt 26:7], and perhaps therefore was reluctant to call her a sinner. According to Luke, a sinner poured ointment on Christ's feet. She cannot be the same woman, lest the Evangelists seem to have contradicted each other.... If you understand this, you will see this woman, and you will certainly see her blessed wherever this gospel is preached. Her memory will never pass away, since she poured the fragrances of good conduct and the ointment of righteous deeds on the head of Christ" (*Exposition of the Gospel of Luke* 6.14–15); cf. Just, *Luke*, 126.

58. "The words that Kassia places in the sinner's mouth draw from Luke's account of the sinful woman anointing and kissing Christ's feet amid tears in the home of the Pharisee Simon [Luke 7:36–38]. Yet this direct speech is chronologically and spatially placed at Christ's tomb ('[she] brings you in tears myrrh before your entombment saying'). Kassia thus creates a 'chronotopos' (Michail Bakhtin) that defies chronological linearity and spatial allocation. The impression of a movement beyond the rules of time and space is further reinforced by the reference to Eve, which previous scholarship struggled to interpret adequately in their readings of the hymn. The lines at first glance seem awkward and misplaced—a mechanical insertion of a standard figure of female identification by means of a relative clause loosely connected to the main clause. Yet scholars have failed to notice a small but important detail: the relative pronoun *hōn* refers to *podas*, thus identifying Christ's feet with the feet of God in the Old Testament. However, in Gen 3:8—the passage to which Kassia alludes—there is

no direct reference to God's feet: having realized that they are naked, Adam and Eve hide from the Lord's face (*apo prosōpou kyriou*), when they hear His voice (*phōnēn*)"; Riehle, "Authorship and Gender (and) Identity," 248.

59. Dyck, "On Cassia," 76.

60. In the Byzantine hymns composed for July 22, when Orthodox Christians commemorate Saint Mary Magdalene, she is called the "Myrrh Bearer and equal to the apostles" (*myrophora kai isapostolos*), the "true [female] Disciple" (*alēthē mathētrian*), and the "First Herald of the gospel" (*prōtē kai euangelistria*). The Magdalene is praised for "being filled with great perception [*syneseōs*] and true knowledge [*gnōseōs*] due to [her] familiarity with the Creator (actually with Christ) . . . and [she] proclaimed his sufferings" (Vespers for July 22, Sticheron for the Myrrh Bearer)—a similar gift (*synesis*, "perception") found in Kassia's female protagonist.

61. A similar case occurs with Jacob, who in the Bible is described as "weeping" (*klaiaō*, Gen 37:34–35) and in hymns as "lamenting" (verb *odyromai*); on "hermeneutical pointers," see the section on "Hermeneutical Procedures" in chapter 7.

62. Cf. Matt 26:12: "By pouring this fragrant ointment on my body, she did it to prepare me for burial [*entaphiasai*]." The basic meaning of *entaphiasmos*, which is commonly rendered "entombment," here may be "laying out for burial," from the verb *entaphiazō*, "to prepare, embalm (one's body) for burial" (Gen 50:2, a hapax legomenon). This meaning is attested in early Christian writings (e.g., Justin Martyr, *Quaestiones et responsiones ad Orthodoxos* 117 [*PG* 100:1093C]).

63. If Kassia's hymn distinguishes clearly between the narrator's voice and the sinful woman's monologue, in Romanos's homily *On the Harlot*, this distinction becomes blurry. One can imagine Romanos seeking to understand the woman's soul so that he may express her feelings and thoughts as his own: "I would like to search the mind of the wise woman and to know how Jesus came to shine in her" (4.1–2); cf. Krueger, *Liturgical Subjects*, 46–47. Something similar occurs in this hymn prescribed for Holy Wednesday Matins; the hymnographer identifies himself with the harlot: "More than the harlot have I transgressed and yet no torrents of tears have I offered you, O good One. But praying in silence, I fell before you, and with longing, I kiss your immaculate feet, so that you, as Master, will grant forgiveness of trespasses to me who cry out to you, O Savior. From the mire of my sinful burdens deliver me" (Holy Wednesday, Matins, Kontakion).

64. Lit. "gadfly, breeze," an insect that infests cattle; another meaning is "a stinging, mad desire." *Oistros* is a very rare word, occurring fewer than fifty times in Classical Greek literature. In Greek mythology, *oistros* designates a type of fly plaguing cattle; it appears as a tormentor of Io, the heifer maiden. Being attracted by Io, Zeus makes her a white heifer so Hera, his wife, may not see her. But after a while, Hera discovers Io and sends a gadfly to torment her so that she roams around far from home (Aeschylus, *Suppliant Women* 539–545: "*Chorus*: I have come here . . . into that pasture, from which Io, tormented by the gad-fly's sting, fled in frenzy, traversing many tribes of men, and according to fate, cut in two the surging strait, marking off the land upon the farther shore"; cf. *Suppliant Women*, ad locum. Metaphorically, *oistros*, occurring also in 4 Macc 2:3; 3:17, could possibly mean a "sting that drives mad" or an

"insane passion" (cf. Herodotus, *Histories* 2.93). One can imagine the sinful woman in Kassia's hymn repeatedly stung or tormented by her maddening inclination for sexual indulgence. With the use of such an elevated lexicon, Kassia proves herself again cultured in Classical literature, which enables her to paint an erudite portrait of the sinful woman.

65. The word *akolasia*, "intemperance, licentiousness, debauchery," is a hapax legomenon in LXX, occurring only in 4 Macc 13:7, with reference to the seven martyrs, who, through reasoning and piety, thought that they could overcome the passions. But the word is absent in the New Testament.

66. A similar phrase is attested in 4 Macc 2:3, *ton tōn pathōn oistron*, "madness of passions" or "maddening sting of passions," with reference to a young Joseph, who "through [his] reasoning [*tō logismō*] reduced the maddening sting of passions to naught"; cf. 3:17 (pertaining to the seven martyr brothers), "a temperate mind [*ho sōphrōn nous*] can quench the flames of insane passions [*tas tōn oistrōn phlegmonas*]." One may notice here a contrast between two figures: Joseph, a symbol of chastity, based on 4 Macc 2:3 and several hymns prescribed for Holy Monday, and the sinful woman of Kassia's hymn, who is driven by the "insane passion of debauchery." This contrast is quite singular because the interconnection or parallelism is between a primarily biblical character (Joseph) and a "liturgized" biblical figure (Luke's "sinner" turned into "the woman who fell in with many sins" by Kassia). This procedure can be termed biblical-liturgical intertextuality or interpretive "intercontextuality," a relation between two different contexts/settings, biblical and liturgical. In any event, this case confirms the holistic character of "liturgical hermeneutics." The liturgical interpretation not only includes diverse media and genres within the liturgical settings, but it also extends to different "contexts" or "settings" where the interpretive process unfolds in its own right and according to its own set of rules.

67. The adjective *zophōdēs*, "dark," is related to *zophos*, "darkness, gloom," used to describe the netherworld, beginning with Homer and up to the time of the New Testament (e.g., 2 Pet 2:4 refers to the "sinful angels" whom God cast in "chains of darkness"; cf. Jude 6). The imagery Kassia proposes here evokes a deathly, inferno-like situation.

68. One of the hymns designated for Holy Wednesday points to the sinful woman's state of despair: "Today, Christ enters the house of the Pharisee. A sinful woman draws near and rolls up [*ekylindouto*] at [his] feet, while crying out, 'See me, a woman submersed in sin. I have fallen in despair [*apēlpismenēn*] due to [my] deeds [*praxeis*]. But I was not abhorred [*bdelychtheisan*] by your very goodness'" (Holy Wednesday, Matins, Apostic: on).

69. According to Leclerc, *Introduction to the Prophets*, 426–427, the Old Testament prophets, as intercessors, use three strategies: prayer, moral blackmail, and moral pressure. For instance, Moses, the model of the prophetic movement, reminds God of the oath he has sworn to Abraham and his duty to adhere to it if he wants the people to do the same (Exod 32:11–14).

70. God bowing down the heavens is part of the Bible's "divine revelation" grammar (cf. Ps 18:9 [17:10]; 144 [143]:5).

71. See Simić, "Kassia's Hymnography," 25–26.

72. In clear contrast to the "woman who fell in with many sins," Romanos's harlot is quite active, planning and rehearsing her conversion, while exhorting herself to come out of her sinful past: "Come then, my soul, see the moment you were seeking, the one who purifies you is at hand. Why do you stand fast in the filth of your deeds?" (4.6–11); cf. Krueger, *Liturgical Subjects*, 47.

73. For Tillyard, "A Musical Study," 432, Eve's presence in the poem is merely a "pedantic" addition.

74. Dyck, "On Cassia," 72, rightly observes, "The two women become for all humanity negative and positive exempla of the behavior of a sinful woman."

75. I agree with Peterson in his remarks that dismissing liturgically the mystery of "delivering," "handing over," through the agency of Judas for some simplistic explanations of his guilt is as dangerous as the recent tendencies (but going back to the Gnostics) to exonerate Judas. One should focus rather on the ambiguity of the verb *paradidōmi* ("to deliver, to hand over") and Jesus's salvific work. Augustine makes a good and daring observation when he writes: "If the Father delivered up the Son and the Son delivered up himself, what did Judas do? Delivering up was done by the Father, delivering up was done by the Son, delivering up was done by Judas; one thing was done.... We find God the Father in the same act in which we find Judas" (*Tractate* 7.7; cf. Peterson, "What Happened on 'the Night?'" 381). Thomas Aquinas explains this paradox: "It was from love that the Father delivered Christ and Christ gave himself up to death; it is for that reason both are praised. Judas, however delivered him out of avarice" (*Summa Theologiae*, 3a.47.2). Earlier and later Church theologians recognize that the motives of God and Judas differ, i.e., faithfulness vs. faithlessness; see Peterson, "What Happened on 'the Night?," 363–383.

76. On Judas as depicted in the four canonical gospels, see Grene, "Cowardice, Betrayal and Discipleship"; see also Oropeza, "Judas' Death," 341–361.

77. MT uses Hithpael of the verb *h-l-k*, "to go, to walk," with a special durative conjugation; cf. Gen 5:22 (with Enoch as a subject of "walking *with* [Heb. *'ēt*] God," v. 24); see Speiser, *Genesis*, 1:24. LXX (*peripateō*, "to walk up and down, to walk about") provides a good match for the Heb. verb. Thus, God is described as walking to and fro, probably to give the first humans the opportunity to reflect on their lapse and come forward remorsefully. The same verb, same conjugation, is used by biblical authors to refer to God's active presence in the Tabernacle (Tent of Meeting), thus linking the Eden imagery to later sanctuaries (Lev 26:12; Deut 23:14 [15]; 2 Sam 7:6–7); cf. Wenham, *Genesis 1–15*, 76. On the same line of thought, Targum Pseudo-Jonathan of Lev 26:12 replaces the somehow anthropomorphic statement "I will walk to and fro" with "I will allow the glory of my dwelling [Shekinah] to reside" (*w-'šry 'yqr škynty*) in the tent sanctuary.

78. MT: *lə-rûᵃḥ hay-yôm*, lit. "in the wind of the day," refers to the breezy time of day, which in the Holy Land would be late afternoon, toward sunset, when the heat of day (cf. Gen 18:1) decreases substantially and a refreshing breeze blows in. LXX reads interpretively *to deilinon*, "afternoon, at twilight, evening." However, there is another interpretive option: to take the first Heb. word *rûᵃḥ* in its basic meaning, "wind"; thus, God appears as (in the midst of) a windstorm (hence Adam and Eve seek shelter among the trees of the garden) similar to the theophany recorded in Job 38:1 (God speaks

to an inquisitive Job "out of the windstorm" [Heb. *min has-sǝᶜārāh*; LXX: *dia lailapos kai nephōn*, "through a hurricane and clouds"]) and Acts 2:2 (the coming of the Holy Spirit upon the apostles is heralded by the "noise like the rush of a violent wind" [*ēchos hōsper pheromenēs pnoēs biaias*] coming from heaven and filling the room).

79. The text allows one to imagine that this was God's daily routine: at the end of the afternoon/beginning of evening, God comes to the Garden of Eden, takes his evening constitutional, and enters into conversation with the first human beings; cf. Skinner, *A Critical and Exegetical Commentary*, 77.

80. Apparently, God does not address the couple but Adam (the male individual) alone, since only Adam heard God's ban on "the tree of knowledge of good and evil" (cf. Gen 2:16–17), and Eve had not yet been fashioned at that time. This was the way LXX understood God's question when it expanded the Hebrew reading: "*Adam*, where are you?"

81. Note the phrase "spiritual/rational paradise" (*logikon paradeison*) used in hymnography as a metaphor for the Holy Virgin Mary and the Church, both considered a fulfillment of what paradise was intended to be, a transparent medium of communication between God and humans: "O Christ, your life-bearing side is a spring that like a river out of Eden flows, and it waters your Church, as though she were a rational paradise [*logikon paradeison*]; and from there it separates into the four gospels as if as many heads. It irrigates the world and it fills creation with joy, and it teaches the Gentiles faithfully to adore and worship your kingdom" (Holy Friday, Matins, Beatitudes, Sticheron). Proclus of Constantinople was one of the earliest writers to use this phrase as a Marian epithet with respect to the Virgin's mediatory role: "Today the holy Mother of God and Virgin Mary has gathered us here. She is the spotless treasure of virginity, the spiritual paradise of the second Adam, the workshop where the two natures were united. This is the feast of the exchange that brought salvation . . . the only bridge for God to reach humankind" (*Homily* 1.1); cf. Constas, *Proclus of Constantinople*, 137.

82. Wenham, *Genesis 1–15*, 76, remarks that God's walking was not at all uncommon, but rather humans' sudden hiding from him was out of the ordinary.

83. According to Ambrose of Milan, God's question should be read as a subtle irony, "What then does he mean by 'Adam, where art thou?' Does he not mean 'in what circumstance' are you; not, 'in what place'? It is therefore not a question but a reproof. From what condition of goodness, beatitude and grace, he means to say, have you fallen into this state of misery? You have forsaken eternal life. You have entombed yourself in the ways of sin and death" (*Paradise* 14.17). Augustine underlines the scolding purpose of the divine question: "This was not asked, of course, because God did not know the answer. Rather, it was asked in order to scold Adam by reminding him that there really was nowhere that he could be, once God was not in him" (*City of God* 13.15). In John Chrysostom's view, God's question was, in fact, an invitation addressed to the first humans to admit their sin and re-enter into dialogue with their Creator (*Homilies on Genesis* 17.22); cf. Louth, *Genesis 1–11*, 84.

84. Sarna, *Genesis*, 26.

85. Brueggemann, *Genesis*, 53.

86. See Pentiuc, *Jesus the Messiah*, 27.

87. Brueggemann, *Genesis*, 53.

88. The word *krotos* (verb *kroteō*, "to strike, to beat") appears fewer than fifty times in ancient Classical Greek. There is no evidence of this word in LXX or the New Testament. The use of such a rare word from the ancient Greek repertoire shows the hymnographer's familiarity with Classical literature.

89. John Chrysostom intimates that the sound was strong enough to make an impact on Adam and Eve: "He [God] wanted to provide them with such an experience as would induce in them a state of anguish, which in fact happened: they had so striking an experience that they tried to hide from the presence of God" (*Homilies on Genesis*, 17.3–4); cf. Louth, *Genesis 1–11*, 82.

90. In Luke 7:36–50, the word *podas*, "feet," occurs six times, whereas in Gen 3:8 (LXX), the same word is only implied by the sentence "When they heard the sound [*phōnēn*] of the Lord God walking to and fro [*peripatountos*] in the garden."

91. Krueger, *Writing and Holiness*, 27.

92. Noticeably, Targum Pseudo-Jonathan replaces "the Lord God" with the "*Word* of the Lord God" (*mymrʾ dyyy ʾlqym*) walking in the garden," thus trying to eliminate from the text any trace of anthropomorphic language. Nevertheless, if one reads the targumist's gloss in a Christian register, it is the Word of God, the Logos, who, prior to its incarnation, was somehow mysteriously walking in the Garden of Eden. And the ancient Jewish interpretive reading is quite similar to the one found in the hymn of Kassia, where Jesus's "feet" (replacing "God walking in the garden") made Eve, unlike the sinful woman, hide herself from his presence. Based on a key New Testament text where Jesus states emphatically, "Before Abraham was, *I am*" (John 8:58), patristic interpreters saw in the Old Testament theophanies the appearances of the Son of God before his incarnation. On the identification of Christ with the Creator in Byzantine hymnography, see Bucur, "The Feet That Eve Heard," 3–26.

93. Same emphasis on sound as a bridge of communication between God and humans is found in Ephrem the Syrian: "It was not only by the patience he exhibited that God wished to help them; he also wished to benefit them by the sound of his feet. God endowed his silent footsteps with sound so that Adam and Eve might be prepared, at that sound, to make supplication before him who made the sound" (*Commentary on Genesis* 2.24.1); cf. Louth, *Genesis 1–11*, 82.

94. In the same vein of thought, Augustine notes that the purpose of God's question to Adam was "to remind him that there really was nowhere that he could be once God was not in him" (*City of God* 13.15; cf. Louth, *Genesis 1–11*, 84).

Chapter 4

1. Ps 114 (113):8 (LXX), "the one who turned the rock [*petran*] into lakes [*limnas*] and the flint [*akrotomon*] into springs of waters [*pēgas hydatōn*]," is the closest scriptural text to the hymn; it has the same nominal forms (*limnas* and *pēgas*) but a different verb (*strephō* instead of *poieō*).

2. The word *barathron* is a happax in LXX, *pēlou barathron*, "a pit of clay" (Isa 14:23), rendering Heb. *mɪʕɪʕ*, "besom, broom." However, *barathron* is found in Classical Greek literature designating "pit, gulf," in Athens a "cleft" behind the Acropolis where criminals were thrown.

3. The word *aithēr*, "ether," is absent in both Testaments but attested in ancient Greek literature, designating the "brighter, purer air" above the common "air" (*aēr*).

4. This high status conferred upon Jesus by the hymnographer may be an interpretation of John's description at the beginning of the foot-washing pericope, portraying Jesus as the one coming out from God: "Knowing that the Father gave everything into his hands, and that he had come out from God [*apo theou exēlthen*] and he was going to God" (John 13:3).

5. Justin Martyr (*Dialogue* 54.1; cf. *PG* 6:593C) uses the same verb to express the washing away of sin through Christ's atoning sacrifice: "He would wash thoroughly those who believe in him with his own blood." Basil of Caesarea (*Homily* 1.2 [*On Fasting*]; cf. *PG* 31:165A) employs *apoplynō*, glossing Jesus's logion: " 'Anoint your head and wash your face' [Matt 6:17]. Thoroughly wash your soul of sin."

6. The adjective *hyperōos*, "lofty, upper, (being) above," found in this hymn is a hapax legomenon in the Old Testament (Ezek 42:5); cf. its substantivized version, *hyperōon*, "upper room" (Judg 3:20, 23, 24; 2 Sam 18:33 [19:1]). In the New Testament, the room where the Last Supper and a few other important events occurred (e.g., first appearance of the risen Lord, descent of the Holy Spirit), is first rendered with *katalyma*, "guest room, dining room," from the verb *katalyō*, "to halt, to rest, to find a lodging" (Mark 14:14; Luke 22:11; cf. 2:7).

7. Similarly, "The Logos said to the disciples: 'Go, prepare the Passover in the upper place [*hyperōō topō*], in which the mind is established [*nous enidrytai*]" (Holy Thursday, Matins, Ode 9, Troparion).

8. There is a textual difference worth mentioning between MT and LXX with respect to Gen 18:4. MT: "Let a little water be brought. Bath [*raḥăṣû*, Qal imperative third person plural] your feet!" LXX: "Let water be taken and let them wash [*nipsatōsan*, imperative aorist active third person plural] your feet." Thus, according to MT, Abraham's guests were expected to wash their own feet in a basin to be provided, while LXX suggests that foot washing was done by "them," likely Abraham's servants. Note the interpretive reading of Gen 18:4 in the *Testament of Abraham* (2:9): "Then Abraham went forward and washed the feet of the commander-in-chief, Michael. Abraham's heart was moved, and he wept over the stranger"; cf. Coloe, "Sources in the Shadows," 75. In the Jewish tradition, Abraham, the one who washed the feet of the three heavenly guests, is considered the model par excellence of hospitality (Gk. *philoxenia*, "love for strangers").

9. Note that another scriptural basis for this hymn about Jesus's washing of the disciples' feet may be Job 26:8, where God is described as "binding water in his clouds" (*desmeuōn hydōr en nephelais*), with "water" functioning as a subtle catchword.

10. Note the word *polon*, "axis; the sphere that revolves on this axis; the vault of heaven, the sky, or the firmament," instead of a more common term, *ouranon*, "sky" (Ps 147 [146]:8).

11. According to Matson, "To Serve as Slave," 114, the foot washing is "a story of the status reversal, but a status reversal that was meant to have paradigmatic significance for his [Jesus's] disciples and subsequent followers."

12. The verb *ekplynō*, "to wash out," implies a stain or dirty spot to be taken out by washing. Note the use of the common verb *niptō*, "to wash," in John 13:5.

13. The word *lention*, "cloth" (a Latin loanword, *linteum*), designating a piece of woven fabric made of cotton, wool, linen, etc., is found only in John 13:4, 5, in the entire Bible.

14. Note the use of the same phrase in a worship context, "bending [their] knees, they worshiped the Lord [*kampsantes ta gonata prosekynēsan tō kyriō*]" (1 Chr 29:20).

15. Clines, *Job 1–20*, 292.

16. LXX reads it as a rhetorical question with emphasis on God's power: "Is not in his hand the life [*ei mē en cheiri autou psychē*] ...?"

17. Clines, *Job 1–20*, 295.

18. While found in the Byz., this line is missing in the other three main text types of the Greek New Testament (Western, Caesarean, Alexandrian).

19. Jewett, *Romans*, 634, argues that a shorter text—"How timely [*hōs hōra*] [are] the feet of those who preach the gospel of the good tidings [*euangelizomenōn [ta] agatha*]," exhibiting *hōra*, "time" (LXX), instead of *hōraioi*, "beautiful" (Syro-Hexapla text type)—might reflect the original reading. In support of his view, Jewett brings LXX and considerable manuscript textual evidence; see Metzger, *A Textual Commentary*, 463.

20. According to Jewett, *Romans*, 639, Paul used a variant of Isa 52:7 close to the Lucianic recension that corrected the LXX, bringing it close to the Heb. text attested by MT.

21. See the sections on "Key Features" in chapter 7.

22. Jewett, *Romans*, 639.

23. Through the use of the verb *exaponizō*, "to wash thoroughly," consisting of *ek-*, *apo-*, and *nizō* (cf. *niptō*), this hymn is quite close to John 13:5, unlike other hymns exhibiting the verb *plynō* or its variants.

24. Although the basic meaning of the adjective *hōraios* (related to *hōra*, "time") is "timely, seasonable, appropriate," I have followed throughout this section the conventional rendition "beautiful," which relies on the parallel with Sir 26:18 ("beautiful legs [*podes hōraioi*] on firm-set heels") and corresponds to Isa 52:7 (MT) reading *nāʾwû*, "beautiful." The Heb. form *nāʾwû* is a Qal perfect deriving from the verb *n-ʾ-h*, "to be beautiful, lovely."

25. Cf. Bray, *Romans*, 279.

26. "Ambrosiaster" is the name coined by Erasmus to designate the author of a lengthy commentary on all Pauline epistles (except Heb), who was previously confounded with Ambrose of Milan.

27. Cf. Bray, *Romans*, 280.

28. Jewett, *Romans*, 636.

29. Blenkinsopp, *Isaiah 40–55*, 344.

30. The prophet Habakkuk (LXX: *Ambakoum*) is commemorated by the Eastern Orthodox Church on December 2.

31. Andersen, *Habakkuk*, 264.

32. MT's priority with respect to Hab was enhanced by the *Wadi Murabbcat* Scroll of the Minor Prophets (*MurXII*), discovered in 1955. *MurXII*, providing much of the book of Habakkuk, agrees almost entirely with MT. LXX is either based on a *Vorlage* different from the one of MT, or it represents an interpretation of Hebrew text. Here are some of the main text witnesses to Hab 3:4:

MT: 4a, *wə-nōgah kā-ʾôr tihyeh*, "And his radiance was [will be like] the sun [light]"; 4b, *qarnayim miy-yādô lô*, "[and he had] horns [coming] from his very hand"; 4c, *wə-šām ḥebyôn ʿuzzōh*, "and there he [un-]veiled his power."

LXX: 4a, *kai phengos autou hōs phōs estai*, "And his brightness will be like light"; 4b, *kerata en chersin autou*, "horns [are] in his hands"; 4c, *kai etheto agapēsin krateian ischyos autou*, "and he has established a mighty love of his strength."

Barberini (Barb.) is a non-LXX Greek translation of Hab 3, which was probably done in Alexandria, Egypt, sometimes during the first century C.E. by a translator who shows a good knowledge of Hebrew. The translation was likely made for liturgical purposes; see Good, "The Barberini Greek Version," 11–30. Barb.: 4a, *diaugasma photos estai autō*, "The brightness/transparency of the light will belong to him"; 4b, *kerata ek cheiros autou hyparchei autō*, "Horns from his hand exist for him (belong to him)"; 4c, *ekei epestēriktai hē dynamis tēs doxēs autou*, "There, the power of his glory is established."

V: 4a, *splendor eius ut lux erit*, "His splendor will be like light"; 4b, *cornua in minibus eius*, "His horns [are] in his hands"; 4c, *ibi abscondita est fortitude eius*, "There, his strength is hidden."

33. The Targum, in its recognizably paraphrastic way, stays close to MT: "And the splendor of his glory was revealed like the splendor of Creation, and sparks issued from his glorious chariot; there [*tmn*] he revealed his Shekinah [*glʾ yt škyntyh*] which was hidden [*d-ḥwt mṭmrʾ*] from the sons of men in the high fastness"; cf. Cathcart and Gordon, *The Targum*, 158–159.

34. See a full discussion in Mulroney, *The Translation Style*, 121.

35. Hos 11:8–9 may be adduced as a convincing argument in support of such covenantal love. Addressing an obstinate people, God raises two rhetorical questions followed by his own answer and final decision. Thus, the constant sin of Israel brings a "conflict state" into God's heart. Unknowingly, Israel makes God's "heart" divide in two: on the one hand, there is God's justice and power to implement this justice or punish when it is not observed by people; on the other hand, there is God's passionate love for Israel. One may notice how God's love "fights" against justice, so that the former eventually come out victorious. Why such a resolution? For God is "holy," says the eighth-century northern Israelite prophet Hosea. In other words, the covenantal love of God, consisting of two basic traits, justice and passionate love, is the expression of God's "holiness," i.e., transcendence, a similar idea to the one found in Hab 3:4c (LXX), where the same unique love of God points to his strength; see Pentiuc et al., *The Word of the Lord*, 259–273.

36. See Levenson, *The Love of God*, who succeeds in putting to rest the long-held misconception (every now and then fraught with anti-Judaic feelings and thoughts) that there is a sharp dichotomy, a real gulf, between the Old and New Testaments;

that is, the Old Testament tirelessly preaches the same boring "observe the Law" sermon, and the New Testament proclaims the ever-refreshing gospel of love and freely offered grace. Such a Marcionite view is unfortunately popular nowadays in not a few Christian circles. Nothing is more erroneous than this, Levenson remarks, reminding us that God's love, which begins with the first pages of the Old Testament and continues deeply into the New, is a "covenantal love," a love that ardently offers itself to everybody; yet, at the same time, it is a love that requires mutual faithfulness (loyalty) and, from the human perspective, a continuous struggle to observe God's commandments.

37. The marital imagery in the book of Hosea is a good example. The prophet Hosea, representing God, or more precisely experiencing God's bitterness toward Israel, is ordered by God to marry a prostitute (Hos 1:2). Hosea does exactly as he is told. Later on, Gomer, the prophet's wife, abandons him, becoming an adulteress. God issues Hosea another command. This time, he asks Hosea to bring his wayward wife back home, and even more odd, he requests his prophet to "love" his adulterous wife (Hos 3:1). The prophet's life story moves, paralleling God's history with Israel, from responsibility (marital contract) to passion (love), but this move is the opposite of the Israel/Gomer attitude: more decadence on the part of the wife (Israel/Gomer) leads to more love on the part of the husband (God/Hosea); see Pentiuc et al., *The Word of the Lord*, 110–121.

38. Cf. Cyril of Alexandria, *Commentary on the Twelve Prophets*, 377.

39. For valuable information regarding the reception history of the book of Habakkuk with emphasis on Hab 3:2, see Bucur and Mueller, "Gregory Nazianzen's Reading."

40. Cf. Ferreiro, *The Twelve Prophets*, 190.

41. Cf. ibid., 190.

42. Cf. ibid., 191. Similarly, Basil of Caesarea urges: "You are perhaps distressed that you are driven outside the walls, but you shall dwell under the protection of the God of heaven. The angel who watches over the church has gone out with you. . . . Therefore, the more have been your trials, look for a more perfect reward from your last judge. Do not take your present troubles ill. Do not lose hope. Yet a little while and your helper will come to you and will not tarry" (*Letter* 238).

43. Bovon, *Luke 1*, 1:50, notes: "It is neither the unusual greeting nor the appearance of the angel that confuses the virgin and leads her to puzzle over it, but rather the content of the message."

44. The suggested composition dates of Hab 1 fluctuate between pre- and post-600 B.C.E.; see Andersen, *Habakkuk*, 173.

45. V: *Deus ab austro veniet, et Sanctus de monte Pharan*, "God comes from the south (wind), and the Holy One from Mount Paran"; V's rendition of Heb. *tymn* (Têmān) with "south" generated a series of patristic interpretations explaining "south" as referring to Bethlehem, south of Jerusalem (Jerome, Cyril of Alexandria, Theophylact of Ohrid). Augustine uses Hab 3:3 to reject the Donatists' claim that God would come "out of Africa." In his response, the Bishop of Hippo underlines the biblically based observation that Christ was born in the "south," Bethlehem, and he ascended to heaven at the "shady mountain," the Mount of Olives: "Where we recognize Christ

in what is written: 'God will come from the south and the holy one from the shady mountain; his strength will cover the heavens,' there we recognize the church in what follows: 'And the earth is full of his praise.' Jerusalem was settled from Africa, as we read in the book of Joshua, son of Nun [Josh 15:8, 14, 18; Acts 1:2]; from there the name of Christ was spread abroad; there is the shady mountain, the Mount of Olives, from which he ascended into heaven, so that his strength might cover the heavens and the church might be filled through all the earth with his praise" (Augustine, *Letter* 105); cf. Ferreiro, *The Twelve Prophets*, 202; similarly, Irenaeus: "And there are also some of them who say, 'the Lord has spoken in Zion, and uttered his voice from Jerusalem,' and 'in Judah is God known'—these indicated his advent, which took place in Judaea. Those, again, who declare that 'God comes from the south, and from a mountain thick with foliage,' announced his advent at Bethlehem, as I have pointed out in the preceding book" (*Against Heresies* 4.33.11); cf. *ANF* 1:509–510.

46. The phrase *kataskion oros*, "shady mountain," has always been used by homilists and hymnographers as a metaphor for the Virgin Mary with no special connotation but with reference to different events in her life turned into liturgical Marian feast days ("Birth," "Presentation of Mary at the Temple," "Falling Asleep"). Here is Germanos of Constantinople (d. 730): "Today Anna too . . . makes it known to the ends of the earth that she has received the fruit. Today the open gate of the Lord's temple receives the ascending gate of Immanuel, closed and looking toward the east [Ezek 44:1–3]. . . . Today we are bid by Mary to pay her homage although none can bring together all the praise. Hail, O rich and shady Mountain of God [Hab 3:3] whereon pastured the True Lamb, who hath taken away our sins and infirmities, mountain, whence hath been cut without hands that Stone [Dan 2:34] which has smitten the altars of the idols, and become the head-stone of the corner, marvelous in our eyes [Ps 118 [117]:22, 23]" (*First Homily on the Presentation of Mary at the Temple*; cf. *PG* 98:291–310). Again with no special connotation but as a generic metaphor for Mary, the "shady mountain" occurs in Andrew of Crete's *Fourth Homily on the Nativity of the Most Holy Mother of God*. Here, Habakkuk's "shady mountain" is allegorically identified with Daniel's "mountain": "It is you that Isaiah of the prophetic vision called 'prophetess and virgin' [Isa 7:14] . . . 'sealed'! . . . It is you that Ezekiel called 'the east side' and 'the closed gate,' that the Lord is to pass through and which therefore will be closed [Ezek 44:1–3]. . . . It is you that Daniel saw as a mountain [Dan 2:45], and that wondrous Habakkuk as 'the high shady hill God desires to dwell in,' he prophetically sang of [Hab 3:3]. . . . It is you that Zechariah most discerning in divine matters saw as 'a candlestick all of gold with seven lamps thereon' [Zech 4:2], lighted by seven charismata of the Holy Spirit. . . . Blessed be the fruit that made the barren and bitter waters good for drinking and fruitful by having Elisha cast salt into them [2 Kgs 2:19–22]. Blessed who in the untouched shoot of a virgin womb flowered as a ripe grape" (*PG* 97:862–882). The rendition of the above two excerpts belongs to Kruk, "The Ἄνωθεν οἱ προφῆται," 58.

47. The words *pneuma*, "spirit," and *dynamis*, "power," in Luke 1:35, occurring sometimes together (Luke 4:14; Acts 1:8; 6:8; 10:38), point to God's miraculous, powerful presence. The verb *episkiazō*, "to throw his shadow, to overshadow," is also found in

Acts 5:15, with reference to Peter's healing "shadow"; in Luke 9:34, regarding a "cloud [that] overshadowed" (*nephelē epeskiasen*) Jesus's disciples during the Transfiguration episode; and in Exod 40:35, describing "a cloud [which] was overshadowing" (*nephelē epeskiasen*) the Tent of Witness; all these occurrences designate God's presence, as is the case with the overshadowing "cloud" in Old Testament times indicating God's powerful presence; see Bovon, *Luke 1*, 1:52.

48. Walter, "The Iconography of Habakkuk," 256.

49. "Hail, shady mountain of virgins, from which the holy one of Israel appeared, according to Habakkuk, whose proclamation was divine" (*Encomium on the Dormition of Our Holy Lady* [*PG* 99:719–729]); cf. Kruk, "The Ἄνωθεν οἱ προφῆται," 64.

50. Note that Byz. reads *eucharistēsas*, "he thanked" (cf. Luke 22:19; 1 Cor 11:24), and the rest of the textual witnesses have *eulogēsas*, "he blessed" (cf. Mark 14:22).

51. Lenzi, "Proverbs 8:22–31," 688.

52. As early as the turn of the eras, one may detect an interpretation pointing to gender distinction between God the Creator (male, father role) and the personified Wisdom (female, mother role): "We can properly say that the Creator who made everything was thus the 'father' of that which was born, while the 'mother' was the knowledge belonging to its maker, with whom God had come together, though not in manner of humans, to engender that which was created" (Philo, *On Drunkenness* 30). A similar interpretation may be found in Wis 7:12 (cf. 8:3–4): "I rejoiced in them all for Wisdom is their leader [*autōn hēgeitai*], but I was unaware that she was their mother [*genetin*]"; see Kugel, *Traditions of the Bible*, 63.

53. Whybray, *The Composition of the Book of Proverbs*, 121.

54. See Lenzi, "Proverbs 8:22–31," 695–696.

55. See the special nuance of the Heb. verb *ḥ-y-l*, Qal, "to writhe, to tremble," perhaps alluding to labor pains, making a mother writhe when the time of delivery arrives. Read in a Christological hermeneutical key and applied to the Father–Son relationship, Prov 8:25 (MT) might convey a certain propensity for self-offering on the Father's part, whose role as begetting the Son is painted in brushes of "labor pains." For more on this intriguing birth imagery in Prov 8:22–31, see Pentiuc, *Jesus the Messiah*, 46–47; Pentiuc, "A Self-Offering God," 255–265.

56. Origen, *Homily on Jeremiah* 9:4; cf. Dowling, "Proverbs 8:22–31," 55.

57. Note the following ancient Jewish interpretation of Heb. *ʾāmôn*, "artisan: "[Wisdom speaking:] 'Then I was beside him as an artisan . . .': The Torah [identified with Wisdom, Sir 24:10] is thus saying, 'I was the instrument of God's workmanship': When a king wishes to build a palace, he usually does not himself design it, but relies on a builder ['artisan'], and even the builder does not simply build it on his own, but he has blueprints and diagrams in order to know how he will make the chambers and little doors. Just so did God look into the Torah and create the world. [Therefore,] the Torah says, 'In the beginning God created . . .,' for the word *beginning* means Torah, as it says, 'God created me the beginning of his dominion'" (*Genesis Rabbah* 1:1); cf. Kugel, *Traditions of the Bible*, 62.

58. Kugel, *Traditions of the Bible*, 49.

59. Anderson, "The Interpretation of Genesis 1:1," 21–29.

60. On the Jewishness of the prologue to John, see Forger, "Divine Embodiment," 223–262, who embarks on a well-informed and enticing scholarly journey to find evidence of a "divine embodiment" theme in the most representative examples of Jewish thought on God's "absolute incorporeality."

61. Boyarin, "The Gospel of the *Memra*," 243–284.

62. Ibid., 261.

63. On such a hotly debated yet unresolved topic, "the parting of the ways," see Boyarin, *Border Lines*. The topic became popular after the publication of Parkes, *The Conflict of the Church and the Synagogue*.

64. *ANF* 1:227–228.

65. Ibid., 10:307.

66. Ibid., 3:601.

67. Cf. Dowling, "Proverbs 8:22–31," 57.

68. Dowling, "Proverbs 8:22–31," 57–58. In addition to Dowling's contribution, those interested in the reception history of Prov 8:22–31 are directed to Gohl, "Performing the Book of Proverbs."

69. Cf. Dowling, "Proverbs 8:22–31," 58.

70. Daley, *God Visible*, 101.

71. See Boyarin, "The Gospel of the *Memra*," 258–259.

72. Cf. *NPNF*² 7:440.

73. Kugel, *Traditions of the Bible*, 676–678.

74. See Kasman, "Breath, Kiss, and Speech," 97–98 and n. 5.

75. In Fox's view, in *Proverbs 1–9*, 96, this puzzling plural (encountered also in 1:20; 14:1; 24:7; Sir 4:11; and Ps 49:3 [48:4]; approximately vocalized *ḥokmôt* by the Massorets; one expects the correct plural vocalization, *ḥăkāmôt*, like ᶜărālôt from ᶜorlāh, "foreskin" [Josh 5:3]) can be explained either as a "phoenicianism" (**ḥukmōt* > Canaanite **ḥukmatu*), or the final *-t* on *ḥokmôt* is not the feminine plural ending but the feminine singular marker; or it can be simply considered a "plural of majesty." I would lean toward the latter explanation, seeing in this odd plural form a "plural of intensity," imitating the generic word for "God" in the Hebrew Bible, *ʾĕlōhîm*, "God," lit. "gods," construed like a plural with singular verbal forms. This explanation might have support in Wisdom's heavy personification and her conspicuous intimacy with God the Creator in Prov 8:22–31.

76. Fox, *Proverbs 1–9*, 297, adduces an intriguing parallel, the Assyro-Babylonian description of one of the primary gods, Apsu, as "the house of wisdom" (*bît nimêqi*). If the notion of Wisdom's house predates Prov 9:1, Fox remarks, one should acknowledge that the biblical writer "reappropriated and demythologized" this image, turning it into a simple metaphor.

77. "The betrayer [*ho prodotēs*] stretches the same hands that received the bread so that he may receive secretly the price [put on] the one who fashioned humanity with his own hands [*plasantos tais oikeiais chersi ton anthrōpon*], and he [i.e. the betrayer] remained unrestored [*adiogthōtos*]." (Holy Wednesday, Matins, Kontakion)

78. Quoted in Theodoret of Cyrus, *Eranistes* 1.50; cf. Wright, *Proverbs*, 73.

79. *ANF* 5:175; see Wright, *Proverbs*, 72.

80. "R. Ahabah b. Kahana opened [his discourse with the Scriptural passage], 'Wisdom has built her house, she has hewn out her seven pillars. [Prov 9:1] . . .' R. Jeremiah b. Ila'i expounded the passage as referring to the creation of the world. 'Wisdom has built her house' refers to the Holy One, blessed be he, as it is said, 'The Lord by wisdom founded the earth' [Prov 3:19]. 'She has hewn out her seven pillars' refers to the seven days at the Beginning, as it is said, 'For in six days the Lord made heaven and earth, the sea, and all that in them is, and rested on the seventh day' [Exod 20:11]" (*Leviticus Rabbah* 11.1); cf. Kantrowitz, *Judaic Classics Library*, ad locum.

81. See Pentiuc, *The Old Testament*, 232–233.

82. Cf. Wright, *Proverbs*, 72–73.

83. On the verb *proslambanō*, "to accept, to assume," related to incarnation lexicon, see the discussion in the section "The Mystical Supper" earlier in this chapter.

84. The second time *hagnē*, "pure," occurs in the New Testament is in relation to the Wisdom of God. Jas 3:17 clearly states, "The Wisdom from above [*anōthen sophia*] is first pure [*hagnē*]." This line fits quite well with the context of our hymn which speaks of the Logos's incarnation from a chaste, pure mother.

85. Here is the targumic rendition-interpretation of Gen 4:1: "And Adam knew about his wife Eve that she had conceived by Sammael the [wicked] angel of the Lord, and she became pregnant and gave birth to Cain. He resembled the upper ones [angels] and not the lower ones, and she [therefore] said, 'I have acquired a man, indeed, an angel of the Lord'" (Targum Pseudo-Jonathan Gen 4:1). Somehow this line of interpretation made its inroad into Christian circles. So, John urges his fellows: "Do not be like Cain who was from the Evil One [*ek tou ponērou ēn*]" (1 John 3:12). Or later, Tertullian, speaking of Eve, writes: "Having been made pregnant by the seed of the devil . . . she brought forth a son" (*On Patience* 5:15); see Kugel, *Traditions of the Bible*, 147–148.

86. Isaac, "1 Enoch," 33.

87. Boyarin, "The Gospel of the *Memra*," 277–278.

88. Ibid., 277.

89. Anderson, "Mary in the Old Testament," 41–42, has convincingly demonstrated the subtle interconnection between signifier and signified with respect to Old Testament temple theology and incarnational Christology. To make his point stronger and clearer, Anderson adduces an excerpt from Athanasius's *Letter to Adelphius* in which the famous Patriarch of Alexandria argues that the biblical temple physically participates in the life of God who dwells in it; the same with the human body that participates in the divinity of the Logos, who "put on all around," to use the hymnographer's favorite verb (*peritithēmi*). Here is Athanasius: "And we do not worship a creature, and neither do we divide the body from the Word and worship it by itself; nor when we wish to worship the Word do we set him far apart from the flesh, but knowing, as we said above, that 'the Word was made flesh' [John 1:14] we recognize him as God also, after having come in the flesh"; cf. *NPNF*[2] 4:577.

90. Cf. Wright, *Proverbs*, 73.

91. On the Last Supper's Sitz im Leben, see Parsenios, *Departure and Consolation*.

92. The wine-to-water ratio in these "mixed wines" varied greatly (e.g., from twenty parts water to one part wine [cf. Homer, *Odyssey* 9.208f.] to as strong as one to one). Drinking wine unmixed was considered a barbarian habit. The rabbis of the Talmudic period ruled that wine unmixed with water could not be blessed. So, the term *oinos*, "wine," in ancient times meant wine mixed with water. Nevertheless, mixing wine with water was sometimes used to make the latter safe for drinking; see Pentecost, *The Words and Works of Jesus Christ*, 116–117.

93. Smith, *From Symposium to Eucharist*, 145–147.

94. See Warren, *Food and Transformation*, 9–14.

95. Winston, *The Wisdom of Solomon*, 298.

96. The association of manna with ambrosia is fairly well attested in ancient Greek literature, since the LXX transliteration *manna* for Heb. *mān* is actually a Gk. generic word denoting a powder made of aromatic botanical substances and used in medical and ritual settings. The semantic area of the Gk. word overlaps the Heb. word *mān*, as one can glean from a first- to third-century C.E. pseudepigraphical Jewish text, mentioning the bird known as the phoenix, a symbol of immortality, feeding on aromatics and dew. The author of 3 Bar 6:11 (Gk. version) asks: "And what does it [the phoenix] eat? . . . The manna of heaven and the dew of earth"; immortality (*ambrosia*) is encoded in the above question as well as in the Greek myth of the phoenix; see Smith, *Relating Religion*, 124–125; see also Nicklas, "Food of Angels," 83–100.

97. Cf. *ANF* 2:242. Irenaeus shares a similar thought with Clement, when he writes: "When, therefore, the mingled cup and the manufactured bread receive the Word of God, and the Eucharist of the blood and the body of Christ is made, from which things the substance of our flesh is increased and supported, how can they affirm that the flesh is incapable of receiving the gift of God, which is life eternal, which [flesh] is nourished from the body and blood of the Lord, and is a member of Him?" (*Against Heresies* 5.2); cf. *ANF* 1:528. Similarly, Theodore of Mopsuestia covers these aspects, i.e., "wine mixed with water" and the Eucharist being "immortal nourishment": "At first [the offering] is laid upon the altar as mere bread and wine mixed with water, but by the coming of the Holy Spirit it is transformed into the body and blood, and thus it is changed into the power of a spiritual and immortal nourishment" (*Catechetical Homilies* 16); cf. Jurgens, *The Faith of the Early Fathers*, 83.

98. Cf. Holmes, *The Apostolic Fathers*, 199.

99. See Perdue, *Proverbs*, 151.

100. According to Dahood, *Proverbs*, 16–17, "maidservants" should be taken as a literary motif rather than reflecting reality, since women would never send maidservants to invite male guests to a feast. Dahood supports his view on comparative Ugaritic literary grounds.

101. See Garrett, *Proverbs*, 115.

102. *ANF* 5:175–176; cf. Wright, *Proverbs*, 74.

103. Fox, *Proverbs 1–9*, 298.

104. See Perdue, *Proverbs*, 151.

105. Among others, see Jonge, "Mark 14:25."

106. Ibid., 128; against Jeremias, *The Eucharistic Words of Jesus*, 210, who argues that Jesus took a Nazarite vow.

107. Cf. Kantrowitz, *Judaic Classics Library*, ad locum.

108. The verb form *phēmi*, "to declare, to say or affirm, to make known," occurs only four times in the entire Bible, all in 1 Cor (7:29; 10:15, 19; 15:50). Its use in this hymn seems to have a declaratory-revelatory overtone.

109. According to an ancient Jewish interpretation, God allowed Israel to roam about in a hostile environment so that the Torah might be well incorporated into its life. "[God said at the Exodus:] If I bring Israel to the[ir] land right away, every man will be taking possession of his field and vineyard and they will neglect the Torah. Therefore I will send them around the desert for forty years so that they will eat manna and drink the water of the well and thus the Torah will be incorporated into their bodies" (*Mekhilta deR. Ishmael, Wayhi* 1); see Kugel, *Traditions of the Bible*, 620.

110. Fisk, "Pseudo-Philo," 117–136.

111. See discussion in Kugel, *Traditions of the Bible*, 620–621.

112. Fisk, "Pseudo-Philo," 133–134.

113. In Ps 81:16 (80:17), "rock," a metaphor for God, is associated with "honey," a metaphor for unexpected and awesome sustenance: "And he fed [*epsōmisen*] them from the finest wheat [*steatos pyrou*], and he satisfied [*echortasen*] them with honey from the rock [*ek petras meli*]"; cf. Deut 32:13: "they sucked honey from a rock [*ethēlasan meli ek petras*]." This imagery, God likened to a mother nursing her children in the wilderness, is reused by a hymnographer who wanted to contrast God/Christ satisfying the Israelites with "honey from the rock" with Jesus's contemporaries offering him "gall" when he was on the cross: "Those who sucked honey from the rock [*ek petras meli thēlasantes*], they offered you gall [*cholēn*]" (Holy Friday, Third Hour, Troparion).

114. It is worthwhile to consider the intrinsic meaning of Ps 82 (81):1–4: the God of the Bible will not tolerate the mistreatment of the marginalized, powerless ones, but he will rather adjudicate whoever does this, be it "god" or human being, whoever abuses one's own power. The God of Israel is truly concerned with the execution of justice; justice is understood primarily as caring for the lost and marginalized. In poetical terms, Ps 82 (81) tells us that the gods' responsibilities are in fact ours, so no one can escape the primordial duty of implementing and defending justice. Ps 82 (81) in this existential reading tells us that there should be a nexus between theology and more earthly concerns and activities. Life and theology are inescapably interconnected.

115. Hossfeld and Zenger, *Psalms 2*, 334.

116. Dahood, *Psalms II*, 270.

117. Neyrey, " 'I Said: You Are Gods,' " 647–663.

118. The equation of "gods" with "angels" is attested in a wide array of ancient interpretations (Targum to the Psalms, Qumran, Peshitta, and Church Fathers).

119. This interpretation is found in *11QMelchizedek* (ca. 100 B.C.E.), a commentary on Jubilees (Lev 25), a fragmentary Dead Sea scroll, mentioning Melchizedek (cf. Gen 14:18–20) as leader of the angels of light battling the angels of darkness.

120. The term "gods" was applied to "judges" by the Talmud (*b. Ber.* 6a) and a midrash on Ps 82 (81). Note that Targum Onkelos of Exod 21:6 renders Heb. *ʾlhym*, "god(s)," as *dynyʾ*, "judges," initiating such an identification. Thus, the Heb. term *ʾlhym*, "god(s)," in Exod 21:6; Judg 5:8; and 1 Sam 2:25 has been conventionally explained as denoting "angels"; see Gordon, "*ʾlhym*," 139–144. However, given the ambiguity of the Heb. phrase *ʾl-ʾlhym ʾl-hdlt*, "to (before) God, to (before) the door" (in a forensic setting), found in the primary proof text (Exod 21:6), such a hurried identification seems quite implausible.

121. The following midrash connects Israel at Sinai with Adam in paradise: "The Holy one, blessed be he, said to them: 'I thought you would not sin and would live and endure forever like me; even as I live and endure forever and to all eternity; I said: You are gods, and all of you sons of the Most High [Ps 82:6], like the ministering angels, who are immortal. Yet after all this greatness, you wanted to die! 'Indeed, you shall die like men' [Ps 82:7]—Adam, i.e., like Adam whom I charged with one commandment which he was to perform and live and endure forever; as it says, 'Behold the man was as one of us' [Gen 3:22]. Similarly, 'And God created man in His own image' [Gen 1:27], that is to say, that he should live and endure like himself. Yet [says God] he corrupted his deeds and nullified my decree. For he ate of the tree, and I said to him: 'For dust you are' [Gen 3:19]. So also in your case, I said: 'You are gods' but you have ruined yourselves like Adam, and so 'Indeed, you shall die like Adam'" (*Numbers Rabbah* 16.24). This ancient Jewish interpretation saw a perfect parallel between Adam and Israel that can be summed up as follows: (1) created/restored in holiness; (2) and deathless; (3) yet sinned (forbidden fruit, golden calf); (4) and died; see Neyrey, "'I Said: You Are Gods,'" 655–657.

122. Mosser, "The Earliest Patristic Interpretations," 30–74.

123. Ackerman, "The Rabbinic Interpretation," 186–191.

124. See Russell, *The Doctrine of Deification*.

125. Excerpts from *Dialogue* 124 reproduced from *ANF* 1:261.

126. Mosser, "The Earliest Patristic Interpretations," 41.

127. Ibid., 49.

128. Ibid., 56.

129. Ibid., 56–57.

130. On Anselm's theology of the atonement and its relation to Greek Byzantine theology, see Lossky, "Redemption and Deification," 97–110.

Chapter 5

1. See Zakovitch, "Inner-Biblical Interpretation," 27–63.

2. MT reads "like a lion my hands and my feet," where *kʾry* was vocalized by Masoretes *kā-ʾărî*, "like a lion," leaving the clause with no verb; LXX reads *ōryxan*, "they gouged (dug)," which presupposes the same consonantal form, *kʾry*, with a different vocalization; based on the LXX reading, one can reconstruct the pre-MT vocalization,

kā(ʾ)rēy, an infinitive absolute of the verb **k-r-y > k-r-h*, "to dig," with an archaic final *-y* and an inserted *-ʾ-* as mater lectionis; see Pentiuc, *Jesus the Messiah*, 159–160.

3. Early Christian writers (e.g., Justin Martyr, Tertullian, Aphrahat, Theodoret of Cyrus, Diodor of Tarsus) follow the gospel tradition by developing the Christological use of Ps 22 (21), especially with respect to the overlooked v. 16b (17b) (LXX), "they gouged my feet and hands." According to Koltun-Fromm, "Psalm 22's Christological Interpretive Tradition," 37–38, the use of Ps 22:16b (21:17b) by early Christian writers is due to the Christian-Jewish polemic and the search for self-identification on the part of early Christianity. To the patristic authors, I would add Diodor of Tarsus: "I mentioned that the resemblance emerged more properly in the Lord's case to the extent of its being possible to see the nails driven into his hands and feet"; cf. Diodor of Tarsus, *Commentary on Psalms 1–51*, 72. And I would also add Theodoret of Cyrus: "This is obvious and clear even to the most contentious: we hear in the sacred Gospels the Lord himself saying to his holy disciples, 'Look at my hands and my feet for proof that I am here in person [Luke 24:39].' And he actually showed Thomas the marks of the nails and the blow of the spear [John 20:27]"; cf. Theodoret of Cyrus, *Commentary on the Psalms*, 150.

4. Patterson, "Psalm 22," 222.

5. Prior to the composition of this hymn, the use of "dogs" in Ps 22:16a (21:17a) as a metaphor for enemies most likely influenced Paul's warning in Phil 3:2, "Look out for the dogs [*kynas*]; look out for the evil workers [*kakous ergatas*]"; see Patterson, "Psalm 22," 228n83. Theodoret of Cyrus explains: "After the passion these former 'dogs' took on the status of children through faith, whereas those who once had enjoyed the care shown to children received the name of dogs for raging against the Lord. . . . Blessed Paul cries about them, 'Beware of the dogs, beware of the evildoers. Beware of mutilation' [Phil 3:2]" (*Commentary on the Psalms* 22.10); cf. Blaising and Hardin, *Psalms 1–50*, 172.

6. Mays, *Psalms*, 109.

7. Dahood, *Psalms I*, 140.

8. "The dogs that surrounded him and the council of the wicked were the rulers of the Jews, the scribes and high priests and the Pharisees, who spurred on the whole multitude to demand his blood against themselves and against their own children. Isaiah clearly calls them dogs when he says, 'You are all foolish dogs, unable to bark' [Isa 56:10]. For when it was their duty, even if they could not acquire the character of the shepherds, to protect like good sheepdogs their master's spiritual flock and the sheep of the house of Israel, and to warn by barking, and to fawn on their master and recognize him, and to guard the flock entrusted to them with all vigilance and to bark if necessary at enemies outside the fold, they preferred like senseless dogs, yes, like mad dogs, to drive the sheep wild by barking, so that the words aptly describe them that say, 'Many dogs have surrounded me; the council of the wicked has hemmed me in.' And all who even now conduct themselves like them in reviling and barking at the Christ of God in the same way may be reckoned their kin; yes, they who like these impious soldiers crucify the Son of God and put him to shame have a character very like theirs. Yes, all who today insult the body of Christ, that is, the church, and attempt to destroy the hands and feet and very bones are of their number" (Eusebius, *Proof of the Gospel* 10.8.505–506); cf. Blaising and Hardin, *Psalms 1–50*, 172–173.

9. Cogan, *I Kings*, 492.

10. Similarly, S: *shdʾ d-ʿwlʾ*; V: *testes iniqui*; but MT reads "violent witnesses" (*ʿēdēy ḥāmās*) (cf. Targum: *shdy ḥṭwpyn*). The term *ḥāmās* means "violence, wrong" (Ps 18:48 [17:49], of a violent man; cf. Gen 16:5, of the "wrong" the maidservant Hagar did to Sarah); see Pentiuc, *Jesus the Messiah*, 163–164.

11. Commonly considered an "individual lament" or "prayer" where the psalmist prays for his own deliverance from personal enemies, Ps 35 (34) is specifically a "royal psalm to be interpreted in an international context"; cf. Craigie, *Psalms 1–50*, 285.

12. Craigie, *Psalms 1–50*, 289.

13. Cf. *NPNF²* 7:90.

14. The LXX verb *kremazō*, "to hang," parallels the hymn's variant *kremamai*.

15. S: "the one who hangs the earth on nothing" (*w-tlʾ ʾrʿ ʿl lʾ mdm*); MT: "the one who stretches the Saphon over chaos [*tōhû*], the one who hangs [*tōlēh*] the earth on nothing [*ʿal-bəlî māh*]"; Targum: "the one who raises up [*zqyp*] the earth on the waters [*ʿly myʾ*] without any support to it [*mdlyt məʾm smyk lh*]."

16. Clines, *Job 21–37*, 635.

17. Pope, *Job*, 183.

18. Interestingly, as early as the sixth century, the Byzantine author of the text *Christian Topography* connects Job 26:7 to Ps 104 (103):5, emphasizing the same idea that the earth hangs on itself: "And with regard to the earth it is again written in Job: '*He that hangs the earth upon nothing*' [Job 26:7] meaning, that it had nothing underneath it. And David in harmony with this, when he could discover nothing on which it was founded, says: '*He that has founded the earth upon its own stability*' [Ps 104 [103]:5] as if he said it has been founded by you upon itself and not upon anything else"; cf. Laderman, "Cosmology, Art, and Liturgy," 126.

19. MT: *tōhû wā-bōhû*, "unformed and void," is a hendiadys, a lexical unit in which one of the terms explains the other, as in "a formless void." This phrase appears again in Jer 4:23–27, depicting a return to the primeval chaos; see Speiser, *Genesis*, 1:5.

20. LXX adds to the psalm's title, "a psalm of David" (MT), the words *tēs mias sabbatou*, "for the first day of the week," mirroring an early Jewish liturgical use of this psalm, read in light of the creation account of Gen 1.

21. As Craigie, *Psalms 1–50*, 212, rightly notices, Ps 24 (23) shows a "transformation of Ugaritic-Canaanite mythological language." As in the Ugaritic myth, where Baal's conquest of Yam leads to the former's renewed kingship, the same occurs in Ps 24 (23), where God's defeat of chaos culminates in the proclamation of his kingship (vv. 7–10).

22. Note that John Chrysostom uses a similar phrase to the one found in our hymn: "I adjure [*horkizō*] you by [*kata*] the one who hanged [*kremasantos*] the earth on [*epi*] the waters; I adjure you by the one who founded [*themeliōsantos*] the heavens in inaccessible spirals [*en abatois eilixin*]; I adjure you on [*eis*] the immovable [*asaleuton*] throne of God; I adjure you by the blessed powers [*makariōn dynameōn*] and the immaterial ranks [*aylōn tagmatōn*]" (Scr. Eccl. *In infirmos* [Sp.] [2062.417], p. 326, line 26; cf. *TLG*, ad locum). The only difference is that Chrysostom employs *epi*, "on," rather than *en*, "in." Was he aware of the targumic reading of Job 26:7 ("the one who raises [*zqyp*]

the earth over/on the waters without any support to it [*ʿly myʾ mdlyt mdʾm smyk lh*]")?
In any event, the presence of the more common preposition *epi*, "on," in Chrysostom's
passage suggests that the hymnographer meant to paint a different picture from that
of the earth floating *upon* the waters, namely, that the earth was hanging, by God's
power, *in* the midst of the waters. An almost identical phrase to the one in our hymn is
found in Didymus the Blind. After quoting fragmentally Ps 136 (135):6 and Job 26:7,
Didymus continues: "For if it [earth] has been founded [*tethemeliōtai*] in the sea [Ps
24 (23]:2), then it has no stiff [*sklēron*] and hard [*antitypon*] foundation, but it has the
characteristic that it hangs [*kremasthai*] *in* the waters [*en tois hydasi*], and any water
[*pan hydōr*] has some ground [*edaphos*] that strives against [*anterizon*] it" (Scr. Eccl.
Commentarii in Psalmos 22–26.10 [2102.017], Codex p. 66, line 8; cf. *TLG*, ad locum).
The renditions of the *TLG* texts are mine.

23. Fragmenta e cod. Vat. gr. 1236. [2934.018]; cf. *TLG*, ad locum. The rendition of the
TLG text is mine.

24. "He who hung the earth is hanging [*ho kremasas tēn gēn krematai*]. He who fixed
[*pēxas*] the heavens in place has been fixed in place [*pepektai*]. He who laid the
foundations [*stērixas*] of the universe has been laid on a tree [*epi xylou estēriktai*]. The
master has been profaned [*parybristai*]. God has been murdered [*pephoneutai*]. The
King of Israel has been destroyed [*anēretai*] by an Israelite right hand" (*Peri Pascha*,
96); cf. "This is the one made flesh in a virgin [*en parthenō sarkōtheis*], who was
hanged on a tree [*ho epi xylou kremastheis*], who was buried in the earth [*ho eis gēn
tapheis*], who was raised from the dead [*ho ek nekrōn anastatheis*], who was exalted
to the heights of heaven [*eis ta hypsēla . . . analēmphthei*]" (*Peri Pascha*, 70); for the
Gk. text, see Méliton de Sardes, *Sur la Pâque et fragments*, 98, 116, 118; for the English
translation, see Melito of Sardis, *On Pascha*, 56, 64.

25. Mays, *Psalms*, 120.

26. Cf. Ps 104 (103):5 (LXX): "He founded [*ethemeliōsen*] the earth on its stability [*epi
tēn asphaleian autēs*]"; MT: "He established [*yāsad*] the earth on its foundation [*ʿl-
məkôneyhā*]"; Targum: "the one who establishes [*dy mysd*] the earth on its foundation
[*ʿlwy bsysh*]."

27. It is worth noting that the Assyro-Babylonian god Apsu, the body of sweet water beneath the earth, where the god Ea-Enki dwells, is called the "house of wisdom"; cf.
Fox, *Proverbs 1–9*, 297.

28. Similarly, Neophytus Inclusus (Scr. Eccl. *Decem homiliae* [3085.004], *Homily 4*, section 40, line 7; cf. *TLG*, ad locum), referring to Jesus's crucifixion, uses the preposition *epi*, "on," and the verb *hedrazō*, "to establish": "For the day light [*to phōs to
hēmerinon*] seeing you crucified [*staurōthenta*], the true light coming into the world
and illuminating any human being, namely the one who believes, turned into darkness [*meteblēthē pros skotos*], hiding itself away [*apekrybē*]. Likewise, the earth shook
thoroughly [*gē synetromaxen*] seeing you hanged [*kremasthenta*] on the cross [*en
tō staurō*], the one who established it [the earth] on waters [*ton autēn epi hydatōn
hedrasanta*]" (my rendition).

29. Note Origen's comments on the symbolism of "scarlet robe" and "crown of thorns": "So
now, in taking up the 'scarlet robe,' he took upon himself the blood of the world, and

in that thorny 'crown' plaited on his head, he took upon himself the thorns of our sins. As to the robe, it is written that 'they stripped him of the scarlet robe.' But as to the crown of thorns, the evangelists mention nothing further. Apparently they wanted us to determine what happened to that crown of thorns placed on his head and never removed. My belief is that the crown of thorns disappeared from the head of Jesus, so that our former thorns no longer exist now that Jesus has removed them from us once and for all on his own distinguished head" (*Commentary on Matthew* 125); cf. Simonetti, *Matthew 14–28*, 285.

30. Cf. Danker, "Purple," 5:557–560.

31. Haenchen, *John 1*, 181.

32. See the section "The Sacred Washing of the Feet" in chapter 4. The only difference between that hymn and the current one is that in the former, the word *polon*, "axis" occurs in place of "sky" ("wraps the *sky* in clouds," *ho nephelais de ton polon periballōn*).

33. Havrelock, *River Jordan*, 162–163.

34. On this *theologoumenon*, see the discussion in chapter 6.

35. For Cyril of Jerusalem, Christ's descent into the Jordan aimed at wrestling with the adverse powers by overpowering them, as in the logion of Luke 11:21–22, and plundering their fortress: "According to Job, there was in the waters the dragon that *draweth up Jordan into his mouth* [Job 40:23]. Since, therefore, it was necessary to break the heads of the dragon in pieces [Ps 74 [73]:14], He [Jesus] went down and bound the strong one in the waters, that we might receive power to *tread upon serpents and scorpions* [Luke 10:19]. The beast was great and terrible.... The Life encountered him, that the mouth of Death might henceforth be stopped" (*Catechetical Lecture* 3; cf. *NPNF²* 7:17).

36. On textual differences between MT and LXX of Isa 7:14 (*^calmāh/parthenos*), as well as the meanings of the phrase *hyios tou anthrōpou*, "son of man" (Dan 7:13), see Pentiuc, *Jesus the Messiah*, 52–55, 95–99.

37. This paradox is masterfully conveyed by the two following hymns: "Today is the summary [*kephalaion*] of our salvation, and the disclosure [*phanerōsis*] of the age-old mystery: The Son of God [*hyios tou theou*] becomes [*ginetai*] the Son of the Virgin [*hyios tou parthenou*], and Gabriel heralds the good news of grace [*tēn charin euangelizetai*]" (March 25, The Annunciation, Vespers, Apolitikion 1); "Equal [*isos*] to the Father, the Son of the Virgin [*hyios tou parthenou*], the Word [*logos*] of God, is a perfect Person [*hypostasis teleia*] in two natures [*en dyo physin*], Jesus the Lord, perfect God and man [*theos teleios kai anthrōpos*]" (Octateochos, Sunday, Matins, Ode 5, Mode 3).

38. This type of hymn, where a monologue/dialogue is introduced by the narrator, goes back as far as the fourth to fifth centuries—Syriac hymnography—a common characteristic of the *Sôgithâ* (the Byzantine kontakion borrows the dramatic decor from these Syriac liturgical productions); cf. Wellesz, "The Nativity Drama," 145.

39. Here is another hymn, written in the third person, where the narrator sets a contrast between God's acts in the past and Israel's present acts toward the crucified Lord: "Israel's senseless [*agnōmones*] children who sucked [*thēlasantes*] the honey

from the rock, offered you, Christ, who worked wonders [*teratourgēsanti*] in the wilderness, gall; instead of manna, they gave you in exchange [*ēmeipsanto*] vinegar for your kindness [*euergesian*]" (Octoechos, Sunday, Matins, Ode 3, Mode 5). The following hymn contrasts Jesus's benevolent acts with his contemporaries' ungratefulness, this time with no reference to the Exodus period: "Oh! How the unlawful [*paranomos*] synagogue condemned [*katedikase*] to death the king of creation [*basilea tēs ktiseōs*], with no respect [*aidestheisa*] for the kind acts [*euergesias*] that he, reminding [*anamimnēskōn*], made previously secure [*proēsphalizeto*], saying to them: 'My people, what have I done to you? Did I not fill Judaea with miracles [*thaumatōn*]? Did I not raise [*exanestēsa*] the dead with but a word? Did I not treat [*etherapeusa*] every weakness [*malakian*] and disease [*noson*]? And what did you give me in return [*antapodidote*]? How did you remember [*amnēmoneite*] me? For healings [*iamatōn*], you inflicted wounds [*plēgas*] on me; for life, you put [me] to death [*nekrountes*]; you hang [*kremōntes*] the benefactor [*euergetēn*] to a tree [*xylō*] as a malefactor [*kakourgon*], the Lawgiver [*nomodotēn*] as an outlaw [*paranomon*], the King of all as a condemned [*katakriton*]: O long-suffering [*makrothyme*] Lord, glory to you" (Holy Saturday, Vespers, Sticheron).

40. Bergren, "Tradition-History," 46.
41. The *Improperia* have a quite intricate history going back as far as the ninth century. The earliest evidence of these hymns known as *Popule meus* (the repeated refrain) is found in a liturgical manuscript dated to 880 and written at the Abbey of Saint Denis for the Cathedral of Senlis in France. Brou, "Les Impropères du Vendredi-Saint" ("Introduction"; "Les formules mozarabes"; "Les formules de Jérusalem"; "Les precedents latins"), argues for a Western origin of the *Improperia*.
42. Karim, "'My People,'" 3. On the history of the *Improperia*, see the classic study by Drumbl, "Die Improperien," 68–100.
43. Koltun-Fromm, "Psalm 22's Christological Interpretive Tradition," 44.
44. "But this suffering was due to his [Jesus's] own choice. It was ordained that he should suffer on a tree, since the inspired writer attributes to him the following words: 'Save me from the sword' [Ps 22:21[21:22]], and, 'Nail through my flesh [*kathēlōson tas sarkas mou*]' [Ps 119 [118]:120], 'because bands of evildoers have risen against me' [Ps 22:16 [21:17]]"; cf. Kleist, *The Didache*, 44; see Koltun-Fromm, "Psalm 22's Christological Interpretive Tradition," 45.
45. Cf. Barnard, *St. Justin Martyr*, 47.
46. Koltun-Fromm, "Psalm 22's Christological Interpretive Tradition," 37–57. Koltun-Fromm notes that "[t]his contextualization within anti-Jewish polemics may also explain why this particular exegesis on Psalm 22 does not appear universally in other ante-Nicene writings, for neither Clement, Ignatius, nor Tatian interpret it thus. While Origen notes in his *De Principiis* that the entire psalm speaks of Jesus, in his commentary on Psalm 22, he makes no remarks concerning verses 17 nor 18" (p. 53).
47. Cf. Jas 2:1. A similar title, *ho basileus tēs doxēs*, "the King of Glory," emphasizing also God's power and majesty, is found frequently in the pages of the Old Testament; e.g., Ps 24 (23):8–10 (LXX): "Who is this King of Glory? The Lord mighty [*krataios*] and powerful [*dynatos*], the Lord, powerful in battle. Raise [*arate*] the gates, O you rulers

[*archontes*]! And be raised up [*eparthēte*], O eternal gates [*pylai aiōnioi*]! And the King of Glory shall enter [*eiseleusetai*]. Who is this King of Glory? The Lord of the powers [*kyrios tōn dynameōn*], he is the King of Glory [*ho basileus tēs doxēs*]."

48. With a polemical twist, Peter, on the day of Pentecost, proclaims essentially the same thing as Paul: "Therefore, let the entire house of Israel know with certainty that God made this Jesus whom you crucified [*estaurōsate*] both Lord [*kyrion*] and Christ [*Christon*]" (Acts 2:36); cf. Ps 29 (28):3, "God of Glory" (*ho theos tēs doxēs*).

49. The same terms occur in each of the two stories: Jacob (Gen 35:3 [*thlipsis*]; 48:16 [*rhyomai*]) and the children of Israel (Exod 4:31 [*thlipsis*]; cf. 3:9 [*thlimmos*, a biform of *thlipsis*]; 6:6 [*rhyomai*]).

50. On Jesus's identification with God the Creator, see Bucur, "Exegesis of Biblical Theophanies," 91–112.

51. See Barkhuizen, "Romanos' Encomium," 91–106.

52. Aus, *Two Puzzling Baptisms*, 16–17.

53. Cf. Ugaritic Baal, "the cloud rider" (*rkb ʿrpt*), *Baal Cycle*. For an interesting analysis of the differences between Baal and Yahweh regarding the attribute of "cloud riding" in the ANE religious context, see Smith, *The Early History of God*, 81–82.

54. Garrett, *Song of Songs/Lamentations*, 423.

55. Similarly, in Byzantine hymnography, the "(pillar of) cloud" symbolizes divine protection and guidance and by consequence is often employed as an attribute for the Theotokos, the Protectress of the Church, as in the following hymn: "The cloud in the Law [Pentateuch] [*nephelē hē nomikē*], that covered [*kalyptousa*] the Tent of Witness [Tabernacle], prefigured [*etypou*] of old your [Theotokos's] holy protection [*skepēn*]; for on each occasion [*ekastote*] you cover [*kalypteis*], besprinkle [*drosizeis*], and warm [*thalpeis*] the Church, O Pure One, with the overshadowing [*episkiasei*] of your veil [*skepēs*]" (October 28, The Holy Protection of the Theotokos, Matins, Ode 1, Canticle 23).

56. Similarly, "In the past, Christ led Israel in the wilderness with a pillar of fire and cloud; and today ineffably he has shone forth in light on Mount Tabor" (The Transfiguration, Matins, Ode 3, Sticheron).

57. On manna, in conjunction with ambrosia, see the section on "The Mystical Supper" in chapter 4.

58. Hagner, *Matthew 14–28*, 834.

59. See the section on "The Mystical Supper" in chapter 4.

60. The Targum Onkelos on Num 21:16 interprets: "At that time the well was given to them, that is the well about which the Lord told Moses, 'Gather the people together, and I will give them water.' So Israel offered this praise, 'Rise O well, sing to it.' The well which the princes dug, the leaders of the people dug, the scribes, with their staffs, and it was given to them, since wilderness. Now since it was given to them, it went down with them to the valleys, and from the valleys it went up with them to the high country. And from the high country to the descents of the Moabite fields, at the summit of the height, which looks out toward Beth Yeshimon"; cf. Grossfeld, *The Targum Onqelos*, 126. Although the targumic reading betrays a degree of elaboration (i.e., the "rock" is replaced by a "well"), the same central idea dating back to the

first century C.E., a movable water source, is found in both 1 Cor 10 and the Targum Onkelos. One may add that Paul's remark "the rock that followed them" is not his own invention but rather relies on a broader Jewish tradition resulting from a midrashic combination of various biblical texts; see Enns, "The 'Moveable Well;'" 28. For more on 1 Cor 10 and the "traveling rock," see chapter 4 of the present volume, under "Hymnography."

61. Chromatius of Aquileia expands on the same idea: "When they had come to Golgotha, the Gospel says, 'They gave him vinegar mixed with gall, but when he tasted it, he refused to drink.' This event was foretold by David when he wrote, 'They gave me gall for food, and they gave me vinegar to slake my thirst' [Ps 69:21/68:22]. Take note of the mystery revealed here. Long ago, Adam tasted the sweetness of the apple and obtained the bitterness of death for the whole human race. In contrast to this, the Lord tasted the bitterness of gall and obtained our restoration from death's sting to the sweetness of life. He took on himself the bitterness of gall in order to extinguish in us the bitterness of death. He received acrid vinegar into himself but poured out for us the precious wine of his blood. He suffered evil and returned good. He accepted death and gave life" (*Tractate on Matthew* 19.7); cf. Simonetti, *Matthew 14–28*, 287.

62. A similar interpretation may be found in Origen: "Just as it sufficed for the Lord only to taste 'vinegar mixed with gall,' so also was it sufficient for our benefit that he only taste death, which lasted no longer than three days. The other wine, however, which was not 'mixed with gall' or with anything else, he took and drank, and 'when he had given thanks' [Matt 26:27] he gave it to his disciples, promising that he would drink it 'anew in the kingdom of God' [Matt 26:29]" (*Commentary on Matthew* 12.7); cf. Simonetti, *Matthew 14–28*, 287.

63. Bergren, "The Structure and Composition of 5 Ezra," 115–139.

64. Luz, *Matthew 21–28*, 626.

65. Bergren, "The Structure and Composition of 5 Ezra," 115.

66. Jerome, *Commentary on Jeremiah*, 11.

67. Holladay, *Jeremiah* 1, 91. The text of Hos 10:10 ("I came to discipline them and peoples will gather against them as they are disciplined for their two injustices") is not very clear: MT (*kativ*) has *ͨēynōtam*, "their springs" (rendered "furrows" by KJV, TNK); many mss. and *qere* of MT read *l-šty ͨwntm*, "for their double iniquity" (similarly, LXX [*adikiais*], S [*sklwthwn*], V [*iniquitates*]).

68. Cf. *PL* 25:908. Church Fathers saw in the "double iniquity" an allusion to apostasy (abandoning God) and idolatry (attachment to idols). Thus, Theophylact of Ohrid interprets: "They abandoned me, their benefactor, and they ran to the senseless and useless idols" (*Exposition on Hosea*, Hos 10:10 [*PG* 126:748A]; similarly, Cyril of Alexandria (*Commentary on Hosea* [*PG* 71:252B]); Julian of Eclanum (*Commentary on Hosea* [*PG* 21:1013C–D]); Theodoret of Cyrus (*Interpretation of Hosea* [*PG* 81:1608B–C]); Theodore of Mopsuestia (*Commentary on Hosea* [*PG* 66:188A]); see Pentiuc et al., *Hosea*, 249–258.

69. Tertullian sees in the darkness an "omen" foretelling the future, claiming that the phenomen was recorded in Roman archives: "And yet, nailed upon the cross, He exhibited many notable signs, by which his death was distinguished from all others.

At his own free will, he with a word dismissed from him his spirit, anticipating the executioner's work. In the same hour, too, the light of day was withdrawn, when the sun at the very time was in its meridian blaze. Those who were not aware that this had been predicted about Christ, no doubt thought it an eclipse. You yourselves have the account of the world-portent still in your archives" (*Apology* 21); cf. *ANF* 3:34–36. Origen explains the "darkness" as an eclipse (during Tiberius's reign, around 29 C.E., felt in other parts of the empire), based on Phlegon of Tralles (second century C.E.): *Against Celsus* 2.23; cf. *ANF* 4:441. In the ninth century, the Byzantine chronicler George Syncellus cites the third-century Christian historian Sextus Julius Africanus, who mentions that another historian, by the name of Thallus, doubted that the darkness that occurred at the crucifixion was an eclipse; see Van Voorst, *Jesus outside the New Testament*, 20–22. However, as Fitzmyer, *The Gospel According to Luke 10–24*, rightly observes, an eclipse at the Passover (full-moon time) would be impossible: "However, it should be noted that Thucydides (*Hist.* 2.28) speaks of an eclipse of the sun at *noumēnia*, 'new moon.' The darkening of the sun is otherwise known in the Mediterranean area, as an effect of the *ḥamsîn* or searing sirocco" (p. 1517).

70. Fitzmyer, *The Gospel According to Luke 10–24*, 1517.

71. If the Jewish reader was accustomed to the "darkness" of the "Day of the Lord," the pagan reader was also familiar with heavenly portents (Gk. *terata*, Lat. *prodigia*) announcing the deaths of princes and heroes; see Bovon, *Luke 3*, 324.

72. MT reads *ywm l*-YHWH *ṣb'wt*, "Day of Yahweh of the Hosts," that is, heavenly hosts (cf. Gen 2:1, of the creation of heavens and earth along with *kl-ṣb'm*, "all their hosts"; LXX: *kosmos autōn*, "all their order").

73. Cf. Ferreiro, *The Twelve Prophets*, 112.

74. On "hermeneutical pointers," see the section on "Hermeneutical Procedures" in chapter 7.

75. Note Ephrem the Syrian's similar interpretation: "That sun also, the lamp of mankind, extinguished itself. He took the veil of darkness and spread it out before his face so that he would not see the shame of the Sun of righteousness [Mal 3:20] in whose light the angels from above shine. Creation staggered and heaven inclined. Sheol vomited the dead people and spat them out" (*De Crucifixione* 4.14); cf. Botha, "The Paradox," 38. Ephrem's hymn *De Crucifixione* 4 underscores the paradox that even though they were intended to humiliate Jesus, the trial and crucifixion brought honor to the one who endured all for the salvation of the world. For instance, nature's participation (e.g., the sun "taking the veil of darkness") eclipses the people's crass ingratitude.

76. Cf. Just, *Luke*, 368.

77. Ibid.

78. Cf. Melito, *On Pascha*, 64. Somehow, similar feelings of "shamefulness" and "horror" experienced by nature at men's "lawless deeds" against men and "unlawful acts" against gods are described in a letter, reproduced by the Jewish historian Josephus, sent by Mark Antony to Hyrcanus, the high priest and leader of the Jews (42 B.C.E.). In his letter, Mark Antony narrates how in one of his battles, he fought against those "who were guilty both of lawless deeds against men [*eis anthrōpous paranomiōn*] and of unlawful acts against the gods [*eis theous hamartēmatōn*], from which we believe

the very sun turned away [*hellion apestraphthai*], as if it too were loath [*aēdōs*] to look upon the foul deed [*to mysos*] against Caesar" (Josephus, *Antiquities* 14:309); cf., Fitzmyer, *The Gospel According to Luke 10–24*, 1518.

79. To paraphrase the title of Richard John Neuhaus's classic *Death on a Friday Afternoon*.

80. Isa 53:7b is part of the so-called Fourth Song of the Servant (Isa 52:13–53:12): "The Suffering Servant of God: His Life, Death and Exaltation. The Rehabilitation of the Servant of God in a Heavenly Court"; see Baltzer, *Deutero-Isaiah*, 392–429.

81. Baltzer, *Deutero-Isaiah*, 414.

82. *Midrash Tanchuma*, 32b notes: "Hadrian said to R. Jehoshua [ca. 90 C.E.]: 'There is something great about the sheep [Israel] that can persist among seventy wolves [the nations]. He replied: Great is the Shepherd who delivers it and watches over it and destroys them [the wolves] before them [Israel]"; cf. Jeremias, "*Amnos*," 1:340.

83. In another hymn, quite similar in content to this one, the word *amnos*, "one-year-old lamb," is used as a metaphor for Jesus: "When the ewe lamb [*amnas*] saw the lamb [*amnon*] and shepherd [*poimena*], and redeemer [*lytrōtēn*] on the cross, she lamented [*ololyze*] with tears and bitterly cried out: 'On the one hand, the world rejoices [*agalletai*] receiving redemption [*lytrōsin*], on the other hand my inward parts are on flame [*splanchna mou phlegontai*] seeing your crucifixion [*staurōsin*]'" (September 9, Matins, Ode 3, Kathisma).

84. Holladay, *Jeremiah 1*, 372.

85. Jeremias, "*Amnos*," 1:339, notes that the designation of Jesus as "lamb" (*amnos*) could arise only in a bilingual territory, hence its exclusive occurrence in the Johannine literature (John 1:29, 36; twenty-nine times in Rev); note that Acts 8:32 and 1 Pet 1:19 compare Jesus with a lamb without designating him as such. In Aramaic, *talyā'* means both "lamb" and "boy, servant"; hence, John the Baptist's reconstructed Aramaic statement *talyā' d-'ĕlāhā'* could have been understood by the gospel writer either way, i.e., "Lamb of God" (*ho amnos tou theou*) or "Servant of God" (*ho pais tou theou*; cf. Josh 14:7, of Moses called "servant of God")—both images are found in Isa 53. John 1:29, 36, chose the former option in its Gk. rendition, though the latter would have been more appropriate with "God" as qualifier. See Haenchen, *John 1*, 152, who considers Jeremias's interpretation unlikely.

86. Cf. Johns, *The Lamb Christology*, 81.

87. According to the ancient Israelite Law, a sacrificial animal should be at least eight days old (Exod 22:29; Lev 22:27). As for the Paschal lamb (*probaton*) of Exod 12:5, it should be a one-year-old male animal from sheep or goats. By choosing the term *arēn*, "young lamb less than one year old," presumably the hymnographer did not intend to identify Jesus expressly with a Paschal lamb.

88. Levine, *Leviticus*, 28.

89. Melito's homily *Peri Pascha* (*On the Pascha*) was probably part of the baptism ritual to be performed on Good Friday. In the time of Melito, the Easter celebration was only one feast day, hence surmising that *On the Pascha* was read on Good Friday is an anachronism. Melito was one of the main representatives of the Quartodecimans (Christians who celebrated Easter on the fourteenth of Nisan at the same time as the Jewish Passover). In style, *On the Pascha* looks like a Passover Haggadah; cf. Manis,

"Meliton of Sardis," 387–401. This homily is a typological interpretation of Easter in relation to the Jewish Passover (e.g., the blood of the Paschal lamb foreshadows the saving blood of Christ).

90. Cf. Gambero, *Mary and the Fathers of the Church*, 49–50; see the critical edition of Melito's Paschal homily, Méliton de Sardes, *Sur la Pâque*.

91. Méliton de Sardes, *Sur la Pâque*, 176.

92. Constas, *Proclus of Constantinople*, 228.

93. Leroy, *L'homilētique de Procles de Constantinople*, 208; Constas, *Proclus of Constantinople*, 240.

94. On the messianic title "Son of Man" (*hyios anthrōpou*; e.g., Mark 2:10; 8:31; Matt 8:20; 25:31; Luke 19:10), going back to Dan 7:13 (Aramaic *bar ʾĕnāš*), see the discussion in chapter 6. One may stress here again that this messianic title points to Jesus's humanity in its defining aspects: weakness and mortality.

95. Winston, *The Wisdom of Solomon*, 273.

96. Cf. Behr, "Irenaeus of Lyons," 53–54.

97. Steenberg, "The Role of Mary," 117–137.

98. Cf. Jer 51 (28):13; Prov 26:22; 2 Macc 9:5, 6; 4 Macc 10:8; Acts 1:18 (of Judas's horrible end) and, metaphorically, "emotions, feelings" (the inward part is the seat of feelings, emotions; Prov 12:10; Wis 10:5; Luke 1:78; 2 Cor 6:12; Phil 2:1; Col 3:12); hence, the denominative verb *splanchnizō* (in LXX, a hapax legomenon, "to share in sacrifices," targeting the animal's entrails, 2 Macc 6:8), attested as *splanchnizomai* in the New Testament, "to have pity, compassion, to feel sympathy," implying a commotion of one's entrails. It points to an almost visceral "compassion, love" that only a mother can feel for her children (e.g., Jesus being moved "viscerally" with "motherly" compassion, Matt 14;14; 18:27; Mark 1:41; 6:34; 8:2; Luke 7:13; a loving father receiving back his prodigal son, Luke 15:20). The adjective *mētrōa*, "of mother, motherly," is a biblical hapax legomenon (4 Macc 13:19, a "motherly womb" [*mētrōas gastros*]). In our hymn, *mētrōa* is construed with *splanchna*, meaning "motherly affections," the two phrases remaining quite close to each other in their basic meaning ("mother's womb/ compassion").

99. See Smith, *Micah-Malachi*, 349.

100. For instance, Ambrose writes: "Do not, therefore, without due consideration put your trust in the sun. It is true that it is the eye of the world, the joy of the day, the beauty of the heavens, the charm of nature and the most conspicuous creation. When you behold it, reflect on its author. When you admire it, give praise to its creator. If the sun as consort of and participant in nature is so pleasing, how much goodness is there to be found in that Sun of justice? If the sun is so swift that in its rapid course by day and night it is able to traverse all things, how great is he who is always and everywhere and fills all things with his majesty [Ps 72 [71]:17–19]! If that which is bidden to come forth is deemed worthy of our admiration of whom we read, 'Who commands the sun and it rises not!' [Job 9:7]. If the sun which the succession of the seasons advances or recedes is mighty, how mighty must he be also who 'when he emptied himself' [Phil 2:7] that we might be able to see him, who 'was

the true light that enlightens every man who comes into this world!' [John 1:9]" (*Six Days of Creation* 4.1.2); cf. Ferreiro, *The Twelve Prophets*, 309.

Chapter 6

1. Mays, *Psalms*, 331.
2. Dahood, *Psalms III*, 33.
3. In Gen 1:3, "light" is differentiated from "luminaries" (sun, moon, stars) which are created on the fourth day (vv. 14–19). Only light is created exclusively by word with no different verb of completion: "Let there be . . . and it was." There is no other creature with which the Creator is so closely associated as the light—he calls the light "good," while on the other days, his creative work (not a specific creature) is labeled "good" (e.g., inter alia, v. 10); see Noort, "The Creation of Light," 11.
4. Referring to God, e.g., Tapharensis, *Disputatio cum Herbano Judaeo* (*PG* 86:784B); Joannes IV Constantinopolitanus, *Sermo de Poenitentia* (*PG* 88:1921A); as a neuter noun, e.g., Theodore the Studite, *Epistularum Libri Duo* 2.121 (*PG* 99:1396C).
5. On the verb *kremannymi*, "to hang," see the section "Hanged on a Tree" in chapter 5.
6. See the discussion on *skotos*, "darkness," and the episode narrated by Luke 23:44–45a in chapter 5.
7. Note Heb 12:18, where *zophos* (Byz. has *skotos*, "darkness") has a positive connotation with reference to the "darkness" concealing God during his conversation with Moses on Mount Sinai (cf. Exod 20:21; MT: ʿǎrāpēl; LXX: *gnophos*]). On *zophōdēs*, "dark," related to *zophos*, "darkness," see the discussion in chapter 3.
8. The phrase *hypo zophon*, "under darkness," is used in Greek poetry to designate the underworld (Homer, *Iliad* 21:56; Hesiod, *Theogony* 729; Aeschylus, *Persians* 839; odes of Solomon 11:37); see Bauckham, *2 Peter*, 53.
9. Note the LXX verb *diarrēssō/diarrēgnymi*, "to rend," in passive, "to be dashed to pieces" (of Judah's enemies); the LXX verb renders the Heb. verb *b-q-ʿ*, "to split, to dash to pieces" (2 Chr 25:12); Mark 15:38: *to katapetasma tou naou eschisthē*, "the curtain of the Temple was torn in two"—the verb *schizō*, "to split, to tear," is used here. The hymnographer's use of *diarrēgnymi* might imply a solid structure or, more probably, suggest an "utter" destruction of the separating curtain, whatever material it might have been made of.
10. Based on extra-biblical sources (primarily Mishnah and Josephus), one learns that in the Herodian Temple, extant in Jesus's time, inside the sanctuary (*naos*) and in front of the Holy of Holies, there was a single "veil" (*katapetasma*; *m. Scheq.* 5.1.2; 8:4; *m. Men.* 3:6; *m. Mid.* 1:1; *m. Tam.* 7:1; yet *Jewish War* 5.5.4, paragraph 212, implies a "door"). Note that not all these sources have the same historical value. For instance, *Middot* is dependent on the vision of Ezekiel (41:24) and not on memory. Since Josephus was present at the siege of Jerusalem by the Romans in 70 C.E., his writings (especially *Jewish War* 5) carry more weight than other sources; see Gurtner, "The Veil of the Temple," 102–103.

11. Schneider, "*Katapetasma*," 3:629–630.

12. Gurtner, "The Veil of the Temple," 111.

13. Ulansey, "The Heavenly Veil Torn," 124.

14. Death as "sleep" occurs forty-one times in the Old Testament (e.g., inter alia, Jer 51 [28]:39, 57; Dan 12:2; Ps 13 [12]:3; 90 [89]:5; 1 Kgs 11:43) and fifteen times in the New Testament (Matt 9:24; 27:52; John 11:11; Acts 7:60; 13:36; 1 Cor 11:30; 15:6, 18, 20, 51; Eph 5:14; 1 Thess 4:13–15; 5:10).

15. Besides Jer 51 (28):39, *hypnoō*, "to sleep," as a metaphor for death appears only in Ps 13:3 (12:4) (*hypnōsō eis thanaton*, "[less] I sleep [the sleep] of death"), being unattested in the New Testament, where the verbs *katheudō*, "to lie down to sleep" (Matt 9:24, of the daughter of Jair), and *koimaomai*, "to fall asleep" (Matt 27:52, of the dead who rose when Jesus yielded his spirit on the cross; John 11:11, of Lazarus's death; 1 Cor 15:6, of eyewitnesses of Jesus's resurrection who subsequently died) are employed. Nevertheless, note that in John 11:13 (of Lazarus's sickness), the noun *hypnos*, "sleep," is used as a euphemism for death.

16. Summing up Jer 51 (28):38–40, God is about to punish Babylon for its excesses. While being in power (i.e., "heat"), compared with lions, God will "give them drink [*potēma*] and made them drunk [*methysō*] in order to be stupefied [*karōthōsin*] and sleep a perpetual sleep and never wake [*mē egerthōsi*]." Here, Jeremiah delivered a prophetic word that happened in reality if one considers the testimony of ancient historians, such as Herodotus (*Histories* 1.191, 211) or Xenophon (*Cyropaedia* 7.5): the Babylonians fell to King Cyrus of Persia, without a fight. They were celebrating when the Persians besieged Babylon. Jeremiah minutely described it as if he were an eyewitness to that final party leading to utter destruction: the Babylonians became drunk, were stupefied, and fell asleep, but under the Persians' attack, that alcohol-induced sleep turned into a "perpetual sleep" (i.e., death). The moral of this historical episode is that under God, even powerful lions can end up like lambs being led to slaugter; see Lundbom, *Jeremiah 37–52*, 391, 477.

17. See the discussion of "The One Who Shut the Abyss" below.

18. MT has *kāraʾ rābaṣ kəʾaryēh û-kəlābîʾ* "like a lion and lioness, he bowed down and crouched."

19. Brueggemann, *Genesis*, 365.

20. Wenham, *Genesis 16–50*, 476.

21. Cf. Sheridan, *Genesis 11–50*, 328.

22. Cf. Sarna, *Genesis*, 336.

23. Aune, *Revelation 1–5:14*, 349.

24. SC 140:46–48; cf. Sheridan, *Genesis 11–50*, 328.

25. On Ps 82 (81), see the discussion in chapter 4. It is worth noting that Jesus, who is about to be stoned by the crowd for claiming that he is the Son of God, makes use of Ps 82 (81):6 ("I said, 'Gods you are, and sons of the Most High'") in self-defense: "Jesus answered them, 'Is it not written in your law, "I said, you are gods"? If he called them gods to whom the Word of God came (and Scripture cannot be broken), do you say of him whom the Father consecrated and sent into the world, "You are blaspheming," because I said, "I am the Son of God"?'" (John 10:34–36 [NRSV]). This Johannine

text reflects a common ancient Jewish interpretation that "gods" in Ps 82 (81) are the Israelites who received the Word from God but did not observe it; see Mays, *Psalms*, 270.

26. Cf. Sheridan, *Genesis 11–50*, 328.

27. Ibid.

28. I.e., a sacrifice offered out of an impulse of the heart (Exod 35:20–29; Lev 22:18 [MT: *ndbh*, "voluntary gift"; LXX *kata pasan hairesin*, "according to any choice"]; 7:16; Deut 16:9–12; 2 Chr 31:14; Ezra 1:4–6; Ezek 46:11–12; Amos 4:5).

29. The Prayer of Manasseh is a short poetic book written in Gk. In Eastern Orthodox tradition, this book is an *anaginoskomenon* ("to be read aloud"). 2 Chr 33:11–13 narrates how the evil king Manasseh, while imprisoned in Babylon, repents for the sin of idolatry and God restores him to Jerusalem. The composition date of Pr Man referred to in 2 Chr 33:18 is placed in the second to the first century B.C.E. The prayer is at the same time a confession and a petition for forgiveness purporting to be uttered or written by Manasseh, king of Judah in the seventh century B.C.E., the successor of King Hezekiah. In LXX, the prayer occurs in the Odes attached to the Psalter. In V, this prayer comes after 2 Chr, and in NRSV, it appears after 1 Esd.

30. See the discussion in Tsumura, "The Doctrine of Creation," 3–22.

31. Perhaps influenced by Plato's *Timaeus* 50–51 (*anoraton . . . amorphon*, "invisible and unformed"); note that the second-century C.E. Jewish Gk. translation by Aquila renders the Heb. phrase as *kenōma kai outhen*, "an emptiness and a nothing"; V has *inanis et vacua*, "void and empty"; the Targums Onkelos and Jonathan have *ṣdy wrwqny*, "desolate and empty," but Targum Pseudo-Jonathan leaves the phrase untranslated; see Tsumura, "The Doctrine of Creation," 12–13, 18.

32. Tsumura, "The Doctrine of Creation," 3.

33. Tromp, *Primitive Conceptions of Death*, 59.

34. While not a loanword from Akk., Heb. *təhôm* and its suggested Akk. counterpart *tiamtum* derive from a proto-Semitic form *tihām*, meaning "ocean" or "many waters"; cf. Tsumura, "The Doctrine of Creation," 8.

35. Gunkel, *Creation and Chaos*, 82.

36. Waschke, "*Tᵉhôm*," 15:577.

37. In LXX, *abyssos*, "abyss," is used to render *təhôm*, "deep." It is used once in the plural (Ps 71 [70]:20) to designate the kingdom of the dead. Under Persian and Hellenistic influence, *abyssos* came to connote the abode of the runagate spirits (Jubilees 5:6ff.; Ethiopian version of En 10:4f); cf. Jeremias, "*Abyssos*," 1:10.

38. Most likely, the Qumran scroll *Community Rule* (previously known as *Manual of Discipline*), dated to between the late first century B.C.E. and the early first century C.E. and asserting that everything in the world is predestined, saw God's creative work painted in Gen 1 as following a preestablished plan or design: "From the God of knowledge stems all there is and all there shall be. Before they existed he established their entire design. And when they have come into being, at their appointed time, they will execute all their works according to his glorious design, without altering anything" (1QS III, 15–16); cf. Martinez and Tigchelaar, *The Dead Sea Scrolls*, 74–75.

39. The wording of Matt 27:66 recalls Dan 6:17 (the sealing of the lions' den into which the exiled Jewish man was thrown).

40. Bovon, *Luke 1*, 320.

41. John Chrysostom touches on this matter when he writes: "You see, in saying at this point that God rested from his works, Scripture teaches us that he ceased creating and bringing from nonbeing into being on the seventh day, whereas Christ, in saying that 'my Father is at work until now and I am at work' [John 5:17], reveals his unceasing care for us: he calls 'work' the maintenance of created things, bestowal of permanence on them and governance of them through all time. If this wasn't so, after all, how would everything have subsisted, without the guiding hand above directing all visible things and the human race as well?" (*Homilies on Genesis* 10.18); cf. Louth, *Genesis 1–11*, 46.

42. Heb. verbal root *š-b-t*, "to cease, to stop, to be at a standstill" (Gen 8:22; with preposition *min*, "from" [Gen 2:2–3]; with preposition *min* plus infinitive [Jer 31 [38]:36]), "to stop working, to take a holiday, to keep the Sabbath" (Exod 16:30; Lev 23:32; 26:34, with "land" as subject; for these occurrences, LXX uses the verb *sabbatizō*, "to keep the Sabbath, to sabbatize," a loanword from Heb. *šābat*, "to keep/observe the Sabbath."

43. The Gk. verb *katapauō*, in ancient Greek literature and LXX, means "to put an end to [an activity, work, task, suffering, etc.]." The connotation, "to rest, to give rest," developed from its primary meaning, i.e., to put an end to suffering, hence to rest or to be given rest on account of the cessation of trouble. Thus, in LXX, *katapauō* occurs with two imports: "to stop" (working) (e.g., Gen 2:2; MT: *w-yšbt*, "he stopped") and "to rest, to give rest" (Exod 20:11 [MT]: *w-ynḥ*, "he rested"; 1 Chr 23:25 [MT]: *hnyḥ*, "he gave rest").

44. Scholars assign Gen 1:1–2:4a to a "priestly" source dated roughly to the period of the Babylonian exile (sixth century B.C.E.) and Gen 2:4b–25 to a "Yahwist" source during the time of David and Solomon (about 950 B.C.E., in Jerusalem). On the authorship of Gen 1–2, see Friedman, *Who Wrote the Bible?* 47–65.

45. *ANF* 7:495.

46. Heschel, *The Sabbath*, 8.

47. The Gk. verb *prodiatypoō* connotes "to express by a type beforehand, to imagine perfectly beforehand, to prefigure" (Philo); in LXX, there is a hapax legomenon *diatypoō*, "to form, to fashion" (Wis 19:8); note the Byzantine Gk. verb *diatypoō*, "to form perfectly, to mold," and *prodiatypoō*, "to prefigure."

48. For instance, Clement of Alexandria writes: "He is Isaac (for the narrative may be interpreted otherwise), who is a type of the Lord, a child as a son; for he was the son of Abraham, as Christ the Son of God, and a sacrifice as the Lord, but he was not immolated as the Lord. Isaac only bore the wood of the sacrifice, as the Lord the wood of the cross. And he laughed mystically, prophesying that the Lord should fill us with joy [*de mystikōs emplēsai hēmas prophēteuōn charas ton kyrion*], who have been redeemed from corruption by the blood of the Lord [John 8:56]. Isaac did everything but suffer, as was right, yielding the precedence in suffering to the Word. Furthermore, there is an intimation of the divinity of the Lord in his not being slain. For Jesus rose again

after his burial, having suffered no harm, like Isaac released from sacrifice" (*The Pedagogue* 1.5); cf. *ANF* 1:215.

49. The Gk. verb *sabbatizō*, "to keep the Sabbath" or "to sabbatize," is a loanword from the Heb. verb *šābat*, occurring several times in LXX (Exod 16:30; Lev 23:32; 26:34, 35; 2 Chr 36:21; 1 Esd 1:58 [55]; 2 Macc 6:6).

50. The word *oikonomia*, found in Eph 1:10 with an active force meaning "ordering" or "administering," is attested in patristic writings with the sense of "plan of salvation." Similarly, in our hymn, as in this following poem, *oikonomia* refers to the management plan: "What is this spectacle [*theama*] we see? What is this present rest [*parousa katapausis*]? The king of the ages, having accomplished the plan [*telesas oikonomian*] through Passion [*dia pathous*], he sabbatizes in the tomb [*en taphō sabbatizei*], granting us a new Sabbath [*kainon sabbatismon*]" (Holy Saturday, Matins, Lauds, Sticheron).

51. The participial form *stenōn*, "groaning," occurs six times in the Bible, the first time in the story of Cain. After Adam's firstborn son commits fratricide, God promises that Cain will be "groaning and trembling" (Gen 4:12 [LXX]: *stenōn kai tremōn*; MT: *nāᶜ wā-nād*, "tottering and wandering"). Groaning can be an expression of a "soul's bitterness" (*pikria psychēs*, Job 10:1), the incompatibility between righteous and impious (Prov 28:28; 29:2), or a mere preamble to crying (Job 30:28), as in our hymn.

52. Hades is envisioned in the Bible as supplied with "gates" (Isa 38:10 [Odes 11:10]: *pylais hadou*; Wis 16:13; Matt 16:18: the gates of Hades will not "prevail" [*katischysousin*] over the Church) and "gatekeepers" (Job 38:17: *pylōroi*), both images conveying Hades's vigilance and indestructibility.

53. Allen, *Psalms 51–100*, 89.

54. Note that the verb *katechō*, "to confine," occurs in Gen 39:20 (cf. 42:19) with reference to Pharaoh's prison, where prisoners, including Joseph, were "confined."

55. On the insatiable appetite of Hades (Isa 5:14; Hab 2:5; Prov 27:20; 30:15, 16), in the context of Sheol's ANE background, see Pentiuc, "'Renewed by Blood,'" 535–564.

56. Andersen, *Habakkuk*, 260.

57. Constas, "The Last Temptation of Satan," 139.

58. In the *Homily on the Passion and the Cross*, attributed to Athanasius of Alexandria, the author applies the "divine deception" theme to the last days of Jesus: "The devil wanted to know what he was unable to know when he tempted him [i.e., Christ] on the mountain, namely, 'whether or not he is the Son of God' [Luke 4:3]. At that time he was put to shame, and kept watch [*etērei*; cf. Gen 3:15 [LXX]: *tērēseis*, "you will watch [his heel]" for the time [*kairos*] of his death. For it is written in Luke that, 'When the devil completed all his temptations, he departed from him until an opportune time' [*achri kairou*, Luke 4:13]. This [i.e., the Passion] is now that time" (lines 25–32; *PG* 28:209); cf. Constas, "The Last Temptation of Satan," 150 and n. 29.

59. On Hebrew Sheol in its ANE religious-literary context, see Pentiuc, "'Renewed by Blood,'" 535–564.

60. On the Aramaic phrase in Dan 7:13, see Pentiuc, *Jesus the Messiah*, 54–56.

61. Even though the Christological connotation of this phrase will emerge in the second century, keeping "*the* Son of Man" idiolect in the canonical gospels shows the early Church's genuine respect for the very sayings of Jesus the Lord (*kyrios*); see Hurtado, *Lord Jesus Christ*, 304–306.

62. Cf. Gen 15:12; Dan 8:17; 10:8. For extra-biblical evidence, see, e.g., the case of Gilgamesh who wakes from his sleep during the night, asking, "Why am I startled? Did some god go by? Why is my flesh a quiver?" (*Gilgamesh* 5.4.11–12); cf. Clines, *Job 1–20*, 130.

63. The Heb. verbal root *r-q-m*, "to weave," evokes a multicolored textile brocaded with raised images. Emphasis is placed here on the intricacy of the multicolored textile, complex yet well knitted (cf. Ps 139 [138]:13: *s-k-k*, "to knit together"); the verb *r-q-m* occurs eight times in Exodus priestly texts with reference to Tabernacle's curtains in various colors, purple, crimson, etc. (Exod 26:36; 27:16; 28:39; 35:35; 36:37; 38:18, 23; 39:29).

64. That each individual is created by God without any decisive human participation can be seen in the speech of the mother of the seven Maccabees to her children urging them to stick to their faith and oppose the persecutor Antiochus IV Epiphanes: "I do not know how you came into being in my womb. It was not I who gave you life and breath, nor I who set in order the elements within each of you. Therefore the Creator of the world, who shaped the origin of man and devised the origin of all things, will in his mercy give life and breath back to you again, since you now forget yourselves for the sake of his laws" (2 Macc 7:22–23).

65. According to Dahood, *Psalms III*, 294–295, there are several Old Testament texts (e.g., Gen 2:7; 3:19; Ps 90 [89]:3; Eccl 3:20; 12:7; Sir 40:1; Job 1:21) that might suggest a peculiar tradition that "man originated and pre-existed in the nether world." Nevertheless, such a preexistent humanity has no basis in the Bible, and Dahood's view is quite challenged. However, Allen, *Psalms 101–150*, 329, notes the parallel between "secret" (*str*) and "lowest [parts] of the earth" in Ps 139 (138):15 and Job 14:13 (LXX) ("Oh that you had guarded [*en hadē me ephylaxas*] me in Hades, and had concealed me [in a secret place, *ekrypsas*] until your anger had ceased"), which makes one think of the "secret [place]" (*kryphē*) as a metaphor of Hades (cf. Isa 45:19).

66. See Köster, "*Hypostasis*," 8:572–589.

67. Brotherton, "Hans Urs von Balthasar," 177–178.

68. On Prov 8:22–31, see the section on "The Mystical Supper" in chapter 4.

69. Note the related verb *hypodyō*, "to slip in under, to slip into," a hapax legomenon (Jdt 6:13, of the men of Bethulia "having slipped away beneath the mountain" [*hypodysantes hypokatō tou orous*] and capturing the Ammonite mercenary Achior).

70. Wis 17:4–5: "For not even the innermost place [*mychos*] that holds [*ho katechōn*] them, kept [them] [*diephylatten*] fearless [*aphobous*], but sounds [*ēchoi*] reverberated [*periekompoun*] throwing them into confusion [*ektarassontes*], and dreary phantoms with gloomy faces [*phasmata ameidētois katēphē prosōpois*] made their appearance [*enephanizeto*]. And no force [*bia*] of fire [*pyros*] was able [*katischyen*] to give light [*phōtizein*], nor did the very bright flames [*eklamproi phloges*] of the

stars continue [*hypemenon*] to illuminate [*kataugazein*] that horrible night [*stygnēn nykta*]." Wis 17:14 (13)–15 (14): "But they, throughout the night that was really powerless [*adynaton*] and came upon [*epelthousan*] them from the innermost parts [*mychōn*] of powerless Hades, sleeping [*koimōmenoi*] the same sleep, now were vexed [*ēlaunonto*] by the monsters of phantoms [*terasin phantasmōn*], now were paralyzed [*parelyonto*] by the[ir] soul's surrender [*prodosia*], for sudden [*aphnidios*] and unexpected [*aprosdokētos*] fear poured over [*epechythē*] them."

71. As Winston, *The Wisdom of Solomon*, 22, remarks, some thirty-five words distributed almost uniformly throughout the book of Wisdom were unknown prior to 100 B.C.E., which pushes the dating of this writing to the first half of the first century C.E.

72. See Enns, "Wisdom of Solomon," 212–225.

73. Note the contemptuous ridicule ("Let us therefore enjoy the good things that exist, and let us use the creation as in youth hastily. . . . These things they reasoned, and they were led astray for their malice blinded them" [Wis 2:6, 21]) of Eccl's exhortation: "Rejoice, young man, in your youth, and let your heart do good to you in the days of your youth, and walk in the ways of your heart and in the sight of your eyes, and know that for all these things God will bring you into judgment" (Eccl 11:9).

74. See Winston, *The Wisdom of Solomon*, 303.

75. Maguire, *Art and Eloquence*, 98–99.

76. Achtemeier, *1 Peter*, 249.

77. Speaking of entombment, John of Damascus notes that Jesus "as God [*hōs theos*] was uncircumscribed [*aperigraptos*] . . . [but] in the tomb, he was bodily circumscribed [*sōmatikōs perigraptos*]" (*Homily* 4.29 [*PG* 18:372C]).

78. *PG* 91:1044CD; cf. Maximus the Confessor, *On Difficulties in the Church Fathers*, 26–27.

79. The Heb. word *derek*, "way," designates a personal behavior or attitude. The form *darkēy*, "ways," is a plural of intensity denoting a wide array of ways through which the adulteress of Prov 7 could seduce a young man.

80. The word *tamieion* (spelled also *tameion*) occurs in LXX and the New Testament with two basic meanings, "storeroom" (from *temieuō*, "to store up, to reserve") and "hidden, secret, innermost room." LXX occurrences (spelled *tamieion* and commonly rendering Heb. *ḥeder*, "chamber, room"): Gen 43:30 (innermost room, of Joseph weeping privately); Exod 7:28 (secret places of the bedrooms); Deut 32:25 (inner chambers); Judg 3:24 (retreat of the bedroom); 15:1 (bedroom); 2 Sam 13:10 (inner room); 1 Kgs 1:15 (inner room, of Bathsheba); 1 Kgs 20:30 (inner room); Prov 7:27 ("chambers of death"). New Testament occurrences (spelled *tameion*): Matt 6:6; 24:26; Luke 12:3 (secret room); Luke 12:24 (storeroom).

81. Fox, *Proverbs 1–9*, 251.

82. Among the ancient interpreters who saw in Eph 4:8–9 a locus classicus for Jesus's "descent to Hades" (*ad Inferos*) are: Tertullian, Irenaeus, Chrysostom, Theodoret, and Jerome; see Barth, *Ephesians 4–6*, 433.

83. John Chrysostom explains: "The 'lower parts of the earth' here means death, by a human metaphor [Gen 44:29]. . . . And why does he mention this region here? What sort of captivity is he speaking of? That of the devil. He has taken captive the tyrant,

the devil and death, the curse and sin" (*Homily on Ephesians* 11.4.9–10); cf. Edwards, *Galatians*, 164.

84. The verb used here, *poreuomai*, "to go," is generic with no further directional meaning, e.g., "up" or "down." However, read in conjunction with Eph 4:9 (see above), this Petrine text might allude to Jesus's "going down" to the netherworld.

85. The Heb. word *nōᶜam* designates God's favors for petitioners; see Hossfeld and Zenger, *Psalms 2*, 423; Levenson, "A Technical Meaning," 51–100.

86. Nikodemus the Hagiorite, *Eortodromion*, 394–396.

87. In LXX, *typos* occurs four times meaning: "model" (Heb. *tabnît*, Exod 25:40), "idol" (Heb. *ṣelem*, Amos 5:26), "wording, text" of a decree (3 Macc 3:30), "example" (4 Macc 6:19). The New Testament employs this term on various occasions denoting "mark" (John 20:25: "mark of the nails" [*typon tōn hēlōn*] in Jesus's hands; cf. 20:20), "idol" (Acts 7:43; cf. Amos 5:26), "text" of a letter (Acts 23:25); in Pauline epistles, "example, model" (Rom 6:17). Paul describes the events of the Old Testament as *typoi*, "types"; here not the scriptural texts but rather the Old Testament events are called *typoi*, "types" (1 Cor 10:6), and *typikōs*, "typical" (1 Cor 10:11) as foreshadowing God's further acts. These are the two New Testament places where the word *typos*, "type," is used for the first time as a hermeneutical term in the way it will be used in later Christian writings. Likewise, the same sense is required in Rom 5:14, where Adam is the foreshadowing of the new Adam to come, Christ. Adam is an "advanced presentation" of Christ, which raises the relationship between Adam and Christ to a higher level of correspondence; here the nature of correspondence is antithetical. It is due to Paul's influence that Christian literature subsequent to him adopted and used *typos* as a default hermeneutical term. 1 Pet 3:21 uses the term *antitypos*, "antitype," as "corresponding, counterpart"; thus, baptism is the counterpart (*antitypos*) to the deliverance of Noah from the flood (Acts 7:44; Heb 8:5, of the heavenly "original pattern" [*typos*] of the sanctuary [cf. Exod 25:40]) vs. its earthly "copy" (*antitypos*) (Heb 9:24); see Goppelt, "*Typos*," 248–259; on allegory and typology, see Pentiuc, *The Old Testament*, 181–186.

88. Cf. Sasson, *Jonah*, 26.

89. On Jonah in gospel traditions, see Chow, *The Sign of Jonah*.

90. Luz, *Matthew 8–20*, 2:216.

91. Bovon, *Luke 2*, 139–140.

92. Kannengiesser, *Handbook of Patristic Exegesis*, 329–330.

93. Köster, "*Synechō*," 7:877–882.

94. Hanse, "*Echō*," 2:829.

95. Cf. Ferreiro, *The Twelve Prophets*, 139.

96. Ibid.

97. MT of Jonah 1:17 (2:1) reads: "And Yahweh appointed [verb *m-n-h*] a big fish [*dg gdwl*] to swallow [*b-l-ᶜ*] Jonah, and Jonah was [*w-yhy*] in the entrails [*mᶜy*] of the fish three days and three nights."

98. *PG* 46:604B; see Reddish, *Does God Always Get What God Wants?*, 31–32.

99. On the Gk. verb *paschō*, "to suffer," and its interesting relationship with the Aramaic *Paschaʾ*, "Passover festival" (cf. Luke 22:15), see the discussion in chapter 1.

100. Cf. Ferreiro, *The Twelve Prophets*, 138.

101. Kitchen, "Jonah's Oar," 36.

102. Cf. Ferreiro, *The Twelve Prophets*, 135.

103. Nikodemus the Hagiorite, *Eortodromion*, 395.

104. E.g., *Anebiō gar ek nekrōn, anethore te pros Patera meta sarkos*: "Having returned to life from the dead, he [Jesus] *sprang up*, in [his flesh] to the Father" (Cyril of Alexandria, *Glaphyra on Exodus* 2; cf. *PG* 69:476C; emphasis added).

105. On the Gk. word *mychos*, "inner part of a house," see the discussion above of the hymn "Streams of Life in Hades."

106. Kitchen, "Jonah's Oar," 35.

107. Sasson, *Jonah*, 195.

108. Ibid., 197.

109. Stuart, *Hosea-Jonah*, 478.

110. In a sentence where there is a second plural verbal form, *enkatalipete*, "you have abandoned," one would expect a second-person plural *hymōn* qualifying the direct object *eleos*, "[your] mercy." Instead, there is a dative plural with a smooth breathing mark ('), *autois*, "for/to them," hence our gloss placed within the brackets, "[intended] for them." Nikodemus's quoted text has a rough breathing mark ('), *hautois*, "for themselves," but the problem remains with the third- instead of second-person plural.

111. Nikodemus the Hagiorite, *Eortodromion*, 395.

112. Watts, *Isaiah 1–33*, 171.

113. Throughout the lengthy and intricate book of Isaiah, the theme of light is employed within a wider soteriological context. Note Isa 49:6, where the Servant of the Lord (a messianic agent) is portrayed as having a double mission, namely, to be a "covenant of a nation" and a "light of nations": "Lo, I placed you as covenant of a race/nation [*eis diathēkēn genous*], a light of nations [*eis phōs ethnōn*] so that you may be as salvation until the end of the earth"; cf. Isa 60:1 "Shine [*phōtizou*], shine, O Jerusalem, for your very light has come [*hēkei . . . sou to phōs*], and the glory [*doxa*] of the Lord has risen [*anatetalken*] upon you."

114. Although unattested in the Bible, the phrase "never-setting light" (*phōs anesperon*) corresponds to "eternal light" in Isa 60:19, 20: "The Lord will be to you an everlasting light [*phōs aiōnion*], and God will be your glory." The adjective *anesperon*, "never-setting," absent in the Bible, appears in Hesychus (fifth century B.C.E.) along with an explicative gloss, *askoteinon*, "free from darkness." Note the use of this adjective in Christian writings with regard to Christ, the "never-setting light" (Epiphanius, *Homilies* 2 [*PG* 53:440D); the "eternal day" (Basil, *Hexaemeron* 2.8 [*PG* 29:52A], *On Isaiah* 87 [*PG* 30:260B]); "in the never-setting day of your Kingdom" (*en tē anespera hēmera tēs basileias sou*) (John of Damscus, *Carmina* 125 [*PG* 96:844B]).

115. Blenkinsopp, *Isaiah 1–39*, 249.

116. The term *theophaneia*, "God's appearance," unattested in the Bible, occurs in ancient Greek literature ("vision of God") and is exceedingly employed in ancient Christian writings in reference to the first coming of Christ (e.g., *tēs prōtēs tou sōtērou*

theophaneias antrō, "of the first appearance of the Savior in a cave" (Eusebius, *De vita Constantini* 3.41 [*PG* 20:1001A]) as prophesied in the Old Testament, "the one that was according to the economy [*oikonomian*] of the Word of God . . . [and] on the one hand, was preannounced [*prokatangeltheisan*] through the prophets, and on the other hand, was made visible [*phanerōtheisan*] through a theophany [*theophaneias*] according to the Son's flesh [*sarka*]" (Gregory of Nyssa, *Homily on Song of Songs* 5 [*PG* 44:860D]).

117. Note that the verb *sympatheō*, "to suffer along with, to co-suffer, to sympathize," from which *sympathikōs*, "compassionately," derives, is more frequently used than *sympaschō*.

118. Watts, *Isaiah 1–33*, 342. The belief in the final bodily resurrection is clearly stated around the mid-second century B.C.E. in Dan 12:2 (LXX): "And many of those lying down [*katheudontōn*] in the flat of the earth will stand up [*anastēsontai*], some for eternal life [*zōēn aiōnion*], but others to shame, but others to dispersion and eternal shame."

119. *The Zohar*, 356n291. In chapter 32 of *Pirqei de-Rabbi Eli'ezer*, there is a "prayer for dew" to be read on the first day of Passover, so vital was dew in the Holy Land during those dry months following the annual Passover festival.

Chapter 7

1. On different levels of literacy in Byzantium, see the classical study of Browning, "Literacy," 39–54.
2. Pentiuc, *The Old Testament*, 161, 360n26.
3. Parpulov, "The Bibles of the Christian East," 314–315.
4. Parpulov, "Psalters and Personal Piety," 77–105.
5. Our knowledge of Old Testament Septuagint manuscripts relies on Rahlfs, *Verzeichnis der griechischen Handschriften des Alten Testaments*; Rahlfs and Fraenkel, eds., *Verzeichnis der griechischen Handschriften des Alten Testaments*.
6. Parpulov, "The Bibles of the Christian East," 321–322; see Blake, "The Athos Codex," 33–56.
7. On lectionaries, see Engberg, "The Greek Old Testament Lectionary," 39–48.
8. Parpulov, "The Bibles of the Christian East," 316–317.
9. On the Old Testament in Byzantium, see Miller, "The Prophetologion," 55–76. The critical edition of the Prophetologion, based on a detailed analysis of seventy-one manuscripts of the ninth through fourteenth centuries, was published by Carsten Høeg, et al., *Prophetologium*.
10. Engberg, "The *Prophetologion*," 89–91.
11. Miller, "The Prophetologion," 62n18.
12. Ibid., 65–66 and n. 30.
13. On Eastern Orthodox views of the Septuagint vs. Hebrew text, see Pentiuc, *The Old Testament*, 90–100.

14. Parpulov, "The Bibles of the Christian East," 310–311. Parpulov argues that it was only for expensive books that scribes would seek the most recent exemplars and add textual notes on different readings. For instance, the Praxapostolos codex produced for Emperor Michael VII and dated to 1072 includes a good number of original readings. Interestingly, ecclesiastical authorities in Constantinople never showed a desire to declare a certain textual transmission as the "official" one. For Eastern Orthodoxy, the Septuagint has become with time a *textus receptus* rather than an officially decreed authoritative text, as occurred, for instance, with Jerome's Vulgate, which became the authoritative version of the Bible for the Roman Catholic Church at the Council of Trent (1546).

15. Bucur, "Exegesis of Biblical Theophanies," 92–112.

16. These midrashic techniques can be detected as early as the targumic tradition, whose roots go back to pre-Christian times. For instance, Gen 1:1 [MT], "In the beginning, God created the heavens and earth," is interpretively rendered into Aramaic: "*With wisdom [bhkmh]*, the Lord created and *perfected* the heavens and the earth" (Fragment Targum on Gen 1:1). The targumist expanded the original Hebrew text in his Aramaic translation by replacing "beginning" with an explicative gloss ("wisdom"), based on Prov 8:22 [MT] (where "beginning" can be read as a nickname of "wisdom"), and adding (inserting) another verb ("perfected"). The Neophyti Targum has "*From* the beginning [*mlqdmyn*], *with wisdom [bhkmh]*, the Lord created . . .," where the same explicative gloss ("wisdom") is this time inserted into the biblical text.

17. The content of Jubilees can be divided into seven sections: (1) chap. 1, introduction; (2) chaps. 2–10, stories about Adam and Noah; (3) chaps. 11–23:8, stories about Abraham; (4) chaps. 23:9–32, appendix following Abraham's death; (5) chaps. 24–45, stories about Jacob and his sons; (6) chaps. 46–49, stories in Egypt and the Exodus; (7) chap. 50, conclusion. Sections 2, 3, 5, and 6 are based on and follow the Pentateuch's sequentiality, except for the story of Joseph being sold by his brothers, which was moved earlier (Jubilees 34), prior to Isaac's death (Jubilees 36:18), in contrast with the sequence in Genesis, where this story (Gen 37) follows the death of Isaac (Gen 35:29); cf. Segal, *The Book of Jubilees*, 3.

18. Here is a comparison between Gen 6 and Jubilees 5, showing textual alterations and additions (in italics). Gen 6:5a: "The Lord saw how great was man's wickedness on earth"; Jubilees 5:2: "Wickedness increased on earth." Gen 6:12b: "for all flesh has corrupted its ways on earth"; Jubilees 5:2: "All animate beings corrupted their way." Gen 6:12b: "for all flesh had corrupted its ways on earth"; Jubilees 5:2: "All of them corrupted their way *and their prescribed course, they began to devour one another*." See Segal, *The Book of Jubilees*, 105.

19. O'Brien, "Cubism: Art and Philosophy," 30.

20. Florovsky, *Bible, Church, Tradition*, 47.

21. Quoted in O'Brien, "Cubism: Art and Philosophy," 33.

22. Parpulov, "The Bibles of the Christian East," 322–323.

23. O'Brien, "Cubism and Kant," 482–506.

24. Rubin, *Picasso and Braque*, 44.

25. Pentiuc, *The Old Testament*, 199–232 (i.e., chaps. 6 ["Aural"] and 7 ["Visual"]).

26. Ibid., 329.

27. On these hymns and their generative biblical episode, see the detailed discussion in chapter 2.
28. I first mentioned this distinction between the classical vertical paradigm and my proposed new horizontal paradigm in Pentiuc, *Jesus the Messiah*.
29. On the Semitic views on "end of time," see Pentiuc, "Behind the Days," 3–21.
30. On the delicate matter of various views on supersessionism, see Pentiuc, *The Old Testament*, 39–52.
31. See discussion of this hymn in chapter 6.
32. See discussion of this hymn in chapter 5.
33. On Kassia's hymn and the *chronotopos*, see chapter 3.
34. On "intertextuality," see the section below on "Hermeneutical Procedures."
35. On the detailed discussion of this hymn, see chapter 4.
36. As rightly noted by Clines, "Biblical Hermeneutics," 65.
37. On the assumptions of patristic exegesis, see Pentiuc, *The Old Testament*, 170–176.
38. On this hymn, see chapter 5.
39. On this hymn, see comments in chapter 1.
40. Published in Kristeva, *Sēmiōtikē*, 143–173. The English version, "Word, Dialogue and Novel," was published in Kristeva, *Desire in Language*, 64–91. On Kristeva's contribution to the theory of intertextuality, see Alfaro, "Intertextuality," 268–285.
41. Kristeva, *Desire in Language*, 65.
42. On "inner biblical interpretation" as an example of intertextuality, see Meek, "Intertextuality," 280–291; see also the magisterial study by Fishbane, *Biblical Interpretation*.
43. On this hymn, see comments in chapter 5.
44. On this hymn, see comments in chapter 5.
45. For more on biblical typology, including the differences between allegorical and typological interpretations, see Pentiuc, *The Old Testament*, 169–198.
46. Young, *Biblical Exegesis*, 153.
47. On the identification of the site of the transfiguration with Mount Tabor, see O'Connor, *The Holy Land*, 412–415.
48. See Pentiuc, "Above All His Friends," 179–185.
49. See discussion of the hymn in chapter 1.
50. See the section on "Hermeneutical Pointers."
51. See discussion of the hymn in chapter 1.
52. See discussion of the hymn in chapter 2.
53. See discussion of the hymn in chapter 6.
54. See discussion of the hymn in chapter 2.
55. See discussion of the hymn in chapter 3.
56. See discussion of the hymn in chapter 2.
57. Benvindo, *On the Limits of Constitutional Adjudication*, 177.
58. Louth, "Tradition and the Icon," 150–151.

Bibliography

Achtemeier, Paul J. *1 Peter*. Hermeneia. Minneapolis: Fortress, 1996.

Ackerman, James S. "The Rabbinic Interpretation of Psalm 82 and the Gospel of John." *HTR* 59 (1966): 186–191.

Alfaro, Mariá Jesús Martínez. "Intertextuality: Origins and Development of the Concept." *Atlantis* 18, nos. 1–2 (1996): 268–285.

Allen, Leslie C. *Psalms 51–100*. Word Biblical Commentary 20. Dallas: Word, 2002.

———. *Psalms 101–150*. Word Biblical Commentary 21. Dallas: Word, 2002.

Ambrose. *Letters 1–91*. Translated by Mary Melchior Beyenka. The Fathers of the Church 26. Washington, DC: Catholic University of America Press, 1954.

———. *Seven Exegetical Works*. Translated by Michael P. McHugh. The Fathers of the Church 65. Washington, DC: Catholic University of America Press, 1985.

Andersen, Francis I. *Habakkuk: A New Translation with Introduction and Commentary*. The Anchor Yale Bible Commentaries. New Haven, CT: Yale University Press, 2008.

Anderson, Gary. "The Interpretation of Genesis 1:1 in the Targums." *CBQ* 52, no. 1 (1990): 21–29.

———. "Mary in the Old Testament." *Pro Ecclesia* 16, no. 1 (2007): 49–55.

———. *Charity: The Place of the Poor in the Biblical Tradition*. New Haven, CT: Yale University Press, 2013.

Arentzen, Thomas. "Sex in the City: Intercourse in Holy Week." *JECS* 28, no. 1 (2020): 115–147.

Argyle, A. W. "Joseph (Le Patriarche)." In *Dictionnaire de spiritualité*, 8:1276–1289. Ascétique et Mystique Doctrine et Histoire. Paris: Beauchesne, 1974.

Attridge, Harold W. *The Epistle to the Hebrews: A Commentary on the Epistle to the Hebrews*. Hermeneia. Minneapolis: Fortress, 1989.

Aune, David E. *Revelation 1–5:14*. Word Biblical Commentary 52A. Dallas: Word, 1997.

Aus, Roger D. *Two Puzzling Baptisms: First Corinthians 10:1–5 and 15:29: Studies in Their Judaic Background*. Studies in Judaism. New York: Hamilton, 2017.

Balthasar, Hans Urs von. *Theo-Drama*, Vol. 3: *Theological Dramatic Theory: The Dramatis Personae: Persons in Christ*. San Francisco: Ignatius, 1992.

Baltzer, Klaus. *Deutero-Isaiah: A Commentary on Isaiah 40–55*. Hermeneia. Mineapolis: Fortress, 2001.

Barkhuizen, Jan H. "Romanos' Encomium on Joseph: Portrait of an Athlete." *Jahrbuch der Österreichischen Byzantinistik* 40 (1990): 91–106.

Barnard, Leslie William. *St. Justin Martyr: The First and Second Apologies*. New York: Paulist, 1997.

Barth, Markus. *Ephesians 4–6*. The Anchor Yale Bible Commentaries. New Haven, CT: Yale University Press, 1998.

Bartlett, John R. "The Books of the Maccabees." In *The Oxford Companion to the Bible*, edited by Bruce M. Metzger and Michael D. Coogan, 475–482. New York: Oxford University Press, 1993.

Basil. *Letters*, Vol. 1: *Letters 1–58*. Translated by Roy J. Deferrari. Loeb Classical Library 190. Cambridge, MA: Harvard University Press, 1989.

Bathrellos, Demetrios. "The Temptations of Jesus Christ According to St. Maximus the Confessor." In *Papers Presented at the Fourteenth International Conference on Patristic Studies Held in Oxford 2003*, edited by F. Young, M. Edwards, and P. Parvis, 45–49. Studia Patristica 42. Leuven: Peeters, 2006.

Bauckham, Richard J. *2 Peter, Jude*. Word Biblical Commentary 50. Dallas: Word, 1983.

Behr, John. "Irenaeus of Lyons." In *Christian Theologies of Salvation: A Comparative Introduction*, edited by Justin S. Holcomb, 41–58. New York: New York University Press, 2017.

Benvindo, Juliano Zaiden. *On the Limits of Constitutional Adjudication: Deconstructing Balancing and Judicial Activism*. Heidelberg: Springer, 2010.

Berger, Albrecht, trans. *Accounts of Medieval Constantinople: The Patria*. Dumbarton Oaks Medieval Library 24. Cambridge, MA: Harvard University Press, 2013.

Bergren, Theodore A. "The Tradition History of the Exodus-Review in 5 Ezra 1." In *Of Scribes and Sages: Early Jewish Interpretation and Transmission of Scripture*, Vol. 2: *Later Versions and Traditions*, edited by Craig A. Evans, 34–50. Studies in Scripture in Early Judaism and Christianity 10. Library of Second Temple Studies 51. London: T. and T. Clark, 2004.

——. "The Structure and Composition of 5 Ezra." *Vigilae Christianae* 64 (2010): 115–139.

Bertonière, Gabriel. *The Historical Development of the Easter Vigil and Related Services in the Greek Church*. Orientalia Christiana Analecta 193. Rome: Pontificium Institutum Studiorum Orientalium, 1972.

Bertschmann, Dorothea H. "Hosting Jesus: Revisiting Luke's 'Sinful Woman' [Luke 7.36–50] as a Tale of Two Hosts." *Journal of the Study of the New Testament* 40, no. 1 (2017): 30–50.

Blaising, Craig A., and Carmen S. Hardin, eds. *Psalms 1–50*. ACCS OT 7. Downers Grove, IL: InterVarsity, 2008.

Blake, Robert P. "The Athos Codex of the Georgian Old Testament." *HTR* 22 (1929): 33–56.

Blenkinsopp, Joseph. *Isaiah 1–39*. The Anchor Yale Bible Commentaries. New Haven, CT: Yale University Press, 2000.

——. *Isaiah 40–55*. The Anchor Yale Bible Commentaries. New Haven, CT: Yale University Press, 2002.

Blum, Georg Günter. "Oikonomia und Theologia: Der Hintergrund einer konfessionellen Differenz zwischen östlichen und westlichen Christentum." *Ostkirchliche Studien* 33 (1984): 281–301.

Boersma, Hans. *Scripture as Real Presence: Sacramental Exegesis in the Early Church*. Grand Rapids, MI: Baker Academic, 2017.

Botha, Phil J. "The Paradox between Appearance and Truth in Ephrem the Syrian's Hymn *De Crucifixione IV.*" *Acta Patristica et Byzantina* 12 (2002): 34–49.

Bovon, François. *Luke 1: A Commentary on the Gospel of Luke 1:1–9:50*. Hermeneia. Minneapolis: Fortress, 2002.

——. *Luke 3: A Commentary on the Gospel of Luke 19:28–24:53*. Hermeneia. Minneapolis: Fortress, 2012.

——. *Luke 2: A Commentary on the Gospel of Luke 9:51–19:27*. Hermeneia. Minneapolis: Fortress, 2013.

Bowen, Matthew L. "'They Came and Held Him by the Feet and Worshipped Him': Proskynesis before Jesus in Its Biblical and Ancient Near Eastern Context." *Studies in the Bible and Antiquity* 5 (2013): 63–68.

Boyarin, Daniel. "The Gospel of the *Memra*: Jewish Binitarianism and the Prologue to John." *HTR* 94, no. 3 (2001): 243–284.

———. *Border Lines: The Partition of Judeo-Christianity.* Philadelphia: University of Pennsylvania Press, 2004.

Bradshaw, Paul F. "Cathedral vs. Monastery: The Only Alternatives for the Liturgy of the Hours?" In *Time and Community: In Honor of Thomas Julian Talley*, edited by J. Neil Alexander, 123–126. NPM Studies in Church Music and Liturgy. Washington, DC: Pastoral, 1990.

———. "The Origins of Easter." In *Between Memory and Hope: Readings on the Liturgical Year*, edited by Maxwell E. Johnson, chapter 7. Kindle ed. Collegeville, MN: Liturgical, 2000.

Bray, Gerald L. *Romans.* ACCS NT 6. Downers Grove, IL: InterVarsity, 1998.

Brayford, Susan. *Genesis.* Septuagint Commentary Series. Leiden: Brill, 2007.

Brock, Sebastian P. "Dramatic Dialogue Poem." In *IV Symposium Syriacum 1984: Literary Genres in Syriac Literature*, edited by H. J. W. Drijvers, 135–147. Rome: Pontificium Institutum Orientalium Studiorum, 1987.

———. "The Sinful Woman and Satan: Two Syriac Dialogue Poems." *Oriens Christianus* 72 (1988): 21–62.

Brotherton, Joshua R. "Hans Urs von Balthasar on the Redemptive Descent." *Pro Ecclesia* 22, no. 2 (2013): 167–188.

Brou, Louis. "Les Impropères du Vendredi-Saint: Introduction; les improperes; le vocable; la formule romaine des Impropères." *Revue grégorienne* 20 (1935): 161–179.

———. "Les Impropères du Vendredi-Saint: Les formules mozarabes; les autres analogies mozarabes; les formules françaises." *Revue grégorienne* 21 (1936): 8–16.

———. "Les Impropères du Vendredi-Saint: Les formules mozarabes; les autres analogies mozarabes; les formules françaises." *Revue grégorienne* 21 (1936): 8–16.

———. "Les Impropères du Vendredi-Saint: Les formules de Jérusalem; les autres analogies orientales." *Revue grégorienne* 22 (1937): 1–9.

———. "Les Impropères du Vendredi-Saint: Les precedents latins des Impropères." *Revue grégorienne* 22 (1937): 44–51.

Brown, Raymond, Karl Donfried, Joseph Fitzmyer, and John Reumann, eds. *Mary in the New Testament: A Collaborative Assessment by Protestant and Roman Catholic Scholars.* New York: Paulist, 1978.

Browning, Robert. "Literacy in the Byzantine World." *Byzantine and Modern Greek Studies* 4 (1978): 39–54.

Brueggemann, Walter. *Genesis.* Interpretation. Louisville, KY: Westminster John Knox, 1982.

Buchinger, Harald. "Was There Ever a Liturgical Triduum in Antiquity? Theological Idea and Liturgical Reality." *Ecclesia Orans* 27 (2010): 257–270.

———. "On the Early History of Quadragesima: A New Look at an Old Problem and Some Proposed Solutions." In *Liturgies in East and West: Ecumenical Relevance of Early Liturgical Development, Acts of the International Symposium Vindobonense I, Vienna, November 17–20, 2007*, edited by Hans-Jürgen Feulner, 99–117. Österreichische Studien zur Liturgiewissenschaft und Sakramententheologie 6. Berlin: LIT, 2013.

——. "'Let the Wise Listen and Add to Their Learning' (Prov 1:5)." In *Festschrift for Günter Stemberger on the Occasion of his 75th Birthday*, edited by Constanza Cordoni and Gerhard Langer, 481–501. Studia Judaica 90. Berlin: De Gruyter, 2016.

——. "Breaking the Fast: The Central Moment of the Paschal Celebration in Historical Context and Diachronic Perspective." In *Sanctifying Texts, Transforming Rituals: Encounters in Liturgical Studies, Essays in Honour of Gerard A. M. Rouwhorst*, edited by Paul van Geest, Marcel Poorthuis, and Els Rose, 191–205. Brill's Studies in Catholic Theology. Leiden: Brill, 2017.

Bucur, Bogdan G. "Exegesis of Biblical Theophanies in Byzantine Hymnography: Rewritten Bible?" *Theological Studies* 68 (2007): 92–112.

——. "The Feet That Eve Heard in Paradise and Was Afraid: Observations on the Christology of Byzantine Festal Hymns." *Philosophy and Theology* 18, no. 1 (2007): 3–26.

——. "The Mountain of the Lord: Sinai, Zion, and Eden in Byzantine Hymnographic Exegesis." In *Symbola caelestis: Le symbolisme liturgique et paraliturgique dans le monde chrétien*, edited by B. Lourié and A. Orlov, 129–172. Piscataway, NJ: Gorgias, 2009.

Bucur, Bogdan G., and Elijah N. Mueller. "Gregory Nazianzen's Reading of Habbakuk 3:2 and Its Reception: A Lesson from Byzantine Scripture Exegesis." *Pro Ecclesia* 20, no. 1 (2011): 86–103.

Bucur, Bogdan G. "Christophanic Exegesis and the Problem of Symbolization: Daniel 3 (The Fiery Furnace) as a Test Case." *Journal of Theological Interpretation* 10, no. 2 (2016): 227–244.

——. "The Son of Man and the Ancient of Days: Observations on Early Christian Reception of Daniel 7." *Phronema* 32, no. 1 (2017): 1–27.

——. "Anti-Jewish Rhetoric in Byzantine Hymnography: Exegetical and Theological Contextualization." *SVTQ* 61 (2017): 39–60.

——. "Anti-Jewish Rhetoric in Byzantine Hymnography: Exegetical and Theological Contextualization." *SVTQ* 61 (2017): 39–60.

Caesarius of Arles. *Sermons*, Vol. 2: *81–186*. Translated by Mary Magdaleine Mueller. The Fathers of the Church. Washington, DC: Catholic University of America Press, 1981.

Calivas, Alkiviadis C. *Great Week and Pascha in the Greek Orthodox Church*. Brookline, MA: Holy Cross Orthodox, 1997.

Cathcart, Kevin, and Robert P. Gordon. *The Targum of the Minor Prophets*. Collegeville, MN: Liturgical, 1990.

Chow, Simon. *The Sign of Jonah Reconsidered: A Study of Its Meaning in the Gospel Traditions*. Coniectanea Neotestamentica or Coniectanea Biblica: New Testament Series 27. Stockholm: Almqvist and Wiksell, 1995.

Christ, W., and M. Paranikas, eds. *Anthologia Graeca Carminum Christianorum*. Leipzig: n. p., 1871.

Clines, David J. A. "Biblical Hermeneutics in Theory and Practice." *Christian Brethren Review* 31, no. 32 (1982): 65–76.

——. *Job 1–20*. Word Biblical Commentary 17. Nashville: Thomas Nelson, 1989.

——. *Job 21–37*. Word Biblical Commentary 18. Nashville: Thomas Nelson: 2006.

Cogan, Mordechai. *I Kings: A New Translation with Introduction and Commentary*. The Anchor Yale Bible Commentaries. New Haven, CT: Yale University Press, 2001.

Collins, John J. *Daniel: A Commentary on the Book of Daniel*. Hermeneia. Minneapolis: Fortress, 1993.

——. "The Son of God Text from Qumran." In *From Jesus to John: Essays on Jesus and New Testament Christology in Honor of Marinus de Jonge*, edited by M. de Boer,

65–82. Journal for the Study of the New Testament Supplement 84. Sheffield, UK: Sheffield Academic, 1993.

Coloe, Mary L. "Sources in the Shadows: John 13 and the Johannine Community." In *New Currents through John: A Global Perspective*, edited by Francisco Lozada Jr. and Tom Thatcher, 69–82. Atlanta: SBL, 2006.

Constas, Nicholas. *Proclus of Constantinople and the Cult of the Virgin in Late Antiquity: Homilies 1–5*. Texts and Translations. Leiden: Brill, 2003.

———. "The Last Temptation of Satan: Divine Deception in Greek Patristic Interpretations of the Passion Narrative." *HTR* 97, no. 2 (2004): 139–163.

Coogan, Michael D. *Stories from Ancient Canaan*. Philadelphia: Westminster, 1978.

Craddock, Fred B. *Luke*. Interpretation. Louisville, KY: Westminster John Knox, 1990.

Craigie, Peter C. *Psalms 1–50*. Revised by Marvin Tate. Word Biblical Commentary 19. Nashville: Thomas Nelson, 2004.

Cramer, J. A. *Catena in Matthaeum et Marcum*. Oxford: n.p., 1840.

Cross, Frank Moore. *Canaanite Myth and Hebrew Epic. Essays in the History of the Religion of Israel*. Cambridge, MA: Harvard University Press, 2009.

Croy, N. Clayton. *3 Maccabees*. Septuagint Commentary Series 2. Leiden: Brill, 2006.

Cunningham, Mary B., trans. *Wider Than Heaven: Eighth-Century Homilies on the Mother of God*. Popular Patristic Series 35. Crestwood, NY: St. Vladimir's Seminary Press, 2008.

Custer, Jack. "Inspired Word and Spiritual Worship: How Byzantine Hymnography Interprets Sacred Scripture." In *Symbola caelestis: Le symbolisme liturgique et paraliturgique dans le monde chrétien*, edited by B. Lourié and A. Orlov, 173–198. Piscataway, NJ: Gorgias, 2009.

Cyril of Alexandria. *Commentary on the Twelve Prophets*, Vol. 1. Translated by Robert C. Hill. Fathers of the Church. Washington, DC: Catholic University of America Press, 2013.

Dahood, Mitchell. *Proverbs and Northwest Semitic Philology*. Scripta Pontificii Instituti Biblici 113. Rome: Pontifical Biblical Institute, 1963.

———. *Psalms III: 101–150: A New Translation with Introduction and Commentary*. The Anchor Yale Bible Commentaries. New Haven, CT: Yale University Press, 1970.

———. *Psalms I, 1–50: A New Translation with Introduction and Commentary*. The Anchor Yale Bible Commentaries. New Haven, CT: Yale University Press, 1995.

———. *Psalms II, 51–100: A New Translation with Introduction and Commentary*. The Anchor Yale Bible Commentaries. New Haven, CT: Yale University Press, 1995.

Daley, Brian E., trans. *On the Dormition of Mary: Early Patristic Homilies*. Crestwood, NY: St. Vladimir's Seminary Press, 1998.

———. *God Visible: Patristic Christology Reconsidered*. Changing Paradigms in Historical and Systematic Theology. New York: Oxford University Press, 2018.

Danby, Herbert, ed. *The Mishnah Translated from the Hebrew with Introduction and Brief Explanatory Notes*. Oxford: Oxford University Press, 1993.

Danielou, Jean. *From Shadows to Reality: Studies in the Biblical Typology of the Fathers*. Translated by Wulstan Hibberd. London: Burns and Oates, 1960.

Danker, Frederick W. "Purple." In *ABD*, 5:557–560.

Dedes, Seraphim. "Ecclesiastical Translations, Texts, and Music." https://www.agesinitiatives.com/dcs/public/dcs/dcs.html.

Diodor of Tarsus. *Commentary on Psalms 1–51*. Translated with introduction and notes by Robert C. Hill. Writings from the Greek-Roman World 9. Leiden: Brill, 2005.

Dionysius of Alexandria. *Letters and Treatises*. Edited by Charles Lett Feltoe. Translation of Christian Literature, Series I: Greek Texts. New York: Macmillan, 1918.

Dix, Gregory. *The Shape of the Liturgy.* London: Dacre, 1949.

Dowling, Maurice. "Proverbs 8:22–31 in the Christology of the Early Fathers." *Perichoresis* 8, no. 1 (2010): 47–65.

Dreyfus, François. "La condescendance divine (*synkatabasis*) comme principe herméneutique de l'Ancien Testament dans la tradition juive et dans la tradition chrétienne." *VTSup* 36 (1985): 96–107.

Drumbl, Johann. "Die Improperien der lateinischen Liturgie." *Archiv für Liturgiewissenschaft* 15 (1973): 68–100.

Dulaey, Martine. "Les trois Hébreux dans la fournaise (Dan 3) dans l'interprétation symbolique de l'église ancienne." *RSR* 71, no. 1 (1997): 33–59.

Dyck, Andrew R. "On Cassia, Kyrie, he en pollais." *Byzantion* 56 (1986): 63–76.

Edwards, Mark J. *Galatians, Ephesians, Philippians.* ACCS NT 8. Downers Grove, IL: InterVarsity, 1999.

Égérie, *Journal de voyage (Itinéraire).* Translated with introduction, critical text, notes, and index, by Pierre Maraval. SC 296. Paris: Cerf, 1982.

Engberg, Sysse G. "The Greek Old Testament Lectionary as a Liturgical Book." *Cahiers de l'Institut du Moyen-Âge grec et latin* 54 (1987): 39–48.

———. "The *Prophetologion* and the Triple-Lection Theory: The Genesis of a Liturgical Book." *Bollettino della Badia greca di Grottaferrata,* 3 (2006): 67–92.

Enns, Peter. "The 'Moveable Well' in 1 Cor 10:4: An Extrabiblical Tradition in an Apostolic Text." *Bulletin for Biblical Research* 6 (1996): 23–38.

———. "Wisdom of Solomon and Biblical Interpretation in the Second Temple Period." In *The Way of Wisdom: Essays in Honor of Bruce K. Waltke,* edited by J. I. Packer and Sven K. Soderlund, 212–225. Grand Rapids, MI: Zondervan, 2000.

Etheridge, J. W. *The Targums of Onkelos and Jonathan Ben Uzziel on the Pentateuch with the Fragments of the Jerusalem Targum: Genesis and Exodus.* London: Longman, 1862.

Ferreiro, Alberto. *The Twelve Prophets.* ACCS OT 14. Downers Grove, IL: InterVarsity, 2003.

Fishbane, Michael. *Biblical Interpretation in Ancient Israel.* Oxford: Oxford University Press, 1985.

Fisk, Bruce N. "Pseudo-Philo, Paul and Israel's Rolling Stone: Early Points along an Exegetical Trajectory." In *Israel in the Wilderness: Interpretations of the Biblical Narratives in Jewish and Christian Traditions,* edited by Kenneth E. Pomykala, 117–136. Themes in Biblical Narrative. Leiden: Brill, 2008.

Fitzmyer, Joseph A. *The Gospel According to Luke 1–9: Introduction, Translation, and Notes.* The Anchor Yale Bible Commentaries. New Haven, CT: Yale University Press, 1970.

———. *The Gospel According to Luke 10–24: Introduction, Translation, and Notes.* The Anchor Yale Bible Commentaries. New Haven, CT: Yale University Press, 1985.

Florovsky, Georges. *Bible, Church, Tradition: An Eastern Orthodox View.* Vol. 1 of *The Collected Works of Georges Florovsky.* Belmont, MA: Nordland, 1972.

Forger, Deborah L. "Divine Embodiment in Philo of Alexandria." *Journal for the Study of Judaism* 49 (2018): 223–262.

Fox, Michael V. *Proverbs 1–9: A New Translation with Introduction and Commentary.* The Anchor Yale Bible Commentaries. New Haven, CT: Yale University Press, 2000.

———. "Wisdom in the Joseph Story." *VT* 51, no. 1 (2001): 26–41.

Frayer-Griggs, Daniel. *Saved through Fire: The Fiery Ordeal in New Testament Eschatology.* Eugene, OR: Wipf and Stock, 2016.

Freedman, R. D. "'Put Your Hand under My Thigh'—Patriarchal Oath." *BAR* 2, no. 2 (1976): 2–4, 42.

Friedman, Richard E. *Who Wrote the Bible?* New York: Harper & Row, 1987.

Frøyshov, Stig Simeon R. "The Cathedral-Monastic Distinction Revisited, Part I: Was Egyptian Desert Liturgy a Pure Monastic Office?" *Studia Liturgica* 37 (2007): 198–216.

——. "Greek Hymnody." In *The Canterbury Dictionary of Hymnology*, edited by J. R. Watson and Emma Hornby. London: Canterbury, 2013. http://www.hymnology.co.uk/g/greek-hymnody.

Gambero, Luigi. *Mary and the Fathers of the Church: The Blessed Virgin Mary in Patristic Thought.* San Francisco: Ignatius, 1999.

Garrett, Duane A. *Proverbs, Ecclesiastes, Song of Songs.* New American Commentary. Nashville: Broadman and Holman, 2001.

——. *Song of Songs/Lamentations.* Word Biblical Commentary. OT 23B. Nashville: Thomas Nelson, 2004.

Gavrilyuk, Paul L. *The Suffering of the Impassible God: The Dialectics of Patristic Thought.* Oxford Early Christian Studies. New York: Oxford University Press, 2004.

Gieschen, Charles A. *Angelomorphic Christology: Antecedents and Early Evidence.* Leiden: Brill, 1998.

——. "The Real Presence of the Son before Christ: Revisiting an Old Approach to Old Testament Christology." *Concordia Theological Quarterly* 68, no. 2 (2004): 105–126.

Ginzberg, Louis. *Legends of the Jews*, Vol. 1: *Bible Times and Characters, from the Creation to Moses in the Wilderness.* Vol. 2: *Bible Times and Characters, from Moses in the Wilderness to Esther.* Translated by Henrietta Szold and Paul Radin. Philadelphia: JPS, 2003.

Gohl, Justin M. "Performing the Book of Proverbs: Engaging Proverbs as Christian Scripture." PhD diss., Lutheran Theological Seminary at Philadelphia, 2013.

Golitzin, Alexander. "A Monastic Setting for the *Syriac Apocalypse of Daniel.*" In *To Train His Soul in Books: Syriac Asceticism in Early Christianity*, edited by Robin D. Young and M. J. Blanchard, 66–98. Catholic University of America Studies in Early Christianity. Washington, DC: Catholic University of America Press, 2011.

Gonosová, Anna. "Epitaphios," *ODB*, 1:720–721

Good, Edwin M. "The Barberini Greek Version of Habakkuk III." *VT* 9, no. 1 (1959): 11–30.

Goppelt, Leonhard. "*Typos.*" In *TDNT*, 8:246–259.

Gordon, Cyrus H. "ᵓlhym in Its Reputed Meaning of *Rulers, Judges.*" *JBL* 54, no. 3 (1935): 139–144.

Greeven, H. "*Proskyneō.*" In *TDNT*, 6:758–766.

Grene, Clement. "Cowardice, Betrayal and Discipleship: Peter and Judas in the Gospels." PhD diss., University of Edinburgh, 2016.

Grossfeld, Bernard. *The Targum Onqelos to Leviticus and the Targum Onqelos to Numbers.* Aramaic Bible 8. Wilmington, DE: Michael Glazier, 1988.

Gunkel, Hermann. *Creation and Chaos in the Primeval Era and the Eschaton: A Religio-Historical Study of Genesis 1 and Revelation 12.* Translated by K. William Whitney Jr. Biblical Resource Series. Grand Rapids, MI: Eerdmans, 2007.

Gurtner, Daniel M. "The Veil of the Temple in History and Legend." *JETS* 49, no. 1 (2006): 97–114.

Haenchen, Ernst. *John 1: A Commentary on the Gospel of John, Chapters 1–6.* Translated by R. Funk. Hermeneia. Minneapolis: Fortress, 1984.

Hagner, Donald A. *Matthew 14–28.* Word Biblical Commentary. NT 33B; Dallas: Word, 1995.

Hamilton, Victor P. *The Book of Genesis: Chapters 18–50.* The New International Commentary on the Old Testament. Grand Rapids, MI: Eerdmans, 1995.

Hanse, Hermann. "*Echo*." In *TDNT*, 2:816–832.

Havrelock, Rachel. *River Jordan: The Mythology of a Dividing Line*. Chicago: University of Chicago Press, 2011.

Hays, Richard B. *Echoes of Scripture in the Letters of Paul*. New Haven, CT: Yale University Press, 1989.

Heal, Kristian S. "Joseph as a Type of Christ in Syriac Literature." *BYU Studies Quarterly* 41, no. 1 (2002): 29–49.

Hengel, Martin. *Judaism and Hellenism: Studies in Their Encounter in Palestine during the Early Hellenistic Period*. 2 vols. Translated by John Bowden. Minneapolis: Fortress, 1974.

Hengstenberg, Ernst Wilhelm. *Christology of the Old Testament*. Grand Rapids, MI: Kregel, 1970.

Henze, Matthias. *The Syriac Apocalypse of Daniel: Introduction, Text, and Commentary*. Studien und Texte zu Antike und Christentum/Studies and Texts 11. Tübingen: Mohr Siebeck, 2001.

Heschel, Abraham Joshua. *The Sabbath: Its Meaning for Modern Man*. New York: Farrar, Straus and Giroux, 1951.

Høeg, Carsten, Günter Zuntz, and Sysse Engberg, eds. *Prophetologium*. Monumenta Musicae Byzantinae Lectionaria. Copenhagen: Munksgaard, 1939–1981.

Holladay, William L. *Jeremiah 1: A Commentary on the Book of the Prophet Jeremiah (Chapters 1–25)*. Hermeneia. Minneapolis: Fortress, 1986.

Holmes, Michael W., ed. *The Apostolic Fathers: Greek and English Translations*. Grand Rapids, MI: Baker Academic, 2007.

Holy Week. Translated from Greek by the Holy Transfiguration Monastery. Brookline, MA: Holy Transfiguration Monastery, 2016.

Hossfeld, Frank L., and Enrich Zenger. *Psalms 2: A Commentary on Psalms 51–100*. Translated by Linda M. Maloney. Hermeneia. Minneapolis: Fortress, 2005.

Hunt, Hannah. "Sexuality and Penitence in Syriac Commentaries on Luke's Sinful Woman." *Studia Patristica* 44 (2010): 189–194.

Hurtado, Larry W. *Lord Jesus Christ: Devotion to Jesus in Earliest Christianity*. Grand Rapids, MI: Eerdmans, 2003.

Isaac, Ephraim, trans. "1 Enoch [Ethiopic Apocalypse of Enoch]." In *Old Testament Pseudepigrapha*, Vol. 1: *Apocalyptic Literature and Testaments*, edited by James H. Charlesworth, 5–90. Garden City, NY: Doubleday, 1983.

Janeras, Sebatià. *Le Vendredi-Saint dans la tradition liturgique byzantine: Structure et histoire de ses offices*. Studia Anselmiana 99; Analecta Liturgica 13. Rome: Benedectina-Edizioni Abbazia S. Paolo, 1988.

——— . "Les lectionnaires de l'ancienne liturgie de Jérusalem." *Collectanea Christiana Orientalia* 2 (2005): 71–92.

Jeffreys, Elizabeth M. "Kanon." In *ODB*, 2:1102.

——— . "Kontakion." In *ODB*, 2:1148.

——— . "Troparion." In *ODB*, 3:2124.

Jeremias, Joachim. *The Eucharistic Words of Jesus*. Translated by Norman Perrin. Minneapolis: Fortress, 1977.

——— . "*Abyssos*." In *TDNT*, 1:9–10.

——— . "*Amnos, arēs, arnion*." In *TDNT*, 1:338–341.

——— . "*Nymphē*." In *TDNT*, 4:1099–1106.

Jerome. *Commentary on Jeremiah*. Translated with an introduction and notes by Michael Graves. Edited by Christopher A. Hall. Ancient Christian Texts. Downers Grove, IL: InterVarsity, 2011.

Jewett, Robert. *Romans*. Hermeneia. Minneapolis: Fortress, 2006.

Johns, Loren L. *The Lamb Christology of the Apocalypse of John: An Investigation into Its Origins and Rhetorical Force*. Wissenschaftliche Untersuchungen zum Neuen Testament. Eugene, OR: Wipf and Stock, 2015.

Johnson, Maxwell E. "From Three Weeks to Forty Days: Preparation and the Origins of Lent." In *Living Water, Sealing Spirit: Readings on Christian Initiation*, edited by Maxwell E. Johnson, 118–136. Collegeville, MN: Liturgical, 1995.

———. "Preparation for Pascha? Lent in Christian Antiquity." In *Between Memory and Hope: Readings on the Liturgical Year*, edited by Maxwell E. Johnson, chapter 12. Kindle ed. Collegeville, MN: Liturgical, 2000.

Johnson, Scott F. "The Sinful Woman: A *Memra* by Jacob of Serug." *Sobornost* 24 (2002): 56–88.

Jonge, Marinus de. "Mark 14:25 among Jesus' Words about the Kingdom of God." In *Sayings of Jesus: Canonical and Non-Canonical. Essays in Honour of Tjitze Baarda*, edited by William L. Petersen, Johan S. Vos, and Henk J. Jonge, 123–135. *NT*Sup 89. Leiden: Brill, 2014.

Jurgens, William A. *The Faith of the Early Fathers*, Vol. 2. Collegeville, MN: Liturgical, 1979.

Just, Arthur A. *Luke*. ACCS. NT 3. Downers Grove, IL: InterVarsity, 2003.

Kannengiesser, Charles. *Handbook of Patristic Exegesis: The Bible in Ancient Christianity*. Leiden: Brill, 2006.

Kantrowitz, David. *Judaic Classics Library*. Version 2.2 (computer software). Chicago: Institute for Computers in Jewish Life, Davka & Judaic, 2001.

Karim, Armin. "'My People, What Have I Done to You?': The Good Friday *Popule Meus* Verses in Chant and Exegesis, c. 380–880." PhD diss., Case Western Reserve University, 2014.

Kasman, Admiel. "Breath, Kiss, and Speech as the Source of the Animation of Life: Ancient Foundations of Rabbinic Homilies on the Giving of the Torah as the Kiss of God." In *Self, Soul and Body in Religious Experience*, edited by Albert I. Baumgartner, Jan Assmann, and Guy Stroumsa, 91–124. Studies in the History of Religions 78. Leiden: Brill, 1998.

Khazdan Alexander, and Nancy Patterson Ševčenko. "Stylite." In *ODB*, 3:1971.

King, Daniel. "The Textual History of the New Testament and the Bible Translator." *Bible Translator* 68, no. 1 (2017): 20–37.

Kitchen, Robert A. "Jonah's Oar: Christian Typology in Jacob of Serug's *Mēmrā* 122 On Jonah." *Hugoye* 11, no. 1 (2011): 29–62.

Kleist, James A. *The Didache, the Epistle of Barnabas, the Epistles and the Martyrdom of St. Polycarp, the Fragments of Papias and the Epistle of Diognetus*. New York: Newman, 1948.

Koltun-Fromm, Naomi. "Psalm 22's Christological Interpretive Tradition in Light of Christian Anti-Jewish Polemic." *JECS* 6, no. 1 (1998): 37–58.

Köster, Helmut. "*Synechō*." In *TDNT*, 7:877–882.

———. "*Hypostasis*." In *TDNT*, 8:572–589.

Kristeva, Julia. *Sēmiōtikē: Recherches pour une sémanalyse*. Paris: Éditions du Seuil, 1969.

———. *Desire in Language: A Semiotic Approach to Language and Art*. Edited by Leon S. Roudiez, translated by T. Gora. New York: Columbia University Press, 1980.

Krueger, Derek. *Writing and Holiness: The Practice of Authorship in the Early Christian East.* Divinations: Rereading Late Ancient Religion. Philadelphia: University of Pennsylvania Press, 2004.

———. *Liturgical Subjects: Christian Ritual, Biblical Narrative, and the Formation of the Self in Byzantium.* Philadelphia: University of Pennsylvania Press, 2014.

Krueger Derek, and Robert Nelson, eds. *The New Testament in Byzantium.* Dumbarton Oaks Byzantine Symposia and Colloquia. Washington, DC: Dumbarton Oaks Research Library and Collection, 2016.

Kruk, Miroslaw P. "The Ἄνωθεν οἱ προφῆται in Dionysius's Hermeneia: A Source for the Iconography of the Mother of God Surrounded by the Prophets?" *Museikon* 1 (2017): 53–68.

Kugel, James L. *In Potiphar's House: The Interpretive Life of Biblical Texts.* San Francisco: Harper, 1990.

———. *Traditions of the Bible: A Guide to the Bible as It Was at the Start of the Common Era.* Cambridge, MA: Harvard University Press, 1998.

Külzer, Andreas, and Claudia Rapp, eds. *The Bible in Byzantium: Appropriation, Adaptation, Interpretation.* Part 6 JAJ Supplements, Reading Scripture in Judaism and Christianity 25. Göttingen: Vandenhoeck & Ruprecht, 2019.

Laderman, Shulamith. "Cosmology, Art, and Liturgy." In *Between Judaism and Christianity,* edited by Katrin Kogman-Appel and Mati Meyer, 121–138. Leiden: Brill, 2009.

Lash, Ephraim, trans. "Ephrem the Syrian: Sermon on the Most Virtuous Joseph." http://web.archive.org/web/20060911201927/http://anastasis.org.uk/Joseph.pdf

———. "Holy Week Hymns." http://web.archive.org/web/20060911201927/http://anastasis.org.uk/.

Layton, Richard A. "Origen and Didymus on the Origin of the Passions." *Vigilae Christianae* 54, no. 3 (2000): 262–282.

Leclerc, Thomas L. *Introduction to the Prophets: Their Stories, Sayings and Scrolls.* New York: Paulist, 2017.

Lenten Triodion (in Greek *Triōdion Katanyktikon*). Edited by the Church of Greece. Athens: Apostoliki Diakonia. 2003.

The Lenten Triodion. Translated from the original Greek by Mother Mary and Archimandrite Kallistos Ware. Service Books of the Orthodox Church. London: Faber and Faber, 1978.

Lenzi, Alan. "Proverbs 8:22–31: Three Perspectives on Its Composition." *JBL* 125, no. 4 (2006): 687–714.

Leroy, F.-J. *L'homilétique de Proclus de Constantinople: Tradition manuscrite, inédits, études connexes.* Studi e testi 247. Vatican City: Biblioteca Apostolica Vaticana, 1967.

Levenson, Jon D. "A Technical Meaning for n'm in the Hebrew Bible." *VT* 35 (1985): 61–67.

———. *The Love of God: Divine Gift, Human Gratitude and Mutual Faithfulness in Judaism.* Library of Jewish Studies. Princeton, NJ: Princeton University Press, 2016.

Levine, Baruch A. *Leviticus.* JPS Torah Commentary. Philadelphia: JPS, 1989.

Lingas, Alexander. "The Liturgical Place of the Kontakion in Constantinople." In *Liturgy, Architecture and Art of the Byzantine World, Papers of the XVIII International Byzantine Congress (Moscow, 8–15 August 1991), and Other Essays Dedicated to the Memory of Fr. John Meyendorff,* edited by Constantin C. Akentiev, 50–57. Byzantinorossica 1. St. Petersburg: St. Petrsburg Society for Byzantine and Slavic Studies, 1995.

Long, Phillip J. "The Origin of the Eschatological Feast as a Wedding Banquet in the Synoptic Gospels: An Intertextual Study." PhD diss., Andrews University, 2012.

Lossky, Vladimir. "Redemption and Deification." In *In the Image and Likeness of God*, edited by Vladimir Lossky, 97–110. Crestwood, NY: St. Vladimir's Seminary Press, 1985.

Louth, Andrew, ed. *Genesis 1–11*. ACCS. OT 1. Downers Grove, IL: InterVarsity, 2001.

Louth, Andrew. "Tradition and the Icon." *The Way* 44, no. 4 (2005): 147–159.

Louth, Andrew, and Augustine Cassiday, eds. *Byzantine Orthodoxies: Papers from the Thirty-sixth Spring Symposium of Byzantine Studies, University of Durham, 23–25 March 2002*. Society for the Promotion of Byzantine Studies. Aldershot, UK: Ashgate Variorum, 2006.

Louth, Andrew. "John of Damascus on the Mother of God as a Link between Humanity and God." In *The Cult of the Mother of God in Byzantium*, edited by Leslie Brubaker and Mary B. Cunningham, 153–161. Farnham, UK: Ashgate, 2011.

Lundbom, Jack R. *Jeremiah 37–52*. The Anchor Yale Bible Commentaries. New Haven, CT: Yale University Press, 2004.

Lunn, Nicholas P. "Allusions to the Joseph Narrative in the Synoptic Gospels and Acts: Foundations of a Biblical Type." *JETS* 55, no. 1 (2012): 27–41.

Luz, Ulrich. *Matthew 8–20*. Hermeneia. Minneapolis: Fortress, 2001.

———. *Matthew 21–28*. Hermeneia. Minneapolis: Fortress, 2005.

Magdalino, Paul, and Robert Nelson, eds. *The Old Testament in Byzantium*. Dumbarton Oaks Byzantine Symposia and Colloquia. Washington, DC: Dumbarton Oaks Research Library and Collection, 2010.

Maguire, Henry. *Art and Eloquence in Byzantium*. Princeton Legacy Library. Princeton, NJ: Princeton University Press, 2019.

Manis, Andrew M. "Meliton of Sardis: Hermeneutic and Context." *GOTR* 32, no. 4 (1987): 387–401.

Martinez, Florentino Garcia, and Eibert J. C. Tigchelaar, eds. *The Dead Sea Scrolls: Study Edition*, Vol. 1: *1Q1–4Q273*. Grand Rapids, MI: Eerdmans, 1997.

Matson, Mark A. "To Serve as Slave: Footwashing as Paradigmatic Status Reversal." In *One in Christ Jesus: Essays on Early Christianity and "All That Jazz," in Honor of S. Scott Bartchy*, edited by David L. Matson and K. C. Richardson, 113–131. Eugene, OR: Wipf and Stock, 2014.

Maximus the Confessor. *On Difficulties in the Church Fathers*, Vol. 1: *The Ambigua*. Edited and translated by Nicholas Constas. Dumbarton Oaks Medieval Library 28. Cambridge, MA: Harvard University Press, 2014.

Mays, James L. *Psalms*. Interpretation. Louisville, KY: Westminster John Knox, 2011.

McCarty, V. K. "Illuminating the Incarnation: The Life and Work of the Ninth Century Hymnographer Kassia." *International Congregational Journal* 16, no. 1 (2017): 165–178.

McDonough, Sean M. *Christ as Creator: Origins of a New Testament Doctrine*. New York: Oxford University Press, 2009.

McGowan, Anne, and Paul F. Bradshaw. *The Pilgrimage of Egeria: A New Translation of the Itinerarium Egeriae with Introduction and Commentary*. Alcuin Club Collections 93. Collegeville, MN: Liturgical, 2018.

Meek, Russell L. "Intertextuality, Inner-Biblical Exegesis, and Inner-Biblical Allusion: The Ethics of a Methodology." *Biblica* 95, no. 2 (2014): 280–291.

Méliton de Sardes. *Sur la Pâque et fragments*. Introduction, text criticism, translation, and notes by Othmar Perler. *SC* 123. Paris: Cerf, 1966.

Melito of Sardis. *On Pascha, with the Fragments of Melito and Other Material Related to the Quartodecimans*. Translated, introduced, and annotated by Alistair Stewart-Sykes. Popular Patristic Series 20. Crestwood, NY: St. Vladimir's Seminary Press, 2001.

Metzger, Bruce M. *A Textual Commentary on the Greek New Testament: A Companion Volume to the United Bible Societies' Greek New Testament*. Stuttgart: Deutsche Bibelgesellschaft, 1994.

Michaelis, Wilhelm. "*Myron, Myrixō*." In *TDNT*, 4:800–801.

Michalak, Alexander R. *Angels as Warriors in Late Second Temple Jewish Literature*. Wissenschaftliche Untersuchungen zum Neuen Testament 2. Reihe 330. Tübingen: Mohr Siebeck, 2012.

Miller, James. "'Let us sing to the Lord': The Biblical Odes in the Codex Alexandrinus." PhD diss., Marquette University, 2006.

———. "The Prophetologion: The Old Testament of Byzantine Christianity?" In *The Old Testament in Byzantium*, edited by Paul Magdalino and Robert Nelson, 55–76. Washington, DC: Dumbarton Oaks Research Library and Collection, 2010.

Moberly, R. W. L. *Genesis 12–50*. Old Testament Guides. Sheffield, UK: Sheffield Academic, 1995.

Morozowich, Mark M. "Historicism and Egeria: Implications of *In eo typo*." *Ecclesia Orans* 27 (2010): 169–182.

Mosser, Carl. "The Earliest Patristic Interpretations of Psalm 82, Jewish Antecedents, and the Origin of Christian Deification." *JTS* new series 56, no. 1 (2005): 30–74.

Moyise, Steve. "Intertextuality and Biblical Studies: A Review." *Verbum et Ecclesia* 23, no. 2 (2002): 418–431.

Mulroney, James A. E. *The Translation Style of Old Greek Habakkuk: Methodological Advancement in Interpretive Studies of the Septuagint*. Forschungen zum Alten Testament 2. Reihe 86. Heidelberg: Mohr Siebeck, 2016.

Neuhaus, Richard John. *Death on a Friday Afternoon: Meditations on the Last Words of Jesus from the Cross*. New York: Basic Books, 2000.

Neyrey, Jerome H. "'I Said: You Are Gods': Psalm 82:6 and John 10." *JBL* 108, no. 4 (1989): 647–663.

Nicklas, Tobias. "Food of Angels (Wis 16:20)." In *Studies in the Book of Wisdom*, edited by Géza G. Xeravits and József Zsengellér, 83–100. Supplements to the Journal for the Study of Judaism 142. Leiden: Brill, 2010.

Nikodemus the Hagiorite. *Eortodromion, or the Exposition of Sung Canons Which Are Sung on the Eve of Feasts of the Lord and the Mother of God* [in Greek]. Venice: n.p., 1836.

Nolland, John. *Luke 1–9:20*. Word Biblical Commentary 35A. Dallas: Word, 1989.

Noort, Edward. "The Creation of Light, Genesis 1:1–5: Remarks on the Function of Light and Darkness in the Opening Verses of the Hebrew Bible." In *The Creation of Heaven and Earth*, edited by G. H. van Kooten, 3–20. Leiden: Brill, 2004.

Notley, Steven R. "8 Luke 5:35: 'When the Bridegroom Is Taken Away'—Anticipation of the Destruction of the Second Temple." In *The Gospels in First-Century Judaea: Proceedings of the Inaugural Conference of Nyack College's Graduate Program in Ancient Judaism and Christian Origins, August 29th, 2013*, edited by Steven R. Notley and Jeffrey P. Garcia, 107–121. Jewish and Christian Perspectives Series 29. Leiden: Brill, 2015.

Novello, Henry L. *Death as Transformation: A Contemporary Theology of Death*. Burlington, VT: Ashgate, 2011.

O'Brien, Dan. "Cubism: Art and Philosophy." *Espes* 7, no. 1 (2018): 30–37.

———. "Cubism and Kant." *Proceedings of the European Society for Aesthetics* 10 (2018): 482–506.

O'Connor, Jerome Murphy. *The Holy Land: An Oxford Archeological Guide from Earliest Times to 1700*. New York: Oxford University Press, 2008.

Olariu, Daniel. "Textual History of Daniel." In *The Hebrew Bible*, Vol. 1C: *Writings*, edited by Armin Lange and Emmanuel Tov, 517–527. Leiden: Brill.

Olyan, Saul. *A Thousand Thousands Served Him: Exegesis and the Articulation of the Angelic Host in Ancient Judaism*. Tübingen: Mohr Siebeck, 1993.

Origen. *Commentarii in Epistulam ad Romanos*. Edited by T. Heither. 5 vols. Freiburg im Breisgau: Herder, 1990–1995.

———. *Homilies on Genesis and Exodus*. Translated by Ronald E. Heine. The Fathers of the Church 71. Washington, DC: Catholic University of America Press, 2002.

Oropeza, B. J. "Judas' Death and Final Destiny in the Gospels and Earliest Christian Writings." *Neotestamenica* 44, no. 2 (2010): 341–361.

Panagopoulos, Spyros P. "Kassia: A Female Hymnographer of 9th Century Byzantium and Her Hymnographic Poem on the Vesper of Holy Tuesday." *De Medio Aevo* 7, no. 1 (2015): 115–128.

Papagiannis, K. *Corrections and Observations on the Triodion* [*Diortōseis kai Paratērēseis eis to Triōdion*]. Thessaloniki: University Studio, 2008.

Parker, Victor L. "Judas Maccabaeus' Campaigns against Timothy." *Biblica* 87, no. 4 (2006): 457–476.

Parkes, James. *The Conflict of the Church and the Synagogue: A Study in the Origins of Antisemitism*. London: Soncino, 1934.

Parpulov, Georgi R. "Psalters and Personal Piety in Byzantium." In *The Old Testament in Byzantium*, edited by Paul Magdalino and Robert Nelson, 77–105. Washington, DC: Dumbarton Oaks Research Library and Collection, 2010.

———. "The Bibles of the Christian East." In *The New Cambridge History of the Bible*, Vol. 2: *From 600 to 1450*, edited by Richard Marsden and E. Ann Matter, 309–324. Cambridge: Cambridge University Press, 2012.

Parsenios, George L. *Departure and Consolation: The Johannine Farewell Discourses in Light of Greco-Roman Literature*. NTSup 117. Leiden: Brill, 2005.

Patria Konstatinopoleōs: Scriptores Originum Constantinopolitanarum. Edited by Theodorus Preger. Leipzig: n.p., 1907.

Patterson, Richard D. "Psalm 22: From Trial to Triumph." *JETS* 47, no. 2 (2004): 213–233.

Pentecost, Dwight J. *The Words and Works of Jesus Christ: A Study of the Life of Christ*. Grand Rapids, MI: Zondervan, 2000.

Pentiuc, Eugen J. "Above All His Friends: Paradoxical Language in the Messianic Prophecies of the Old Testament." *GOTR* 44 (1999): 179–185.

———. "A Self-Offering God and His Begotten Wisdom (Prov 8:22-24)." *GOTR* 46 (2001): 255–65.

———. *Long-Suffering Love: A Commentary on Hosea with Patristic Annotations*. Brookline, MA: Holy Cross Orthodox, 2002, 2008.

———. *Jesus the Messiah in the Hebrew Bible*. New York: Paulist, 2005.

———. "'Renewed by Blood': Sheol's Quest in 2 Baruch 56:6." *RB* 114, no. 4 (2007): 535–564.

———. *The Old Testament in Eastern Orthodox Tradition*. New York: Oxford University Press, 2014.

———. "Il perdono nell'Antico Testamento: Giuseppe e i suoi fratelli." In *Misericordia e pardon: Atti del XXIII Convegno ecumenico internazionale di spiritualità ortodossa, Bose, 9-11 settembre 2015*, edited by L. d'Ayala Valva, L. Cremaschi, and A. Mainardi, 102–132. Spiritualità orientale. Bose: Editione Qyqajon, 2016.

———. "Behind the Days: A Semitic Way of Looking at the End of Time." In *Perceptions du temps dans la Bible*, edited by Marc Leroy and M. Staszak, 3–21. Études bibliques. Nouvelle série 77. Leuven: Peeters, 2018.

Pentiuc, Eugen J., Gad Barneea, Étienne Méténier, and Lukasz Popko. *Hosea: The Word of the Lord That Happened to Hosea*. La Bible en ses traditions 3. Leuven: Peeters, 2017.

Perdue, Leo G. *Proverbs*. Interpretation. Louisville, KY: Westminster John Knox, 2000.

Peterson, Brian K. "What Happened on 'the Night'? Judas, God, and the Importance of Liturgical Ambiguity." *Pro Ecclesia* 20, no. 4 (2011): 363–383.

Pitra, Jean-Baptist-François. *L'hymnographie de l'église grecque*. Rome: n.p., 1867.

———. *Analecta sacra spicilegio Solesmensi parata*. Vol. 1. Paris: n.p., 1876.

Pope, Marvin H. *Job*. The Anchor Yale Bible Commentaries. New Haven, CT: Yale University Press, 1965.

Puech, Emile. "Fragment d'une Apocalypse en Araméen (4Q246 = pseudo-Dan^d) et le 'Royanume de Dieu." *RB* 99 (1992): 98–131.

Rad, Gerhard von. "Josephgeschichte und ältere Chokma." *VTSup* 1 (1953): 121–127.

Rahlfs, Alfred., ed. *Verzeichnis der griechischen Handschriften des Alten Testaments: Für das Septuaginta-Unternehmen*. Berlin: Weidmannsche Buchhandlung, 1914.

Rahlfs, Alfred, and Detief Fraenkel, eds. *Verzeichnis der griechischen Handschriften des Alten Testaments: Die Überlieferung bis zum VIII. Jahrhundert*. Göttingen: Vandenhoeck & Ruprecht, 2004.

Reddish, Tim. *Does God Always Get What God Wants? An Exploration of God's Activity in a Suffering World*. Eugene, OR: Cascade, 2018.

Regan, Patrick. "The Three Days and the Forty Days." In *Between Memory and Hope: Readings on the Liturgical Year*, edited by Maxwell E. Johnson, chapter 8. Kindle ed. Collegeville, MN: Liturgical, 2000.

Reynolds, Benjamin E. *The Apocalyptic Son of Man in the Gospel of John*. Wissenschaftliche Untersuchungen zum Neuen Testament 2. Reiche 249. Tübingen: Mohr Siebeck, 2008.

The Rhetorical Exercises of Nikephoros Basilakes: Progymnasmata from Twelfth-Century Byzantium. Translated and edited by Jeffrey Beneker and Craig A. Gibson. Dumbarton Oaks Medieval Library 43. Cambridge, MA: Harvard University Press, 2016.

Riehle, Alexander. "Authorship and Gender (and) Identity: Women's Writing in the Middle Byzantine Period." In *The Author in the Middle Byzantine Literature: Modes, Functions and Identities*, edited by Aglae Pizzone, 245–262. Göttingen: De Gruyter, 2014.

Rochow, Ilse. *Studien zu der Person, den Werken und dem Nachleben der Dichterin Kassia*. Berliner Byzantinistische Arbeiten 38. Berlin: Akademie, 1967.

Romanos le Mélode. *Hymnes I: Ancien Testament*. Introduction, critical text, translation, and notes by José Grosdidier de Matons. SC 99. Paris: Cerf, 1964.

———. *Hymnes II: Nouveau Testament*. Introduction, critical text, translation, and notes by José Grosdidier de Matons. SC 110. Paris: Cerf, 1965.

Rubin, William. *Picasso and Braque: Pioneering Cubism*. New York: Museum of Modern Art, 1989.

Russell, Norman. *The Doctrine of Deification in Greek Patristic Tradition*. Oxford Early Christian Studies. New York: Oxford University Press, 2004.

Russo, Nicholas V. "A Note on the Role of Secret Mark in the Search for the Origins of Lent." *Studia Liturgica* 37, no. 2 (2009): 181–197.

———. "The Early History of Lent." Lent Library. Waco, TX: Center for Christian Ethics at Baylor University, 2013. http://www.baylor.edu/content/services/document.php/193181.

Sarna, Nahum M. *Genesis*. JPS Torah Commentary. Philadelphia: JPS, 1989.

Sasson, Jack M. *Jonah*. The Anchor Yale Bible Commentaries. New Haven, CT: Yale University Press, 1995.

Schaberg, Jane. *The Resurrection of Mary Magdalene: Legends, Apocrypha and the Christian Testament*. New York: Continuum, 2002.

Schaper, Joachim. "The Pharisees." In *The Cambridge History of Judaism*, Vol. 3: *The Early Roman Period*, edited by William Horbury, W. D. Davies, and John Sturdy, 401–427. Cambridge: Cambridge University Press, 1999.

Schatkin, Margaret. "The Maccabean Martyrs." *Vigilae Christianae* 28 (1974): 97–113.

Schiroò, G. "La seconda leggenda di Cassia." *Diptycha* 1 (1979): 303–315.

Schlier, Heinrich. "*Elaion*." In *TDNT*, 2:470–473.

Schmemann, Alexander. *Great Lent: Journey to Pascha*. Crestwood, NY: St. Vladimir's Seminary Press, 1969.

———. *Introduction to Liturgical Theology*. Crestwood, NY: St. Vladimir's Seminary, 1975.

——— . *Great Lent, a School of Repentance: Its Meaning for Orthodox Christians*. New York: Department of Religious Education, Orthodox Church of America, 1977.

Schmidt, T. C., trans. "Hippolytus of Rome: Commentary on Daniel." Scotts Valley, CA: CreateSpace, 2010

Schneider, Carl. In *TDNT*, 3:629–630.

Seeliger, Hans Reinhard. "ΠΑΛΛΑΙ ΜΑΡΤΥΡΕΣ: Die drei Jünglinge im Feuerofen als Typos in der spätantiken Kunst, Liturgie und patristischen Literatur." In *Liturgie und Dichtung: Ein interdiziplinàres Kompendium II*, edited by H. Becker and R. Kaszynski, 257–334. Pietas Liturgica 1. St. Ottilien: EOS, 1983.

Segal, Michael. *The Book of Jubilees: Rewritten Bible, Redaction, Ideology and Theology*. Supplements to the Journal for the Study of Judaism 117. Leiden: Brill, 2007.

The Services for Holy Week and Easter. Translated by Leonidas C. Contos, edited by Spencer T. Kezios. San Francisco: Narthex, 1994.

Sheridan, Mark, ed. *Genesis 11–50*. ACCS. Old Testament 2. Downers Grove, IL: InterVarsity, 2002.

Sherry, Kurt. *Kassia the Nun in Context: The Religious Thought of a Ninth Century Byzantine Monastic*. Gorgias Eastern Christian Studies 14. Piscataway, NJ: Gorgias, 2013.

Simić, Kosta. "Kassia's Hymnography in the Light of Patristic Sources and Earlier Hymnographical Works." *Zbornik Radova Vizantološkog Instituta* 48 (2011): 7–37.

Simonetti, Manlio. *Matthew 14–28*. ACCS. NT 1b. Downers Grove, IL: InterVarsity, 2002.

Skinner, John. *A Critical and Exegetical Commentary on Genesis*. International Critical Commentary. New York: Scribner, 1910.

Smith, Dennis E. "Table Fellowship as a Literary Motif in the Gospel of Luke." *JBL* 106 (1987): 613–638.

——— . *From Symposium to Eucharist: The Banquet in the Early Christian World*. Minneapolis: Fortress, 2003.

Smith, Jonathan Z. *Relating Religion: Essays in the Study of Religion*. Chicago: University of Chicago Press, 2004.

Smith, Mark S. *The Early History of God: Yahweh and the Other Deities in Ancient Israel*. Dearborn, MI: Dove, 2002.

Smith, Murray. "The Lord Jesus and His Coming in the Didache." In *The Didache: A Missing Piece of the Puzzle in Early Christianity*, edited by J. A. Draper and C. N. Jefford, 363–407. Early Christianity and Its Literature 14. Atlanta: SBL, 2015.

Smith, Ralph L. *Micah-Malachi*. Word Biblical Commentary 32. Dallas: Word, 1984.

Smith, Warren J. "Ambrose, Paul, and the Conversion of the Jews." *Exod Auditu* 25 (2009): 175–198.

Smyth, Herbert Weir, transl. *Aeschylus*. Loeb Classical Library 145–146. Cambridge, MA: Harvard University Press, 1926.

Snodgrass, Klyne R. *Stories with Intent: A Comprehensive Guide to the Parables of Jesus*. Grand Rapids, MI: Eerdmans, 2018.

Speiser, Ephraim A. *Genesis: Introduction, Translation, and Notes*. 2 vols. The Anchor Yale Bible Commentaries. New Haven, CT: Yale University Press, 1964.

Steenberg, Matthew C. "The Role of Mary as Co-Recapitulator in St. Irenaeus of Lyons." *Vigiliae Christianae* 58, no. 2 (2004): 117–137.

Stewart-Sykes, Alistair. *The Lamb's High Feast: Melito, Peri Pascha and the Quartodeciman Paschal Liturgy at Sardis*. Leiden: Brill, 1998.

Stokes, Ryan E. "The Throne Visions of Daniel 7, 1 'Enoch' 14, and the Qumran 'Book of Giants' (4Q530): An Analysis of Their Literary Relationship." *Dead Sea Discoveries* 15, no. 3 (2008): 340–358.

Stuart, Douglas. *Hosea-Jonah*. Word Biblical Commentary 31. Dallas: Word, 1987.

The Synaxarion of the Monastery of the Theotokos Evergetis. 3 vols. Text and translation by Robert H. Jordan. Belfast Byzantine Texts and Translations 6.6. Belfast: Byzantine Enterprises, 2000–2005.

Taft, Robert. "A Tale of Two Cities: The Byzantine Holy Week Triduum as a Paradigm of Liturgical History." In *Time and Community: In Honor of Thomas Julian Talley*, edited by J. Neil Alexander, 21–41. NPM Studies in Church Music and Liturgy. Washington, DC: Pastoral, 1990.

———. "In the Bridegroom's Absence: The Paschal Triduum in the Byzantine Church." In *La celebrazione del Triduo pasquale: Anamnesis e mimesis, Atti del III Congresso Internazionale di Liturgia, Roma, Pontificio Istituto Liturgico, 9–13 maggio 1988*, edited by Ildebrando Scicolone, 71–97. Analecta Liturgica 14. Rome: Pontificio Ateneo S. Anselmo, 1990.

———. "Holy Week." In *ODB*, 2:943.

———. "Lent." In *ODB*, 2:1205–1206.

———. "Triodion." In *ODB*, 3:2118–2119.

———. "Cathedral vs. Monastic Liturgy in the Christian East: Vindicating a Distinction." *Bolletina della Badia Greca di Grottaferrata* 3, no. 62 (2005): 173–219.

Talley, Thomas J. *The Origins of the Liturgical Year*. Collegeville, MN: Liturgical, 1991.

———. "History and Eschatology in the Primitive Pascha." In *Between Memory and Hope: Readings on the Liturgical Year*, edited by Maxwell E. Johnson, chapter 6. Kindle ed. Collegeville, MN: Liturgical, 2000.

Theodoret of Cyrus. *Commentary on the Psalms: Psalms 1–72*. Translated with introduction and commentary by Robert C. Hill. Fathers of the Church 101. Washington, DC: Catholic University of America Press, 2000.

———. *Commentary on Daniel*. Translated with introduction and notes by Robert C. Hill, edited by Richard Price. Writings from the Greco-Roman World 7. Leiden: Brill, 2007.

Thurn, Hans. *Oikonomia von der frühbyzantinischen Zeit bis zum Bilderstreit: Semasiologische Untersuchungen einer Wortfamilie*. Munich: Steinbauer, 1961.

Tillyard, Henry J. W. "A Musical Study of the Hymns of Cassia." *Byzantinische Zeitschrift* 20 (1911): 420–485.

Topping, Eva Katafygiotou. "Women Hymnographers in Byzantium." *Diptycha* 3 (1982–1983): 98–111.

Torrance, Thomas F. *Divine Meaning: Studies in Patristic Hermeneutics*. Edinburgh: T. and T. Clark, 1995.

Touliatos-Miles, Diana. "Kassia (ca. 810–843 and 867)." In *New Historical Anthology of Music by Women*, edited by James R. Briscoe, 6–13. Bloomington: Indiana University Press, 2004.

Treadgold, Warren. "The Problem of the Marriage of the Emperor Theophilus." *Greek, Roman and Byzantine Studies* 16 (1975): 325–341.

Tripolitis, Antonia, ed. and trans. *Kassia: The Legend, the Woman and Her Work*. Garland Library of Medieval Literature Series A, 84. New York: Garland, 1992.

Tromp, Nicholas J. *Primitive Conceptions of Death and the Nether World in the Old Testament*. Biblica et Orientalia 21. Rome: Pontifical Biblical Institute, 1969.

Tsumura, David Toshio. "The Doctrine of Creation *Ex Nihilo* and the Translation of *TŌHŪ WĀBŌHŪ*." In *Pentateuchal Traditions in the Late Second Temple Period: Proceedings of the International Workshop in Tokyo, August 28–31, 2007*, edited by Akio Moriya and Gohei Hata, 3–22. Supplements to the *Journal for the Study of Judaism* 158. Leiden: Brill, 2012.

Ulansey, David. "The Heavenly Veil Torn: Mark's Cosmic Inclusio." *JBL* 110 (1991): 123–125.

Van Voorst, Robert E. *Jesus outside the New Testament: An Introduction to the Ancient Evidence*. Grand Rapids, MI: Eerdmans, 2000.

Wallis, Faith, ed. and trans. *Bede: The Reckoning of Time*. Translated Texts for Historians. Liverpool: Liverpool University Press, 1999.

Walter, Christopher. "The Iconography of Habakkuk." *Revue des études byzantines* 47 (1989): 251–260.

Warren, Meredith J. C. *Food and Transformation in Ancient Mediterranean Literature*. Writings from the Greco-Roman World Supplement Series 14. Atlanta: SBL, 2019.

Waschke, Ernst-Joachim. "Tehôm." In *TDOT*, 15:574–581.

Watts, John D. W. *Isaiah 1–33*. Word Biblical Commentary 24. Nashville: Thomas Nelson, 2005.

Wellesz, Egon. "Melito's Homily on the Passion: An Investigation into the Sources of Byzantine Hymnography." *JTS* 44 (1943): 41–52.

———. "The Nativity Drama of the Byzantine Church." *Journal of Roman Studies* 37, nos. 1–2 (1947): 145–151.

———. *A History of Byzantine Music and Hymnography*. Oxford: Oxford University Press, 1961.

Wenham, Gordon J. *Genesis 1–15*. Word Biblical Commentary 1. Dallas: Word, 1987.

———. *Genesis 16–50*. Word Biblical Commentary 2. Dallas: Word, 1987.

Wevers, J. W., ed. *Exodus*. Septuaginta Vetus Testamentum 2/1. Göttingen Vandenhoeck & Ruprecht, 1991.

Whybray, Roger N. *The Composition of the Book of Proverbs*. JSOTSup 168. Sheffield, UK: JSOT, 1994.

Wilkinson, John. *Egeria's Travels in the Holy Land: Newly Translated with Supporting Documents and Notes*. Warminster, UK: Arts and Phillips, 1981.

Winston, David. *The Wisdom of Solomon: A New Translation with Introduction and Commentary.* The Anchor Yale Bible Commentaries. New Haven, CT: Yale University Press, 1979.

Woolfenden, Gregory. "From Betrayal to Faith: The Themes and Theology of Holy Week in Byzantine Orthodoxy." *Eastern Churches Journal* 8, no. 1 (2002): 59–84.

Wright, Robert J. *Proverbs, Ecclesiastes, Song of Songs.* ACCS OT 9. Downers Grove, IL: InterVarsity, 2005.

Young, Frances M. *Biblical Exegesis and the Formation of Christian Culture.* Cambridge: Cambridge University Press, 1997.

Zakovitch, Yair. "Inner-Biblical Interpretation." In *A Companion to Biblical Interpretation in Early Judaism*, edited by Matthias Henze, 27–63. Grand Rapids, MI: Eerdmans, 2012.

The Zohar. Translation and Commentary by Daniel C. Matt. Stanford, CA: Stanford University Press, 2006.

Zugravu, Gheorghita. "Kassia the Melodist and the Making of a Byzantine Hymnographer." PhD diss., Columbia University, 2013.

Index of Names and Topics